ENCYCLOPEDIA OF INDIAN PHILOSOPHIES

ENCYCLOPEDIA OF INDIAN PHILOSOPHIES

General Editor, Karl Potter

The following volumes are published:

I. Bibliography, 2nd ed. (1984)

II. Indian Metaphysics and Epistemology: The Tradition of Nyāya-Vaiśeṣika up to Gaṅgeśa (1978)

III. Advaita Vedānta up to Śaṃkara and His Pupils (1982)

IV. Sāṃkhya: A Dualist Tradition in Indian Philosophy (1987)

ENCYCLOPEDIA OF INDIAN PHILOSOPHIES

Sāṃkhya
A Dualist Tradition in
Indian Philosophy

EDITED BY
GERALD JAMES LARSON
AND
RAM SHANKAR BHATTACHARYA

PRINCETON UNIVERSITY PRESS
Princeton, New Jersey

Published by Princeton University Press, 41 William Street,
Princeton, New Jersey 08540

In the United Kingdom: Princeton University Press, Guildford, Surrey

Library of Congress Cataloging in Publication Data will
be found on the last printed page on this book

ISBN: 0-691-07301-5

This book has been composed in India by Shantilal Jain at
Shri Jainendra Press, A-45, Naraina, Phase I, New Delhi 110 028

Clothbound editions of Princeton University Press books are
printed on acid-free paper, and binding materials are
chosen for strength and durability

Printed in the United States of America
by Princeton University Press, Princeton, New Jersey.

Contributors:

Dayanand Bhargava, Department of Sanskrit, University of Jodhpur (Rajasthan), India
Kalidas Bhattacharya, Department of Philosophy, Visva-Bharati University, Santiniketan (Bengal), India
Harsh Narain, Department of Philosophy, University of Lucknow (UP), India
Kapil Deo Pandey, Department of Sanskrit, Arya Mahila Degree College, Lahuravir Chowmuhani, Varanasi (UP), India
Ṣangamlal Pandey, Department of Philosophy, Allahabad University, Allahabad (UP), India
Karl H. Potter, Department of Philosophy, University of Washington, Seattle, USA
Anima Sen Gupta, Department of Philosophy, Patna University, Patna (Bihar), India
Prabal Kumar Sen, Department of Philosophy, University of Calcutta (Bengal), India
Raghunatha Sharma, Sampurnananda Sanskrit University, Varanasi (UP), India
Shiv Kumar Sharma, Department of Sanskrit, University of Poona, Poona (Maharashtra), India
Esther A. Solomon, Department of Sanskrit, University of Gujarat, Ahmedabad (Gujarat), India
Kedaranatha Tripathi, College of Oriental Learning, Banaras Hindu University, Varanasi (UP), India

CONTENTS

PREFACE

Many years ago when I met the great Gopinath Kaviraj for the first time in Varanasi, he inquired about my work. I commented that I was working on one of the ancient systems of Indian philosophy, namely, the Sāṃkhya. He impatiently waved his hand to interrupt me. "Sāṃkhya," he said, "is not *one* of the systems of Indian philosophy. Sāṃkhya *is* the philosophy of India!" He was referring, of course, to the ancient period, but he also went on to stress the remarkable influence that Sāṃkhya has had on almost every phase of Indian culture and learning. Philosophy, mythology, theology, law, medicine, art, and the various traditions of Yoga and Tantra have all been touched by the categories and basic notions of the Sāṃkhya. This is not at all to claim that these various areas of learning and cultural practice have accepted the dualist metaphysics of Sāṃkhya or its overall classical systematic formulation. To the contrary, there have been intense polemics over the centuries against the Sāṃkhya position. What is striking, however, is the ubiquitous presence of the Sāṃkhya network of notions, functioning almost as a kind of cultural "code" (to use a semiotics idiom) to which intellectuals in every phase of cultural life in India have felt a need to respond.

The present volume of the *Encyclopedia of Indian Philosophies* attempts to trace the history and to interpret the meaning of Sāṃkhya philosophy from its beginnings in the ancient period to the present time, a period of some twenty-five hundred years. As might well be imagined, it has not been an easy task to accomplish this in one volume. Ram Shankar Bhattacharya and I have had to make some difficult editorial decisions by way of limiting the boundaries of our undertaking. One such decision concerned the manner in which we would treat ancient and/or "popular" (nontechnical) Sāṃkhya passages. For a time we considered the possibility of including summaries of Sāṃkhya passages in the Upaniṣads, the *Mahābhārata* (including the *Bhagavadgītā*), the Purāṇas, the medical literature, and so forth. As we proceeded in our work, however, it became clear that these passages could be best treated in the Introduction to the present volume. More than that, it became clear that these passages represent what could be called "Proto-Sāṃkhya" and should be clearly distinguished from what we are calling in the present volume "Pre-Kārikā-Sāṃkhya," "Kārikā-Sāṃkhya," "Pātañjala-Sāṃkhya," "Kārikā-Kaumudī-Sāṃkhya," "Samāsa-Sāṃkhya," and "Sūtra-Sāṃkhya" (and see Introduction).

A second editorial decision concerned the manner in which we would deal with the extensive number of passages in Indian philosophical literature that criticize Sāṃkhya from the perspective of other traditions, passages, for example, from Nyāya, Vaiśeṣika, Buddhist, Jaina, Mīmāṃsā, and Vedānta works. Again, for a time we considered the possibility of including at least some of these passages, but we ultimately determined that such passages appropriately belong in their own respective volumes in the *Encyclopedia* series and not in the Sāṃkhya volume itself.

A third editorial decision concerned the manner in which we would deal with the issue of the literature of Yoga. Our own view is that "Pātañjala-Sāṃkhya" is an important type of Sāṃkhya philosophy and deserves to be treated as such, but we encountered the practical difficulty of some seventy Sanskrit texts on Yoga that should be considered. The only sensible solution appeared to be, therefore, to prepare a separate volume of the *Encyclopedia* series for the Yoga materials with appropriate cross-references in both the Sāṃkhya and Yoga volumes. Eventually, then, when both volumes are published, they can be used in tandem.

Apart from such external editorial decisions, that is to say, what to exclude from the volume, we also had to make a number of decisions regarding the internal boundaries of the volume. It was obvious from the beginning, for example, that three of our texts required special treatment, namely, the *Sāṃkhyakārikā*, the *Tattvasamāsasūtra*, and the *Sāṃkhyasūtra*. These are the three fundamental and primary texts of the tradition upon which most other texts are based, and each presented a unique problem. Because the *Sāṃkhyakārikā* is the oldest systematic text available, we thought it appropriate to present an extensive treatment of it. Indeed, the so-called "summary" of the *Sāṃkhyakārikā* in the volume is considerably longer than the original text itself! In our view, however, since our task was not that of translation but, rather, that of presenting an overview of the systematic philosophical arguments in the text, we felt justified in taking some liberties in unpacking those arguments. Regarding the *Tattvasamāsasūtra*, the problem was the reverse. The *Tattvasamāsa* is not really a text in any sense. It is a checklist of topics upon which several commentaries have been written. We have, therefore, presented it in its entirety as a checklist. The *Sāṃkhyasūtra*, as is well known, is a late compilation, and there is no authoritative tradition either for the sequence of *sūtras* or their intepretation apart from the reading and interpretation offered, first, by Aniruddha, and then later by Vijñānabhikṣu (who generally follows Aniruddha throughout). We have, therefore, presented the *sūtras* themselves in a bare, outline form. We have, then, presented a full summary of Aniruddha's reading and interpretation followed by a shorter summary of Vijñānabhikṣu's reading and interpretation (stressing only those views of Vijñānabhikṣu that clearly differ from Aniruddha).

In three instances in the volume we have presented unusually detailed summaries, namely, those for the *Sāṃkhyavṛtti*, the *Sāṃkhyasaptativṛtti*, and the *Yuktidīpikā*. The former two texts are those recently edited by Esther A. Solomon, and because they have been unknown in Sāṃkhya studies until now, we invited Professor Solomon to prepare full treatments of both. The latter text, the *Yuktidīpikā*, is undoubtedly the most important text for understanding the details of the Sāṃkhya system, but until now no translation has been available. We thought it appropriate, therefore, to include as full a treatment of it as possible. The summary of the *Yuktidīpikā* in this volume is not by any means exhaustive, but it does provide a wealth of information that has until now been unavailable.

Dr. Ram Shankar Bhattacharya and I would like to take this opportunity to thank all of those who helped to bring this volume to completion. First, of course, our thanks to the many contributors (see List of Contributors) who prepared the published summaries. Second, a special word of thanks and acknowledgment to those who prepared summaries of passages that could not be included in the final published version of the volume—passages, for example, from Jaina, Buddhist, or epic literature that, based on our final editorial decisions, finally fell outside of the boundaries of the volume, or summaries in which it became apparent that a particular text was simply repeating what had been said earlier in terms of philosophical interpretation. In this regard, we would like to thank and acknowledge the help of Dr. Biswanath Bhattacharya (Calcutta Sanskrit College), Dr. Sabhajit Misra (University of Gorakhpur), Dr. A. N. Pandey (Kashi Vidyapith), Dr. R. R. Pande (Banaras Hindu University), Dr. R. K. Tripathi (Banaras Hindu University), and Dr. S. P. Verma (Kuruksetra University).

Several research assistants have helped us in our work along the way, and we would like to thank and acknowledge them as well: Dr. Jayandra Soni, formerly of Banaras Hindu University and currently at McMaster University in Ontario, Canada; Dr. Paul Muller-Ortega, Dr. Wade Dazey, Dr. Michiko Yusa, and Dr. James McNamara, former doctoral students in religious studies at the University of California, Santa Barbara. Also, a special word of thanks for the research assistance of Dr. Edeltraud Harzer, of the University of Washington, Seattle. Our thanks, furthermore, to the American Institute of Indian Studies and the Indo-U.S. Subcommission for Education and Culture for financial assistance to our various contributors and to the coeditors, and, finally, our thanks and appreciation to Karl H. Potter for his continuing patience, encouragement, and help in his capacity as general editor of the *Encyclopedia of Indian Philosophies*.

For the nonspecialist reader of the volume, it should be noted that the Index provides brief definitions of many technical Sāṃkhya terms before listing page numbers and may be used, therefore, as a glossary for those unfamiliar with the Sanskrit terminology of the Sāṃkhya system. An additional glossary for classical Sāṃkhya terminology may also be found in Gerald J. Larson, *Classical Sāṃkhya* (2nd edition, Delhi: Motilal Banarsidass, 1979), pp. 237-247.

Full diacritical marks are given only for all primary entries of texts and authors in the volume. In the case of modern Indian scholars, namely, authors of secondary works, summarizers, and other contributors, names are cited without diacritical marks, in accordance with current convention in modern India, Likewise, the names of modern Indian cities are given without diacritical marks.

GERALD JAMES LARSON
January 1987 Santa Barbara, California, USA

PART ONE

INTRODUCTION TO THE PHILOSOPHY OF SĀṂKHYA

THE HISTORY AND LITERATURE OF SĀṂKHYA

I. Proto-Sāṃkhya and Pre-Kārikā-Sāṃkhya

The term "*sāṃkhya*" means "relating to number, enumeration, or calculation." As an adjective, the term refers to any enumerated set or grouping and can presumably be used in any inquiry in which enumeration or calculation is a prominent feature (for example, mathematics, grammar, prosody, psychology, medicine, and so forth). As a masculine noun, the term refers to someone who calculates, enumerates, or discriminates properly or correctly. As a neuter noun, the term comes to refer to a specific system of dualist philosophizing that proceeds by a method of enumerating the contents of experience and the world for the purpose of attaining radical liberation (*mokṣa*, *kaivalya*) from frustration and rebirth.

These three dimensions of meaning in the word "*sāṃkhya*" are not simply synchronic distinctions but indicate as well the diachronic or historical development of the word in the ancient period. That is to say, in the ancient history of South Asian culture there appear to be three identifiable phases of development of the term "*sāṃkhya*" that roughly correspond to these three basic meaning dimensions.[1] These can be briefly characterized as follows:

(1) Intellectual inquiry in the oldest learned traditions of ancient India (from the Vedic period, ca. 1500 before the Common Era [B.C.E.], through the Mauryan period in the fourth and third centuries B.C.E.) was frequently cast in the format of elaborate enumerations of the contents of a particular subject matter — for example, the principles of statecraft as preserved in Kauṭilya's *Arthaśāstra*, the principles of medicine as preserved in the *Carakasaṃhitā* and *Suśrutasaṃhitā*, and so forth. The Vedic corpus itself exhibits this tendency as do traditions of law (*nītiśāstra*) and politics (*rājadharma*), and it is in such environments that one finds some of the early references to *sāṃkhya*. Kauṭilya, for example, refers to

sāṃkhya as one of three traditions of *ānvīkṣikī*.[2] The notion of *ānvīkṣikī* in these ancient contexts means something like the enumeration of the contents of a particular subject matter by means of systematic reasoning.[3] The practice of *ānvīkṣikī* is not really "philosophy" in our usual senses of the term; it is, rather, a kind of general "scientific" inquiry by means of the systematic enumeration of basic principles.[4] Such enumerations appeared in a variety of intellectual subject areas, including phonology, grammar, statecraft, medicine, law, cosmology, and iconography, and the compilations of these subject-area enumerations sometimes came to be called "*tantras*" (meaning a scientific work, and synonymous with such terms as "*śāstra*," "*vidyā*", and so forth). Moreover, certain stylistic rules or "methodological devices" (*yuktis*) came to be accepted in composing scientific works—for example, a brief statement of a position (*uddeśa*), a lengthy exposition of a position (*nirdeśa*), an etymological explanation (*nirvacana*), the proper order or sequence in enumerating a subject (*vidhāna*), and so forth.[5] Kauṭilya's *Arthaśāstra* provides a list of such methodological devices, and the author illustrates how his work uses the various methodological devices, thereby establishing that his treatise is a scientific work. The medical texts (*Caraka* and *Suśruta*) are also scientific works in this sense and likewise provide lists of methodological devices. This may well explain why the later technical Sāṃkhya philosophy is frequently referred to as a *tantra*, and it helps in understanding the reasons why the long introduction to the *Yuktidīpikā* (the most important commentary on the *Sāṃkhyakārikā*), contains a detailed discussion of the methodological devices essential for any systematic inquiry. In this oldest period, however, it is undoubtedly an anachronism to interpret references to *sāṃkhya*, *ānvīkṣikī*, or *tantra* as themselves completed or distinct systems of thought, as some older scholars have suggested (Garbe, for example).[6] It is more plausible to interpret these references in a much more general sense as the first and groping attempts at systematic thinking, which proceeded by determining and enumerating the components of anything (whether it be the components of the human body, the components of the sacrificial ritual, the components of the heavens, or the components of grammar).

(2) A second phase in the development of the term "*sāṃkhya*" begins from the period of the oldest, pre-Buddhistic Upaniṣads, ca. eighth or seventh centuries B.C.E., and can be traced through traditions of the early ascetic spirituality in South Asia, namely, the various monastic (*śramaṇa* and *yati*) groups, the early Jain and Buddhist movements, and so forth, reaching a culmination in the sorts of speculative thinking one finds in the *Mokṣadharma* portion of the *Mahābhārata*, in the *Bhagavadgītā*, and in the cosmological descriptions of the oldest Purāṇas (or, in other words, reaching into the first centuries of the Common Era). If in the oldest period the term "*sāṃkhya*" could refer generally to any

enumerated set of principles (in an environment of *ānvīkṣikī* for the sake of constructing a scientific work), in this second period the notion becomes linked to a methodology of reasoning that results in spiritual knowledge (*vidyā*, *jñāna*, *viveka*) that leads to liberation from the cycle of frustration and rebirth. It is possible, of course, perhaps even likely, that in the oldest period the term "*sāṃkhya*" in its general sense of intellectual enumeration was applied on occasion in contexts of meditation and religious cosmology — the enumerations in *Ṛg Veda* I.164, X.90, or X.129, or the enumerations of the parts of the body or the breaths in the *Atharva Veda* or in the Brāhmaṇa literature would suggest as much — but there is little doubt that it is primarily in this second period that "*sāṃkhya*" becomes a prominent notion in those environments in which meditation, spirititual exercises, and religious cosmology represent the crucial subject matters.

The archaic ontology of *Chāndogya Upaniṣad* VI.2-5, for example, with its emphasis on primordial Being (*sat*) in its tripartite manifestations as fire (red), water (white), and food (black), correlated with speech, breath, and mind, probably foreshadows the later Sāṃkhya ontological notions of *prakṛti*, the three *guṇas*, and the preexistence of the effect. On one level, of course, this kind of reflection echoes older Vedic notions (for example, some of the number sequences and symbolism of RV.X.164), but, on another level, it represents a transition to later formulations such as those in *Śvetāśvatara Upaniṣad* — for example, "The One unborn, red, white, and black... ." (*Śvet. Up.* IV.5), and "Two birds, companions (who are) always united, cling to the selfsame tree..." (*Śvet. Up.* IV.6-7) — a text in which the older Vedic symbolism is clearly present and yet a text in which the terms "*sāṃkhya*" and "*yoga*" are actually used. Cosmological speculations such as these are combined with elaborate descriptions of yogic experience in such texts as *Kaṭha Upaniṣad*, *Mokṣadharma*, *Bhagavadgītā*, and *Buddhacarita*. The same sorts of speculation are used in the medical literature (*Carakasaṃhitā* and *Suśrutasaṃhitā*), and the hierarchical ordering of basic principles (*tattva*) is given a cosmological turn with respect to the periodic creation and dissolution of the manifest world in *Manusmṛti* and in most of the oldest Purāṇas. Certain characteristic notions become associated with Sāṃkhya, but throughout the period *Sāṃkhya* is primarily a methodology for attaining liberation and appears to allow for a great variety of philosophical formulations. Edgerton has expressed the matter well: "Any formula of metaphysical truth, provided that knowledge thereof was conceived to tend towards salvation, might be called Sāṃkhya.[7] ... It appears, then, that Sāṃkhya means in the Upaniṣads and the Epic simply the way of salvation by knowledge, and does not imply any system of metaphysical truth whatever."[8]

On one level, Sāṃkhya as a methodology for attaining salvation by knowing carries further many of the older cosmological notions of the oldest Upaniṣads as set forth in *Chāndogya Upaniṣad* VI, and so forth. On another level, Sāṃkhya as a methodology for attaining salvation by knowing carries further the various psychological analyses of experience that first appear in the oldest Upaniṣads and then become dominant motifs in Jain and Buddhist meditation contexts and in such later Upaniṣads as *Kaṭha* and *Śvetāśvatara*. The enumeration of basic principles in a hierarchical order is a fundamental aspect of the methodology, but the precise number of enumerated items varies widely. In some passages seventeen basic principles are enumerated;[9] in other passages twenty;[10] or twenty-four;[11] or the later, standard listing of twenty-five[12] are enumerated. On occasion the highest principle is the old Upaniṣadic *brahman* or *ātman*, or, again, the highest principle is God (*iśvara*). In some contexts the Sāṃkhya methodology implies a monistic perspective, in others a theistic or dualist perspective. Throughout the period, however, a characteristic terminology and a recurrent set of intellectual issues begin to develop around the methodology: reflections about a primordial materiality (*pradhāna*); enumerations of psychic states or conditions (*bhāvas*, *guṇas*) that can be construed psychologically and/or cosmologically; analyses of the various aspects of intellectual experience in terms of intellect/will (hereafter translated simply as "intellect") (*buddhi*), egoity (*ahaṃkāra*), and mind (*manas*); speculations about the nature of the inner self (*puruṣa*) in terms of a cosmic Self (*ātman*) or the self in the body or in the manifest world (*jiva*, *bhūtātman*); elaborations of the five sense capacities (*indriya*) correlated with the five gross elements (*bhūta*), the five action capacities (*karmendriya*), and the five contents or "objects" (*viṣaya*) of the senses; and a general polarity between subjectivity and objectivity in terms of "the knower of the field" (*kṣetrajña*) and "the field" (*kṣetra*). Clearly there is a system (or systems) in the process of developing, but the focus in this second period is rather on the process or methodology itself and not on the contents that result from the process.

In contrast to methods of spiritual discipline (*yoga*) that emphasize posture, breathing, recitation, and ascetic practices (*tapas*), *sāṃkhya* is the intellectual or reasoning method. The follower of *sāṃkhya* is one who reasons or discriminates properly, one whose spiritual discipline is meditative reasoning. This is probably the sense of the term "*sāṃkhya*" in the compound *sāṃkhya-yoga-adhigamya* ("to be understood by proper reasoning and spiritual discipline") in *Śvetāśvatara Upaniṣad* VI.13. It is probably also the sense meant in the twelfth chapter of Aśvaghoṣa's *Buddhacarita*, in which reference is made to older spiritual methodologies studied by Gotama the Buddha prior to the discovery of his own unique method of meditation. Regarding the specific contents of this reasoning methodology, J.A.B. van Buitenen has offered the following comment:

> There must have existed scores of more or less isolated little centres where parallel doctrines were being evolved out of a common source. Occasional meetings at pilgrimages and festivals, reports from other and remote *āśramas* brought by wandering ascetics, polemic encounters with other preachers must have resulted in a laborious process of partial renovation and conservation, more precise definitions of doctrines and eclecticisms, readjustments of terminology, etc. At this stage to credit these little centres with the name "schools" is to do them too much or too little honor. . . . Most of the process must elude us necessarily, but we stand a better chance of recovering the little that is left by allowing for the greatest diversity, rather than the greatest uniformity of doctrine.[13]

In the *Mokṣadharma* portion of the *Mahābhārata* various names of ancient teachers are associated with these developing traditions, including Kapila, Āsuri, Bhṛgu, Yājñavalkya, Sanatkumāra, Vasiṣṭha, Śuka, Asita Devala (or Asita and Devala), Vyāsa, Janaka, and Pañcaśikha. Some of these names can be traced back to the older Upaniṣads, and many of them also appear in the later Purāṇic literature. Three of them are frequently referred to in the later technical philosophical literature as important precursors of Sāṃkhya philosophy, namely, Kapila, Āsuri, and Pañcaśikha. The *Sāṃkhyakārikā* and its commentaries refer to Kapila and Āsuri as the founders of the philosophical system and to Pañcaśikha as a teacher who greatly expanded or revised the original teachings. Unfortunately, all three teachers are lost to antiquity. References to Kapila and Āsuri are brief and largely eulogistic, and the situation is not much better with Pañcaśikha. Fragments here and there are attributed to a certain "Pañcaśikha," and Pañcaśikha on occasion is referred to as the author of a massive treatise in verse on Sāṃkhya philosophy called *Ṣaṣṭitantra.* The views attributed to Pañcaśikha in the *Mokṣadharma,* however, appear to be clearly different from the views that can be pieced together from the fragments, suggesting that there was more than one Pañcaśikha or that the name Pañcaśikha was a revered name in the tradition to which a variety of views were ascribed.[14] Moreover, the claim that Pañcaśikha is the author of the *Ṣaṣṭitantra* is contradicted by other references that attribute authorship of *Ṣaṣṭitantra* to Kapila or to a certain Vārṣagaṇya. It is reasonable to suppose, however, that Pañcaśikha was a revered teacher of *sāṃkhya* in the sense that has been indicated in this second period, that is, *sāṃkhya* not yet as a fixed philosophical system, but as a general methodology of salvation by knowing or reasoning. It is also reasonable to suppose that practitioners of *sāṃkhya* in this sense represent various kinds of ancient lines of teachers (*guruparamparā*) that traced their lineages to archaic figures such as Kapila and Āsuri (in much the same fashion as Jains and Buddhists claimed archaic precursors for their traditions).

What is missing in all of these environments, however, is a critical appreciation for the need to argue for or establish an intellectual basis for these speculative intuitions. Reasoning, to be sure, is being used, but it is a reasoning not yet distinguished from the immediacy of personal experience and the accumulated heritage of ritual performance and priestly wisdom. There is, of course, some groping for independence and a growing recognition that thinking itself may be a unique human activity that can exert its own identity against the established and received ordering of things. The very fact that much Upaniṣadic speculation appears to have been developed in princely (*rājanya*) or warrior (*kṣatriya*) circles (as opposed to priestly groups) and that the early independent ascetic movements (Jains, Buddhists, and so forth) were especially successful among the newly emerging commercial classes in towns where commerce and a monied economy were developing, certainly suggest that thoughtful persons were in need of new and independent ways of thinking and behaving. Moreover, that the political consolidation achieved under the Mauryans appears to have been legitimized by a notion of *dharma* and a theory of the state that owed more to Jain and Buddhist paradigms than to older Vedic models is also symptomatic of changes that were occurring in other areas of intellectual life. Similarly, the rise of devotional and theistic movements (the Kṛṣṇa cult, and so forth) in the last centuries before the beginning of the Common Era is an additional symptom of a broadly based cultural need to develop new and different patterns of intellectual formulation. Many of these tensions and changes come together intellectually in the *Bhagavadgītā*, and it is surely no accident that the so-called "philosophy" of the *Gītā* is little more than a potpourri of Upaniṣadic speculation, cosmological and psychological *sāṃkhya* reasoning, Jain and Buddhist ascetic motifs, *varṇāśramadharma* as *karmayoga*, tied together with an apologia for early Vaiṣṇava *bhaktiyoga* — a potpourri that confuses a modern reader almost as much as it confused Arjuna.

In older German scholarship there was an interesting debate as to whether the kind of "philosophy" one finds in the epics (including the *Gītā*) and the Purāṇas is pure syncretism (*Mischphilosophie*, as in Garbe) or transitional philosophy (*Übergangsphilosophie*, as in Oldenberg).[15] The resolution of the debate is surely the correctness of both, or possibly neither, for the crucial point is that there is no evidence of serious independent philosophizing of any kind in these texts. Whether one wishes to call these traditions syncretistic religion (or what we usually mean when we use the terms "Hinduism" and "Buddhism") or prephilosophical speculation on the way to becoming philosophy (or what we usually mean when we use the expressions "the philosophy of the Vedas and Upaniṣads" in regard to the Vedic corpus or "early Buddhist philosophy" in regard to the Buddhist canonical texts of the *Tripiṭaka*) makes little difference. They all have in common a predilection for speculative intuition in an environment of received authority. Returning, however, to Sāṃkhya, the point to be stressed is that in this ancient period there is only a Proto-Sāṃkhya. There was, of course, an incipient philosophical Sāṃkhya gradually distilling itself out of this diffuse and varied intellectual heritage, but the evidence suggests that it was not at first taken very seriously. Whenever it is referred to (in the *Mokṣadharma* or the *Gītā*, for example), it is simply discounted and characterized as not really being different from Yoga.[16] Taken overall, then, it is heuristically permissible to refer to this second period of development of Sāṃkhya as Kapila-Pañcaśikha-Sāṃkhya, or to carry through the association of the term "*sāṃkhya*" with the term "*tantra*" from the oldest period, to refer to this second period as Kapila-Pañcaśikha-Tantra, or simply as Kapila-Tantra.

(3) The third phase in the development of the term "*sāṃkhya*" marks the beginning of the technical philosophical tradition and coincides with the end of the second period, namely, from about the last century B.C.E. through the first several centuries C.E. Until recently this third phase was as shrouded in obscurity as the second phase, and Edgerton, for example, in 1924 claimed that Sāṃkhya as a technical philosophical system was not really in existence prior to Īśvarakṛṣṇa's *Sāṃkhyakārikā*.[17] Since then, however, three sources have become available that clearly indicate that Sāṃkhya as a technical system existed prior to Īśvarakṛṣṇa, and that Īśvarakṛṣṇa's own formulation comes at the end of the normative period of formulation rather than at the beginning. These three sources are (A) the publication of a previously unknown commentary on the *Sāṃkhyakārikā* called *Yuktidīpikā* (edited by P. Chakravarti in 1938, and edited a second time by R. C. Pandeya in 1967);[18] (B) the reconstruction of a pre-*Kārikā* interpretation of Sāṃkhya epistemology based on quotations from older Sāṃkhya texts cited in Dignāga, Jinendrabuddhi, Mallavādin, and Siṃhasūri by E. Frauwallner;[19] and (C) the reconstruction of a Sāṃkhya "emanation text" or a "short instructional tract" from the earliest Purāṇas and the *Mokṣadharma*, which Purāṇic editors then brought into conformity with the normative view of an established Sāṃkhya philosophical system, by P. Hacker.[20]

(A) From the *Yuktidīpikā* it becomes clear that there was a tradition of philosophical Sāṃkhya in the early centuries of the Common Era that was more than a methodology of liberation by knowing (that is to say, more than the rather diffuse Sāṃkhya-Yoga traditions characteristic of the second period described above), and, specifically, that this tradition (1) attempted to establish certain instruments of knowledge (*pramāṇas*) and to offer careful definitions of these instruments;

(2) developed a special interest in inference (*anumāna*) and constructed a sequence for making inferences made up of ten members (*avayavas*); (3) attempted, after much debate, to fix the number of basic principles, together with the precise order of their enumeration, including the technical term "subtle element" (*tanmātra*); (4) fully developed the related notions of *prakṛti*, the three *guṇas*, the transformation of the *guṇas* (*guṇapariṇāma*), and the effect's preexistence in the cause (*satkārya*); (5) finally accepted after much controversy one primordial *prakṛti* but a plurality of *puruṣas*; (6) maintained a rich fabric of internal debate involving such teachers as Paurika, Pañcādhikaraṇa, Patañjali, Vārṣagaṇya, and various schools such as the "followers of Vārṣagaṇya," including Vindhyavāsin and Īśvarakṛṣṇa,[21] and (7) maintained as well a vigorous polemic of external debate with certain Buddhist philosophers and with the followers of early Vaiśeṣika. (8) It also identified itself with a tradition known as *ṣaṣṭitantra*, which apparently referred to a scheme of sixty topics made up of ten principal topics (*mūlikārtha*) and fifty subsidiary categories (*padārtha*) and which also apparently referred to a text (or possibly texts, that is to say, more than one version) by the same name (*Ṣaṣṭitantra*); and (9) it received its final normative formulation in Īśvarakṛṣṇa's *Sāṃkhyakārikā*, which, though a brief text, nevertheless encompassed all of the important issues of the system in a concise and cogent fashion.

(B) From Frauwallner's reconstruction it becomes clear that Pre-*Kārikā* philosophical Sāṃkhya operated with a definition of perception ("the functioning of the ear, etc.", *śrotrādi-vṛttiḥ*) and a definition of inference ("because of the perception of one aspect of an established relation, one is able to infer the other aspect of a relation," *sambandhād ekasmāt pratyakṣāt śeṣasiddhir anumānam*, based on a scheme of seven established relations, or *saptasambandha*) that Īśvarakṛṣṇa clearly built upon and improved. Frauwallner speculates that this older Sāṃkhya epistemology derives from a revised version of *Ṣaṣṭitantra* composed by Vārṣagaṇya at the beginning of the fourth century of the Common Era. Such may or may not be the case, but the reconstructed passages do point to a pre-*kārikā* philosophical Sāṃkhya epistemology.[22]

(C) Finally, from Hacker's reconstruction it becomes clear that there was an older Sāṃkhya ontology-cosmology that, again, formed the bases for Īśvarakṛṣṇa's normative conceptualization in the *Sāṃkhyakārikā*.[23]

Apparently, this philosophical tradition of Sāṃkhya developed some time between the sorts of speculation one finds in the *Mokṣadharma* and the *Bhagavadgītā*, on the one hand, and the sort of normative conceptualization one finds in the *Śāṃkhyakārikā*, on the other. Moreover, it appears to coincide with the development of comparable conceptualizations within traditions of early Buddhist thought and early Vaiśeṣika. It is tempting to suggest with Frauwallner that this

Sāṃkhya philosophical tradition is the oldest of the technical schools of Indian philosophy (Hindu, Buddhist, or Jain) and that Buddhist ontology, Vaiśeṣika atomism, and Nyāya epistemology may all have arisen out of an earlier Sāṃkhya philosophical environment, but this is perhaps to claim too much. To be sure, all of the later technical systems undoubtedly derive from the sorts of fluid speculation one finds in the "middle"-verse Upaniṣads (*Kaṭha*, and so forth), the *Mokṣadharma*, and the *Bhagavadgītā*, in which Sāṃkhya is primarily a methodology for liberation by knowing. When the term "sāṃkhya" becomes linked with a technical philosophical system, however, one has the impression that there has been a definite turn away from the older diffuse speculations and that philosophical Sāṃkhya has become a parallel or sibling intellectual movement alongside Vaiśeṣika and the early Buddhist schools, rather than a parental tradition to these schools.

Unfortunately, although the *Yuktidīpikā* refers to a number of older Sāṃkhya philosophical teachers, it is difficult to ascertain even rough approximations of their dates. Paurika, who evidently accepted a plurality of *prakṛtis* along with a plurality of *puruṣas*, was probably an older teacher whose views were finally rejected during the final stages of normative consolidation. Similarly, Pañcādhikaraṇa, who accepted only ten organs instead of the normative thirteen, was also probably an older teacher. Moreover, Pañcādhikaraṇa appears to have had a somewhat eccentric view concerning the subtle body, which later teachers rejected. Also, Patañjali (not to be confused with the compiler of the *Yogasūtra* and/or the grammarian) is apparently an older figure, for his views that there was a new subtle body for each rebirth and that egoity has no separate existence as a basic principle apart from the intellect were discounted in the final formulation of the *Sāṃkhya* system.

Vārṣagaṇya, however, and the followers of Vārṣagaṇya, including Vindhyavāsin, appear to have been closer to the time of Īśvarakṛṣṇa. Indeed, it could well be the case that Īśvarakṛṣṇa was himself in the lineage of Vārṣagaṇya. Frauwallner has suggested, basing his opinion primarily on citations of Vārṣagaṇya's views in the works of Vācaspati Miśra, that Vārṣagaṇya was the author of a revised version of the *Ṣaṣṭitantra*, older versions of which had been attributed to Kapila or Pañcaśikha. Vindhyavāsin is said to have been a pupil of Vārṣagaṇya, to have revised the developing system further, and, according to Paramārtha's "Life of Vasubandhu," to have defeated Vasubandhu's teacher (Buddhamitra, according to Paramārtha, or Manoratha, according to Hsüan Tsang's pupil, Kuei-chi) in a debate during the reign of Candragupta II (ca. fourth century).[24] Vasubandhu, according to Chinese sources, then composed a rejoinder to Vindhyavāsin. Also, Hsüan-tsang (seventh century) refers to a later debate between Guṇamati and a certain Sāṃkhya teacher, Mādhava, by name.[25] It is interesting to observe, however, that the views of Vindhyavāsin (as set forth in the *Yuktidīpikā*) and Mādhava (as set forth in Dignāga) diverge considerably from the views of Īśvarakṛṣṇa. Vindhyavāsin clearly preceded Īśvarakṛṣṇa, for the author of the *Yuktidīpikā* indicates that Īśvarakṛṣṇa refrained from discussing the tenfold inference, since it had already been discussed by Vindhyavāsin. Moreover, the author of the *Yuktidīpikā* claims that Vindhyavāsin rejected the notion of a subtle body (because the sense capacities are ubiquitous and do not, therefore, require a subtle vehicle for transmigration); and that he accepted neither the contention that the subtle elements emerge out of egoity (since they emerge, rather, along with egoity from the intellect) nor the notion of a thirteenfold instrument (*trayodaśakaraṇa*) (since he argued instead that experience occurs in the mind, thus reducing intellect, egoity, and mind to one organ of internal experience, which, along with the ten sense capacities make a total of eleven organs instead of thirteen). These variant views of Vindhyavāsin are suspiciously similar to the views of Vyāsa in his *Yogasūtrabhāṣya*, a similarity that has inclined both Chakravarti and Frauwallner to suggest that the Vārṣagaṇya-Vindhyavāsin line of Sāṃkhya is preserved in the Pātañjala-Sāṃkhya of classical Yoga philosophy.[26]

Mādhava, on the other hand, appears to have been later than Īśvarakṛṣṇa, for the reported debate with Guṇamati occurred around the time of Dignāga (ca. 480-540) a period in which the normative view of Sāṃkhya was already established. Moreoever, Dignāga refers to Mādhava as a Sāṃkhya heretic or "destroyer of Sāṃkhya" (*sāṃkhya-vaināśika*, *sāṃkhya-nāśaka*) because he interprets the notion of *prakṛti* and the three *guṇas* as a plurality of primordial materialities (thus taking *prakṛti* in the direction of Vaiśeṣika atomism). Then, too, Mādhava appears to have believed that action (*karman*) resides in this plurality of kinds of stuff and that the cycle of rebirth (*saṃsāra*) is beginningless (thereby implicitly denying the Sāṃkhya notion of emanation).

In all of this, it is quite clear that Sāṃkhya was a vigorous and polemical philosophical system, and one is tempted to believe the old Chinese claim that there were as many as eighteen schools of philosophical Sāṃkhya (though the parallel with the eighteen Buddhist schools is probably no accident). This must have been intellectually a remarkable stage in the development of Sāṃkhya, and of Indian philosophy generally, for it was evidently in this creative and formative period in the first several centuries of the Common Era that the main issues of Indian philosophy were first formulated and polemically discussed: the number and definition of .the instruments of knowledge, theories of ontology and causation, the role and function of knowing and ignorance, the theory of error, the problem of selfhood, the problem of action and rebirth, and the problem of freedom and bondage. All of these issues had been discussed earlier, but the crucial task in this first philosophical period was that of systematic formulation, overall intellectual coherence, and persuasive presentation. Earlier diffuse traditions were brought together and codified in collections of *sūtras* and *kārikās* — one thinks, for example, not only of the *Sāṃkhyakārikā* but of Nāgārjuna's, and, later, Gauḍapāda's *kārikās*, and, of course, the early *sūtra* collections of Vaiśeṣika, Nyāya, Mīmāṃsā, and Vedānta; patterns of training students were being established; commentaries were being composed explaining the emerging technical terminology; and rules for discussion and debate were being formulated. These developments in Indian philosophy mirrored similar developments in literature, art, law, medicine, and social reality generally. The older Mauryan political hegemony had collapsed centuries earlier and the resulting decentralized regionalism had generated a resurgence of local traditions that now found themselves in creative tension with one another as the Gupta political unification (beginning in the fourth century under Candra Gupta [ca. 320]) reopened once again a broader cultural environment that transcended the older provincialism.

Taking all of these disparate (and admittedly problematic) historical observations together, one might suggest a tentative chronology for early philosophical Sāṃkhya:

(1) *Ṣaṣṭitantra*, a tradition of "sixty topics" that was either a format for the treatment of philosophical Sāṃkhya or the actual name of a text, an old form of which was attributed either to Kapila or Pañcaśikha—ca. 100 B.C.E.-200 C.E.[27]

(2) Paurika, Pañcādhikaraṇa, Patañjali, and other early philosophical *ācāryas*—100-300 C.E.

(3) Vārṣagaṇya, who composes a revision of the *Ṣaṣṭitantra*—ca. 100-300 C.E.

(4) Followers of Vārṣagaṇya, including
  (a) Vindhyavāsin, ca. 300-400, who further revises the Sāṃkhya system and who carries on a vigorous polemic with the Buddhists, and
  (b) Īśvarakṛṣṇa, ca. 350-450, who composes a definitive summary of the Sāṃkhya position, the *Sāṃkhyakārikā*, based on Vārṣagaṇya's *Ṣaṣṭitantra* but corrected as a result of the Buddhist debates and the work of Vindhyavāsin.

(5) Mādhava, the "destroyer of Sāṃkhya," who goes even further in adjusting the views of Sāṃkhya to Vaiśeṣika and Buddhist thought—ca. 450-500.

(6) Patañjali's *Yogasūtra* and Vyāsa's *Yogasūtrabhāṣya*, which possibly preserve the older Vārṣagaṇya-Vindhyavāsin interpretation of Sāṃkhya in the format of Pātañjala-Sāṃkhya—ca. 500-700.

This, then, brings us to the threshold of the beginning of technical philosophical Sāṃkhya as set forth in the normative account of Īśvarakṛṣṇa's *Sāṃkhyakārikā*. Up to this point there has been no available Sāṃkhya textual tradition, and the historical account has been based on reconstructions and occasional references in the ancient literature. Nevertheless, we have been able to identify (at least heuristically) three phases in the development of Sāṃkhya that roughly parallel the three basic meanings of the term, namely, *sāṃkhya* as any enumerated set or grouping (Tantra); *sāṃkhya* as a method properly employed by a discriminating person (Kapila-Tantra); and *sāṃkhya* as an early tradition of dualist philosophizing (Ṣaṣṭi-Tantra), which attained a normative formulation in the work of Īśvarakṛṣṇa.

From this point on there is an identifiable textual tradition, and the task of writing a history of Sāṃkhya thought is on somewhat firmer ground.[28]

II. The Sāṃkhya Textual Tradition

Because we have now reached the beginning of the Sāṃkhya textual tradition, summaries of the contents of which make up the main part of the volume, it may be useful, first of all, to present a Checklist of Texts and Authors of the Sāṃkhya tradition as a whole and then to comment in some detail about the historical development of the textual tradition in its various parts. We are dealing, of course, with a sweep of intellectual history that covers nearly two thousand years (indeed, more than two thousand years if one includes the Proto-Sāṃkhya and Pre-Kārikā traditions already briefly discussed), so it will only be possible to discuss the high points of Sāṃkhya's intellectual history. It is important, however, to provide at least a rough outline of the history of the tradition so that the philosophical discussions in the sequel have an appropriate historical framework.

CHECKLIST OF TEXTS AND AUTHORS

TEXT	*AUTHOR*	*DATE*
(PROTO-SĀṂKHYA):		
Chāndogya Upaniṣad	?	ca. 800-600 B.C.E.
Kaṭha Upaniṣad	?	400-200
Śvetāśvatara Upaniṣad	?	400-200
Arthaśāstra	Kauṭilya	300 (core text)
Mokṣadharma (*Mahābhārata*)	?	ca. 200 B.C.E.-200 C.E.
Bhagavadgītā (*Mahābhārata*)	?	200 B.C.E.-200 C.E.
Manusmṛti (and other lawbooks)	?	200 B.C.E.-200 C.E.
Buddhacarita	Aśvaghoṣa	ca. 100 C.E.

TEXT	*AUTHOR*	*DATE*
Carakasaṃhitā (Āyurveda)	Caraka	100-200 C.E.
Suśrutasaṃhitā (Āyurveda)	Suśruta	200-300 C.E.
Purāṇas (*Mārkaṇḍeya*, *Vāyu*, etc.)	?	300 C.E. and after
?	(Kapila, Āsuri, and Pañcaśikha are names frequently linked with the old Sāṃkhya traditions mentioned in the above texts)	?
(PRE-KĀRIKĀ-SĀṂKHYA):		
Ṣaṣṭitantra (either a text or systematic format for discussing Sāṃkhya)	Pañcaśikha (but also attributed to Kapila and Vārṣagaṇya)	ca. 100 B.C.E.-200 C.E.
?	Paurika	?
?	Pañcādhikaraṇa	?
?	Patañjali (other than the Patañjali of the Yoga tradition)	?
Ṣaṣṭitantra (possibly a revised version or format of an older tradition)	Vārṣagaṇya (but also attributed, as noted above, to Kapila and Pañcaśikha)	ca. 100-300 C.E.
?	Vindhyavāsin	ca. 300-400 C.E.
?	Mādhava (referred to as a Sāṃkhya heretic by Dignāga)	? (but probably later than Īśvarakṛṣṇa)
(KĀRIKĀ-SĀṂKHYA and PĀTAÑJALA-SĀṂKHYA):		
Sāṃkhyakārikā (SK)	Īśvarakṛṣṇa	ca. 350-450 C.E.
* (*Yogasūtra*)	(Patañjali)	(ca. 400-500 C.E.)
Suvarṇasaptati (SS)	? (translated by Paramārtha into Chinese)	translated into Chinese, 557-569C.E. composed ca. 500C.E.
Sāṃkhyavṛtti (SV)	?	ca. 500-600

*A few important Yoga texts are included in the résumé for comparative purposes. They are not dealt with in detail, however, since another volume in this series will be given over to the history of Yoga philosophy.

TEXT	*AUTHOR*	*DATE*
Sāṃkhyasaptativṛtti (SSV)	?	ca. 500-600
Bhāṣya (GB)	Gauḍapāda	ca. 500-600
* (*Sāṃkhyapravacana-bhāṣya*) (on *Yoga-sūtra*)	(Vyāsa)	(ca. 500-700) (?)
Yuktidīpikā (YD)	?	ca. 600-700
Jayamaṅgalā (J)	? (Śaṃkara or Śaṃkarārya)	ca. 700 or later
* (*Yogasūtrabhāṣya-vivaraṇa*)	(Śaṃkarabhagavat)	(ca. 700 or later)
Māṭharavṛtti (M)	Māṭhara	ca. 800 or later

(KĀRIKĀ-KAUMUDĪ-SĀṂKHYA; SAMĀSA-SĀṂKHYA; and SŪTRA-SĀṂKHYA):

Sāṃkhyatattvakaumudī (STK)	Vācaspati Miśra	ca. 850 or 975 C.E.
* (*Tattvavaiśāradī*)	(Vācaspati Miśra)	(ca. 850 or 975 C.E.)
* (*Rājamārtaṇḍa*)	(Bhojarāja)	(ca. 1150)
Tattvasamāsasūtra	?	ca. 1300-1400
Kramadīpikā (on *Tattvasamāsa*)	?	ca. 1300-1400
Sāṃkhyasūtra	?	ca. 1400-1500
Sāṃkhyasūtravṛtti	Aniruddha	ca. 1400-1500
Sāṃkhyapravacanabhāṣya (on *Sāṃkhyasūtra*)	Vijñānabhikṣu	ca. 1550-1600
* (*Yogavārttika*)	(Vijñānabhikṣu)	(ca. 1550-1600)
Sāṃkhyasāra	Vijñānabhikṣu	ca. 1550-1600
* (*Yogasārasaṃgraha*)	(Vijñānabhikṣu)	(ca. 1550-1600)
Tattvayāthārthyadīpana (on *Tattvasamāsa*)	Bhāvagaṇeśa	ca. 1550-1600
Vṛttisāra (on *Sāṃkhyasūtra*)	Mahādeva Vedāntin	ca. 1650-1700
Guṇatrayaviveka	Svayaṃprakāśayati	ca. 1650-1700
Sāṃkhyacandrikā (on *Sāṃkhyakārikā* as read by Gauḍapāda)	Nārāyaṇatīrtha	ca. 1680-1720
Sāṃkhyasūtravṛtti (on *Sāṃkhyasūtra*)	Nāgoji Bhaṭṭa, or Nāgeśa	ca. 1700-1750
Sāṃkhyatattvavibhākara (on *Tattvakaumudī*)	Vaṃśidhara	ca. 1750

(KĀRIKĀ-KAUMUDĪ-SĀṂKHYA; SAMĀSA-SĀṂKHYA; and SŪTRA-SĀṂKHYA continued)

Sāṃkhyatattvavivecana (on *Tattvasamāsa*)	Ṣimānanda (or Kṣemendra)	ca. 1700-1900
Sarvopakāriṇīṭīkā (on *Tattvasamāsa*)	?	ca. 1700-1900
Sāṃkhyasūtravivaraṇa (on *Tattvasamāsa*)	?	ca. 1700-1900
Sāṃkhyatattvapradīpa	Kavirāja Yati	ca. 1700-1900
Sāṃkhyataruvasanta	Muḍumba Narasiṃhasvāmin	ca. 1700-1900

TEXT	*AUTHOR*	*DATE*
(KĀRIKĀ-SĀṂKHYA; SAMĀSA-SĀṂKHYA; and SŪTRA-SĀṂKHYA continued):		
Sāṃkhyatattvavilāsa (on *Tattvasamāsa*)	Raghunātha Tarkavāgīśa	ca. 1800-1900
Sāṃkhyataraṅga	Devatīrtha Svāmin	ca. 1850
Upodghāta (on *Tattvakaumudī*)	Tārānātha Tarkavācaspati	ca. 1865
Tattvasamāsabhāṣya	Narendranātha Tattvanidhi	ca. 1871
Tattvakaumudīvyākhyā	Bhāratī Yati	ca. 1889
Amalā (on *Sāṃkhyasūtravṛtti*)	Pramathanātha Tarkabhūṣaṇa	*ca. 20th century (published edition, 1900)
Āvaraṇavāriṇī (on *Tattvakaumudī*)	Kṛṣṇanātha Nyāyapañcānana	ca. 20th century (1902)
Vṛtti (on *Sāṃkhyasūtra*)	Hariprasāda	ca. 20th century (1905)
Vidvattoṣiṇī (on *Tattvakaumudī*)	Bālarāma Udāsīna	ca. 20th century (1907)
Pūrṇimā (on *Tattvakaumudī*)	Pañcānana Tarkaratna	ca. 20th century (1919)
Tattvabodhinī (on *Sāṃkhyasūtravṛtti*)	Kuñjavihāri Tarkasiddhānta	ca. 20th century (1919)
Kiraṇāvalī (on *Tattvakaumudī*)	Kṛṣṇavallabhācārya	ca. 20th century (1924)
Sāṃkhyakārikābhāṣya	Kṛṣṇavallabhācārya	ca. 20th century (1933)
Tattvakaumudīṭīkā	Rājeśvara Śāstrī Drāviḍa	ca. 20th century (1932)
Guṇamayī	Rameścandra Tarkatīrtha	ca. 20th century (1935)
Vivekapradīpa (on *Sāṃkhyasāra*)	Rameścandra Tarkatīrtha	ca. 20th century
Sāraprabhā (on *Sāṃkhyasāra*)	Kālīpada Tarkācārya	ca. 20th century
Sāṃkhyatattvāloka	Hariharānanda Āraṇya	ca. 20th century (1936)
Suṣamā (on *Tattvakaumudī*)	Harirāma Śukla	ca. 20th century (1937)
Sārabodhinī (on *Tattvakaumudī*)	Śivanārāyaṇa Śāstrin	ca. 20th century (1940)
Sāṃkhyavasanta	Naraharinātha	ca. 20th century (1946)
Abhinavarājalakṣmī (on *Tattvakaumudī*)	Sītarāma Śāstrī	ca. 20th century (1953)
Sāṃkhyasūtrabhāṣya	Brahmamuni	ca. 20th century (1955)
Sāṃkhyatattvapradīpikā	Keśava	ca. 20th century (1969)

*Here and following are works of the twentieth century. Specific dates indicate available published editions in libraries and bookstores.

TEXT	*AUTHOR*	*DATE*
Tattvamīmāṃsā	Kṛṣṇa Miśra	ca. 20th century (1969)
Sāṃkhyaparibhāṣā	?	ca. 20th century (1969)
Sāṃkhyasiddhāntaparāmarśa	M.V. Upādhyāya	ca. 20th century (1972)
Sāṃkhyarahasya	Śrī Rāma Pāṇḍeya	ca. 20th century

The Checklist begins with a sequence of texts that clearly are not Sāṃkhya philosophical texts but represent, rather, the probable intellectual environments from which the later Sāṃkhya philosophy arose. These may be conveniently designated as Proto-Sāṃkhya environments. Sāṃkhya philosophy proper begins with what the Checklist calls Pre-Kārikā-Sāṃkhya, including the tradition known as *ṣaṣṭitantra*, older teachers such as Paurika, Pañcādhikaraṇa, Vārṣagaṇya, Vindhyavāsin, and so forth. As already suggested, this was undoubtedly an exciting and crucial period in the development of Sāṃkhya philosophy. Unfortunately, however, the important details of this formative period escape us, for no texts remain and the interpreter is forced to reconstruct what might have occurred from stray references and occasional quotations in the later literature.

A. Kārikā-Sāṃkhya and Pātañjala-Sāṃkhya

What is available and what perforce must represent the beginning of the Sāṃkhya textual tradition are two summary compilations, namely, Īśvarakṛṣṇa's *Sāṃkhyakārikā* and Patañjali's *Yogasūtra*, truly remarkable works by any measure, but nevertheless reflecting the end products of a process of intellectual formulation rather than the process itself. These are two victors, as it were, in an intellectual war whose memories of specific battles have become hazy, reflecting, on one level, the arrogance of victory that attracts fellow travellers who in many cases were not part of the original conflict (namely, copyists and commentators) and, on another level, the security of peace that inevitably allows for endless scholastic recapitulation and a mindless defensiveness that can only finally be dislodged by yet another major conflict. Both of these summary compilations have many commentaries attached to them, but with the exception of the *Yuktidīpikā* and the *Tattvakaumudī* on the *Sāṃkhyakārikā* and Vyāsa's *Bhāṣya*, Śaṃkara's *Vivaraṇa*, and Vācaspati's *Tattvavaiśāradī* on the *Yogasūtra*, all of the commentaries are less than satisfactory. To be sure, here and there each commentary offers valuable explanations of basic terms or helpful illustrations on a particular issue, but the reader gains an unmistakable sense that somehow the commentator neglects to come to grips with the deeper issues or fundamental rationality of the Sāṃkhya system. One possible explanation is that the commentators are simply assuming a knowledge of the basic system itself and construing their task as one of providing notations on this or that point. Another possible explanation, perhaps more likely, is that there was a definite break in the tradition at an early point and that the commentators are themselves at a loss in understanding the deeper issues of the system. In any case, what comes through is that there is a basic and normative Sāṃkhya philosophy, concisely yet completely set forth in Īśvarakṛṣṇa's *Sāṃkhyakārikā* and appropriated with a somewhat different inflection in Patañjali's *Yoga-sūtra* for the sake of yogic praxis. The former can be called simply the tradition of Kārikā-Sāṃkhya and the latter, Pātañjala-Sāṃkhya.

From a historical point of view we know very little about this early textual period extending from the fourth to the eighth century. The precise date of Īśvarakṛṣṇa's *Sāṃkhyakārikā* is unknown, but the text together with a commentary was translated into Chinese by Paramārtha during the last phase of his literary activity, 557-569. Little is known about Īśvarakṛṣṇa beyond the passing reference in the Chinese commentary to his being a Brahmin of the Kauśika family and the reference in the *Jayamaṅgalā* that he was a *parivrājaka*. If we assume with Frauwallner and others that a normative Sāṃkhya philosophical system was known in the time of Dignāga (ca. 480-540) and that the views of a certain Sāṃkhya teacher, Mādhava, were judged to be heretical from the perspective of the normative system, this would suggest that a philosophical school of Sāṃkhya must have been in existence well before the middle of the fifth century. Moreover, if we accept the evidence of the *Yuktidīpikā* that Vārṣagaṇya and Vindhyavāsin preceded Īśvarakṛṣṇa, and if we accept Frauwallner's view that Vārṣagaṇya worked probably at the beginning of the fourth century (ca. 300) or earlier, this would indicate that Īśvarakṛṣṇa's *Sāṃkhyakārikā* may be reasonably placed in the middle of the fourth century (ca. 350). It must be admitted, however, that the date for a so-called "normative" Sāṃkhya — the term "normative" referring to the Sāṃkhya system as reflected in the *Sāṃkhyakārikā* — may be older than Īśvarakṛṣṇa. The *Sāṃkhyakārikā* by its own admission is only a summary account of an older tradition or text called *ṣaṣṭitantra*, and it could well be the case that Īśvarakṛṣṇa in his *Sāṃkhyakārikā* is summarizing an old normative Sāṃkhya system that predates both Vārṣagaṇya and Vindhyavāsin. In other words, simply because Īśvarakṛṣṇa postdates Vārṣagaṇya and Vindhyavāsin (as suggested in the *Yuktidīpikā*), it does not at all follow that his account of the Sāṃkhya is later than theirs conceptually. To the contrary, according to the *Yuktidīpikā*, Īśvarakṛṣṇa appears to have disagreed with some of the views of Vārṣagaṇya and Vindhyavāsin and may have cast his summary account of the Sāṃkhya system using an older model. In any case, it appears likely that Īśvarakṛṣṇa was familiar with the views of Vārṣagaṇya and Vindhyavāsin and, more than that, was familiar with the various debates that were taking place in the first centuries of the Common Era with the Buddhist and early Vaiśeṣika thinkers, and it is reasonable to assume that he was attempting a final definitive statement of the Sāṃkhya position in his *Sāṃkhyakārikā*. Whether other Sāṃkhya teachers of the time accepted Īśvarakṛṣṇa's account or even considered it a faithful summary of the whole system is an open question, although there can be no doubt that in subsequent centuries the *Sāṃkhyakārikā* became the definitive and normative statement of the Sāṃkhya position. To place the *Kārikā* account of Sāṃkhya in the middle of the fourth century, therefore, or to link the normative views of Sāṃkhya with the *Kārikā* is only to offer a reasonable interpretation of the extant evidence. The normative system may, in fact, be much older, and there must have surely been fuller accounts of the normative system than that found in the *Kārikā*. Current evidence, however, relegates such suggestions to the realm of scholarly speculation.

There are eight available commentaries on the *Sāṃkhyakārikā* from this early commentarial period, namely, (1) *Suvarṇasaptati* (Paramārtha's Chinese translation), (2) *Sāṃkhyavṛtti*, (3) *Sāṃkhyasaptativṛtti*, (4) Gauḍapāda's *Bhāṣya*, (5) *Yuktidīpikā*, (6) *Jayamaṅgalā*, (7) *Māṭharavṛtti*, and (8) Vācaspati Miśra's *Sāṃkhyatattvakaumudī*. Reliable dates are only available for the first and last texts on the list. As already mentioned, Paramārtha's Chinese translation of the *Suvarṇasoptati* was completed by the middle of the sixth century (557-569). It is also known that the famous Vācaspati Miśra did his work in the ninth or tenth century (either 841 or 976).[29] Apart from these two approximations, unfortunately, there is little reliable evidence for dating the other commentaries, although there are suggestive hints here and there. The *Yuktidīpikā* for example, probably precedes Vācaspati Miśra, for the latter quotes some verses regarding the makeup of the *ṣaṣṭitantra*, verses that are also quoted in the opening section of the *Yuktidīpikā*. Moreover, the *Yuktidīpikā* quotes both Dignāga (ca., 480-540) and Bhartṛhari (ca., fifth to early sixth century) but does not seem to quote directly Dharmakīrti (ca., 650), thus making it plausible to suggest that it is a work of the beginning of the seventh century (ca., 600). Regarding Gauḍapāda, if one accepts that the Gauḍapāda of the *Bhāṣya* on the *Kārikā* is the same as the early Vedāntin Gauḍapāda of the *Māṇḍūkya-Kārikā*, a sixth-century date for the *Bhāṣya* is not implausible. The problem, however, is that the views in the two texts attributed to Gauḍapāda diverge widely, although it must be conceded that Gauḍapāda may well have avoided expressing his own philosophical views when composing his elementary commentary on the *Sāṃkhyakārikā*. There is insufficient evidence, unfortunately, to make a clear judgment either way.

Regarding the *Māṭharavṛtti*, it was suggested long ago by Belvalkar that it is the original commentary on the *Kārikā* and the one on which the Chinese commentary (*Suvarṇasaptati*) was based.[30] Moreover, Belvalkar suggested that the *Bhāṣya* is simply a plagiarized version of the *Māṭharavṛtti*. This would make the *Māṭharavṛtti* the oldest commentary on the *Kārikā*. Unfortunately, however, Belvalkar's claims have been challenged for a variety of reasons including (a) the *Māṭharavṛtti* quotes the *Bhāgavatapurāṇa* and the *Viṣṇupurāṇa*, both of which are later texts; (b) the *Māṭharavṛtti's* discussion of Sāṃkhya epistemology in verses 4 through 6 of the *Kārikā* presupposes a number of distinctions regarding the nature of inference that appear to come from later Nyāya technical discussions; and (c) perhaps most telling, in almost every instance in which the *Māṭharavṛtti* has common content with other *Kārikā* commentaries, the discussion in the *Māṭharavṛtti* is fuller and more systematic.[31] These are not by any means conclusive arguments, but it is difficult to avoid the judgment that the *Māṭharavṛtti* is a very late commentary (possibly ninth century or later) and represents an explicit attempt to expand and systematize the older commentarial tradition. With the question whether there were one or two Gauḍapādas, so also here the evidence is insufficient to warrant an unambiguous conclusion.

The existence of the commentaries *Sāṃkhyavṛtti* and *Sāṃkhyasaptativṛtti*, recently edited by E. A. Solomon (Ahmedabad, Gujarat University, 1973), only exacerbates the problem of dating the various *Kārikā* commentaries.[32] Solomon argues that the *Sāṃkhyavṛtti* is the original commentary upon which the *Suvarṇasaptati*, the *Sāṃkhyasaptativṛtti*, the *Bhāṣya*, and the *Māṭharavṛtti* are based, and she has based her conclusion on a painstaking and valuable comparative analysis of all the commentaries on the *Kārikā*.[33] What Solomon has demonstrated, however, is a remarkable common core of content that appears in all five works. On the basis of this evidence one can plausibly argue for (a) the priority of the *Sāṃkhyavṛtti*, (b) the priority of the *Suvarṇasaptati*, or (c) some sort of original *Ur*-commentary upon which all five commentaries are based. Given the present state of the evidence, it is impossible to choose any one of these alternatives as being better than the other two, or, to put the matter somewhat differently, problems relating to the common content in the various *Kārikā* commentaries have not yet been satisfactorily solved.

Finally, regarding the *Jayamaṅgalā*, it has been argued that it precedes the *Sāṃkhyatattvakaumudī*, for Vācaspati Miśra refers to an alternative explanation of the *siddhis* in verse 51 of the *Kārikā* that is remarkably similar to the explanation of the *Jayamaṅgalā*. Moreover, the *Jayamaṅgalā* is possibly somewhat later than the *Yuktidīpikā*, for the *Jayamaṅgalā* refers to an interpretation of the expression "*kāraṇakāryavibhāgāt*" in *Kārikā* 15 that mirrors a similar view in the *Yuktidīpikā*.[34]

It may be noted, furthermore, that the *Jayamaṅgalā* (in verse 5) appears to preserve the old Sāṃkhya view of the "sevenfold inference" (*saptadhā sambandha*) (which is also found, by the way, in the *Sāṃkhyavṛtti*). This is hardly evidence for suggesting an early date, however, because the *Jayamaṅgalā* may well be a late text that preserves some older views. Kaviraj has suggested, interestingly, that the author of the *Jayamaṅgalā*, a certain Śaṃkara, or Śaṃkarārya, may be the same as a Hindu author of commentaries (one of which is called *Jayamaṅgalā*) on the *Kāmandakanītisāra* and *Kāmasūtra* from the fourteenth century.[35] This suggestion is undercut, however, by the benedictory verse of the *Jayamaṅgalā* (" . . . *lokottaravādinaṃ praṇamya munim*"), which suggests that the author of the *Jayamaṅgalā* was a Buddhist. Clearly, then, the date and authorship of the *Jayamaṅgalā* remains something of a mystery in Sāṃkhya studies, although its anteriority to the *Sāṃkhyatattvakaumudī* and its posteriority to the *Yuktidīpikā* is perhaps not an unreasonable suggestion.

Pulling together these various hints and suggestions, then, it can be reasonably asserted that the commentarial tradition on the *Kārikā* extends from about the beginning of the sixth century, assuming that the *Suvarṇasaptati* that Paramārtha translated had been known in the tradition for some time prior to his work, through the ninth or tenth century (the time of Vācaspati Miśra's *Sāṃkhyatattvakaumudī*). The *Sāṃkhyavṛtti*, *Sāṃkhyasaptativṛtti*, and *Bhāṣya* are probably contemporary or slightly later than the *Suvarṇasaptati*. The *Yuktidīpikā* and *Jayamaṅgalā* are most likely products of the seventh century with the *Jayamaṅgalā* being slightly later than the *Yuktidīpikā*. Finally the *Māṭharavṛtti* appears to be a late expansion of the *Suvarṇasaptati*, *Sāṃkhyavṛtti*, *Sāṃkhyasaptativṛtti*, and *Bhāṣya* and may have been composed in the ninth century (or later).

The situation regarding date and authorship for the early textual tradition of Pātañjala-Sāṃkhya is even murkier than that for the *Kārikā* tradition. The *Yogasūtra* is obviously a compilation of older *sūtra* collections, and it is highly unlikely that the extant ordering of the *sūtras* is reliable. We know nothing about Patañjali, and attempts to link the Patañjali of the *Yogasūtras* with the grammarian Patañjali of the *Mahābhāṣya* are generally unconvincing. Keith may well have been correct in suggesting that the appearance of the *Sāṃkhyakārikā* may have been the occasion for an attempt by the followers of Yoga to systematize their own older traditions. The so-called *Bhāṣya* of Vyāsa is also a mystery. The name "Vyāsa" is obviously incorrect, and the highly condensed and aphoristic *Bhāṣya* is hardly an exhaustive commentary in the traditional sense.

The *Yogasūtrabhāṣyavivaraṇa*, attributed to the great Vedāntin Śaṃkara, is, if authentic, a most important text on Yoga. Unfortunately, its authenticity is not yet established.[36] It is only with Vācaspati

Miśra's *Tattvavaiśāradī* in the ninth or tenth century that one reaches a historically identifiable text. As already mentioned, the views of Pātañjala Sāṃkhya appear to be similar to the views of Vārṣagaṇya and Vindhyavāsin, and it may well be the case that the early textual tradition of Yoga philosophy represents their particular school of Sāṃkhya philosophizing.[37]

These early centuries of Sāṃkhya textual tradition saw a series of external invasions (the Hūṇas) and internal rivalries in India that had, by the middle of the sixth century, resulted in the disappearance of the Gupta political consolidation and ushered in centuries of feudal regionalism. This decentralization of political power was accompanied by the progressive decline of Buddhist traditions (as described, for example, by Hsüan Tsang in the seventh century) and the progressive strengthening of Hindu orthodoxy and rigid social stratification (the caste system). This trend toward a narrow orthodoxy was, however, tempered by popular syncretistic religion (the Tantra, Śāktism, and so forth) and exuberant *bhakti* spirituality (beginning in the south by the seventh century) that provided some personal relief from the ponderous presence that the established order was becoming. We know that other systems of Indian philosophy (Nyāya, Mīmāṃsā, early Vedānta, the philosophy of language of Bhartṛhari, and so forth) were undergoing vigorous development, and one part of that development in each case involved polemical encounter with Sāṃkhya philosophy, but little remains of the Sāṃkhya response, if indeed there was a Sāṃkhya response.

Although Kārikā-Sāṃkhya and Pātañjala-Sāṃkhya are available only through the summary compilations of Īśvarakṛṣṇa and Patañjali (together with the commentaries already mentioned), there is sufficient evidence to indicate that both were systematic philosophical systems. They may be summarized as follows:

KĀRIKĀ-SĀṂKHYA:

1. *Ontology*: A dualism of two all-pervasive ultimate principles, namely, pure consciousness (*puruṣa*), construed pluralistically, and one primordial materiality (*mūlaprakṛti*).
    (A) Primordial materiality is made up of three constituent processes (*guṇa*), that is, intelligibility (*sattva*), activity (*rajas*), and inertia (*tamas*).
    (B) Because of the all-pervasive copresence of the two ultimate principles, the three constituent processes of primordial materiality undergo a continuing transformation (*pariṇāma*) and combination (*saṃghāta*) for the sake of consciousness (*puruṣārtha*). Viewed analytically, the various transformations and combinations of primordial materiality are simply parts of a totally functioning

whole. Viewed synthetically, primordial materiality (with its constituents) is construed as a basic unmanifest material cause (*kāraṇa*, *avyakta*) from which twenty-three preexistent effects become manifest (*vyakta*); they are (1) intellect; (2) egoity; (3-7) a group of five subtle elements, all of which are described as being both creative (*prakṛti*) and created (*vikṛti*); (8-23) a group of sixteen additional emergents, including mind, the five sense capacities, the five action capacities, and the five gross elements described as being only created (*vikṛti*). The five subtle elements, the five sense-capacities, the five action capacities and mind emerge from and make up the structure of egoity. Egoity emerges from intellect. Gross elements emerge from the five subtle elements and together constitute the natural body and the phenomenal world.

2. *Epistemology*: A critical realism based upon three distinct instruments of knowledge (*pramāṇa*), that is, perception (*dṛṣṭa*), inference (*anumāna*), and reliable verbal testimony (*āptavacana*).
   (A) Awareness (*jñāna*) is a fundamental predisposition (*bhāva*) characteristic of intellect whereby the intellect assumes the form of that which is to be known (termed *buddhivṛtti*, or intellectual operations) assisted by the self-awareness (*abhimāna*) of egoity, the intentionality (in the sense of purposive intellectual activity [*saṃkalpa*]) of the mind, and the various mere sensings (*ālocanamātra*) by the sense capacities in immediate perception. These mere sensings arise from present or immediate intellectual operations, but the intentionality of mind, the self-awareness of egoity and the basic determinations of intellect encompass the operations of past, present, and future (including, for example, memory, imagination, fantasy, dreaming, and so forth).
   (B) Awareness by means of the three instruments of knowledge issues in reflective discerning (*adhyavasāya*) by the intellect, which is possible because of the presence of consciousness, which, though distinct from the intellect, is nevertheless an essential catalyst in the process of the occurrence of awareness.
   (C) Although inferences are in some sense always related to perception, it is nevertheless possible to make valid inferences regarding matters that are imperceptible in principle. Such inferences are called *sāmānyatodṛṣṭa* and make possible the inference of the two ultimate unmanifest principles of *puruṣa* and *prakṛti*. The inference of

primordial materiality is based upon (1) the presence of the three constituents in both the unmanifest and manifest transformations of primordial materiality; and (2) a corollary observation that the transformations and combinations of the constituents, whether construed analytically or synthetically, must be in a relation of preexistent identity with an original "material cause." The inference of *puruṣa* is based upon the need for a catalytic consciousness, itself distinct from intellect and primordial materiality, but the presence of which is essential for the occurrence of the awareness function of intellect and the transformations of primordial materiality. The former inference (namely, the inference to primordial materiality) provides the realism in Sāṃkhya epistemology. The latter inference (namely, the inference to *puruṣa*) provides a critical basis for Sāṃkhya epistemology in the absence of which Sāṃkhya would be a reductive materialism unable to account for its own rationality.

3. *Psychology/Physiology*: An organic psycho-physiology in which the polarity of mind-body or thought-extension is interpreted as a polarity between, on the one hand, a detachable "subtle body" capable of transmigration and rebirth, and on the other hand, a one-time-only "gross body" born of father and mother.
   - (A) There is a subtle, material "internal organ" (*antaḥkaraṇa*) made up of intellect, egoity, and mind.
   - (B) The internal organ is within a larger framework of a thirteenfold instrument made up of the threefold internal organ together with the five sense capacities and the five action capacities.
   - (C) The thirteenfold instrument together with the five subtle elements make up the eighteenfold subtle body (*liṅga-śarīra*), which transmigrates and undergoes a sequence of rebirths impelled by the effects of varying predispositions that reside in the intellect and that represent the karmic heritage of the organism.
   - (D) The eighteenfold subtle body is reborn sequentially in one-time-only "gross bodies" (*sthūlaśarīra*) produced genetically by father and mother.
   - (E) Common to the organism as a whole is a sequence of five vital breaths (*pañcavāyu*), namely, *prāṇa*, *apāna*, *udāna*, *samāna*, and *vyāna*, which regulate such varied functions as respiration, swallowing, speaking, digestion, excretion, sexual activity, circulation of bodily fluids, and the general homeostasis of the organism.

4. *Phenomenology* (meant here only in the sense of the apparent everyday world of ordinary experience): A dynamic, projective phenomenalism based upon a network of fundamental predispositions that generate the everyday, phenomenal world of ordinary experience (*upabhoga*) made up of fifty categories (*padārthas*) and referred to as the "intellectual creation" (*pratyaya-sarga*).
   (A) There are eight fundamental predispositions (*bhāvas*), four of which are *sāttvika*: meritorious behavior (*dharma*), knowledge (*jñāna*), nonattachment (*vairāgya*), and power (*aiśvarya*); and four of which are *tāmasa*, the opposites of the above four: *adharma, ajñāna, avairāgya*, and *anaiśvarya*. All these eight predispositions reside in intellect. The projective force of these fundamental predispositions is determined by the activities of the organism in past lives and determines in turn the trajectory of the organism in present and future lives.
   (B) In any given rebirth the projective force of the fundamental predispositions results in a particular constellation of categories that provides a sort of grid through which an organism experiences its world. The particular constellation of categories for a given organism is made up of five kinds of misconception (*viparyaya*), twenty-eight kinds of dysfunction (*aśakti*), nine kinds of contentment (*tuṣṭi*), and eight kinds of perfection (*siddhi*).
   (C) The projective force of the fundamental predispositions, together with the subtle body, generates not only the human realm but also an eightfold divine or cosmic realm and a fivefold animal and plant realm. Taken together, the projected realms are referred to as the external world (*bhautikasarga*), with *sattva* predominating in the divine realm, *rajas* in the human realm, and *tamas* in the animal and plant realm.
5. *Ethics*: A rational renunciation of ordinary experience based upon a psychological hedonism that generates an awareness that the entire pleasure-pain continuum must finally be overcome.
   (A) The experience of frustration (*duḥkha*) is threefold: internal or personal (whether mental or physical) (*ādhyātmika*), external (whether from other persons, animals, objects in the world, and so forth) (*ādhibhautika*), and celestial (whether from supernatural beings, astrological phenomena, cosmic forces, and so forth) (*ādhidaivika*).
   (B) Such frustration is inescapable in ordinary experience and generates the desire to know (*jijñāsā*) the means for overcoming it.

(C) Frustration is an experience of discomfort and may be contrasted with two other typical feelings that occur in ordinary experience, that is, satisfaction (*sukha*) and confusion (*moha*). Satisfaction is an experience of restful tranquillity (*śānta*), and confusion is an experience of bewilderment or alienation (*mūḍha*). All three experiences occur in the specific (*viśeṣa*) contexts of ordinary life, but it is the experience of frustration that arouses the faculty of awareness (the intellect) to discriminate the reasons for frustration and to pursue the means for overcoming it.

(D) Reflection reveals that the satisfaction-frustration-confusion continuum refers to three constituent dimensions that permeate the manifest world, namely, reflective intelligibility (*prakhyā*, *prakāśa*), externalizing activity (*pravṛtti*, *cala*), and reifying inertia (*sthiti*, *āvaraṇa*), or, in other words, *sattva*, *rajas*, and *tamas*.

(E) Further reflection (by means of perception, inference, and reliable authority) reveals that the three constituents together make up primordial materiality in its manifest and unmanifest aspects.

(F) To overcome frustration, therefore, it is necessary to transcend the transformations and combinations of primordial materiality altogether (including even reflective intelligibility or *sattva*).

(G) The ethical goal of Sāṃkhya, then, is to discriminate the presence of a transcendent consciousness, distinct from primordial materiality and its three constituents, and thereby to attain a radical isolation (*kaivalya*) or liberation from ordinary human experience.

PĀTAÑJALA-SAṂKHYA

1. *Ontology*: Basically the same as Kārikā-Sāṃkhya with three important exceptions, namely:

   (A) Intellect, egoity, and mind are brought together into a single all-pervasive cognitive faculty called awareness (*citta*).

   (B) The notions of transformation and combination are interpreted in terms of momentary manifestations or aspects of primordial materiality that exhibit changes in external property (*dharma*), present functioning (*lakṣaṇa*), and state of development (*avasthā*).[38]

   (C) The existence of God is admitted, although the Lord is not considered to be an additional principle of the system. Rather, He is a particular kind of *puruṣa*.

2. *Epistemology*: Basically the same as Kārikā-Sāṃkhya, although the process of awareness is called *cittavṛtti* instead of *buddhivṛtti* or *antaḥkaraṇavṛtti*.
3. *Psychology/Physiology*: Basically the same as Kārikā-Sāṃkhya with the important exception that there is no subtle, transmigrating body. Because the *citta* is all-pervasive, a subtle body is unnecessary.
4. *Phenomenology*: Similar in intent to Kārikā-Sāṃkhya, but the explanatory mode is dramatically different. Whereas Kārikā-Sāṃkhya develops its phenomenology using the notion of the eight predispositions and the fifty categories (misconceptions, incapacities, contentments, and perfections), Pātañjala-Sāṃkhya develops its phenomenology around the notion of the five cognitive conditions (*vṛtti*) of awareness, namely, knowledge (*pramāṇa*) error (*viparyaya*), conceptual construction (*vikalpa*), sleep (*nidrā*), and memory (*smṛti*). These conditions may be afflicted (*kliṣṭa*) or unafflicted (*akliṣṭa*). The former conditions generate latent dispositions (*vāsanā, saṃskāra*) and karmic residues (*karmāśaya*) that exacerbate "ignorance" (*avidyā*) and progressively lead to further frustration, rebirth, and transmigration. The latter conditions generate latent dispositions that counteract the afflicted dispositions, gradually destroy the residues that exacerbate ignorance, and progressively lead to the discriminative realization (*vivekakhyāti*) of the distinction between *sattva* and *puruṣa*. Finally, all cognitive conditions (both afflicted and unafflicted) must be stopped, for Pātañjala-Sāṃkhya defines the term "*yoga*" as "the cessation of the cognitive conditions of awareness" (*cittavṛttinirodha*).
5. *Ethics*: Basically the same ethical goal as Kārikā-Sāṃkhya, although the methodology for attaining the goal is different. Whereas Kārikā-Sāṃkhya appears to recommend a progressive sequence of reflective discriminations that naturally or spontaneously leads to the desired goal of liberation, Pātañjala-Sāṃkhya stresses a systematic and rigorous meditative *praxis* that is a prerequisite for reflective discrimination. To some extent the difference is only one of perspective, with Kārikā-Sāṃkhya focusing on the final stages of reflective discrimination and Pātañjala-Sāṃkhya focusing on the requisite preparatory discipline. On another level, however, the difference appears to relate to divergent interpretations with respect to the role and function of the intellect and the cognitive faculty. Whereas Kārikā-Sāṃkhya focuses primarily on the "intellect" dimension of *buddhi* Pātañjala Sāṃkhya focuses primarily on the "will" dimension of *citta*. In Pātañjala-Sāṃkhya the yogin practices personal austerities (*tapas*), recitation and study (*svādhyāya*), and devotion to God (*īśvarapraṇi-*

dhāna) in order to discipline body and mind (*kriyāyoga*). The yogin also pursues a systematic eightfold program of discipline (*yogāṅgas*) made up of external and internal cleansing (*yama* and *niyama*), controlled posture (*āsana*), controlled breathing (*prāṇāyāma*), the restraint of capacities (*pratyāhāra*), focused concentration (*dhāraṇā*), continuous meditation (*dhyāna*), and the cultivation of altered states of awareness (*samādhi*). Pātañjala-Sāṃkhya provides detailed accounts of the various levels of altered states of awareness (including *savitarka*, *savicāra*, *sānanda*, and *sāsmita*), referred to as "altered states of awareness that have content or support" (*saṃprajñātasamādhi*), and Pātañjala-Sāṃkhya also provides an account of a final *samādhi* that transcends all content or support (*asaṃprajñātasamādhi*). According to Pātañjala-Sāṃkhya, the attainment of the advanced levels of awareness requires continuous and rigorous effort (*abhyāsa*) and the total nonattachment (*vairāgya*) to ordinary experience. Also, devotion to God is strongly recommended, since the object of devotion (namely, the transcendent consciousness of the Lord) is the perfect model or exemplar of what the yogin is seeking to achieve in his own discipline.

B. *Kārikā-Kaumudī-Sāṃkhya*

By the eighth and ninth centuries a crucial development had occurred that paradoxically both salvaged and destroyed the old Sāṃkhya philosophy, namely, the emergence of Advaita Vedānta in the work of Śaṃkara and his successors.[39] Vedānta salvaged and destroyed Sāṃkhya philosophy in much the same manner as Christian theology in the medieval period both salvaged and destroyed Plato and Aristotle. That is to say, while polemically regretting the errors of the older tradition, the newly emerging tradition unashamedly stole many of the essential features of the conceptual structure of the heretics. Vedānta, stripped of its scripture-based monistic *brahman-ātman*, is in many ways a warmed-over Sāṃkhya ontology and epistemology spooned up with the philosophical methodology of the old negative dialectic of the Mādhyamika Buddhists. What Śaṃkara could not intellectually tolerate, however, was the Sāṃkhya notion of an independent material (*pradhāna* or *prakṛti*) apart from consciousness (*puruṣa*), and even more difficult to accept was the crucial role for inference apart from scriptural authority that the Sāṃkhya notion of materiality permitted. Sāṃkhya had never denied reliable verbal testimony (*āptavacana* or *śruti*) as a legitimate and important means of knowing, but Sāṃkhya clearly gave pride of place in knowing to independent reasoning, even in the area of *samyagdarśana* and *adhyātmavidyā* (that is to say, in the area of ultimate truth and the science of liberation).

One has the impression in reading Śaṃkara's *Brahmasūtrabhāṣya* that the author is not especially vexed by the naive realism and the neat, logical distinctions of Nyāya, or by the quaint atomism of Vaiśeṣika, or by the action-orientation of Mīmāṃsā, or by the harmless devotion of the theological *bhakti* enthusiasts. The genuine enemy is the *pradhāna-kāraṇavāda* (namely, the Sāṃkhya), because Sāṃkhya offers an alternative account of the role and function of philosophy on precisely the same ground and for precisely the same purpose (liberation) as does Vedānta.[40] To allow Sāṃkhya to stand is to threaten the entire edifice of the received tradition. Moreover, as Śaṃkara himself points out, to demolish Sāṃkhya is to demolish by implication the other systems of Indian thought that harbor the pretence of the adequacy of independent reasoning.

> . . . we have taken special trouble to refute the *pradhāna* doctrine, without paying much attention to the atomic and other theories. These latter theories, however, must likewise be refuted, as they also are opposed to the doctrine of Brahman being the general cause. . . . Hence the Sūtrakāra formally extends, in the above Sūtra, the refutation already accomplished of the *pradhāna* doctrine to all similar doctrines which need not be demolished in detail after their protagonist, the *pradhāna* doctrine, has been so completely disposed of.[41]

Apart from this crucial disagreement, however, Vedānta adopts many of the Sāṃkhya conceptualizations (with, of course, numerous variations in nuance): the theory of causation (which becomes *vivartavāda* with the collapse of the Sāṃkhya dualism), the notion of the three *guṇas*, the importance of the science of liberation and nondiscrimination (*aviveka*), the notion of a subtle body, technical terms such as "*buddhi*," "*ahaṃkāra*," "*manas*," and so forth.

This tendency of Vedānta to absorb the conceptual structure of Sāṃkhya had the double effect of, on one level, decisively destroying the old Sāṃkhya dualism (through the refutation of the Sāṃkhya notion of primordial materiality on the basis of independent reasoning), but, on another level, of reviving and refurbishing many of the old Sāṃkhya notions. This latter effect helps to explain why an important thinker such as Vācaspati Miśra, composed a major commentary on the *Sāṃkhyakārikā* (the *Sāṃkhyatattvakaumudī*) in the ninth or tenth century. Vācaspati, of course, composed a variety of commentaries on many of the older schools of Indian philosophy (including Nyāya, Mīmāṃsā, Yoga, and Vedānta), but his work on Sāṃkhya is especially significant in the sense that it triggered a subsequent commentarial Sāṃkhya tradition that reaches down to the present day and that probably would otherwise not have existed. In other words, whereas his work on Nyāya, Mīmāṃsā, and Vedānta represents an important contribution to each of these systems, his work on Sāṃkhya actually inaugurated an independent tradition. As the Checklist clearly shows, many of the Sāṃkhya texts after the tenth century are based on Vācaspati's reading of the *Sāṃkhyakārikā*. This is true everywhere in India in recent centuries but especially so in Bengal, where many pandits refuse to take the *Sāṃkhyasūtra* or Vijñānabhikṣu's work as serious Sāṃkhya texts. Vaṃśīdhara's *Tattvavibhākara*, Kavirāja Yati's *Tattvapradīpa*, Śrī Bhāratī Yati's *Tattvakaumudīvyākhyā*, Nyāyapañcānana's *Āvaraṇavāriṇī*, Bālarāma Udāsīna's *Vidvattoṣiṇī*, Pañcānana Tarkaratna's *Pūrṇimā*, Kṛṣṇavallabhācārya's *Kiraṇāvali*, Rameścandra Tarkatīrtha's *Guṇamayī*, Harirāma Śukla's *Suṣamā*, Śivanārāyaṇa Śāstri's *Sārabodhini*, and Sītārāma Śāstri's *Abhinavarājalakṣmī*, works ranging from the 17th to the 20th centuries, are all important later texts that interpret the Sāṃkhya system through Vācaspati Miśra's *Tattvakaumudī*.

What must be noted, however, is that Vācaspati's reading of Sāṃkhya is more than a little influenced by the emerging Advaita Vedānta and its characteristic network of intellectual issues, and in this sense it should be distinguished from Pre-Kārikā-Sāṃkhya, Kārikā-Sāṃkhya and Pātañjala-Sāṃkhya. For convenience it can be designated simply as Kārikā-Kaumudī-Sāṃkhya, that is to say, the *Sāṃkhyakārikā* as read through Vācaspati's *Tattvakaumudī*.

Some of the characteristic emphases in Vācaspati Miśra's interpretation may be outlined as follows (using the same format that was used earlier in the outlines of Kārikā-Sāṃkhya and Pātañjala-Sāṃkhya):

KĀRIKĀ-KAUMUDĪ-SĀṂKHYA:

1. *Ontology*: Whereas Vācaspati closely follows Kārikā-Sāṃkhya, he is much more concerned with discussing the problem of the relation between intellect (as a manifestation of primordial materiality) and consciousness. According to Vācaspati, a theory of reflection (*pratibimba*) is required in order to explain how intellect is able to have experience. Consciousness becomes reflected in the intellect, thus making it appear as if the intellect were conscious. Experience actually occurs only in intellect, but it appears as if consciousness experiences, because its image (*chāyā*) has become reflected in the intellect (see summary of *Tattvakaumudī* under *Kārikās* 5 and 37). Such a theory of reflection is only hinted at in the *Kārikā* itself (and the other early commentaries), and it is undoubtedly the Vedānta preoccupation with the problem of consciousness and its reflection that explains Vācaspati's concern about the issue.
2. *Epistemology*: Again, Vācaspati closely follows Kārikā-Sāṃkhya, but there are at least two important extensions beyond what is found in the *Kārikā* itself (and the other early commentaries). First, regarding the problem of inference, Vācaspati discusses

the threefold inference in terms of positive (*vīta*) and exclusionary (*avīta*) types, placing both *pūrvavat* and *sāmānyatodṛṣṭa* under *vīta*, and *śeṣavat* under *avīta*. Vācaspati's discussion shows a familiarity with logical problems and technical logical issues that arose considerably later than the time of the *Kārikā* itself, problems and issues that were especially prominent in Nyāya philosophy and were becoming prominent as well in the various traditions of Vedānta philosophy after Śaṃkara. Second, regarding the problem of perception, Vācaspati argues that the sense capacities are only capable of mere sensing (*ālocanamātra*), for they apprehend sense objects without any mental ordering or verbal characterization (*nirvikalpa*), whereas the mind performs the task of ordering and verbalizing (*savikalpa*) the impressions of the senses. Such a distinction had perhaps been hinted at in the earlier texts, but it was Vācaspati who spelled out this important distinction.

3. *Psychology/Physiology*: Vācaspati accepts the basic psychology/physiology of the *Kārikā* and indicates specifically that the subtle body is made up of the five subtle elements, which accompany the thirteenfold instrument in the cycle of transmigration.
4. *Phenomenology*: Vācaspati provides no new explanations of the predispositions or the intellectual creation, although he indicates that the five misconceptions, (*tamas*, *moha*, *mahāmoha*, *tāmisra*, and *andhatāmisra*) of the intellectual creation are equivalent to the five afflictions (*kleśas*) (*avidyā*, *asmitā*, *rāga*, *dveṣa*, and *abhiniveśa*) of Pātañjala-Sāṃkhya.
5. *Ethics*: Again, Vācaspati closely follows the presentation of Kārikā-Sāṃkhya, but throughout he appears to be casting Sāṃkhya notions into a Vedānta idiom. Vācaspati begins his commentary with a clear allusion to the *Śvetāśvatara Upaniṣad*, indicating thereby that the Sāṃkhya concern for overcoming frustration has a firm Upaniṣadic base. Moreover, in his interpretation of the Sāṃkhya rejection of Vedic means for the alleviation of frustration (under *Kārikā* 2), Vācaspati is quick to point out that only the ritual portion of the Veda is intended, and in his discussion of the perfections (under *Kārikā* 51) he correlates Sāṃkhya meditational techniques with the Vedānta triad hearing (*śravaṇa*), considering (*manana*), and meditating (*nididhyāsana*).

C. *Samāsa-Sāṃkhya*

Yet another independent tradition of Sāṃkhya philosophy is that found in a cryptic little text entitled *Sāṃkhyatattvasamāsa*.[42] Because it is not mentioned in Mādhava's *Sarvadarśanasaṃgraha* (from the fourteenth century) and because none of its commentaries appears to be much earlier than the medieval period, it is usually assigned a late date (that is to say, some time after the fourteenth century). Max Müller, however, suspected that it may well be much earlier, and more recently Frauwallner has described the Sāṃkhya of Vārṣagaṇya as having close parallels with the *Tattvasamāsa*. Some of the notions of the *Tattvasamāsa* (for example, the five sources of action and the presentation of materiality in terms of eight generative principles) are either not mentioned in the *Sāṃkhyakārikā* or are explained in a different manner, whereas the presentation of Sāṃkhya as found in the *Yuktidīpikā*, an authentically older Sāṃkhya text, does mirror to some extent the *Tattvasamāsa*.[43] Possibly, then, the *Tattvasamāsa* may represent an older formulation. In any case, the *Tattvasamāsa* does have a modern (largely Vedāntin) commentarial tradition reaching from the fourteenth or fifteenth century down to the present day, including such texts as the *Kramadīpikā* (possibly of the fourteenth century or even earlier), the *Tattvayāthārthyadīpana* of Bhāvāgaṇeśa (sixteenth century), the *Sarvopakāriṇīṭīkā* (eighteenth or nineteenth century), the *Sāṃkhyasūtravivaraṇa* (eighteenth or nineteenth century), the *Sāṃkhyatattvavivecana* (eighteenth or nineteenth century), and the *Sāṃkhyatattvavilāsa* (nineteenth century).

According to Max Müller, the *Tattvasamāsa* has been especially popular among the *paṇḍitas* of Varanasi and presents Sāṃkhya philosophy in a manner notably different from the traditions of Kārikā-Sāṃkhya, Pātañjala-Sāṃkhya, and Kārikā-Kaumudī-Sāṃkhya. The important differences may be outlined as follows:

SAMĀSA-SĀṂKHYA:

1. *Ontology*: There is a distinct difference in emphasis. Whereas the *Kārikā* begins by calling attention to the three kinds of frustration and then moves on to discuss the instruments of knowledge and the various inferences for establishing primordial materiality and consciousness, the *sūtras* of the *Tattvasamāsa* begin with the ontology and cosmology of Sāṃkhya (*sūtras* 1-6). Instead of discussing primordial materiality and its seven basic emergents (intellect, etc.), which are described in the *Kārikā* as being both creative (*prakṛti*) and created (*vikṛti*), the *Tattvasamāsa* refers to "eight *prakṛtis*" (*sūtra* 1), "sixteen emergents" (*sūtra* 2), and "consciousness" (*puruṣa*) (*sūtra* 3). The presentation of the *Tattvasamāsa* calls to mind older nonphilosophical or popular accounts of Sāṃkhya such as those found in the *Mahābhārata* (the *Gītā* and the *Mokṣadharma*) and the *Purāṇas*. Moreover, in *sūtras* 5 and 6 reference is made to the creation or emergence of the manifest world (*sañcara*) and its periodic dissolution (*pratisañcara*), again calling to mind older, cosmological account

of Sāṃkhya common to popular texts such as the Purāṇas and the *Mānavadharmaśāstra*.

2. *Epistemology*: Except for one brief reference (*sūtra* 23) to the three instruments of knowledge, epistemological notions are not enumerated in the *Tattvasamāsa*. This may simply mean, of course, that the compiler of the *sūtras* is presupposing the fully developed Sāṃkhya epistemology, but it may also mean that the *Tattvasamāsa* form of Śāṃkhya represents an older, cosmological form of Sāṃkhya that did not concern itself with epistemological issues.
3. *Psychology/Physiology*: The *Tattvasamāsa* mentions none of the characteristic psychological notions of Kārikā-Śaṃkhya apart from a reference to the five "breaths" (*vāyus* or *prāṇas*). Instead, it introduces a set of distinctively new notions that are not mentioned at all in the *Kārikā* account of Śāṃkhya, namely, the "five functions of the *buddhi*" (*abhibuddhi*, i.e., *vyavasāya*, *abhimāna*, *icchā*, *kartavyatā*, and *kriyā*), the "five sources of action" (*karmayoni*, i.e., *dhṛti*, *śraddhā*, *sukha*, *vividiṣā*, and *avividiṣā*), and the "five essences of action" (*karmātman*, i.e., *vaikārika*, *taijasa*, *bhūtādi*, *sānumāna*, and *niranumāna*).
4. *Phenomenology*: The *Tattvasamāsa* refers to the "five misconceptions" (*avidyā*), the "twenty-eight dysfunctions" (*aśakti*), the "nine contentments" (*tuṣṭi*), and the "eight perfections" (*siddhi*)together with the "ten principal topics" (*daśamūlikārthas*), thus making a total of sixty topics, which evidently represent the enumerated components of the Sāṃkhya *ṣaṣṭitantra* ("the system of sixty topics"). The *Tattvasamāsa* then introduces the expression "*anugrahasarga*" (*sūtra* 19), which means something like "the supporting creation" and is probably synonomous with the more common expression "*pratyayasarga*" (or "intellectual creation"). Interestingly, the expression "*anugrahasarga*" is found in a number of Purāṇic texts, again suggesting that the *Tattvasamāsa* may represent an old cosmological form of Sāṃkhya.
5. *Ethics*: Unlike Kārikā-Sāṃkhya, which apparently refers only to one kind of bondage and one kind of release, the *Tattvasamāsa* refers to a "threefold bondage" (*trividho bandaḥ*) and a "threefold liberation" (*trividho mokṣaḥ*). Presumably these tripartite notions relate to the "threefold instrument of knowledge" (*sūtra* 23) and the "threefold frustration" (*sūtra* 24), but the commentaries on the *Tattvasamāsa* do not elucidate any correlation. This may be because the notions are archaic formulations that the later commentators failed to understand, or it may possibly be because these enumerations are heuristic learning devices that have no particular conceptual significance for the system as a whole. The former explanation is probably correct, since there

are references in some of the commentaries on the *Kārikā*, in some Purāṇas, and in other older literature to a "threefold bondage" and a "threefold liberation," suggesting that these were older formulations that were simplified or eliminated in later accounts of the system.

D. *Sūtra-Sāṃkhya*

Finally, there is one additional independent tradition of philosophical Sāṃkhya, that of the *Sāṃkhyasūtra* and its attendant commentaries. As is the case with the *Tattvasamāsa*, possibly many or at least some of the *sūtras* may be very early, perhaps reaching back to the formative period. Unfortunately, however, there is no old commentarial tradition that would enable us to sort out the earlier from the later *sūtras*. We have only a series of modern commentaries and subcommentaries composed mainly by various Vedāntins, the chief among whom is Vijñānabhikṣu. Commentaries on the Sāṃkhyasūtra include the following: the *Sāṃkhyasūtravṛtti* of Aniruddha (fifteenth century), the *Sāṃkhyapravacanabhāṣya* of Vijñānabhikṣu (sixteenth century), the *Vṛttisāra* of Mahādeva Vedāntin (seventeenth century), the *Sāṃkhyasūtravṛtti* of Nāgoji Bhaṭṭa or Nāgeśa (eighteenth century), the *Amalā* of Pramathanātha Tarkabhūṣaṇa (early twentieth century), the *Vṛtti* of Hariprasāda (twentieth century), the *Tattvabodhinī* of Kuñjavihāri Tarkasiddhānta (twentieth century), and the *Sāṃkhyasūtrabhāṣya* of Brahmamuni (twentieth century).

In this tradition the process of what might be called the Vedāntinization of Sāṃkhya is carried much further than it had been by Vācaspati. Vijñānabhikṣu construes Sāṃkhya in terms of a grand metaphysical cosmology on analogy with Vedānta, with a highest self (*paramātman*), a creative God (*īśvara*), and gradations of reality in terms of the old Sāṃkhya basic principles. Moreover, he documents his interpretation of Sāṃkhya with extensive quotations from the theistic portion of the *Mokṣadharma*, the *Gītā* and the Purāṇas (that is to say, largely from Proto-Sāṃkhya references). He freely offers his own views on a variety of Sāṃkhya notions (for example, the three *guṇas*, the relation between *puruṣa* and *prakṛti*, and so forth), and he argues at length that the atheistic orientation of philosophical Sāṃkhya can really be read in terms of Vedānta theism. Sāṃkhya becomes, in other words, a variation on a theme of Vijñānabhikṣu's own Vedānta, and he deals with all of the older schools of Indian philosophy (Nyāya, Vaiśeṣika, and Mīmāṃsā) in much the same manner. The differences between the older schools of Indian philosophy are transcended in the direction of a grand Vedānta synthesis, and Sāṃkhya is assigned its rung (but interestingly, a very high rung) on a ladder of Indian philosophical truth, the highest rung of which is the Vedānta philosophy.[44] Some of the more distinctive features of this late form of Sāṃkhya may be outlined as follows:

SŪTRA-SĀṂKHYA:

1. *Ontology*:

(A) As was noted earlier in the discussion of Kārikā-Kaumudī-Sāṃkhya, so also for the Sūtra-Sāṃkhya of Vijñānabhikṣu (and the other commentators on the *Sāṃkhyasūtra*), the problem of the relation between intellect (as a manifestation of primordial materiality) and pure consciousness is a dominant theme in ontological discussions. Vijñānabhikṣu argues, however, that Vācaspati's theory of reflection is not a sufficient explanation of the problem. Vācaspati had argued that pure consciousness and intellect are not in contact and that pure consciousness becomes reflected in the intellect, thus making the latter appear as if it were conscious. According to Vijñānabhikṣu, this explanation deprives pure consciousness of experience and does not adequately elucidate the subtlety of the Sāṃkhya dualism. Instead of Vācaspati's simple theory of reflection, therefore, Vijñānabhikṣu introduces his own theory of "mutual reflection" (*anyonyapratibimba*, mainly in his discussion under *sūtra* I.99 but *passim* as well), in which pure consciousness becomes reflected in intellect (whereby the *buddhi* becomes "intelligized," as it were) but in which *buddhi*'s transactions (including satisfaction, frustration, confusion, awareness, etc.) in turn become reflected back in pure consciousness as limiting adjuncts (*upādhi*)—thus making it possible for pure consciousness to "have" experience (albeit a mistaken or distorted experience). There is, therefore, a mutual contact (through this double reflection) between pure consciousness and intellect, but such contact does not in any way involve any change or activity in pure consciousness.

(B) In addition, in Sūtra-Sāṃkhya the problem of the plurality of pure consciousness is taken further. Kārikā-Sāṃkhya and Kārikā-Kaumudī-Sāṃkhya had simply asserted the classical Sāṃkhya notion of plurality. The Vedānta discussions of one ultimate Self, however, in the later centuries had obviously posed a challenge to the old Sāṃkhya view. In Sūtra-Sāṃkhya the problem is handled by arguing (primarily under I.154 but *passim* as well) that Vedic references to nonduality (*advaita*) imply only a simple, generic essence (*jāti*) of selfhood and need not be taken to mean that there is only one undivided Self. In other words, there is a plurality of selves, but they all have one, simple, generic essence. Uncovering or discriminating the limiting adjuncts that distort this simple, generic essence of selfhood is the goal both of Sāṃkhya philosophy and the Vedic scripture.

(C) Also, in the Sūtra-Sāṃkhya of Vijñānabhikṣu, there is an inclination to make room for the notion of a God (*īśvara*). Although the *sūtras* themselves (see I.92-99 and V. 1-12) appear to be clearly non-theistic, Vijñānabhikṣu goes to great length to show that God is not really a problem for Sāṃkhya. The apparently nontheistic arguments only show that the notion of God is not really essential for establishing the rationality of Sāṃkhya. This does not at all mean, according to Vijñānabhikṣu, that God need be denied, and Vijñānabhikṣu proceeds to quote extensively from pre-Kārikā epic and Purāṇic passages to document that God has a useful role to play in the Sāṃkhya tradition.

(D) Perhaps the most significant innovation of Vijñānabhikṣu's Sūtra-Sāṃkhya, however, is his interpretation of the *guṇas*. Unlike the earlier Sāṃkhya traditions, which describe the *guṇas* as constituent processes and affective states, Vijñānabhikṣu interprets the *guṇas* as subtle substances (*dravyas*) that are originally in a condition of homogeneous equilibrium (*sāmyāvasthā*) and then combine in various heterogeneous collocations of manifest principles (*tattva*) when the equilibrium is disrupted by the presence of pure consciousness (see I.61, VI.39 and *passim*). In other words, Vijñānabhikṣu develops an elaborate metaphysical ontology/cosmology of periodic manifestation and dissolution, more reminiscent of epic and Purāṇic cosmologies than of the older Sāṃkhya traditions as found in Kārikā-Sāṃkhya, Pātañjala-Sāṃkhya or Kārikā-Kaumudī-Sāṃkhya. Whereas the older Sāṃkhya traditions had focused largely on epistemology, psychology/physiology, and ethics, the Sūtra-Sāṃkhya of Vijñānabhikṣu focuses on a metaphysical cosmology centering on the interaction of *guṇas* as substances. One may well argue (as, for example, S. Dasgupta argues) that Vijñānabhikṣu's metaphysical *guṇa* substances were implicit even in the earlier traditions, but there is little or no support for such an argument in the earlier Sāṃkhya texts themselves. The only support for such an argument is to be found in prephilosophical epic and Purāṇic passages, which is probably the primary reason why Vijñānabhikṣu quotes so extensively from the old cosmological literature.

(E) One further innovation of Vijñānabhikṣu's Sūtra-Sāṃkhya relates to the threefold structure of egoity (*vaikṛta*, *taijasa*, and *bhūtādi*, from *Sāṃkhyakārikā* 25). Older interpretations had suggested that *vaikṛta* is *sattva* and encompasses the elevenfold cognitive apparatus (the five sense capacities, the five action capacities, and mind); *bhūtādi* is *tamas* and encompasses the five subtle elements; and *taijasa* is *rajas*, which pertains both to *vaikṛta* and *bhūtādi* (thereby assisting both in cognition and material development). According to Vijñānabhikṣu (see under II.18), however, this is not correct. Rather, *vaikṛta* as *sattva* pertains only to *manas* or mind; *taijasa* as *rajas* pertains to the five sense capacities and the five action capacities; and *bhūtādi* as *tamas* pertains to the five subtle elements. The reference in the *Kārikā* verse to *taijasa* or *rajas* pertaining to "both" means simply that the sense capacities and action capacities mediate between *sattva* (mind) and *tamas* (matter). Vijñānabhikṣu quotes some verses from the *Bhāgavata Purāṇa* in support of his view, but it should be noted that this interpretation is not to be found in any of the older, extant Sāṃkhya philosophical traditions.

2. *Epistemology*:

(A) The only innovative epistemological argument of importance in Vijñānabhikṣu's Sūtra-Śāṃkhya relates to the role and function of the sense capacities in perception. Kārikā-Sāṃkhya and Pātañjala-Sāṃkhya refer respectively to *buddhivṛtti* and *cittavṛtti* but do not spell out the specific functions in the cognitive process. Vācaspati Miśra carried the discussion further by attributing bare awareness without mental elaboration (*nirvikalpa*) to the sense capacities and mental elaboration (*savikalpa*) to mind. Vijñānabhikṣu disagrees with Vācaspati (under II.32), arguing that the sense capacities are capable of both *nirvikalpa* and *savikalpa* perception. Mind only plays a role of focusing attention (*saṃkalpa*) and initiating conceptual constructions (*vikalpa*). Perception, then, according to Vijñānabhikṣu, is primarily a result of the interaction of intellect/ will and the sense capacities. Mind, as a result, plays a very minor role in Sūtra-Sāṃkhya.

(B) Although there are few other epistemological innovations by Vijñānabhikṣu, it should be noted that there are elaborate polemical discussions against other schools of Indian philosophy. There is much of interest in these discussions, but it is difficult to know if the Sāṃkhya views expressed are those of the earlier tradition or simply possible interpretations that Vijñānabhikṣu himself favored. One has the strong sense that the latter is the case rather than the former. At V.51ff., for example, there are elaborate discussions of the validity of knowledge, *sphoṭa* theory, and the theory of error. According to Vijñānabhikṣu, Sāṃkhya philosophy accepts (V.51) the theory that knowledge is intrinsically valid (*svataḥ prāmāṇya*), rejects the theory of *sphoṭa* (V.57), and accepts a theory of error known as *sadasatkhyāti* (V. 56) (wherein the basic *tattvas* are existent, or *sat*, but certain relations superimposed on the *tattvas* are nonexistent, or *asat*). All of these views are reasonable implications regarding the Sāṃkhya philosophical position, and Vācaspati Miśra in earlier times had strongly suggested the intrinsic validity argument. Overall, however, one has the sense that these discussions reflect a later philosophical period long after Sāṃkhya had attained its normative formulation.

3. *Psychology/Physiology*: Sūtra-Sāṃkhya extends the old Sāṃkhya psychology/physiology in a cosmological direction. Intellect/will becomes a cosmic entity (*hiraṇyagarbha*, *Brahmā*, and so forth), and the various cognitive principles (sense organs, and so forth) are linked up with various deities on analogy with the old epic and Purāṇic cosmologies.
4. *Phenomenology*: Sūtra-Sāṃkhya conflates the old Kārikā-Sāṃkhya and Pātañjala-Sāṃkhya. Whereas Kārikā-Sāṃkhya describes ordinary experience in terms of the eight predispositions and fifty categories (misconceptions, dysfunctions contentments and perfections) and Pātañjala-Sāṃkhya describes ordinary experience in terms of *cittavṛttis*, *saṃskāras*, and *vāsanās*, Vijñānabhikṣu's Sūtra-Sāṃkhya uses both explanatory approaches and does not distinguish one from the other. Moreover, the Sūtra-Sāṃkhya of Vijñānabhikṣu presents the various explanations in an apparently haphazard manner, which has led most interpreters to conclude that the *sūtras* either are not in proper order or represent a compilation of a variety of old Sāṃkhya traditions.
5. *Ethics*: The ethical thrust of Vijñānabhikṣu's Sūtra-Sāṃkhya is akin to the other Sāṃkhya traditions already outlined, although Vijñānabhikṣu's tendency to emphasize Sāṃkhya as a metaphysical cosmology and his predilection for quoting older, nonphilosophical theistic passages from the epics and Purāṇas gives a characteristic flavor or tone to his presentation that is clearly different from the older Sāṃkhya philosophical texts. More-

over, Vijñānabhikṣu's synthetic perspective in which Sāṃkhya and Yoga (along with the other orthodox schools) represent a *preparatio evangelium* for Vedānta strikes a distinctively different posture from the older Sāṃkhya literature.

Śaṃkara's encounter with Sāṃkhya had been intense and polemical, even bitter. Vācaspati's had been more dispassionate and descriptive, an obvious effort to lay out those dimensions of Sāṃkhya philosophy that could be appropriated with respect to the set of philosophical issues that had become pressing in his time. Vijñānabhikṣu's encounter with Sāṃkhya was generous and clearly synthetic, symptomatic probably of Vedānta philosophy's having emerged as the most favored variety of systematic reflection. There were, of course, numerous varieties of Vedānta, just as there were numerous varieties of theology among Christian groups in medieval Europe, but intellectual athletics had largely become intramural. The task now was to place the various older traditions in an appropriate hierarchical network that reflected the new intellectual environment. Vijñānabhikṣu was an expert in this task, and much of the tone and flavor of Indian philosophy in modern times is traceable to the kind of intellectual synthesizing that Vijñānabhikṣu represents. It is apparent in most of the Sanskrit philosophical texts of the modern period, and it is noticeable even in the Western-style scholarly treatments of Indian philosophy of Dasgupta, Radhakrishnan, Simha, and others. It has had a profound impact not only on the way Indian intellectuals think of their tradition but also on the entire tradition of the European scholarly treatment of Indian thought. The Vedānta bias is almost everywhere in modern Indian thought. There is no use in regretting this, however (except perhaps for the occasional old soul who wonders what Sāṃkhya was before the Vedāntins got their hands on it), because, for better or worse, India has allowed Sāṃkhya to subsist as an appendage to its modern Vedānta bias in much the same way as Christian thought has been characterized as a "Platonism for the masses" (Nietzsche) for generations of European and American believers.

To summarize this overview, then, it is useful to distinguish the following types of Sāṃkhya in India's intellectual heritage:

(1) Proto-Sāṃkhya: 800 B.C.E.—100 C.E.
(2) Pre-Kārikā Sāṃkhya: 100-500 C.E.
(3) Kārikā-Sāṃkhya: 350-850 C.E.
(4) Pātañjala-Sāṃkhya: 400-850 C.E.
(5) Kārikā-Kaumudī-Sāṃkhya: 850 (or 975)-present
(6) Samāsa-Sāṃkhya: 1300-present
(7) Sūtra-Sāṃkhya: 1400-present

The original philosophical formulation occurs with the emergence of Pre-Kārikā Sāṃkhya, and the normative formulations in summary form appear in Kārikā-Sāṃkhya and Pātañjala-Sāṃkhya. Somewhere in these ancient traditions there appears to have been a clear break with the original genius and vitality of the system, and the later traditions of Kārikā-Kaumudī-Sāṃkhya, Samāsa-Sāṃkhya, and Sūtra-Sāṃkhya present the system through a Vedānta prism, a prism, to be sure, that frequently irritates the Sāṃkhya interpreter, but nevertheless a prism without which one of the truly remarkable traditions of ancient philosophizing would possibly have vanished from India's intellectual heritage and from the general history of cross-cultural philosophy.

THE PHILOSOPHY OF SĀṂKHYA

Preliminary Remarks

Although the main outlines of the history and literature of Sāṃkhya are reasonably clear, the same cannot be said about the details of the system qua philosophical system. As was mentioned in the last chapter, there appears to have been a break in the Sāṃkhya textual tradition at an early date. Beginning with Īśvarakṛṣṇa's *Sāṃkhyakārikā* and thereafter, there are only summaries and digests of the system, and many of the commentators are almost as much at a loss to explain the full system as is a modern interpreter. This is unfortunate, for in many ways the evidence suggests that Sāṃkhya philosophy stands at the fountainhead of systematic Indian reflection, somewhat on analogy with Pythagoreanism and other pre-Socratic systems in ancient Greece. As is well known, the influence of Sāṃkhya is ubiquitous in South Asian cultural life, not only in philosophy but in medicine, law, statecraft, mythology, cosmology, theology, and devotional literature. Sāṃkhya was evidently a direct descendent of older and unsystematic Upaniṣadic speculation, a precursor of much of India's scientific literature and an older sibling of the first philosophical efforts in South Asia (including Jain, Buddhist, Vaiśeṣika, Mīmāṃsā, and Yoga traditions).

To be sure, certain characteristic philosophical notions are continually attributed to Sāṃkhya in the history of Indian philosophy—for example, the dualism of consciousness and materiality (*puruṣa* and *prakṛti*), the *guṇa* theory, the theory that the effect preexists in the cause in a potential state (*satkāryavāda*), the plurality of *puruṣa*s, and so forth—but there is a notable absence of the larger conceptual and speculative framework from which these characteristic Sāṃkhya notions are derived, and more than that, an absence of any firm sense that these so-called characteristic notions were, in fact, central within the Sāṃkhya tradition itself. Regarding this latter point, one has the impression that many of the characteristic notions of Sāṃkhya were central largely to the later issues in Indian philosophy and were probably much less prominent within the original Sāṃkhya speculative environment. In other words, later commentators were interrogating Sāṃkhya philosophy from the perspective of their own philosophical agendas—for example, Nyāya argumentation, Buddhist logic, Vedānta metaphysics, and so forth—and were simply uninterested in, or unaware of, Sāṃkhya's own speculative agenda. K. C. Bhattacharya has expressed the matter well:

> Much of Sāṃkhya literature appears to have been lost, and there seems to be no continuity of tradition from ancient times up to the age of the commentators. In such systematic works as we have, one seems to have a hazy view of a grand system of speculative metaphysics.... The interpretation of all ancient systems requires a constructive effort; but while in the case of some systems where we have a large volume of literature and a continuity of tradition, the construction is mainly of the nature of translation of ideas in to modern concepts, here in Sāṃkhya the construction at many places involves supplying of missing links from one's imagination. It is risky work, but unless one does it one cannot be said to understand Sāṃkhya as a philosophy. It is a task that one is obliged to undertake. It is a fascinating task because Sāṃkhya is a bold, constructive philosophy.[1]

The Sāṃkhya system qua system, then, is an interesting lacuna in our understanding of ancient India's first systematic philosophizing, an intriguing intellectual puzzle that requires a "constructive effort" (to use K. C. Bhattacharya's idiom) in order to piece it together, but a puzzle that if even partly unscrambled could provide many valuable perspectives for the cultural historian, the historian of philosophy, and the pure philosopher. For the cultural historian, a fuller grasp of Sāṃkhya could possibly provide improved interpretive perspectives for understanding the complex symbol systems that underlie so much of Indian religion, art, law, mythology, and medical theorizing. For the historian of Indian philosophy, a fuller grasp of the Sāṃkhya system could possibly provide a sharper awareness of the network of archaic notions and values that launched many of the first systematic reflections in Indian philosophy. For the pure philosopher, a fuller grasp of the Sāṃkhya system could possibly provide a better grasp of that set of primordial intuitions by means of which South Asians first addressed questions about being, nonbeing, change, causation, and so forth, in a systematic way—a South Asian surrogate, as it were, for a context of primordial philosophizing that thinkers such as Heidegger have pursued among the pre-Socratic traditions of the Western philosophical tradition.

In any case, the task of discussing Sāṃkhya as a philosophical system involves a good deal more than historical research, philological investigation, and comparison and contrast with the agenda items of classical Indian philosophy, though, of course, such conventional approaches are a prerequisite for reaching the threshold of the system. Historical research provides some helpful bits and pieces of the puzzle, glimpses, and hints of how the Sāṃkhya methodology of enumeration slowly emerged into a conceptual system, even though the final system qua system is nowhere fully exposed in an extant text in other than a summary fashion. Philological work takes one a bit further, helping to determine the relevant set of technical terms and providing some sense of which lists and enumerations are more important than others. The Sāṃkhya texts, however, are largely laconic lists, and the later commentators are remarkably unhelpful in explaining the relevance or meaning of the various lists (and, in this sense, notably unlike the later commentators on the other systems of classical Indian philosophy). Further progress can be made by examining the manner in which Sāṃkhya is criticized in later philosophical traditions—for example, by Dignāga, Jinendrabuddhi, Mallavādin, Siṃhasūri, Śaṃkara, Rāmānuja, and so forth—but as was mentioned earlier this later agenda of Indian philosophy has moved considerably beyond the older Śāṃkhya speculative environment. Moreover, there remains not a single Sāṃkhya rejoinder to these ripostes by Sāṃkhya's opponents—with the possible exception of the *Yuktidīpikā*, which is clearly a Sāṃkhya polemic vis-à-vis Buddhist and Naiyāyika critiques of Sāṃkhya. Sāṃkhya's role in the history of classical Indian philosophy is comparable, *mutatis mutandis*, to that of Cārvāka materialism, that is to say, a sort of philosophical "whipping boy" abused by all but never allowed to respond—or to shift metaphors, an intellectual "paper tiger" seldom taken seriously but providing a convenient point of departure for doing other things.

In discussing Sāṃkhya philosophy, then, after one has pursued historical work as far as possible, after one has read all of the extant texts, and after one has studied all of the criticisms of Sāṃkhya in the larger classical philosophical literature, one has only attained what K. C. Bhattacharya has aptly called "... a hazy view of a grand system of speculative metaphysics." To sharpen the view, the interpreter must engage in "... supplying of missing links from one's imagination." This cannot mean, of course, inventing notions or projecting a favored perspective on the evidence that is unwarranted. The "supplying of missing links from one's imagination" means, rather, searching for relations, bundles of relations, and possible interpretive perspectives that may not be directly expressed in the texts but that bring together the various Sāṃkhya enumerations into more coherent patterns.

To some extent, of course, the textual tradition itself offers some halting steps in this direction. The *Yuktidīpikā*, for example, offers several intriguing interpretations that provide a larger view of the Sāṃkhya system as a whole, certainly more so than the *Kārikā* itself and all of its other commentaries. Similarly, Bhāvāgaṇeśa in his *Tattvayāthārthyadīpana* (on the *Tattvasamāsa*) provides a "constructive effort" in Bhattacharya's sense, as does Vijñānabhikṣu in his *Sāṃkhyapravacanabhāṣya*, although both of them, unfortunately, Vedānticize Sāṃkhya more than would seem warranted. Such efforts are important, however, in providing helpful clues about the manner in which the indigenous philosophical tradition interpreted the old Sāṃkhya system, as well as in warning against the dangers of bias, excessive polemic, and anachronism in any constructive undertaking.

Among modern scholarly "constructive efforts" (apart, of course, from the standard summaries of Sāṃkhya that one finds in numerous textbooks), one can identify four distinct approaches to reconstructing the Sāṃkhya system, namely, those of Richard Garbe, Surendranath Dasgupta, Erich Frauwallner, and K. C. Bhattacharya.[2] Garbe construes the old Sāṃkhya system as primarily an ancient philosophy of nature, a unique system that must have been the product of a single mind (either Kapila or Pañcaśikha) in ancient times. There is, therefore, neither a "preclassical Sāṃkhya" nor a postclassical Sāṃkhya. There is one ancient system, and one can range freely throughout the entire scope of Sāṃkhya literature in reconstructing that system.[3] Surendranath Dasgupta approaches his construction from the opposite direction. The old Sāṃkhya-Yoga texts are notoriously difficult to interpret, and it is only with Vijñānabhikṣu in his *Sāṃkhyapravacanabhāṣya* (in the medieval period) that one reaches a firm basis for piecing together the contours of the Sāṃkhya system as a whole. The key notions of the system, therefore, are presented through the interpretive perspective of Vijñānabhikṣu's Vedāntin metaphysics.[4] Erich Frauwallner (following the anti-Garbe polemic of Hermann Oldenberg) focuses primarily on Sāṃkhya as an important position in the history of epistemological discussions within Indian philosophy. Frauwallner construes Sāṃkhya's philosophy of nature as deriving largely from Pañcaśikha with its epistemological grounding given by Vārṣagaṇya and Vindhyavāsin. Īśvarakṛṣṇa's *Kārikā* is only a later summary of the system and fails to provide an adequate account of the old Sāṃkhya epistemology, which, therefore, must be reconstructed from other sources. Frauwallner relies heavily on the *Yuktidīpikā* in his construction of the final Sāṃkhya system and reconstructs Sāṃkhya cosmology from the old Purāṇas.[5] Finally, K. C. Bhattacharya construes the Sāṃkhya system as a bold "philosophy of the subject" that is ". . . based on speculative insight" and that ". . . demands imaginative-introspective effort at every stage on the part of the interpreter." Like Dasgupta, Bhattacharya relies heavily on Vijñānabhikṣu, although Bhattacharya is much more critical in his use of Vijñānabhikṣu than is Dasgupta.[6]

Each approach is clearly a "constructive effort" and has offered important new insights in understanding the system as a whole. Striking, however, is the divergence in perspective that each approach represents. There is usually, in the history of scholarship, an overall convergence of scholarly views, but in the case of Sāṃkhya philosophy a scholarly consensus has not obtained. Garbe and Frauwallner cannot both be correct. K. C. Bhattacharya's ". . . grand system of speculative metaphysics" bears little resemblance to Garbe's ancient philosophy of nature or Frauwallner's view of Sāṃkhya as an elementary and simplistic, though nevertheless important, epistemology. Dasgupta and Bhattacharya come close to convergence in their common use of Vijñānabhikṣu, but, whereas Dasgupta sees the genius of Sāṃkhya in the explanatory power of its *guṇa* theory (as interpreted by Vijñānabhikṣu and given an updated scientific explanation by B. N. Seal), K. C. Bhattacharya identifies the genius of Sāṃkhya in its emphasis on "reflection as spiritual function" and on its being a philosophy of spontaneous freedom.

In the present chapter, rather than following any one of these ancient or modern approaches, the Sāṃkhya system is constructed in a somewhat different manner. While, of course, benefiting from, and using where appropriate the approaches already mentioned, the "constructive effort" in the present context seeks to present Sāṃkhya philosophy as a total functioning system, on analogy with what Wittgenstein calls a "complete system of human communication." or a "form of life," or a "system of thought and action" for purposes of communicating a way of life.[7] The focus, in other words, is on grasping Sāṃkhya philosophy as a systemic, synchronic, and paradigmatic network of notions in which the various transactions within the larger system come to be exhibited in a more coherent intrasystemic way. Admittedly, such an interpretive approach is not as useful for comparing and contrasting Sāṃkhya with other kinds of modeling systems in Indian philosophy (for example, Vaiśeṣika, Buddhist, or Vedānta models), nor is it an especially useful approach if one is attempting a historical treatment of Sāṃkhya. It is to be noted, however, that these latter shortcomings are notoriously typical of Sāṃkhya literature itself. That is to say, the usual intersystemic polemics of Indian philosophy are glaringly absent in most Sāṃkhya literature, and more than that, there is no concern whatever in the Sāṃkhya literature for dealing with the history of the tradition. In other words, a systemic, synchronic, and paradigmatic approach may, in fact, more accurately reflect an original and authentic Sāṃkhya method of philosophizing.

At the same time, of course, it is clear enough that the Sāṃkhya system did not emerge fully grown, like Athena from the head of Zeus, even though the Sāṃkhya texts make precisely such claims for the founder of the system, Kapila.[8] Sāṃkhya philosophy was hardly the product of a single mind in ancient times, *pace* Garbe, nor was it a blurred set of intuitions that finally got its house in order through the genius of Vijñānabhikṣu, *pace* Dasgupta. The history of the tradition has already been surveyed in the last chapter and need not be repeated here, but it may be useful to summarize briefly the diachronic, locations for the synchronic system that is to be presented in the sequel, namely:

(1) There was a coherent Sāṃkhya conceptual system, often referred to as the *ṣaṣṭitantra* ("the system or science of sixty topics"), that was widely known by the year 400 of the Common Era (that is to say, the interim period that is post-Īśvarakṛṣṇa and pre-Dignāga).

(2) The conceptual system had been in existence for some centuries earlier and had been undergoing considerable modification through the work of Pañcaśikha, Vārṣagaṇya, Vindhyavāsin, and so on.

(3) There were probably a variety of attempts in this early period to summarize the basic contours of the system, but one summary came to be accepted as a standard presentation, namely, that summary as set forth in Īśvarakṛṣṇa's *Sāṃkhyakārikā*.

(4) This system, modified in some important respects (along the lines of Vārṣagaṇya's and Vindhyavāsin's views) is the basis of Patañjali's *Yogasūtra* and its commentaries.

(5) The commentaries on the *Kārikā* come considerably later, and apart from the *Yuktidīpikā*, appear to lack a firsthand grasp of the system qua system, and even the *Yuktidīpikā* presupposes the full content of the system instead of presenting that content.

(6) The *Tattvasamāsa* and the *Sāṃkhyasūtra* together with their commentaries, though undoubtedly preserving much old material, are nevertheless late texts (post-1000) that tend to interpret the old Sāṃkhya system with a notable Vedānta bias.

I. Sāṃkhya as Enumeration

Because the term "*sāṃkhya*" means "enumeration" or "relating to number," one reasonable point of departure for presenting the Sāṃkhya philosophical system as a "complete system of human communication" is to outline the more prominent sets of enumerations.

(A) *Enumerations relating to the basic principles (tattvas)*

The set of 25. First and foremost, of course, is the set of 25 that encompasses the basic principles of the system, namely:

(1) pure consciousness (*puruṣa*),
(2) primordial materiality (*mūlaprakṛti*),
(3) intellect (*buddhi* or *mahat*),
(4) egoity (*ahaṃkāra*), and
(5) mind (*manas*)—both a sense capacity and an action capacity;

(6) hearing (*śrotra*), (7) touching (*tvac*), (8) seeing (*cakṣus*), (9) tasting (*rasana*), and (10) smelling (*ghrāṇa*);	the five sense capacities (*buddhīndriyas*)
(11) speaking (*vāc*), (12) grasping/prehending (*pāṇi*), (13) walking/motion (*pāda*), (14) excreting (*pāyu*), and (15) procreating (*upastha*);	the five action capacities (*karmendriyas*)
(16) sound (*śabda*), (17) contact (*sparśa*), (18) form (*rūpa*), (19) taste (*rasa*), and (20) smell (*gandha*);	the five subtle elements (*tanmātras*)
(21) "space"/ether (*ākāśa*), (22) wind/air (*vāyu*), (23) fire (*tejas*), (24) water (*ap*), and (25) earth (*pṛthivī*).	the five gross elements (*mahābhūtas*)

According to Sāṃkhya philosophy, among these twenty-five principles, only the first two are independent existents, namely, pure consciousness (*puruṣa*) and primordial materiality (*mūlaprakṛti*). In other words, only items (1) and (2) exist in some sense as "distinct" or "separate" from one another. The two are described in Sāṃkhya philosophy as being ungenerated, outside of ordinary space and time, stable, simple, unsupported, nonmergent (or nondissolvable), without parts, and independent (SK 10).[9] The relation between them is one of simple copresence (SK 19). Pure consciousness is inherently inactive, but primordial materiality is inherently generative in the sense that it is capable of generating a set of discrete or manifest subdivisions when activated by the catalytic presence of pure consciousness. Items (3) through (25) make up the various subdivisions of primordial materiality and are, thus, internal to primordial materiality or represent "parts" of a totally functioning "whole," which is primordial materiality. These twenty-three subdivisions are described as being generated, temporal, spatial, unstable, composite, supported, mergent (or dissolvable), made up of parts, and contingent (SK 10). Seven of the subdivisions of primordial materiality, namely, intellect, egoity, and the five subtle elements are described as being both generated, that is to say, emergents from primordial materiality, and generative, that is to say, capable of generating subsequent subdivisions. The remaining sixteen subdivisions, namely, the mind, the five sense capacities, the five action capacities, and the five gross elements are only generated, that is to say, incapable of generating additional subdivisions. Intellect is generated out of primordial materiality but also generates egoity. Egoity is generated out of intellect but also generates the mind, the five sense capacities, the five action capacities, and the five subtle elements. The five subtle elements are generated out of egoity but also generate the five gross elements. Subtle elements are so called because they are the generic (*aviśeṣa*) material essences for all specific (*viśeṣa*) elements. They are imperceptible to ordinary persons, whereas gross elements can be perceived by ordinary persons.

The subtle elements are the generic presuppositions for the experience of all specific objectivity. Five kinds of specific sensations may be experienced, namely, specific vibrations via the ear (speaking, music, sounds, and so forth), specific contacts via the skin (hot, cold, and so forth), specific forms via the eyes (colors, shapes), specific tastes via the tongue (bitter, sweet), and specific smells via the nose. According to Sāṃkhya, the apprehension of a specific vibration is only possible if there is an undifferentiated generic receptivity for sound, or put differently, if the experiencer is in some sense actually constituted by the generic, material essence of sound, that is, actually made up of a subtle sound element. The subtle sound element itself is not any particular sound. It is the generic essence of sound, the presupposition for all particular sounds, the universal possibility of sound-as-such. Similarly, the apprehension of a specific contact is only possible if there is an undifferentiated generic receptivity for touch, the universal possibility of touch-as-such, namely, the subtle touch element, and so forth. The subtle elements, therefore, are not functions or capacities (as are, for example, the five senses or the motor capacities of an organism) nor are they the actual sense organs (eye, ear, and so forth) which, of course, are aggregates of gross elements. They are, rather, subtle, material essences or presuppositions with which perceptual and motor functioning correlate and through which certain aspects of the material world become differentiated. If such subtle, material essences or presuppositions were not present, no specific objects could possibly be experienced or become manifest, and in this sense the subtle elements correlate with and may be said to "generate" the gross elements. In the absence of subtle elements, in other words, there would only be an unmanifest mass of primordial materiality. Some have suggested that the subtle elements might be usefully compared to Platonic ideas or universals, but it must be kept in mind that for Sāṃkhya all such ideas or universals have some sort of subtle, material basis (requiring, in other words, a reconceptualization of idealism in terms of reductive materialism, as will be discussed further in the sequel).[10]

Regarding the manner in which gross elements are derived from subtle elements, the important Sāṃkhya texts differ, suggesting that the manner of derivation was an open issue even in the classical period. The *Kārikā* itself simply asserts that the five gross elements are derived from the five subtle elements (SK 22 and 28). Some commentaries (*The Tattvakaumudī*, *Māṭharavṛtti*, *Jayamaṅgalā*, and so forth) argue for a so-called "accumulation theory" of derivation, according to which each successive subtle element combines with the preceding ones in order to generate a gross element.[11] The subtle sound element generates the space/ether gross element (*ākāśa*); the subtle touch element and the subtle sound element generate the gross air/wind element (*vāyu*); the subtle form element with the subtle sound and touch elements generate the gross fire element (*tejas*); the subtle taste element with subtle sound, touch, and form elements generate the gross water element (*āp*); and the subtle smell element with the subtle sound, touch, form, and taste elements generate the gross earth element (*pṛthivī*). According to the *Yuktidīpikā* (Pandeya edition, p. 91 and pp. 117-118, and hereafter all page references are to the Pandeya edition), this "accumulation theory" is attributed to Vārṣagaṇya. The commentary of Gauḍapāda argues, however, that each subtle element is capable of generating each gross element singly. The Chinese commentary on the *Kārikā* offers yet another interpretation.[12] According to it, each subtle element generates not only a respective gross element but a respective sense capacity as well. Thus, the subtle sound element generates not only *ākāśa* but also the sense capacity of hearing (*śrotra*), and so forth. Although an attractive idea, it tends to confuse the actual physical sense organ with an actual sense capacity. This may well be an old notion, but it is hard to imagine that the final philosophical system would have settled for such a view. Still other East Asian commentaries offer further interpretations, according to one of which the five subtle elements generate not only gross elements (in an accumulation manner) but the entire set of eleven sense and action capacities as well.[13] For Īśvarakṛṣṇa and the classical tradition, however, it is clear enough that the five subtle elements are only generative of the five gross elements (and not the various sense and action capacities), although the manner of derivation was evidently a continuing matter of debate. All specific objects (*viṣaya*) in the phenomenal empirical world of ordinary experience are collocations or aggregations of the various gross elements and are never themselves numbered as basic principles.

Given these various distinctions regarding their derivation, the initial listing of 25 principles may now be more precisely exhibited in a chart.

(1) consciousness / (2) primordial materiality

↓

(3) intellect

↓

(4) egoity

↙ ↘

(5) mind			
(6) hearing	(11) speaking	(16) sound	(21) space
(7) touching	(12) grasping	(17) touch	(22) wind
(8) seeing	(13) walking	(18) form →	(23) fire
(9) tasting	(14) excreting	(19) taste	(24) water
(10) smelling	(15) procreating	(20) smell	(25) earth
(the elevenfold capacities: sensing, motor functioning, and mind)		(the five subtle elements)	(the five gross elements)

Principles (5) through (15), and (21) through (25) are generated products (*vikāra*, SK 3).[14] Principles (3), (4), and (16) through (20) are both generative and generated (*prakṛti-vikṛti*, SK 3). Principle (2) is generative but ungenerated (*avikṛti*), and (1) is neither generative nor generated (*na prakṛtir na vikṛtiḥ puruṣah*, SK 3).

The set of 3. Principles (3), (4), and (5), namely, intellect, egoity, and mind, taken together are referred to as the "internal organ" (*antaḥkaraṇa*, SK 33), and their three respective functions are "reflective discerning" (*adhyavasāya*), "self-awareness" (*abhimāna*), and "intentionality" (*saṃkalpaka*). Together they perform the task of intellectual awareness, which functions not only in immediate experience but encompasses the past and future as well (SK 33).

The set of 10. Items (6) through (10), and (11) through (15), namely, the five sense capacities and the five motor functions, taken together are referred to as the "external organ" (*bāhyakaraṇa*, SK 33), and their respective activities provide mere sensings (*ālocanamātra*, SK 28), namely, hearing, touching, and so forth; and basic motor skills, namely, speaking, grasping, and so forth (SK 28). These operate only in immediate or present experience (SK 33).

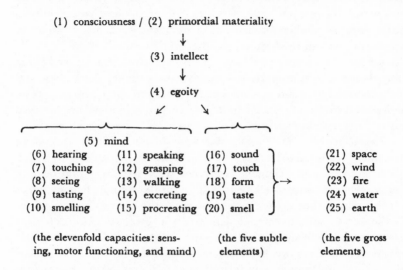

The set of 13. Items (3) through (15), namely, intellect, egoity, mind, the five sense capacities, and the five motor functions, taken together are referred to as the "thirteenfold instrument" (*trayodaśakaraṇa*, SK32), or what is often called simply the "essential core" (*liṅga*, SK 40), which is the presupposition for all experience. The "thirteenfold instrument" or *liṅga* functions as a whole by "seizing" (*āharaṇa*) (presumably through the motor capacities), "holding" (*dhāraṇa*) (presumably through the sense capacities), and "illuminating" (*prakāśa*) (presumably through the "internal organ") (SK 32).[15] The tenfold "external" divisions of the *liṅga* are referred to as the "doors" (*dvāra*) of awareness, and the three divisions of the "internal organ" are referred to as the "door-keepers" (*dvārins*) (SK 35).

The set of 17. Items (4) through (20) represent the structure of egoity (*ahaṃkāra*), and it should be noted, therefore, that "self-awareness," according to Sāṃkhya philosophy, is a complex phenomenon encompassing mental states (mind, sense capacities, and motor functioning) and physical components (the subtle elements).[16]

The set of 18. Items (3) through (20), namely, intellect, egoity, mind, the five sense capacities, the five motor functions, and the five subtle elements, taken together are referred to as the "subtle body" (*liṅgaśarīra* or *sūkṣmaśarīra*), which is detachable from any particular gross body and is, therefore, capable of transmigration in a continuing series of gross embodiments.[17] Gross bodies (*sthūlaśarīra*) are one-time-only aggregations of gross elements. In the case of human gross bodies, these are genetically derived from mother and father (with hair, blood, and flesh from the maternal line, and bone, tendon, and marrow from the paternal line). Such human gross bodies are "womb born" (*jarāyuja*) and become enlivened when linked with a transmigrating "subtle body." There are also "egg born" (*aṇḍaja*), "seed born" (*udbhijja*) and "moisture born" (*svedaja*) gross bodies for other sorts of sentient beings (and see *Yuktidīpikā*, p. 120 on SK 39).

(B) *Enumerations relating to the fundamental predispositions* (*bhāva*).

The set of 8. Inherent to the intellect, in addition to its basic *tattva* nature of reflective discerning, is a set of 8 fundamental predispositions (*bhāva*) or instinctual tendencies that guide the life-trajectory of a sentient being, namely:

(1) the predisposition toward meritorious behavior (*dharma*),
(2) the predisposition toward knowledge (*jñāna*),
(3) the predisposition toward nonattachment (*vairāgya*),
(4) the predisposition toward power (*aiśvarya*),
(5) the predisposition toward demeritorious behavior (*adharma*),
(6) the predisposition toward ignorance (*ajñāna*),
(7) the predisposition toward attachment (*avairāgya*), and
(8) the predisposition toward impotence (*anaiśvarya*) (SK 23).

Whereas reflective discerning represents the material dimension of *buddhi*, the fundamental predispositions represent the "efficient" possibilities of the *buddhi*. The fundamental predispositions, therefore, are called "efficient causes" (*nimittas*) and are correlated with eight resulting (*naimittika*) trajectories, namely:

(1) the tendency to move upward in the cycle of transmigration (*ūrdhva*),
(2) the tendency to move toward final release (*apavarga*),
(3) the tendency to move toward merger in primal materiality (*prakṛtilaya*),
(4) the tendency to move toward increasing control over life (*avighāta*),
(5) the tendency to move downward in the cycle of transmigration (*adhastāt*),
(6) the tendency to move toward increasing attachment and bondage (*bandha*),
(7) the tendency to move toward further involvement in transmigration (*saṃsāra*),
(8) the tendency to move toward declining control over life (*vighāta*) (SK 42-45).

The fundamental predispositions are innate or inherent (*sāṃsiddhika* or *prākṛtika*), but they can be modified (*vaikṛta*) in terms of intensity or dominance of one (or more) over another (or others) through the cycle of continuing transmigration (SK 43). The "essential core" (*liṅga*) or the subtle body carries a particular constellation of these predispositions as it proceeds in the process of rebirth, and a particular sentient being, which becomes enlivened by the coalescence of a *liṅga* with a gross body, is, as it were, "coded" or "programmed" at birth by these tendencies and, hence, predisposed to a certain life trajectory.

Comparing this set of 8 predispositions with the earlier set of 25 basic principles, it is perhaps helpful to use a computer or a linguistic metaphor. Regarding a computer metaphor, it might be suggested that the set of 25 basic principles is the "hardware" of the Sāṃkhya system, whereas the set of 8 predispositions with the resultant trajectories represents the "software" of the Sāṃkhya system. Or, using a metaphor from linguistics, it might be suggested that the set of 25 basic principles represents the deep structural "syntactic" component of the Sāṃkhya system, whereas the set of 8 predispositions with the resultant trajectories represents the deep structural "semantic" component of the Sāṃkhya system. In any case, the Sāṃkhya system asserts that these two sets are fundamental and presuppose one another.

> The *liṅga* (namely the realm of *tattvas*) cannot function without the *bhāvas*. The *bhāvas* cannot function without the *liṅga*. Therefore, a two fold creation (*sarga*) operates (or functions) called *liṅga* and *bhāva*. (SK 52).

The set of 5 *life breaths* (*vāyu prāṇa*). In addition to the set of 8 fundamental predispositions that determine the life trajectory of an organism, a particular life-support system is also necessary for the maintenance of a given life. According to Sāṃkhya philosophy, this support system is provided by a network of five "winds" or "breaths," namely:

(1) "respiration" or "breathing" (*prāṇa*), located in the heart primarily, but also circulating in the mouth, nose, and lungs,
(2) "excretion" or "disposing breath" (*apāna*), located in the navel and lower portions of the body,
(3) "digestion" or "nutrient breath" (*samāna*), located primarily in the region between the navel and the heart, but carrying nutrients equally to all parts of the body,
(4) "cognition" or "up breath" (*udāna*), located primarily in the nose and brain and enabling an organism to utter intelligible sounds (communication, language, and so forth), and
(5) "homeostasis" or "diffused breath" (*vyāna*), pervading the entire body and presumably maintaining the general physical and emotional balance of an organism (SK 29).

The author of the *Yuktidīpikā*, interestingly, further relates these biological "winds" or "breaths" to certain external or social tendencies as well, with *prāṇa* being related to social obedience, *apāna* being related to striving for a higher or lower social status, *samāna* being associated with social cooperation, *udāna* being related to a sense of social superiority, and *vyāna* being linked with a strong sense of devotion or any deep bond of love (*Yuktidīpikā*, p. 106 on SK 29).

The set of 5 *sources of action* (*karmayoni*). Although the *Kārikā* does not mention the set of 5 *karmayonis*, the author of the *Yuktidīpikā* indicates that the set of sources of action is related to the set of 5 "winds" or "breaths" just enumerated (*Yuktidīpikā*, pp. 107-108). The set explains the basic motivations for the maintenance of life, namely:

(1) "perseverance" (*dhṛti*), an organism's innate urge to follow through over a given period of time on a particular trajectory,
(2) "faith" (*śraddhā*), an organism's innate urge to maintain a trajectory on the basis of belief or trust in the validity of a social or religious heritage,
(3) "the desire for satisfaction" (*sukha* or *icchā*,) an organism's innate urge to seek its own self-gratification.
(4) "the desire to know" (*vividiṣā*), an organism's innate urge to be curious and critical, and
(5) "the desire not to know" (*avividiṣā*), an organism's innate urge to be insufficiently discriminating.

The sources of action are also mentioned in the *Tattvasamāsa* (*sūtra* 9) and appear just before the five "breaths" or "winds," lending perhaps some support to the *Yuktidīpikā's* claim that the sources of action should be construed together with the breaths. The commentaries vary widely in their interpretations of the sources of action, possibly suggesting that they are very old notions that eventually became less important as the system developed. In any case, the sources of action appear to be related to the same sorts of concerns that find expression in the set of 8 predispositions, that is to say, basic attitudes and dispositions that propel an organism in a given direction. Unlike the predispositions, however, which are quite unconscious and represent the inherited karmic propensities of an organism, the sources of action appear to be conscious and could presumably represent the dispositional possibilities available to an organism in any given life. Furthermore, it would appear that these sources of action can be construed either positively or negatively.[18] Positively, they would suggest that an organism can be disciplined, faithful, pleasant, thoughful, and circumspect in avoiding matters that cannot be known. Negatively, they would suggest that an organism can be stubborn, gullible, pleasure seeking, overly critical, or skeptical, and insensitive or thick headed regarding obvious truths.

(C) *Enumerations relating to the phenomenal, empirical world of ordinary life* (*pratyayasarga*) (*bhautikasarga*).

The set of 50 "*categories*" (*padārthas*). The set of 25 basic principles interacting with the set of 8 predispositions within the intellect generate what the Sāṃkhya system calls the "phenomenal creation" (*pratyayasarga*), made up of the set of 5 fundamental "misconceptions" (*viparyayas*), the set of 28 "dysfunctions" (*aśaktis*), the set of 9 "contentments" (*tuṣṭis*) and the set of 8 "spiritual attainments" (*siddhis*). Taken together, they are referred to as the set of 50 "categories," namely:

(1-5) the five categories of fundamental misconception (*viparyaya*) with the ancient technical names *tamas, moha, mahāmoha, tāmisra,* and *andhatāmisra* (or, according to Pātañjala-Sāṃkhya, called the five "afflictions" or *kleśas*, namely, *avidyā, asmitā, rāga, dveṣa,* and *abhiniveśa*):[19]

(1) "darkness" (*tamas*) or "ignorance" (*avidyā*), described as having 8 subdivisions in the sense that there is a failure to discriminate (*aviveka*) pure consciousness (*puruṣa*) from the eight generative principles (or, in other words, the failure to distinguish *puruṣa* from primordial materiality, intellect, egoity, and the five subtle elements) (SK 48),

(2) "confusion" (*moha*) or preoccupation with one's own identity (*asmitā*), also described as having 8 subdivisions in the sense that finite beings seek to overcome their finitude by pursuing the eight well-known omnipotent or supernatural powers (*siddhis*) (including becoming atomic in size, becoming exceedingly large in size, becoming light or buoyant, becoming heavy, becoming all-pervasive, attaining all desires, gaining lordship over elemental forces and immediate gratification) (SK.48),

(3) "extreme confusion" (*mahāmoha*) or passionate attachment (*rāga*), described as having 10 subdivisions either (a) in the sense that one becomes attached to the five subtle elements and the five gross elements (according to most of the *Kārikā* commentaries) or (b) in the sense that one becomes attached to the 10 basic social relationships (including father, mother, son, brother, sister, wife, daughter, teacher, friend, or colleague) (according to the *Yuktidīpikā* under SK 48), (4) "gloom" (*tāmisra*) or aversion (*dveṣa*), described as having 18 subdivisions in the sense that one becomes frustrated and cynical because of the failure to attain the eight conventional *siddhis* or supernatural attainments and one becomes angry or hateful toward the tenfold material existence (subtle and gross) or the 10 basic social relationships (SK 48), and (5) "utter darkness" (*andhatāmisra*) or the instinctive fear of death (*abhiniveśa*), described also as having 18 subdivisions in the sense that although one has become cynical about material and social life one nevertheless clings to it tenaciously (SK 48). These five fundamental "misconceptions" with their 62 subdivisions are characteristic of most conventional sentient life and represent the core afflictions of ordinary finite existence;

(6-33) the twenty-eight categories of perceptual, motor, and mental dysfunction (*aśakti*), 11 of which are correlated with disorders of the five sense capacities (for example, deafness, blindness, and so forth), the five motor capacities, and the mind, and 17 of which are correlated with disorders of the intellect (the number 17 representing the negation of the 9 *tuṣṭis* and 8 *siddhis* next to be described) (SK 49);

(34-42) the nine categories for a reasonably balanced and conventional mendicant life, the contentments (*tuṣṭi*), described as referring to certain more advanced forms of sentient life who have not yet overcome the first of the fundamental misconceptions but who have made considerable progress in understanding sentient existence, both internally (in terms of a proper conception of primordial materiality, a proper conception of the appropriate means for living a conventional mendicant existence, a proper conception of delayed gratification, and the ability to withstand the vicissitudes of ordinary existence) and externally (in terms of not being excessively attached to the fivefold structure of material existence and thereby not being involved in the acquisition, preservation, waste, enjoyment, or injury of ordinary worldly life) (SK49);

(43-50) the eight categories that represent the authentic attainments (*siddhi*) (in contrast to the conventional supernatural attainments as already described above under "confusion") that are conducive to final discrimination and release, namely:

(43) rational reflection and reasoning (ūha),

(44) appropriate verbal instruction from a qualified teacher (*śabda*),

(45) careful study (*adhyayana*),

(46) thoughtful discussion with appropriate peers (*suhṛtprāpti*),

(47) an open yet disciplined temperament (*dāna*),

(48) a progressive overcoming of the frustrations of body and mind,

(49) a progressive overcoming of the frustrations of material and social existence, and

(50) a progressive overcoming of the frustrations related to the cycle of rebirth and transmigration (the three being construed together and referring to overcoming the three kinds of frustration or *duḥkhatraya*) (SK 51).[20]

The author of the *Yuktidīpikā* correlates this set of 50 categories with the set of the 8 predispositions in the following fashion: the primacy of the predisposition toward ignorance (*ajñāna*) accompanied by nonmerit (*adharma*), passionate attachment (*avairāgya*), and impotence (*anaiśvarya*) generates the fundamental misconceptions (*viparyaya*) that are at the core of most ordinary sentient life; the primacy of the predisposition toward impotence (*anaiśvarya*), accompanied by *adharma*, *ajñāna*, and *avairāgya* generates the disorders of perceptual, motor, and mental functioning (*aśakti*); the primacy of the predisposition toward non-attachment (*vairāgya*), accompanied by *dharma* and *aiśvarya*, generates conventional mendicant life (*tuṣṭi*); and the predisposition toward knowledge (*jñāna*) generates the spiritual attainments (*siddhi*) conducive to final discrimination and release (*Yuktidīpikā*, pp. 124-136). The author of the *Yuktidīpikā* also relates the set of 50 categories to an old creation myth, thereby linking the *pratyayasarga* or "phenomenal creation" to what is apparently an archaic cosmogony reminiscent of the old Upaniṣads. According to the myth, at the beginning of the world cycle, the Great Being (*māhātmyaśarīra*, presumably Brahmā or Hiraṇyagarbha), though endowed with all the requisite organs, was nevertheless alone and needed offspring to perform his work (*karman*). Meditating, he first created from his mind a set of 5 "fundamental streams" (*mukhyasrotas*), but he found them insufficient for satisfying his needs. He next created a set of 28 "horizontal streams" (*tiryaksrotas*) but again was dissatisfied. He then created a set of 9 "upward moving streams" (*ūrdhvasrotas*), but his work still could not be accomplished. Finally, he created a set of 8 "downward streams" (*arvāksrotas*), which did fulfil his needs. These streams (*srotas*), of course, are the

5 *viparyayas*, the 28 *aśaktis*, the 9 *tuṣṭis* and the 8 *siddhis*. The fundamental streams are characteristic of the plant realm (or the simplest forms of life). The twenty-eight horizontal streams are characteristic of the realm of animals, birds, and insects. The nine upward streams are characteristic of the divine realm, and the eight downward streams are characteristic of the human realm (*Yuktidīpikā* on SK 46, p. 127).

The set of 14 *types* (*caturdaśavidha*) *of sentient life* (*bhautikasarga*). There are fourteen levels or realms of sentient creatures "from Brahmā down to a blade of grass" (SK 53-54):

(1) the realm of Brahmā,
(2) the realm of Prajāpati,
(3) the realm of Indra,
(4) the realm of the Pitṛs,
(5) the realm of the Gandharvas,
(6) the realm of the Yakṣas or Nāgas,
(7) the realm of the Rakṣases, and
(8) the realm of the Piśācas.

} The eightfold celestial realms (*daiva*)

(9) the human realm (*mānuṣaka*)

(10) the realm of (domestic) animals (*paśu*),
(11) the realm of (wild) animals (*mṛga*)
(12) the realm of birds and flying insects (*pakṣin*),
(13) the realm of crawling creatures (*sarīsṛpa*), and
(14) the realm of plants and immovables (*sthāvara*).

} fivefold animal and plant realms (*tairyagyona*)

The set is obviously a hierarchical cosmology or cosmogony encompassing the divine or celestial realm (*adhidaiva*), the external natural world (*adhibhūta*) apart from the human condition, and the human realm (*adhyātma*), and it is within these realms that one encounters the three kinds of frustration (*duḥkhatraya*) SK 55 and SK 1). The human realm and the animal/plant realm are relatively easy to understand. The divine or celestial realm, however, is not as clear, but there are some passages in the *Yuktidīpikā* that offer some clarification. From one point of view, the divine realm is the realm of the *māhātmyaśarīras*, Brahmā, Hiraṇyagarbha, Prajāpati, and so forth, who perform specific tasks (*adhikāra*) in the cosmos and who are able to generate their own bodies by a simple act of will. From another point of view, the divine realm is the realm of the great Sāṃkhya precursors, especially Kapila who emerges at the beginning of the world cycle fully endowed with the positive fundamental predispositions of meritorious behavior, knowledge, renunciation, and power. Kapila passes on his knowledge to six other great Sāṃkhya *sādhus*, namely, Sanaka, Sanandana, Sanātana, Āsuri, Voḍhu, and Pañcaśikha, and an old verse refers to the group together as the "seven great seers" (*saptamaharṣis*) (quoted by Gauḍapāda under SK. 1). From still another point of view, the divine realm is clearly linked up with the process of transmigration through the heavenly spheres. The author of the *Yuktidīpikā*, in explaining the adjectives "*sāṃsiddhika,*" "*prākṛta,*" and "*vaikṛta*" as modifiers of the term "*bhāva*" in verse 43 of the *Kārikā* (*Yuktidīpikā*, p. 124) comments that those beings endowed with "modified" (*vaikṛta*) predispositions transmigrate in the usual fashion through a continuing process of rebirth, (b) those beings endowed with "inherently powerful" (*prākṛta*) predispositions (namely, the *māhātmyaśarīras*, or Great Beings) can generate whatever bodies they wish; and (c) those beings endowed with "innate" (*sāṃsiddhika*) or perfect predispositions have subtle bodies that transmigrate among "the planets, the lunar mansions, and the stars" (*grahaṇakṣatratārādi*). Furthermore, the author of the *Yuktidīpikā* introduces a mythical scheme of "six ways of reproduction" (*ṣaṭsiddhi*) that was presumably an ancient way of explaining the manner in which divine realm reproduction differs from natural reproduction. According to the myth (*Yuktidīpikā*, pp.120-121), in the time prior to creaton, spiritual entities simply willed or desired themselves into existence. Such is the *manaḥsiddhi* or the "spiritual power of simple willing or desire." When this capacity became weakened, entities reproduced themselves with the "spiritual power of amorous glances" (*cakṣuḥsiddhi*). When this became weakened, reproduction occurred by the "spiritual power of speaking with one another" (*vāksiddhi*). When this weakened, reproduction took place by the "spiritual power of touching" (*hastasiddhi*). When this weakened, reproduction occurred through the "spiritual power of embracing" (*āśleṣasiddhi*). Finally, when even this weakened, reproduction required the "spiritual power of sexual intercourse" (*dvandvasiddhi*), and from then onward the ordinary process of transmigration was in operation.[21]

The *daiva* realm is given a further explication in the late text, *Kramadīpikā*, and although it is difficult to be sure if the interpretation therein is an authentic reading of the old Sāṃkhya philosophy, it nevertheless provides an interesting set of correlations. In explaining *sūtra* 7 of the *Tattvasamāsa* (namely, "*adhyātmam adhibhūtam adhidaivataṃ ca*") the author of the *Kramadīpikā* offers the following correlations:[22]

	adhyātma	*adhibhūta*	*adhidaiva*
(1)	intellect (*buddhi*)	what can be ascertained (*boddhavya*)	Brahmā
(2)	egoity (*ahaṃkāra*)	what can be thought (*mantavya*)	Rudra
(3)	mind (*manas*)	what can be intended (*saṃkalpitavya*)	Candra

(4)	hearing	what can be heard	Diś
(5)	touching	what can be touched	Vāyu
(6)	seeing	what can be seen	Āditya
(7)	tasting	what can be tasted	Varuṇa
(8)	smelling	what can be smelled	Pṛthivī
(9)	speaking	what can be spoken	Agni
(10)	grasping	what can be grasped	Indra
(11)	walking	what can be gone to	Viṣṇu
(12)	excreting	what can be expelled	Mitra
(13)	procreating	what can be sexually enjoyed	Prajāpati

The scheme in the *Kramadīpikā* is clearly different from the scheme of Īśvarakṛṣṇa in *Kārikā* 53, but both schemes may well have in common a tendency to make the divine realm recapitulate the human realm (or vice versa, of course). In this regard one wonders if Īśvarakṛṣṇa's scheme in *Kārikā* 53 might be a recapitulation, for example, of the old eightfold *prakṛti*,[23] namely:

(1)	primordial materiality (*avyakta* or *prakṛti*)	(1)	Brahmā
(2)	intellect (*buddhi*)	(2)	Prajāpati
(3)	egoity (*ahaṃkāra*)	(3)	Indra
(4)	sound-*tanmātra* or space/ether (*bhūta*)	(4)	Pitṛs
(5)	touch-*tanmātra* or wind (*bhūta*)	(5)	Gandharvas
(6)	form-*tanmātra* or fire (*bhūta*)	(6)	Yakṣas or Nāgas
(7)	taste-*tanmātra* or water (*bhūta*)	(7)	Rakṣases
(8)	smell-*tanmātra* or earth (*bhūta*)	(8)	Piśācas

Or possibly the first three levels of the divine realm may be a recapitulation of the threefold "internal organ" in the following fashion:[24]

(1)	intellect	(1)	Brahmā
(2)	egoity	(2)	Prajāpati
(3)	mind	(3)	Indra
(4)	sound or space/ether	(4)	Pitṛs
(5)	touch or wind	(5)	Gandharvas
(6)	form or fire	(6)	Yakṣas or Nāgas
(7)	taste or water	(7)	Rakṣases
(8)	smell or earth	(8)	Piśācas

One also wonders if a similar recapitulation may be operating with respect to the action capacities in relation to the mythical notion of "the six ways of reproduction" in the following fashion:[25]

(1)	*buddhi/ahaṃkāra/manas*	(1)	*manaḥsiddhi*
(2)	speaking	(2)	*vāksiddhi*
(3)	grasping	(3)	*hastasiddhi*
(4)	walking	(4)	*cakṣuḥsiddhi*
(5)	expelling	(5)	*āśleṣasiddhi*
(6)	procreating	(6)	*dvandvasiddhi*

Such reconstructions are admittedly risky and may well be wrong, but there is ample evidence in the texts that the old Sāṃkhya teachers did make methodological use of correlations and recapitulations in their speculative attempts to synthesize an overall view of the world.

Thus far, three kinds of Sāṃkhya enumerations have been presented, and it may be useful to pause at this point to summarize in outline form the material that has been covered.

(A) Enumerations relating to the basic principles:
- (1) The set of 25 principles;
  - (a) The set of 2 principles that are actually distinct or separate, namely, pure consciousness and primordial materiality;
  - (b) The set of 23 subdivisions of primordial materiality;
    - (i) The set of 7 that are generated and also generative, including intellect, egoity, and the five subtle elements;
    - (ii) The set of 16 products that are generated but not generative, including mind, the five senses, the five motor capacities, and the five gross elements;
- (2) The set of 3 making up the "internal organ," including intellect, egoity, and mind;
- (3) The set of 10 making up the "external organ," including the five senses and the five motor capacities;
- (4) The set of 13 making up the "essential core" that is a prerequisite for experience, a combination of the threefold internal organ and the tenfold external organ;
- (5) The set of 17 representing the complex mental and physical structure of egoity;

(6) The set of 18 making up the "subtle body" that transmigrates through successive rebirths, including the thirteenfold *liṅga* together with the five subtle elements;[26]
(7) Collocations of gross elements that generate one-time-only gross bodies that are womb-born, egg-born, seed-born, and moisture-born.

(B) Enumerations relating to the fundamental predispositions:
(1) The set of 8 predispositions inherent in the intellect, carried by the essential core in the course of transmigration, "coding" or "programming" a particular life trajectory in successive rebirths, including meritorious behavior, knowledge, nonattachment, power, demeritorious behavior, ignorance, attachment, and impotence—called also "efficient causes";
(2) The set of 8 resultant life trajectories, including moving upward, final release, dissolution in primordial materiality, nonrestraint, moving downward, bondage, transmigration, and declining control;
(3) The set of 5 "winds" or "breaths" that support the embodied condition;
(4) The set of 5 sources of action that enable an organism to persevere through an embodiment;

(C) Enumerations relating to the phenomenal, empirical world of ordinary life:
(1) The set of 50 categories or the phenomenal creation;
(a) The set of 5 fundamental misconceptions; 62 subdivisions;
(b) The set of 28 dysfunctions;
(c) The set of 9 contentments;
(d) The set of 8 spiritual attainments;
(2) The set of 50 "streams," which cosmologically recapitulate the 50 *padārthas*;
(a) The set of 5 *mukhyasrotas* (plant and other simple life forms);
(b) The set of 28 *tiryaksrotas* (animal life);
(c) The set of 9 *ūrdhvasrotas* (divine or celestial realms);
(d) The set of 8 *arvāksrotas* (human realm);
(3) The set of 14 levels of sentient life, including the eightfold celestial realm, the one human realm, and the fivefold animal and plant realm, or, in other words, *adhidaiva*, *adhyātma*, and *adhibhūta*;[27]
(4) The set of 6 "spiritual powers, of reproduction" (*ṣaṭsiddhis*) (in descending order from mind-only, amorous glances, speaking, touching, embracing and, finally, sexual intercourse).

When one inquires into the manner in which these three kinds of enumerations are related to one another, a crucial clue is available from the *Yuktidīpikā*. In referring to the various levels of creation in the Sāṃkhya system (*Yuktidīpikā*, p. 21, on SK 2), the author of the *Yuktidīpikā* offers the following observation concerning the manifest world (*vyakta*):

> The manifest world has three dimensions: (1) a "form (*rūpa*) dimension, (b) a "projective" (*pravṛtti*) dimension, and (c) a "consequent" (*phala*) dimension. To be specific, the "form" dimension is made up of intellect, egoity, the five subtle elements, the eleven sense and motor capacities, and the five gross elements. The "projective" dimension, generally speaking, is twofold: getting what is advantageous (*hitakāmaprayojana*) and avoiding what is disadvantageous (*ahitakāmaprayojana*). Specifically, it involves the various functions of the "sources of action" and the maintenance of life (*prāṇa*, and so forth) in terms of the five "winds." The "consequent" dimension is (likewise) twofold, namely, the perceptible, manifest, or apparent (*dṛṣṭa*) and the imperceptible or latent (*adṛṣṭa*). The perceptible or manifest relates to the attainments, contentments, dysfunctions, and fundamental misconceptions. The imperceptible or latent relates to the acquisition of a particular body in the cycle of rebirth (*saṃsāra*) within the hierarchy of manifest life from the realm of the gods (Brahmā, and so forth) to simple plant life.[28]

Elsewhere, the author of the *Yuktidīpikā* refers to the three dimensions of the manifest world with a slightly different terminology, namely, under SK 56 (p. 140):

> (There is a dimension) called *tattva*, made up of intellect and so forth; (a dimension) called *bhāva*, made up of meritorious behavior, and so forth; (and a dimension) called *bhūta*, made up of the atmosphere, and so forth.[29]

Bringing together, then, the three kinds of enumerations presented thus far with these references from the *Yuktidīpikā*, there would appear to be three distinct yet related dimensions in the full Sāṃkhya system:

(A) The "constitutive" dimension, referred to as the "form" (*rūpa*), the "principle" (*tattva*) or the "essential core" (*liṅga*) realm;

(B) The "projective" dimension, referred to as the "projecting" or the "intentional" (*pravṛtti*), the "predispositional" (*bhāva*), or the "efficient cause and effect" (*nimittanaimittika*) realm; and

(C) The "consequent" dimension, referred to as the "resultant" (*phala*), the "creaturely" or "what has become" (*bhūta*), or the "phenomenal creation" (*pratyayasarga*) realm, or, in other words, the phenomenal, empirical world of ordinary experience (*bhautikasarga*).

Dimensions (A) and (B) interact or combine with one another in generating dimension (C). Referring once again to the computer and linguistic metaphors mentioned earlier, if (A) is the "hardware" of the Sāṃkhya system and (B) the "software," then dimension (C) is, as it were, the "printout" of the functioning system. Or, again, if dimension (A) is the deep-structural "syntactic" component of the Sāṃkhya system, and dimension (B) the deep-structural "semantic" component of the system, then dimension (C) is, as it were, the surface-structural phonological component. Such metaphors, of course, are only rough approximations, but they have at least a heuristic value in directing attention to the systemic aspects of the old Sāṃkhya philosophy.

II. Sāṃkhya as Process Materialism

At the outset of the discussion of Sāṃkhya enumerations, primordial materiality was described as being inherently generative, but attention was thereafter focused on the various principles, predispositions, and categories of the Sāṃkhya world view, or what the *Yuktidīpikā* calls the "constitutive" or "form" (*rūpa*) realm, the "projective" or "intentional" (*pravṛtti*) realm, and the "consequent" or "resultant" (*phala*) realm. As a result, the basic components and core structures of the Sāṃkhya world have been exhibited, but little has been said about the Sāṃkhya conceptualization of the inner essence or the underlying reality of primordial materiality itself. Regarding this latter issue, Sāṃkhya philosophy makes use of a formulation that is unique in the history of Indian philosophy (and unique, for that matter, in the general history of philosophy as well), namely, the notion of *triguṇa* or *traiguṇya*, which may be translated in this context as "tripartite constituent process."

The word "*guṇa*" in Sanskrit usually means a "cord," "string," or "thread." The term can refer to a "rope" or to the various "strands" that make up a rope. Moreover, the word can be used in the sense of "secondary" or "subordinate," and in much of Indian philosophical discussion (for example, especially in Nyāya-Vaiśeṣika) the term is used to refer to the notion of a "quality" or "attribute" of a "substance" (*dravya*) or thing. The term also comes to be employed in moral discourse, so that "*guṇa*" may refer to "outstanding merit" or "moral excellence."

In Sāṃkhya philosophy, however, the term takes on a peculiar technical sense, which combines many of the above meanings but goes much further as well. On one level in Sāṃkhya, *guṇa* is a "cord" or "thread," a constituent "strand" of primordial materiality. On another level, *guṇa* is "secondary" or "subordinate" in the sense that it is secondary to what is primary or principal (*pradhāna*). On still another level, *guṇa* implies moral distinctions in that it refers to the activity of *prakṛti* as the basis of satisfaction, frustration, and confusion, or moral excellence, moral decadence, and amoral indifference. On yet other levels, *guṇa* refers to aesthetic and intellectual matters and is said to pervade the entire sphere of ordinary experience. The term "*guṇa*," in other words, comes to encompass, according to Sāṃkhya, the entire range of subjective and objective reality, whether manifest (*vyakta*) or unmanifest (*avyakta*). It becomes the "thread" that runs through all of ordinary experience and throughout the natural world, tying together, as it were, the *tattva* realm, the *bhāva* realm, and the *bhūta* realm.

In attempting to understand the Sāṃkhya notion of *guṇa*, it is important to recognize at the outset that *guṇa* is never enumerated or counted as a *tattva*, a *bhāva*, or a *bhūta* (that is to say, *guṇa* is never included within the list of 25 *tattvas*). It is not an "entity," a "predisposition," or a phenomenal "structure," nor is it any combination of these, although, to be sure, it is presupposed in the formulation of all entities, predispositions, and structures. Moreover, although three *guṇas* are mentioned, namely, *sattva*, *rajas*, and *tamas*, the basic Sāṃkhya conceptualization is that of one, continuous and unique process with three discernible "moments" or "constituents." There is one continuous process of transformation (*pariṇāma*), which is the inherent generativity of primordial materiality, but this one continuous process manifests itself in three inextricably related "constituents" that intensionally define the unique, continuous process itself. Rather than referring to "three" *guṇas*, therefore, it is perhaps more accurate to refer to a "tripartite process," which the Sanskrit language permits with such expressions as "*triguṇa*" or another word meaning the same thing, "*traiguṇya*" (meaning "possessed of three constituents" or "the state or condition of being made up of three constituents").

This tripartite process, which *is* primordial materiality, may be described either with reference to objectivity or with reference to subjectivity, because, according to Sāṃkhya philosophy, the tripartite process underlies both sorts of descriptions. From an objective perspective, Sāṃkhya describes the tripartite process as a continuing flow of primal material energy that is capable of spontaneous activity (*rajas*), rational ordering (*sattva*), and determinate formulation or objectivation (*tamas*). Primal material energy can activate or externalize (*pravṛtti*, *cala*) itself in a manner that is transparent or intelligible (*laghu*, *prakāśaka*) and substantial or determinate (*guru*, *niyama*), and all manifestations of primary material energy are, therefore, purposeful, coherent, and objective. From a subjective perspective, Sāṃkhya describes the tripartite process as a continuing flow of experience that is capable of prereflective spontaneous desiring or longing (*rajas*), reflective discerning or discriminating (*sattva*), and continuing awareness of an opaque, enveloping world (*tamas*). The continuing flow of experience actively seeks continuing gratification (*cala*, *upaṣṭambhaka*), reflectively discerns the intelligible dimensions within the flow of experience (*prakhyā*, *prakāśa*), and continually encounters contents within experience that are opaque (*varaṇaka*) and oppressive (*viṣāda*). Moreover, the quest for gratification is frequently frustrated (*duḥkha*), and, although there are occasional times of reflective discernment that bring satisfaction (*sukha*), there are also moments when experience is completely overwhelmed by the sheer plenitude of the world (*moha*). In everyday, ordinary life, therefore, experience tends to vacilate between the discomforting failure (*ghora*) to attain gratification, occasional moments of reflective comprehension that bring a sense of comfort (*śānta*), and moments of confused (*mūḍha*) uncertainty.

Philosophy (*jijñāsā*) begins, according to Sāṃkhya, as a result of the experience of failure and frustration and represents a desire to overcome that frustration. Reflection reveals, however, what might be called a double-bind problem. There is, first of all, the recognition of tripartite process within the flow of experience itself, that is to say, the realization that frustration (*ghora, duḥkha*) is but a moment or modality inextricably linked with occasional other moments of comfort (*śānta, sukha*) and confused uncertainty (*mūḍha, moha*). There is no possibility, in other words, of permanently overcoming frustration without also relinquishing the other constituents of the tripartite process that are inextricably allied with it. The constituents of the tripartite process presuppose one another in a dialectical fashion. There can be no gratification unless there is something external to be appropriated; there can be no reflective discerning in the absence of discernibles; and there can be no confused uncertainty in the absence of someone seeking discernment. Thus, the constituents of the tripartite process are described as being "mutually dominant over, dependent upon, generative of, and cooperative with, one another" (*anyonyāśrayajananamithunavṛttayaś ca guṇāḥ*, SK 12). Although apparently distinct and contradictory in function to one another, the constituents of tripartite process nevertheless operate together as the wick, oil, and flame of a lamp operate together in producing light (SK13). More than this, however, there is, secondly, the recognition that the subjective dilemma of the flow of experience is the obverse side of the inherent objective dilemma of primordial materiality itself. That is to say, according to Sāṃkhya philosophy, there is no polarity or bifurcation of subjective and objective within tripartite process, no ontological distinction between "mind" and "matter" or "thought" and "extension." The subjective flow of experience is simply another way of describing the objective primal material energy that unfolds in a continuing tripartite process of spontaneous activity, rational ordering, and determinate formulation. Put another way, the subjective flow of experience that is at one and another time frustrating, pleasurably discernible, and overwhelmingly encompassing is nondifferent from the primal material energy that is at one and another time purposeful, coherent, and objective. The tripartite process of *mūlaprakṛti* is, in other words, a sort of philosophical Klein bottle or Möbius strip in which the usual distinctions of subjective/objective, mind/body, thought/extension simply do not apply. Therefore, the subjective dilemma of frustration is an inherent dilemma of the world itself, or as the refrain in the *Gītā* puts it, "...*guṇā guṇeṣu vartanta iti*," or "...the constituents (primordial materiality) flow on (endlessly)."[30]

From the perspective of the analysis of the inner essence or underlying reality of primordial materiality itself, therefore, the notion of tripartite process in Sāṃkhya philosophy is clearly tending in the direction of a reductive materialism in the sense that it "reduces" our usual notions of mind, thinking, ideas, sensations, feelings, and so forth, to constituents of primal material energy.[31] Intellect, egoity, or mind are as much manifestations of tripartite process as are trees, stones, or other manifestations of gross matter. Ordinary awareness or thinking (*antaḥkaraṇavṛtti, cittavṛtti, buddhi*) is but a "moment," or constituent, of continuous tripartite process that is inextricably linked with spontaneous activity and determinate formulation.

The constituents of tripartite process (*sattva, rajas, tamas, guṇapariṇāma, triguṇa, traiguṇya*) encompass manifest and unmanifest reality from "Brahmā down to a blade of grass" (*brahmādistambaparyanta*, SK 54). Therefore, the three realms described in the previous section on Sāṃkhya enumerations (namely, the "constitutive," the "projective," and the "consequent") have tripartite process as their underlying reality or essence, but, according to Sāṃkhya, actual transformation (*pariṇāma*) only occurs in the first realm (the *rūpa* or *tattva* realm). In the other two realms, that is to say, in the "projective" and "consequent" realms, there is apparently only simple "continuing activity" (*praspanda*).

The transactions in the first or *tattva* realm represent what K. C. Bhattacharya has aptly called actual "causal" or "noumenal" transformations.[32] That is to say, the *tattvas* (*buddhi*, and so forth) that emerge from *mūlaprakṛti* (because of the catalytic presence of *puruṣa*) are actual material transformations of primordial materiality made up of the constituents of tripartite process. The set of 23 "evolutes" or emergents are called material effects (*kārya*) of a primary material cause (*kāraṇa*), which is *mūlaprakṛti* or *pradhāna*. These 23 effects preexist (*satkārya*) in the material cause in the sense, described earlier, that they are specifications of the inherent generativity of primordial materiality. Put another way, they are actual manifestations (*vyakta*) of the unmanifest (*avyakta*) potencies that reside inherently in primordial materiality. Moreover, because materiality itself is construed primarily in terms of tripartite process, it follows that the emegence of the various effects together with the causal matrix from which they derive is characterized in terms of continuing dynamic transformation. Because tripartite process encompasses both "subjective" and "objective" (or "mind" and "matter" or "thought" and "extension"), dynamic transformation is both analytic and synthetic (or both a priori and a posteriori). Analytically, each manifest component is a "part" of the "whole" that is primordial materiality. Synthetically, each emergent is the manifestation of an actual "effect" that preexists in the unmanifest potentiality of the primary material "cause." The tripartite process of emergence is, thus, both "logical" and "natural."[33]

From the perspective of the "logic" of tripartite process, it would appear that Sāṃkhya wishes to argue that prereflective spontaneous activity (*rajas*) implies an inherent, though latent, rational ordering (*sattva*) and determinate formulation (*tamas*), for an awareness of spontaneous activity could not arise in the absence of reflective discerning vis-à-vis some kind of formulation. Reflective discerning (*sattva*) implies an inherent, though latent, determinate formulation (*tamas*) and spontaneous activity (*rajas*), for reflective discerning could not occur in the absence of a content discernible through some kind of process of appropriation. Determinate formulation (*tamas*) implies an inherent, though latent, reflective discerning (*sattva*) and spontaneous activity (*rajas*), for a determinate formulation could not arise in the absence of a spontaneous process that allows for reflective discerning. All three constituents of tripartite process are always present to, or presuppose, one another. If one refrains from attempting to formulate an interpretation of tripartite process, then the process is simply "unmanifest" (*avyakta*). When, however, any attempt at formulation takes place, a logical sequence manifests (*vyakta*) itself in which each constituent implies or presupposes the other two.[34]

From the perspective of the "nature" of tripartite process, it would appear that Sāṃkhya wishes to argue that, although it must be conceded that prereflective spontaneous activity (*rajas*) is a prerequisite for all process (whether logical or natural), reflective discerning (*sattva*) is nevertheless first in the emergence of manifest "effects" insofar as tripartite process only begins to be aware of itself in that constituent. Thus, intellect as a principle or an effect is said to be the first manifestation of primordial materiality. Its unique function is reflective discerning, ascertainment, or determination (*adhyavasāya*, SK 23), largely derivative, in other words, of *sattva* as reflective discerning or rational ordering but presupposing the latent possibilities of spontaneous activity (*rajas*) and determinate formulation (*tamas*). It reflects, therefore, or encompasses the complete content of tripartite process, at least implicitly, so that the entire order of manifest being is present in it as the reflective constituent of primordial materiality. It is presubjective (or intersubjective) and preobjective in the sense that it is at one and the same time the inherent reflective discerning and the inherent rationality of tripartite process. Moreover, to the extent that its discerning reveals the necessity for prereflective spontaneous activity (*rajas*) as preceding (at least logically) its inherent discerning, the *buddhi* also becomes the locus for what might be called prereflective "willing," not in the sense of egoistic willing (which comes "later" with the emergence of egoity), but in the sense of being predisposed to certain kinds of activity, and in the sense of being capable of initiating or creating new courses of action and various transformations within experience. The *buddhi*, in other words, is also the locus of the fundamental predispositions and is capable of generating the *pratyayasarga* or "phenomenal creation." Reflective discerning by the intellect, therefore, is both passive and active, passive in the sense that it reflectively discerns the ongoing transactions of tripartite process and active in the sense that it is able to project its own destiny and its own formulation of itself.

Egoity is implicit in intellect as reflective discerning becoming aware that it functions as only one constituent of tripartite process, which also implies spontaneous activity and determinate formulation or objectivation. Reflective discerning loses its innocence, as it were, as it recognizes that its pure reflecting function cannot be disembodied from that which it reflects. Egoity, therefore, is "self-awareness" (*abhimāna*, SK 24), not in the sense of free-floating and creative discerning, but, rather, in the sense that creative discerning is dependent upon and derivative of embodiment. The pleasure or joy of reflective discerning gives way to the emergence of a sense of finitude or, as K. C. Bhattacharya puts it, egoity is "...the mind as active I becoming the standing me." Egoity, in other words, is ordinary subjectivity in which reflective discerning is always revealed as being inextricably involved with spontaneous activity (*rajas*) and determinate formulation (*tamas*), that is to say, the "...I *becoming* the standing me." As a result, egoity is the locus of frustration and is largely derivative of *rajas*, for it is on this level that tripartite process begins to reveal itself as the embodied specifications upon which both reflective discerning (*sattva*) and determinate formulation (*tamas*) are dependent. Egoity generates (*taijasād ubhayam*, SK 25) a "twofold creation" (*dvividhasarga*, SK 24), the "specified" or "modified" (*vaikṛta*, SK 25) presuppositions for all reflective discerning (*sattva*), namely, the functions of conceptualizing or "explicating" (*saṃkalpaka*, SK 27) or thinking (*manas*) together with sensing (the five *buddhīndriyas*) and motor functioning (the five *karmendriyas*), and the first (*bhūtādi*, SK 25) determinate formulation (*tamas*) or objectivation, namely, the five subtle elements (*tanmātras*). Finally, the five subtle elements, generated out of egoity in its *tamas* modality as determinate formulation, generate the further *tamas* specifications of the gross elements (*mahābhūtas*).

That the five subtle elements as *tamas* or determinate formulation are derived from egoity and in turn generate gross material existence underscores in the most radical fashion the Sāṃkhya claim that tripartite process is overall a closed, causal system of reductive or process materialism in which the most pleasurable reflective discerning (*sattva, sukha, buddhi*) differs neither in essence nor in kind from the most painful transactions of frustrated gratification (*rajas, duḥkha, ahaṃkāra*) nor from the most oppressive presence of opaque formulation (*tamas, moha, tanmātra/bhūta*). Ordinary thinking, willing, and feeling are but the "subjective" obverse side of the "objective" ongoing transactions of tripartite process in its constituent unfoldings as *sattva, rajas,* and *tamas.* It has been said that the intention of Hegelian philosophy is to show that, finally, substance is subject. The Sāṃkhya conceptualization of the tripartite process appears to intend precisely the opposite. For Sāṃkhya the apparent subject (namely, internal awareness in terms of *buddhi, ahaṃkāra, manas,* and so forth) is really substance (*mūlaprakṛti* as *triguṇa*).[35]

Such, then, is the underlying nature of the "causal" or "noumenal" *tattva* (or *rūpa*) realm with its transactions as the tripartite process. The transactions in the second and third realms (that is to say, the *bhāva* and *bhūta* realms) are also related to tripartite process but presumably not in terms of the "causal" tripartite process. The *bhāva* and *bhūta* realms are secondary or derivative constructions that can be generated or projected by the ongoing simple "continuing activity" (*praspanda*) of the tripartite process. Again, to use K. C. Bhattacharya's idiom, if the *tattva* realm is the realm of "causal" or "noumenal" transformations, then the *bhāva* and *bhūta* realms are the realms of "non-causal" or "phenomenal" transactions.[36] Residing in the *buddhi,* in other words, in addition to its constitutive *tattva* identity as reflective discerning or ascertainment is a special projective capacity (the *bhāvas*) capable of generating a derivative, secondary set of manifestations, constituted to be sure by *sattva, rajas,* and *tamas,* (as are all manifestations), but not unfolding in terms of the tripartite process. This derivative, secondary set of manifestations unfolds, presumably, by simple continuing activity, and its components are related to one another as *nimittanaimittika* (efficient causes and effects), or, in other words, the karmic transactions of ordinary life and experience (*bhoga, upabhoga*). The *Yuktidīpikā* provides some documentation for such an interpretation in its discussion of the inherent activity of *triguṇa*:

> ...activity or change can be construed in two ways, namely (a) fundamental transformation and (b) simple continuing activity. When there emerges a new state or condition of manifestation that has distinctly different characteristics, there is a fundamental transformation. The maintenance of ordinary life and its ongoing activities, like speaking, and so forth, may be referred to as simple continuing activity.[37]

Fundamental transformation is chiefly characteristic of the *rūpa* or *tattva* realm. Simple continuous activity is characteristic of the *pravṛtti* (*bhāva*) and *phala* (*bhūta*) realms. Or, putting the matter in terms of causation, the *rūpa* or *tattva* realm is that realm in which material (*kāraṇakārya*) causation operates, the *pravṛtti* and *phala* realms are those realms in which efficient (*nimittanaimittika*) causation operates.

Within the predispositional or projective realm (*bhāva* or *pravṛtti*), those predispositions of the intellect that evoke the inherent reflective discerning of the *buddhi* principle are referred to as its *sāttvika* predispositions (namely, meritorious behavior, knowledge, nonattachment, and power, SK 23). Those predispositions of the *buddhi* which evoke the objectifying or reifying tendencies of the *buddhi* principle are referred to as its *tāmasa* predispositions (namely, demeritorious behavior, ignorance, attachment, and impotence). Presumably, as mentioned earlier, the predispositions themselves, as the active or creative capacity of intellect in contrast to its passive tattvic constitution as reflective discerning, are derivative of the spontaneous externalizing activity of prereflective *rājasa* tendencies within primordial materiality, though this is nowhere directly stated in the extant Sāṃkhya texts. In any case, the constellation of predispositions residing in the *buddhi* principle in any particular rebirth predisposes the transmigrating *liṅga* to project a resultant phenomenal creation with its fifty categories of ordinary experience, with *sattva* tendencies dominant in the divine or celestial regions, *rajas* tendencies dominant on the human level and *tamas* tendencies dominant in the external gross world.[38]

Whereas the progression of fundamental principles in terms of the tripartite process and material causality cannot be changed inasmuch as they constitute the "causal" or "noumenal" reality of everything that is, the transactions of the projective (*bhāva*) and consequent (*phala*) realms inasmuch as they are "noncausal" (in a material, constitutive sense) or "phenomenal" tendencies in terms of *guṇapraspanda* and efficient causality, are subject to change. In other words, one cannot change what is, but one can change one's perspective or one's predisposition toward what is. Thus, knowledge or knowing (*jñāna*) and insufficient discriminating or ignorance (*ajñāna*), according to Sāṃkhya philosophy, pertain only to the projective and consequent realms. Knowledge and ignorance are only predispositions. They are never principles. Put another way, knowing can never change or reconstitute being; it can only change our predisposition toward what is and the manner in which we pursue our life trajectories.

Before proceeding to discuss the Sāṃkhya notion of *puruṣa* and the Sāṃkhya epistemology, it may be useful to offer a chart, which brings together the material presented thus far.

(1) consciousness / (*puruṣa*) (2) primordial materiality (*mūlaprakṛti*) = the unmanifest (*avyakta*) = *traiguṇya* (*sattva, rajas, tamas*)

"the manifest world" (*vyakta*) = *triguṇa*

The constitutive realm	The projective realm	The consequent realm
(A) *rūpa*-realm	(B) *pravṛtti*-realm	(C) *phala*-realm
tattva realm	*bhāva* realm	*bhūta* realm
liṅga realm	*nimittanaimittika*	*pratyayasarga*
buddhi	*buddhibhāvas*	50 *padārthas*
ahaṃkāra	*dharma/adharma*	5 *viparyayas*
11 *indriyas*	*jñāna/ajñāna*	28 *aśaktis*
5 *tanmātras*	*vairāgya/avairāgya*	9 *tuṣṭis*
5 *mahābhūtas*	*aiśvarya/anaiśvarya*	8 *siddhis*

LIṄGA + *BHĀVA* ⟶ *BHAUTIKASARGA*

LIṄGA	*BHĀVA* ⟶ *BHAUTIKASARGA*
triguṇa/pariṇāma	*triguṇa/praspanda*
kāraṇa/kārya, satkārya	*nimittanaimittika*
nirupabhoga (devoid of ordinary experience)	*upabhoga, apavarga* (ordinary experience *and* the experience of release)
aviśeṣa (with the exception of the *bhūtas*)	*viśeṣa*
"causal" or "noumenal"	"noncausal" or "phenomenal"
	pratyakṣa, anumāna, āptavacana
	karman and *saṃsāra*
	duḥkha and/or *kaivalya*

III. Sāṃkhya as Contentless Consciousness

The discussion of the Sāṃkhya system has thus far focused almost exclusively on the notion of primordial materiality, its underlying essence as tripartite process, its "causal" or "noumenal" transformation into the manifest *tattva* realm, and its "noncausal" or "phenomenal" projections and permutations in terms of the fundamental predispositions, the intellectual creation, and the spheres of rebirth and transmigration. Thus, although twenty-four of the twenty-five basic principles have been discussed, in reality, according to Sāṃkhya, only one "thing" or "entity" or "existent" has been described, namely, primordial materiality. The twenty-three fundamental principles (intellect, and so forth) that "manifest" (*vyakta*) themselves from "unmanifest" (*avyakta*) primordial materiality are all "parts" of a totally functioning "whole," which is primordial materiality, or material "effects" (*kārya*) of a primal material "cause" (*kāraṇa*). The "thread" that ties the "whole" together is tripartite process.

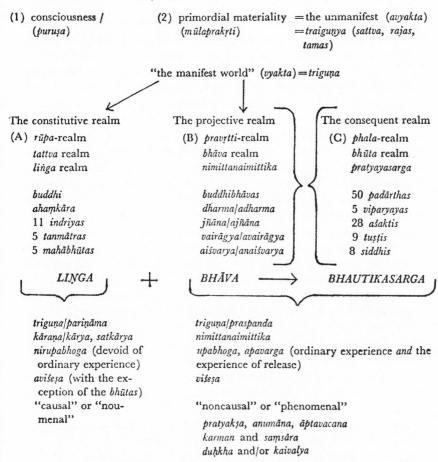

The Sāṃkhya notion of tripartite process was an attractive and powerful solution to many of the older speculative problems in South Asian thought, attractive and powerful because it pulled together so many loose ends from the older speculative potpourri of random theorizing, but attractive and powerful also because it provided an independent rational basis for serious reflection quite apart from received revelation, but nevertheless very much in harmony with the received heritage. There had been a variety of speculations in the ancient brahmanical and heterodox periods regarding the notion of selfhood, ranging from the cosmic *ātman* of the oldest Upaniṣads through such notions as *kṣetrajña, bhūtātman, mahān ātman* the Jain notion of *jīva,* and, of course, archaic Buddhist notions of no-self (*anātman*).[39] Similarly, there had been a variety of speculations concerning the cosmos, the process of rebirth and transmigration, and the manner in which the physical world had come into existence—including archaic element lists in the Upaniṣads, the atomism of the early Vaiśeṣika, the *pratītyasamutpāda* of the Buddhists, theories about a creative "Lord" or *īśvara* among early *bhakti* followers, and even "arguments" about random chance among materialists.[40] Moreover, the issue of the relation between selfhood, on the one hand, and the phenomenal, empirical world, on the other, was a pressing issue even in the earliest phases of speculation. What Sāṃkhya philosophy accomplished with its conceptualization of the tripartite process was an intuitively cogent intellectual synthesis of many of these older strands of speculation. The transactions of intellect, egoity, and mind were now construed as rational manifestations of an intelligible, uniform, and real world "from Brahmā down to a blade of grass," and the process of rebirth and transmigration was given a meaningful interpretation. More than this, however, as already indicated, this was accomplished largely on the basis of independent reasoning, aided to be sure by the "reliable testimony" of the *ṛṣis* and the pronouncements of scripture, but independently derived nevertheless. It is perhaps hardly surprising, therefore, that Sāṃkhya philosophy should have been so influential in ancient Indian culture. Its conceptualization of the tripartite process became a kind of intellectual charter for many aspects of scientific and rational endeavour, widely used both in its technical sense and as a useful heuristic device in such divergent fields as medicine, law, ethics, philosophy, and cosmology.

In addition to the twenty-four principles that make up the one "entity" or "existent" that is primordial materiality as tripartite, however, the Sāṃkhya system also asserts that there is a second kind of "existent," distinct from primordial materiality and uninvolved in its transactions, yet nevertheless a crucial component for the manifest functioning of that materiality. The Sāṃkhya system refers to this second kind of "existent" as "*puruṣa.*" The term "*puruṣa,*" though in origin meaning "man" or "person" and used synonymously in prephilosophical contexts with the old Upaniṣadic notion of *ātman* or Self, came to have a peculiar technical meaning in philosophical Sāṃkhya in much the same way as the old word "*guṇa*" was reinterpreted and given a new sense by the Sāṃkhya teachers.[41] It is quite likely, in fact, that the two technical notions of the constituent process and consciousness developed in tandem, for it is clear enough that the precision and comprehensiveness of the notion of *triguṇa* would require a fundamental rethinking of the old Upaniṣadic "ghost in the machine".[42] To be sure, one might anticipate that the notion of the constituent process with its tendency toward a "reductive materialism" might well have rendered the older Upaniṣadic notions of selfhood superfluous. In other words, one might anticipate that Sāṃkhya would have moved in the direction of some sort of no-self theory on analogy with comparable developments within archaic Buddhist traditions or in the direction of a thoroughgoing materialism. This did not happen, however. Instead, the Sāṃkhya teachers worked out an eccentric form of dualism with primordial materiality or the tripartite constituent process (encompassing twenty-four fundamental principles) as one kind of "existent," and pure consciousness (*puruṣa*, a twenty-fifth *tattva*) as a second kind of "existent."

The term "eccentric" is meant to indicate simply that the Sāṃkhya dualism does not fit the usual or conventional notions of dualism. If one looks, for example, at the classic expression of the dualist position in Western thought, namely, that of Descartes, one realizes immediately that the Sāṃkhya somehow misses the mark. In his *Principles of Philosophy* Descartes comments as follows about the dualist position:

> Thus extension in length, breadth and depth, constitutes the nature of corporeal substance; and thought constitutes the nature of thinking substance. For all else that may be attributed to body presupposes extension, and is but a mode of this extended thing; as everything that we find in mind is but so many diverse forms of thinking.[43]

In his *Meditations* Descartes sets forth the essence of the dualist perspective as follows:

> ...because, on the one side, I have a clear and distinct idea of myself inasmuch as I am only a thinking and unextended thing, and as, on the other, I possess a distinct idea of body, inasmuch as it is only an extended and unthinking thing, it is certain that this I (that is to say, my soul by which I am what I am), is entirely and absolutely distinct from my body and can exist without it.[44]

A modern statement of the conventional dualist position is that of the analytic philosopher Kai Nielsen, who puts the matter as follows:

> The core of the dualist claim...could...be put in this way: There are at least two radically different kinds of reality, existence or

> phenomena: the physical and the mental.... Physical phenomena or realities are extended in space and time and are perceptually public, or, like electrons and photons, are constituents of things that are perceptually public .... Mental phenomena or realities, by contrast, are unextended, not in space, and are *inherently* private.[45]

Whether one considers the Cartesian position or the modern, analytic restatement of it, according to Kai Nielsen, the interpreter of Sāṃkhya must admit that the Sāṃkhya is not a dualism in these senses. Similarly, if one considers the theological or ethical dualism of Christian thought — in the manner of Pauline theology or later treatments such as those of Augustine, and so forth — again, the Sāṃkhya is not a dualism in these senses. Similarly, if one considers the dualistic analyses in Plato or Aristotle, or the Kantian dualism of noumenon and phenomena, or a phenomenological dualism of *noesis* and *noema*, the Sāṃkhya is not really dualist in any of these senses. Even within the framework of Indian philosophy, the garden-variety dualisms of the later Vedānta schools or the older archaic *jīva-ajīva* dualism of the Jains do not adequately fit the Sāṃkhya case. Regarding all of these positions, Sāṃkhya philosophy with its notion of tripartite process would be a critique of the traditional or conventional dualist position and approaches, rather, as has been shown in the preceding section, the opposite position or what modern Western philosophy of mind would call "reductive materialism," that is to say, a philosophical view that "reduces" "mind" talk, or "mentalistic" talk to "brain-process" talk, or, in other words, construes mind, thought, ideas, sensations, and so forth, in terms of some sort of material stuff, or energy, or force (as has been argued, for example, by such thinkers as H. Feigl, J. J. C. Smart, Kai Nielsen, and others).[46] For, according to Sāṃkhya philosophy, the experiences of intellect, egoity, and mind, and the "raw feels" such as frustration or satisfaction — or, in other words, what conventional dualists would consider to be "inherently private"— are simply subtle reflections of a primordial materiality, a primordial materiality undergoing continuous transformation by means of its constituent unfolding as spontaneous activity, reflective discerning, and determinate formulation. Thus, the modern reductive materialists' claim that "sensations are identical with certain brain processes" would have a peculiar counterpart in the Sāṃkhya claim that "awarenesses" (*antaḥkaraṇavṛtti* or *cittavṛtti*) are identical with certain *guṇa* modalities. Or again, the modern reductive materialists' claim that the conventional notions of the "inherently private" or the "mental" are only linguistic fictions that inhibit a more correct understanding of the human situation would find its peculiar counterpart in the Sāṃkhya claim that the notion of the discreet "individual" or the "individual ego" seriously inhibits a more correct understanding of an organism as a composite constellation of a subtle material transmigrating *liṅga* (made up of intellect, egoity, mind, and so forth) periodically being reborn in gross physical bodies. Both positions, in other words, appear to criticize the notion of an inherently private, mentalistic "ghost in the machine" as being a product of verbal carelessness (*vikalpa*) brought about by the failure to make relevant distinctions (*aviveka, avidyā*).

At this point, however, the comparison of Sāṃkhya philosophy with reductive materialism breaks down, for instead of expelling the traditional or conventional "ghost in the machine" and getting on with the task of describing the world and experience without "ghost talk," Sāṃkhya as it were refurbishes the "ghost," stripping it of its conventional attributes and reintroducing it in the framework of an "eccentric" dualism in the sense that the "ghost" no longer has to do with "mind talk, "mentalist" talk, or "ego" talk, all of which latter are fully reducible to *guṇa* talk in good reductive materialist fashion. Sāṃkhya designates its eccentric ghost as "consciousness" (*cetana, puruṣa*), thus introducing a fundamental distinction between "awareness" (*antaḥkaraṇavṛtti, cittavṛtti*) and "consciousness" (*cetana, puruṣa*) and requiring a radically different kind of dualism, namely, a dualism between a closed, causal system of reductive materialism (encompassing "awareness" or the "private" life of the mind), on the one hand, and a nonintentional and contentless consciousness, on the other. Whereas awareness (*antaḥkaraṇavṛtti*) (namely, intellect, egoity and mind) is active, intentional, engaged and at every moment a reflection of subtle materiality; consciousness (*puruṣa*) cannot think or act and is not ontologically involved or intentionally related in any sense to primordial materiality other than being passively present. Consciousness, in other words, is sheer contentless presence (*sākṣitva*). Sāṃkhya philosophy thereby rejects idealism without giving up an ultimately transcendent "consciousness." It also rejects conventional dualism by reducing "mentalist" talk to one or another transformation of material "awareness"; and it modifies reductive materialism by introducing a unique notion of "consciousness" that is nonintentional and has nothing to do with ordinary mental awareness.

This eccentric Sāṃkhya dualism is set forth in verses 3, 10, and 11 of the *Sāṃkhyakārikā*. The dualism is introduced in the following fashion: Primordial materiality is ungenerated; the seven — intellect, and so forth — are both generated and generative. The sixteen are generated. Consciousness is neither generated nor generative. (SK 3)

The four hemistichs of the verse may be exhibited as follows:

(I) Primordial materiality is ungenerated (*mūlaprakṛtir avikṛtir*);
(II) The seven — intellect, and so forth — are both generated and generative (*mahadādyāḥ prakṛtivikṛtayaḥ sapta*);
(III) The sixteen are generated (*ṣoḍaśakas tu vikāro*);

(IV) Consciousness is neither generated nor generative (*na prakṛtir na vikṛtiḥ puruṣaḥ*).[47]

The *puruṣa* is clearly distinguished from all other fundamental principles in the sense of not being implicated in what is generating or generated. Moreover, the first hemistich is a negation of the third hemistich, and the fourth hemistich is a negation of the second hemistich. It follows, then, that whatever is predicated of the second part will provide a negative description of the fourth part, and whatever is predicated of the third part will provide negative descriptions of both the first part and the fourth part (inasmuch as the fourth part is similar to the first part to the extent that it too is ungenerated). The sequences of predications are then presented in verses 10-11 and may be exhibited in the accompanying chart.

Consciousness (*purusa*) — Primordial Materiality (*mūlaprakṛti*)

Primordial Materiality (*mūlaprakṛti*) → Unmanifest (*avyakta*); Manifest (*vyakta*)

	(*jña* or *puruṣa*) (*avyakta*)	(*vyakta*)
(Predications of the third part that provide a negative description of the first and fourth parts)	uncaused (*ahetumat*)	caused (*hetumat*)
	nontemporal (*nitya*)	temporal (*anitya*)
	nonspatial (*vyāpin*)	spatial (*avyāpin*)
	stable (*akriya*)	unstable (*sakriya*)
	simple (*eka*)	complex (*aneka*)
	unsupported (*anāśrita*)	supported (*āśrita*)
	nonmergent (*aliṅga*)	mergent (*liṅga*)
	without parts (*anavayava*)	having parts (*avayava*)
	independent (*aparatantra*)	contingent (*paratantra*)

	(*jña* or *puruṣa*)	(*avyakta*) (*vyakta*)
(Predications of the second part that provide a negative description of the fourth part)	without tripartite process (*atriguṇa*)	tripartite process (*triguṇa*)
	differentiated (*vivekin*)	undifferentiated (*avivekin*)
	non-content (*aviṣaya*)	content (*viṣaya*)
	uncharacterizable (*asāmānya*)	characterizable (*sāmānya*)
	conscious (*cetana*)	nonconscious (*acetana*)
	unproductive (*aprasavadharmin*)	productive (*prasavadharmin*)

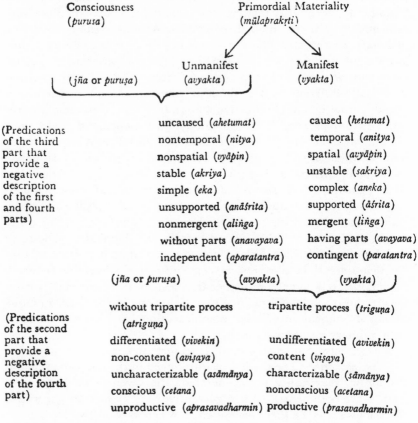

The first sequence establishes the manner in which the manifest world differs both from unmanifest materiality and consciousness. Both unmanifest materiality and consciousness, in other words, are alike in the sense of being uncaused, nontemporal, nonspatial, and so forth.[48] The second sequence establishes the manner in which unmanifest and manifest taken together differ from consciousness, the crucial difference having to do with the tripartite process. Because both the unmanifest and manifest dimensions of primordial materiality are inherently tripartite process, it follows, according to Sāṃkhya, that primordial materiality is uniform overall (*avivekin*) in the sense that it is one "existent" in which "parts" and "whole" or "effects" and "cause" make up one undifferentiated entity; that it is, therefore, a content of consciousness (*viṣaya*); that it can be rationally or relationally characterized (*sāmānya*); that it is not conscious (*acetana*); and that it is inherently productive (*prasavadharmin*).[49] Consciousness, therefore, according to Sāṃkhya, refers to an "existent" that is distinct from tripartite process and thus differentiated from all of the transactions of awareness (intellect and so forth), transcending all objectivity whether specific or unspecific, utterly unique or uncharacterizable, sentient or intelligent, and incapable of producing anything.

According to Sāṃkhya philosophy, such a notion of contentless consciousness is essential for several important reasons (SK 17). First, because the combinations (*saṃghāta*) of tripartite process appear to be purposeful (*parārthatva*) overall and because these transactions are themselves finally only objective or manifestations of primal material energy, there must be some ultimate grounding for such purposefulness that is itself not objective, or, in other words, not implicated in tripartite process. This ultimate grounding is pure consciousness and it is that *for* which primordial materiality functions. Second, although pure consciousness is nonintentional and incapable of producing anything, nevertheless, there must be a sentient principle that by its mere presence exercises a function of passive overseeing (*adhiṣṭhāna*). Third, there must be a substratum that is the recipient or beneficiary (*bhoktṛbhāva*) of the various awarenesses of primordial materiality. Finally, because the quest or urge for liberation is such a crucial component in all experience, there must be a principle of sentience apart from the closed causal system of reductive materialism that renders such a quest intelligible. All of these arguments amount to one basic claim, namely, that the very notion of tripartite process itself becomes unintelligible in the absence of a distinct principle of sentience. In other words, tripartite process, although a powerful intellectual synthesis or conceptualization, cannot stand alone in and of itself, for even the awareness of the concept presupposes a ground or basis, or perhaps better, a "medium" through which and for which the concept becomes meaningful. Otherwise what appeared to be a uniform, rational, and meaningful world "from Brahmā down to a blade of grass" would finally show itself as an endless mechanical process in which the transactions of ordinary experience would amount to little more than occasional pleasurable respites from an endlessly unfolding tragedy. Or, putting the matter another way, one would come upon the remarkable paradox that an apparently uniform, rational, and meaningful world is finally pointless.

Moreover, according to Sāṃkhya philosophy, the notion of contentless consciousness requires that it be construed pluralistically (*bahutva*). That is to say, because consciousness is a contentless, nonintentional presence incapable of performing any activity, it, therefore, cannot know or intuit itself. The presence of contentless consciousness can only be intuited by the intellect in its reflective discerning (*sattva*) and in an intuition by the intellect that in itself is *not* consciousness. The presence of consciousness, thus, is an awareness that occurs within intellect, an awareness that the intellect itself is not consciousness. According to the *Yuktidīpikā*, this realization of the presence of consciousness emerges as an awareness of the difference between tripartite process and consciousness (*jñānaṃ guṇapuruṣāntaraupalabdhilakṣaṇam*). Because there is a plurality of intellects engaging in reflective discernment; because these intellects are following various life trajectories; and because they are functioning, therefore, at various times and under varying circumstances in accordance with the varied manifestations of tripartite process, contentless consciousness can only be disclosed pluralistically (SK 18), or, putting the matter somewhat differently, there may be as many disclosures of contentless consciousness as there are intellects capable of reflective discernment. Sāṃkhya philosophy, therefore, rejects the old cosmic *ātman* of the Upaniṣads and argues instead that contentless consciousness accompanies every intellect, stressing thereby that the awareness of consciousness is an achievement of the intellect and is a negative discernment of what the intellect is not. The Sāṃkhya arguments for a plurality of pure consciousnesses, in other words, appear to be directed at epistemological concerns rather than ontological matters. Because contentless consciousness can never be a content and cannot be characterized as are materiality or the tripartite process, it is hardly likely that the Sāṃkhya teachers were thinking of the plurality of consciousnesses as a set of knowable entities to be counted.[50] They were thinking, rather, of a plurality of intellects through which the disclosure of contentless consciousness occurs. Vijñānabhikṣu (in his commentary on *Sāṃkhyasūtra* I.154) makes a somewhat comparable point when he suggests that the Sāṃkhya plurality of consciousnesses does not contradict the evidence of the Veda that there is only one Self or subject. In the Veda, according to Vijñānabhikṣu, oneness or uniformity refers to the essential nature (*svarūpa*) of selfhood in terms only of genus (*jāti*). Vedic references to oneness need not be construed as implying entirety or undividedness. There are numerous passages in the Veda that show that selfhood shows itself under limiting adjuncts (*upādhi*), and, hence, there is no contradiction between Vedic testimony and the Sāṃkhya notion of the plurality of consciousnesses. Whether in fact Vedic references can be so construed, of course, is a matter for debate and textual interpretation. (Generally speaking, it would appear that Vijñānabhikṣu is wrong. Vedic references to selfhood do seem to imply entirety or undividedness.) Vijñānabhikṣu is probably correct, however, in suggesting that Sāṃkhya's intention with its notion of a plurality of consciousnesses was largely epistemological.

Putting all of this together, contentless consciousness, according to Sāṃkhya philosophy, is (a) pure passive presence (*sākṣitva*); (b) distinct from the tripartite process (*kaivalya*); (c) uninvolved in the transactions of the three *guṇas* except for its passive presence (*mādhyasthya*); (d) the foundation for subjectivity or pure consciousness (*draṣṭṛtva*); and (e) incapable of activity (*akartṛbhāva*) (SK 19).

It is outside the realm of causality, outside space and time, completely inactive, utterly simple, unrelated apart from its sheer presence, uninvolved in emergence or transformation, without parts, completely independent, transcendent yet always immanent by reason of its presence, the presupposition for all apparent discrimination or differentiation, neither an object nor a subject (in any conventional sense), verbally uncharacterizable, a pure witness whose only relation to primordial materiality is sheer presence, utterly isolated, completely indifferent, the presupposition for apprehending unmanifest or manifest being, a nonagent, and potentially present in the awareness of all intellects as *not* being that awareness.

Sāṃkhya philosophy strips consciousness of most of the usual attributes of a mutable subject. Even the discrimination (*viveka*) of its very presence is delegated to the intellect as a negative apprehension that intellect is not contentless consciousness (*nāsmi, na me, nāham ity apariśeṣam*, SK 64). As the *Sāṃkhyasūtra* (III.75) puts it, "The attainment of the discrimination (of *puruṣa*) occurs as a result of the meditative analysis (*abhyāsa*) of the fundamental principles through which one progressively abandons (*tyāga*) all contents, saying 'It is not this,' 'It is not that.'"

Such an unusual notion of consciousness entails, of course, some equally unusual corollaries. First of all, if consciousness is inactive and distinct from the tripartite process, then consciousness is neither the material nor the efficient cause of the transactions of primordial materiality, and yet all causal transactions occur in the presence of consciousness and are illuminated by consciousness. Second, if consciousness is only a contentless passive presence, it can only appear as what it is not, passively taking on all content (whether subjective or objective) as a transparent witness. Third, tripartite process appears to be conscious until such time as it is realized that consciousness is the radical absence of content (whether subjective or objective). A double negation occurs, in other words, whereby contentlessness appears to have content (*guṇakartṛtve 'pi tathā karte 'va bhavaty udāsīnaḥ*, SK 20) and content appears to be conscious (*acetanaṃ cetanāvad iva liṅgam*, SK 20). Fourth, when contentless consciousness is present to primordial materiality, this double negation occurs quite spontaneously or naturally and becomes the occasion for the manifest world and experience to occur. Hence, because consciousness and primordial materiality (in any given world cycle) are all-pervasive "existents" it can be said that this spontaneous double negation is beginningless. Fifth, the manifest world and experience, therefore, though fully real, are nevertheless distorted appearances in which pure consciousness appears to be bound up in the transactions of tripartite process (and hence caught in the closed causal system) and tripartite process appears to be conscious (and hence lacking any basis outside of the closed causal system for the possibility of freedom or release). Whether this double negation is construed with a simple theory of reflection (*pratibimba*), whereby consciousness becomes reflected in intellect (thereby occasioning experience) — as in Vācaspati Miśra — or with a double theory of reflection (*anyonyapratibimba*), whereby consciousness becomes reflected in intellect and intellect in turn is reflected back on consciousness — as in Vijñānabhikṣu — makes little difference in terms of the basic thrust of the Sāṃkhya position, which is that there is a basic epistemological distortion at the root of experience.[51] Vācaspati Miśra's interpretation is perhaps cleaner in the sense that all transactions of experience occur only in intellect after it has been "intelligized" by consciousness. Vijñānabhikṣu's interpretation has the merit of ascribing experience to consciousness (because the contents of intellect awareness are reflected back on consciousness). In either case, however, the crucial point is that intellect is only a surrogate for contentless consciousness, and only proper discrimination (*viveka*) by the intellect is sufficient finally to eliminate the beginningless distortion (*aviveka*). Finally, and most important, bondage and release, according to Sāṃkhya philosophy, are never ontological problems. The two ultimate "existents" (pure consciousness and primordial materiality) in fact both exist, and their presence to one another cannot be changed. What can change is the fundamental epistemological distortion that is the occasion for the appearance of the manifest world and experience. The intellect is capable finally of discriminating the presence of contentless consciousness, thereby intuiting a radical foundation for liberation that dissipates the pain or frustration of ordinary experience. Both bondage and freedom, in other words, pertain to intellect, the former being the case when beginningless nondiscrimination, occasioned by the natural copresence of consciousness and materiality, obtains and the intellect is on a trajectory toward ordinary experience (*upabhoga*), the latter being the case when discrimination (*viveka*) arises — occasioned by the intellect's sufficiently distinguishing itself from consciousness — and the intellect is predisposed toward liberation and/or isolation. As Īśvarakṛṣṇa puts the matter in verse 62: "Therefore, it is surely the case that (*puruṣa*) is never bound, nor released nor subject to transmigration. Only *prakṛti* in its various forms transmigrates, is bound and is released." Primordial materiality, therefore, provides both ordinary experience and the extraordinary knowledge that consciousness exists.

Ultimately, of course, contentless consciousness and primordial materiality go beyond what can be reasonably described in ordinary discourse. Both the notions of consciousness and materiality (or the tripartite process) are like certain ultimate notions in Plato's thought for which Plato turned to the language of myth, metaphor, and simile. It is hardly surprising, then, that Sāṃkhya philosophy should also make use of metaphor and simile regarding its ultimate conceptions. To some extent, of course, such metaphors and similes were often used in Indian philosophy as "illustrations" (*dṛṣṭānta*) in framing the so-called Indian syllogism, but metaphors and similes were also used as vivid images for evoking a brief intuitive glimpse of an idea that did not easily lend itself to rational formulation.[52] Thus, the relation between contentless consciousness and primordial materiality is like that between a lame man and a blind man, whereby each functions for the other in accomplishing a common goal. Or again, consciousness is the crystal; materiality the China rose that distorts the clarity of the crystal and makes it appear as what it is not. Consciousness is the spectator; materiality is the dancer performing for him until such time as the aesthetic performance has been completed. Consciousness is the young calf; materiality the nourishing milk. Consciousness is the young lover; materiality is the shy virgin who withdraws from his sight having been seen by him in her nakedness. Consciousness is the master; materiality is the obedient servant. (See SK 13, 21, 36, 41, 42, 56, 57, 58, 59, 61, 65, 66, and 67; see also Book IV of the *Sāṃkhyasūtra*, which is given over to reciting various narratives, metaphors, and similes about the basic Sāṃkhya conceptions.)

IV. Sāṃkhya as Rational Reflection

Now that the basic components and overall contours of the Sāṃkhya system have been presented, attention can be directed, finally, to the manner in which the Sāṃkhya teachers argued their case. That is to say, it is appropriate now to address such issues as the philosophical methodology, logic, and epistemology of the Sāṃkhya. To some extent, of course, such matters have been implicit throughout the preceding sections, for it has become clear enough that the genius of the Sāṃkhya in the ancient Indian context was its success in formulating a tight set of conceptualizations that pulled together a great variety of speculative loose ends from the older heritage. The notions of *triguṇa*, *buddhi*, *ahaṃkāra*, *manas*, *mūlaprakṛti*, *puruṣa*, and so forth, set forth in a systematic pattern that rendered the world and human experience intelligible was a remarkable intellectual achievement by any measure, and it is no accident, therefore, that Sāṃkhya exercised an enormous influence in so many areas of ancient Indian intellectual life. To be sure, Sāṃkhya was vigorously criticized by later and more sophisticated philosophical traditions, but that in itself is a measure of its stature in the formative phase of Indian intellectual history. As Frauwallner and others have eloquently argued, Sāṃkhya's contribution to Indian philosophy was evidently fundamental and basic, perhaps even seminal.[53] That its later opponents were quick to pounce on the obvious weaknesses of the system should not deflect our attention from an appreciation for Sāṃkhya's crucial contribution in its own time. Only Vaiśeṣika, early Nyāya, and early Buddhist thought came even close to exercising a comparable influence in terms of Indian systematic philosophizing. Yoga, Vedānta, and Mīmāṃsā in these early centuries had not yet (and perhaps really never did) adequately differentiate themselves from their religious roots. Moreover, even when these latter traditions did finally emerge as philosophical (cum religious) movements, the influence of Sāṃkhya in them was extensive (to the extent that "Yoga philosophy" can really only be taken as itself a theme and variation on Sāṃkhya). As was mentioned in Chapter One, later Vedānta is really only a warmed over Sāṃkhya, upgraded somewhat with the sophisticated dialectic of Mādhyamika and Nyāya but in most respects a regression to prephilosophical religious intuition and scriptural authority.

Be that as it may, the task now is to piece together in as systematic a way as possible Sāṃkhya's contribution in such areas as philosophical methodology, logic, and epistemology. In many ways, unfortunately, this is the most difficult dimension of Sāṃkhya to uncover, for the extant Sāṃkhya textual evidence contains very little information. Unlike the other systems of classical Indian philosophy, there is no lengthy ancient Sāṃkhya *sūtra* collection, which would be the normal source for uncovering such issues (if not in the *sūtras* themselves, certainly in the detailed commentaries that accompany such collections). There is, of course, a *Sāṃkhyasūtra*, commented on by Aniruddha, Vijñānabhikṣu, and others, but this is a medieval tradition (fifteenth or sixteenth century) that is largely useless for purposes of studying the old Sāṃkhya system. Whether Sāṃkhya, in fact, ever had a set of ancient *sūtras* is difficult to know. There are fragments quoted here and there in the general philosophical literature of India (attributed to Pañcaśikha, Vārṣagaṇya, and so on) that suggest there may have been *sūtra* collections that were subsequently lost or discarded. There is also the little *Tattvasamāsasūtra*, which may well be very old, but its laconic presentation makes it impossible to decipher without commentaries; and the extant commentaries on the text are very late (with the possible exception of the *Kramadīpikā*). In any case, the *Tattvasamāsa* offers little of importance about matters of methodology, logic, or epistemology.

What evidence is available tends to indicate that Sāṃkhya probably did not have an ancient *sūtra* collection. Instead, there are numerous references to a so-called *ṣaṣṭitantra* or "system or science of sixty topics," which, as suggested earlier, may refer to an extensive literature or to a tradition of presenting Sāṃkhya in terms of sixty topics. Authorship of the *ṣaṣṭitantra* has been attributed variously to Kapila, Pañcaśikha, or Vārṣagaṇya, suggesting, according to Frauwallner, that there were several editions or reworkings of an original *ṣaṣṭitantra*. Possibly the *ṣaṣṭitantra* was originally a collection of verses (on analogy perhaps with a *sūtra* collection), later greatly expanded in verse and prose by Pañcaśikha and Vārṣagaṇya as the system developed. Another possibility, of course, as has already been mentioned, is that Sāṃkhya in ancient times was simply known as *ṣaṣṭitantra* ("the system of sixty topics") and that, therefore, there may have been a variety of texts with that appellation.[54]

What presumably happened was that Īśvarakṛṣṇa's *Sāṃkhyakārikā*, which is purportedly a summary of the *ṣaṣṭitantra* tradition, supplanted the older material in classical times (namely, after the fifth and sixth centuries) and came to be accepted as an adequate account of the old Sāṃkhya philosophy, which by classical times had already had its day and was being superseded by newer philosophical developments. Unfortunately, however, whereas Īśvarakṛṣṇa neatly summarized the components of the system as a whole, he dealt with the philosophical methodology, logic, and epistemology of the system only in the most cursory fashion in the first twenty-one verses of his text. According to the author of the *Yuktidīpikā*, Īśvarakṛṣṇa dealt only briefly with these matters, because they had been exhaustively dealt with by other Sāṃkhya *ācāryas* (Vārṣagaṇya, Vindhyavāsin, and others.) and, hence, did not require extensive treatment in his summary compilation. In other words, the reason for his cursory treatment was not that methodology, logic, and epistemology were unimportant. Quite the contrary, they had been dealt with extensively in the tradition of *ṣaṣṭitantra* and were so well known as not to require further elucidation. Thus, there appears to have occurred a most unfortunate historical anomaly, namely, that one of the crucial aspects of Sāṃkhya philosophy became lost because the summarizer of the system in later times, whose work has come down to us, had simply assumed that everyone knew this dimension of the system.

Whether the methodology, logic, and epistemology of Sāṃkhya can ever be adequately recovered is still an open question in Sāṃkhya studies. Frauwallner and Oberhammer have devoted much attention to the problem, and in more recent times Nakada and Wezler have addressed these issues.[55] The *Yuktidīpikā* has been an important new source of information, and some progress has been made in reconstructing the old Sāṃkhya epistemology from occasional references to Sāṃkhya views in the classical philosophical literature (for example, in the work of Dignāga, Jinendrabuddhi, Candramati, Kumārila, Jayanta Bhaṭṭa, Kamalaśīla, Mallavādin, Siṃhasūri, and others). It is clear enough, especially as a result of the research of Frauwallner with respect to crtitiques of Sāṃkhya in Dignāga and Candramati (and related commentaries), that Sāṃkhya philosophy as set forth in the *ṣaṣṭitantra* tradition made some important contributions to the formulation of the "instruments of knowledge" (*pramāṇa*), the definitions of these means, the theory of inference, and the manner in which inferences are to be framed.[56] These contributions are usually linked to the names Vārṣagaṇya and Vindhyavāsin, but the relation of these latter names to the work of Īśvarakṛṣṇa remains obscure. Presumably Īśvarakṛṣṇa knew about these contributions, but, as indicated above, passed over them in a cursory manner because they had been written about extensively and were generally well known.

In reconstructing the methodology, logic, and epistemology of Sāṃkhya in what follows, therefore, it is important to keep in mind that these matters are far from clear and may require considerable revision or refinement as further research proceeds.

Philosophical methodology: *dyads, triads and pentads*. In examining the extant texts of the Sāṃkhya tradition, one is impressed, first of all, with the predilection for enumeration (from which predilection, of course, the term "*sāṃkhya*" itself derives). Although the method of enumeration is common in Indian philosophy (primarily for mnemonic reasons relating to the aphoristic style of Indian scientific writing), and although Sāṃkhya enumerations encompass a variety of what appear to be random sequences, it is notable that the preponderance of enumeration tends to be dyadic, triadic, and pentadic.[57]

Some of the more common dyadic analyses include the following:

Consciousness (*puruṣa*)	/	Materiality (*prakṛti*)
Unmanifest (*avyakta*)	/	Manifest (*vyakta*)
(Material Cause) (*kāraṇa*)	/	(Material Effect) (*kārya*)
Generative (*prakṛti*)	/	Generated (*vikṛti*)
"Causal" (*liṅga*)	/	"Projective" (*bhāva*)
Subtle (*sūkṣma*)	/	Gross (*sthūla*)
Nonspecific (*aviśeṣa*)	/	Specific (*viśeṣa*)
Noumenal (*nirupabhoga*)	/	Phenomenal (*upabhoga*)

Internal Organ (*antaḥkaraṇa*)	/	External Organ (*bāhyakaraṇa*)
(Efficient Cause) (*nimitta*)	/	(Efficient Effect) (*naimittika*)
Merit (*dharma*)	/	Demerit (*adharma*)
Knowledge (*jñāna*)	/	Ignorance (*ajñāna*)
Nonattachment (*vairāgya*)	/	Attachment (*avairāgya*)
Power (*aiśvarya*)	/	Impotence (*anaiśvarya*)
Upward Going (*ūrdhva*)	/	Downward Going (*adhastāt*)
Liberation (*apavarga*)	/	Bondage (*bandha*)
Dissolution in *prakṛti*	/	Transmigration
(*prakṛtilaya*)	/	(*saṃsāra*)
Nonrestraint (*avighāta*)	/	Restraint (*vighāta*)

Moreover, the sequence of predications for establishing the basic Sāṃkhya dualism, which was presented in the preceding section on *puruṣa*, is also dyadic in structure.

Some of the triadic analyses include the following:

Intelligibility (or reflective discerning) (*sattva*)	/	Activity (or spontaneous unfolding) (*rajas*)	/	Inertia (or determinate formulation) (*tamas*)
Illuminating (*prakāśa*)	/	Externalizing (*pravṛtti*)	/	Objectifying (*niyama*)
Intellect/will (*buddhi*)	/	Egoity (*ahaṃkāra*)	/	Subtle Elements (*tanmātra*)
Divine/Celestial (*daiva*)	/	Human (*mānuṣya*)	/	Animal/Plant (*tairyagyona*)
Generated (*vaikṛta*)	/	Fiery (*taijasa*)	/	Elemental (*bhūtādi*)
Satisfaction (*sukha*)	/	Frustration (*duḥkha*)	/	Confusion (*moha*)
Agreeable (*prīti*)	/	Disagreeable (*aprīti*)	/	Depressing (*viṣāda*)
Peaceful (*śānta*)	/	Uncomfortable (*ghora*)	/	Confusion (*mūḍha*)

Furthermore, most of the ethical and epistemological notions of the Sāṃkhya system appear to be discussed in triadic analyses:

Internal Frustration (*ādhyātmika*)	/	External Frustration (*ādhibhautika*)	/	Celestial Frustration (*ādhidaivika*)

Natural Bondage (*prakṛtibandha*)	Generated Bondage (*vaikārikabandha*)	Sacrificial or Celestial Bondage (*dakṣiṇābandha*)
Final Liberation (*mokṣa* or *jñāna*)	Release from Passion (*rāgakṣaya*)	Release as Total Destruction (*kṛtsnakṣaya*)
Perception (*dṛṣṭa*, *pratyakṣa*)	Inference (*anumāna*)	Reliable Authority (*āptavacana*)
Inference from cause to effect (*pūrvavat*)	Inference from effect to cause (*śeṣavat*)	Inference based on general correlation (*sāmānyatodṛṣṭa*)
Reflective discerning (*adhyavasāya*)	Self-awareness (*abhimāna*)	Intentionality (*saṃkalpa*)

Finally, some of the common pentadic analyses include the following:

Sound (*śabda*)	Touch (*sparśa*)	Form (*rūpa*)	Taste (*rasa*)	Smell (*gandha*)
Space-Ether (*ākāśa*)	Wind (*vāyu*)	Fire (*tejas*)	Water (*ap*)	Earth (*pṛthivī*)
Hearing (*śrotra*)	Touching (*tvac*)	Seeing (*cakṣus*)	Tasting (*rasana*)	Smelling (*ghrāṇa*)
Speaking (*vāc*)	Grasping (*pāṇi*)	Walking (*pāda*)	Procreat-ing (*upastha*)	Expelling (*pāyu*)
Life Breath (*prāṇa*)	Up Breath (*udāna*)	Diffuse Breath (*vyāna*)	Digestive Breath (*samāna*)	Down Breath (*apāna*)
Steadfastness (*dhṛti*)	Faith (*śraddhā*)	Pleasure (*sukha*)	Desire to Know (*vividiṣā*)	Desire not to Know (*avividiṣā*)

In addition, the arguments presented for proving the basic Sāṃkhya conceptualizations are presented in the format of pentads. There are five arguments for the notion of the "preexisting" effect (*satkārya*) (SK 9); five arguments for proving that the "unmanifest" (*avyakta*) is the cause (*kāraṇa*) (SK 15); five arguments for the existence of *puruṣa* (SK 17); five arguments for establishing the plurality of *puruṣas* (*puruṣa-bahutva*) (SK 18); five predications of *triguṇa* (SK 11); and five basic predications of *puruṣa* (SK 19).

Dyadic, triadic, and pentadic analyses are, of course, common in the older Indian religious literature (Brahmanical, Buddhist, and Jain), and in this sense Sāṃkhya is clearly a descendent from those older speculative contexts. Whereas those older analyses represent what Edgerton once aptly called an archaic "logic of identification," however, the Sāṃkhya analyses appear to represent something more sophisticated. The dyadic analyses in Sāṃkhya appear to be concerned with ontology and with the logic of basic relations. The triadic analyses in Sāṃkhya are clearly concerned with tripartite process, ethics, and epistemology. The pentadic analyses in Sāṃkhya appear to be concerned primarily with the natural world and the psychophysiology of biological life or what might be called the phenomenal, empirical world of ordinary life. This is also true for the various pentadic arguments given for establishing the basic Sāṃkhya conceptualizations, for in each instance the arguments are derived from ordinary empirical experience.

Taken together, the dyads, triads, and pentads appear to provide a mechanism of mediation. The goal of Sāṃkhya is to intuit or discriminate certain basic relations, the primary one of which is the ontological distinction between consciousness and materiality. Experience occurs, however, within the fivefold realm of ordinary awareness and life (through the senses, motor capacities, and an organism's encounter with the external world). That which mediates between the ordinary (pentadic) phenomenal realm and the extraordinary (dyadic) ontological realm is the epistemological (triadic) mediating realm. This latter mediating realm encompasses tripartite process, thereby positively defining materiality and negatively defining consciousness and serving as the locus both for (a) the awareness of satisfaction, frustration, and confusion characteristic of all ordinary life and (b) the awareness of liberation. The basic ontic dyad (consciousness and materiality) activates the basic epistemic triad (*sattva*, *rajas*, *tamas* or *sukha*, *duḥkha*, *moha* as the internal structure of materiality), and the dyad and triad together generate the basic phenomenal pentad (*tanmātra*, *bhūta*, *buddhīndriya*, *karmendriya*). In such fashion is the realm of ordinary experience generated, but the very process of generation cloaks or hides the basic ontic dyad (or, in other words, makes it appear as an epistemic triad). From the other side, ordinary (pentadic) experience generates the epistemological triad of frustration, which issues in the desire to know (*jijñāsā*) or discriminate, which in turn may finally reveal the basic ontic dyad but which also reveals that the structure of frustration itself is only epistemic. Sāṃkhya philosophy, then, would not deny the existence of consciousness or the natural world; but it would argue that our epistemic perspectives concerning what is real are seriously distorted or insufficiently discriminating and that the task of philosophy is to clarify the nature of what is (namely, *puruṣa* and *prakṛti*) and thereby to eliminate epistemological distortions that generate frustration.

Sāṃkhya numbers. The numbers 2, 3, and 5 (presupposed in the dyads, triads and pentads) are, of course, the first three prime numbers, 3 being the arithmetic mean between 1 and 2, and 5 being the arithmetic mean between 2 and 3. When one combines this observation with the further observation that other prime numbers are prominent among the 25 Sāṃkhya fundamental principles—for example, 7 as the principles that are both generative and generated; 11 as the principles that make up the set of capacities; 13 as the number of principles that make up the *liṅga*; 17 as the number of principles relating to egoity;

and 23 the total number of principles that are subdivisions or components of primordial materiality—it is difficult to avoid the suspicion that Sāṃkhya philosophy was making use of some sort of archaic mathematical methodology perhaps not unlike the mathematical theorizing characteristic of Pythagoreanism in the ancient Greek tradition.[58] Unfortunately, there is at the present time insufficient evidence for making any strong claims along these lines one way or the other. The predilection for prime numbers on the principles level may have had some deeper meaning that the ancient Sāṃkhya teachers were consciously using in building their system (on analogy with Pythagorean attempts to link "numbers" with "things"). On the other hand, such numbers may have been well known in learned religious circles as having some sort of religious or mystical significance that could naturally be employed for speculative purposes. In other words, the use of such numbers may not have had any rational purpose whatever.

One suspects, however, that the former, rather than the latter, is the case, not only because the predilection for primes suggests a rational motivation rather than a purely religious motivation but also because other Sāṃkhya numbers also appear to be more than random mnemonic sequences. It appears to be hardly accidental, for example, that the intellectual creation and its 50 categories, which the *Yuktidīpikā* characterizes as the "consequent" (*phala*) creation, is a doubling or replication of the 25 fundamental principles. Moreover, just as there are 1+7 principles that generate the form or "causal" (*rūpa*) level, so there are 1+7 predispositions (namely, knowledge and the other 7 predispositions) that generate the "noncausal" or phenomenal world. Furthermore, the numbers within the 50 "categories" appear to be more than random lists. There are 62 subvarieties of the 5 misconceptions, 28 varieties of dysfunction, and 9 varieties of contentment, all of which numbers have astronomical significance.[59] Twelve lunar months make only 354 days, and the conflict between the lunar year and the solar year was dealt with in ancient India by inserting an extra month every thirty months. Sixty-two lunar months are approximately equivalent to 60 solar months, and so by inserting an extra month every 30 months, the problem was solved. Twenty-eight (specifically, 27 days plus 8 hours) is, of course, the approximate number of solar days needed for the moon to pass through its cycle of relations to the fixed stars, and the heavens were divided into 27 or 28 portions (*nakṣatra*) to mark this cyclic progression. The number 9 is likewise common in ancient India as the number of "planets" (sun, moon, the five basic planets, plus Rāhu and Ketu). The numbers 62, 28, and 9, in other words, appear to be largely nocturnal and/or lunar variants of diurnal and/or solar numbers such as 30 and 60. In ancient India there were 360 days in the solar year, 30 days in the month and 7 days in the week. Seasons were determined by combining months in dyads (of 60 days each), making a total of 6 seasons for one year (or, in other words, 360 days).[60] The ancient Indians, of course, learned most of their astronomy from the Greeks and from ancient Near Eastern sources, and one important system of calculation for astronomical purposes was the sexagesimal system (as opposed to the decimal system) in which 1 = 60 (and which comes down even to modern times in our 60-minute hour and 60-second minute).[61] One cannot help but wonder if the Sāṃkhya use of the number 60 (*ṣaṣṭitantra*) ("the system or science of 60 topics") may be somehow related to archaic astronomical traditions such as this.

Some further hints about the possible significance of Sāṃkhya numbers may also be found in the apparently unlikely context of ancient acoustical theory. Ernest McClain in his *Myth of Invariance* has shown that the ancient Greek-Hindu diatonic scale with two similar tetrachords encompasses D e^b f G A b^b (b) c D (when rising) and D c# b A Gf# (f) e D (when falling).[62] The octave increment is a ratio of 1:2, and if one wishes to give expression to the ratios between the 7 tones of the scale in the smallest possible whole numbers, the sequence is 30, 32, 36, 40, 45, 48, (50), 54, 60 or the ratio 30:60. Moreover, if one wishes to reduce this sequence to its smallest integers in a formulaic manner, one has the formula $2^p.3^q.5^r.\leq 60$.[63] That is to say, all of the tones in the basic scale can be reduced to 2, 3, and 5 in the following manner: $30 = 2\cdot 3\cdot 5$; $32 = 2^5$; $36 = 2^2\cdot 3^2$; $40 = 2^3\cdot 5$; $45 = 3^2\cdot 5$; $48 = 2^4\cdot 3$; $50 = 2\cdot 5^2$; $54 = 2\cdot 3^3$ and $60 = 2^2\cdot 3\cdot 5$.[64] Similarly, if one wishes to give expression to the 11 semitones of the chromatic scale, one needs a multiple of 60, namely, 360, and the resulting set of smallest whole numbers to express the ratios would be 360, 384, 400, 432, 450, 480, 540, 576, 600, 648, 675, and 720, and a revised formula $2^p\cdot 3^q\cdot 5^r \leq 720$.[65] McClain argues that both formulas were widely known in the ancient world, and that the Ṛg Vedic poets knew of these sequences (as can be seen in the number sequences of such hymns as RV I.164). McClain also argues that many of the large cosmological numbers in the epics and Purāṇas reflect these ancient acoustical or "tonal" formulas.[66] The former formula ($2^p\cdot 3^q\cdot 5^r \leq 60$) is basic to ancient Greek and Indian tonal theory. The latter formula $2^p\cdot 3^q\cdot 5^r \leq 720$) was the "tonal basis" for astronomical extensions based on the 360-day solar year.

Returning, however, to Sāṃkhya philosophy, the only thing that can be said with certainty is that the system is built largely on dyads, triads, and pentads with other prime numbers playing an important role on the principles level, and the system overall is referred as "the system or science of 60 topics." The formula $2^p\cdot 3^q\cdot 5^r \leq 60$, in other words, does appear to fit the Sāṃkhya case in an intriguing and provocative way, and one wonders if such ancient traditions of mathematical (and astronomical/musical) theorizing represent the intellectual environment in which the ancient Sāṃkhya teachers first began their philosophical work. Moreover, we know that Sāṃkhya philosophy did involve cosmology and/or astronomy and that some of the Sāṃkhya numbers reflect possible astronomical phenomena. We know, furthermore, that Sāṃkhya philosophy (along with other traditions of ancient Indian speculation) sought to correlate macrocosmic and microcosmic phenomena so that each appears to recapitulate the other. Then, too, from the evidence of Yoga and Tantric materials, which frequently make use of Sāṃkhya notions, we know that there were elaborate speculations about the role and function of certain "tones," *mantras*, and patterns of recitation. In this connection, it might be briefly noted, one wonders if the Sāṃkhya conceptualization of "subtle element" (*tanmātra*) may be related to older phonetic speculation in which attempts were made to measure the length of sounds in terms of *mātrās*.[67] The term "*mātrā*" is, of course, also well known in Yoga traditions, in which the Yogin's breathing discipline is measured in *mātrās*.

It could be the case, therefore, that the Sāṃkhya enumerations overall are far from being arbitrary or random. There may have been operating some sort of archaic, but nevertheless rational, mathematical theorizing in which prime numbers, archaic acoustical theory (in music and sacred recitation), and cosmological/astronomical observation were crucial concerns. Again, of course, the possible parallel with Pythagoreanism in the ancient Greek tradition is obvious, for the Pythagoreans were likewise keen on relating number theory, musical acoustics, and astronomy to philosophy.[68]

It must be stressed once more that all of this is highly speculative and that further research is essential for building a plausible case. As Frauwallner, Hacker, and others have noted, however, the origins of Sāṃkhya appear to be very different from many of the other traditions of Indian philosophy.[69] Whereas much of Indian philosophy appears to have emerged from religious meditation and dialectical disputation, Sāṃkhya may well have derived from older "scientific" traditions. That Sāṃkhya does not appear to have a set of ancient *sūtras*, that it refers to itself as a *tantra* (specifically, *ṣaṣṭitantra*) and makes use (according to the *Yuktidīpikā*) of *tantrayuktis* or systematic "methodological devices," that it has affinities with cosmology/astronomy and medical theorizing, and that it unfolds seemingly endless patterns of enumeration may all suggest that the point of origin for Sāṃkhya is to be found in early scientific theorizing (in such subject areas as mathematics, astronomy, acoustics, and medicine). If such is the case, then a basic philosophical methodology focusing on rational enumeration would not at all be surprising.

Logic and epistemology. In attempting to piece together Sāṃkhya's logic and epistemology, a convenient point of departure is to refer to what the Sāṃkhya teachers themselves considered to be the ten "fundamental matters" (*mūlikārtha*) requiring rational elucidation. These matters are as follows (using the formulations set forth in the *Jayamaṅgalā*, the *Tattvakaumudī*, and the *Yuktidīpikā*):

(1) The existence of materiality and consciousness (*astitva*);
(2) The uniformity or oneness of materiality (*ekatva*);
(3) The objectivity of materiality (*arthavattva*);
(4) The purposefulness or inherent teleology of materiality (*pārārthya*);
(5) The ontological distinction of consciousness (from materiality) (*anyatva*);
(6) The nonagency or nonactivity of consciousness (*akartṛbhāva*);
(7) The transactions that occur when materiality and consciousness are not distinguished from one another (*yoga*);
(8) The transactions that occur when materiality and consciousness are distinguished from one another (*viyoga*);
(9) The plurality of consciousnesses (*puruṣabahutva*);
(10) The continuous functioning of gross and subtle things even after consciousness and materiality have been distinguished (*sthitiḥ śarīrasya...śeṣavṛttiḥ*).[70]

These matters evidently pertain both to the "basic principle" realm and to the "predispositional" or "projective" realm (or, in other words, the "twofold creation" mentioned in SK 52). They also obviously refer to Sāṃkhya's two fundamental existents, consciousness and materiality. Items (2), (3), and (4), according to most commentators, deal with materiality in and of itself. Items (5), (6), and (9) deal with consciousness. Items (1), (7), (8), and (10) deal with the relation between consciousness and materiality. Commentaries inform us, further, that item (2) refers to preexistence of the effect and material causality or, in other words, the twenty-three inherent subdivisions of materiality; item (3) refers to the tripartite process; item (4) refers to the predispositions; items (5) and (6) refer to the absence of the tripartite process in consciousness; and items (7), (8), and (10) refer to the experience of frustration or liberation when materiality and consciousness are in relation to one another.[71]

These ten "fundamental matters" (*mūlikārtha*), making up the "form" realm and the "projective" realm (*tattva* and *bhāva*), when combined with the fifty "categories" (*padārtha*) of the "consequent" (*phala*) or "intellectual creation" (*pratyayasarga*), made up of the five misconceptions, the twenty-eight dysfunctions, the nine contentments, and the eight attainments, represent the "system or science of sixty topics" (*ṣaṣṭitantra*). The *ṣaṣṭitantra*, in other words, appears to be a shorthand way of referring to the three realms (*tattva*, *bhāva*, and *bhūta*) that have been referred to throughout this exposition, the *tattva* realm being the ontological dyad, the *bhāva* realm being the epistemological triad, and the *bhūta* realm being the phenomenal, empirical pentad. Referring again to the computer and linguistic metaphors mentioned earlier, the *tattva* and *bhāva* realms represent as it were the hardware and software of the Sāṃkhya system, and the *bhūta* realm, the resulting printout; or, the *tattva* and *bhāva* realms represent as it were the deep-structural syntactic and semantic components of the Sāṃkhya system, and the *bhūta* realm the level of surface structure.

From an epistemological standpoint, the *bhūta* realm would obviously be the sphere of perception (*pratyakṣa*, *dṛṣṭa*) for this is the realm of ordinary experience. The *tattva* and *bhāva* realms, however, transcend ordinary experience (or are *nirupabhoga*) and can only be established on the basis of inferential reasoning (*anumāna*). Inference, therefore, must have had pride of place among the "instruments of knowledge" to the early Sāṃkhya teachers, for the ten "fundamental matters" could not persuasively be established in any other way. Moreover, if the sequence of inferences establishes that frustration itself is epistemic, then it certainly would follow that release from frustration is only possible by means of the path of inferential reasoning pursued in an appropriate meditative context. As Īśvarakṛṣṇa puts the matter in *Kārikā* 2.

> The revealed (or scriptural, means of removing frustration) are like the perceptible (that is to say, ultimately inadequate), for they are connected with impurity, destruction, and excess (or, in other words, are bound up with finite relations); a superior means, different from both, is the (discriminative) knowledge of the manifest, the unmanifest and the knower (*jña* or *puruṣa*).

It is reasonable to conclude, therefore, that a significant portion of the so-called *ṣaṣṭitantra* would involve careful consideration of the logic of inference, and Frauwallner has provocatively shown that this was probably the case.[72] Piecing together quotations of Sāṃkhya authors from the work of Dignāga, Jinendrabuddhi, Mallavādin, and Siṃhasūri, Frauwallner was able to reconstruct portions of an older Sāṃkhya discussion regarding the logic of inference. Frauwallner argues that his reconstructed text is a portion of Vārṣagaṇya's *Ṣaṣṭitantra* and can be dated about the beginning of the fourth-century of the Common Era.[73] Whether or not one agrees with Frauwallner's conclusions regarding authorship and date of the reconstructed material, the content of the discussion is interesting and provides useful insights into early Sāṃkhya discussions of epistemology.

According to the reconstructed material, Sāṃkhya philosophy assigned primary status to inference among the instruments of knowledge but also accepted perception and reliable testimony.[74] With respect to inference, the task is one of identifying what sort of relation (*sambandha*) is relevant in a given instance and then to infer an appropriate imperceptible or unknown relatum on the basis of a given perceptible relatum (*saṃbandhād ekasmāt pratyakṣāc cheṣasiddhir anumānam*). In Sāṃkhya philosophy, according to the reconstructed material, seven types or kinds of relation (*saptasambandha*) were basic and fundamental, namely:

(1) "The relation between possession and possessor" (*svasvāmibhāvasaṃbandha*)—for example, a king and his servant;
(2) "The relation between primary and derivative" or "principal and secondary" (*prakṛtivikārasaṃbandha*)—for example, sweet milk and sour milk;
(3) "The relation between material effect and cause" (*kāryakāraṇasaṃbandha*)—for example, a wagon and its parts;
(4) "The relation between efficient cause and effect" (*nimittanaimittikasaṃbandha*)—for example, a potter and a pot;
(5) "The relation between source and offspring" (*mātrāmātrikasaṃbandha*)—for example, a tree and its branch;
(6) "The relation of cooperation or association" (*sahacārisaṃbandha*)—for example, two Cakravāka birds;
(7) "The relation of opposition or hostility" (*vadhyaghātakasaṃbandha*)—for example, a snake and an ichneumon.

Regarding the application of these relations to the fundamental principles of Sāṃkhya, the following would appear to be the case, according to Frauwallner's reconstruction:

(1) Possession and possessor—the relation between consciousness and materiality;
(2) Principal and secondary—the relation between materiality and its twenty-three subdivisions;
(3) Material effect and cause—the relation between *sattva*, *rajas*, and *tamas*;
(4) Efficient cause and effect—the relation between *sattva*, *rajas*, and *tamas* in their predispositional projections;
(5) Source and offspring—the relation between the subtle elements and the gross elements;
(6) Cooperation or association—the cooperating modality of the tripartite process; and
(7) Opposition or hostility—the negating modality of the tripartite process.[75]

Furthermore, according to the reconstructed discussion, various types of inference can be framed. Basically, there are two fundamental types, namely, inferences based on a specific perception in one situation (*viśeṣato dṛṣṭa*) and inferences based on a specific perception in more than one situation (*sāmānyato dṛṣṭa*). The former would be the inference of fire because of the presence of smoke in a sepecific location so that each time one perceives the same smoke in that location, one infers the presence of fire. The latter would be the more general inference of the relation between fire and smoke so that whenever one perceives smoke, one infers the presence of fire. This more general inference, that is to say, inference based on general correlation (*sāmānyato dṛṣṭa*) in turn, is twofold, namely, *pūrvavat* and *śeṣavat.* The former is inference-from-cause-to-effect : the imminent occurrence of rain may be inferred from the perception of gathering storm clouds. The latter is inference-from-effect-to-cause: when one perceives the rising level of water in a river, one infers that it has rained upstream. Moreover, it is also possible to infer what is in principle imperceptible (*atīndriya*) by means of inference based on general correlation, and such inferences may be framed directly (*vīta*) or through exclusion (*avīta*). The direct *sāmānyato dṛṣṭa* inference is when an argument for a specific conclusion is set forth in its own form without reference to its opposing thesis. Such an inference follows a fivefold format of (a) an assertion to be proved (*sādhya*); (b) an appropriate reason (*sādhana*); (c) a concrete example (*nidarśana*); (d) an explanation relating the example to the assertion (*upasaṃhāra*); and (e) a drawing of the appropriate conclusion (*nigamana*). An exclusionary (*avīta*) *sāmānyato dṛṣṭa* inference establishes a conclusion as a definite possibility or a distinct remaining possibility. One proceeds by refuting an opposing thesis and establishing one's own as a distinct remaining possibility. A *vīta* inference in Sāṃkhya philosophy, for example, might argue that sensations (hearing, touching, and so forth) give rise to experiences of pleasure, pain, and indifference. An *avīta* inference, for example, might seek to refute those who argue that the manifest world arises out of nonbeing and to seek to establish the existence of a primordial undifferentiated materiality as a distinct remaining possibility.[76]

Unfortunately, Īśvarakṛṣṇa's *Sāṃkhyakārikā* and the subsequent commentarial tradition add little if anything to the Sāṃkhya treatment of the discussion of inference. Īśvarakṛṣṇa simply asserts that there are three varieties of inference (*anumāna*) (SK 5) and that inference is based on a relation between a "characteristic mark" (*liṅga*) and that which possesses or bears such a mark (*liṅgin*). He mentions only *sāmānyato dṛṣṭa* as one of the three types, and he indicates that *sāmānyato dṛṣṭa* can be used for establishing matters that are in principle imperceptible (*atīndriya*) (SK 6). He also comments that primordial materiality is imperceptible in principle because of its subtlety but that its existence can be inferred on the basis of its effects (SK 8). The various commentaries on the *Kārikā* suggest that the three types of inference Īśvarakṛṣṇa had in mind were *pūrvavat, śeṣavat,* and *sāmānyato dṛṣṭa*, but, generally speaking, the commentators seem to be following later Nyāya accounts of inference. Overall it must be admitted that the various discussions of inference in the Sāṃkhya literature proper are less than satisfactory and are not as informative as the reconstructed material that Frauwallner has put together from citations in the work of Sāṃkhya's opponents. Gauḍapāda suggests that *pūrvavat* is inference-from-cause-to-effect, *śeṣavat* is inference from a part to a whole (as when one infers that sea water is salty because a drop of it tastes salty), and *sāmānyato dṛṣṭa* is inference based on analogy (Gauḍapāda under SK 5). The *Jayamaṅgalā* (under SK 5) suggests that *pūrvavat* is inference-from-cause-to-effect and has to do with the future; *śeṣavat* is inference-from-effect-to-cause and has to do with the past; and *sāmānyato dṛṣṭa* is inference by analogy that has to do with the present. The *Māṭharavṛtti* (under SK 5) follows Gauḍapāda. Vācaspati Miśra's, *Tattvakaumudī* (under SK 5) appears to be following yet another approach when it is suggested that *pūrvavat* and *sāmānyato dṛṣṭa* inferences are of the *vīta* type and *śeṣavat* is only *avīta* or exclusionary. The *Yuktidīpikā* suggests that *pūrvavat* is inference-from-cause-to-effect (for example, rain from gathering storm clouds), *śeṣavat* is inference-from-effect-to-cause (for example, seeing a child one infers a prior parental act of intercourse), and *sāmānyato dṛṣṭa* is inference related to generalities (*jāti*) that pertain at various times and places (for example, the general observation that where there is smoke, there is fire) (p. 38).

Regarding the manner in which inferences are to be framed, the discussions in the various Sāṃkhya texts are also less than satisfactory. Īśvarakṛṣṇa himself says nothing about the issue. The *Māṭharavṛtti* (SK 4-5) suggests that inferences may be framed with three members (namely, the assertion to be proved, or *pratijñā*, the reason, or *hetu*, and an appropriate illustration, or *udāharaṇa*) or with the standard five members (*pratijñā, hetu, udāharaṇa*, plus application, or *upasaṃhāra*, and conclusion, or *nigamana*). The latter more elaborate format is for convincing others (*parārtham anumānam*). The *Yuktidīpikā* suggests interestingly that older Sāṃkhya teachers used a ten-membered inferential format, the first five members of which provide a preliminary explication of a problem (*vyākhyāṅgabhūta*) in terms of (1) the desire to know (*jijñāsā*), (2) the occasion for doubt (*saṃśaya*), (3) the purpose for the undertaking (*prayojana*), (4) the likelihood of a solution (*śākyaprāpti*), and (5) the elimination of extraneous doubts (*saṃśayavyudāsa*), and the last five members of which constitute a persuasive demonstration or proof (*parapratipādanāṅgabhūta*), namely (6) the basic assertion to be proved (*pratijñā*), (7) the reason (*hetu*), (8) an appropriate illustration (*dṛṣṭānta*), (9) an appropriate application (*upasaṃhāra*) and (10) the drawing of a final conclusion (*nigamana*).[77]

As is well known, later classical Indian philosophy pursues the logic of inference in a much more sophisticated and detailed manner, but very little remains of any important Sāṃkhya contribution to these discussions. It is perhaps clear enough, however, that Sāṃkhya's early concern for defining certain precise and important relations (*sapta saṃbandha*) and its concern for giving pride of place to inference (*anumāna*) and the proper formulation of the types of inference, all represent important bits of evidence for suggesting that Sāṃkhya philosophy played an important role in the formative stages of the history of epistemological and logical reflection in India.

Epistemology, of course, is not simply philosophical methodology, the logic of relations, and the framing of persuasive inferences, important as these matters were to the early Sāṃkhya teachers. Equally important were such issues as the number and definition of the instruments of knowledge, the functioning of the senses, mind, egoity, and intellect/will in the process of experience, the actual content of the arguments for such key notions as *satkārya*, *kāraṇakārya*, and *triguṇa*, the manner in which nondiscrimination occurs, the status of the external world, the manner in which knowing affects being, the relation between awareness (the transactions of intellect, egoity, and mind) and consciousness, and most important, the function of knowing with respect to ordinary experience and the ultimate experience of liberation from frustration. Most of these matters have been discussed in passing throughout this essay on the philosophy of Sāṃkhya, and the only remaining task is to bring them together in a systematic manner so that the Sāṃkhya epistemology is shown to be an integral part of the system as a whole.

Regarding the instruments of knowledge, Sāṃkhya philosophy accepts a threefold classification, namely, perception, inference, and reliable authority. Because knowing as reflective discerning is a constituent of tripartite process, there is a basic uniformity in the knowing process "from Brahmā down to a blade of grass," and it would be a mistake, therefore, to interpret the threefold classification as suggesting separate kinds of knowing. The process of knowing is uniform, according to the author of the *Yuktidīpikā* (p. 29), but because of limiting conditions certain methodological variations can be described. Reflective discerning occurs through ascertainment or determination by the intellect, assisted by the self-awareness of egoity, the explication or intellectual elaboration of mind, and the functioning of the various sense and action capacities. Specific awarenesses (*vṛtti*), whether derivative from external objects or internal states, are processed through contacts with the sense capacities, mind, and egoity, and a determinate judgment is accomplished by the intellect. To the extent that reflective discerning occurs in immediate experience (SK 33) as a result of the contact of a sense capacity with an object (or a mind with an internal feeling), such reflective discerning is known as perception. For ordinary persons such perceptions are limited to "specific" (*viśeṣa*) awarenesses related to the gross aspects of experience, but Yogins and other higher beings (for examples, gods) are also able to perceive "nonspecific" (*aviśeṣa*) matters such as the subtle elements (*Yuktidīpikā*, p. 35). To the extent that reflective discerning occurs as a result of reasoning from ordinary experience to the more general principles or relations invariably associated with ordinary experience and required in order to have ordinary experience, such reflective discerning is known as inference. There are three varieties of inference, as already described, and inferences, though dependent on perception, may extend, if properly framed, to matters that are imperceptible in principle (for example, establishing the existence of such matters as materiality and consciousness). To the extent that reflective discerning occurs as a result of the trustworthy verbal testimony of the Veda and *smṛti* teachings, or from the *ṛṣis* or holy men, who are free from personal biases, such reflective discerning is known as reliable authority and concerns matters that transcend perception and cannot be framed in a proper inference (for example, the precise sequence and ordering of the fundamental principles and matters relating to higher beings like the *māhātmyaśarīras*, and so forth).

All knowing transactions, however, whether from perception, inference, or reliable authority are for the sake of the consciousness (*puruṣārtha*) (SK, 31, 37, and 57).[78] That is to say, reflective discerning as the *sattva* constituent of tripartite process is but a part of its total functioning as a teleological but unconscious (*acetana*) material process, in much the same way, says Īśvarakṛṣṇa in *Kārikā* 57, as unconscious milk nourishes a young calf. The results of all knowing transactions, therefore, together with the total functioning of primordial materiality, are ascribed or belong finally to consciousness (*puruṣārtha*).

Moreover, because reflective discerning (*sattva*) is a constituent of a continuous tripartite process, Sāṃkhya describes the knowing process in terms of intellect, egoity, mind, and the various sense capacities actually assuming or becoming the various forms or manifestations that appear. Hearing assumes or becomes the vibration or sound heard; seeing becomes the color or form seen, and so forth. So, likewise, mind becomes the idea elaborated; egoity is the assimilation of the contents of experience to oneself (so that egoity, as it were, "makes" or "forms" itself, *ahaṃkāra, ahaṃ karomi*); and intellect becomes the final, total configuration insofar as it can be reflectively discerned in a pure *sattva* transparency.[79] Put another way, the process of knowing is simply a subtle material process in which reflective discerning (through intellect, egoity, mind, and the capacities) is inextricably allied with spontaneous activity (*rajas*) and determinate formulation (*tamas*, *tanmātra*, *bhūta*). Hence, according to Sāṃkhya, all experience deriving from the pentadic or fivefold realm (*indriya*, *tanmātra*, *bhūta*) manifests itself initially as specific (*viśeṣa*) comfortable (*śānta*), uncomfortable (*ghora*), or bewildering (*mūḍha*) experiences, which upon reflection will finally reveal themselves as one or another constituent of tripartite process. The apparent subject-object dichotomy of ordinary experience will progressively show itself through the process of reflective discerning as *not* being a dichotomy. That is to say, ordinary or apparent subjectivity (intellect, egoity, mind, and the other internal capacities) will show itself as a modality of objectivity (*triguṇa* as *viṣaya*). Perception, inference, and reliable authority, then, represent one continuous process of reflective discerning (*sattva*) that progressively reveals the absence of consciousness, or perhaps better, that reveals the process of knowing as a material process "for the sake of another" (*parārtha*, *puruṣārtha*). As mentioned earlier, Sāṃkhya philosophy is, therefore, the antithesis of Hegelian philosophy. For Hegel, knowing is the progressive revelation of substance as subject. For Sāṃkhya, knowing is the progressive revelation of the ordinary or apparent subject (*antaḥkaraṇa*, *citta*, *buddhi*, *ahaṃkāra*, *manas*) as substance![80]

Primordial materiality as tripartite process is, according to Sāṃkhya, (a) undifferentiated (*avivekin*), (b) a content (*viṣaya*) (c) general (*sāmānya*) and, hence, intelligible in principle, (d) unconscious (*acetana*), and (e) inherently productive (*prasavadharmin*) (SK 11).

Moreover, primordial materiality can be shown to exist as the ultimate material cause,

(a) because that which is manifest is perceived to be limited (*parimāṇa*) (and no limited thing can itself serve as an ultimate cause without getting into an infinite regress),

(b) because all manifest things, insofar as their characteristics are uniform and/or homogeneous (*samanvaya*), require a single, ultimate cause as their causal source,

(c) because the emergence and/or process of that which is manifest presupposes a causal capacity (*śakti*) that enables emergence or process to occur,

(d) because that which is manifest is just a transformation and, hence, presupposes an ultimate cause different from it which is not a transformation, and

(e) because that which is manifest and, hence, defined in terms of ordinary space and time, presupposes an ultimate cause that is not so defined, and, hence, in which the manifest can reside prior to manifestation (SK 15-16).

Furthermore, according to Sāṃkhya, all manifest material effects (*kārya*) already exist (*satkārya*) in the primal material cause in a potential state or condition prior to manifestation, because (a) something (namely, any material effect) cannot arise from nothing, (b) any material effect must have a common material basis (namely, a real relation) with its cause, (c) anything (namely, any manifest effect) cannot arise from just everything, (d) something (namely, an ultimate cause) can only produce what it is capable of producing, and (e) the very nature or essence of the cause is nondifferent from the effect (as, for example, a cloth and its threads) (SK 9).

The manifest world, then, is a series of material effects from a primal material cause. The effects preexist potentially in the cause and, thus, are only manifest transformations of one basic "existent" (viz, primordial materiality). That which links material effect to material cause is tripartite process, which first shows itself as specific satisfying, frustrating, and confusing experiences but is finally reflectively discerned as a closed causal system of reductive materialism in which consciousness is absent.

As mentioned earlier in the section on contentless consciousness, Sāṃkhya presumably could have settled with the elimination of the old Upaniṣadic "ghost in the machine" and developed itself as a pure materialism or as a variant of Buddhist no-self theorizing. Such moves, however, would have required a rejection of the Vedic heritage or a rejection of any significant notion of freedom or release. More than that, however, it would have required reducing its epistemology to some sort of epiphenomenal status within an overall materialist position. Sāṃkhya philosophy rejected such moves and introduced, instead, its "eccentric" dualism and its anomalous notion of contentless or nonintentional consciousness, which has already been described.

Epistemologically, the introduction of consciousness means a shift from reductive materialism to critical realism.[81] Knowing and the content of knowing are separated from an uncharacterizable (*asāmānya*) "presupposition for knowing" (*jña, puruṣa*) that is neither the material nor efficient cause of the manifest world and can only be pointed to as being "not this, not that" (*neti, neti*). Moreover, the "presupposition of knowing" cannot really know, because the process of knowing resides finally in intellect as the focus of reflective discerning (*sattva*). Consciousness is only a mysterious, transcendent, yet immanent, presence (*sākṣitva*) that enables knowing to function but finally reveals that knowing itself falls outside of consciousness or, put another way, that knowing itself is only a dimension of manifest being. Thus, finally, for Sāṃkhya, the manifest external world is fully real, as is the mysterious presence of transcendent consciousness, and the final discrimination (*viveka*) of the intellect is the realization that the two "existents" are distinct (*guṇapuruṣāntraopalabdhi*, as the *Yuktidīpikā* characterizes it), with knowing itself being reduced to the *guṇa* side of the dualism.

What shows itself as being unreal for Sāṃkhya are the misconstrued relations (*anyathākhyāti*, *sadasatkhyāti*) projected on what is real prior to the discrimination of the triparite process from consciousness. Because consciousness is contentless and nonintentional, it appears to take on the content of the tripartite process, and that process appears as if possessing consciousness. There is a beginningless predisposition towards nondiscrimination, which leads naturally towards the experiences of bondage and frustration (SK 55), and this beginningless predisposition towards nondiscrimination functions in Sāṃkhya almost like a Kantian a priori form of intuition—in the sense that ordinary experience always shows itself under this limitation or condition. This basic nondiscrimination is a fundmental predisposition of the intellect and generates along with the other predispositions the "intellectual creation" and the phenomenal, empirical world of ordinary space, time, and causality (the *phala* realm or the *bhūta* realm). Also inherent in the intellect, however, is a natural tendency towards discrimination that reflects the true or real *tattva* dimension of what is. Seven of the predispositions, in other words, foster the primal nondiscrimination and predispose the transmigrating intellect to become further involved in the experiences of bondage and frustration; only one predisposition (namely, knowledge) fosters a predisposition towards a correct apprehension of what truly is, namely, the tripartite process and pure consciousness (SK 63), in which ordinary space, time, and causality show themselves as the ongoing transformations (*pariṇāma*) and combinations (*saṃghāta*) of an undifferentiated (*avivekin*) or uniform primordial materiality (*mūlaprakṛti* as *triguṇa*, *satkārya*, and *kāraṇakārya*) in which consciousness is absent and to which consciousness is indifferent (*udāsīna*, *mādhyasthya*). Sāṃkhya, in other words, wants to make a clear distinction between "phenomenal" and "noumenal," almost in a Kantian sense, but with the important difference, of course, that the Kantian "noumenal" is knowable.[82] For Sāṃkhya what is finally truly "noumenal" is consciousness, but unlike Kant, Sāṃkhya dissociates "consciousness" from "awareness" ontologically, thereby making a claim that Kantian philosophy or Western philosophy in general does not address.[83]

Finally, however, *both* frustration and liberation are shown to be related to the epistemological transactions of the intellect in its ongoing functioning. In other words, bondage and release pertain only to the tripartite process, never to consciousness, although the presence (*sākṣitva*) of consciousness allows all transactions to become manifest. Knowing, therefore, cannot change what is; it can only create interpretive perspectives that either perpetuate conventional views about the world that are insufficiently discriminating, or that reflect the true nature of things. Knowing, then, when insufficiently pursued, is at the root of our bondage to frustration and rebirth (*duḥkha, saṃsāra, bandha*), but it may also become the occasion, when properly cultivated, for a glimpse of the true nature of things, one aspect of which is an intelligible, coherent, and determinate world (*triguṇa, mūlaprakṛti*) and the other aspect of which is the presence of nonintentional consciousness (*puruṣa*) *for* which the world exists.

PART TWO

SUMMARIES OF WORKS
(arranged chronologically)

KAPILA, ĀSURI

In verse 69 of the *Sāṃkhyakārikā*, Īśvarakṛṣṇa indicates that the Sāṃkhya system has been "fully enumerated" or "explained" by the "supreme sage" (*paramarṣi*), who is unanimously identified within the Sāṃkhya tradition as the sage Kapila. In verse 70 of the *Kārikā*, Īśvarakṛṣṇa informs us further that out of compassion Kapila transmitted the knowledge of Sāṃkhya to Āsuri who in turn passed on the system to Pañcaśikha. Moreover, according to Īśvarakṛṣṇa in verse 70, the Sāṃkhya system (*tantra*) was "expanded" or "widely disseminated" (*bahudhā kṛta*) by Pañcaśikha. Various attempts have been made in the commentarial tradition to trace the line of teachers from Pañcaśikha to Īśvarakṛṣṇa. *Māṭharavṛtti*, for example, mentions the sequence "Bhārgava, Ulūka, Vālmīkin, Hārīta, Devala, and many others (*prabhṛti*)" (under SK 71). *Jayamaṅgalā* offers the sequence "Garga, Gautama, and many others" (under SK 71). Paramārtha's Chinese translation (under SK 70) suggests the sequence "Hokia, Ulūka, Po-p'o-li, Īśvarakṛṣṇa," the name "Hokia" possibly meaning "Garga" and the name "Po-p'o-li" possibly meaning "Varṣa" (according to Takakusu), Devala (according to Belvalkar), or "Kapila" (or "derived from Kapila," according to R. C. Pandeya). *Yuktidīpikā* refers to "Hārīta, Bāddhali, Kairāta, Paurika, Ṛṣabheśvara, Pañcādhikaraṇa, Patañjali, Vārṣagaṇya, Kauṇḍinya, Mūka, and so forth" (under SK 71). Revealing, however, is another comment by the author of the *Yuktidīpikā* (under SK 70) that the lineage of Sāṃkhya teachers, unlike the lineage of other *śāstras*, cannot be adequately calculated even in terms of hundreds and/or thousands of years (*varṣaśatasahasra*), implying, in in other words, either that the Sāṃkhya tradition is very old indeed or that its origin is divine. It is permissible to conclude, therefore, that by the sixth-century of the Common Era (the approximate date of the Chinese translation) and thereafter, the writers of Sāṃkhya texts (a) identified Kapila as the founder of the system, (b) recognized Āsuri as someone who inherited the teaching, (c) considered Pañcaśikha as someone who further formulated the system (*tantra*) and widely disseminated it, and (d) described Īśvarakṛṣṇa as someone who summarized and simplified the old system after an interval of some centuries (Paramārtha's Chinese translation) or more (*Yuktidīpikā*).

As was already pointed out in the Introduction, Kapila and Āsuri are only vague memories. According to the oldest commentary on the *Kārikā* (Paramārtha's Chinese translation), Kapila is a "wise ascetic," "born of heaven," "innately endowed with the four fundamental predispositions of virtue, knowledge, renunciation, and supernatural power," who takes pity on suffering humanity and selects a Brahmin, Āsuri by name, as an appropriate person to whom to reveal the knowledge (of Sāṃkhya). Kapila approaches Āsuri, who is described as being a Brahmin householder (*gṛhastha*) and as having been "performing sacrifices for a thousand years" (*varṣasahasrayājin*), but Āsuri does not heed the call of Kapila. Kapila returns on two additional occasions, each one after an additional interval of a thousand years, and finally Āsuri renounces the life of a householder, commences ascetic observances, and becomes a disciple of Kapila. According to *Māṭharavṛtti* (under SK 1), Kapila is a "great sage" (*maharṣi*), born of Manu Svāyaṃbhuva's daughter, Devahūtī, and Prajāpati's son, Kardama. According to the *Bhāṣya* of Gauḍapāda (under SK 1), Kapila is one of the seven "great sages" or "seers" (*sapta maharṣi*) (along with Sanaka, Sananda, Sanātana, Āsuri, Voḍhu, and Pañcaśikha). Vyāsa in his *Yogasūtrabhāṣya* I.25, quotes an old statement that describes Kapila as the "primal wise man" or "knower" (*ādividvān*) who assumes an "artifical mind" (*nirmāṇacitta*) in order to instruct Āsuri about the Sāṃkhya system (*tantra*). Vācaspati Miśra, in his commentary on the passage, asserts that this old statement is from Pañcaśikha. Moreover, according to Vācaspati Miśra, Kapila was born at the beginning of creation, attained complete knowledge immediately from Maheśvara, and may be considered one of the incarnations (*avatāra*) of Viṣṇu. As such, Kapila is also known as "self-existent" (*svayaṃbhū*) Hiraṇyagarbha, the Lord (*iśvara*) of the descendants of Svayaṃbhū ("*svāyaṃbhuvānām . . . iśvara iti bhāvaḥ*," *Tattvavaiśāradī* on *Yogasūtrabhāṣya* I.25). References such as these and others persuaded Albrecht Wezler to suggest that Kapila may have himself been considered to be the Lord (*iśvara*) or God of Sāṃkhya.[1] Kapila is also credited with authorship of the *Ṣaṣṭitantra* ("the science of sixty topics"), according to the author of the *Yuktidīpikā* (in the introductory verses of his commentary) and according to the *Ahirbudhnyasaṃhitā* (XII.30), but other texts ascribe authorship of the *Ṣaṣṭitantra* to Pañcaśikha or Vārṣagaṇya (see below under separate entries).

In older Sanskrit literature there are various references to Kapila and Āsuri, but it is difficult to determine if the older citations can be linked with the later Sāṃkhya references mentioned above. The term "*kapila*" appears already in the *Ṛg Veda* (X.27.16), ". . . one tawny one among the ten. . . ." (*daśānām ekam kapilam*), and is apparently only a term for the color "tawny" or "reddish brown." Similar color references may also be found in *Bṛhadāraṇyaka Upaniṣad* VI.4.15, *Maitrī* VI.30, *Atharvaśiras* 5 and *Garbha* 1. In *Śvetāśvatara Upaniṣad* V.2, however, a text in which the term *sāṃkhya* appears for the first time in Indian literature, *kapila* as a color reference is also linked with a "seer" (*ṛṣi*) who is born at the beginning of creation (*ṛṣiṃ prasūtaṃ kapilam . . . tam agre. . . .*). When this reference is compared with other *Śvetāśvatara* references, namely, IV.12, VI.1-2, VI.18 and III.4, it becomes clear that *kapila* is to be construed with reference to Hiraṇyagarbha and Rudra. In *Aitareyabrāhmaṇa* VII.17, reference is made to the "clans of Kapila" (*kāpileya*), and there was evidently a Kapila *śākhā* of the *Yajurveda*. In the "addenda" (*pariśiṣṭa*) to the *Atharvaveda*, Kapila, along with Āsuri and Pañcaśikha, is mentioned in connection with the *tarpaṇa* or "libation" ritual (at XLIII.3.4). In the *Baudhāyanagṛhyasūtra* (IV.16.1) a system of rules for pursuing the ascetic life is linked with Kapila (*kapilasannyāsavidha*). Kapila is also referred to in the canonical literature of the Jains, specifically in *adhyāya* VIII of the *Uttarādhyayanasūtra*, a poetical discourse entitled "Kāvilīyam" (or "Kapila's Verses"). Śāntisūri's commentary on the discourse reports that Kapila Muni was the son of a Brahmin, Kāśyapa, and his wife, Yaśā. The verses extol the ascetic life, but both Winternitz and Jacobi have commented that there is nothing especially Sāṃkhyan about the verses. In the *Anuyogadvārasūtra* of the Jains, however, there is a specific reference to "Kāvila," along with references to "Saṭṭhitantam," "Kanagasattati," and a certain "Māḍhara," which appear to be respectively Kāpila ("derived from Kapila"), Ṣaṣṭitantra ("the science of sixty topics"), Kanakasaptati (the "Gold-Seventy," an old name of the *Sāṃkhyakārikā*), and Māṭhara or Mādhava (old Sāṃkhya teachers). The latter reference appears to be late, however, and there is apparently no connection with the "Kāvilīyam" section of the *Uttarādhyayana* other than an identity of name. From early Buddhist environments, the only reference to Kapila is, of course, the well-known reference to Kapilavastu, the birthplace of the Buddha. Garbe construed the name Kapilavastu to mean "the place of Kapila," thereby suggesting that Kapilavastu was a center for Sāṃkhya or at least a center for certain specific ascetic traditions, but Oldenberg argued to the contrary that the term "*kapila*" is best taken as a description of the place. Garbe's interpretation presupposes that there could have been an existent Sāṃkhya system in the pre-Buddhistic period, a presupposition for which there is little or no evidence. Oldenberg's interpretation presupposes that there was no Sāṃkhya system in this ancient period, a presupposition that subsequent research has shown to be largely correct.

There are also a number of references to Āsuri in the older literature, especially in the *Śatapathabrāhmaṇa*, namely, I.6.3.26, II.1.4.27, II.6.1.-33, II.6.3.17, and IV.3.4.33 (the latter in the Kāṇva recension), all of which refer to a certain Āsuri who was a specialist in the sacrificial ritual (and which parallel, interestingly, the later Sāṃkhya epithet of Āsuri, namely, *varṣasahasrayājin*, "performing sacrifices for a thousand years"). Moreover, Āsuri is regularly mentioned in the lists of teachers enumerated in the *Bṛhadāraṇyaka* (at II.6.3, IV.6.3, and VI.5.2.). These old references to Kapila and Āsuri became the basis for B. Barua's claim (in *A History of Pre-Buddhistic Indian Philosophy*) that it is useful to trace four periods in the development of Sāṃkhya, namely (a) the Kapila phase as found in Vedic speculations such as *Ṛg Veda* X.90 and X.129; (b) the Āsuri phase as found in the Fourth Brāhmaṇa of the *Bṛhadāraṇyaka* (thereby linking Āsuri with both Yājñavalkya and Uddālaka); (c) the Pañcaśikha phase as found in the *Śāntiparvan* portions of the *Mahābhārata*; and (d) the final summation of the system in Īśvarakṛṣṇa's *Sāṃkhyakārikā*. The reason for linking Kapila with the first phase, according to Barua, is that in the *Mudgala Upaniṣad* the Puruṣasūkta (RV X.90) is said to be the starting point of Sāṃkhya. Moreover, according to the later Sāṃkhya texts, Kapila's first teaching to Āsuri was "In the beginning there was just darkness. . . ." (*tama eva khalu idam agra āsīt. . . .*) (cited by *Māṭharavṛtti* and *Jayamaṅgalā* under SK 70 and cited in a slightly different manner in *Maitrī* V.2), obviously calling to mind RV X.129. Although Barua's periodization for the Pañcaśikha phase and the Īśvarakṛṣṇa phase is reasonable enough, the same cannot be said for his Kapila phase and his Āsuri phase. Here again the issue comes down to whether one can reasonably argue for an existent Sāṃkhya system that is pre-Buddhistic or at least pre-Mokṣadharma. The textual evidence clearly suggests that one cannot. The oldest reference to what can reasonably be construed as important Sāṃkhya notions or the rudiments for some kind of Sāṃkhya system are to be found in the *Kaṭha* and *Śvetāśvatara Upaniṣads*. The former does not include the term "*sāṃkhya*," but there are a number of technical terms in a general environment of yogic praxis that render it plausible that some kind of Sāṃkhya system may have been congealing. The latter does include the term "*sāṃkhya*" (VI.13) along with the term "*triguṇa*" (V.7) together with a variety of "enumerations" that can be construed as being identifiably Sāṃkhyan. In both texts, however, there is a lack of systematic treatment or presentation that seriously calls into question any claim that the authors of the texts were aware of any kind of established system. Much more likely is that both texts, which may be roughly dated in the fourth or third century B.C.E., represent further specifications of the kinds of speculations one finds in older Upaniṣads such as the *Chāndogya* and the *Bṛhadāraṇyaka*. Somewhat more systematic reflection of a Sāṃkhya kind begins to appear in the *Mokṣadharma* and the *Bhagavadgītā* (both of which develop between 200 B.C.E. and 200 C.E.), reflection that has striking analogues in such texts as Aśvaghoṣa's *Buddhacarita* (ca., first century of the Common Era), *Carakasaṃhitā* (ca. second century), the earliest *Purāṇas* (*ca.*, the first centuries of the Common Era), and *Mānavadharmaśāstra* (the cosmological portions of which probably derive from the first centuries of the Common Era). Even in these textual environments, however, one is still a long way from the Sāṃkhya system as summarized by Īśvarakṛṣṇa, although it is plausible to suggest that some kind of Sāṃkhya system(s) was in existence in this period. Moreover, the name Pañcaśikha becomes prominent in this period, although the texts clearly indicate that his views were only one tradition among many that were developing. In any case, prior to the *Kaṭha*, *Śvetāśvatara*, *Mokṣadharma*, and *Bhagavadgītā*, there is no evidence whatever for a Sāṃkhya system, and even in these environments (*Kaṭha*, and so forth) one should properly speak only of Proto-Sāṃkhya traditions. Barua's Kapila phase or Āsuri phase, therefore, cannot be taken seriously.

In the *Mokṣadharma* and *Bhagavadgītā* of the *Mahābhārata*, Kapila and Āsuri are regularly mentioned as important precursors of the Sāṃkhya tradition, but there is no uniformity whatever about their identity or about their views. In the *Bhagavadgītā* (X.6) Kapila is referred to as a *muni* among the "perfected ones" (*siddha*). In the *Mokṣadharma* Kapila is linked variously with Agni, Viṣṇu, and Śiva, but generally in the epic Kapila and Āsuri are referred to as two teachers in the Sāṃkhya lineage of teachers. At XII.306.56-60, for example, the following list of Sāṃkhya teachers is given: Jaigīṣavya, Asita Devala, Parāśara, Vārṣagaṇya, Pañcaśikha, Kapila, Śuka, Gautama, Arṣṭiṣeṇa, Garga, Nārada, Āsuri, Pulastya, Sanatkumāra, Śukra, and Kāśyapa. In XII.211, Āsuri and Pañcaśikha (and see below under Pañcaśikha entry) are associated with the doctrine of Brahman, and the term "*kāpileya*," is derived from the feminine, *kapilā*, who is said to have been Āsuri's (*brāhmaṇī*) wife, from whom Pañcaśikha received the pure milk of the knowledge of Sāṃkhya. One has the impression that Kapila and Āsuri are little more than honored names in the *Mokṣadharma* and that any specific content about them has been long forgotten. This possibly explains the tendency for them to become mythological figures as the tradition develops further, with Kapila coming to be linked to Hiraṇyagarbha and Āsuri coming to be viewed as a culture hero who perseveres over thousands of years with the sacrificial ritual, eventually abandoning it for the life of an ascetic.

There is, finally, a long passage in the *Mokṣadharma* purporting to be a dialogue between Kapila and Āsuri about the basic principles of

Sāṃkhya. The form of Sāṃkhya discussed therein is closely related to the Sāṃkhya system attributed to Pañcaśikha in XII.211-212 (see the Pañcaśikha entry below). This "Kapila-Āsuri dialogue," however, appears only in the southern recension of the *Mahābhārata* (the Kumbhakonam edition) and is not included by the editors of the critical edition in the main text of the epic. It is printed as appendix I, no. 29 in the critical edition, pages 2075 following. It is probably a late interpolation and cannot be taken seriously as a representation of the views of Kapila and Āsuri. Likewise, the reference by Guṇaratnasūri in his commentary on Haribhadrasūri's *Ṣaḍdarśanasamuccaya* to an old verse of Āsuri can hardly be taken as a reliable quotation. The verse asserts that *puruṣa* comes to be the locus of experience when the transactions of the *buddhi* become reflected in it, just as the crystal takes on the color of the flower reflected in it and just as the moon becomes reflected in the water. The content of the verse is clearly related to later Sāṃkhya debates about the nature of experience and probably postdates even Īśvarakṛṣṇa's discussion.

In conclusion, then, all that can be said is that Kapila and Āsuri are linked with the beginning of the Sāṃkhya tradition. There is little reliable information about them apart from Kapila's linkage with ancient ascetic traditions and Āsuri's association with the brahmanical sacrificial system. That the later Sāṃkhya teachers unanimously refer to Kapila and Āsuri as the founders of the system probably reflects the Sāṃkhya tradition's attempts to appropriate traditions of ascetic speculation as its own and to relate that ascetic speculation to dissatisfaction with the older sacrificial religion. Moreover, what might be called the upgrading of Kapila to the status of Hiraṇyagarbha or one or another mythological figure (Agni, Rudra, Śiva, and so forth) together with efforts to list Kapila, Āsuri, and other Sāṃkhya teachers in enumerations of the "great seers" in the epic and Purāṇic literature may be taken as further attempts to establish a proper lineage for the Sāṃkhya philosophy.

PAÑCAŚIKHA

If Kapila and Āsuri are only vague memories in the Sāṃkhya tradition, then it must be said that Pañcaśikha, the third teacher within the tradition, is a confused memory. There are a number of references to Pañcaśikha in the older literature, and it is quite clear that Pañcaśikha is a revered teacher for both the Sāṃkhya and Yoga traditions, or, put somewhat differently, Pañcaśikha may well represent a period in which Sāṃkhya and Yoga had not yet become separate or distinct traditions. The name "Pañcaśikha" appears already in the Pāli Canon (in the *Sakkapañhasutta* I.2 of the *Dīghanikāya*) wherein a certain "*pañcasikho gandhabbadevaputto*", one of the celestial musicians attendant upon the King of the Gods, serenades the Buddha prior to his discourse with the great Sakka on the Vediya mountain, but the passage as a whole has nothing whatever to do with Sāṃkhya or Yoga. A more intriguing Pāli reference, however, appears in the *Indriyabhāvanāsutta* (III.52) of the *Majjhimanikāya*, in which the doctrine of a certain Pārāsariya Brahmin is refuted (" . . . *pārāsariyassa brāhmaṇassa vacanam.*"). The doctrine of the Pārāsariya Brahmin is that yogic meditation leads to the total cessation of the functioning of the senses, whereas the Buddha emphasizes only control over the senses. The reference to the Pārāsariya Brahmin may well be to Pañcaśikha, for in Aśvaghoṣa's *Buddhacarita* (XII.67) the name Vṛddha Pārāśara is mentioned along with Janaka and Jaigīṣavya as old teachers of Yoga, and from *Mokṣadharma* XII.308.24 we know that *pārāśarya* is a *gotra* name for Pañcaśikha ("*pārāśaryasagotrasya vṛddhasya sumahātmanaḥ bhikṣoḥ pañcaśikhasya* . . . .). *Buddhacarita* and *Mokṣadharma* can both be reasonably dated from the first (*Buddhacarita*) through the third or fourth centuries of the Common Era, and it is reasonable to conclude, therefore, that the name "Pañcaśikha" was linked to Sāṃkhya and Yoga by at least this period. Whether it is possible to push Pañcaśikha back to the time of the Buddha (as the Pāli reference would suggest) is a more difficult matter to determine. As is well known, there were ascetic, Yoga-like traditions flourishing in the period of the Buddha (*śramaṇa* and *yati* traditions, Ājīvikas, Jains, and so forth). Moreover, the older Buddhist literature indicates clearly that Gotama studied various meditation techniques prior to the discovery of his own unique approach to meditation, and Aśvaghoṣa's *Buddhacarita* (chapter XII) would have us believe that Arāḍa Kālāma's tradition of meditation was indeed an old form of Sāṃkhyayoga. Garbe, Jacobi, Barua, and others, on the basis of these traditions concluded, therefore, that some form of Sāṃkhya and Yoga was known at the time of the Buddha. Moreover, they also tried to show possible influences of Sāṃkhya and Yoga on early Buddhist thought. Subsequent research has tended to show, however, that these older assumptions about a pre-Buddhistic or even a pre-Mokṣadharma form of Sāṃkhya and Yoga are probably anachronistic. The work of Oldenberg, Edgerton, Keith, Johnston, Frauwallner, and van Buitenen has cogently shown that there are no systematic forms of Sāṃkhya and Yoga before the period of the *Bhagavadgītā*, the *Mokṣadharma*, the *Carakasaṃhitā*, and the *Buddhacarita*, all of which texts derive from the first centuries of the Common Era (at least in their extant forms). Moreover, even in these texts one hardly finds a full-blown systematic Sāṃkhya or Yoga. One can also find Sāṃkhya and Yoga references in Upaniṣads such as the *Kaṭha*, *Śvetāśvatara*, *Maitrī*, and so forth, but these references, taken separately or together, only show that there were a variety of incipient Sāṃkhya and Yoga reflections in the process of formulation. Thus, the preponderance of evidence would seem to suggest that the most reliable date for Pañcaśikha would be the *milieu* of the *Buddhacarita* and the *Mokṣadharma* or, in other words, the first century of the Common Era and thereafter. What Pañcasikha appears to represent, then, is the conclusion of what might be called a period of Proto-Sāṃkhya traditions or, putting the matter somewhat differently, Pañcaśikha brings us to the threshold of Sāṃkhya philosophy proper. As already indicated, the Sāṃkhya textual tradition itself tends to support such a view of Pañcaśikha, for Īśvarakṛṣṇa in SK 70 states that, although the tradition was founded by Kapila and transmitted through Āsuri, it was really Pañcaśikha who consolidated, "expanded," or "widely disseminated" (*bahudhā kṛta*) the tradition (*tantra*).

Before turning to the various views and quotations attributed to Pañcaśikha, it may be useful, first of all, to clarify somewhat what is meant by saying that Pañcaśikha represents the end of the period of proto-Sāṃkhya traditions and/or the threshold of Sāṃkhya philosophy proper. Put simply, the name "Pañcaśikha" is more important as a symbolic designation of a certain phase in the history of prephilosophical Sāṃkhya than as a designation of an historic teacher. Regarding the latter, the actual teacher, although there is no reason to doubt that there was such an historic figure, there is no satisfactory way to reconstruct what his views were. Like Kapila and Āsuri, the historic Pañcaśikha is lost to antiquity. Regarding the former, however, the symbolic Pañcaśikha, a great deal can be said to flesh out what Sāṃkhya represented at the threshold of its becoming a philosophical position. As was pointed out in the Introduction, it appears to be reasonably clear that the intellectual environments of the oldest Upaniṣads (the *Bṛhadāraṇyaka, Chāndogya,* and so forth) represent the context out of which the earliest Sāṃkhya and Yoga speculations were to arise, although it is also reasonably clear that there were no identifiable forms of Sāṃkhya and Yoga in this ancient context. It was most likely the period after the oldest Upaniṣads (possibly from the fifth through the third or second centuries B.C.E.) that proto-Sāṃkhya and proto-Yoga traditions begin to develop, a period roughly contemporaneous with the rise of early Buddhist and Jain thought. According to the testimony of Kauṭilya's *Arthaśāstra* (the oldest portion of which can be dated about 300 B.C.E.), there were three traditions of *ānvīkṣikī* or "systematic reflection" in this period, namely, ". . . *sāṃkhyaṃ yogo lokāyataṃ ca* . . . ." According to some old verses in the *Mokṣadharma* portion of the *Mahābhārata* (XII.337.59 ff.), five traditions of systematic reflection are mentioned: "*sāṃkhyaṃ yogaṃ pāñcarātraṃ vedāḥ pāśupataṃ tathā* . . . ." This reference appears to be later than the Kauṭilya reference, for it obviously reflects a speculative environment in which theistic traditions are coming to the fore and taking their place alongside Vedic speculations and incipient Sāṃkhya and Yoga. In any case, both references indicate clearly that the terms "*sāṃkhya*" and "*yoga*" were being used to refer to distinct traditions of speculation. Regarding the content of these distinct traditions in this ancient period (the fifth through the second century B.C.E.), the only reliable clues are to be found in the so-called "middle" Upaniṣads, the *Kaṭha, Śvetāśvatara, Maitrī,* and so forth, in which one finds various enumerations (sets of 2, 3, 5, 8, 16, 50, etc.) and a developing technical terminology (*triguṇa, prakṛti, puruṣa,* and so forth) in a general environment of Yogic praxis. At the same time, however, one also finds in these texts the old Upaniṣadic *brahman* and *ātman,* one or another kind of theistic speculation, and many of the general themes (ritual performance, mythology, and so forth) from the older Vedic heritage. Sāṃkhya and Yoga are clearly in the process of being formulated, but there is obviously no uniform or systematic metaphysical system present or implied. The fact that there is no systematic formulation present prompted Franklin Edgerton to argue that the terms "*sāṃkhya*" and "*yoga*" are best construed in these contexts as methodological notions rather than metaphysical notions; hence, "*sāṃkhya*", says Edgerton, means "reason-method" and "*yoga*" means "discipline-method." This is also what prompted J.A.B. van Buitenen's important observation that the the interpreter is best guided by "allowing for the greatest diversity, rather than the greatest uniformity of doctrine." The evidence indicates, in other words, that there was a great variety of diffuse spiritual methodologies in the process of developing, a plethora of speculative traditions, some of which were focusing on theoretical issues and others of which were emphasizing various types of practical meditation. To quote van Buitenen again: "At this stage to credit these litlte centres with the name "schools" is to do them too much or too little honor. . . ." This fluid, pluralistic *sāṃkhya-cum-yoga* environment reaches its culmination by the first century of the Common Era and thereafter and is expressed in such texts as the *Mokṣadharma*, the *Bhagvadgītā*, the *Buddhacarita* of Aśvaghoṣa, the *Carakasaṃhitā*, the speculative portions of the *Manusmṛti*, the early Purāṇas, the *Sanatsujātiya*, and the *Anugītā*. Taken together, all of these texts reflect the general condition of Indian reflection at the beginning of the Common Era. From a religious point of view, they represent what we usually mean by the term "Hinduism." From a philosophical point of view, they represent a prephilosophical threshold of speculation from which all of the later traditions of Hindu philosophy derive. If from one point of view they represent Proto-Sāṃkhya and Proto-Yoga, it can also be said that they likewise represent Proto-Vedānta, Proto-Mīmāṃsā, Proto-Vaiśeṣika, and so forth. The fluid and pluralistic quality of this speculation is perhaps best revealed in the *Mokṣadharma* portion of the *Mahābhārata*, the specifically Sāṃkhya and Yoga portions of which are to be found in XII.187-188, 211-212, 228, 231, 232, 233, 238, 240-242, 244, 261, 267, 289, 290-291, 293-296, 298, 303-304, 306, 308, 337-339, all of which passages have been nicely summarized by V. M. Bedekar[1] and most of which have been translated by Edgerton.[2] One might add to this the "Kapila-Āsuri dialogue," referred to earlier, which the editors of the critical edition relegate to appendix I, no. 29, pages 2075 following. The Proto-Sāṃkhya of *Carakasaṃhitā* has been aptly summarized by S. N. Dasgupta.[3] The Proto-Sāṃkhya and Proto-Yoga of Aśvaghoṣa's *Buddhacarita* have been treated in detail by E.H. Johnston,[4] and in Johnston's translation of Canto XII.[5] Erich Frauwallner has closely studied *Mokṣadharma* XII.187 and its variants in XII.239-241, claiming that these passages represent the *Ur* form of Sāṃkhya in which an evolution theory is absent,[6] but J.A.B. van Buitenen[7] was able to reconstruct from the same passages a "little text" that "definitely gives the lie to a primitive Sāṃkhya without evolution." Claims by S. N. Dasgupta and P. Chakravarti that the form of Sāṃkhya found in *Mokṣadharma* XII.211-212 (the so-called "Pañcaśikhavākya", and see further below) and in *Carakasaṃhitā* (*śarīrasthāna* portion) are the same in accepting only 24 *tattvas* (instead of 25), thereby coalescing *puruṣa* and *avyakta*, is cogently refuted by V.M. Bedekar.[8] Dasgupta, Frauwallner, Johnston, van Buitenen, and others have all attempted to outline various historic stages in this Proto-Sāṃkhya and Proto-Yoga material, and these various attempts have been summarized in detail in Gerald J. Larson.[9] All such efforts to delineate a precise historical sequence, although frequently ingenious, must nevertheless be judged to have failed. There is simply insufficient evidence for tracing historical stages. Put more strongly, there is a mistake in historical judgment in such efforts. That is to say, the evidence strongly suggests that there were a variety of parallel traditions developing, no one of which can be considered more important than another. To impose a linear development on these traditions is seriously to distort the available evidence.

In the early centuries of the Common Era, the fluid, pluralistic *sāṃkhya-cum-yoga* traditions just described begin to form themselves into distinct "schools," most likely through the work of such teachers as Vārṣagaṇya, Vindhyavāsin, Mādhava, and Īśvarakṛṣṇa (see the respective entries below). To some extent it is plausible to believe that this tendency toward systematic formulation was triggered by the appearance of systematic Buddhist philosophy, but it is equally plausible to believe that the general cultural environment was simply ripe in the first centuries of the Common Era for a turn from the older diffuse religious-cum-philosophical speculation to a more technical, precise treatment of intellectual matters in a variety of subject areas (including religion, law, cosmology, medicine, philosophy, and so forth). In any case, it appears that the later systematic Sāṃkhya teachers looked back upon the older diffuse traditions as having been consolidated and widely disseminated by a certain Pañcaśikha. All of the later teachers, however, clearly indicate that there was a gap between the work of Pañcaśikha and their own systematic work. The various commentaries, as was pointed out earlier, give different lists of intervening teachers between Pañcaśikha and Īśvarakṛṣṇa, strongly suggesting that Pañcaśikha is functioning more as a heuristic link with an older heritage than as a contemporary colleague. Hence, the relevance of a distinction between an "historic" and a "symbolic" Pañcaśikha. From *Mokṣadharma* XII.306.56-60 (quoted above under the Kapila and Āsuri entries), of course, it is clear enough that there was an ancient Sāṃkhyayoga teacher named Pañcaśikha, but one has the strong impression from the later Sāṃkhya texts proper that the name "Pañcaśikha" represents an ancient revered figure to whom one might attribute a great variety of hallowed Sāṃkhya or Yoga notions. This is certainly true for all of the quotations attributed by Vācaspati Miśra to Pañcaśikha in his *Tattvavaiśāradī* on *Yogasūtrabhāṣya*. It is also surely true of Vijñānabhikṣu's references to Pañcaśikha in his *Sāṃkhyapravacanabhāṣya* and in the references to Pañcaśikha in the late *Sāṃkhyasūtra*. It is probable also that, even in the *Mokṣadharma* portion of the *Mahābhārata*, Pañcaśikha is functioning more as a heuristic, symbolic name, perhaps not unlike the revered Kapila and Āsuri, although it must be conceded that at least some portions of *Mokṣadharma* (perhaps especially XII.211-212) may be representing the views of an historic teacher. Finally, the attribution of the famed *Ṣaṣṭitantra* to Pañcaśikha (by the

Chinese commentary and the *Jayamaṅgalā*) appears to be more symbolic and honorific than reliably historic. In much the same fashion the *Yuktidīpikā* and *Ahirbudhnyasaṃhitā* attribute *Ṣaṣṭitantra* to Kapila !

Keeping in mind, then, that most of what follows is to be assigned to a "symbolic" Pañcaśikha, the specific references to Pañcaśikha are:

(A) *Mokṣadharma* XII.211-212: "Pañcaśikha-Janadeva Janaka Dialogue";

(B) Quotations attributed to Pañcaśikha by Vācaspati Miśra in the *Yogasūtrabhāṣya* of Vyāsa, namely, at I.4, I.25, I.36, II.5, II.6, II.13, II.17, II.18, II.20 (and repeated again at IV.22), II.22 and III.41;

(C) Quotations attributed to Pañcaśikha in the *Sāṃkhyasūtra* at V.32 and VI.68;

(D) Quotation attributed to Pañcaśikha by Vijñānabhikṣu in his *Sāṃkhyapravacanabhāṣya* at I.127;

(E) Quotation of a verse attributed to Pañcaśikha by Bhāvāgaṇeśa and Haribhadrasūri and cited at numerous places in the Sāṃkhya literature, including Gauḍapāda's *Bhāṣya* (under K.1), *Māṭharavṛtti*, (under K.22) and *Jayamaṅgalā* (under K.1).

(A) *Mokṣadharma* XII.211-212 has been summarized by V. M. Bedekar: "Janadeva Janaka (the king of Mithilā) was pre-occupied with the question as to what happened to the soul after death. A hundred teachers had assembled at his court and put forth different views on the subject. Some of these were heretical and did not satisfy the king. At this juncture, there arrived at the king's court a great sage named Pañcaśikha Kāpileya (from *kapilā*, the *brāhmaṇī* wife of Āsuri), who was the first pupil of Āsuri. Pañcaśikha joined in the debate and overwhelmed all the hundred teachers by means of his logical reasoning. Janaka, therefore, sent away all the teachers and followed Pañcaśikha for instruction. Pañcaśikha then expounded to him the doctrine which led to liberation. He emphasized that everything other than the Self was subject to decay and death and that it was wrong to identify the Self with the non-self...Pañcaśikha expounds what is said to be the highest Sāṃkhya doctrine leading to Mokṣa (211.19). He propounds, in particular, the important entities of which a human being is constituted. The five elements . . . come together on account of their *svabhāva* (inherent nature) and dissolve by *svabhāva*. The body, which is the result of the conglomeration of the elements, functions through *jñāna*, *ūṣman*, and *vāyu*. The entities which are essential for the life of an individual are: the senses, the objects of senses, *svabhāva*, *cetanā*, *manas*, *buddhi*, *prāṇa*, *apāna*, and other modifications (*vikāra*). The *buddhi* experiences threefold experience—pleasure, pain, and non-pleasure-pain—which is the result of the three *guṇas*.

The body, which is the conglomeration of the elements, is the *kṣetra* ("field") and the entity which indwells the *manas* is the *kṣetrajña* ("field-knower") (212.40). Sorrow results from the identification of the *guṇas* with the Ātman. To realize the error of this identification by means of right thinking and discrimination and also to realize the true nature of the Ātman as an entity, which is pure and characterless, leads one to the highest happiness of Brahman. As rivers falling into the ocean lose their identity, so also does one who has realized the Self lose himself in Brahman".[10]

(B) Vyāsa in his *Yogasūtrabhāṣya* quotes extensively from an older source, and Vācaspati Miśra in his *Tattvavaiśāradī* attributes many of these quotations to Pañcaśikha. The quotations are as follows (in the order in which they appear in the *Yogasūtrabhāṣya* and as translated by J.H. Woods,[11] *The Yoga System of Patañjali*, Harvard Oriental Series, volume 17, *passim*):

(1) "There is only one appearance (for both) (that is to say, for both *puruṣa* and *buddhi*)—that appearance is knowledge (*khyāti*)". (YSB I.4, in a discussion of how consciousness or *puruṣa* appears as if it were *buddhi*)

(2) "The First Knower (Kapila), assuming a created mind-stuff (*nirmāṇacitta*) through compassion, the Exalted, the supreme Sage, unto Āsuri who desired to know, declared this doctrine." (YSB I.25, in a discussion of God or *īśvara* in which Vācaspati Miśra points out that Kapila, though himself not *īśvara*, is nevertheless Hiraṇyagarbha and an incarnation of Viṣṇu)

(3) "Pondering upon this self which is a mere atom (*aṇumātra*) (or possibly exceedingly small or subtle), one is conscious in the same way as when one is conscious to the extent that one says 'I am.' "
(YSB II.36, in a discussion of the altered states of awareness growing out of Yoga praxis)

(4) "He who counts any existing thing, whether phenomenalized (*vyakta*) or unphenomenalized (*avyakta*) (primary matter), as himself; or who rejoices in the success of these (*tasya*) things, deeming it his own success, or who grieves at the ill-success of these (things), deeming it his own ill-success—these are all unenlightened."
(YSB II.5, in a discussion of difficulties that arise by reason of confusing *buddhi* and *puruṣa*)

(5) "He who should fail to see that the Self is other than the thinking-substance (*buddhi*), distinct in nature and in character and in consciousness and in other respects, would make the mistake of putting his own thinking-substance (*buddhi*) in the place of that (Self)."

(YSB II.6, in a discussion of the failure to distinguish *buddhi* and *puruṣa*)

(6) "Should there be a very slight admixture of guilt in the sacrifice, it is either to be removed or to be overlooked. (Therefore this admixture) is not enough to remove the good-fortune (won by merit). Why not? Because in my case there is much other good-fortune. Where then this (admixture of guilt) is cast away (into the dominant karma), even in heaven it will make only a slight reduction of merit."

(YSB II.13, in a discussion of the effects of *karman*)

(7) "By avoidance of the cause of correlation with this (thinking-substance, *buddhi*) the antidote for pain would be absolute."

(YSB II.17, in a discussion of discriminating *buddhi* from *puruṣa*)

(8) "But he who in the three aspects (*guṇa*) which are agents and in the Self which is not an agent—but which is of the same kind in some respects and of a different kind in other respects—sees all the produced states presented to the fourth, the witness of their action—he has no suspicion that there is another kind of knowledge (the pure intelligence)."

(YSB II.18, in a discussion of the difference between the internal organ and pure consciousness).

(9) "For the power of the enjoyer enters not into mutation (*pariṇāma*) nor unites (with objects). Seeming to unite with a thing in mutation (the thinking-substance or *buddhi*) it conforms itself to the fluctuations (which that thinking-substance undergoes). And it is commonly termed a fluctuation of the thinking-substance in so far as it resembles a fluctuation of thinking-substance that has come under the influence (*upagraha*) of intelligence (*caitanya*)."

(YSB II.20 and again at IV.22, in a discussion of the difference between *buddhi* and *puruṣa*)

(10) "The substances being in correlation from the time without beginning, the external-aspects in general are also in correlation from time without beginning."

(YSB II.22, and although the quotation is introduced in the same manner as all of the preceding, Vācaspati Miśra does not directly attribute it to Pañcaśikha; it is, however, so attributed by Vijñānabhikṣu)

(11) "All those whose processes of hearing (*śravaṇa*) are in the same place have the same kind-of-hearing (*ekaśrutitvam*)."

(YSB III.41, in a discussion of the functioning of the sense-capacities)

(C) Two *sūtras* from the *Sāṃkhyasūtra* appear as direct quotations from Pañcaśikha (following the translation of N. Simha):

(1) ("Logical pervasion" or "concomitance," *vyāpti*) (is) connection with the power of that which is contained (*ādheya-śaktiyoga iti Pañcaśikha*)."[12]
(*Sāṃkhyasūtra* V.32 in a general discussion of *vyāpti*)

(2) "Or, (it is the same if the relation of the owned and the owner) be, as says Pañcaśikha, due to the instrumentality of non-discrimination (*avivekanimitto vā Pañcaśikha*)."[13]
(*Sāṃkhyasūtra* VI.68, in a discussion of *svasvāmibhāvasaṃbandha*, one of the seven basic relations dealt with in older Sāṃkhya discussions, and see Introduction to the present volume for a full discussion)

(D) Vijñānabhikṣu in his discussion of the doctrine of *triguṇa* in *Sāṃkhyapravacanabhāṣya* attributes the following quotation to Pañcaśikha:

> "What is called Sattva, is of infinite variety under the forms of purity or clearness, lightness, love, agreeableness, renunciation, contentment, etc., which are summed up by the word Pleasant. Similarly, Rajas also possesses many varieties, such as grief, etc., which are summed up by the word Painful. So, also, does Tamas possess many varieties, such as sleep, etc., which are summed up by the word Bewildering."[14]

(E) Finally, an old verse frequently cited in Sāṃkhya literature (in Gauḍapāda's *Bhāṣya*, *Māṭharavṛtti*, *Jayamaṅgalā*, and so forth) is attributed to Pañcaśikha:

> "There can be no doubt in this that a knower of the twenty-five principles, in whatever order of life he may be and whether he wears braided hair (*jaṭin*), a top-knot only (*śikhin*), or be shaven (*muṇḍin*), is liberated from existence."[15]
> *pañcaviṃśatitattvajño yatra tatrāśrame vaset,*
> *jaṭī muṇḍī śikhī vāpi mucyate nātra saṃśayaḥ.*
> (*Jayamaṅgalā* under K.1 cites the second *pada* of the verse as "*yatra kutrāśrame rataḥ*"; and *Māṭharavrtti* cites the second *pada* as "*yatra tatrāśrame rataḥ*.")

Even a casual study of the above attributions makes it clear that we are dealing with a "symbolic" Pañcaśikha. That is to say, it is quite unlikely that the quotations derive from one historic teacher. The material in section (A) from the *Mokṣadharma* exhibits the fluid, pluralistic *sāṃkhya-cum-yoga* pre-philosophical Proto-Sāṃkhya, and it is precisely the sort of speculation one finds also in the *Carakasaṃhitā* and the twelfth canto of Aśvaghoṣa's *Buddhacarita*. It is also reminiscent of the Sāṃkhya and Yoga material found in the *Bhagavadgītā*. V.M. Bedekar has nicely summarized the differences between this sort of fluid Sāṃkhya and Yoga and later philosophical Sāṃkhya:

"(i) In the *Mokṣadharma* Sāṃkhya, there is not always emphasized an absolute and clear-cut dualism as in the classical Sāṃkhya. Many of the teachers of the Sāṃkhya in the *Mokṣadharma* appear generally to posit, at the apex, one single Principle or entity which overrides the dualism. (ii) The *Mokṣadharma* Sāṃkhya, often, speaks of the doctrine of the eight Prakṛtis, as against the one Prakṛiti of the classical Sāṃkhya. (iii) The doctrine of the *tanmātras* (subtle elements) does not seem to have yet developed. There is, however, a mention of the five objects of senses or the five qualities of the elements. (iv) The teaching regarding the number, place and functions of the psychical faculties like *manas*, *ahaṃkāra* and *buddhi* does not appear to have been consolidated in the *Mokṣadharma*. Different teachers have expressed different views on the subject. (v) The origin or the source of the five senses of knowledge has not been fixed as in the classical Sāṃkhya."[16]

The quotations attributed to Pañcaśikha in sections (B), (C), and (D), however, breath a totally different air. A distinct dualism is clearly emphasized. The doctrine of *triguṇa* and *pariṇāma* is definitely present. Issues of logical pervasion and the manner in which inferences are to be framed are prominent, and discussions of the manifest world and the manner in which the sense capacities function appear to be much more sophisticated. One has the strong sense that the quotations in sections (B), (C), and (D) derive from a systematic and philosophical form of Sāṃkhya and/or Yoga. Moreover, there is even some evidence in the texts that suggests that the quotations in sections (B), (C), and (D) come from a later period. Vyāsa's *Yogasūtrabhāṣya* under III.13 quotes a passage in which the relation between *rūpa* or *bhāva*, on the one hand, and *vṛtti*, on the other, is discussed. Vācaspati Miśra in his *Tattvavaiśāradī* informs us that this is yet another quotation from Pañcaśikha, but the author of the *Yuktidīpikā*, an older and more reliable source, indicates that the quotation really comes from Vārṣagaṇya, one of the later systematic Sāṃkhya teachers (and see below under the Vārṣagaṇya entry). P. Chakravarti,[17] noting this mistake by Vācaspati Miśra, proceeds to argue that all of the longer quotations in prose attributed to Pañcaśikha should really be ascribed to Vārṣagaṇya. Frauwallner[18] largely follows Chakravarti in this regard, arguing that there was a later prose revision of an older poetic *Ṣaṣṭitantra* and that this prose revision was carried through by Vārṣagaṇya. Frauwallner claims to have reconstructed portions of this prose *Ṣaṣṭitantra* of Vārṣagaṇya from occasional quotations in later Buddhist and Jain texts. Frauwallner claims,[19] further, that the form of Sāṃkhya one finds in Pātañjala-Yoga is largely that of the Vārṣagaṇya-Vindhyavāsin variety together with influences from early Vaiśeṣika and early Buddhist meditation traditions. These matters will be discussed further in the sequel. It need only be pointed out in this context that the so-called "Pañcaśikha" quotations, at least those found in sections (B), (C), and (D) above, are probably a good deal later than the old Sāṃkhya teacher mentioned in the *Mokṣadharma*. Whether Chakravarti and Frauwallner are correct in assigning them to Vārṣagaṇya or Vindhyavāsin, or in deriving Pātañjala Yoga generally from Vārṣagaṇya-Vindhyavāsin, is difficult to know with certainty. There are a variety of hints here and there that this may well be the case, but no definitive conclusions can be drawn at the present time.

ṢAṢṬITANTRA

The "Science of Sixty Topics" (*ṣaṣṭitantra*) appears to represent either (a) one or more philosophical texts of Sāṃkhya by that name, or (b) a sort of stereotyped format for discussing Sāṃkhya, that is to say, the "system of sixty topics," or even a proper name for the system in the early philosophical period. Regarding the enumeration of the sixty topics, there are two divergent accounts in the literature. According to the Sāṃkhya philosophical texts proper, namely, *Suvarṇasaptati*, *Sāṃkhyavṛtti*, *Sāṃkhyasaptatativṛtti*, *Yuktidīpikā*, *Jayamaṅgalā*, *Māṭharavṛtti*, and *Sāṃkhyatattvakaumudī*, *ṣaṣṭitantra* breaks down as follows: ten "principal topics" (*mūlikārtha*), and fifty "categories" (*padārtha*), including five "fundamental misconceptions" (*viparyaya*) twenty-eight "dysfunctions" (*aśakti*) nine "contentments" (*tuṣṭi*) eight "attainments" (*siddhi*).

These have all been discussed at length in the Introduction and require no further comment in this context. According to the *Ahirbudhnyasaṃhitā*, an Āgama (ca. 800) of the Pāñcarātra school of early Vaiṣṇavism, *ṣaṣṭitantra* or "the system of sixty topics" is made up of two sections: (1) a "principal" network of notions (*prākṛtamaṇḍala*) with thirty-two subdivisions, and (2) a "derived" network of notions (*vaikṛtamaṇḍala*) with twenty-eight subdivisions. The subdivisions of the "principal" network are called *tantras* and include the following: (1) *brahman*, (2) *puruṣa*, (3) *śakti*, (4) *niyati*, (5) *kāla*, (6-8) *sattva*, *rajas*, *tamas*, (9) *akṣara*, (10) *prāṇa*, (11) *kartṛ*, (12) *sāmi* or *svāmin*, (13-17) the five *buddhīndriyas*, (18-22) the five *karmendriyas*, (23-27) the five *tanmātras*, and (28-32) the five *bhūtas*. The subdivisions of the "derived" network are called *kāṇḍas* and include the following: (1-5) the five *kṛtyas* (possibly the *karmayonis*), (6) *bhoga*, (7) *vṛtta*, (8-12) the five *kleśas*, (13-15) the three *pramāṇas*, (16) *khyāti*, (17) *dharma*, (18) *vairāgya*, (19) *aiśvarya*, (20) *guṇa*, (21) *liṅga*, (22) *dṛṣṭi*, (23) *ānuśravika*, (24) *duḥkha*, (25) *siddhi*, (26) *kāṣāya*, (27) *samaya*, and (28) *mokṣa*. These enumerations are given at *Ahirbudhnyasaṃhitā* XII.20-30, but the text also informs the reader (in verse 30) that there are many versions (*nānāvidha*) of *ṣaṣṭitantra*.

There can be no serious doubt that the former enumeration of "the system of sixty topics"—the ten principal topics plus the five fundamental misconceptions, the twenty-eight dysfunctions, the nine contentments and the eight attainments—represents the normative formulation of classical, philosophical Sāṃkhya. All extant Sāṃkhya philosophical texts unanimously agree in this regard. The latter enumeration (as found in the *Ahirbudhnya*) is clearly a later reworking of *ṣaṣṭitantra* in Vaiṣṇava theological circles, very much on analogy with other reworkings of Sāṃkhya notions among Śaiva theologians (for example, in Śaiva Siddhānta and Kashmir Saivism). This tendency to appropriate Sāṃkhya notions for theological purposes probably explains also the reference in *Ahirbudhnya* XII.30 to the "many versions" of *ṣaṣṭitantra*. F. Otto Schrader, it should be noted to the contrary, argues that the *Ahirbudhnya* account of *ṣaṣṭitantra* is earlier than the classical, philosophical enumeration, since the *Ahirbudhnya* account parallels the description of ancient philosophical systems as found in *Mokṣadharma* XII.337.59ff.[1] Both Keith[2] and Dasgupta[3] follow Schrader in this regard. In both the *Ahirbudhnya* and the *Mokṣadharma* passage, Sāṃkhya is mentioned along with four other systems, namely, the Vedas, Yoga, Pāñcarātra (or Sātvata), and Pāśupata. Nothing is said, however, about the content of Sāṃkhya (or any of the other systems) in the *Mokṣadharma* passage (which may be dated in the first few centuries of the Common Era), whereas the *Ahirbudhnya* account of the content of the systems comes from many centuries later (ca. the ninth century). Schrader's argument, therefore, that the content of the Sāṃkhya as set forth in the *Ahirbudhnya* may be taken as a reliable account of the Sāṃkhya mentioned in the *Mokṣadharma* appears to be anachronistic. A more plausible view is that in the first centuries of the Common Era (roughly the time of the *Mokṣadharma*) the Sāṃkhya along with other systems of Indian philosophy proper were taking shape, and the Sāṃkhya systematization eventually issued in a "system of sixty topics" made up of ten principal topics plus fifty subsidiary "categories" (5 misconceptions, 28 dysfunctions, 9 contentments, and 8 attainments). At about the same time, but more likely somewhat later, various sectarian theologians appropriated "the system of sixty topics" for their own theological purposes; hence, the divergent enumeration of the sixty topics and the reference to the "many versions" of the *ṣaṣṭitantra*. This is not to deny, of course, yet older formulations of the "sixty topics" that precede the philosophical account. It is only to deny that the *Ahirbudhnya* account is older than the philosophical account. As already mentioned, it may well be the case that the *ṣaṣṭitantra* is simply a proper name for the old Sāṃkhya system(s) and that the "sixty topics" may have been construed in a great variety of schemes.

Turning now to the philosophical account of *ṣaṣṭitantra*, namely the ten principal topics and the fifty subsidiary categories, the Sāṃkhya literature provides varying accounts of its nature and authorship. The *Yuktidīpikā* indicates in its introductory verses that the scheme was handed down by Kapila himself and that it involved a huge treatise that could not be mastered even in a hundred years; hence, the need for Īśvarakṛṣṇa's summary. Paramārtha's Chinese translation (under SK 71), on the other hand, tells us that *ṣaṣṭitantra* was devised by Pañcaśikha in a treatise of sixty thousand verses. The *Jayamaṅgalā* (under SK 70) agrees with the Chinese translation that the scheme was devised by Pañcaśikha, but *Jayamaṅgalā* indicates that its extent was only sixty chapters. Vācaspati Miśra in his *Tattvavaiśāradī* identifies a quotation in Vyāsa's *Yogasūtrabhāṣya* (under IV.13 and see below under Vārṣagaṇya) as deriving from a work entitled *Ṣaṣṭitantra*, and Vācaspati, in his commentary on *Brahmasūtra* II.1.3., identifies the same quotation as coming from a *śāstra* of Yoga composed by Vārṣagaṇya, thereby leading to the conclusion that *ṣaṣṭitantra* was a Yoga *śāstra* authored by Vārṣagaṇya. The "system of sixty topics," therefore, is attributed variously to Kapila, Pañcaśikha, and Vārṣagaṇya. More than that, it is said to be a Sāṃkhya scheme, according to the *Yuktidīpikā*, *Jayamaṅgalā*, and Paramārtha, but Vācaspati Miśra holds it to be a *śāstra* of Yoga. To make matters worse, Gauḍapāda (under SK 17) and *Māṭharavṛtti* (under SK 17) quote a passage from a certain *Ṣaṣṭitantra*—"*puruṣādhiṣṭhitaṃ pradhānaṃ pravartate*," or "primordial materiality performs its function controlled by consciousness"—that appears to be a prose statement, but the *Yuktidīpikā* and Vācaspati Miśra quote passages from the *Ṣaṣṭitantra* that are clearly in *gāthās*, or verses. Frauwallner has argued that these varying references indicate that there was more than one *ṣaṣṭitantra*, perhaps an original verse *ṣaṣṭitantra* by Pañcaśikha and a later, more systematic prose revision of *ṣaṣṭitantra* by Vārṣagaṇya. Moreover, as has been discussed at some length in the Introduction, Frauwallner claims to have reconstructed important parts of the later prose revision of *ṣaṣṭitantra* by Vārṣagaṇya.[4] Chakravarti argues along similar lines, suggesting an original verse *ṣaṣṭitantra* by Kapila, greatly expanded in verse by Pañcaśikha and finally revised into a verse-*cum*-prose treatise by Vārṣagaṇya.[5] Both theories, Frauwallner's and Chakravarti's, are plausible possibilities, but there is insufficient evidence at the present time to prove either of them.

What is clear, however, is that *ṣaṣṭitantra* brings us into Sāṃkhya philosophy proper. That is to say, the scheme of ten principal topics and fifty subsidiary categories appears to be a fundamental framework or format in which the Sāṃkhya philosophy is discussed in classical and later times. According to all of the commentaries on Īśvarakṛṣṇa's *Sāṃkhyakārikā*, the format of *ṣaṣṭitantra* is what Īśvarakṛṣṇa was following. Likewise in the *Tattvasamāsa* and in the later *Sāṃkhyasūtra*, the "system of sixty topics" is presupposed throughout. Whether *ṣaṣṭi-*

tantra was one particular treatise, a group of treatises or simply a stereotyped format or proper name for the Sāṃkhya philosophical system itself cannot, at least at the present time, be definitely determined. What can be said, however, is that when a system of twenty-five *tattvas* is presented in terms of ten principal topics and fifty subsidiary categories we have moved beyond the Proto-Sāṃkhya of Kapila-Āsuri-Pañcaśikha into classical Sāṃkhya philosophy proper.

PAURIKA, PAÑCĀDHIKARAṆA PATAÑJALI (the Sāṃkhya teacher)

From the evidence of the *Yuktidīpikā* (and see below under separate entry) it is now clear that there were a number of teachers of Sāṃkhya philosophy proper (as distinct from the Proto-Sāṃkhya traditions discussed thus far) prior to Īśvarakṛṣṇa, including such as Paurika, Pañcādhikaraṇa, Patañjali (the Sāṃkhya teacher), Vārṣagaṇya, and Vindhyavāsin. These teachers are mentioned in passing throughout the *Yuktidīpikā* as exponents of Sāṃkhya whose views diverged from Īśvarakṛṣṇa or whose views were synthesized by Īśvarakṛṣṇa. It is difficult to offer even approximate dates for these older teachers (especially Paurika, Pañcādhikaraṇa, and Patañjali, and see separate entries below for Vārṣagaṇya and Vindhyavāsin), but it is reasonable to suppose that they were active in a period shortly after or contemporaneous with the latest period of epic (*Mokṣadharma*) speculation, that is, the first centuries of the Common Era. Moreover, it is reasonable to suppose that they represent Sāṃkhya as a technical philosophical position, since they are mentioned by the author of the *Yuktidīpikā* at those points in his commentary in which purely philosophical issues are addressed (for example, the definition of perception, the number and sequence of the emergence of the *tattvas*, the problem of the subtle body, and so forth). Finally, if one combines these names with the emergence of the "system of sixty topics" (*ṣaṣṭitantra*) (consisting of 10 principal topics and 50 subsidiary categories), one is able to posit a tradition (or traditions) of Pre-Kārikā Sāṃkhya as distinct, on the one hand, from older traditions of Proto-Sāṃkhya, and, on the other, from the later summary-formulations of Kārikā-Sāṃkhya (Īśvarakṛṣṇa) and Pātañjala-Sāṃkhya (Patañjali, the Yoga teacher).

Paurika is mentioned by the author of the *Yuktidīpikā* at two places (under SK 56, p. 141; and under SK 71, p. 145), the former referring to Paurika's view that there are a plurality of *prakṛtis* (one accompanying each *puruṣa*), a view that may have paved the way for the later Mādhava's reinterpretation of the *guṇa* theory in terms of a plurality of *pradhānas* (as discussed by Dignāga in section 5 of his chapter on perception in his *Pramāṇasamuccaya*, and see below under Mādhava entry), and the latter referring to Paurika's place in the sequence of Sāṃkhya teachers, namely, Hārīta, Bāddhali, Kairāṭa, Paurika, Ṛṣabheśvara, Pañcādhikaraṇa, Patañjali, Vārṣagaṇya, Kauṇḍinya, Mūka, "and so forth." Pañcādhikaraṇa is mentioned as one of a group of Tāntrikas (under SK 32, p. 112), and his views are mentioned at a number of points in the *Yuktidīpikā*, including (a) his view that the sense capacities are composed of gross elements (under SK 22, p. 91); (b) his view that there are only ten capacities (as opposed to Īśvarakṛṣṇa's view that there is a thirteenfold set of organs) (under SK 32, p. 112); (c) his view that the subtle body is called "*vaivartaśarīra*" and created by materiality but transmigrates according to the influences of *dharma* and *adharma* (under SK 39, p. 121); (d) his view that "knowledge" (*jñāna*) is twofold (*prākṛta* and *vaikṛta*), the former of which breaks down into three subvarieties, namely, "knowledge identical with the *tattva* itself" (*tattvasama*), "knowledge that is inherent when *sattva* is pure" (*sāṃsiddhika*), and "knowledge that arises spontaneously when there is an appropriate stimulus" (*ābhiṣyandika*), and the latter of which breaks down into two subvarieties, "derived knowledge from within" (*svavaikṛta*) and "derived knowledge from without" (*paravaikṛta*) (under SK 42, p. 123); and (e) his view that the organs cannot function on their own (but require being empowered by materiality) (under SK 43, p. 124 and also under SK 22, p. 91). Patañjali, a certain old Sāṃkhya teacher, is credited by the author of the *Yuktidīpikā* with the following views: (a) that egoity is not a separate principle but should be construed as part of intellect/will (under SK 3, p. 27); (b) that there are, therefore, twelve capacities (instead of Īśvarakṛṣṇa's thirteen or Pañcādhikaraṇa's ten) (under SK 32, p. 112); (c) that there is a subtle body but that it is created anew with each embodiment and lasts only as long as a particular embodiment (under SK 39, p. 121); and (d) that the capacities are able to function on their own from within (in contrast to Pañcādhikaraṇa's view that they can only function from without and in contrast to Vārṣagaṇya who argues a synthetic both/and position; see also under Vārṣagaṇya entry below) (under SK 43, p. 124).

Although these various references in the *Yuktidīpikā* do not provide by any means a complete picture of these older interpretations of the Sāṃkhya philosophical system as a whole, they do offer intriguing glimpses of the sorts of issues that were being discussed in the pre-Kārikā period.

VĀRṢAGAṆYA or Vṛṣagaṇa, Vṛṣagaṇavīra or Vārṣagaṇa

The earliest reference to a certain Vārṣagaṇya is to be found in *Mokṣadharma* XII.306.57, in which the name figures as one among many older teachers of Sāṃkhya and Yoga. The list is as follows: Jaigīṣavya, Asita, Devala (sometimes Asita Devala), Parāśara, Vārṣagaṇya, Pañcaśikha, Kapila, Śuka, Gautama, Arṣṭiṣeṇa, Garga, Nārada, Āsuri, Pulastya, Sanatkumāra, Śukra, and Kaśyapa. The listing is obviously not meant to be chronological and indicates little more than that, in the first centuries of the Common Era (the approximate date for the later portions of the epic), the name Vārṣagaṇya was linked with older Sāṃkhya and Yoga traditions.

Further references to Vārṣagaṇya, albeit muddled, appear in Chinese Buddhist sources. Paramārtha, who translated the *Sāṃkhyakārikā* together with a prose commentary into Chinese during the last period of his literary activity (557-569C.E.) in Canton, also composed a biography of the well-known Vasubandhu ("Life of Vasubandhu") in which the following is set forth:

> Nine hundred years after the death of the Buddha, there was a heretic named P'in-chö-ho-p'o-so (Vindhyavāsa). P'in-chö-ho (Vindhya) is the name of a mountain, and P'o-so (*vāsa*) means "living in." This heretic was so called because he lived on this mountain. There was a king of the Nāgas, named P'i-li-cha-kia-na (Vṛṣagaṇa or Vārṣagaṇa), who lived by a pond at the base of this mountain. The king of the Nāgas was very knowledgeable in the Sāṃkhya-śāstra. The aforementioned heretic, realizing that the Nāga was very knowledgeable (in the doctrine), desired to study under him.[1]

Paramārtha then goes on to describe how Vindhyavāsa became Vṛṣagaṇa's pupil, learned the *śāstra*, and finally put together a complete revision of it. Eventually, Vindhyavāsa travels to Ayodhyā in order to engage some great Buddhist "masters" in debate, for, according to the text, Buddhism was the supreme philosophy of the time. Unfortunately, the truly great "doctors of the law," that is, Manoratha and Vasubandhu, were traveling outside of Ayodhyā when Vindhyavāsa arrived in the city with his challenge for a debate, but one old monk was present, namely, Buddhamitra, the teacher of Vasubandhu. Though feeble, Buddhamitra accepted Vindhyavāsa's challenge but was quickly vanquished in the debate by Vindhyavāsa. Vindhyavāsa was rewarded for his victory with three lakhs of gold by the reigning king, Vikramāditya. Vindhyavāsa then returned to the Vindhya mountains and died soon after. Vasubandhu was enraged when he learned that his old teacher had been humiliated in the debate. He searched for Vindhyavāsa in order to stage another debate but discovered that Vindhyavāsa had, in the interim, died. He did, however, compose a rejoinder called *Paramārthasaptati* ("Seventy Verses on Ultimate Truth") that refuted the *Sāṃkhyaśāstra* of Vindhyavāsa and for which he was rewarded by the successor of Vikramāditya with three lakhs of gold.

Hsüan-tsang (seventh century), however, asserts that the teacher of Vasubandhu was Manoratha, and Hsüan-tsang's direct disciple, Kuei-chi, in one of his commentaries, reports the following:

> There was a master-heretic named Kapila, which means "red". He was so called because his complexion and his hair were of red color; even now the most honored Brahmins of India are all of red color. And at that time one called him (that is to say, Kapila) "the red hermit". Among his disciples, the principal ones were made up of eighteen groups whose chief was called Fa-li-cha (Varṣa), which means "rain", because he was born in the rainy season. His companions were called the heretics of the "rain-group" (Vārṣagaṇya). "Sāṃkhya" in Sanskrit means "number", that is to say, "calculating by means of knowledge". This name is used since the notion of number is fundamental for calculation, that is to say, the discussion proceeds from number and hence one calls it "discourse on numbers", or perhaps better: the discussion produces number and so one calls it "discourse on numbers". Those who compose the discourse on Sāṃkhya or who study it are called "discoursers of Sāṃkhya". The work of this master [Vārṣagaṇya] is called *Suvarṇasaptati* ("Gold-Seventy").[2]

Kuei-chi goes on to point out that the *Suvarṇasaptati* was occasioned by a debate with a Buddhist monk (unnamed) in which the Sāṃkhya teacher was victorious and for which he was rewarded with a gift of gold—hence, the title of the text, "Gold-Seventy." Kuei-chi also points out that the great Vasubandhu composed a prose commentary on the "Gold-Seventy" in which he both explained the basic meaning of the text and discussed its fundamental flaws. According to Kuei-chi (and East Asian Buddhist traditions generally), in other words, the prose commentary on the *Sāṃkhyakārikā*, translated by Paramārtha in the middle of the sixth century, was the work of Vasubandhu.

If one follows the account of Paramārtha, then the following would appear to be the case: an original teacher, Vṛṣagaṇa or Vārṣagaṇa, instructs a pupil, Vindhyavāsa, who revises the work of his teacher and composes a *Sāṃkhyaśāstra*. Vindhyavāsa then defeats a Buddhist monk, Buddhamitra (the teacher of Vasubandhu), in a debate, and Vasubandhu, after the death of Vindhyavāsa, composes a rejoinder called *Paramārthasaptati*. If one follows the account of Hsüan-tsang and his disciple, Kuei-chi, the following is the case: the original Sāṃkhya teacher is Kapila (the "red hermit"), whose followers in subsequent centuries divide into eighteen "groups" the chief abbot of which is a certain Varṣa (meaning "rain" since he was born in the rainy season) and who are referred to as the "followers of Varṣa" (or, in other words, Vārṣagaṇya, the "rain-group"). One of these followers wins a debate against a Buddhist monk, and the Sāṃkhya text that marks that debate is called the "Gold-Seventy" (*Suvarṇasaptati*). Somewhat later, the great Vasubandhu composes a prose commentary on the "Gold-Seventy" that, on one level, explains the meaning of the Sāṃkhya text but, on another level, points out its basic flaws.

Takakusu resolves the conflict between the two accounts in an ingenious (but alas wrong) manner as follows: The original teacher is a certain Varṣa or Vṛṣagaṇa. His followers are called Vārṣagaṇya (that is to say, "belonging to Vṛṣagaṇa" or "followers of Vṛṣagaṇa"), one of whom is a certain Vindhyavāsa, an appellation meaning simply "living in the Vindhya mountains." This Vindhyavāsa revises the work of his teacher and composes the *Sāṃkhyaśāstra* otherwise known as the *Suvarṇasaptati* ("Gold-Seventy") or the *Sāṃkhyakārikā*. This "follower of Vṛṣagaṇa" (Vārṣagaṇya), who is "living in the Vindhya mountains" (Vindhyavāsa), is none other than the Kauśika Brahmin whose proper name is Īśvarakṛṣṇa. In other words, "Vārṣagaṇya," "Vindhyavāsa," and "Īśvarakṛṣṇa" all refer to the same person.[3] Takakusu also argues that it is highly unlikely that Vasubandhu is the author of the prose commentary on the *Kārikā*. This wrong attribution, says Takakusu, was introduced into the East Asian tradition by Kuei-chi. Paramārtha, who is more reliable, nowhere claims that Vasubandhu is the author of the commentary. He claims only that Vasubandhu composed a refutation of the *Kārikā* called *Paramārthasaptati* some time after the death of Vindhyavāsa. The prose commentary on the *Kārikā*, translated by Paramārtha into Chinese, was, according to Takakusu, composed either by Īśvarakṛṣṇa himself or one of his early pupils probably some time in the fifth century (because it would have taken about a century for the text to be sufficiently well known for Paramārtha to have translated it between 557 and 569).

As already indicated, Takakusu's solution, though ingenious, is clearly wrong, although for many years it was widely accepted by, among others, A.B. Keith and N. Aiyaswami Sastri. The discovery of the commentary *Yuktidīpikā* radically changed the nature of the evidence upon which the resolution of the Chinese accounts depends, for in the *Yuktidīpikā* there is incontrovertible testimony that Vārṣagaṇya, Vindhyavāsa, and Īśvarakṛṣṇa are three distinct teachers whose views diverge on a number of crucial points. There is no way, therefore, that Takakusu's hypothesis of the identity of Vindhyavāsa and Īśvarakṛṣṇa (as a "follower of Vṛṣagaṇa" or Vārṣagaṇya) can stand.

Before turning to the divergent views of the three, however, it may be useful to clarify the forms of the names involved. In the *Yuktīdipikā* the following names are mentioned: Vārṣagaṇya, Vārṣagaṇa, Vṛṣagaṇavīra, Vindhyavāsin and Īśvarakṛṣṇa. The latter, of course, presents no problem. The next to the last, that is, Vindhyavāsin, is cited throughout the *Yuktidīpikā* (at least in the editions prepared by Chakravarti and Pandeya) as Vindhyavāsin, and there are no serious grounds for doubting that Vindhyavāsa and Vindhyavāsin refer to the same person (see below under Vindhyavāsin). The case of Vārṣagaṇya, however, is not as clear. E. Frauwallner refers to Vṛṣagaṇa as the proper name and accepts Vārṣagaṇya or Vārṣagaṇa as forms referring to the "followers of Vṛṣagaṇa." P. Chakravarti, however, has cogently argued that Vārṣagaṇya is the correct proper name. The form "*vṛṣagaṇavīra*" (under SK 30, p. 110) simply means "son of Vṛṣagaṇa" (or Vārṣagaṇya) and does not at all imply that the father, Vṛṣagaṇa, was a Sāṃkhya teacher. The form "*vārṣagaṇa*," according to Chakravarti, refers to the "followers of Vārṣagaṇya," and it is to be noted that all of the references in the *Yuktidīpikā* to "*vārṣagaṇa*" are without exception to be construed as plurals (or, in other words, *vārṣagaṇāḥ*) and are most often introduced in the stereotyped formulation "*tathā ca vārṣagaṇāḥ paṭhanti*. . . . " It would appear to be a reasonable conclusion, then, that Vārṣagaṇya is the correct proper name; *vṛṣagaṇavīra* simply means "son of Vṛṣagaṇa" (and not implying that the father was a Sāṃkhya teacher); and *vārṣagaṇa* (*vārṣagaṇāḥ*) refers to the "followers of Vārṣagaṇya."

The detailed views of Vārṣagaṇya, Vindhyavāsin, and Īśvarakṛṣṇa will be set forth at the appropriate places (later in this entry and in the sequel), but it may be useful at this point to summarize the most important differences by way of making clear that there can be no question that we are dealing with three distinct Sāṃkhya teachers: (1) Vārṣagaṇya defines perception simply as "the functioning of the ear, etc." (*śrotrādivṛttir iti*); Vindhyavāsin extends the definition to the "functioning of the ear, etc., without construction or verbalization" (*śrotrādivṛttir avikalpikā*); but Īśvarakṛṣṇa defines perception as "the ascertainment of specific objects" (*prativiṣayādhyavasāyo dṛṣṭam*, SK 5), implying, according to the *Yuktidīpikā* (under SK 5, pp. 37-38), both external and internal contents and thereby being an improvement over the definitions of both Vārṣagaṇya and Vindhyavāsin (in the sense that the latter two definitions do not account for internal contents). (2) Vārṣagaṇya speaks of an elevenfold set of sense capacities that are limited in extent, thereby requiring a subtle body for transmigration; Vindhyavāsin also argues for an elevenfold set but claims that they are all-pervasive, thereby obviating the need for a subtle body; but Īśvarakṛṣṇa accepts a thirteenfold set of capacities of limited extent, thereby disagreeing with both Vārṣagaṇya (in terms of the number of the capacities) and Vindhyavāsin (in terms of the need for a subtle body). (3) Vārṣagaṇya defines inference as "on account of the perception of one aspect of an established relation, one is able to infer the other aspect of a relation" (*saṃbandhād ekasmāt pratyakṣāt śeṣasiddhir anumānam*) and develops a scheme of seven basic relations (*saptasaṃbandha*); Vindhyavāsin and others develop the logic of inference by means of the tenfold syllogism (the ten *avayavas*, *Yuktidīpikā* under the introduction, p. 3); but Īśvarakṛṣṇa refers to a scheme of "threefold inference" involving a relation between a "mark" and "that which bears the mark" (*trividham anumānam ākhyātaṃ tallingalingipūrvakam*, SK 5), and the author of the *Yuktidīpikā* points out that Īśvarakṛṣṇa did not repeat what had been said by Vārṣagaṇya and Vindhyavāsin (and others) since these matters had been adequately discussed by them. There can be no doubt, therefore, that the author of the *Yuktidīpikā* was familiar with three distinct teachers whose view on important issues in Sāṃkhya philosophy were clearly divergent.

Turning now to the difficult problem of the date of Vāṛsagaṇya, there is much uncertainty, but at least some intelligent guesses are possible. As was mentioned in the entry under "*Ṣaṣṭitantra*" and as was discussed in detail in the Introduction, Frauwallner claims that Vārṣagaṇya revised an older *ṣaṣṭitantra*. Moreover, Frauwallner claims to have reconstructed the epistemological portions of that revision (from quotations and extracts in Dignāga, Jinendrabuddhi, Mallavādin, and Siṃhasuri), and he suggests that Vārṣagaṇya probably lived around 300 of the Common Era. On the basis of the Chinese Buddhist evidence (that is, the comments of Paramārtha, Hsūan-tsang, and Kuei-chi), although there is much confusion about the specific forms of names and about the attribution of particular texts, it is clear enough that Vārṣagaṇya and Vindhyavāsin (or the traditions they represent) were in polemical contact with the (Sautrāntika) Vasubandhu of *Abhidharmakośa*, who can be dated either in the first part of the fifth century (Frauwallner) or some time in the fourth century (Warder). On the basis of the evidence in the *Yuktidīpikā* it appears to be clearly the case that Vārṣagaṇya precedes both Vindhyavāsin and Īśvarakṛṣṇa, and that Īśvarakṛṣṇa himself is either contemporary or slightly later than Vindhyavāsin. Paramārtha, as has been mentioned several times, translated the *Sāṃkhyakārikā* together with a prose commentary in the middle of the sixth century (557-569), and it is reasonable to infer, therefore, that the work of all three Sāṃkhya teachers, namely, Vārṣagaṇya, Vindhyavāsin and Īśvarakṛṣṇa, was generally well known by the end of the fifth century (ca. 500). This is further confirmed by the work of Dignāga (ca. 480-540), who identifies the later Sāṃkhya teacher, Mādhava (ca. 500, and see entry below), as a Sāṃkhya "destroyer" (*Sāṃkhyanāśaka*: one who deviates so much from the standard Sāṃkhya position as to destroy it), implying that there was a standard Sāṃkhya philosophical position that was fully known and understood at that time. Given all of this, it is probably not far from the truth to place Vindhyavāsin and Iśvarakṛṣṇa between 300 and 450 with Vindhyavāsin (ca. 300-400) being an older contemporary of Īśvarakṛṣṇa (ca. 350-450). It must be noted, however, that Īśvarakṛṣṇa, though probably somewhat later than Vindhyavāsin, does not at all follow Vindhyavāsin's interpretation of Sāṃkhya. Though the *Yuktidīpikā* gives evidence that Īśvarakṛṣṇa knew of the work of Vindhyavāsin, Īśvarakṛṣṇa's summary of the Sāṃkhya position appears to harken back to an older form of the doctrine. Regarding the date of Vārṣagaṇya, it would appear that Frauwallner's suggestion that he lived around 300, errs on the side of being too late. Frauwallner's recnstruction of the revised form of *ṣaṣṭitantra* need not be the work of Vārṣagaṇya himself but may well be, rather, the work of the "followers of Vārṣagaṇya" (the *vārṣagaṇāḥ* of *Yuktidīpikā*). Vārṣagaṇya himself, then, might be placed back in the second and possibly even the first century of the Common Era, a date that would correlate nicely with the reference to Vārṣagaṇya in the *Mokṣadharma*. Also, an early date for Vārṣagaṇya would make plausible Vācaspati Miśra's claim in his *Tattvakaumudī* (under SK 47) that the expression "*pañcaparvā avidyā*" is attributable to Bhagavān Vārṣagaṇya, an expression that appears, interestingly as the twelfth utterance in the *Tattvasamāsasūtra*, and is quoted, even more interestingly, at XII.33 in Aśvaghoṣa's *Buddhacarita* (from the first century of the Common Era).

Although references to Vārṣagaṇya and the "followers of Vārṣagaṇya" are not sufficient to provide a complete picture of this early tradition of Sāṃkhya philosophy, enough references are present in the literature to offer at least a glimpse of this old tradition. The most important of these are :

(1) As mentioned previously, Vārṣagaṇya's definition of perception is simply "the functioning of the ear, etc." (*śrotrādivṛtti*), and his definition of inference is "on account of the perception of one aspect of an established relation, one is able to infer the other aspect of a relation" (*saṃbandhād ekasmāt śeṣasiddhir*). Both definitions are quoted by the author of the *Yuktidipikā* in his introduction (p. 3), but they are not attributed to Vārṣagaṇya at that point. Under SK 5, however, the above defi-

nition of perception is ascribed to the "followers of Vārṣagaṇya." For a full discussion of Vārṣagaṇya's notion of inference and his general theory of knowledge, see Frauwallner.[4]

(2) In a discussion of the process of manifestation, the followers of Vārṣagaṇya are quoted to suggest that, although the entire manifest world (*trailokya*) disappears from manifestation (from time to time), it does not follow that the world actually loses its existence, since Sāṃkhya philosophy does not accept the notion that existence can be destroyed (*tad etat trailokyaṃ vyakter apaiti, na sattvād apetam apy asti, vināśapratiṣedhāt*) (YD, under SK 10, p. 57). The same quotation with a slight expansion in wording may be found in *Yogasūtrabhāṣya* III.13.

(3) Regarding the problem of how the three *guṇas*, though apparently so different, can cooperate together to bring about manifestation, the author of the *Yuktidīpikā* quotes "Lord Vārṣagaṇya" (*bhagavān vārṣagaṇyaḥ*) as follows: "When the *rūpas* (namely, fundamental dispositions) and *vṛttis* (namely, transformations of awareness in terms of pleasure, pain, and so forth) are developed to their full extent, they, of course, oppose one another, but ordinary *rūpas* and *vṛttis* (that is to say, the transactions of ordinary experience) are able to function in cooperation with the more intense or fully developed ones (*rūpātiśayā vṛttyatiśayāś ca virudhyante; sāmānyāni tu atiśayaiḥ saha vartante*)." (YD under SK 13, p. 61) The same quotation appears also in the *Yogasūtrabhāṣya* under II.15, but it should be noted that Vācaspati Miśra in his *Tattvavaiśāradī* attributes the quotation wrongly to Pañcaśikha. This has suggested to P. Chakravarti that most of the long prose quotations in the *Yogasūtrabhāṣya*, attributed by Vācaspati to Pañcaśikha (and see above under Pañcaśikha entry), should really be ascribed to Vārṣagaṇya.[5]

(4) In a discussion of the relationship between *puruṣa* and *buddhi*, the followers of Vārṣagaṇya are quoted to the effect that the *puruṣa*, having come upon the *vṛttis* of *buddhi*, conforms itself to those transformations (*buddhivṛttyāviṣṭo hi pratyayatvena anuvartamānām anuyāti puruṣa iti*, YD under SK 17, p. 79).

(5) In a discussion of the "isolation" (*kaivalya*) or non-involvement of *puruṣa* in the transactions of the *guṇas*, the followers of Vārṣagaṇya are quoted as claiming that materiality functions from the very beginning of creation quite independently of *puruṣa* (*pradhānapravṛttir apratyayā puruṣeṇa aparigṛhyamānā ādisarge vartante*—probably *vartante* should be *vartate* here, according to Pandeya) (YD under SK 19, p. 85).

(6) The author of the *Yuktidīpikā* ascribes to Vārṣagaṇya the accumulation theory for the genesis of the subtle elements,

that is to say, each subsequent subtle element is made up of its own unique essence in combination with the essences of its predecessors so that *śabda* is pure sound, *sparśa* is pure contact plus pure sound, *rūpa* is pure form plus pure contact plus pure sound, and so forth (*ekarūpāṇi tanmatrāṇi iti anye*; *ekottarāṇi iti Vārṣagaṇyaḥ*) (YD under SK 22, p. 91).

(7) As opposed to Pañcādhikaraṇa, who accepts a tenfold set of capacities, and Patañjali (the Sāṃkhya teacher), who accepts a twelvefold set, and, of course, Īśvarakṛṣṇa, who accepts a thirteenfold set, the followers of Vārṣagaṇya are said to believe in an elevenfold set of capacities (*ekādaśavidham iti vārṣagaṇāḥ*, YD under SK 32, p. 112).

(8) In a discussion of the transmigrating *liṅga* under SK 40 in which it is said that a *liṅga* accompanies each *puruṣa* throughout the process of transmigration, the author of the *Yuktidīpikā* says that it is nevertheless the view of the followers of Vārṣagaṇya that there is one general or common *mahat* derived from *prakṛti* (and which presumably resides in all *liṅgas*) (*sādhārano hi mahān prakṛtitvād iti vārṣagaṇānāṃ pakṣaḥ*, YD under S K 40, p. 121).

(9) In a discussion of the simile in SK 57 involving *prakṛti* functioning for the sake of *puruṣa* just as the unconscious milk serves the needs of the calf, the author of the *Yuktidīpikā* mentions a *dṛṣṭānta* (an illustrative example) from the followers of Vārṣagaṇya, namely, that the interaction between *prakṛti* and *puruṣa* might be compared to the manner in which men and women become sexually aroused by contemplating or noticing their unconscious bodies (*vārṣagaṇānāṃ tu yathā strīpuṃśarīrānām acetanānām uddiśya itaretaram pravṛttis tathā pradhānasya iti ayaṃ dṛṣṭāntaḥ*, YD under SK 57, p. 142).

(10) Regarding the disagreement between Pañcādhikaraṇa and Patañjali (the Sāṃkhya teacher) concerning whether the organs function on their own or are empowered from without by *prakṛti* (and see above under Paurika, Pañcādhikaraṇa, and Patañjali), the author of the *Yuktidīpikā* suggests that Vārṣagaṇya takes a both-and view, namely, that extraordinary accomplishments of the capacities are empowered from without through the inherent power of *prakṛti*, whereas ordinary functioning occurs from within (*karaṇānāṃ mahatī svabhāvātivṛttiḥ pradhānāt, svalpā ca svata iti vārṣagaṇyaḥ*, YD under SK 22, p. 91).

(11) Vyāsa in his *Yogasūtrabhāṣya*, in a discussion comparing the Vaiśeṣika theory of atoms with the Sāṃkhya notion of *mūlaprakṛti*, quotes the following utterance of Vārṣagaṇya: "Since there is no difference as to limitation-in-extent or by reason

of intervening-space or of species there is no distinction in the (primary) root (of things) [*mūrtivyavādhijātibhedabhāvān na asti mūlapṛthaktva, Yogasūtrabhāṣya*] " (III. 53).[6]

(12) Vyāsa in his *Yogasūtrabhāṣya*, in a discussion of the difference between the *guṇas* in their ultimate constitutive nature, on the one hand, and the realm of ordinary perception, on the other, quotes the following verse, as rendered by J.H. woods:

The aspects from their utmost height
Come not within the range of sight.
But all within the range of sight
A phantom seems and empty quite.[7]

The Sanskrit is as follows:

guṇānāṃ paramaṃ rūpaṃ na dṛṣṭipatham ṛcchati,
yat tu dṛṣṭipathaṃ prāptaṃ tanmāyā iva sutucchakam.

Vyāsa does not mention the source of the quotation, but Vācaspati Miśra in his *Bhāmatī* on *Brahmasūtra* II.1.2.3 claims that it is from the *Yogaśāstra* of Vārṣagaṇya.

(13) Vācaspati Miśra under SK 47 of his *Tattvakaumudī* claims that the quotation "there are five kinds of ignorance" (*pañcaparvā avidyā*) comes from Vārṣagaṇya. The same quotation can be found in *sūtra* 12 of the *Tattvasamāsasūtra* and in XII.33 of Aśvaghoṣa's *Buddhacarita*. Since these five kinds of ignorance are the same as the five misconceptions of the fiftyfold intellectual creation of Īśvarakṛṣṇa, and since this fiftyfold scheme is part of the classical Sāṃkhya formulation of *ṣaṣṭitantra*, Frauwallner (*Geschichte der indischen Philosophie*, I, pp. 319ff.) has speculated that Vārṣagaṇya may be credited with the classical Sāṃkhya formulation of *ṣaṣṭitantra*. This is an intriguing suggestion, but the evidence is hardly compelling.

(14) Vasubandhu in his *Abhidharmakośa*, in a discussion of the Sarvāstivāda theory of causation comments as follows: "In the end it comes to the same as the theory of the followers of Vārṣagaṇya. According to them 'there is neither production of something new nor extinction of something existent: what exists is always existent, what does not exist will never become existent.'"[8] The first portion, namely, "there is neither. . .", is quoted also by *Yogasūtrabhāṣya* at the beginning of IV.12 ("*na asati sataḥ saṃbhavaḥ, na ca asti sato vināśa iti*"). Vātsyāyana (in *Nyāyasūtrabhāṣya* under I.1.29) quotes a comparable statement with slightly different wording: "*na asata ātmalābhaḥ, na sata ātmahanam . . . iti Sāṃkhyānām.*"[9] One is reminded also, of course, of the first half of śloka 16 of the second chapter of the *Bhagavadgītā*: "*na asato vidyate bhāvo, na abhāvo vidyate sataḥ.*"

(15) The *Yogācārabhūmi* of Asaṅga or Maitreya-Asaṅga from some time in the fourth century comments as follows regarding Vārṣagaṇya: "As to the nature of the doctrine according to which the effect exists in the cause, a certain Śramaṇa or Brāhmaṇa holds this opinion saying that the effect in fact exists in the cause perpetually through perpetual time and constantly through constant time, such a one is Vārṣagaṇya." See D. Seyfort Ruegg, "Note on Vārṣagaṇya and the *Yogācārabhūmi*," *Indo-Iranian Journal* 6 (1962), pp. 137-140. This reference strongly suggests that Vārṣagaṇya's views were generally known by the beginning of the fourth century. As has already been mentioned several times, there are numerous other references to Vārṣagaṇya and the followers of Vārṣagaṇya in Buddhist and Jain texts (Dignāga, Jinendrabuddhi, Mallavādin, Siṃhasūri, and so forth), most of which have been collected and pieced together by Frauwallner in order to reconstruct what he takes to be the epistemological portion of Vārṣagaṇya's revised version of *ṣaṣṭitantra* (and see Introduction to the present volume for a full discussion.

VINDHYAVĀSIN, or Vindhyavāsa

Although it is true with regard to the Chinese Buddhist evidence mentioned at the outset of the entry on Vārṣagaṇya, that is, the accounts of Paramārtha, Hsüan-tsang, and Kuei-chi, that Takakusu's suggested identification of Vārṣagaṇya, Vindhyavāsin and Īśvarakṛṣṇa is clearly incorrect, Takakusu has nevertheless persuasively shown that Paramārtha's "Life of Vasubandhu" can be taken seriously as a reasonably accurate (albeit rough) account of events relating to Sāṃkhya. Kuei-chi's account is, on the other hand, highly suspect, for he appears to have confused a number of matters. His reference, for example, to eighteen schools of Sāṃkhya is suspiciously similar to Buddhist traditions of eighteen schools. His interpretation of "Kapila" as the "red hermit" shows a lack of familiarity with the Indian tradition. His claim that the *Suvarṇasaptati* (the Chinese designation of the *Sāṃkhyakārikā*) was a text used in debate is impossible to believe, as is his further claim that Vasubandhu is the author of the prose commentary on the *Kārikā* ! Paramārtha, however, provides quite a different picture, one that correlates in significant ways with the Indian evidence. According to Paramārtha, Vārṣagaṇya's (or Vārṣagaṇya's followers') formulation of Sāṃkhya was revised by a certain Vindhyavāsin, and Vindhyavāsin took part in a debate with Buddhamitra, a teacher of Vasubandhu. Vindhyavāsin was successful in the debate and received a gift of gold from the then reigning king, who was known as Vikramāditya. Later, after Vindhyavāsin had died, Vasubandhu composed a rejoinder to the *Sāṃkhyaśāstra* of Vindhyavāsin, entitled *Paramārthasaptati*, for which Vasubandhu himself received a gift of gold from the successor of Vikramāditya. What rings true in Paramārtha's account, apart from a great variety of legendary detail, is the sequence that emerges, that is, Vārṣagaṇya or the followers of Vārṣagaṇya; a revision of *Sāṃkhyaśāstra* by Vindhyavāsin; a debate (or debates) with Buddhist philosophers who precede Vasubandhu; and a definitive rejoinder to the *Sāṃkhyaśāstra* of Vindhyavāsin by Vasubandhu called *Paramārthasaptati*. As was suggested in the preceding discussion of Vārṣagaṇya, Paramārtha is probably mistaken in suggesting that Vārṣagaṇya was himself the direct teacher of Vindhyavāsin. It would appear more plausible from the Indian evidence that Vindhyavāsin revised the form of Sāṃkhya that was characteristic of the followers of Vārṣagaṇya (namely, the *vārṣagaṇāḥ* of the *Yuktidīpikā*), thereby allowing for a greater time span between Vārṣagaṇya himself and Vindhyavāsin. In this sense, of course, Vindhyavāsin himself becomes a "follower of Vārṣagaṇya" (in other words, one of the *vārṣagaṇāḥ*), but one who considerably changed the doctrines of the school. It is interesting to note, by the way, that Paramārtha's "Life of Vasubandhu" does not mention Īśvarakṛṣṇa or the *Sāṃkhyakārikā* in the context of Vindhyavāsin's debate with Buddhamitra and Vasubandhu's final rejoinder. Paramārtha's account only tells us that Vindhyavāsin's revision of Sāṃkhya was known as "Sāṃkhyaśāstra." It is usually assumed that because Vasubandhu entitled his rejoinder *Paramārthasaptati* ("Seventy Verses on Ultimate Truth"), that it was probably directed against the so-called "Gold-Seventy" or *Suvarṇasaptati*, the Chinese version of Īśvarakṛṣṇa's *Sāṃkhyakārikā*. It may well have been Kuei-chi who first made this assumption, drawing the conclusion, therefore, that Vindhyavāsin's revised form of Sāṃkhya used in debate was none other than the *Sāṃkhyakārikā*. He evidently also assumed, therefore, that the prose commentary on the *Kārikā* was composed by Vasubandhu as the rejoinder. In view of the Indian evidence, however, all of these assumptions are unlikely. It is now clear that Īśvarakṛṣṇa's views are clearly different from Vindhyavāsin's (as will be documented in the sequel) and that Vasubandhu is not the author of the prose commentary to the *Kārikā* that was translated into Chinese. Most important, it is obvious even to a casual reader that the *Sāṃkhyakārikā* is not a polemical, debating text. Indeed, *Kārikā* 72 (admittedly a later, interpolated verse but nevertheless one that was already added by the time Paramārtha translated the *Kārikā* and its commentary into Chinese in the middle of the sixth century) directly states that the *Sāṃkhyakārikā* is devoid of the discussion of polemical views (". . . *paravādavivarjitāś ca api*"). The *Sāṃkhyakārikā* claims, rather, that it is a brief summary of the tradition of *ṣaṣṭitantra* (see *Kārikās* 70-72). One likely possibility is that the *Sāṃkhyakārikā* is a later summary of the Sāṃkhya position overall, which attempts to reconcile and synthesize what had been happening in the Sāṃkhya tradition since the time of Vārṣagaṇya, or, in other words, a final summary formulation of *ṣaṣṭitantra* that attempts to mediate the views of Paurika, Pañcādhikaraṇa, Patañjali (the Sāṃkhya teacher), Vārṣagaṇya, the followers of Vārṣagaṇya, Vindhyavāsin, and the various critiques of Sāṃkhya that had been pressed by Vaiśeṣikas and Buddhists. It should be stressed, however, that the *Sāṃkhyakārikā* gives every appearance of being an "in-house" document, a document, in other words, whose audience was made up of followers (students?) of Sāṃkhya, and not at all directed at the system's opponents. The primary evidence for this possibility, of course, is the *Yuktidīpikā*, which begins by showing that the *Kārikā*, though brief, is a full and complete statement of the *tantra* (Sāṃkhya system) and which throughout attempts to show how Īśvarakṛṣṇa's account of the system brings together all of the older lines of discussion into one final systematic formulation.

A plausible chronology for all of this, then, is the following:

(a) Paurika, Pañcādhikaraṇa, and Patañjali (the Sāṃkhya teacher) first or second century of the Common Era;

(b) Vārṣagaṇya ca. 100-300 but probably earlier rather than later;

(c) Followers of Vārṣagaṇya (*vārṣagaṇāḥ*) ca., 300-400;

(d) Vindhyavāsin ca. 300-400;

(e) Īśvarakṛṣṇa ca. 350-450, the final synthesizer of earlier developments.

Such a chronology agrees in large measure with both Frauwallner and Chakravarti, although in contrast to Frauwallner it places Vārṣagaṇya at an earlier date, and in contrast to Chakravarti it dissociates the *Sāṃkhyakārikā* from the unlikely context of debate and allows it to stand instead as a final "in-house" summary of the Sāṃkhya *tantra* (or *ṣaṣṭitantra*). Such a chronology also places Vindhyavāsin's revisions of Sāṃkhya ideas during the period of Brahmanical revival under the Gupta kings and just prior to the work of Vasubandhu (that is to say, some time in the fourth century) and makes Īśvarakṛṣṇa possibly a younger contemporary of Vindhyavāsin (as well as a full contemporary of Vasubandhu, whose rejoinder against Vindhyavāsin may have become the occasion for Īśvarakṛṣṇa's own attempt at some sort of further systematic statement of the Sāṃkhya position).

With regard to the specific views of Vindhyavāsin, the task is, as with Vārṣagaṇya, one of reconstruction or pulling together occasional remarks and quotations that appear in the literature. Again, although a complete picture cannot be reconstructed, one can formulate an illuminating glimpse of what Pre-*Kārikā* Sāṃkhya encompassed.

(1) As has been mentioned previously, Vindhyavāsin's definition of perception is "the functioning of the ear, etc., without construction or verbalization" ("*śrotrādivṛttir avikalpikā iti vindhyavāsipratyakṣalakṣaṇam*. . .," from Siddhasena Divākara's *Sanmatitarka*).[1]

(2) Vindhyavāsin evidently wrote a treatise on the ten-membered "syllogism" in Sāṃkhya logic, for the author of the *Yuktidīpikā* indicates that Īśvarakṛṣṇa did not discuss these matters in his text since they had been discussed in earlier authoritative treatises ("*kiñca tantrāntarokteḥ; tantrāntareṣu hi vindhyavāsiprabhṛtibhir ācāryair upadiṣṭāḥ; pramāṇaṃ ca nas te ācārya ity ataś ca anupadeśo jijñāsādīnāṃ iti*," YD in the introduction, p. 3).

(3) Unlike the views of those who derived the subtle elements from egoity, Vindhyavāsin held the view that the six specific forms (namely, egoity and the five subtle elements) all emerged directly out of *buddhi* or *mahat* ("*mahataḥ ṣaḍaviśeṣaḥ sṛjyante pañca tanmatrāṇi ahaṃkārās ca iti vindhyavāsimatam*," YD under SK 22, p. 91).

(4) Unlike those who argued that the sense capacities are pervasive but nevertheless limited in extent, Vindhyavāsin held the view that the sense capacities (including mind) are all-pervasive (*indrīyāṇi . . . vibhūni iti vindhyavāsimatam*," YD under SK 22, p. 91).

(5) Like Vārṣagaṇya, but unlike Pañcādhikaraṇa, Patañjali (the Sāṃkhya teacher), and Īśvarakṛṣṇa, Vindhyavāsin thought that there was an elevenfold set of organs (and not ten, twelve, or thirteen) ("*ekādaśakam iti vindhyavāsi*," YD under SK 22, p. 91).

(6) Unlike others who held that apprehension takes place finally on the level of *mahat* or *buddhi*, Vindhyavāsin took the position that experience occurs in the mind ("*tathā anyeṣāṃ mahati sarvārthopalabdhiḥ, manasi vindhyavāsinaḥ*," YD under SK 22, p. 91).

(7) Unlike others who thought that *saṃkalpa*, *abhimāna*, and *adhyavasāya* are three distinct functions (of *manas*, *ahaṃkāra*, and *buddhi*, respectively) Vindhyavāsin held the view that all three are simply modalities of one ("*saṃkalpābhimānādhyavasāyanānātvam anyeṣām, ekatvaṃ vindhyavāsinaḥ*," YD under SK 22, p. 91).

(8) Because Vindhyavāsin held the view that the sense capacities are all-pervasive, he therefore also denied the need for a subtle body in transmigration ("*vindhyavāsinas tu vibhutvād indriyāṇaṃ bījadeśe vṛttyā janma; tattyāgo maraṇam; tasmān na asti sūkṣmāśarīram*," YD under SK 39, p. 121).

(9) Pañcādhikaraṇa (see above under Pañcādhikaraṇa entry) had suggested that knowledge is twofold, that is, *prākṛta* and *vaikṛta*, the former of which has three subvarieties, *tattvasama*, *sāṃsiddhika*, and *ābhiṣyandika*, and the latter of which has two subvarieties, *svavaikṛta* and *paravaikṛta*. Vindhyavāsin, however, rejected both *tattvasama* (or knowledge that is the same as the *tattva*) and *sāṃsiddhika* (or knowledge that is inherent), arguing that knowledge always requires an outside stimulus and is thus largely derived and not inherent ("*vindhyavāsinas tu na asti tattvasamaṃ sāṃsiddhikaṃ ca*," YD under SK 43, p. 123).

(10) According to Kumārila in his *Ślokavārttika* and his commentator, Umbeka (*ākṛtivāda*, 76 and 65),[2] Vindhyavāsin accepted Vārṣagaṇya's interpretation of *vyaktivāda*, or the notion of

particularity (in contrast to *ākṛti* or "genus" or "class") with respect to the meaning of words, and Vindhyavāsin also held the view that the notions of *sāmānya* and/or *jāti* (that is, commonness or universality) are not separate categories or entities but can be interpreted simply as a general similarity (*sārūpya*) among things belonging to the same group or genus ("... *vindhyavāsinas* ... *piṇḍasārūpyaṃ sāmānyam iti*. . ."). Interestingly, both of these views are similar to the views of an ancient grammarian, Vyāḍi, a coincidence that has raised the question as to whether Vyāḍi and Vindhyavāsin are the same person. Such an identification is unlikely, however, since Vyāḍi lived many centuries before the Sāṃkhya Vindhyavāsin. Possibly, of course, as Chakravarti suggests, both the grammarian and the Sāṃkhya teacher were given the same appellation, "Vindhyavāsin."[3]

(11) Bhojarāja in his commentary, *Rājamārtaṇḍa*, on *Yogasūtra* IV.23 attributes to Vindhyavāsin the quotation: "*sattvatapyatvam evaṃ puruṣatapyatvam*," which means simply that the discriminating activity of *buddhi* appears to be that of the *puruṣa*.

(12) Medhātithi in his commentary on *Manusmṛti* I.55 comments that some Sāṃkhyans, Vindhyavāsin, and others, do not accept a subtle body: "*sāṃkhyā hi kecin na antarābhavam icchanti vindhyavāsaprabhṛtayaḥ*." A similar comment is made by Kumārila (*Ślokavarttika, ātmavāda*, 62): "*antarābhavadehas tu niṣiddho vindhyavāsinā*."[4] These attributions are now confirmed, of course, in view of the evidence of the *Yuktidīpikā* (and see item 8 above in this listing of Vindhyavāsin's views).

(13) Finally, Guṇaratna, in his commentary on *Ṣaḍdarśanasamuccaya*, attributes the following verse to Vindhyavāsin: "*puruṣo 'vikṛtātmā eva svanirbhāsaṃ acetanam manaḥ karoti sānnidhyād upādheḥ sphuṭiko yathā*. The *puruṣa*, though inactive, by its mere proximity makes the unconscious mind appear to be conscious, just as a pure crystal (appears to be red) because of being near the limiting condition or presence (of the rose)."[5]

It is clear enough from these various fragments and attributions that Vindhyavāsin, though very much in the tradition of Vārṣagaṇya (and therefore in an important sense one of the followers of Vārṣagaṇya [*vārṣagaṇāḥ*]), nevertheless considerably revised the tradition of the older school. By the same token, it is also clear that Īśvarakṛṣṇa's *Sāṃkhyakārikā* likewise owes a great deal to Vārṣagaṇya (thereby also making Īśvarakṛṣṇa one of the followers of Vārṣagaṇya), although Īśvarakṛṣṇa also considerably revised the older doctrines albeit in a manner clearly different from that of Vindhyavāsin. We know, of course, what happened to Īśvarakṛṣṇa's revision: it became the standard or normative formulation of what we now know as classical Sāṃkhya philosophy. What happened, however, to Vindhyavāsin's revision? The obvious guess (and it can only be a guess, given the present state of the evidence) is that Vindhyavāsin's revision of Sāṃkhya eventually became the classical Yoga philosophy of Patañjali and Vyāsa (or, in other words, what we have referred to as Pātañjala-Sāṃkhya in contrast to Kārikā-Sāṃkhya). P. Chakravarti[6] has cogently argued that such is the case, and Frauwallner[7] has expressed the same view. Some of the more obvious points of contact include the following:

(a) The reduction of the functions of *buddhi*, *ahaṃkāra*, and *manas* to *ekatva*, or oneness, appears to correlate with Yoga's emphasis on the notion of *citta*.

(b) The consequent all-pervasiveness of the sense capacities, which eliminates the need for a subtle body, is paralleled in Yoga philosophy by the all-pervasiveness of *citta*, which also eliminates the need for a subtle body.

(c) The interpretation of *sāmānya* and *jāti* as *sārūpya*, or similarity, appears to be common to both Vindhyavāsin and Yoga philosophy.

Beyond this there are numerous expressions throughout the *Yogasūtrabhāṣya* that appear to be strikingly parallel with both Vārṣagaṇya's and Vindhyavāsin's manner of discussing basic Sāṃkhya notions. These are described in detail by Chakravarti.[8]

MĀDHAVA

Another well-known name of a Sāṃkhya teacher coming down from ancient times is that of Mādhava. Mādhava is mentioned by Hsüan-tsang, Dignāga, Jinendrabuddhi, Kumārila, Karṇagomin, Śāntarakṣita, and Bhāsarvajña as being an eminent Sāṃkhya teacher but one who seriously deviated from the Sāṃkhya position, so much so that he is frequently called "*Sāṃkhyanāśaka*," or "a destroyer of the Sāṃkhya." Hsüan-tsang refers to a debate that Mādhava held (and lost) against the Buddhist teacher, Guṇamati, and Frauwallner dates this debate near the year 500 of the Common Era.[1] Hattori suggests that Mādhava was, therefore, an older contemporary of Dignāga (480-540) and had probably died by the time Dignāga wrote his *Pramāṇasamuccaya*.[2] If, as has been suggested earlier, Īśvarakṛṣṇa can be dated roughly between 350 and 450, Mādhava may have been a younger contemporary, living some time between 400 and 500.

On the basis of section 5 of Dignāga's *Pramāṇasamuccaya* (the section on the Sāṃkhya theory of perception) and Jinendrabuddhi's commentary thereon,[3] we know that Mādhava introduced a major innovation with respect to the Sāṃkhya theory of *triguṇa*. According to the standard Sāṃkhya view, there is only one primordial materiality, which is *triguṇa*. All objects, therefore, whether "mental" or "physical," represent collections of *triguṇa*, and there are five basic "configurations" (*saṃsthāna*) of *guṇa*-collocations corresponding to objects of sound, contact, form, taste, and smell that can then be apprehended by a particular sense capacity (hearing, touching, seeing, tasting, and smelling). Dignāga argues (as presumably do other Buddhists) that the Sāṃkhya theory is unacceptable because it does not adequately account for specific sense awarenesses. If it is true that all objects are simply configurations of *triguṇa*, then this appears to entail either (a) that there are an infinite variety of sensations (thereby making unintelligible any limitation to five types) or (b) that any one sense capacity should be capable of apprehending all objects (since all objects are simply configurations of *triguṇa*). In either case the Sāṃkhya is incapable of accounting for specifically five kinds of perception (hearing, touching, seeing, tasting, and smelling). Mādhava, according to Dignāga and his commentator, gets around this problem (and thereby greatly improves the Sāṃkhya position, in their view) by arguing that there are five different types of *guṇa*-configurations already on the level of primordial materiality. That is to say, there are sound-*guṇas*, touch-*guṇas*, etc., as heterogeneous atoms within *prakṛti* from the beginning, and therefore, the apprehension of five distinct types of objects becomes fully intelligible. Moreover, says Dignāga, Mādhava calls these "quanta" or atoms of distinct *guṇas* "*pradhānas*," or material constituents (using the plural). In other words, Mādhava has given up the unity of *prakṛti* and has reworked the notion of *triguṇa* into a theory of atomism that moves the Sāṃkhya view suspiciously close to the atomism of Vaiśeṣika. As is obvious, this is a radical innovation in the Sāṃkhya view of a unified cosmic *prakṛti* (and hence the antithesis of atomism), and it is surely not an accident that Mādhava came to be known as "the destroyer of Sāṃkhya."

Very little more is known about Mādhava. Frauwallner suggests that Mādhava also rejected the older Sāṃkhya view of the periodic emergence and disappearance of the world, arguing instead for a beginningless process of manifestation impelled by *karman*.[4] Also, according to Frauwallner, he made a distinction between the qualities of things (*dharma*) and that in which the quality resides (*dharmin*), again taking Sāṃkhya in the direction of Vaiśeṣika.

E.A. Solomon has conveniently collected all of the various references to Mādhava.[5] She speculates that Mādhava may be the same as Māṭhara, the commentator of *Māṭharavṛtti* and an ancient authority on Sāṃkhya. Our present *Māṭharavṛtti*, however, says Solomon, is a late revision of an original *Māṭharavṛtti*, which is now lost. Her own recently edited text, *Sāṃkhyasaptativṛtti*,[6] however (see appropriate entry below), called "V_1," may be the original *Māṭharavṛtti*, and Solomon cautiously suggests that this V_1 may be the work of Māṭhara or Mādhava. This is an interesting suggestion, but the views of V_1, though admittedly diverging somewhat from other Sāṃkhya commentaries, do not seem to warrant authorship by someone as radical as Mādhava. V_1, as will become apparent in the sequel, is a "garden-variety" commentary on *Sāṃkhyakārikā*, far removed from the sorts of incisive philosophical discussions that appear to be characteristic of the great Sāṃkhya heretic Mādhava and his Buddhist critics.

ĪŚVARAKṚṢṆA

We have already discussed (see above entries on Vārṣagaṇya and Vindhyavāsin) the approximate date of Īśvarakṛṣṇa (350-450) and have suggested that Īśvarakṛṣṇa's work, the *Sāṃkhyakārikā*, represents an "in-house" final summary formulation of the "system of sixty topics" (*ṣaṣṭitantra*). About Īśvarakṛṣṇa himself, nothing is known beyond the testimony of the Chinese translation that he was a Brahmin of the Kauśika *gotra*, or family, and the testimony of *Jayamaṅgalā* that he was a *parivrājaka*. From the evidence of the *Yuktidīpikā* it is fair to say that he was in the tradition of the followers of Vārṣagaṇya, and in view of the fact that he does not follow the innovations of Vindhyavāsin it is also fair to suggest that his final summary formulation harkens back to some of the older views of that tradition. Also, if the testimony of *Yuktidīpikā* is to be believed, Īśvarakṛṣṇa considered his role to be one of mediator among the many opposing views within the developing Sāṃkhya tradition. For better or worse, his summary formulation of the Sāṃkhya position proved to be definitive, for all later texts within the tradition, including not only the commentarial tradition up through Vācaspati Miśra but also the tradition of the *Sāṃkhyasūtra* and its commentaries, consider Īśvarakṛṣṇa's formulation to be normative. The one possible exception is the little *Tattvasamāsasūtra*, which includes material not mentioned in the work of Īśvarakṛṣṇa, but all of the commentaries on the *Tattvasamāsa* are fully aware of and make extensive use of the *Sāṃkhyakārikā*.

SĀṂKHYAKĀRIKĀ

The *Sāṃkhyakārikā* is hardly a "philosophical" text as that designation is understood in an Indian intellectual environment. There is very little of the polemical give and take so typical of *darśana* or philosophical literature. Instead, the *Sāṃkhyakārikā* is a philosophical poem, laying out the contours of the Sāṃkhya system in a relaxed and artful manner, presenting its content in serious and elegant *ārya* verses that flow easily and make use of striking similes and metaphors throughout.

If the term "*darśana*" is to be taken in its original sense as an "intuitive seeing" that nurtures a quiet wisdom and invites ongoing thoughtful meditation, then surely the *Sāṃkhyakārikā* must stand as one of the most remarkable productions of its class, far removed, on one level, from the laconic *sūtra* style that glories in saying as little as possible and presupposing everything, and even further removed, on another level, from the frequently petty and tedious quibbling of Indian philosophy. (It should be noted, however, that the *Yuktidīpikā* (p. 2, lines 18-19) suggests that the SK is composed in *sūtra* style). But alas, philosophers are seldom poets, and it is hardly surprising, therefore, that more prosaic minds both ancient and modern have faulted the text for its lack of precision and incisive polemic. In any case, the seventy verses of Īśvarakṛṣṇa have been remarkably influential both as a summary of the Sāṃkhya position and as a symptom of Sāṃkhya's contribution to India's philosophical and cultural heritage. It is surely appropriate, therefore, that the present volume begins its sequence of full summaries with this ancient philosophical poem.

As has been mentioned, the text together with a full prose commentary was translated into Chinese by Paramārtha during the last phase of his literary activity in Canton, between 557 and 569, and it is fair to infer, therefore, that the text was reasonably well known by about 500 of the Common Era. Since the text is referred to in Chinese as *Suvarṇasaptati* (the "Gold-Seventy"), it is also reasonable to infer that the original text of the poem had precisely seventy verses. This has proved to be something of a problem, however, since the *Kārikā* has been transmitted with varying numbers of verses. The commentary of Gauḍapāda, for example, though it reads seventy-two verses, comments only on the first sixty-nine. The Chinese translation of Paramārtha, *Suvarṇasaptati*, reads seventy-one verses but omits verse 63. The commentaries *Jayamaṅgalā*, *Yuktidīpikā*, and *Tattvakaumudī* read seventy-two verses, but *Māṭharavṛtti* reads seventy-three verses. The two newly edited commentaries on the *Kārikā* by E.A. Solomon, namely, *Sāṃkhyasaptativṛtti* (V_1) and *Sāṃkhyavṛtti* (V_2), read respectively seventy-three verses and seventy-one verses. As early as 1915 Lokamanya B. G. Tilak argued that verses 70-72 in the Gauḍapāda text are later additions, since Gauḍapāda does not comment upon them.[1] The original text, then, represents the sixty-nine verses commented upon by Gauḍapāda plus a missing verse. Tilak argues further that the missing verse may be reconstructed from the last portion of Gauḍapāda's commentary on verse 61 as follows:

kāraṇam īśvaram eke bruvate kālaṃ pare svabhāvaṃ vā
prajāḥ kathaṃ nirguṇato vyaktaḥ kālaḥ svabhāvaś ca

Some argue that *īśvara* is the ultimate cause; others suggest time or inherent nature;

(But) how can finite creatures be said to derive from that which is without attributes (namely *īśvara*); (moreover,) time and inherent nature are manifest entities (and hence cannot be the ultimate cause).

Tilak suggests that this verse was dropped because it denies *īśvara* as creator. Though an ingenious suggestion, most scholars have hesitated to follow Tilak's reconstruction, mainly because the commentary on verse 61 in Gauḍapāda appears to fit quite naturally within the total framework of his continuing discussion and shows no signs of having been tampered with. Others have suggested that verses 70-72, since they simply enumerate the tradition of Sāṃkhya teachers and stress that the text is a complete summary of the *ṣaṣṭitantra*, require no comment, and hence Gauḍapāda felt no need to comment beyond verse 69. This is unlikely, however, since most commentators would comment on the *guruparamparā* of a tradition, especially on one as problematic as that of the Sāṃkhya. Suryanarayana Sastri has proposed perhaps the best suggestion.[2] He argues that the earliest commentary is the one translated by Paramārtha into Chinese in the middle of the sixth-century, and that in this commentary verse 63 is missing. It is interesting to note, says Sastri, that verse 63 simply repeats what has already been said in verses 44-45, and more than that, the progression between verse 62 and 64 is a natural one, with verse 63 suddenly referring back to the doctrine of eight predispositions. In other words, says Sastri, verse 63 looks very much like a later interpolation. In addition, the Chinese translation reads just seventy-one verses and indicates in its introduction to verse 71 that this final verse was uttered by an "intelligent man" (*medhāvin*) of the school (or, in other words, someone other than Īśvarakṛṣṇa). In other words, the original seventy verses of the *Sāṃkhyakārikā* include verses 1-62 and 64-71 (for a total of 70). Verses 63 and 72, as also verse 73 (as read by *Māṭharavṛtti* and V_1), are later interpolations.

Variant readings of the verses of the *Sāṃkhyakārikā* in the various commentaries are conveniently collected by R. C. Pandeya in Appendix I of his edition of the *Yuktidīpikā*.[3] E. A. Solomon in her *The Commentaries of the Sāṃkhya Kārikā—A Study*, pages 194-207, cites additional variants from the *Sāṃkhyasaptativṛtti* (V_1) and *Sāṃkhyavṛtti* (V_2)."

The edition and translation (ET) used for the following summary is that of Gerald J. Larson, translation, *Classical Sāṃkhya*, second edition, revised (Delhi: Motilal Banarsidass, 1979), pp. 255-277.

(*Summary by Karl H. Potter and Gerald J. Larson*)

I. Introductory Verses: The Scope and Task of the Sāṃkhya

(*Kārikā* 1) (ET255) Because of the affliction occasioned by the three kinds of frustration (*duḥkhatraya*: explained by all commentators as internal [*ādhyātmika*], external and/or natural [*ādhibhautika*], and divine and/or celestial [*ādhidaivika*]), there arises in experience a desire to know what will eliminate that affliction.

Objection: One might argue that a philosophical inquiry into that which will eliminate the affliction is useless, since there are ordinary remedies (medicines, etc.) available.

Answer: This is not the case, however, because all such ordinary remedies are only temporary palliatives that treat the symptoms of the affliction. Such remedies fail to deal with the underlying cause of the affliction and, hence, provide only limited and temporary relief. The issue is to remove the ultimate cause of the affliction and thereby provide relief that is permanent (*atyanta*) and complete (*ekānta*). This can only be accomplished by philosophical analysis—hence, the occasion for the Sāṃkhya.

(*Kārikā* 2) (ET256) Scriptural remedies (as, for example, the performance of sacred rituals, etc.) are like ordinary remedies in the sense that they also provide only limited and temporary relief. This is so because the scriptural remedies are connected with impurity (*aviśuddhi*), destruction (*kṣaya*), and excess or surpassibility (*atiśaya*). In contrast to this, a better method for the elimination of affliction is available, namely, the discriminative understanding of the difference between the manifest (*vyakta*), the unmanifest (*avyakta*), and the absolute knower (*jña*) (i.e., *vyaktāvyaktajñavijñāna*).

(*Kārikā* 3) (ET256) Primordial materiality (*mūlaprakṛti*) is ungenerated (*avikṛti*). (That is to say, it subsists by and in itself.) The seven, namely, the "great one" or intellect (*mahat* or *buddhi*), egoity (*ahaṃkāra*), and the five subtle elements (*tanmātra*), are generated products (*vikṛti*) as well as generative principles (*prakṛti*). (That is to say, the seven are modifications of primordial materiality and, hence, are derived; but they also in turn generate subsequent principles [*tattva*] and in that sense are creative.) Sixteen of the principles are simple derived products, namely, mind (*manas*), the five sense capacities (*buddhīndriya*), the five action capacities (*karmendriya*), and the five gross elements (*bhūta*). Consciousness (*puruṣa*) is neither a generating principle nor generated.

II. The Instruments of Knowledge

(4) (ET256-257) There are three instruments of knowing (*pramāṇa*): (a) perception (*dṛṣṭa*); (b) inference (*anumāna*) and (c) reliable authority (*āptavacana*). All other instruments of knowing can be reduced to one of these three. (That is to say, other so-called separate instruments of knowing as put forth by other schools of Indian thought can be reduced to perception, inference, or reliable authority.) Any-

thing that can be known (*prameya*) must be demonstrably established *vis-à-vis* one of these three reliable instruments of knowing.

(5) (ET257) Perception is the reflective discerning (*adhyavasāya*) that arises through (sense contact with) the particular contents (*viṣaya*) of sensing. Inference is of three varieties and is based on a characteristic mark (*liṅga*) and that which bears a characteristic mark (*liṅgin*). Reliable authority is reliable scriptural testimony and/or reliable utterance.

(6) (ET257) Knowledge of what is beyond the senses arises through the variety of inference known as "inference based on general correlation" (*sāmānyatodṛṣṭa*). That which can be known but not established even through this kind of inference is to be established through reliable authority (*āptāgama*).

(7) (ET257-258) Something that can be known may not be known through perception for the following reasons: it is too far away; it is too close; a sense capacity may not be functioning adequately; the mind may be inattentive; the thing is too subtle; it is hidden (as, for example, an object behind a veil or wall); it is overpowered by something else (as, for example, something overcome by darkness or overcome by the brightness of the sun, etc.); or it is mixed with similar things (as, for example, a grain of rice in a heap of rice or a drop of water in the ocean, etc.).

(8) (ET258) With respect to materiality, it is not perceived not because it does not exist; it is not perceived because of its subtlety. Materiality is known through its effects, namely, the "great one" (*mahat*) or intellect (*buddhi*), etc., whose effects are both similar to and different in form from materiality. (That is to say, primordial materiality is to be established through inference.)

III. The Notion of Preexistent Effect

(9) (ET258) The effect (*kārya*) exists or resides (*satkārya*) in the cause in a potential state or condition prior to the operation of the cause for the following reasons: (a) something cannot arise from nothing; (b) any effect requires a material basis (*upādāna*); (c) anything cannot arise from just everything; (d) something can only produce what it is capable of producing; and (e) the very nature or essence of the cause is nondifferent from the effect.

IV. The Manifest and Unmanifest Aspects of Materiality

(10) (ET258-259) Materiality as manifest is characterized as (a) having a cause (*hetumat*); (b) impermanent (*anitya*); (c) nonpervasive (*avyāpin*); (d) mobile (*sakriya*); (e) multiple (*aneka*); (f) supported (*āśrita*); (g) mergent (*liṅga*); (h) being made up of parts (*sāvayava*);

and (i) dependent (*paratantra*). Materiality as unmanifest is the reverse (that is to say, uncaused, permanent, pervasive, etc.). (Compare commentaries for alternative explanations.)

(11) (ET259) Although the manifest and unmanifest have these contrary characteristics, nevertheless, they are alike in the sense that they share certain common characteristics, namely, (a) both are constituted by the tripartite constituent process (*triguṇa*); (b) neither can be clearly distinguished from the other in a final sense (*avivekin*); (c) both are objects or objective (*viṣaya*) ; (d) both are general (*sāmānya*, that is to say, capable of objective apprehension either by perception or inference); (e) both are non-conscious (*acetana*); and (f) both are productive (*prasavadharmin*). With respect to these common characteristics of the manifest and unmanifest, consciousness (*puruṣa*, or the specific term used here, *puṃs*) is the reverse of these characteristics. It should be noted, however, that consciousness shares certain characteristics with the unmanifest—specifically, those characteristics as set forth in verse 10 (see above).

V. The Three Constituents

(12) (ET259) The constituents or constituent processes (*guṇa*) are experienced as agreeable (*prīti*), disagreeable (*aprīti*), and oppressive (*viṣāda*). Moreover, these constituents have as their purpose illumination (*prakāśa*), activity (*pravṛtti*), and restriction (*niyama*). Finally, with respect to the operation of the constituents, they mutually and successively dominate, support, activate, and interact with one another.

(13) (ET259-260) The intelligibility constituent (*sattva*) is lightweight (*laghu*) and illuminating (*prakāśaka*) (that is to say, it provides the intellectual clarity and/or the intelligibility of primal, creative nature); the activity constituent (*rajas*) is stimulating (*upaṣṭambhaka*) and moving (*cala*) (that is to say, it provides the capacity for change and/or the continuing process of primal, creative nature); the inertia constituent (*tamas*) is heavy (*guru*) and enveloping (*varaṇaka*) (that is td say, it provides the substance and/or the "thingness" of primal, creative nature). These three, though different in operation and makeup, nevertheless function together for a purpose just as the wick, oil, and flame of a lamp, though different in their makeup, nevertheless function together for the purpose of illumination.

VI. The Inferences that Establish the Existence and Makeup of Primordial Materiality and Consciousness

(14) (ET260) It can be argued that the characteristics of that which is manifest (namely, that the manifest cannot be distinguished, is objective, general, nonconscious, and productive as was described

in verse 11) are established or determined primarily because the manifest is made up of the three constituents. It would follow by inference, therefore, that consciousness is *not* made up of the three constituents insofar as it has been described as being the reverse of the manifest (see verse 11). Moreover, it can be inferred further that the unmanifest is made up of the three constituents because of the argument of verse 9 in which it is established that the effect preexists in the cause (in a subtle form) prior to the operation of the cause. (That is to say, in so far as the unmanifest and manifest are related to one another as cause and effect, it follows that if the manifest has the three constituents, then the unmanifest must also have them.) (Compare commentaries for alternative explanations.)

(15-16) (ET260-261) The unmanifest is the ultimate cause because (a) that which is manifest is perceived to be limited in size (*parimāṇa*) (and no limited thing can itself serve as an ultimate cause); (b) all manifest things, in so far as their characteristics are uniform and/or homogeneous (*samanvaya*), require a single, ultimate cause as their causal source; (c) the emergence and/or process of that which is manifest presupposes a causal efficiency (*śakti*) that enables emergence or process to occur; (d) that which is manifest is just a modification and, hence, presupposes an ultimate cause different from it that is not a modification (but, rather, is the source or presupposition for modification); and (e) that which is manifest and, hence, defined in terms of ordinary space and time, presupposes an ultimate cause that is not so defined, and, hence, in which the manifest can reside prior to manifestation—that is to say, although cause and effect differ with respect to the contraries manifest/unmanifest, they are identical when there is no manifestation, or, putting the matter another way, the effect disappears when there is no manifestation, but it continues to exist because the effect always preexists in the cause prior to the operation of the cause. Moreover, this unmanifest functions because of the three constituents that individually and together constitute its very being. These constituents undergo continuing transformation, which can be accounted for by the respective capacities that reside in each of the constituents. This notion of the unmanifest undergoing transformation because of its constituent capacities is like (the taste of) water (which, though basically of one taste, is modified in various transformations into a sour taste, a bitter taste, a sweet taste, etc.).

(17) (ET261) Consciousness exists because of the following inferences: (a) all aggregates exist for the sake of something else (*parārthatva*) (as, for example, the components of a bed either as a whole or in its respective parts serve the needs of something else, namely, the person who uses the bed for sleeping); (b) since it has been established (in verses 14, 15, and 16) that the manifest and unmanifest are both aggregates in the sense that they are made up of the three constituents,

it must be inferred further, in order to avoid an infinite regress, that the "something else" referred to in the first inference must be distinct from that which has the three constituents (that is to say, one cannot argue that aggregates serve only the needs of other aggregates without getting caught in an infinite regress, for any given aggregate posited as that for which another aggregate exists will itself require another aggregate, and so on;) (c) moreover, this "something else" different from the constituents must be inferred because there is a "standing-place," "controlling factor", or "*basis*" (*adhiṣṭhāna*) required for both the manifest and unmanifest (that is to say, there must be a principle that "accompanies" all composite aggregates and thus provides a raison d'être and, hence, an authoritative motive for primal, creative nature's activity or its objective transformations); (d) in addition, this "something else" different from the constituents must be inferred because there is a need for a ground or basis for all subjective experience (*bhoktṛbhāva*) (that is to say, insofar as the unmanifest encompasses all subjective aggregates as well as objective aggregates, there must be "something else" that provides the basis for subjectivity as well as objectivity); and finally (e) this "something else" different from the constituents must be inferred because there is an inclination in experience to seek freedom or "isolation" (that is to say, there must be "something else" distinct from the manifest and the unmanifest, for otherwise the inclination to seek freedom would be unintelligible or pointless).

(18) (ET261) Moreover, (a) since there are varieties of births, deaths, and functional capacities; and (b) since these three divergent manifestations do not occur simultaneously; and (c) since these three differentiations are to be accounted for because of the diversity occasioned by the constituents, consciousness, insofar as it is that for which all such manifestations and transformations occur, must be construed pluralistically.

(19) (ET261-262) Finally, because consciousness is the reverse of that which has the three constituents (namely, the manifest and unmanifest as described in verse 11), it follows that consciousness can be characterized as that which is the basis for there being a witness (*sākṣitva*); as that which is "isolation" or liberation; as that which is the condition of neutrality (or, in other words, the condition of being separate from all specific experience) (*mādhyasthya*); and as that which is the condition of nonagency (*akartṛbhāva*).

VII. The Association or Proximity of Materiality and Consciousness

(20) (ET262) Because of the association or proximity (*saṃyoga*) of

primordial materiality and pure consciousness, that which is manifest appears as if it is characterized by consciousness, and, similarly, even though all agency or activity occurs only in the constituents, consciousness (here the term "*udāsīna*" is used) appears as if characterized by agency or activity.

(21) (ET262) Moreover, this association or proximity is like the association of the lame man and the blind man (that is to say, both are quite distinct, but they come together in order to benefit from the capacities of one another). Materiality "performs its task," as it were, so that consciousness may have content, and consciousness "performs its task", by revealing itself as radically distinct or isolated from all subjective and objective transformations. Because of this association, the manifest and experiential world has come into being.

VIII. The Derivation of the Basic Principles (tattva)

(22) (ET262-263) The "great one," that is, the intellect, arises from materiality. Egoity arises from the intellect. The mind, the sense capacities, the action capacities, and the subtle elements arise from the ego. The five gross elements arise from the five subtle elements.

IX. The Functioning of the Thirteenfold Instrument (trayodaśakaraṇa)

(23) (ET263) Intellect is characterized by reflective discerning (*adhyavasāya*). When its intelligibility constituent (*sattva*) is dominent, it is characterized by four forms (*rūpa*): (1) the basic predisposition toward meritorious behavior (*dharma*); (2) the basic predisposition toward discriminating knowledge (*jñāna*); (3) the basic predisposition toward nonattachment (*virāga*); and (4) the basic predisposition toward mastery or control (*aiśvarya*). When its inertia constituent (*tamas*) is dominant, it is characterized by the four opposite forms or predispositions (namely, (5) *adharma* or "demeritorious behavior," (6) *ajñāna* or "ignorance," (7) *rāga* or "attachment," and (8) *anaiśvarya* or "impotence").

(24) (ET263) Egoity is characterized by self-awareness (*abhimāna*). A twofold creation comes forth from it, namely, the elevenfold aggregate (made up of the mind, the sense capacities and the action capacities) and the fivefold subtle aggregate (made up of the five subtle elements).

(25) (ET263-264) The elevenfold aggregate, dominated by the intelligibility constituent emerges out of egoity and is called "modified" (*vaikṛta*).[5] The fivefold subtle aggregate dominated by the inertia constituent emerges from what is called "the source of the gross elements" (*bhūtādi*). Both aggregates are able to manifest themselves

because of what is called "the fiery one" (*taijasa*) (that is to say, both come into manifestation because of the capacity for change or activity that is provided by the activity constituent).

(26) (ET264) The sense capacities are those of seeing, hearing, smelling, tasting, and touching. The action capacities are speaking, grasping, walking or locomotion, excreting, and sexual functioning.

(27) (ET264) The mind is similar to both the sense capacities and the action capacities and so is also a capacity. Its function is intentionality (*saṃkalpaka*); it apprehends the contents of the various action capacities and sense capacities. The variety of the capacities and the external differences (among things apprehended by the mind) arise because of the particular transformations of the constituents.

(28) (ET264) The function of the five sense capacities is bare awareness (*ālocanamātra*), or perhaps better, the ' indeterminate sensing" of sound, etc. The functions of the five action capacities are speaking, grasping, walking, excretion, and orgasm.

(29) (ET264-265) As already pointed out, intellect, egoity, and mind have specific and separate functions, namely, reflective discerning, self-awareness, and intentionality which, set forth in verses 23, 24, and 27, are also their essential characteristics. Taken together, however, they also have a common function or common essential characteristic, and that is the (support or maintenance of the) five vital breaths (*prāṇa*, etc.) (that is to say, the common function or common essential characteristic of the intellect, ego, and mind is the maintenance of life).

(30) (ET265) When perception of something takes place, the four (intellect, egoity, mind, and one of the capacities) function either simultaneously or successively. Similarly, when awareness occurs of something unperceived (as, for example, in conceptualization, inference, etc.), the intellect/will, egoity, and mind function on the basis of prior perceptions (retained in memory, imagination, etc.).[6]

(31) (ET265) All of these capacities in their respective ways function coordinately with one another. The reason for the functioning is always one "for the sake of consciousness" (*puruṣārtha*) (that is, for the sake of the two purposes of consciousness: experience (*bhoga*) and liberation (*apavarga*)). None of these capacities ever functions for any other purpose.

(32) (ET265-266) This, then, is the "thirteenfold instrument" (namely, intellect, egoity, mind, and the sense and action capacities), and it functions with respect to seizing (*āharaṇa*), holding (*dhāraṇa*), and illuminating (*prakāśa*). The objects, or in other words, the things to be seized, held, and illuminated, are tenfold.

(33) (ET266) The internal organ (*antaḥkaraṇa*, or intellect, egoity, and mind taken together) is threefold. The external (*bāhya*, or the five sense capacities and the five action capacities) is tenfold and

provides the sense contents (*viṣaya*) of experience. The external functions in present time, whereas the internal functions in all three times (*trikāla*).

(34) (ET266) The five sense capacities have or provide both specific (*viśeṣa*) and nonspecific (*aviśeṣa*) sense contents. The action capacity of speech has or provides only the content of sound. The other four action capacities have or provide the contents of all five kinds of sensing and their contents.

(35) (ET266) Because intellect together with the other components of the internal organ comprehends every content, the threefold internal organ, therefore, can be said to be the "door-keeper," (*dvārin*) whereas the tenfold external organ can be said to be the "doors" (*dvāra*).[7]

(36) (ET267) Egoity, mind, the five sense capacities and the five action capacities, all of which are differentiated by reason of the specific modifications of the constituents, and all of which function together like the components of a lamp, thereby illuminating or providing access to all of reality, present or deliver up to intellect that which has been illuminated. They do all of this for the sake of the entire purpose of consciousness (namely, experience and liberation).

(37) (ET267) Intellect provides certitude (*sādhayati*) regarding every aspect of experience for consciousness and, even more than that, reveals the subtle difference between primordial materiality and consciousness.

X. The Subtle and Gross Elements

(38) (ET267) The subtle elements are nonspecific. The five gross elements (*mahābhūtas*), which are specific, arise from these. The five gross elements are experienced as being comfortable (*śānta*), uncomfortable (*ghora*), and confusing (*mūḍha*).

(39) (ET267-268) There are three kinds of specific aggregates in the manifest world: (a) subtle bodies (*sūkṣma*); (b) gross bodies born of maternal and paternal seeds (*mātāpitṛja*); and (c) various objects made up of gross elements (*prabhūta*). Of these, the subtle body persists from one existence to another, whereas the gross bodies born of parents cease.

XI. Thr Subtle Body

(40) (ET268) The subtle body (*liṅga*), which is preexistent to all other bodies (*pūrvotpanna*), unconfined (*asakta*), persistent (*niyata*) (for each individual in the course of transmigration), and made up of intellect, egoity, mind, the five sense capacities, the five action capacities, and the five subtle elements, and which in itself is devoid of experience,

transmigrates, permeated or "perfumed" (*adhivāsita*) (and, hence, given a characteristic "scent" as it were) by its basic predispositions.

(41) (ET268) Just as a painting cannot exist without a canvas or just as a shadow cannot exist without a pillar or post, in a similar manner the subtle body cannot exist without an appropriate support.

(42) (ET268-269) The subtle body, motivated for the purpose of consciousness, behaves like a dramatic actor, functioning by means of the efficient causes and effects (*nimittanaimittika*) derived from the inherent power of materiality.[8]

XII. The Basic Predispositions

(43) (ET269) The innate (*sāṃsiddhika*) predispositions (*bhāva*), namely, meritorious behavior etc. are either natural (*prākṛtika*) or acquired (*vaikṛta*). The predispositions reside in the subtle body (and, specifically, in intellect, as was stated in verse 23). These innate predispositions determine the quality of life of the gross embryo, etc. (that is to say, the predispositions, which reside on the level of the subtle body, nevertheless bring about certain effects on the level of the gross, perishable body).

(44) (ET269) By means of (the predisposition toward) meritorious behavior one transmigrates into higher forms of life; by means of (the innate predisposition toward) demeritorious behavior, one transmigrates into lower forms of life; by means of (the predisposition toward) knowledge, one comes to liberation; and by means of (the predisposition toward) the opposite of knowledge, one comes to bondage.

(45) (ET269) By means of (the predisposition toward) nonattachment, one attains dissolution in materiality; by means of (the predisposition toward) passionate attachment, one attains transmigration; by means of (the predisposition toward) power, one attains control over life; by means of (the predisposition toward) impotence, one attains declining control over life.

(46) (ET270) This is the "intellectual creation" (*pratyayasarga*), and it manifests itself on the level of ordinary experience in fifty divisions that arise because of the varying collocations (occasioned by the unequal distributions) of the constituents. The fifty divisions are broadly classified into four groups: misconceptions (*viparyaya*), dysfunctions (*aśakti*), contentments (*tuṣṭi*), and attainments (*siddhi*).

(47) (ET270) There are five kinds of misconception; twenty-eight kinds of dysfunction due to defects in the functioning of one's capacities; nine kinds of contentment; and eight attainments.

(48) (ET270) The five kinds of misconception are darkness (*tamas*), confusion (*moha*), great confusion (*mahāmoha*), gloom (*tāmisra*), and blind gloom (*andhatāmisra*). Among these five kinds of misconception, there are eight varieties of darkness, eight varieties of delu-

sion, ten varieties of great delusion, eighteen varieties of gloom, and eighteen varieties of blind gloom.

(49) (ET270) The twenty-eight kinds of dysfunction include injuries to the eleven capacities (namely, the mind, the five sense capacities and the five action capacities) together with seventeen kinds of injury to intellect. The list of seventeen injuries to intellect refers to the reverse of the nine contentments and the eight attainments.

(50) (ET271) The nine kinds of contentment are divided into two groups: (a) the internal, including belief in primordial materiality as ultimate, belief in a material basis (*upādāna*) as ultimate, belief in time (*kāla*) as ultimate, and belief in destiny (*bhāgya*) as ultimate; and (b) the external, including the turning away from the contents of the five kinds of activity that relate to the five sense capacities.

(51) (ET271) The eight attainments are reflective reasoning (*ūha*), oral instruction, study, removal of the three kinds of frustration (see verse 1), association with appropriate persons, and an open yet disciplined temperament (*dāna*). The misconceptions, dysfunctions, and contentments all hinder the development of the attainments.

(52) (ET271) The subtle body cannot function without the predispositions; likewise the predispositions cannot function without the subtle body. Therefore, a "twofold creation" (*dvividhasarga*) operates, referred to as the "subtle creation" (*liṅga*) and the "predisposition creation" (*bhāva*).

XIII. The Empirical World

(53) (ET271-272) The divine order has eight varieties; the animal and plant order has five varieties; and the human order is of one variety. Such, briefly, is the scope of the total, empirical world experience (*bhautikasarga*).

(54) (ET272) In the upper (divine) order there is a preponderance of the intelligibility constituent (*sattva*); in the animal/plant order the inertia constituent (*tamas*) is preponderant; and in the middle, human order, the activity constituent (*rajas*) is preponderant. This classification applies to all of creation from Brahmā down to a blade of grass.

(55) (ET272) Consciousness in this empirical world comes upon frustrations that are occasioned by old age and death.[9] So long as the subtle body continues to function (by means of the lack of discrimination), just so long suffering will appear to be a completely natural part of experience.

(56) (ET273-274) This entire manifest world, from intellect down to the gross elements, has been constructed by materiality. The entire effort, though it appears to be for her own benefit, is really for the sake of another, namely, for the sake of the liberation of each consciousness.

XIV. Similes Illustrating the Role and Function of Materiality

(57) (ET272-273) Just as unconscious milk functions for the nourishment of a calf, so materiality functions for the sake of the freedom or liberation of consciousness.

(58) (ET273) Just as in the world someone acts so as to bring about the cessation of a desire, so the unmanifest (materiality) functions for the sake of the liberation of consciousness.

(59) (ET273) Just as a dancer ceases from the dance after having been seen by the audience, so materiality ceases after having shown herself to consciousness.

(60) (ET273) Materiality, made up of the constituents, helps consciousness in various ways and behaves selflessly toward consciousness, who does not return the favor (that is to say, materiality behaves like a servant or like a generous man who assists all).

(61) (ET273-274) In my view, there is nothing more sensitive and delicate than primal, creative nature, who, having realized that she has been seen, withdraws and never again comes into the sight of consciousness (that is to say, primordial materiality behaves like a lovely and shy young virgin who, having been seen in her nakedness by a man, quickly withdraws from his view).

XV. Liberation and Isolation (mokṣa and kaivalya)

(62) (ET274) Not any (consciousness), therefore, is really bound, is liberated or transmigrates. Only materiality in her various manifestations is bound, is liberated or transmigrates.

(63) (ET274) Materiality binds herself by herself by means of the seven predispositions (described in verses 43-45 and 46-51). She releases herself by means of one form (*ekarūpa*) or one predisposition (namely, the predisposition toward knowledge or *jñāna*) for the sake of consciousness (*puruṣārtha*).[10]

(64) (ET274) As a result of the meditative analysis (*abhyāsa*) on the principles (of the Sāṃkhya), the discriminating knowledge (*jñāna*) arises, "I am not (conscious), (consciousness) does not belong to me, the 'I' is not (conscious)." This discriminating knowledge is complete (*apariśeṣa*), pure (*viśuddha*) because it is free from error (*viparyaya*), and not mixed with any other thing (*kevala*).

(65) (ET275) Then, consciousness like a spectator sees materiality, for at that moment materiality has turned away from the other seven predispositions.

(66) (ET275) The indifferent one (namely, consciousness) thinks, "I have seen her." The other (namely, materiality) thinks, "I have been seen," and ceases. Though the two continue to be in proximity with one another, no new transformations take place.

(67) (ET275) When the seven predispositions no longer operate because of the realization of correct, discriminating knowledge (*samyag-jñāna*), nevertheless, the subtle body (associated, with *puruṣa*) continues to subsist because of the force of latent dispositions (*saṃskāra*), just as the potter's wheel continues for a time even after the potter ceases exerting force.

(68) (ET275) When distinction from the body (and its attendant processes) has been attained (that is to say, when materiality has ceased to function after having accomplished her purpose), there is the realization of isolation that is both complete (*aikāntika*) and permanent (*ātyantika*).

(69) (ET276) This profound (*guhya*) discriminating knowledge, which brings about the realization that consciousness is the radical foundation for freedom or isolation, has been expounded by the sage. The very nature of all of reality, its duration in time (*sthiti*), its origin (*utpatti*), and its final dissolution (*pralaya*) has been analyzed herein.

XVI. The Transmission of the Śaṃkhya Tradition

(70) (ET276) This excellent and pure (discriminating knowledge) was given out of compassion to Āsuri. He, in turn, passed it on to Pañcaśikha. By Pañcaśikha the doctrine (*tantra*) was widely disseminated and/or variously expanded (*bahudhā*).

(71) (ET276) And this (knowledge) handed down by a succession of pupils has been summarized in these verses by the noble-minded Īśvarakṛṣṇa who has understood the doctrine correctly.

(72) (ET276-277)[11] Moreover, it is to be noted that in these seventy verses all of the sixty topics (*ṣaṣṭitantra*) of the traditional Sāṃkhya have been included. Only illustrative tales and polemics against opposing views have been excluded.

(73) (ET277)[12] Thus, this briefly summarized system of thought (*śāstra*) is not defective with respect to the complete subject matter of the Sāṃkhya. It is a reflected mirror image of the vast (Sāṃkhya) doctrine (*tantra*).

PATAÑJALI (the Yoga teacher)

YOGASŪTRA

The literature of the philosophy of Yoga will be treated in a separate volume of the *Encyclopedia*, so, there is no need to discuss it in detail here. Because we have construed Yoga philosophy as one type of Sāṃkhya, however—Pātañjala-Sāṃkhya—and because there are some indications that this divergent form of Sāṃkhya may represent the Vindhyavāsin revision of the followers of Vārṣagaṇya, it may be useful to offer chronological approximations for some of the more important texts of Yoga.

Concerning the compiler of the *Yogasūtra*,[1] namely Patañjali the Yoga teacher, there is no clear consensus. The later Indian tradition (beginning perhaps with Bhojarāja and Cakrapāṇidatta in the eleventh century and thereafter) tends to identify Patañjali the Yoga teacher with the famous grammarian Patañjali of the *Mahābhāṣya*. This identification has been rejected by J. H. Woods, partly because the notion of substance or *dravya* in the two Patañjalis appears to be clearly different and partly because the *Yogasūtra* appears to reflect a philosophical environment of a period much later than that of the grammarian Patañjali (of the second century before the Common Era).[2] S. N. Dasgupta, however, disputes Woods, arguing instead that the notion of *dravya* is not very different in the two Patañjalis and that the supposed later philosophical milieu is more a reflection of the commentators on the *Yogasūtra* than it is a reflection of the *sūtras* themselves.[3] Moreover, Dasgupta sees Book IV of the *Yogasūtra*, which contains most of the later Buddhist material, as a later interpolation. J. W. Hauer in *Der Yoga* has argued that the *Yogasūtra* is a composite text, the oldest portion of which the *yogāṅga* section (from II.28 through III.55) may indeed harken back to the time of the grammarian Patañjali, but the most recent portion of which the *nirodha* section (or I.-1-22) appears to be much later.[4] Frauwallner, perhaps wisely, has refused to comment one way or the other about the *sūtras* themselves or Patañjali, claiming that there is simply insufficient evidence to offer even a guess.[5] Frauwallner is inclined to suggest, however, as is also Chakravarti,[6] that the

Yogasūtrabhāṣya of Vyāsa appears to be dependent in important respects on the work of Vindhyavāsin (whom we have tentatively placed between 300 and 400 of the Common Era). Frauwallner ventures the further suggestion (only in the most tentative fashion) that the *Yogasūtrabhāṣya* of Vyāsa may have been composed some time around 500. Woods is inclined to date the Yogasūtrabhāṣya somewhat later, that is to say, some time between 650 and 850.[7]

All of this leaves us with little more than the suggestion that there is virtually no evidence of a philosophical literature of Yoga much before the sixth century of the Common Era (if one accepts Frauwallner's tentative dating for the *Yogasūtrabhāṣya* and its dependence on Vindhyavāsin). Prior to the sixth century, there is only the older pre-kārikā Sāṃkhya and the yet older *sāṃkhya-cum-yoga* proto-Sāṃkhya of texts such as the *Mokṣadharma* and the *Bhagavadgītā*. This does not rule out the possibility that there were older *sūtra* collections on Yoga, some of which may have been current in the time of the grammarian Patañjali (per Hauer's suggestion). One gets an overall impression, however, that the present form of the *Yogasūtra* probably took shape during or after the time of Vindhyavāsin and that its attribution to Patañjali (or Hiraṇyagarbha) is somewhat on analogy with the Sāṃkhya tradition's attribution of its founding to Kapila, Āsuri, and Pañcaśikha. A. B. Keith is probably not far off the mark when he suggests that the final compilation of the *Yogasūtra* may have been occasioned by the appearance of Īśvarakṛṣṇa's *Sāṃkhyakārikā*.

SUVARṆASAPTATI

(Paramārtha's Chinese Translation of the *Sāṃkhyakārikā* with a Prose Commentary)

Among the eight commentaries on the *Sāṃkhyakārikā*, five of them are so alike in overall content and specific wording as to suggest an identity among one or more of them, an extensive borrowing of one from another, or that all five stem from a common original (some sort of *Ur*-commentary, now lost). The five commentaries with common content are Paramārtha's *Suvarṇasaptati*, Gauḍapāda's *Bhāṣya*, the *Māṭharavṛtti*, the *Sāṃkhyasaptativṛtti* (V_1), and the *Sāṃkhyavṛtti* (V_2). It was originally thought that Paramārtha's Chinese version (translated by Paramārtha between 557 and 569) was the same as the *Bhāṣya* of Gauḍapāda, but Takakusu's exhaustive (and still important) work with the Chinese text and the Gauḍapāda *Bhāṣya* in 1904 clearly proved that the two commentaries, though having much in common, are not identical.[1] Takakusu argues that the original of the Chinese commentary may have been written by the author of the *Kārikā* himself and that Gauḍapāda borrowed from the author of Paramārtha's original when he composed his *Bhāṣya* at a later date. When the commentary called *Māṭharavṛtti* was discovered, the problem of the original commentary on the *Kārikā* became even more exacerbated, for it was realized that the *Māṭharavṛtti* had even more in common with the Chinese commentary and with the *Bhāṣya* of Gauḍapāda. S. K. Belvalkar then argued that the *Māṭharavṛtti* was the original commentary upon which the Chinese translation is based and that Gauḍapāda's *Bhāṣya* is a shorter and largely plagiarized version of *Māṭharavṛtti*.[2] A. B. Keith expressed considerable skepticism about Belvalkar's proposal, because there was at least some content in Paramārtha's commentary, and in the *Bhāṣya* of Gauḍapāda, and the *Māṭharavṛtti* that was clearly not common to all.[3] This in turn inspired S. S. Suryanarayana Sastri to pursue a detailed comparison of the *Māṭharavṛtti* and Paramārtha's Chinese version in which he argued that the two commentaries are clearly different at important points and that our extant *Māṭharavṛtti* cannot be taken as Paramārtha's original.[4] S. S.

Suryanarayana Sastri also prepared a complete English translation of Takakusu's French translation of the Chinese original.[5] Umesha Mishra meanwhile set about the task of showing that the *Māṭharavṛtti* and Gauḍapāda's *Bhāṣya* differ in interesting ways and that one cannot dismiss the latter as a plagiarized form of the former.[6] Then in 1944 N. Aiyaswami Sastri published a reconstruction of the original Sanskrit of the Chinese version.[7] In his introduction to the book he carries through a detailed and exhaustive comparison between the *Māṭharavṛtti* and the Chinese commentary. He clearly proves that the present text of the *Māṭharavṛtti* is not the same as the Chinese commentary (contra Belvalkar), and he also cogently argues that the author of the Chinese original was different from the author of the *Sāṃkhyakārikā* (contra Takakusu). Regarding the original of the Chinese version, Aiyaswami Sastri offers an interesting suggestion. Already in the *Anuyogadvārasūtra* (ca. fifth century of the Common Era) of the Jains, mention is made of a certain "Māḍhava" in the context of a listing of early works and teachers on Sāṃkhya (including a revised version of *ṣaṣṭitantra*, and *Sāṃkhyakārikā*). Māḍhava is probably none other than Māṭhara. Guṇaratna in his commentary on *Ṣaḍdarśanasamuccaya* also makes reference to a certain Māṭhara text, which he refers to as "*māṭharaprānta*" (a text coming from the Māṭhara "corner" or school). According to Aiyaswami Sastri, Guṇaratna quotes one verse from the *māṭharaprānta* that also appears in our extant *Māṭharavṛtti*.[8] It is clear, however, that this *māṭharaprānta* is a later, expanded, and revised version of an older Māṭhara tradition. In other words, there may have been an original *Māṭharabhāṣya*, now lost, and a later expanded version of Māṭhara, called "*māṭharaprānta*," which is none other than our extant text called *Māṭharavṛtti*. This suggestion has the obvious merit of explaining the common content between our extant *Māṭharavṛtti* and the Chinese version (and also Gauḍapāda for that matter), but it also posits a later revised version of Māṭhara, which explains why the present *Māṭharavṛtti* contains so much obviously later material (quotations from the *Purāṇas*, much fuller discussions of logical issues, and so forth). Aiyaswami Sastri's work, in other words, tends to support the view, long since held by A. B. Keith and S.S. Suryanarayana Sastri, that there is an original or *Ur*-commentary, now no longer extant, to which many of the later commentaries on the *Sāṃkhyakārikā* are indebted.

To all of these discussions must now be added the recent work of E. A. Solomon, who has recently edited two additional commentaries, the *Sāṃkhyasaptativṛtti* (V_1) and the *Sāṃkhyavṛtti* (V_2)[9], and a painstaking comparative analysis of all of the commentaries on the *Sāṃkhyakārikā*.[10] Solomon frankly admits that the two new commentaries do not solve any of the old problems, but she is personally inclined to think that V_2 could be an original commentary by the author of the *Sāṃkhyakārikā* (and hence the original upon which Paramārtha based his translation) and that V_1 is the original upon which our extant *Māṭharavṛtti* is based. She also suggests, as has been mentioned earlier, that the Māṭhara of V_1 may be the same as the famous Sāṃkhya *nāśaka* ("destroyer of Sāṃkhya"), mentioned by Dignāga and other Buddhists. All of this is highly speculative, as Solomon herself admits, and cannot be definitely proved in the absence of considerable additional evidence.

In any case, given the present state of the evidence, it appears likely that Paramārtha's Chinese translation can still be said to be the earliest extant commentary available on the *Kārikā* (having been translated between 557 and 569), that its author is different from the author of the *Sāṃkhyakārikā*, and that it and the *Bhāṣya* of Gauḍapāda, the *Māṭharavṛtti*, the *Sāṃkhyavṛtti* (Solomon's V_2), and the *Sāṃkhyasaptativṛtti* (Solomon's V_1) are all apparently dependent on an original or *Ur*-commentary that is no longer extant. One might wish that there were more to say about the chronology and ordering of these commentaries, but Frauwallner is surely right when he comments: "Über die Zeit der Kommentare zur Sāṃkhya-*Kārikā* vor allem der *Māṭharavṛttih* und des *Gauḍapādabhāṣyam* ist mehr geschrieben worden, als ihrem inhaltlichen Wert entspricht," or, in other words, too much has been written already ![11]

The edition (E) for the following summary is that of N. Aiyaswami Sastri, editor, *Suvarṇasaptati Śāstra, Sāṃkhya Kārikā Saptati of Īśvara Kṛṣṇa with a Commentary Reconstructed into Sanskrit from the Chinese Translation of Paramārtha* (Tirupati: Tirumalai-Tirupati Devasthanams Press, 1944; Sri Venkatesvara Oriental Series No. 7). The translation (T) used for the summary is that of S. S. Suryanarayana Sastri, *The Sāṃkhya Kārikā studied in the Light of its Chinese Version*, by M. Takakusu (rendered from the French into English) (Madras: The Diocesan Press Vepery, 1933). Both of the above are based largely on M. J. Takakusu, editor and translator, "La Sāṃkhyakārikā étudiée à la lumière de sa version chinoise (II)," *Bulletin de l'École Française d'Extrême-Orient*, Vol. IV, Hanoi (1904), pp. 978-1064.

In this summary and those of other commentaries on the *Sāṃkhyakārikā*, section headings parallel the headings of the summary of the *Sāṃkhyakārikā*, which should be consulted as one reads the summaries of the commentaries.

(*Summary by Gerald J. Larson*)

I. Introductory Verses: The Scope and Task of the Sāṃkhya (E1-6; T1-6)

(*Kārikā* 1) A wise ascetic, Kapila, heaven-born and innately possessed of the four constructive predispositions, namely, meritorious behavior, discriminating knowledge, nonattachment, and power, noticed that all creatures in the world were abiding in the darkness of ignorance. Out of compassion he approached the Brahmin householder, Āsuri, who for a thousand years had been making sacrifices to heaven. Kapila spoke to Āsuri, calling into question the value of the householder's life, but Āsuri offered no reply. After another thousand years, Kapila approached Āsuri again. On this second occasion Āsuri commented that he enjoyed the life of a householder. Later, Kapila approached Āsuri yet a third time and inquired whether Āsuri had the requisite discipline and fortitude to pursue the life of an ascetic. Āsuri finally accepted the invitation of Kapila, abandoned his family, and became Kapila's disciple. Hence, the origin of the Sāṃkhya tradition.

One is compelled ultimately to pursue the life of an ascetic because of the three kinds of frustration: internal, external and celestial. Internal frustration includes both mental and physical illness. External frustration is that brought about by other men, birds, beasts, serpents, and so forth. Celestial frustration includes such natural phenomena as cold, wind, rain, and thunder. There are various ordinary remedies (medicine, and so forth) for alleviating frustration, but no ordinary remedy is certain and final. Even the remedies available from Vedic sacrifices and sacred tradition are problematic. The Vedic verse, "We have drunk soma, we have become immortal . . . ," is quoted.

(*Kārikā* 2) Whereas ordinary remedies for the alleviation of frustration are neither certain nor final, the remedies available from Vedic sacrifice and sacred tradition have the defects of (a) being impure (because they involve killing, and so forth), (b) being impermanent (because even the heavenly realm is subject to time), and (c) being uneven (because of the inequitable rewards of the sacrificial rites).

There is another, superior way, however, for overcoming frustration, which is (a) certain, (b) final, (c) pure, (d) permanent, and (e) universal. This superior way involves the discriminating knowledge (*vijñāna*) of the manifest, the unmanifest, and the knower. The manifest world is made up of:

(a) the "great one" or intellect;
(b) egoity;
(c) the five subtle elements;
(d) the five sense capacities;
(e) the five action capacities;
(f) the mind; and
(g) the five gross elements.

The unmanifest is materiality. The "knower" is consciousness. There is an ancient verse (here quoted) asserting that anyone who truly knows these twenty-five principles attains liberation regardless of the stage of life or the particular group to which he belongs.

(3) Primal creative nature produces all manifestations without itself being produced. For this reason the term "*prakṛti*" also appears as "*mūlaprakṛti*" or primordial materiality. Intellect, egoity, and the five subtle elements are both generative principles and generated products. They are generated products because they are all produced from materiality. They are generating principles because intellect generates egoity, egoity generates the five subtle elements, and the five subtle elements generate both the five gross elements and the five sense capacities.[12] The five gross elements, the five sense capacities, the five action capacities and the mind are all simply derived products (*vikāra*). Consciousness is neither a generative principle nor a generated product.

II. The Instruments of Knowledge (E7-12, T6-12)

(5) Inference is dependent on perception and is of three kinds: (a) prior or antecedent inference (*pūrvavat*) based upon the perception of a cause, for example, when one perceives a black rain-cloud, one infers that it will rain; (b) subsequent or posterior inference (*śeṣavat*) based upon the perception of an effect, for example, when one perceives that a river is swelling and muddy, one infers that it has rained further up the river; and (c) inference based upon general correlation (*sāmānyatodṛṣṭa*), for example, when one perceives that mangoes are flowering in Pāṭaliputra, one infers that they are also flowering in Kośala. These three kinds of inference also clearly relate to the three times: (a) *pūrvavat* is an inference of what will occur; (b) *śeṣavat* is an inference of what has occurred; and (c) *sāmānyatodṛṣṭa* is an inference of what is now occurring under certain comparable and general conditions.

(6) The third kind of inference (namely, *sāmānyatodṛṣṭa*) also allows one to infer that which in principle is beyond perception (*atīndriya*), and it is this kind of inference that enables one to establish the imperceptible principles of materiality and consciousness. In order to account for the experiences of satisfaction, frustration, and confusion, which accompany all awareness, there must be some root-cause that is so constituted. Therefore, one is able to infer the existence of materiality as constituted by the intelligibility constituent (*sattva*), the activity constituent (*rajas*), and the inertia constituent (*tamas*). Moreover, since all experience requires an experiencer *for* which all experience is constituted, one is able to infer the existence of consciousness as distinct from materiality.

(7) In addition to these eight conditions that prevent ordinary perception, there are also four additional things that do not *now* exist but can be talked about in terms of their absence (*abhāva*): (a) "prior nonexistence" (*prāgabhāva*) as, for example, a utensil that is to be made from a lump of clay but has not yet been made; (b) "consequent non-

existence" (*pradhvaṃsābhāva*) as, for example, a pitcher that has been broken and thus no longer exists as a pitcher; (c) "mutual nonexistence" (*anyonyābhāva*) as, for example, a cow that is not a horse and a horse that is not a cow; and (d) "absolute nonexistence" (*atyantābhāva*) as, for example, the second head or third arm of an ordinary mortal.

(8) There are three views regarding the problem of cause and effect: (a) the correct Sāṃkhya view that the effect already resides or exists potentially in the cause; (b) the Buddhist view that the effect neither exists nor does not exist in the cause; and (c) the Vaiśeṣika view that the effect does not reside in the cause but rather arises later or subsequent to the cause. The Buddhist view can be disposed of quickly, since it is obviously self-contradictory. To say that the effect neither exists nor does not exist in the cause is like saying that a certain man is neither dead nor living. Such self-contradictions cannot be admitted in a serious philosophical discussion. The Vaiśeṣika view will be discussed in the next portion of the commentary (that is, in verse 9).

III. The Notion of Preexistent Effect (E12-13, T12-13)

(9) Illustrations for the five arguments in favor of the Sāṃkhya theory that the effect preexists in the cause are that (a) something cannot arise from nothing—e.g., oil cannot be derived from sand, only from sesamum; (b) any effect requires an appropriate material cause or basis—e.g., curds can only be derived from milk, not from water; (c) anything cannot arise from just anything—e.g., grass, gravel, or stones cannot produce gold; (d) something can only produce what it is capable of producing—e.g., a potter makes a pot from a lump of clay, not from plants or trees; and (e) the very essence of the cause is nondifferent from the effect—e.g., barley plants derive from barley seeds, not from the seeds of beans. For all of these reasons the effect must necessarily exist in the cause, and the Vaiśeṣika view that the effect is not preexistent in the cause is, therefore, inadmissible.

IV. The Manifest and Unmanifest Aspects of Materiality (E13-15, T13-16)

(11) The term "*avivekin*" or "undifferentiated" is taken to mean "inseparable." That is to say, materiality and its products are inseparable from the three constituents. Consciousness is dissimilar from the six characteristics (namely, *triguṇa*, *avivekin*, *viṣaya*, *sāmānya*, *acetana*, and *prasavadharmin*) that describe the manifest and the unmanifest. On the other hand, consciousness is similar to eight of the nine characteristics of materiality described in verse 10. In other words, consciousness is similar to materiality in being uncaused, eternal, all-pervasive, not characterized by transmigration, not capable of dissolution, partless,

not related to another, and self-sufficient. Unlike materiality, which is one, however, consciousness is multiple.

V. The Three Constituents (E16-19, T17-19)

(12) The constituents interact with one another in five ways, namely, in terms of dominance, mutual dependence, origination (or one occasioning another to become dominant), pairing, and intervention (one for another), or substitution (one for another).

VI. The Inferences That Establish the Existence and Makeup of Primordial Materiality and Consciousness (E19-28, T20-28)

(16) Two kinds of production are ordinarily distinguished: (a) production that involves significant transformation (*pariṇāma*) as when milk produces cream; and (b) production that does not involve significant transformation (*apariṇāma*) as when parents produce a child. When Sāṃkhya philosophy refers to the productivity of materiality, production in the former sense is intended. That is to say, the productivity of materiality involves significant transformation.

(17) (In the Chinese text, according to S. S. Suryanarayana Sastri, the *Ṣaṣṭitantra* is referred to as the "Treatise of the Sixty Categories," suggesting, therefore, that Paramārtha considered *Ṣaṣṭitantra* to be a text and not simply a conventional list of topics.) In order to give an intelligible account of purposeful activities such as religious rites, it is necessary to infer the existence of consciousness. Also, we know that consciousness exists because of the testimony of sages (and a verse from the ancient sages is quoted here, suggesting that the nerves, bones, blood, and flesh of the body is like the earth and plaster of a house in which consciousness resides).

(18) (a) If consciousness were one, then when one person is born, all would be born, etc. Also, (b) if consciousness were one, then the varying collocations of the constituents would be unintelligible or meaningless.

(19) Consciousness is a passive spectator. Only the constituents engage in activities, and consciousness is separate from the activity of the constituents.

VII. The Association or Proximity of Materiality and Consciousness (E29-31, T28-30)

(20) Just as gold becomes hot when placed in fire and cold when placed in water and just as a person is sometimes taken to be a thief because he associates with thieves, so both materiality and

consciousness appear to take on the characteristics of one another when they are in proximity. Consciousness appears to be active, like the constituents, and materiality appears to be conscious.

(21) Consciousness is able to see and to know. Materiality is able to act. Consciousness sees and knows the constituents. The instinctual activities of the constituents spontaneously function for the sake of consciousness. The interaction of consciousness and materiality can be heuristically compared to the story of the cooperation between the blind man and the lame man. A caravan was attacked by a group of thieves. The merchants fled and left behind a blind man and a paralytic. The paralytic mounted the shoulders of the blind man, and the two together were able to get to their homes, after which they separated. Or, again, just as a male and female come together to produce offspring, so the association of consciousness and materiality brings about creation.

VIII. The Derivation of the Basic Principles (E31-32, T30-31)

(22) Synonyms for "*mahat*" are "intellect" (*buddhi*), "intelligence" (*mati*), "idea" or "assertion" (*khyāti*),[13] "knowledge" (*jñāna*), or "wisdom" (*prajñā*). The commentary then simply enumerates the various principles.

IX. The Functioning of the Thirteenfold Instrument (E33-55, T31-46)

(26) The sense capacities and the gross elements are derived from the subtle elements in the following manner. The subtle element of sound gives rise to the organ of hearing and is related to the gross element ether. The subtle element of touch gives rise to the organ of touch and is related to the gross element air. The subtle element of form gives rise to the eyes and is related to the five gross elements. The subtle element of taste gives rise to the tongue and is related to the gross element water. The subtle element of odor gives rise to the nose and is related to the gross element earth.[14] Each action capacity (the organ of speech, and so forth) functions with the various sense capacities.

(27) Among the ten senses, two (seeing and hearing) are for avoiding danger, since they function over great distances. The other eight are localized and function largely to protect the body.

(32) The thirteenfold instrument functions with respect to the ten objects of the five sense capacities and the five action capacities. Overall there are three classes of functioning, namely, seizing (*āharaṇa*), holding (*dhāraṇa*), and illuminating (*prakāśa*). Seizing is the primary function of intellect, ego, and mind. Holding is the primary func-

tion of the five action capacities. Illuminating is the primary function of the five sense capacities.

(34) Specific objects are those constituted by all three constituents. Nonspecific objects are those constituted by only one constituent.

X. The Subtle and Gross Elements (E55-58, T46-49)

(38) The subtle elements are nonspecific, and are characterized by the constituent *sattva*. They are devoid of *rajas* and *tamas*. The gross elements are specific, and are characterized by all three constituents.[15]

(39) The subtle body is made up of the five subtle elements only. It enters into the gross body born of father and mother and is nourished by the gross body. The subtle body transmigrates from life to life, but the gross body perishes at the time of death.

XI. The Subtle Body (E58-60, T49-51)

(40) The subtle body is made up of intellect, egoity, and the five subtle elements. It transmigrates accompanied by the eleven capacities (namely, the five sense capacities, the five action capacities and mind).[16]

(41) The transmigrating entity is supported by the five subtle elements, which are "nonspecific."

(42) The "causes and effects" referred to in the verse relate to the innate predispositions, which will be discussed further in verses 43-52.

XII. The Basic Predispositions (E61-80, T52-69)

(46) The story of the Brahmin with his four disciples is recounted in order to illustrate the notions of "misconception," "dysfunction," "contentment," and "attainment." Before sunrise the Brahmin and his disciples notice an object on the road in front of them. The Brahmin asks his disciples to find out what the object is. The first disciple expresses doubt as to whether the object is a post or a man. The second disciple claims that he is incapable of approaching the object. The third disciple says that he is content to wait until sunrise before approaching the object. The fourth disciple goes over to the object, examines it closely, and returns to tell the Brahmin that the object is a post. The first disciple illustrates misconception; the second, dysfunction; the third, contentment; and the fourth, attainment. The intellectual creation is said to be made up of sixteen causes and effects. The eight causes are the eight predispositions (*dharma*, and so forth). These eight effects are rebirth in heaven, release, absorption in primordial materiality, and are as enumerated in verses 44-45. These sixteen causes and effects are either *sāttvika* or *tāmasa*. The causes *dharma*, *jñāna*, *virāga*, and *aiśvarya* together with

their effects are made up of the intelligibility constituent (*sattva*). The remaining causes and effects are made up of the inertia constituent (*tamas*). When these two sets of causes and effects interact with one another, they generate fifty subdivisions, and the fifty subdivisions are to be classified into five kinds of misconception, twentyeight kinds of dysfunction, nine kinds of contentment, and eight kinds of attainment.

(51) In realizing the attainments one must practice the eight divisions of knowledge and the six contemplations. The eight divisions of knowledge include the following:

(1) listening with joy (*prīti*);
(2) listening with focused attention (śraddhā);
(3) grasping (what is said) (*grahaṇa*);
(4) remembering (*smṛti*);
(5) comprehending the basic principles (*padārtha*);
(6) reasoning (*ūha*);
(7) denying what is not true (*apohana*); and
(8) acting in accordance with what is true (*yathābhūta*).

The six contemplations include the following:

(1) understanding the level of gross reality (*mahābhūta*) and turning away from it (or the contemplation called *ūhapada*);
(2) understanding the reality of the sense capacities, the action capacities and the mind (in other words, understanding the eleven organs) and turning away from them (or the contemplation called (*dhṛtipada*);
(3) understanding the level of subtle reality (*tanmātra*) and turning away from it (or the contemplation called *upagatasamapada*);
(4) understanding the ego (*ahaṃkāra*) and the eight supernormal powers (*aṇiman*, etc.) and turning away from them (or the contemplation called *prāptipada*);
(5) understanding the intellect (*buddhi*) and turning away from it (or the contemplation called *nivṛttipada*); and
(6) understanding primal creative nature (*pradhāna*) and turning away from it to abide in contentless consciousness (or the contemplation called *kaivalyapada*).

At this point in the commentary, a subcommentary is added (presumably by Paramārtha himself), explaining the meaning of the eight attainments on the basis of their ancient names. These ancient names are, according to N. Aiyaswami Sastri's Sanskrit reconstruction:

(1) *svatāra*,
(2) *sutāra*,
(3) *tāratāra*,
(4) *pramodatāra*,
(5) *pramuditatāra*,
(6) *mohanatāra* (or perhaps better *modana* or *pramodamāna*),

(7) *ramyakatāra*,
(8) *sadāpramuditasiddhi*.

The interpretation is the following:

(1) "crossing by oneself": attaining wisdom (*prajñā*) by one's own unaided reasoning;
(2) "crossing well": attaining wisdom and release by one's own effort as well as by the help of another;
(3) "crossing all": attaining wisdom solely through the instruction of another;
(4) "crossing with joy": overcoming internal suffering and also attaining wisdom and release from a master of Sāṃkhya;
(5) "crossing with an excessive joy": overcoming internal and external suffering and also attaining wisdom and release from a master of Sāṃkhya;
(6) "crossing with full joy": overcoming internal, external, and divine or celestial suffering and also attaining wisdom and release from a master of Sāṃkhya;
(7) "crossing by love": attaining wisdom and release solely through the love or compassion of the master;
(8) "crossing by universal love": attaining wisdom and release by giving away all one has and thereby making oneself universally loved.[17]

XIII. The Empirical World (E81-84, T69-71)

(53) The eightfold divine realm is made up of Brahmā, Prajāpati, Indra, Gandharva, Asura, Yakṣa, Rakṣas, and Piśāca.[18]

XIV. Similes Illustrating the Role and Function of Materiality (E84-90, T72-76)

(61) Only materiality is the cause of release. Those who argue that God, own-being (*svabhāva*), time (*kāla*), or consciousness itself is the cause are wrong. Why? God has no constituents and, thus, cannot be the cause. Own-being cannot be established by means of perception, inference, or reliable authority and, thus, cannot be the cause. Time does not exist; it is only a modality of the manifest world. Consciousness cannot be the cause because it cannot do anything.

XV. Liberation and Isolation (E90-97, T76-83)[19]

(69 or, according to Paramārtha, 68) The reference to the duration, origin, and dissolution of the world means the following:

(a) duration: the period during which the subtle body transmigrates influenced by the predispositions;

(b) origin: the productive power of primordial materiality;
(c) dissolution: the condition of isolation attained by means of the eight attainments.

(70-71 or, according to Paramārtha, 69-70) The knowledge of Sāṃkhya was established even before the four Vedas. The Vedas and all the important schools were based on that knowledge. Kapila was the original sage, and the line of transmission was as follows: Kapila, Āsuri, Pañcaśikha (who composed a treatise of 60,000 verses, thereby greatly expanding the treatment of the Sāṃkhya, (Vindhyavāsa),[20] Ho-Kia (Gārgya), Ulūka, Po-p'o-li (possibly Vṛṣā or the Vārṣagaṇya school), and finally Īśvarakṛṣṇa (of the Brahmin family named Kauśika). A quotation attributed to Kapila is cited: "In the beginning there was just darkness (*tamas*); in this darkness, the field knower (*kṣetrajña*) dwelled; the field knower was *puruṣa*; *puruṣa* was, but knowledge did not exist; hence, only a "field" was spoken about."[21] Pañcaśikha wrote a treatise of about 60,000 verses and Īśvarakṛṣṇa summarized the content of Pañcaśikha's work in these seventy verses known as the *Sāṃkhyakārikā*.

(72 or, according to Paramārtha, 71).[22] The *Sāṃkhyakārikā* is a precise and careful summary of the *Ṣaṣṭitantra*. The reference to "sixty topics" (*ṣaṣṭi*) includes the five misconceptions, the twenty-eight dysfunctions, the nine contentments and the eight attainments together with ten additional important subjects, namely:

(1) the existence of the effect in the cause;
(2) the uniqueness (or oneness) of materiality;
(3) the goal of consciousness;
(4) the five reasons for the existence of primordial materiality;
(5) the five reasons for the existence of consciousness;
(6) isolation;
(7) the proximity of consciousness and materiality;
(8) the separation of consciousness and materiality;
(9) the plurality of consciousnesses;
(10) the continual transmigration of the subtle body until release is attained.[23]

SĀṂKHYAVṚTTI

This manuscript was edited for the first time by E. A. Solomon and published by Gujarat University in 1973.[1] The edition is based on a single palm-leaf manuscript preserved in the Jesalmere Grantha Bhandara. The first seventy-one verses of the *Kārikā* are commented upon by the *Sāṃkhyavṛtti*. The name of the author of the commentary is not mentioned, but Solomon has ventured the hypothesis that this may be the earliest of the extant commentaries on the *Kārikā*, possibly written by Īśvarakṛṣṇa himself (hence making it a *svopajñavṛtti* or autocommentary) and thereby representing the original Sanskrit commentary upon which Paramārtha based his Chinese translation (see above entry on *Suvarṇasaptati*). Solomon is quick to point out, however, that her hypothesis is only an impressionistic hunch and that a good deal of additional evidence and further research would be required before asserting her hypothesis as a firm conclusion. In support of Solomon's hypothesis there are indeed many similarities between *Sāṃkhyavṛtti* and the Chinese version of Paramārtha. At the same time, however, there are also a number of differences (for example, *Sāṃkhyavṛtti* reads and comments upon verse 63, which is not read by Paramārtha), suggesting that *Sāṃkhyavṛtti* and Paramārtha's Chinese version are both dependent on a common source (or sources?) that they have used selectively. In any case, *Sāṃkhyavṛtti* does appear to be an old text and may well be roughly contemporary with the Chinese *Suvarṇasaptati* (or, in other words, some time in the sixth century of the Common Era).

The following summary of the text is based on the E. A. Solomon edition (E) of the manuscript.

(*Summary by Esther A. Solomon*)

I. Introductory Verses: The Scope and Task of the Sāṃkhya (E1-8)

(1) The *Sāṃkhyavṛtti* does not have any introductory stanza or *namaskāra* to Kapila. It begins immediately with the story of Āsuri's encounter with the great Kapila. The threefold frustration is respon-

sible for the desire to know (a) what is ultimate, (b) what is not, (c) what is truth, (d) what is the final good, and (e) what must be done. This threefold frustration is (i) internal (both physical and mental; the physical being due to the disorder or imbalance of the three bodily humors, viz., wind (*vāta*), bile (*pitta*), and phlegm (*kapha*), and the mental being due to separation from what is dear, association with what one dislikes, and not attaining what one wants to attain); (ii) external, caused by man's natural environment (e.g., men, animals, etc.); and (iii) celestial (caused by forces constituting nature, namely, cold, heat wind, etc., and also by some evil influences, e.g., possession by spirits). Āsuri asks if there is any cause or remedy that can eradicate this threefold frustration, and whether this frustration is related to the body or to consciousness. If there is a means to get rid of these frustrations, he would apply himself to it; and if there were not, he would endure without uttering a word. Prompted by such a spirit of inquiry, Āsuri approaches the revered Kapila.

A doubt may arise as to how an inquiry deriving from frustration can itself also eradicate frustration. One born of the mother does not usually kill her. The answer to this is that sometimes this is exactly what we find in the world. A prince born of a king sometimes kills his father. Another doubt may arise: since there are well-known and easily accessible means for the removal of frustration, this inquiry becomes meaningless. The science of medicine (*āyurveda*) with its eight branches can cure physical ailments. Gaining an object of desire brings an end to mental frustration. A secure dwelling protects people from external forces. Religious rituals can bring an end to frustration due to cosmic and supernatural factors. Hence, what is the need for this inquiry? The answer is that the cure by these means is not definite or necessary (*ekānta*) and is not final (*atyanta*); the desired result may or may not occur, and there is no guarantee that the frustrations will not return.

(2) A follower of the Veda may suggest that the Veda provides a definite means for removing frustration. According to *Ṛg Veda* VIII. 48.3, the gods have drunk *soma* and become immortal; they will not have to suffer from disease, old age, or death. If such remedies are available, what is the need for renunciation and the knowledge of Sāṃkhya? It is said in the Veda that by sacrificing an animal, one wins all worlds. Scriptural means, however, are like perceptible means (e.g., Āyurveda) incapable of definitely and finally bringing an end to frustration, since they involve impurity (killing of animals, etc.), destruction (on the fruit being destroyed the sacrificer falls from that state which has been attained), and excess (there is a hierarchy in the fruits of sacrifices, and this leads to jealousy and consequent suffering). Thus, the means enjoined in the Veda are of no avail. Something that is the reverse of scriptural and perceptible means, that is to say, something that is definite, final, pure, and free from destruction and excess, would

obviously be superior. Such a means leading to the final elimination of suffering is the discriminative knowledge of the manifest, the unmanifest, and the knower, which together account for the twenty-five principles of Sāṃkhya philosophy. Intellect (*buddhi*), egoity, the five subtle elements, the eleven organs, and the five gross elements constitute the manifest; primordial materiality is the unmanifest, and "the knower signifies consciousness. It is said that if one knows these twenty-five principles, in whatever stage of life, whether he has matted hair, or a shaven head, or a tuft of hair, he would be released.

(3) These twenty-five principles can be further classified into a fourfold scheme as follows: ungenerated, generated and also generating, generated but not generating, and neither generated nor generating.

II. The Instruments of Knowledge (E8-14)

(4) According to this commentary, *arthāpatti* (presumption), *abhāva* (nonapprehension), *pratibhā* (intuition), and *ceṣṭā* (activity) can be subsumed under inference. *Aitihya* (tradition) and *aupamya* (analogy) are included in reliable authority. Illustrations are given for all these. The recognition of the three instruments of valid knowledge is essential, because the objects of knowledge (*prameya*) can be established by these.

The term "*pramāṇa*" presupposes (a) one direct instrument of knowing (namely, perception) and (b) and (c) two indirect instruments of knowing (namely, inference and reliable authority). Similarly, the term "*prameya*" presupposes (a) one direct object to be known (namely, manifest objects) and (b) and (c) two indirect objects to be known (namely, the unmanifest and the knower). Thus, the term "*pramāṇa*" stands for the class of the various instruments of knowledge, and the term "*prameya*" stands for the class of things to be known.

Sound, touch, color, taste, and smell are the objects of knowledge that are perceived by the sense capacities. What cannot be grasped by the five sense capacities is to be established by inference (e.g., fire from seeing smoke); and what cannot be established by either of these is established by reliable verbal testimony (e.g., Indra is the king of the gods; the Kuru country is in the north; and there are *apsaras(es)* in heaven). Reliable authority refers to the statements of someone who has no faults and, therefore, cannot utter a false statement. Thus, the twenty-five principles are the cognizables cognized by these three sources of knowledge.

(5) Perception is the reflective discerning by the five sense capacities of their respective objects. Inference is threefold: (i) *pūrvavat*, inference from what precedes, e.g., seeing a cloud in the rainy season,

one infers that it will rain. (ii) *śeṣavat*, inference about the whole from a part, e.g., tasting a drop of ocean water and inferring that the rest also is salty. (iii) *sāmānyatodṛṣṭa*, e.g., seeing a mango tree in bloom in this city, one infers that mango trees are in bloom elsewhere. Inference is based on the knowledge of the characteristic mark (*liṅga*) and that to which the mark belongs (*liṅgin*). For instance, seeing the triple staff, one establishes that the wandering mendicant (*parivrājaka*) is the *liṅgin*, that the staff belongs to him; or seeing the wandering mendicant as possessed of the mark, one infers the mark, namely, the triple, staff. The relation of the *liṅga* and the *liṅgin* can be any of the following types: (a) ownership (*svasvāmi*); (b) whole-part (*prakṛtivikṛti*); (c) material cause-effect (*kāraṇakārya*); (d) measure-measured (*mātrā-mātrikā*); (e) opposition (*pratidvandvi*); (f) companionship (*sahacara*); and (g) efficient cause-effect (*nimittanaimittika*). Reliable authority is unimpeachable verbal testimony. It is *āptaśruti* (i.e., the hearing of that which is intuitively known by the *āptas* namely, Hari, Hara, Hiraṇyagarbha, etc.) and *āptavacana* (the statement of the *āptas*, namely, the authors of the lawbooks, Manu and others).

(6) Which object is known by which source of knowledge? The answer is that the imperceptible materiality and consciousness are established by the *sāmānyatodṛṣṭa* (inference). The *liṅga* (mergent, characteristic mark), comprehending intellect, etc., is constituted of the three constituents, so primordial materiality from which intellect, etc., are produced must also be constituted of the three constituents. Likewise, consciousness is established by inference—there must be a consciousness for whom materiality produces the *liṅga* (intellect, etc.). Reliable, authoritative statements give knowledge with regard to that which cannot be established by perception or inference, e.g., Indra is the king of the gods, etc.

(7) It may be argued that what is not perceived in the world is not existent, and since materiality and consciousness are not perceived, they must be nonexistent. The answer to this is that, even though something is not apprehended, it does not necessarily follow that it is nonexistent. There are eight causes accounting for the nonperception of an existent thing.

(8) Of these eight causes accounting for the nonperception of an existent thing, it is due to subtlety that primordial materiality is not perceived. It is not nonexistent, for one can know of its existence on the basis of its effects, intellect, etc. Seeing that the effect is possessed of the three constituents, it is inferred that primordial materiality also is possessed of three constituents. The effect (intellect, etc.) is similar in certain respects to primordial materiality and dissimilar in others just as the son may be like his father with respect to physical form, but not with respect to virtue, etc.

III. The Notion of Preexistent Effect (E14-15)

(9) There is much difference of opinion among the venerable teachers of different schools regarding the relation between cause and effect. The Vaiśeṣikas are of the opinion that the pot does not exist in the lump of clay before its production. The Jainas say that it both exists and does not exist; and the Buddhists that it neither exists nor does not exist. The Jaina view is not tenable, for existence and nonexistence are contradictory, and if a thing is existent it cannot be nonexistent and vice versa. The Buddhists do not take up any position, so there can be no dialogue with them. The Vaiśeṣikas, however, represent an apparently cogent view that the effect is nonexistent (*asatkārya*) before its production, but this view must be repudiated.

The effect (intellect, etc.) is existent in primordial materiality before its production: (a) because what is nonexistent cannot be produced (otherwise oil could have been produced from grains of sand); (b) because of the need for an appropriate material cause (e.g., one desirous of curds uses milk); (c) because of the impossibility of all things coming from all things (e.g., gold, silver, and diamonds could be produced from grass, sand, and pebbles); (d) because something can produce only what it is capable of (e.g., a capable potter produces a pot from a lump of clay); and (e) because the effect is of the nature of the cause (e.g., rice is produced from rice seeds, not from *kodrava* seeds).

IV. The Manifest and Unmanifest Aspects of Materiality (E15-19)

(11) Thus is explained the dissimilarity between manifest and unmanifest. The points of similarity are as follows: both are characterized by the three constituents; both cannot be clearly discriminated from the constituents of which they are constituted; both are objects of enjoyment for all the consciousnesses; both are common (objects of enjoyment) to all the consciousnesses, both are nonconscious, and both are productive. Consciousness is said to have the opposite characteristics in certain respects, and to be like the manifest and the unmanifest in other respects. Consciousness is not constituted of the three constituents; it can be clearly distinguished from the constituents; it is not an object but, rather, is the subject; it is not general but is particular; it is conscious and it is nonproductive. But like primordial materiality it is uncaused, permanent, pervasive, immobile, unsupported, nonmergent, noncomposite, and independent.[2]

V. The Three Constituents (E19-24)

(12) The constituents dominate, support, activate, and interact with one another. When one of these constituents becomes powerful,

it overpowers the other two. They support each other and work together, just as three sticks supporting each other serve to support a basin. These constituents rouse each other, and each one makes the others do their own function, as also its own; thus they form a unity. They also interact and work in association. Various parables are given to illustrate the manner in which the constituents work together.

(13) Each constituent has its unique characteristic: *sattva* is light and illuminating, *rajas* is stimulating and dynamic, and *tamas* is heavy and enveloping. Yet they also function jointly as do the oil, wick, and flame of a lamp in illuminating objects like a pot in the inner recesses of a mansion. When the limbs are light and the organs are pure and capable of grasping their objects, *sattva* is dominant. When one is scattered and fickle minded but also inquisitive, *rajas* is dominant. On the other hand, when *tamas* is dominant, the limbs are heavy and the organs are inert, incapable of grasping any object. Yet the three constituents, though having differing characteristics, work in unison for the sake of consciousness, just like the parts of a lamp.

VI. The Inferences that Establish the Existence and Makeup of Primordial Materiality and Consciousness (E24-32)

(14) The unmanifest is characterized by the three constituents. If the effect is present, the cause must invariably be there. Moreover, the effect is of the same nature as the cause. If the threads are black, the cloth also is black. Thus, the cause (primordial materiality) also must be known to have these characteristics. In other words, the ultimate cause is inferred from its effects.

(15) Yet how can it be said that the unmanifest exists and is the cause of the manifest when it is not apprehended? The answer to this is that the unmanifest is existent and is the cause: (a) because of the finiteness of specific things in the world that require a nonfinite ultimate cause; (b) because of homogeneity (e.g., seeing a Brahmin boy one understands that his parents also must be Brahmins); (c) because of the potency of the cause that the process of production implies (e.g., people are active in respect of that alone of which they are capable); and (d) because of the separation or distinction between cause and effect (e.g., clay is the cause, pot is the effect). (e) Because of the uniformity of the universe (three worlds) (e.g., curds and milk).

(16) How can one primordial materiality produce a multiple world? One thread does not produce a cloth; one grass fibre does not make a mat. The answer is: creative nature can produce a multiple world because of the joint interaction of the three constituents. The constituents are transformed by the process of modification, so that the effect is nondifferent from the cause. This production is

not like parents producing a child, but is like milk being transformed into curds. This results in a variegated world. Water drunk by a serpent turns into poison, that drunk by a cow turns into milk, and that drunk by a camel into urine. Rain water as it falls from the sky is the same but assumes different tastes in accordance with the place where it falls. Thus, because of the differences among the three constituents, there is diversity in the world, depending on whether *sattva* or *rajas* or *tamas* is predominant.

(18) The plurality of *puruṣas* can be inferred for the following reasons: (a) There is great diversity in births, deaths and faculties. If there were only one consciousness, a number of pregnant women would give birth to one child. If one were born, all would be born; and if one died, all would die. Similarly, there is diversity in faculties. Some are deaf or dumb or have impaired capacities, whereas others are not impaired. (b) The actions of different individuals take place at different times. One strives for merit (*dharma*), another for love (*kāma*), a third for wealth (*artha*), and a fourth for liberation (*mokṣa*). (c) There is a difference in the predominance of the constituents. The three sons of a Brahmin are born in the same, family and yet one has *sattva* predominant in him, another *rajas*, and the third *tamas*. Had there been one consciousness, this would not have been so.

(19) The followers of Sāṃkhya argue that consciousness is a nondoer. According to Kaṇāda, Akṣapāda, and others, however, he is a doer. Nonphilosophers also suggest consciousness is a doer of action; there is a superimposition of action on consciousness, e.g., *puruṣa* walks, he runs, he does this and that. The correct view, however, is that he is a nondoer. Since consciousness is different from the three constituents, etc., consciousness is simply a witnessing presence and is, thus, isolated, indifferent, a spectator and a nondoer. This can be explained by an analogy. A wandering mendicant comes to live in a village. The village folk keep on doing or not doing their work in the field, but the mendicant remains isolated, indifferent, and a nondoer of their actions. Consciousness is like that, a nondoer, whereas the constituents are active. Thus the existence of consciousness is established together with the plurality of consciousnesses.

VII. The Association or Proximity of Materiality and Consciousness (E32-34, verses 20-21)

(20) Because of the proximity of creative nature and consciousness, the unconscious *liṅga* (intellect, etc.) appears to be characterized by consciousness, just as a pot that is neither hot nor cold in touch appears to be intrinsically cold or hot when in contact with cold or

hot water. Likewise, the indifferent consciousness appears to be characterized by activity because of the activity of the constituents. A parable illustrates this. Some robbers were going to their own village after completing their work. A learned Brahmin happened to be going the same way along with them. When the robbers were caught by the police and accused of being robbers, the Brahmin also was caught and similarly accused. Though not a robber, he appeared to be one because of his association with the robbers. In a similar manner, consciousness appears to be active because of association with the constituents, and the constituents appear to be conscious because of the presence of consciousness.

(21) Consciousness enables creative nature to be seen, and creative nature finally provides the means of liberation for consciousness. Thus, the two principles become associated, just as a king and a servant become associated with each other. One wants someone to work for him, and the other wants someone who can provide the means of maintenance. Or, again, it is like the association of the lame man and the blind man. One is able to see, and the other is able to move. Together they attain a common purpose. Creation occurs because of the association.

The commentary indicates here that the discussion of the ten fundamental topics of Sāṃkhya is now basically complete, although "separation" (*viyoga*) and "the continuation of life after the attainment of knowledge" (*śeṣavṛtti*) will also be discussed later.

VIII. The Derivation of the Basic Principles (E34-35)

(22) The manifest, experiential world (*sarga*) referred to in verse 21 is threefold : elemental or essential creation (*tattvasarga*), predispositional creation (*bhāvasarga*), and consequent or gross creation (*bhūtasarga*). Since the process of emergence is fundamental, essential creation (*tattvasarga*) is described first of all. Intellect emerges from creative nature. Egoity emerges from intellect ; the group of sixteen (namely, the eleven sense capacities and the five subtle elements) emerges from ego; and the five gross elements emerge from the five subtle elements. These are the basic twenty-five principles the true knowledge of which leads to release.

IX. The Functioning of the Thirteenfold Instrument (E35-52)

(23) Meritorious behaviour is characterized by restraint (*yama*) and restriction (*niyama*). The five restraints are: not to kill, to practice continence, to speak the truth, not to indulge in vulgar worldly mundane activities (*avyavahāratā*), and not to steal. The five restrictions are: not to become angry, to serve one's preceptor, purity, to

be moderate in eating, and not to be irresponsible or careless (*apramāda*).[4] Knowledge is twofold: external (that of musical instruments, sculpture, grammar, etc.) and internal (that of the difference between the constituents and consciousness). By external knowledge the cultural world is maintained, and by internal knowledge liberation is attained. Nonattachment is also twofold. Seeing the drawbacks in the activities of acquiring, protecting, and so on, one becomes nonattached and gives up worldly life. Such a person is not liberated, however, for such nonattachment is external. If a person has discriminative knowledge of materiality and consciousness, however, and turns away from worldly life, then this nonattachment is due to internal knowledge and leads to liberation. Power is eightfold: one becomes very minute and subtle in form (*aṇiman*); one becomes light and moves like the wind (*laghiman*); one is adored and worshiped in the three worlds (*mahiman*); one gets whatever one wants (*prāpti*) ; one moves about being the master of the three worlds (*īśitva*); one has profuse ambition, and has sufficient potency to enjoy the objects of enjoyment (*prakāmya*); one brings others under one's control (*vaśitva*); and one is undeterred in whatever condition desired (*yatrakāmāvasāyitva*), whether among the gods or among insentient things. The forms of intellect with *tamas* preponderant are the opposite.

(25) Egoity itself is threefold: (i) "modified" (*vaikṛta* or *vaikārika*) with a preponderance of *sattva* from which the pure *sāttvika* sense and action capacities emerge; (ii) "elemental" (*bhūtādi*) with a preponderance of *tamas*, from which the five subtle elements emerge; and (iii) "fiery" (*taijasa*) with a preponderance of *rajas*. The "fiery one" assists the "modified" and "elemental" by providing force or energy, and without it the "modified" and "elemental" egos would not be able to function.

(27) The mind is both a sense capacity and an action capacity, because it determines or arranges the impulses and sensations coming from these capacities—just as a man may be a wrestler among wrestlers and a cowherd among cowherds. Intentionality is the peculiar function of the mind. It functions with respect to objects in the past, present, and future.[5]

A question arises: by whom are the eleven organs created—by consciousness, or by God or naturally (*svabhāva*)? Sāṃkhya rejects all such causal entities and ascribes all creative activity to materiality and the three constituents.

(28) The term "*ālocana*" signifies awareness, and the term "*mātra*" (bare) specifies a particular or unique grasping (e.g., seeing, hearing, etc.).

(29) Intellect decides; egoity gives rise to self-awareness; and the mind reflects or analyzes. Each has, in other words, its unique function, but the three together also have a common function. This com-

mon function is the maintenance of life, constituted by the five breaths. That which comes out of the mouth and nostrils and operates with respect to external objects is *prāṇa*. The function of *apāna* is to go away or down, of *udāna* to rise, of *samāna* to stay together, and of *vyāna* to pervade the body up to the hair and nails.

(30) In perception the internal organ (namely, intellect, egoity and mind) and one of the senses function either simultaneously or successively. The four function simultaneously, but they can function one after the other also. Walking along a road, Devadatta sees a post, and he thinks, "Is it a post, or could it be a man?" If he sees a creeper going up the post he has the certain knowledge that it is a post, but if he sees movements like contracting, walking, etc., he decides, "It is a man." The post is seen and yet not seen, and there is successive functioning with respect to it. Regarding the experience of the past and future, there is simultaneous functioning of intellect, ego, and mind, but such experiences always presuppose some kind of prior perception.

(31) The thirteenfold instrument (intellect, egoity, mind, and the ten sense capacities) functions for the sake of consciousness. By nothing else is the thirteenfold instrument actuated. An illustration will explain this: a band of a hundred dacoits intends to raid a village. The leader of the band determines certain signs or hints to be followed, namely, "If someone says, 'Hā, Hā,' you enter," etc. Here the leader is like the intellect, and the robbers are like the capacities. They do their respective jobs knowing the intention of the intellect. The organs do this not for themselves but for the sake of consciousness, but they are not controlled by God or by consciousness.

(32) Seizing and holding are the functions of the organs of action, and manifesting, that of the organs of knowledge.

(33) The internal organ is threefold, and the external tenfold organ is subservient to the threefold internal organ. The external sense and action capacities function with respect to present objects, and the internal organ with respect to objects in all three times (past, present, and future).

(34) The five sense capacities function with respect to objects that are specific and nonspecific. In the case of the gods, objects are characterized by satisfaction, and are nonspecific; on the other hand, in the case of mortals, objects are characterized by frustration and confusion also, and they are specific. Of the organs of action, speech alone has sound as its object. The remaining organs of action have all five (sound, touch, color, taste, odor) as their sphere of operation.

(35) Intellect, egoity, and mind comprehend all objects in all three worlds; so this threefold internal organ is the doorkeeper (that for which the doors exist; principal) and the remaining ten organs are

the doors (that is to say, subsidiary to them) through which the former grasps objects.

(36) The eleven organs and egoity are different from each other inasmuch as all have their own objects and are distinct specifications of the constituents.[6] They illuminate (manifest) whatever there is in the three worlds just as a lamp lighted in the interior of a house illuminates the interior. They present the object to the intellect, and consciousness apprehends the object in the intellect, the object being characterized by pleasure and pain.

(37) All objects are grasped and presented by the organs to the intellect, and the intellect presents the objects to consciousness, just as a minister who receives information from spies, conveys it to the king. It is the intellect, moreover, that distinguishes the subtle difference between materiality and consciousness. Thus, the intellect enlightens consciousness, and he attains liberation. The intellect, therefore, provides both experience and liberation for consciousness.

X. The Subtle and Gross Elements (E52-53)

(38) The commentator clarifies what is meant by "nonspecific" and "specific," thus throwing light on what was said in verse 34—that the sense organs have both of these as their objects. The subtle elements operate in the sphere of the gods. They are nonspecific, because they are characterized by pleasure, and not by pain or delusion. From these evolve the five gross elements (*ākāśa* from *śabdatanmātra*, *vāyu* from *sparśatanmātra* and so on), which are said to be specific because they are comfortable, uncomfortable, and bewildering. Each of the five elements (namely, space, wind, fire, water, and earth) may bring about satisfaction, frustration, or confusion, depending on the circumstances.

XI. The Subtle Body (E53-55)

(40) The subtle body is made up of intellect, egoity, mind, the five sense capacities, the five action capacities, and the five subtle elements, and was produced from creative nature before the world became manifest. The subtle body is not confined to a particular place. It is constant, that is to say, fixed in transmigration, depending on the level of ignorance. It is devoid of experience when separated from the gross body. It is influenced by the predispositions. At the time of world dissolution, the subtle body along with the organs is dissolved into creative nature and is referred to as mergent (*liṅga*).

XII. The Basic Predispositions (E55-58)

(45) Nonattachment leads to dissolution in primordial materiality.

Nonattachment is the instrumental cause (*nimitta*) and dissolution in materiality that which is brought about (*naimittika*). From attachment that is passionate (*rājasa*) comes transmigration. Because of *rajas*, a person performs sacrifice and gives alms so that he can be happy in the next world. This attachment gives rise to transmigration. From power consisting of the eight attainments comes nonobstruction. A person can go unobstructed anywhere in the world. From the reverse of this, i.e., lack of power, there is the reverse situation. One is obstructed and frustrated in all respects. Thus, there are eight causes and eight consequences. This is the sixteenfold "consequent creation" (*naimittika sarga*).

(46) This is also known as the intellectual creation (*pratyayasarga*), since it arises out of the intellect. The intellectual creation is fourfold: misconceptions, dysfunctions, contentments, and attainments. A parable (cited above in verse 46 of the Chinese edition) illustrates the four.

XIV. Similes Illustrating the Role and Function of Materiality (E60)

(61) Some say nature (*svabhāva*) is the cause of the world. The knowers of the Veda differ and say that consciousness is the cause. Sāṃkhya asserts, however, that primordial materiality (made up of the three constituents) is the cause. The constituents—*sattva*, *rajas*, *tamas*—exist in all manifest things and, therefore, the manifest world is produced from materiality. We get white cloth from white threads and black cloth from black threads. Thus, the world possessed of constituents is produced from materiality having the three constituents. Such worlds cannot reasonably be produced from God or from consciousness, both of which are devoid of constituents. Moreover, there is no such entity as nature (*svabhāva*). Some say that time is the cause of everything. According to the Sāṃkhya however, there is no entity like time. It is not distinct from materiality.

XV. Liberation and Isolation (E61-67)

(62) Consciousness cannot be said to transmigrate, since it is devoid of constituents. Being unmodified and inactive, consciousness is not an agent, and, thus, it cannot be bound; if it is not bound, it cannot be said to be freed. Ever free as it is, it never undergoes transmigration. Consciousness is ubiquitous (omnipresent), so it cannot transmigrate. It is materiality that is bound and that is released. It puts itself in bondage and frees itself. The subtle body made up of the subtle elements, along with the thirteenfold instrument is bound by a triple bondage, namely, "personal" (*dākṣiṇa*), "natural" (*prākṛta*), and

"acquired" (*vaikārika*). When knowledge arises, it is released. Materiality, which is the support of many, i.e., of the three worlds, is bound, transmigrates, and is released. Here, by "materiality" is meant the subtle body constituted by materiality.

(64) From meditative analysis on the twenty-five principles arises the knowledge "I am not just a body; I am different from it; the body is not mine; I am different from it." This knowledge is complete and free from doubt, and thus, is pure and isolated; that is to say, this pure absolute knowledge is liberation.

(66) Since both materiality and consciousness are ubiquitous, is it not likely that another body would emerge again as a result of their association? The answer is that no further creation takes place, since the motives for the individual "dance" of life have been fulfilled (namely, experience and emancipation). Now that materiality has been seen by consciousness, both have their purposes achieved. Even though both are ubiquitous and, hence, will remain conjoined, there is no purpose served by the production of another individual body. This can be explained by the parable of the creditor and the debtor. The creditor keeps on approaching the debtor for his money and finally after the lapse of considerable time the debtor repays it. Both have their purposes fulfilled; the debtor is free from debt, and the creditor gets his money. Subsequently, they may come into contact again, but no purpose is served thereby. So also, the later association of materiality and consciousness does not give rise to another individual body.

(67) When true knowledge of the twenty-five principles has been achieved, the seven predispositions that lead to bondage (namely, merit, nonattachment, power, demerit, ignorance, attachment, and impotence) can no longer give rise to anything. As seeds being scorched by fire are incapable of sprouting forth, so with the rise of knowledge, the other predispositions cannot produce any new fruit. They no longer have causal efficacy. Yet consciousness (associated with body) continues to remain by virtue of latent dispositions. The body is produced by reason of merit or demerit achieved from a previous birth. This residue does not come to an end without yielding its fruit, and, thus, the body does not immediately perish when someone has attained knowledge. The body continues to remain for a time by virtue of merit and demerit even in the case of a man of knowledge, just as the potter's wheel continues to revolve even after the potter has finished his work.

XVI. The Transmission of the Sāṃkhya Tradition (E67-68)

(70) The great sage Kapila imparted this knowledge to the one born in the family of Āsuri. Āsuri in turn gave it to the Brahmin

Pañcaśikha, and by him it was expanded. The knowledge in brief was as follows: "In the beginning there was darkness (*tamas*) alone. In that darkness there was a field (*kṣetra*) (or *kṣetrajña*?). Darkness (*tamas*) signifies *prakṛti* and *kṣetra* (or *kṣetrajña*) signifies *puruṣa*." In this concise form it came down to Pañcaśikha who expanded it. A Brahmin of Kośala, Īśvarakṛṣṇa,[7] summarized the *Ṣaṣṭitantra* for the benefit of students.

(71) The list of descent (*paramparā*) by which this knowledge was handed down is as follows: Kapila, Āsuri, Pañcaśikha, Gārgya, Khūkacañcali (Ulūka-Bāddhali) and others, a hundred, Īśvarakṛṣṇa. Īśvarakṛṣṇa of noble understanding (*āryamati*) gave it a concise form in a text of seventy verses beginning from "*duḥkhatraya*. . ." (verse 1) to "*etat pavitram*. . ." (verse 70), after having understood the doctrine properly.

(This commentary ends with verse 71)

SĀṂKHYASAPTATIVṚTTI

This is the second of two newly edited texts (see preceding entry on *Sāṃkhyavṛtti*) prepared by E.A. Solomon and published by Gujarat University.[1] The edition is based on a single palm-leaf manuscript preserved in the Jesalmere Grantha Bhandara. The name of the author of this commentary starts with the syllable "ma" but the manuscript leaf is broken after that point and the full name cannot be recovered. The commentary is nearly identical to the extant version of *Māṭharavṛtti* (and see below under appropriate entry). In fact, argues Solomon, our present *Māṭharavṛtti* appears to be an expanded version of this commentary. Unlike the *Māṭharavṛtti*, however, it does not quote extensively from the *Purāṇas*, and this suggests that it is earlier than *Mṭāharavṛtti*. Interestingly, it quotes extensively from an Āyurvedic text. There are seventy-three verses commented upon here as in the *Māṭharavṛtti*. Verses 72 and 73—the latter being found only here and in the *Māṭharavṛtti*—may be, according to Solomon, the composition of the author of the commentary, for Paramārtha quotes verse 72 and indicates that it is a verse composed by an "intelligent man of this (school)." The *Yuktidīpikā* (see below under appropriate entry) also seems to think that verse 72 is not an original part of the text, yet in the *Jayamaṅgalā* and the *Tattvakaumudī* the verse is included in the original text.[2]

Regarding date, a reasonable guess is that this commentary is also an old text, possibly a bit later than *Sāṃkhyavṛtti* (and hence dependent on it) but roughly contemporary with *Sāṃkhyavṛtti* and Paramārtha (and thus composed some time in the sixth century). If it is the original of *Māṭharavṛtti*—and it must be said that the similarities are many and striking—it would nicely confirm N. Aiyaswami Sastri's suggestion (discussed in the *Suvarṇasaptati* entry above) that our present *Māṭharavṛtti* (referred to by Guṇaratna as a later, revised text of the *māṭharaprānta* or Māṭhara "school") is different from an older commentary by Māṭhara.

The following summary of the text is based upon the E. A. Solomon edition (E) of the manuscript.

(*Summary by Esther A. Solomon*)

I. Introductory Verses: The Scope and Task of the Sāṃkhya (E1-10)

(1) The commentary begins with an obeisance to Kapila, who, out of compassion for the world that was drowning in the ocean of ignorance, made a boat of Sāṃkhya for crossing over. Then the introductory episode of Kapila—with *dharma*, etc., manifest in him from his birth, and desirous of rescuing the world from ignorance—and a reputed Brahmin (Āsurisagotra and Varṣasahasrayājin) is given. The discussion of physical and mental suffering includes many references to Āyurveda. The places of the different humors are mentioned—the place of wind is up to the navel, of bile up to the heart, of phlegm up to the head. A list of diseases resulting from the imbalance of these humors is given at the end of the discussion of personal physical frustration. Mental frustration may be (a) due to separation from what is dear (e.g., Devadatta is separated from someone dear to him and because he continues to think of the person, personal mental frustration arises), (b) due to association with what is unpleasant (e.g., Devadatta captured by his enemies in a battle thinks, "What will they do to me?" and mental frustration arises), (c) due to nonattainment of what one desires (e.g., once Devadatta had ample prosperity, but destiny was perverse, and as he keeps on pondering over past joys, he does not get what he wants and thus experiences mental frustration). The commentary raises the question as to whom these frustrations affect—is it the body, or is there a consciousness different from the body that is affected? Āsuri also asks if these sufferings can be eliminated. If not, one must suffer silently like an ox. As Devadatta, bitten by a scorpion, inquires as to who could remove the poison and finds the right person, so Āsuri resorted to the revered Kapila, confident that he would show him the means of removing the cause of the threefold frustration.

Now one may raise a doubt as to how inquiry arising from frustration could eradicate it as well; the son born of the mother does not kill her. The answer is that we find in the world that one destroys the one from whom one is born, e.g., certain insects kill their mothers.

An objection may be raised that when the cause for the removal of these frustrations is visible (e.g., Āyurveda with its eight branches, and the like), this inquiry becomes meaningless. Satisfying objects of the senses could bring an end to mental frustration. Similarly, visible causes of the removal of the frustration due to external and celestial factors are mentioned. Hence this inquiry is meaningless. The answer to this objection is that there are two drawbacks in Āyurveda—"*naikāntabhāva*" (it is not definite, or the result does not necessarily follow) and "*nātyantabhāva*" (it is not final, the disease may return).[3] So also, the remedies in the case of the other frustrations do not bring about a definite and final cure.

(2) There is another remedy, prescribed by the Veda, and the Veda tells us of a definite result—"by sacrificing animals one attains all desires." If a Vedavādin were, therefore, to say that the injunctions of the Veda are capable of eradicating frustrations definitely and finally, the Sāṃkhya teacher's answer is: Scriptural means is like the visible means, incapable of definitely and finally bringing an end to suffering. A woman may observe all that is enjoined in the Veda and yet not have a son. One may pray for a life of a hundred years, and yet the child may die in the womb itself. Moreover, Vedic remedies involve impurity, for slaughter of animals and men, impure practices (incest, etc.) and falsehood (on occasions) are enjoined or permitted. As to the drinking of *soma*, we know that Nahuṣa, Indra, and Yayāti had drunk *soma* but also fell from the enjoyment of the fruits of their rites. And when these rites last for a day or two. . . or for a year and so are limited, how could what they have brought about be unlimited? A limited lump of clay produces a pot of limited size. Thus the fruits of Vedic rites are limited and perish. Moreover, there is a hierarchy among them, one fruit exceeding another. We know that in the world a poor person is frustrated on seeing a rich man, an ugly man on seeing a handsome one, a fool on seeing a wise man; so also in the world of the gods. Something that is the reverse of this—definite, final, pure, unexhausted, of infinite fruits, and unsurpassed because of being isolated—is necessary. Such a means is the discriminative knowledge of the manifest, unmanifest, and knower. It necessarily gives rise to its fruit so it is definite; because of the knowledge of primordial materiality it is final; since it consists of restraints and restrictions it is pure; on the body being disintegrated one does not return to the mundane world, so its fruit is unending; because it is isolated and because there is nothing superior to it, it is unexcelled.[4] (The second line is different from the well-known one—"*prakṛtijño vikārajñaḥ sarvair duḥkhair vimucyate.*")

II. The Instruments of Knowledge (E11-17)

(4) An alternative definition of reliable testimony is given: "He who is proficient in any work and has not known a fault even in thought is reliable (*āpta*); and what is taught by him is reliable testimony (*āptavacana*)." This commentary includes *arthāpatti*, *sambhava*, *abhāva*, *pratibhā* (or *pratibhāna*), *aupamya*, and *ceṣṭā* in *anumāna*, and *aitihya* in *āptavacana*. *Aitihya* is explained as the proper (correct) recollection of the Vedaśruti in a *śāstra*; that is to say, the *Dharmaśāstras*. Illustrations are given for all these instruments of knowledge. Knowable objects are those that can be known by an instrument of knowledge. Know-

ables consist of 25 principles of which some are known by perception, some by inference, and some by verbal testimony.

(6) On seeing a *vikāra* (child) we infer that the *strī* (woman, mother) must be such, so primordial materiality is established by *sāmānyatodṛṣṭa* inference. Similarly, consciousness is established by inferences, as, e.g., it is consciousness for whom materiality produces the *liṅga* (intellect, etc.). Thus the supersensuous materiality and consciousness can be established by inference, and what is manifest can be established by perception.

(8) Primordial materiality is "subtle" because it is not characterized by words, etc., and it is by reason of this subtlety that it is not apprehended, and not because it is nonexistent. How is it then apprehended? Seeing the effect we infer the existence of the cause, just as seeing the Nyāgrodha tree we infer that there is something powerful that gives rise to the Nyāgrodha tree which is its effect. But there is no effect of a hare's horn from which it could be inferred. Therefore, primordial materiality is existent and is inferred from its effects.

III. The Notion of Preexistent Effect (E17-18)

(9) The discussion here is meant to refute the *asatkāryavādins*. The following five reasons prove that the effect (intellect, etc.) exists in materiality before its production: (a) because what is nonexistent cannot be produced, e.g., oil from sand, the daughter of a barren woman, etc., (b) because of the need for an appropriate material cause—one desirous of curds uses milk. If the effect were nonexistent, he would have used water for getting it, but he does not do so. We therefore know that the effect (intellect, etc.) is existent in materiality. (c) Because of the impossibility of all things coming from all things. In this world, a thing is produced from that in which it exists, e.g., oil from sesamum; ghee from curds, etc. If the effect were nonexistent, everything could be produced from everything: silver, gold, pearls, coral, etc., could have been produced from grass, dust, sand, etc. (d) Because something can produce only what it is capable of, e.g., an artisan being equipped with instruments, material, time, and means, produces from an adequate cause that which is capable of being produced, and not what cannot be made from an inadequate cause. For example, a capable potter produces a pot out of a lump of clay. A pot cannot be produced from a jewel, etc. (e) Because the effect is of the nature of the cause; *kodrava* grows from *kodrava* seeds, and rice from rice seeds; otherwise rice could have been produced from *kodrava* seeds.

IV. The Manifest and Unmanifest Aspects of Materiality (E19-23)

(10) Materiality is the cause (*hetu*), and intellect, etc., are the

effects (*hetumat*). The intellect is derived from primordial materiality, egoity from intellect, and so on. Cause (*hetu*) is twofold: *kāraka* (productive) and *jñāpaka* (cognitive). Materiality, intellect, egoity, and the subtle elements are the fourfold productive causes; and misconception, dysfunction, contentment, attainment, and the supporting creation (*anugraha*) are the fivefold cognitive causes. What results from this twofold cause is the "effect" (*hetumat*). At the time of transmigration, the effect (intellect, etc.) belonging to the subtle body associated with the thirteenfold organ, transmigrates, so it is "mobile." A thing is "supported" in that from which it is produced: intellect is supported in primordial materiality, egoity in intellect, and so on. The five gross elements are dissolved in the subtle elements and so on. Thus, the effect (intellect, etc.) is mergent (*liṅga*). As in the world, so long as the father is living the son is not independent, so intellect, etc., are dependent (*paratantra*); intellect is dependent on primordial materiality, egoity on intellect and so on. After explaining these characteristics of the manifest, the commentary says that the unmanifest has the opposite characteristics. It comments on the reverse nature in each case.

(11) The points of similarity between manifest and unmanifest are shown. The effects (intellect and so forth) are possessed of three constituents (*sattva, rajas, tamas*); so also is materiality possessed of them; for it is said that the effect is of the nature of the cause. Black cloth only can be produced out of black threads. So, seeing that the manifest world is possessed of three constituents, one infers that primordial materiality also has three constituents. No clear-cut division can be made between the manifest and the constituents, for what are the constituents is the manifest, and what is the manifest are the constituents. So also, materiality cannot be distinguished. Hence, the manifest and the unmanifest are not distinctively different (*avivekin*). This commentary, although showing that the consciousness has the opposite characteristics, and is like the manifest or unmanifest in others, specifically states that consciousness is not common or one: One consciousness is not common as an enjoyer to different bodies. Rather, consciousnesses are many.

V. The Three Constituents (E23-26)

(12) Various qualities are mentioned as being characteristic of each constituent: (a) intelligibility constituent (*sattva*): agreeableness, (*prīti*), satisfactoriness (*sukha*), propriety (*ārjava*), kindness (*mārddava*), truth (*satya*), honesty (*śauca*), modesty (*hrī*), intelligence (*buddhi*), purity (*śuddhi*), patience (*kṣamā*), compassion (*anukampā*), knowledge (*jñāna*), etc.—all these are characteristic of the predominance of *sattva*; (b) activity constituent (*rajas*): disagreeableness (*aprīti*), frustration

(*duḥkha*), hatred (*dveṣa*), malice (*droha*), envy (*matsara*), blame (*nindā*), pride (*stambha*), sexual desire (*utkaṇṭha*), dishonesty (*nikṛti*), murder (*vadha*), binding (*bandhana*), cutting (*chedana*), etc.; (c) inertia constituent (*tamas*): oppressive (*viṣāda*), confusion (*moha*), ignorance (*ajñāna*), intoxication (*mada*), sloth (*ālasya*), fear (*bhaya*), depression (*dainya*), heterodoxy (*nāstikya*), insanity (*unmāda*), sleep (*svapna*), etc.

(13) An opponent objects that *sattva, rajas,* and *tamas* should not be regarded as distinct when their nature is such that one can produce the functions of all. This is wrong, however. Each constituent has its exclusive characteristic and so it is different from the other two.

VI. The Inferences that Establish the Existence and Makeup of Primordial Materiality and Consciousness (E26-35)

(14) It has been said that the manifest is made up of three constituents, not distinctly different, etc.: how can it be known that the unmanifest also has these characteristics? This is proved from the possession of the three constituents. What is constituted is not distinctively different (*avivikta*), what is not distinctly different is objective (*viṣaya*), what is objective is general (*sāmānya*), what is general is nonconscious (*acetana*), and what is nonconscious is productive in nature (*prasavadharmin*). Thus all these characteristics are established just on the basis of the constituted nature of the unmanifest. The effect and the cause are present together. Where the threads are, the cloth is; and where the cloth is, the threads are. He who sees the threads sees the cloth and vice versa. So also is the relation between manifest and unmanifest. Primordial materiality is distant and the manifest is close. He who sees the manifest sees the unmanifest and the Yogin who sees primordial materiality sees also the manifest. Thus, since the effect and the cause are found together, it is established that the unmanifest is endowed with the characteristics of not being clearly distinct, etc. Moreover, the effect is of the same nature as the cause. This is what we see in the world. From a bitter *nimba* tree, we get bitter juice, and from a sweet tree we get the sweet juice of grapes, etc.

(15) But how can it be said that primordial materiality and pure consciousness exist when they are not apprehended? Things may exist even when not apprehended, e.g., the peak of the Himālaya.

(16) The one primordial materiality produces manifold effects because of the interaction of the three constituents. As the streams come together to form the Gaṅgā, and as threads unite to produce the cloth, so the three constituents in creative nature together produce the manifest. It is to be noted that a cause produces an effect by (a) undergoing modification or (b) not undergoing modification. A lump of clay, a stick and threads, etc., are the cause of a pot without undergoing modifications, whereas milk is the cause of curds by a process

of modification. What sort of cause is materiality? It is a cause that works by means of transformation. (How then can the diversity be accounted for?) As water turns into snow in the Himālayas or as sugarcane juice is modified into different kinds of sugar, etc., or as milk is turned into whey, curds, etc., so one unmanifest materiality is turned into the (personal) intellect, egoity, etc., and into the (external) cold, heat, etc., and into the (celestial) gods, *gandharvas*, etc.

If it is asked how the three worlds produced from one materiality are so unlike each other—gods are happy, human beings are miserable, and lower beings stupefied or deluded—the answer is: because of the difference in the respective substrata of the constituents. As water of uniform nature falls from the sky and reaching the earth assumes different tastes and conditions, so the three worlds produced from one materiality become different owing to the unevenness of the constituents, *sattva* being predominant among the gods, *rajas* among human beings, and *tamas* among lower beings, which accounts for their happiness, misery, and delusion respectively.

(17) Some teachers say that there is not a supreme self (*paramātman*) different from the body, organs, intellect, etc. The answer is: as in the case of a sheath for a sword, so there is a self different from the body, and it is subtle like materiality. In the explanation of "basis" (*adhiṣṭhāna*) a quotation from *Ṣaṣṭitantra* is given: "Materiality is active, having consciousness as its basis" (*puruṣādhiṣṭhitaṃ pradhānaṃ pravartate*). "Subjective experience" is explained thus: there are six tastes: seeing food possessed of these, an enjoyer is established—there is an enjoyer whose food this is. So, seeing the manifest and unmanifest materiality, it is established that there is this highest self or consciousness of whom the manifest and the unmanifest is the object of enjoyment (*bhojana*).

(18) By means of the above-mentioned five reasons we understand that there is consciousness over and beyond the body. A question arises: is there one consciousness in all the bodies, or is there a consciousness in each body? This doubt arises because teachers hold different views. The followers of the Veda say that one consciousness is apprehended in all bodies like one thread running through all the beads (jewels). Or are there consciousnesses like the "*jalacandra*" (moon in the water)—i.e., numerous moons seen in the river, well, pond, sea, etc.? Is there one consciousness according to the first analogy, or are there many consciousnesses like the numerous moons? The answer is: there are many consciousnesses: (a) because of the individual restriction seen in respect of birth, death, and organs. Some are of low birth, some of middling, and some of high birth. If there were one consciousness, one and the selfsame would be of low birth and high birth; but some are low, some middling, and some high. Hence, there is a plurality of consciousnesses. This individual restric-

tion is seen in the case of death. "My brother is dead," "My father is dead" (that is to say, death pertains individually to each). Hence, there is a plurality of consciousnesses. Some interpret the first reason (a) differently. In this world when at some time someone dies, exactly then another dies. If there be one consciousness, all would die on one dying, and all would be born on one being born, but we find that others die. Hence, there is a plurality of consciousnesses. "Functional capacities" (*karaṇaniyama*) signifies the sense capacities. Some are deaf, others are not deaf, some blind, others not, and so on. So those with impaired capacities are different and those with unimpaired capacities are different. Thus, because of the individual restriction in respect of the sense capacities we see that there are many consciousnesses. (b) The actions of different individuals take place nonconcurrently. There are people with different motives. One acts being motivated by merit (*dharma*), another by desire (*kāma*), and a third by liberation (*mokṣa*). A Brahmin is engaged in the work of a Brahmin, a Kṣatriya in that of a Kṣatriya and so on. Thus, consciousnesses are many. (c) There is difference in the respective predominance of the constituents. A Brahmin had three sons—all costudents and born of the selfsame parents. Yet one was dominated by *sattva* and was intelligent, happy, and pure. The second had *rajas* predominant, was miserable, and was of wicked intellect; and the third had *tamas* predominant and was deluded. Hence, there is a plurality of consciousnesses.

(19) Is consciousness a doer or a nondoer? We hear in the world: consciousness goes, runs, stands; this was done by consciousness. The teachers who are followers of the Veda say that consciousness is a doer; and so also the *Vaiśeṣikas*. Because of this difference of opinion there is doubt. The (Sāṃkhya) answer is that consciousness is a nondoer. Devoted to restraints and restrictions, an ascetic is living in a town. Whereas the citizens are performing their functions—sacrificing, agriculture, trade, etc.—he is just a witness; he experiences cold and heat that come according to the seasons. Similarly, consciousness (*kṣetrajña*) in the midst of the manifold modifications of the constituents is just a witness. Unlike the monk telling the quarreling citizens that their action was good or bad, he is just indifferent and has nothing to do with anyone. He is neither a doer, nor one who provokes to action.

VII. The Association or Proximity of Materiality and Consciousness (E35-37)

(20) Various kinds of mutual contact (*saṃyoga*) are listed (see *Māṭharavṛtti* for enumeration), but all are rejected in favor of the Sāṃkhya teleological view (*arthahetuka*).

(21) The word "*tat*" in "*tatkṛtaḥ sargaḥ*" is explained as referring to the association between materiality and consciousness. As by the union of a woman and a man, a son is born, so there is the production of the empirical world by the contact of materiality and consciousness.

IX. The Functioning of the Thirteenfold Instrument (E38-53)

(23) Intellect is characterized by reflectively discerning, e.g., "This is a post; this is a man." Meritorious behavior (*dharma*) is characterized by *yama* (restraint) and *niyama* (restriction) and is taught to the people of different *varṇas* and *āśramas*. The five restraints and restrictions are explained as in *Sāṃkhyavṛtti*. Continence (*brahmacarya*) is broadly defined as desisting from the attachment to all pleasures—sexual or others. In the exposition of the *tāmasa* form of intellect, the commentary is quite elaborate. The ten vices contrary to the restraints and restrictions are mentioned as constituting demeritorious behavior. "Ignorance" signifies the lack of apprehension of materiality and consciousness and obsession for grammar and similar worldly pursuits; "attachment" signifies passion for or attachment to objects and to materiality. Impotence signifies not having the eight attainments. From intellect possessed of four *sāttvika* forms and four *tāmasa* forms is produced egoity.

(27) Mind is an organ of action among the organs of action and an organ of knowledge among the organs of knowledge, as Devadatta does the work of a cowherd among cowherds, of a Brahmin among Brahmins, and of a wrestler among wrestlers. The mind is such because it operates with respect to the functioning both of the organs of knowledge and of the organs of action. It is an organ because of similarity of characteristics, for like the organs of knowledge and the organs of action, the mind also is produced from the *sāttvika* egoity.

A question arises: by whom are the eleven capacities created—by consciousness, by God, or by a thing's own nature? It may be argued that primordial materiality, intellect, and egoity are insentient, so the organs grasping their respective objects must have been created by the sentient consciousness of God or nature. According to Sāṃkhya, the difference of the organs is in accordance with the particular modifications that the constituents undergo. The eleven capacities grasp their respective objects. Another questions arises: Who put these organs in their own places? Was it consciousness or God or nature? This is refuted as above, the Sāṃkhya answer being that it was the constituents present in egoity that located the organs in their own places. Therefore, it is owing to the particular modification of the constituents and owing to the difference of the external objects of the organs that the organs are different.

(30) In perception, intellect, egoity, mind, and one of the senses function simultaneously or successively. In fact, the functioning is always successive, but the time between the functioning is so little that the functioning is said to be simultaneous. To illustrate this, the example of Devadatta going on a road and having a doubt whether a thing at a distance is a post or a man is given. The eye sees form; the mind reflects on it; egoity conceives; and intellect arrives at decisive knowledge. Such is the case with the other senses also.

(32) "Seizing" refers to the capacities, "holding" refers to egoity, and "illuminating" refers to the intellect; but surprisingly, immediately afterward the action capacities are said to seize and hold the thing manifested by the sense capacities; e.g., the hand seizes and holds a pot manifested by a light.

X. The Subtle and Gross Elements (E53-55)

(38) The subtle elements are nonspecific inasmuch as they are characterized by happiness and are the objects of the gods. Even among the gods, of course, *rajas* and *tamas* are certainly present, but *sattva* is predominant. The objects of the gods are nonspecific, whereas those of human beings are physical (gross) and are characterized by happiness, misery, and delusion, and are specific.

(39) At the beginning of the creation of all three worlds, subtle bodies are constituted out of the five subtle elements. This subtle body enters the mother's womb; and the mother's blood and the father's semen are assimilated with it. The juice of what the mother eats or drinks is assimilated to what is contributed by the father and the mother. This enables the child's body to grow. The shape of the subtle body becomes like that of the external body—hands, feet, etc. The learned say that the external body has six constituents—blood, flesh, and hair are generated from the mother, and muscles, bones, fat from the father. Thus, this external body is assimilated with the subtle body. When the child emerges from the mother's womb at the time of birth, it begins to assimilate unto itself the external world. Thus, the specific components of the human body are threefold—(a) the subtle, (b) what is generated by the parents, and (c) the gross elements. The prefix "*pra*" in "*prabhūtaiḥ*" ("gross elements") signifies that earth (the external gross elements), etc., are meant. These are the threefold specific components and are the basis for comfortable, uncomfortable, and bewildering experiences. The subtle bodies produced in the initial creation are constant. They transmigrate, impelled by the merit and demerit accrued in the course of gross embodiments. At the time of death the part contributed by the parents leaves the subtle body and perishes, and the subtle body transmigrates. The subtle body remains constant so long as transmigration continues. So long

as knowledge is not produced, the subtle body continues transmigrating. When knowledge arises, it ceases to exist.

XI. The Subtle Body (E56-58)

(41) The relation between the thirteenfold instrument and the subtle body is that of supporter-supported. The supported cannot remain without the support. The picture cannot remain without the support of wall or canvas (on which it is painted), so the thirteenfold organ cannot remain without the support of the subtle body made of the nonspecific subtle elements.

(42) The subtle body, in order to achieve the goal of consciousness, assumes many roles in the context of the efficient causes (*nimitta*) (viz., meritorious or demeritorious behavior, etc.) and what is achieved thereby (*naimittika*, viz., birth as gods, men, etc.).

XII. The Basic Predispositions (E58-67)

(43) The predispositions that determine rebirth are threefold—innate (*sāṃsiddhika*), natural (*prākṛtika*), and derived (*vaikṛtika*). The innate dispositions are four—meritorious behavior, knowledge, nonattachment and power—which were innate in the great sage Kapila born in the initial creation. The natural are the predispositions that arose all of a sudden in the four sons of Brahmā (Sanaka and others), when they were sixteen years of age. The derived are those that arise from the instructions of teachers. Knowledge is derived from the teacher; from knowledge comes nonattachment; from nonattachment, merit; and from merit comes power.

(44) What are the efficient causes and consequences? Merit is the efficient cause by means of which the subtle body goes upward, i.e. assumes a godly existence. The divine realm is eightfold, encompassing the realms of Brahmā, Prajāpati, Indra, Pitṛs, Gandharvas, Yakṣas, Rākṣases, and Piśācas. By means of demerit the subtle body goes downward into the five kinds of lower beings: *paśu* (domestic animals), *mṛga* (wild animals), *pakṣin* (birds), *sarīsṛpa* (reptiles), *sthāvara* (immovables, trees, etc.). Demerit is the efficient cause and going downward is the consequence thereof. By means of the knowledge of the twenty-five principles, the subtle body ceases to exist, that is to say, is finally released. So knowledge is the efficient cause and liberation is the consequence thereof. From the opposite, i.e., from ignorance, when one thinks "I am handsome", etc., one binds oneself to births among the lower beings, human beings, and gods and does not attain emancipation. So ignorance is the efficient cause, and bondage (*bandha*) is the consequence thereof. Bondage is threefold: (i) when one conceives the eight generative principles—the unmanifest, intellect, egoity, and the

five subtle elements—as the highest (*prakṛtibandha*), (ii) when one regards birth in the region of Brahmā, etc., as the final good (*vaikārika-bandha*), (iii) when one uses sacrifices and religious acts for personal gain (*dakṣiṇābandha*).

(45) Nonattachment leads to dissolution in materiality. For example, a person is detached; he has control over his organs; he is not attached to the objects of enjoyment; he is devoted to restraints and restrictions; only he does not have the knowledge of the 25 principles. By virtue of this nonattachment backed by ignorance he does not get liberation. But he regards himself as released when he is just merged in the eight generative principles. Again, at the time of transmigration he transmigrates, a body is produced for him in one of the three worlds. One who has attachment that is passionate (*rājasa*) performs sacrifice, gives gifts (in charity) with the idea that he would be happy in the next world. Due to this attachment there is transmigration—birth among the gods, human beings, lower beings, or inanimate things. Attachment is the efficient cause, and transmigration (*saṃsāra*) is the consequence thereof. By means of power consisting of the eight attainments, there is nonobstruction in respect of all that is desired, but not attachment. Here power is the efficient cause and nonobstruction is the consequence thereof. And from the reverse of this (i.e., from impotence) there is obstruction, i.e., nonobtainment of what is desired. Here impotence is the efficient cause and obstruction the consequence thereof. Thus, there are eight efficient causes and eight consequences resulting from them. This is the sixteen-fold *nimittanaimittika sarga*.

(46) The *nimittanaimittika sarga* is known as the intellectual creation (*pratyayasarga*), because it arises from the intellect. It is again fourfold—misconception, dysfunction, contentment, and perfection. Misconception signifies doubtful knowledge. "Is it a post or a man?" Second, seeing a post, a man does not know the difference. This is dysfunction. Third, he does not want either to doubt or to know. This is contentment. Fourth, the thing being seen, he sees a creeper climbing up the thing and a bird sitting on it and he has the determinate or certain knowledge, "This is a post." This is attainment. Due to the impact of the imbalance of the three constituents, when one or the other of the constituents is predominant, and the others subdued, there arise 50 varieties of these four kinds of intellectual disposition, viz., 5 kinds of misconception, 28 kinds of dysfunction, 9 kinds of contentment, and 8 kinds of attainment.

(48) (a) Darkness (*tamas*) is eightfold. One who recognizes the eight generative principles as the highest merges into these and merged into these thinks that he is liberated. This is the eightfold darkness. (b) Gods like Brahmā, Indra, and others, being attached to power (namely, the eight attainments), do not attain liberation and when power is exhausted, they transmigrate. This is the eightfold confusion

(*moha*). (c) The five objects of sense of the gods are characterized by satisfactoriness, and the five of human beings are characterized by being satisfying, frustrating and confusing. All beings from the gods to the lower beings are attached to these and think that there could not be any higher happiness. They do not try to attain knowledge. This is the tenfold great confusion (*mahāmoha*). (d) A person frustrated with respect to the above-mentioned ten sense objects and eight attainments becomes angry, and this anger is the eighteenfold gloom (*tāmisra*). (e) Blind gloom (*andhatāmisra*) is also eighteenfold. If, while one is enjoying the above eight powers and ten sense objects of the gods and men, one has to leave them and to be taken away by death, one experiences mental anguish. This is the eighteenfold blind gloom. Thus there are 62 sub-varieties of the five misconceptions.

49. Injuries to the 11 organs together with the seventeenfold injuries to the intellect together make up the 28 varieties of dysfunction. Injuries to any of the eleven organs (blindness, etc.) render them incapable of grasping their objects. The 17 injuries to the intellect are due to the failure of the ninefold contentments and eightfold perfections (attainments).

(50) There are four kinds of internal contentment: (a1) Belief in primordial materiality. For example, someone has the knowledge of just materiality, but does not know whether it is eternal or noneternal, sentient or insentient, possessed of constituents or devoid of them, ubiquitous or not. He is contented with the knowledge of just the existence of materiality and renounces worldly life. Such a one does not attain liberation. (a2) Belief in a material basis. Someone acquires the triple staff, basin, gourd, black deer skin, rosary, etc., and hopes to be liberated. Being so contented, he does not acquire knowledge. Such a person is not released. (a3) Belief in time as ultimate. A person does not go to a teacher who knows the principles, for he thinks that there will be liberation by virtue of time (i.e., when the right time comes); he does not acquire knowledge for he feels that it will serve no purpose. For such a person with this complacent disposition there is no release. (a4) Belief in destiny. A person does not approach a teacher who knows the principles, for he thinks there will be release by virtue of destiny or providence; he does not acquire knowledge for he feels that it will serve no purpose. For a man with such an attitude there is no release.

The remaining five contentments are external. (b1) A person feels that in order to acquire objects of enjoyment he has to engage himself in agriculture, cattle rearing, trade, etc., and this means suffering in the form of worry, effort, etc. He keeps himself away from the objects of enjoyment and rests contented. This is the fifth contentment. (b2) One finds that whatever wealth, grains, etc., he acquires have to be protected from the king, thieves, etc., so he desists from them. This is the sixth contentment. (b3) Moreover, even when the earned things are protected, they get exhausted when enjoyed. Thinking thus, a person desists from them. This is the seventh contentment. (b4) One may find ways of ensuring against the evils of earning, protecting, exhausting, but our organs are never satisfied. Thinking thus, a person desists from the objects of enjoyment and attains complacency. This is the eighth contentment. (b5) Even when one can fight against the evils of earning, protecting, exhausting, and nonsatisfaction, the operation of earning, etc., is not free from violence (*hiṃsā*). He has to obstruct and injure other creatures in the process. Thinking thus, a person keeps away from the objects of enjoyment and attains complacency. This is the ninth contentment. These contentments signify that the person feels that he can obtain liberation by virtue of nonattachment alone, even without knowledge; but actually these contentments cannot lead to emancipation. (These contentments are here provided respectively technical names: *ambhas, salila, augha, vṛṣṭi, sutāra, supāra, sunetra, marīcika, andhamāmbhasikam.* The reverse of these are called *atuṣṭis* (noncontentment): *anambhas, asalila, anaugha, avṛṣṭi, asutāra, asupāra, asunetra, amarīcika, anandhamāmbhasikam.*)

(51) The eight attainments are: reflective reasoning, oral instruction, study, the threefold destruction of frustration, acquiring knowledge from friends, and an open temperament. (The exposition of the first four *siddhis* and a part of the exposition of the fifth is missing.) (These attainments have been given the following technical names by the early teachers: *tāra, sutāra, tāranyanta, pramoda, pramudita, modamāna, ramyaka, sadāpramudita.* The reverse of these are the *asiddhis*: *atāra, asutāra, atārayanta, apramoda, apramudita, amodamāna, aramyaka, asadāpramudita.*) As an elephant curbed by a hook can be controlled easily, so one hindered or checked by misconception, dysfunction, and contentment does not attain knowledge. So one must avoid these and resort to the attainments. True knowledge results from the attainments, and from true knowledge there will be emancipation.

(52) Predispositions cannot exist without the subtle body and the subtle body cannot exist with the dispositions. That is to say, the *lingasarga* and *bhāvasarga* arose in the initial creation.

XIII. The Empirical World (E67-70)

(53) There is a third creation known as the empirical world. In it, the divine order is eightfold, relating to Brahmā, Prajāpati, Indra, Pitṛ, Gandharva, Yakṣa, Rākṣasa, and Piśāca. The order of lower beings is fivefold: *paśu* (cattle, animals), *mṛga* (wild animals), *pakṣin* (birds), *sarīsṛpa* (reptiles) and *sthāvara* (immovables). The human order is one from Brahmins to low classes (*cāṇḍāla*).

(54) The upper, eightfold creation from Brahmā to the Piśāca is

dominated by *sattva* (though *rajas* and *tamas* are there), and the gods are mostly happy. The lower, fivefold creation from animal to immovable is dominated by *tamas*, and the middle creation of human beings is dominated by *rajas* (and characterized by frustration). This fourteenfold creation from Brahmā to a blade of grass is the empirical world.

(55) A question arises: who is it among the gods, men, and lower beings who experiences satisfaction and frustration? The answer is given that it is the sentient consciousness that is the basis for the experiences of the suffering of old age and death. Creative nature and its effects are insentient: the consciousnesses are sentient, and, thus, it is consciousness that experiences frustration. How long does the consciousness experience frustration? Until the essential core (*liṅga*) consisting of intellect, etc., recedes or retires. And when the essential core recedes, consciousness attains emancipation.

(56) This creation, starting with intellect and ending with the gross elements, was brought about by materiality. Now, it may be asked why this creation was brought about. It was for the sake of the release of each consciousness so that the consciousnesses in the world of gods, man, and lower beings could atttain emancipation.

XV. Liberation and Isolation (E74-79)

(62) In the world, the *śiṣṭa* (learned, well-instructed) say that consciousness is bound, consciousness is freed, consciousness transmigrates. In fact, consciousness is not bound, because it is ubiquitous, unchanging, immobile and a non-doer. Since it is not bound, it is not freed. It is ubiquitous so it does not transmigrate. Consciousness is all-pervading. Those who do not know consciousness say that it is bound, released, and transmigrates. What, then, is released? What transmigrates? It is materiality that binds itself, frees itself, and transmigrates.

XVI. The Transmission of the Sāṃkhya Tradition (E79-81)

(70) Kapila imparted the doctrine of the Sāṃkhya to Āsuri. Āsuri in turn imparted it to Pañcaśikha, and Pañcaśikha, imparted it to many disciples. A passage is quoted: "In the beginning there was only darkness. In that darkness the 'knower of the field' (*kṣetrajña*) functioned." The darkness refers to materiality. The "knower of the field" refers to consciousness. The term "doctrine" (*tantra*) signifies *Ṣaṣṭitantra*—that *śāstra* in which sixty topics (*padārtha*) are taught. Having mastered the *Ṣaṣṭitantra*, Īśvarakṛṣṇa became proficient. He then summarized the *Ṣaṣṭitantra*.

(71) This knowledge descended in a line of pupils—Kapila, Āsuri,

Pañcaśikha, Bhārgava, Ulūka, Vālmīki, Hārīta, and others. Īśvarakṛṣṇa inherited the tradition from them.

(72) All the subjects that have been stated in the *Ṣaṣṭitantra* have been stated in the *Saptati* (collection of 70 verses). SK 47 speaks of the fifty intellectual dispositions (*pratyaya*); and there are ten fundamental topics, namely, *astitvam, ekatvam, arthavattvam, pārārthyam, anyatvam, nivṛttiḥ, yogaḥ, viyogaḥ, bahavaḥ puruṣaḥ sthitiḥ śarīrasya ca śeṣavṛttiḥ*. (See Introduction to the present volume for translation.) The five reasons in verse 15 establish the *ekatva* (oneness) and *arthatva* (necessity) of primordial materiality. Verse 17 establishes its *parārthatā* (being meant for another), "*tadviparītas tathā ca pumān*" (verse 11) establishes the *anyatva* (difference) between materiality and consciousness. Verse 21 establishes the *nivṛtti* (cessation) of materiality. Verse 21 establishes the *saṃyoga* (contact), and verse 68, the *viyoga* (separation, dissociation). Verse 18 establishes the *bahutva* (plurality) of *puruṣas*; "*cakrabhramavat*" (verse 67) establishes *śeṣavṛtti*. Thus, sixty subjects are taught in the *Ṣaṣṭitantra*. The same sixty are taught in the *Saptati*. Only the parables (illustrative stories) and the dialectical discussions are left out.

(73) How could this tiny text state all the subjects? Since the *Ṣaṣṭitantra* is vast, it has been summarized in this text. It is *śāstra*—that by which people are summoned from the wrong path. There is consideration of doer, enjoyer, object of enjoyment, and emancipation. Or, it is called "*śāstra*" because it teaches about suffering. Regarding content, this *Saptati* is not lacking in anything. As even a huge body can be reflected even in a small mirror, so in this tiny *śāstra* there is the manifestation of the complete *Ṣaṣṭitantra*.

GAUḌAPĀDA

If one does not accept the identity of the Gauḍapāda of the *Sāṃkhya-kārikābhāṣya* with the early Vedāntin Gauḍapāda of the *Māṇḍūkya-kārikā*, then nothing is known about Gauḍapāda the Sāṃkhya writer other than the fact that he wrote a commentary on the *Kārikā* that has much in common with Paramārtha's Chinese translation, and with the *Sāṃkhyavṛtti*, *Sāṃkhyasaptativṛtti* and *Māṭharavṛtti*. As we have been suggesting, these five commentaries bear a strong family resemblance, and, although they are not by any means identical, they all appear to have used a common original and may, in addition, be dependent to some extent on one another. E. A. Solomon, for example, has pointed out that Gauḍapāda's *Bhāṣya* appears to follow both the *Sāṃkhyavṛtti* and Paramārtha's Chinese translation, whereas the *Māṭharavṛtti* appears to be heavily dependent on the *Sāṃkhyasaptativṛtti*.[1] Among the five, the *Māṭharavṛtti* (see below under appropriate entry) is clearly late (ninth century or later) and may well represent a later attempt to systematize and expand the earlier four commentaries with the *Sāṃkhyavṛtti* being used as the core text in the expansion. In any case, in the absence of additional evidence, the *Bhāṣya* of Gauḍapāda can be placed at a date that is roughly contemporary with Paramārtha, the *Sāṃkhyavṛtti* and the *Sāṃkhyasaptativṛtti*, that is to say, some time in the sixth century. As mentioned earlier, Gauḍapāda comments only on the first sixty-nine verses of the *Kārikā*.

If one accepts the identity of Gauḍapāda the Sāṃkhya writer with the early Vedāntin Gauḍapāda of the *Māṇḍūkyakārikā*, then one gains a certain confirmation for the above-suggested dating around 500 or shortly thereafter, for there is now a general consensus that the Vedāntin Gauḍapāda is to be dated about 500 of the Common Era (based upon III.5 of the *Māṇḍūkyakārikā*, cited in Bhāvaviveka's *Tarkajvālā*, which was composed toward the middle of the sixth century). The arguments pro and con for identifying the two Gauḍapādas are not especially strong on either side. The arguments against identity are basically two: (a) the philosophical views of the two Gauḍapādas are clearly different; and (b) the Gauḍapāda of the *Sāṃkhya-*

kārikābhāṣya does not appear to have the philosophical depth of the Gauḍapāda of the *Māṇḍūkyakārikā*. Both arguments are trivial and can be easily answered. Regarding the former, it is hardly surprising that the philosophical views are different, since each text addresses a different philosophical subject area (that is to say, Sāṃkhya and early Vedānta). Regarding the latter, it is hardly surprising that an elementary or introductory commentary on a text would come across as having less philosophical depth (namely, Gauḍapāda's *Sāṃkhyakārikābhāṣya*) than a text in which an author is making a specific effort to set forth his own original philosophical views (namely, Gauḍapāda's *Māṇḍūkyakārikā*). The arguments in favor of identity appear also to be basically two: (a) in this early period in the history of Indian philosophy it is not at all anomalous that someone such as Gauḍapāda should be interested in and influenced by Sāṃkhya just as he appears to have been interested in and influenced by Mādhyamika Buddhism; and (b) there are a number of quotations from the Brahmanical tradition in the *Gauḍapādabhāṣya* (for example, the *Ṛgveda*, *Bhagavadgītā*, and so forth), which suggest that the author may have been an early Vedāntin. These are also trivial arguments because they both beg the question. Anybody studying philosophy in the sixth century would have been interested in Sāṃkhya, and almost anybody writing in Sanskrit (with the possible exception of some Buddhists) would have been inclined to quote from well-known Brahmanical sources. The issue, however, is whether the Gauḍapāda of the *Māṇḍūkyakārikā* can be specifically linked with the author of the *Sāṃkhyakārikābhāṣya* (by a quotation, for example, or even a few vague parallels). Unhappily, such specific evidence is simply not available, and the issue of the identity of the two Gauḍapādas finally comes down to a matter of personal taste or bias.[2]

It might be noted, finally, that Alberuni, in his account of Sāṃkhya in the eleventh century of the Common Era, clearly uses the *Sāṃkhyakārikā*.[3] He also makes reference to a certain anchorite by the name of "Gauḍa" who could well be the Gauḍapāda of the *Sāṃkhyakārikābhāṣya*. Unfortunately, the reference might also be to the Vedāntin Gauḍapāda, for Alberuni also discusses Vedānta and Yoga.

The edition and translation (ET) used for the following summary is that of T. G. Mainkar, translator, *The Sāṃkhyakārikā of Īśvarakṛṣṇa with the Commentary of Gauḍapāda* (Poona : Oriental Book Agency, 1964).

SĀṂKHYAKĀRIKĀBHĀṢYA

(*Summary by Gerald J. Larson*)

I. Introductory Verses: The Scope and Task of Sāṃkhya (ET1-10)

(1) In two introductory verses, homage is made to Kapila who

provided a boat (namely, the Sāṃkhya) for crossing the ocean of ignorance, and this commentary (by Gauḍapāda) is characterized as being a brief and clear statement that clarifies the meaning of the verses for the benefit of students.

Kapila is one of the seven great sages (*maharṣi*) (including, in addition, Sanaka, Sanandana, Sanātana, Āsuri, Voḍhu, and Pañcaśikha). Kapila himself was born already in possession of the four constructive innate predispositions (namely, meritorious behavior, discriminating knowledge, nonattachment, and power), and because of his great compassion, he taught the twenty-five principles of the Sāṃkhya to Āsuri. There is an ancient verse (here quoted) asserting that anyone who truly knows the twenty-five principles attains liberation regardless of the stage of life or the particular group to which he belongs.

Internal frustration encompasses both mental (separation from what is satisfying, etc.) and bodily (fever, etc.) afflictions. External frustration encompasses afflictions arising from external beings and things (including insects, other men, stones, etc.). Divine or celestial frustration encompasses afflictions coming from the gods, fate, natural disasters, etc. To the objection that everyday remedies (Āyurvedic medicine, etc.) are available to cope with these frustrations, the answer is given that such remedies are neither certain (*avaśya*) nor permanent (*nitya*). Hence, a philosophical enquiry (*vividiṣā*) is required.

(2) If everyday remedies are neither certain and permanent, then surely Vedic (*ānuśravika, āgama*) remedies are capable of removing frustration. "We drank the Soma, and have become immortal," etc., and other Vedic passages indicate that frustrations can be overcome by Vedic sacrifices, etc. Unfortunately, however, this is not the case, because sacrificial rites involve (a) the slaughter of animals (and, hence, imply "impurity"); (b) being overcome by time or, in other words, temporality, even on the level of the gods as with, Indra, etc. (and, hence, imply "destruction") and (c) unequal benefits for persons performing the sacrifices (and, hence, imply "excess" or "surpassability").

That which is superior to both everyday remedies and Vedic remedies is the discriminating knowledge (*vijñāna*) of the difference between the manifest (*vyakta*, including intellect, ego, the five subtle elements, the eleven sense capacities and five gross elements), the unmanifest (*avyakta*, or primordial materiality) and the "knower" (consciousness).

(3) With respect to the issue of generation, the following: intellect is generated from primordial materiality, but it, in turn, produces egoity; egoity, produced from intellect, produces, in turn, the five subtle elements. The subtle elements, produced from egoity, in turn, produce the gross elements, each subtle element producing one gross element. Hence, the subtle element of sound produces ether; touch

produces wind; smell produces earth; form produces light; and taste produces water.

II. The Instruments of Knowledge (ET12-25)

(4) It is necessary to establish the instruments of knowing and to determine which things are known by what instruments. Any claim to know the world presupposes that the instruments of knowing have been established. The sense capacities, which make perception possible, are the ear, the skin, the eye, the tongue, and the nose[4] and these perceive respectively sound, touch, form, taste, and smell., An object comprehended neither by perception nor inference may be known through reliable testimony (*āptavacana*). This latter includes such items as "Indra is king of the gods", "there is a country called Kuru in the north" and "there are nymphs in heaven," etc. Also, the Veda is considered to be reliable testimony. A reliable person is someone who does his own work and is free from hatred and attachment. Such a person is to be believed.

Other schools assert additional instruments of knowing, but Sāṃkhya accepts only the three that have been mentioned, because, according to Saṃkhya, these three encompass all of the rest. Jaimini, for example, mentions six additional instruments of knowing: presumption (*arthāpatti*), inclusion (*sambhava*), nonapprehension (*abhāva*), imagination (*pratibhā*), tradition (*aitihya*), and comparison (*upamāna*).[5] In fact, however, these six instruments are encompassed by perception, inference, and reliable authority. Presumption is really a variety of inference. Probability, negation, imagination, tradition, and analogy are all varieties of reliable authority.[6]

That which is to be known by the three instruments of knowing (namely, perception, inference, and reliable testimony) include the twenty-five principles of the Sāṃkhya (the manifest, the unmanifest, and the knower). Some of the principles are established by perception, some by inference, and some by reliable testimony.

(5) With respect to definitions of the three instruments of knowing, (a) perception is the reflective discerning of specific objects by appropriate sense capacities ; (b) inference is that knowledge which is preceded by knowledge of the "characteristic mark" (*liṅga*) and that which bears the mark (*liṅgin*) (as, for example, by perceiving a staff or *daṇḍa*, one infers that there is a mendicant or *yati*, for one invariably finds these two together); and (c) reliable testimony is knowledge made available through authoritative teachers (*āptācārya*) and authoritative Vedic utterances (*āptaśruti*).

The three kinds of inference are prior (*pūrvavat*), consequent (*śeṣavat*), and inference based upon general correlation (*sāmānyatodṛṣṭa*). Prior inference is from cause to effect, as from rising clouds rain being inferred. Consequent inference is from effect to cause, as from a measure of water from the sea being salty, the saltiness of the sea in general is inferred. Inference based on general correlation is arguing for one thing on the basis of another, as from noticing that there must be movement because Caitra is first in one place and then in another, and then arguing that the moon and the stars must move because their positions change (even though the movement itself is not noticeable directly).

(6) That which is unmanifest is established by inference based on general correlation. Consciousness is also established by the same type of inference. That which is manifest (namely, intellect and the other principles that are effects of *prakṛti*) is established by means of perception. Such items of knowledge as "Indra is the king of the gods," etc., are established by means of reliable testimony.

Inference based on general correlation with respect to establishing the existence and makeup of creative nature is based upon the three constituents. Inference based on general correlation with respect to establishing the existence and makeup of consciousness is based on the awareness in ordinary experience of the appearance of consciousness (that is to say, since it is observed that that which is manifest is unconscious (*acetana*), but nevertheless appears to be conscious, so there must be a basis or ground for consciousness apart from creative nature).

III. The Notion of Preexistent Effect (ET25-27)

(9) The five reasons given in support of the theory of the "preexistent effect" (*satkāryavāda*) are meant to answer the opposite theory that the effects are not preexistent in the cause (*asatkāryavāda*) put forth by the Buddhists and others.

IV. The Manifest and Unmanifest Aspects of Materiality (ET29-37)

(10) In SK 8, it was said that primordial materiality, the unmanifest, is similar and yet different from its effects, the manifest. In this verse Īśvarakṛṣṇa explains how the unmanifest and manifest are different from one another. The manifest is caused (*hetumat*) by the unmanifest or primordial materiality. The terms "*upādāna*", "*hetu*", "*kāraṇa*", and "*nimitta*" are synonyms for the word "cause." The manifest is impermanent (*anitya*) in the sense that it is produced, like a jar. It is nonpervading (*avyāpin*) because only primordial materiality and consciousness are all-pervading. It is mobile (*sakriya*) in the sense that it migrates (*saṃsarati*) at the time of creation. It is multiple (*aneka*) in the sense that there is a plurality of principles (intellect, egoity, etc.). It is supported (*āśrita*) in the sense that it is supported

by the cause. It is mergent (*liṅga*) in the sense that at the time of dissolution all of the principles finally merge in primordial materiality. It has parts (*sāvayava*), in the sense that it has sound, taste, touch, etc. It is dependent (*paratantra*) in the sense that all of the principles are governed by materiality. In all of these senses, the unmanifest, primordial materiality, is the opposite of the manifest.

(11) Both the manifest and unmanifest are made up of the three constituents; are not capable simply by themselves of discriminating (*avivekin*) (as, for example, "this is a horse"); are both objects (*viṣaya*) in the sense that they are objects of experience (*bhojya*) for consciousness; are common to all (*sāmānya*) like a harlot; are not conscious (*acetana*) in the sense that they are incapable by themselves of being conscious of satisfaction, frustration, and confusion; and are productive (*prasavadharmin*) in that intellect, ego, and the five subtle elements are productive (as was described earlier in verse 3).

Consciousness is opposite to both the unmanifest and manifest in the sense that consciousness is distinct from the three constituents; is that which enables discrimination to take place; is individual or particular (and not general); is conscious of satisfaction, frustration, and confusion; and is totally unproductive.

From another perspective, however, it can be said that consciousness is similar to the unmanifest. In SK 10, it was said that the unmanifest is uncaused; all pervasive; immobile (in the sense that it does not "migrate"); one; not itself dependent on a cause; nonmergent (in the sense that it does not dissolve at the time of dissolution); not made up of parts; and totally self-subsistent or independent. In all of these senses, consciousness is similar to the unmanifest.

V. The Three Constituents (ET38-43)

(12) The term "purpose" (*artha*) in the verse is expressive of capacity or power. The three constituents mutually suppress, support, produce, consort, and coexist with one another. They mutually "suppress" (*abhibhava*) in the sense of successively dominating one another with, first, the intelligibility constituent (*sattva*) being dominant, second, the activity constituent (*rajas*) being dominant and, finally, the inertia constituent (*tamas*) being dominant. They mutually "support" (*āśraya*) one another like a binary or dyad (*dvyaṇukavat*). They mutually "produce" (*janana*) in the sense that a jar is produced from clay. They mutually "consort," (*mithuna*) as a man and woman make love. *Sattva* is the consort of *rajas*; and *rajas* is the consort of *sattva*. *Tamas* is said to be the consort of both the other two. Finally, the constituents mutually "coexist" (*vṛtti*) in the sense that each constituent produces a condition conducive not only to itself but also to the other two constituents. Thus,

sattva, like a beautiful woman, is a joy to her husband, a trial to her cowives, and arouses passion in other men. In a similar way, *rajas* and *tamas* likewise generate divergent conditions among the constituents.

(13) The intelligibility constituent, when dominant, generates a sense of lightness in the limbs and clarity in the senses. The activity constituent, when dominant, excites or stimulates, as when a bull is excited by another bull. The inertia constituent, when dominant, generates a sense of heaviness in the limbs, and the senses become obtuse and incapable of precise apprehension.

Although the three constituents are, thus, very different from one another, they nevertheless together produce one effect, just as the wick, oil, and flame of a lamp, though different in nature, work together to generate light for the illumination of objects.

VI. The Inferences that Establish the Existence and Makeup of Primordial Materiality and Consciousness (ET44-61)

(14) In verse 11, it was said that the unmanifest and the manifest are similar, and the question naturally arises as to how it can be known that the unmanifest has the same attributes or characteristics as the manifest. This question is answered in this verse with two arguments. First, negatively, it can be established that the unmanifest is similar to the manifest (in having the three constituents etc., as was set forth in verse 11) because the cause cannot be contrary to the effect, just as when one has a cloth one cannot argue that the threads are different from the cloth. In other words, it is not possible for the cause to have a different makeup, than the effect. Second, positively, even though the unmanifest is not perceived, it can nevertheless be established as existing, because whatever is the makeup of the cause is the very same as the makeup of the effect. Black cloth can only be produced from black thread.

(15-16) Five arguments are given to support the existence and makeup of the unmanifest or primordial materiality. The thrust of each of the five arguments is as follows: (a) Because "the manifest is limited" there must be an ultimate cause that is not limited. (b) Because the manifest is "uniform" or "homogeneous," there is "natural sequence," as, for example, when one sees a boy performing Vedic rites, one infers that his parents are Brahmins. (c) Because of the observance of causal efficiency; therefore, it can be said that a thing can only produce what it is capable of producing, as, for example, a potter can make a jar but not a chariot. (d) Because there must be some distinction between cause and effect; therefore, one must have appropriate sequential modification, as, for example, a lump of clay produces a jar, but a jar does not produce a lump of clay. (e) Because there is a final reunion of the universe (*vaiśvarūpya*) in the sense that the gross elements are absorbed in to the subtle elements, and the subtle elements into the ego, and the ego into intellect, and the intellect into primordial materiality; therefore, there must be an ultimate ground or source wherein all of these effects abide in an unmanifest state.

For all of these reasons, "the unmanifest is the ultimate cause," and the unmanifest is made up of the three constituents. Sometimes the constituents are in equivalent mutuality, and sometimes they mutually dominate one another, etc. (as was described above in the commentary on verse 12). The three constituents are like the three streams of the Gaṅgā that come together in the hair of Śiva, or are like threads that come together to make a cloth. The constituents become diversely modified, thereby accounting for the diversity of the manifest world, just as water from the atmosphere, though of one taste, becomes modified into a variety of tastes because of its contact with the earth.

(18) These arguments are given to show that it is not possible to maintain that consciousness is one, for if consciousness were one, all of the issues raised in this verse having to do with the diversity of the manifest world could not be intelligibly interpreted. In other words, the one consciousness or self would be now this, now that, etc., and one would get caught in hopeless contradictions.

(19) Consciousness can be compared metaphorically to the following : a bystander, a middle man, a wandering mendicant, and a spectator.

VII. The Association or Proximity of Materiality and Consciousness (ET62-66)

(20) It appears to be the case that consciousness is the agent, but it has been shown that consciousness is a nonagent. How is this to be explained? Two illustrations are especially helpful in this regard. Just as a jar appears to be cold when filled with cold liquid or hot when filled with something hot, but, in fact, is in itself neither hot nor cold, so consciousness appears to be the agent though, in fact, all agency is accomplished by the constituents. Or again, just as a man who is not a thief is taken to be a thief when he happens to be arrested along with others who are thieves, just so consciousness is taken to be an agent because of its proximity to the agency of the three constituents.

(21) The purpose for the coming together of creative nature and consciousness is to bring about the contemplation (*darśana*) of consciousness and liberation (*kaivalya*). The coming together may be illustrated by the story of the blind man and the lame man.

VIII. The Derivation of the Basic Principles (ET67-69)

(22) Synonyms for the term "*prakṛti*" are "the principal one" (*pradhāna*), "the greatest" (*Brahman*), "the unmanifest" (*avyakta*), "possessing much wealth" (*bahudhānaka?*), and "creative capacity" (*māyā*). Synonyms for *mahat* or the "great one" are "intellect" (*buddhi*), "Āsuri" "intention" or "determination" (*mati*), "discrimination" (*khyāti*), "knowledge" (*jñāna*), and "wisdom" or "insight" (*prajñā*). Synonyms for ego or *ahaṃkāra* are "the first of the elements" (*bhūtādi*), "generated" (*vaikṛta*), "the bright one" or "fiery one" (*taijasa*), and "self-awareness" (*abhimāna*). The five gross elements are produced from the five subtle elements (here called *paramāṇu*) as was described above in the commentary on verse 3.

IX. The Functioning of the Thirteenfold Instrument (ET70-103)

(23) The term *tattva* is a neuter abstract made from the pronoun "*tad*" hence, *tat-tva* or "that-ness" or "principle."

Intellect is said to be reflective discerning and can be glossed by the term "ascertainment" (*adhyavasāya*). Just as a future sprout is contained in a seed, so ascertainment is contained in intellect. "Ascertainment" means definite cognition as, for example, "this is a jar" or "this is a cloth."

Intellect in its "intelligibility mode" (*sāttvika*) has four forms (*rūpa*), namely, meritorious behavior (*dharma*), knowledge (*jñāna*), nonattachment (*vairāgya*), and power (*aiśvarya*).

Meritorious behavior (*dharma*) includes mercy and charity as well as the restraints and restrictions as set forth in *Yogasūtra* II.30 and II.32.

Knowledge has three synonyms: light (*prakāśa*), understanding (*avagama*), and manifestation (*bhāna*). There are two kinds of knowledge: (a) external, including the knowledge of the Vedas, the related six disciplines (of ritual, grammar, etc.), the Purāṇas, the Nyāya, the Mīmāṃsā, and the Dharmaśāstras and (b) internal, including the knowledge of materiality and consciousness. External knowledge brings worldly acclaim. Internal knowledge provides liberation.

Nonattachment is also twofold: (a) external, including freedom from the objects of sense and the correlates of earning, protecting, decreasing, attachment, and injury, etc., and (b) internal, including the desire to be free from materiality.

Power is lordliness (*īśvarabhāva*) and includes the eight attainments.

Intellect in its "inertia mode" (*tāmasa*) is the opposite of these four forms, namely, demerit, ignorance, attachment, and impotence.

(25) The ego in its "intelligibility mode" (*sātvika*) produces the mind, the five sense capacities and the five action capacities. These are called *sāttvika* because they are pure (*viśuddha*) and capable (*samartha*) of apprehension. The ego in its "inertia mode" (*tāmasa*) produces the five subtle elements. The productions of both modes are assisted by the "activity constituent" (*rajas*), because without the "activity constituent" (*rajas*), both the "intelligibility constituent" (*sattva*) and the "inertia constituent" (*tamas*) would be incapable of activity.

The ancient Sāṃkhya teachers named the ego in its *sāttvika* mode by the term "*vaikṛta*" ("generated"), in its *tāmasa* mode by the term "*bhūtādi*" ("the first of the elements"), and in its activity mode by the term "*taijasa*" (the "bright" or "fiery one").

(27) Mind is both a sense capacity and an action capacity, because it elaborates intellectually (*pravṛttiṃ kalpayati*) the functions of both. Moreover, it is similar in structure to the sense capacities and action capacities—that is to say, mind is likewise produced from ego in its "intelligibility mode" (*sāttvika*). Because the mind is responsible for intellectual elaboration, it is referred to as the "intentional" (*saṃkalpaka*) capacity.

The variety of these capacities together with the diversity of the external world is brought about by the modification of the constituents (*guṇapariṇāma*), functioning spontaneously (*svabhāva*). Variety and diversity cannot be explained as the work of God, or egoity, or intellect, or materiality, or consciousness. In the same manner, as unconscious milk functions for the nourishment of the calf (see SK57), so the constituents function spontaneously (*svabhāva*) to bring about all variety and diversity.

(28) The term "*mātra*" is to be construed in the sense of special capacity. That is to say, the eye has the special capacity to see form, but it cannot smell, etc. The apprehensions of form, taste, smell, sound, and touch are the functions of the five sense capacities. The capacities to speak, grasp, walk, excrete, and have sexual relations are the functions of the five action capacities.

(29) The specific functions (and unique characteristics) of intellect, egoity, and mind have now been discussed (in terms of "ascertainment," "self-delusion," and "explicating" in SK 23, 24 and 27). In this verse the common function or common nature of the three is given. This common function (*sāmānyakaraṇavṛtti*) has to do with the five vital breaths or airs (*vāyu*), namely, *prāṇa* (in the mouth and nose, supportive of life itself), *apāna* (the breath that carries away or downward); *samāna* (the digestive breath for assimilating food, located in the center of the body); *udāna* or (the breath that carries upward or ascends between the region of the navel and the head); and, finally, *vyāna* (the breath that circulates or pervades the entire

body). (In other words, in addition to the separate psychological and intellectual aspects of intellect, ego, and mind, the three together function commonly to support the physiological life of the organism as well, including respiration, digestion, the functioning of the nervous system, etc.).

(30) Perception occurs either simultaneously or gradually. It occurs simultaneously when there is a direct cognition, as, for example, in realizing "this is a post." In such an instance, intellect, egoity, the mind and a sense capacity formulate the cognition simultaneously. When there is a doubt, however, as, for example, when one is not sure whether something is a post or a man, then there is gradual functioning. Such is the case with perception in present time.

When, however, cognition occurs with respect to that which is past or future, cognition is always only gradual. With respect to cognition of something past, for example, the functioning of the intellect, ego, and mind is preceded by a prior perception.

(31) It is to be noted that the last sentence, "None of these capacities ever functions for any other purpose," refers to the Sāṃkhya rejection of God (*īśvara*).

(32) The action capacities seize (*āharaṇa*) and hold (*dhāraṇa*). The sense capacities illuminate (*prakāśa*). The reference to "tenfold" (*daśadhā*) means the five action capacities and the five sense capacities taken together.

(34) The sense capacities of human beings apprehend specific, gross objects (sounds, smells, etc.). The sense capacities of the gods are also able to apprehend the nonspecific (that is to say, the subtle elements). The action capacity of speech has sound for its object, and this is true for human beings and gods. The other action capacities have to do with all five sense contents (namely, sound, touch, form, taste, and smell).

(37) The reference to "every aspect" means not only all objects but also all three times (that is, past, present, and future). The reference to "subtle difference" means that which cannot be understood by those who have not performed religious austerities (*tapas*).

X. The Subtle and Gross Elements (ET104-107)

(38) The subtle elements can only be apprehended by the gods, and this apprehension is only pleasurable (hence, unmixed with the experiences of pain and delusion). From the five subtle elements are produced the five gross elements (as was described in the commentary on verse 3), and these gross elements are apprehended by human beings as comfortable, uncomfortable, and bewildering (that is to say, as mixed, respectively, with satisfaction, frustration, and confusion).

(39) The subtle body is made up of intellect, egoity, mind, the

sense capacities, the action capacities, and the five subtle elements. The gross body is the body produced from the mixture of seminal fluids that result because of sexual intercourse between father and mother. The gross body is sustained by the gross elements. Similarly the subtle body is nourished and sustained by food provided to the organism through the umbilical cord of the mother. In this fashion the embryo (made up of subtle body, gross body, and gross elements) slowly begins to develop a stomach, thighs, chest, head, etc., and is endowed with blood, flesh, tendons, semen, bones, and marrow. During the gestation period the embryo is wrapped in six sheaths. When the gestation period is finished, a baby is born from the mother's womb.

Of these specific forms (that is, subtle body, gross body, and gross elements), only the subtle body is permanent and transmigrates from life to life (into the forms of animals, deer, birds, reptiles, or plants). If the subtle body has been impelled continuously by meritorious behavior, it may transmigrate to the divine regions of Indra, etc. Gross bodies and gross elements perish at the moment of death and merge again into the undifferentiated gross elements.

XI. The Subtle Body (ET108-115)

(40) The subtle body is the first creation of primordial materiality. It is unimpeded or unrestrained until it becomes attached to a gross body. Moreover, the subtle body is devoid of experience, for experience only arises through the gross body form of parents. The subtle body is "perfumed" or motivated by certain innate predispositions, but this is to be discussed later (verse 43 and following). The subtle body is referred to as a "*liṅga*" because at the time of dissolution (*pralaya*) it "merges" into primordial materiality and does not reemerge until that materiality begins another creative phase.

(41) The reference to "nonspecific" means the subtle elements. Moreover, "without an appropriate support" refers both to subtle elements as well as to gross elements. The term "*liṅga*" in this verse refers to the "thirteenfold instrument" (namely, intellect, ego, mind, the five sense capacities and the five action capacities).

(42) The reference to "efficient causes and effects" (*nimittanaimittika*) means the innate predispositions of meritorious behavior, etc., which will be described subsequently.

XII. The Basic Predispositions (ET115-138)

(43) In verse 40 it was said that the *liṅga* or subtle body is "perfumed or motivated by basic predispositions." Now, in verse 43 and following, these basic predispositions are to be explained.

The predispositions, meritorious behavior, etc, are of three types: (a) innate (*sāṃsiddhika*), meaning merit, etc., in one's inherent nature; (b) natural (*prākṛtika*), meaning merit, etc., in one's nature as a result of previously virtuous lives, as was the case with the four sons of Brahman (namely, Sanaka, Sanandana, Sanātana, and Sanatkumāra) ; and (c) acquired (*vaikṛtika*), meaning merit, etc., acquired by ordinary human beings in this life because of having learned of the truth from a teacher.

The predispositions reside in the intellect and determine the quality of life of the gross embryo.

(44) In this verse the reference to "efficient causes and effects" *nimittanaimittika* (of verse 42) is explained. The phrase "higher forms of life" (*ūrdhva*) refers to the realms of Brahmā, etc. The phrase "lower forms of life" refers to animals, deer, etc. Liberation is to be attained by means of the basic predisposition called knowledge. The content of knowledge is the twenty-five basic principles of Sāṃkhya. Bondage is attained by means of the basic predisposition called ignorance. It is of three types; natural (*prākṛtika*), acquired (*vaikārika*), and personal (*dākṣiṇaka*). There is a verse in the *Vāyu Purāṇa* (101.59-60) (here quoted) that asserts that these three kinds of bondage can only be overcome by knowledge.

(45) The basic predisposition called "nonattachment," when unaccompanied by knowledge, leads to dissolution (*laya*) into the eight generative principles. Such a person at the moment of death becomes dissolved into primordial materiality, intellect, egoity, and the five subtle elements, but subsequently migration occurs again. Similarly by means of the predisposition called "passion" one becomes caught in worldly transmigration. The predisposition called "power" leads to the lordliness already described (in verse 23), and lack of power or impotence leads to the contrary condition or obstruction.

(46-47) These eight predispositions together with their eight effects (as have been described in verses 44-45) make up what is called the "intellectual creation" (*pratyayasarga*). The expression "*pratyayasarga*" means the creation of the intellect. Because of disparities in the reciprocal influence of the constituents (with, sometimes, *sattva* being dominant and, other times, *rajas* being dominant, etc.), this intellectual creation comes to manifest itself vis-á-vis ordinary experience in fifty varieties. These "fifty varieties" fall under four general types: (a) misconception, which is occasioned mainly by doubt (*saṃśaya*), (b) dysfunction, occasioned by a defect in one's sense or action capacities; (c) contentment, occasioned by indifference or the lack of a desire to know; and (d) attainment, occasioned by correct apprehension.

(48) Misconception, as has been said, is of five varieties. These five are as follows: (a) darkness (*tamas*), which in turn has eight

subdivisions, for "darkness" is the wrong belief that liberation arises because of merging into one of the eight generative principles: materiality, intellect, egoity, or any one of the five subtle elements; (b) confusion (*moha*), which, in turn, also has eight subdivisions for "confusion" means the wrong belief that liberation arises because of the attainment of the eight varieties of power; (c) great confusion (*mahāmoha*), which, in turn, has ten subdivisions, for "great confusion" means the wrong belief that permanent or abiding pleasure can come from the five objects of sense (sound, etc.) both for the gods and for men (that is to say, five objects pertaining to the gods, and five objects pertaining to men, making a total of ten); (d) gloom (*tāmisra*), which, in turn, has eighteen subdivisions, for "gloom" means the wrong belief that the ten objects of sense (both human and divine), together with the eight varieties of power, bring enjoyment; and, finally (e) blind gloom (*andhatāmisra*), which, in turn, also has eighteen subdivisions, for "blind gloom" means the grief that occurs when someone, who wants the ten objects of sense and the eight varieties of power, dies or loses control over power. Altogether, then, the five varieties of misconception have sixty-two subdivisions.

(49) The injuries of the eleven capacities are the following: deafness, blindness, paralysis, inability to taste, inability to smell, dumbness, mutilation, lameness, constipation, impotence, and insanity.

(50) The nine varieties of contentment are subdivided into two groups, internal and external. Four of the contentments are internal or related to the self (*ādhyātmika*). They are (a) belief in primordial materiality, or the tendency to be satisfied with the knowledge of creative nature alone; (b) belief in a material basis, or the tendency to think that the external signs of the ascetic life (e.g., carrying a sacred staff, a water pot, etc.) are sufficient for attaining liberation; (c) belief in time, or the tendency to think that liberation will occur spontaneously in due time for all; and (d) belief in destiny, or the tendency to believe that liberation can arise by chance or without effort. Five of the contentments are external and involve being satisfied with having turned away from the objects of sense (sound, touch, form, taste, and smell) together with turning away from the five evils attached to them, that is, acquisition, protection, waste, attachment, and injury. In another text, these nine "complacencies" are given the following technical names: *ambhas*, *salila*, *ogha*, *vṛṣṭi*, *sutamas*, *pāra*, *sunetra*, *nārikā* and *anuttamāmbhasika*.

(51) "Proper reasoning" means learning to think about philosophical issues like "what is truth here in this world," etc. "Oral instruction" means learning about truth as a result of verbal instruction. "Study" means attending to the Veda and other sacred writings. "Removal of the three kinds of frustration" means attending to a teacher and benefiting from his instruction. "Association with

appropriate persons" means association with those who are able to increase one's knowledge. "Generosity" means making appropriate gifts to holy men. In another text, these eight "perfections" are given the following technical names: *tāra*, *sutāra*, *tāratāra*, *pramoda*, *pramodamāna*, *ramyaka* and *sadāpramudita*.

(52) The predisposition (*bhāva*) creation has now been described, or, in other words, the intellectual creation (from verse 43 through 51). Previously (in verses 40-42) the "subtle" (*liṅga*) creation was described, made up of the subtle elements. The two creations (namely, *bhāva* and *liṅga*) function reciprocally that is to say, each presupposes the other just as the seed and the sprout; and the relationship between the two is beginningless.

XIII. The Empirical World (ET140-146)

(53) The eight divine orders are *brāhma*, *prājāpatya*, *saumya*, *aindra*, *gāndharva*, *yākṣa rākṣasa* and *paiśāca*.

(54) Although a particular constituent dominates in each realm, nevertheless, the three are always present together.

XIV. Similes Illustrating the Role and Function of Materiality (ET147-154)

(57) This simile answers the objection that an unconscious materiality could not serve the purpose of another. In fact, however, there are many examples of unconscious functioning that is purposive.

(58) This simile shows that after a particular task is accomplished, activity ceases.

(61) This simile illustrates that materiality is the sole cause. Those who argue that God is the cause, or that a thing's own nature is the cause, or that time is the cause are wrong. The Sāṃkhya teachers argue that primordial materiality alone is the most intelligible account of manifestation. God must be rejected as cause, because God has no qualities or constituents (*guṇa*) and, hence, it would not be possible to establish a relationship between cause and effect. Own-nature and time are to be rejected as ultimate causes because they are both manifest and, hence, themselves require the unmanifest materiality as ultimate cause.

XV. Liberation and Isolation (ET155-167)

(64) Repeated meditation on the twenty-five principles leads to the knowledge "I am not", etc. This knowledge is referred to as being "pure" and "absolute" because only this knowledge leads to liberation.

(65) "Like a spectator" means like the spectator of a play who perceives the dancer from his own seat in the audience.

(66) Another analogy is that of the debtor and the creditor. When a loan has been repaid, no further money transactions take place between the two, although both continue to exist and may even maintain contact with one another.

(67) Knowledge is capable of destroying the effects of all future acts as well as the effects of acts being performed in the present. Acts performed in the past, however, have left latent dispositions that must work themselves off in the present life, just like the momentum of the potter's wheel, after the potter has completed his work, must run itself off.

(69) The "sage" (*paramarṣi*) mentioned in the verse is Kapila. (Gauḍapāda ends his commentary here at verse 69.)

VYĀSA, or VEDAVYĀSA
YOGASŪTRABHĀṢYA

We have already discussed (see above entry on Patañjali the Yoga teacher) some of the problems relating to the date of the *Yogasūtrabhāṣya* and Frauwallner's tentative guess that it may have been composed by around 500 of the Common Era. The name "Vyāsa" or "Vedavyāsa" is obviously not correct, and there is no way of determining the correct name of the author. P. Chakravarti[1] and Frauwallner[2] are probably on the right track in suggesting that the author of the *Yogasūtrabhāṣya* is indebted to that revision of Sāṃkhya philosophy put forth by Vindhyavāsin (see Vindhyavāsin entry above).

YUKTIDIPIKĀ

As this volume has made abundantly clear, the *Yuktidīpikā* is without doubt our most important extant text for understanding Sāṃkhya in its early and formative philosophical development. No other text compares with it in terms of its detailed treatment of Sāṃkhya arguments and its apparently thorough familiarity with the various teachers and schools that preceded Īśvarakṛṣṇa, and it is no exaggeration to assert, therefore, that it is the *only* commentary on the *Kārikā* that appears to understand the full scope and details of classical Sāṃkhya philosophy. Since its discovery has been comparatively recent—it was first carefully edited and studied by P. Chakravarti,[1] based upon a single manuscript, and then reedited with an additional manuscript by R. C. Pandeya[2]—most of the older historical and philosophical treatments of Sāṃkhya are now outdated and require extensive revision. Even more than that, the contribution of Sāṃkhya to early Indian philosophy (and hence the entire history of early Indian philosophy) must be recast because of the evidence of the *Yuktidīpikā*. Unfortunately, there is still lacking a good critical edition of the text, but that will soon be corrected with the (promised) critical edition of Albrecht Wezler.[3] There is also forthcoming a complete English translation of the *Yuktidīpikā* being prepared by Dayanand Bhargava and S. K. Sharma, and to be published by Motilal Banarsidass.

The title of the text, "A Lamp on the Intellectual Coherence (of the *Sāṃkhyakārikā*)," indicates that the purpose of the commentary is to explain the overall reasoning of the *Kārikā* and to defend the intellectual coherence of the whole from all objections. The author of the text is unknown. The colophon refers to Vācaspati Miśra as author, but it is unlikely that Vācaspati would have written two commentaries on the *Sāṃkhyakārikā*, and, even more than that, the *Yuktidīpikā* appears to be older than the time of Vācaspati Miśra. R.C. Pandeya is inclined to think that the author is a certain Rāja, because Vācaspati Miśra quotes three verses from a text entitled *Rājavārttika* ("A Vārttika composed by Rāja"), and these three verses appear to be the same as three verses in the introductory verses of the *Yuktidīpikā*.[4] Wezler, however, in his article cited just above has argued that the *Yuktidīpikā* is itself a commentary on an old Sāṃkhya Vārttika and that portions of the Vārttika are embedded in the present text of the *Yuktidīpikā*.[5] If this is the case, then Vācaspati's reference to the *Rājavārttika* may not at all be a reference to the *Yuktidīpikā*. In other words, both Vācaspati and the author of the *Yuktidīpikā* may have quoted from the *Rājavārttika*. The identity of the author of the *Yuktidīpikā*, therefore, continues to be a problem.

The date of the text is likewise a problem, although some rough approximations are possible. There are quotations in the *Yuktidīpikā* from Dignāga (ca., 480-540 C. E., according to Frauwallner and Hattori) and from Bhartṛhari (ca., 450-510, according to Frauwallner), and it would seem that the text overall is older than Vācaspati Miśra (who can be placed in the ninth or tenth century). Whether or not the author is familiar with the views of Dharmakīrti (seventh century) is an open question, although it is odd that the views of Dharmakīrti concerning perception are not cited in the *Yuktidīpikā* if the *Yuktidīpikā* is, indeed, later than the seventh century. Frauwallner is persuaded by this latter negative evidence and, therefore, places *Yuktidīpikā* about the middle of the sixth century.[6] One might add to this the additional negative evidence that the *Yuktidīpikā* does not appear to be aware of the rigorous critique of Sāṃkhya by the great Śaṅkara, and, if Śaṅkara's date can now be plausibly put at 700 of the Common Era or slightly earlier (as Allen W. Thrasher has now cogently demonstrated[7]), one is tempted to think that *Yuktidīpikā* cannot be much later than the late seventh or early eighth century. R. C. Pandeya, on the other hand, cautions against accepting such negative evidence and suggests simply that the *Yuktidīpikā* be placed somewhere between the time of Dignāga (the sixth century) and the time of Vācaspati Miśra (the ninth or tenth century).[8] Possibly, when a critical edition of the text has been completed and some of the many quotations identified, one will be able to determine a more precise date.

The author of the *Yuktidīpikā* tends to treat the *Sāṃkhyakārikā* as if written in *sūtra* style and breaks up the *Sāṃkhyakārikā* into four *prakaraṇas*, namely:

(I) verses 1-14 (subdivided into three subsections or *āhnikas*: verses 1-2, 3-8, and 9-14);

(II) verses 15-21 (subdivided into two subsections: 15-16, 17-21);

(III) verses 22-45 (subdivided into three subsections: 22-27, 28-34, and 35-45);

(IV) verses 46-71 (subdivided into three subsections: 46-51, 52-59, and 64-71).

No commentary is available on verses 11-12, 60-63, and 65-66. Verse 72 is mentioned in the *Yuktidīpikā*, but there is no commentary directly upon it. Also, it is introduced in a manner that suggests that it may possibly have not been originally a verse of Īśvarakṛṣṇa's test.

The following summary of the text has been helped along by a number of persons. First, Pandit Raghunath Sharma of Saṃpūrṇānanda Sanskrit University in Varanasi prepared a general summary of the entire text in Sanskrit. Then, V. P. Bhatta, a Sanskrit language consultant at the University of California, Berkeley, prepared a rough English rendering of Sharma's Sanskrit summary. Next, Dayanand Bhargava and S. K. Sharma put together a lengthy summary of the entire text based upon their forthcoming English translation of the text (to be published by Motilal Banarsidass). In addition, Edeltraud Harzer, a doctoral student at the University of Washington, Seattle, who is preparing a dissertation on Sāṃkhya epistemology, offered a number of helpful comments regarding epistemological issues in the text. Finally, Gerald J. Larson and Ram Shankar Bhattacharya put together the final form of the summary. Primary credit for the overall content of the summary, however, belongs to Raghunath Sharma, Dayanand Bhargava, and S. K. Sharma.

For the sake of consistency in the overall volume, we have followed the topic headings that have been used in other summaries, but it should be repeated that the author of the *Yuktidīpikā* has organized his commentary in a different manner—in four *prakaraṇas* and eleven *āhnikas*).

Because a full discussion of this text is not yet available, we have attempted to prepare as full a summary as possible. The text itself, however, is very long and at many points does not lend itself to brief summarization. Many long polemical discussions have been shortened or only briefly alluded to. Every effort has been made, however, to mention important contents of the text that do not appear in other Sāṃkhya texts.

The following summary is based upon the edition of R. C. Pandeya, editor, *Yuktidīpikā*: *An Ancient Commentary on the Sāṃkhya-Kārikās of Īśvarakṛṣṇa* (Delhi: Motilal Banarsidass, 1967).

The text begins with fifteen introductory verses (pp. 1-2) followed by a long introduction (pp. 2-5) in which the author argues that the *Sāṃkhyakārikā* possesses the basic characteristics of an authentic scientific tradition (*tantraguṇa*). The commentary itself begins on page 5. The author tends to break down the *kārikās* into four parts for separate comment, thereby appearing to convert the longer *kārikās* into shorter *sūtras*.[9] The author also tensd to comment, briefly at first, about the meaning of an expression or a phrase and then to expand his brief comment into a longer discussion in which the views of varying opponents are refuted.

(*Summary by Raghunatha Sharma, Dayanand Bhargava, and Shiv Kumar Sharma*)

I. Introductory Verses: The Scope and Task of the Sāṃkhya (E1-29)

(Fifteen introductory verses present a brief synopsis of the occasion and purpose of the *Sāṃkhyakārikā*. Though the text of the *Kārikā* is short, nevertheless it presents a reliable overview of the full Sāṃkhya system and provides an adequate refutation of the views of opponents.)

Sāṃkhya is like an elephant whose two tusks are two of the kinds of inference (namely, positive and exclusionary inference). The elephant is located in a jungle, and it is surrounded by various creepers (namely, opposing views) that threaten to entangle it. In fact, however, the creepers are fragile and can be easily cut through by the tusks of the Sāṃkhya elephant. Reverence is offered to the greatest guru (Kapila) whose sunlike brilliance is able to destroy the darkness of *saṃsāra*. Kapila transmitted the system (*tantra*), which is designed to bring about the cessation of the threefold frustration, to the Brahmin Āsuri, who was desiring to learn the truth (*tattva*). Kapila's teaching was so extensive that it could not be mastered even in a hundred years. Moreover, on account of many opponents (theists, atomists, Buddhists, materialists, and so forth), the basic doctrine was further developed in many smaller works by various eminent teachers. Finally, a point was reached when pupils could no longer understand the intricacies of the system, and at that point Īśvarakṛṣṇa composed his brief text in seventy verses in which all of the basic categories are clearly explained. Īśvarakṛṣṇa's work is a brief summary of the entire *śāstra* of Sāṃkhya. It contains the ten principal topics and the fifty categories, making a total of sixty. The topics are presented in correct order, and the *Sāṃkhyakārikā*, though a small text, nevertheless possesses all of the characteristics of a complete system and is like a reflection in a mirror of the complete Sāṃkhya system. The author indicates that he will provide an explanation of the *Sāṃkhyakārikā* according to correct principles of logic.

If one asks about the basic characteristics of a complete system, there is a verse (here quoted) that enumerates those characteristics as follows:

(A complete science contains) aphoristic statements that indicate the main topics (*sūtra*).
a discussion of the instruments of knowing (*pramāṇa*);
a discussion of the "parts" relevant to a subject matter (*avayava*);
a statement that describes the overall structural components of the system (*anyūnatā*);

a discussion of doubts relating to general principles (*saṃśaya*);
a discussion of specific technical problems (*nirṇaya*);
brief definitions (*uddeśa*);
longer or expanded definitions (*nirdeśa*);
a discussion of basic principles in sequential order (*anukrama*);
a discussion of technical terminology (*saṃjñā*);
a discussion of what is to be done or practical advice that one should follow as a result of following the science (*upadeśa*).

One might also refer to other characteristics as well, but the above ones are the most important. The *Sāṃkhyakārikā* contains all of these characteristics. (Specific quotations are given from the *Kārikā* illustrating each characteristic.) In come instances Īśyarakṛṣṇa does not discuss all of the details. He relies on earlier discussions (in other books) so long as they do not contradict his own views. Also, he relies on reasonable deductions. That is to say, he does not directly express what can be reasonably inferred. At the same time he does not hesitate to express his own views even if they differ from other teachers.

Thus, it can be argued that the *Sāṃkhyakārikā* is not simply a work on a portion of the system (that is to say, a *prakaraṇa*) but is, rather, an independent and coherent account of the entire Sāṃkhya system.[10]

(1) (E5-14) The fact that Kapila explained it to Āsuri indicates that this treatise should be explained only to a worthy disciple who, intelligent and inquisitive, approaches the teacher. The activity constituent (*rajas*) is itself misery, which is alleviated by the intelligibility constituent (*sattva*).

The desire to know arises because of the occurrence of the three types of frustration occasioned by the relationship between the power of consciousness (*cetanāśakti*), on the one hand, and the internal organ (*antaḥkaraṇa*), which is characterized by the threefold frustration, on the other.

The desire to know arises with reference to the alleviation of frustration.[11] The text mentions "frustration" at the outset, but this is not inauspicious, because independent words taken out of a sentence do not convey any particular sense. Bhartṛhari has said that words taken out of a sentence are like senses taken out of the body.[12] The word "frustration" here in the sentence does not convey its own meaning but rather the meaning of the "removal of frustration." The expression "*duḥkha-traya-abhighāta*," therefore, is an auspicious beginning.

Objection: If it is the case that the activity constituent is one, then it is wrong to say that frustration is threefold. To say that the reference to the three types of frustration is meant only loosely in order to characterize frustration that arises externally, internally, and celestially is also wrong, because there are many occasions for frustration. Hence, there should be as many types of frustration as there are occasions for it.

Answer : This is only a broad classification like that of castes into four, even though one caste may have many subcastes.

Objection : If the occurrence of frustration gives rise to the desire to know the means of alleviating it, it should be present in all, and in Āsuri also it should have been present earlier. You should have mentioned that it arises because of the destruction of demerit and because of the ripening of previous acquired merit in the case of any person.

Secondly, liberation means not only emancipation from the divine realm, the human realm, and the animal plant realm but also from the realm of desire (*kāmadhātu*), the realm of form (*rūpadhātu*), and the formless (*ārūpyadhātu*). (These latter three represent Buddhist notions.) Moreover, the desire for knowledge is possible even in a detached person and not always because of the occurrence of frustration. Further, consciousness is devoid of desire, or any other quality (*guṇa*) for that matter, and desire cannot be ascribed to the nonsentient constituents of cosmic matter.

Answer : The desire to know arises only in the case of a nonattached person. All, though afflicted, do not realise the occurrence of frustration because of attachment, nor do they renounce the violence involved in maintaining an ordinary worldly life. The desire to know in Āsuri arose because of the realization of the occurrence of threefold frustration. If you insist upon asking about the reason for this realization of the occurrence of frustration, though the question is irrelevant and involves the danger of infinite regress, nevertheless it can be said that the practice of merit may be adduced as the cause for this realization.

We accept a fourteenfold world—the eight types of divine being, the five types of animal and plant life, and one type of human being (SK 53). Such realms as the three (Buddhist) realms (mentioned above) are not accepted by us.

Regarding the issue of nonattachment, we shall speak of it under the next stanza. Even the satisfactions of meditation do not transcend destruction (*kṣaya*) and excess (*atiśaya*). Hence the proposition that nonattachment also contributes toward the desire for knowledge is acceptable. Desire arises in the constituents of materiality, which though insentient are capable of desire. This will be explained later.

Objection : The term "that" (*tat*) in the statement "there arises the desire to know the means for alleviating *that*" is meaningless. This word cannot refer to the "desire to know" since no one wants to alleviate that desire. If we take occurrence (*abhighāta*) as the meaning of the word "that," for the occurrence is only the effect, the cause therefore will remain intact. Thus, there would be no final alleviation of frustration. The term "that" cannot refer to "triad" (*traya*), since that simply indicates a number and not any objects. If one argues that the term "that" refers to frustration, there are several objections. First, the word "frustration" is separated from the term "that" by many intervening words. Second, in the compound "*duḥkh-atraya*," "*duḥkha*" is a subordinate member. Moreover, frustration is an external fact and can, therefore, never be alleviated. Nor can the functioning of frustration be permanently alleviated so long as its cause, frustration, is present. Further, because the functioning of frustration is identical with its locus, viz, frustration, the objections with reference to frustration hold good with reference to its functioning also.

Answer : The term "that" refers to frustration. Although one word ought not to be related to another distant word (in a sentence), it is possible to have a relation based on the meaning of the words.[13] Moreover, there are examples where even a pronoun is separated from its antecedent by several intervening words. A relation between words based primarily on meaning is also accepted by the grammarians.[14] The word "frustration" is subordinate only as a component of the compound and as such cannot be connected with another word, but it is here taken out of the compound and is thought of as an independent word conceptually and is related to another word as in the usage of the *Mahābhāṣya* (1.1.1): "Hereafter the word-teaching. Of which words?"

As regards "alleviation," it means neither the destruction of the constituents of materiality nor suppression of their functions, but rather that the power of the constituents of materiality continues to exist only in its own form, having no further purpose to function for the sake of consciousness. Thus the statement that "there arises the desire to know the means for alleviating *that* (frustration)" is correct.

Objection : The desire to know is superfluous since there are worldly remedies available. There are drugs for alleviating bodily frustrations; enjoyable worldly pursuits for alleviating mental frustrations; and rituals for alleviating frustrations that arise from the gods or other cosmic forces.

Answer : Perceptible means are neither certain (*ekānta*) nor final (*atyanta*). The satisfactions of life, being only occasional, are difficult to attain and, if attained, they are sustained only with great difficulty. They are all perishable because they are produced. Also, they involve attachment and violence.

The limitations of perceptible means are obvious. Medical science accepts that there are diseases arising from previous births that can be cured only with death, and that there are diseases of old age that are simply symptoms of approaching death. Moreover, the recurrence of disease is common.

Regarding mental frustrations, the attainment of one object of enjoyment leads to the desire for another object. Satisfactions do not lead to the final pacification of desire. They rather intensify desire. Moreover, enjoying satisfactions without sharing them with those who lack them is cruel. If these satisfying objects are shared with others, limited as they are, they become exhausted. Also, it is too much to expect that all satisfying objects will be readily available. The lack of some of them will always cause frustration. Moreover, desires lead to pitfalls and are the source of all frustrations. Thoughtful people condemn worldly enjoyments. Hence the insufficiency of perceptible means.

(2) (E14-24) *Objection* : Why not resort to rituals prescribed by the scriptures ? They are invariably successful provided that their performance is free from defects. In statements such as "I have drunk *soma* and have become immortal" the permanence of the results of scriptural remedies is clearly implied.

Answer : The revealed literature includes the Vedas, the sciences related to the Vedas, and logic, but these are like perceptible means in that they are connected with impurity, destruction, and excess.

Impurity comes from the violence involved. Violence involves destruction of the body of the victim.

Objection : Having once accepted the authority of the Vedas, it is illogical to say that what has been prescribed by the Vedas is impure. The Vedas, being divine, cannot be questioned as a human statement can. After all, the impurity of violence is also to be known through the scriptures. If the same scriptures prescribe violence in the sacrifice, this has to be accepted as an exception to the general rule of nonviolence. Of course, to say that violence is bad because it injures others would imply that inducing a student to pious observations like celibacy and study would also be bad. Similarly, to say that nonviolence is good because it pleases others may make illicit relations with one's teacher's wife good. Consequently, the scriptures and nothing else could decide the goodness or badness of an act.

Answer : The authority of the Vedas is acceptable to us and we accept that sacrifice leads to heaven. We only question the desirability of attaining heaven at the cost of the life of others. The criterion for meritorious behavior is that one should not do to others that which is disagreeable to one's own self.

When we say violence is impure, we speak metaphorically and mean the effect of the violence, i.e., the grief generated in the mind because of the disposition toward compassion. In the next line of the text, knowledge is spoken of as superior to rituals, which implies that rituals themselves are not condemned. They are only considered to be inferior to knowledge.

Objection : How can rituals be held inferior when their life-long performance is recommended ?

Answer : The rituals require association with a wife, which is not always possible. The scriptures also enjoin performance of sacrifice only for one who is capable. This proves that rituals are not always obligatory but can be abandoned under some circumstances (e.g., in extreme old age). Moreover, the scriptures prescribe not only rituals but their renunciation also. For renunciation, one may refer to *Kaivalya Upaniṣad* 3 or *Chāndogya Upaniṣad* 5.10.

Objection : The scriptures prescribe rituals, whereas the statement of renunciation is merely an expression of approval.

Answer : But even an expression of approval implies prescription. An act is approved only for calling attention to it and recommending it. Otherwise the expression of approval would become meaningless. The scriptures cannot just praise something falsely.

Objection : There is no prescription for renunciation as there is for rituals.

Answer : This is so because renunciation means absence of all acts. What, therefore, could be prescribed for renunciation has been prescribed, namely, penance, faith, forest-dwelling, calmness, scholarship, and alms-begging (*Muṇḍaka Upaniṣad* 1.2.11). Manu and others have explained these duties of an ascetic.

Regarding rituals, they do yield a result, but that result is temporary. The means of the sacrifice being limited, it can yield only a temporary result. In fact, we observe that actions lead to transmigration and not liberation.

Objection : The scriptures proclaim that "he crosses death" and "he crosses sin." How, then, can one say that rituals lead only to temporary results?

Answer : The scriptures also declare that the ritualists are involved in the circle of transmigration (*Chāndogya Upaniṣad* 5.10.3-6). In such a situation, to avoid the conflict of scriptural statements, the statement "he crosses death" is to be taken in the metaphorical sense that he is saved from death for a long time.

Objection : But why not take the statement regarding involvement in transmigration as metaphorical to avoid the conflict?

Answer : Because all other instruments of knowledge favor the interpretation offered by us. We perceive worldly existence, and we can infer the fact that an eternal result cannot be achieved by limited means. Scriptural proof has been already quoted to prove our point. The daily metaphorical usages like "always laughing" or "always talking" also favor the view that the meaning accepted by us is correct.

The defect of excess or surpassability (i.e., the fruit of one action being superior to that of the other) is known, first, because we repeat the action. Second, the parts of the sacrifice, such as donations to the Brahmins, involve gradations; their result must also involve gradations. If one argues that it is the presiding deity that is the focus of the sacrifice and not donations, etc., and that the deity has no gradations, then, first it has to be proved that the deity has no gradation and, second, consciousness, neutral as it is, cannot become part of an action.

Moreover, if deity—and not the sacrificial matter—is the focus of the sacrifice, why kill animals? All gods reside in the body, which is invariably a means to any action. Any action would, therefore, suffice; why then is there sacrifice involving violence? Hence the surpassability of one ritual by another.

The means for alleviating frustration "which is contrary to that (*tadviparita*) is superior." Here "that" (*tat*) means heaven, which is achieved by rituals. "Superior" here refers to liberation. It is superior, because it is pure, permanent, and without gradations. Liberation arises out of the dissociation (*asaṃyoga*) of consciousness from materiality. The purpose of the association of the two shall be spoken of later in SK 21.

This dissociation is achieved by "the discriminative knowledge of the manifest, the unmanifest, and the knower." Alternatively, it could be interpreted as "the discriminative knowledge of the knower of the manifest and the unmanifest." This will be explained later in verse 66.

Such knowledge involves discriminating the difference between the manifest, the unmanifest, and the knower. The unmanifest is equivalent to materiality. The knower is equivalent to consciousness. The manifest is the ordinary world of experience, which has three dimensions: (a) a "form" (*rūpa*) dimension; (b) a "projective" (*pravṛtti*) dimension; and (c) a "consequential" (*phala*) dimension. The form dimension is the level of the basic principles, namely, intellect, egoity, mind, the capacities, the subtle elements, and the gross elements. The projective dimension is the level of an organism's basic tendencies (or, in other words, the eight predispositions that will be described later). The projective dimension can be described generally as involving the inclination to pursue what appears to be advantageous and the inclination to avoid what appears to be disadvantageous. More specifically, the projective dimension involves the five sources of action and the five breaths. Finally, the consequential dimension is the manifestation of ordinary experience and can be described as being twofold; "the perceptible" (*dṛṣṭa*) and the "imperceptible" *adṛṣṭa*. The "perceptible" is constituted by the "intellectual" or "intentional" creation (or, in other words, the *pratyayasarga*, and see SK 46) and is made up of the five misconceptions, the twenty-eight dysfunctions, the nine contentments, and the eight attainments. The "imperceptible" is made up of the karmic heritage that results from the activities of the organism and that leaves its impression upon the projective dimension, thereby determining the nature of rebirth in the body of a god or a plant, and so forth. Frustration is caused by the proximity or association (*saṃyoga*) of the manifest, the unmanifest, and the knower. The cause of frustration is the failure to discriminate between these three, and, more specifically, the cause of frustration is the tendency to ascribe the activities of the manifest and unmanifest (namely, materiality and its three constituents) to the power of consciousness. By discriminating (*vijñāna*) between manifest and unmanifest, on the one hand, and between them and consciousness, on the other, one attains liberation. Discrimination is like the distinguishing between darkness and light. In the darkness, objects like pots and so forth are undifferentiated from the darkness, but when the light of a lamp is present the darkness is dispelled and the objects can be correctly differentiated. This is supported by scriptures such as *Taittirīya Upaniṣad* 2.1 and 2.41, *Śvetāśvatara* 3.8, *Chāndogya* 7.1.3, and *Muṇḍaka* 3.2.9.

Objection: If this is the case, then the ritualistic scriptures will become meaningless.

Answer : But what of the scriptures that praise knowledge ? Those will be meaningless.

Objection : Therefore, let there be a combination of the two—ritual (action) and knowledge.

Answer : If actions were to lead to liberation, all would be liberated. Moreover, the scriptural statement that (ritual) actions lead to rebirth will be violated. How can actions and knowledge—leading to diverse results—be combined ? The scriptures declare heaven to be the result of ritual actions.

Objection : Ritual actions are prescribed, and, therefore, let them be accepted as primary.

Answer : Knowledge is equally prescribed in the *Chāndogya Upaniṣad* 8.7.1, and there is no predominance of one over another. The combination of knowledge and action, therefore, is not possible.

Objection : Let us then accept that those who are incapable of performing actions be allowed to follow the path of knowledge.

Answer : We have quoted scriptures saying that a learned man renounces. It nowhere speaks of an incapable man. The fact is that the secret of the Vedas is spoken of in the end (cf. *Chāndogya Upaniṣad* 3.11.4-6). In other words, knowledge is spoken of in the end.

The scriptures no doubt speak of rituals for a knower, but they declare him to be first amongst the wise who renounces actions. Yājñavalkya and others have corroborated this. Those who are attached do not appreciate it. One should, therefore, leave the householder's life and take up the life of an ascetic.

(3) (E25-29) The discriminative knowledge of the triad of the manifest, the unmanifest, and the knower can be described either briefly or in detail and this triad can be discussed in five ways, in terms of: (a) the generative original and its generated transformations (*prakṛti-vikāra*), (b) cause and effect (*kāraṇakārya*), (c) excess and nonexcess (*atiśayānatiśaya*), (d) efficient cause and effect (*nimittanaimittika*), or (e) content and its awareness (*viṣayaviṣayin*).

The first of these, which is the most fundamental, determines four varieties (among the principles); (a) that which is only the cause and not the effect, (b) that which is only the effect and not the cause, (c) that which is the cause as well as the effect and, (d) that which is neither the cause nor the effect.

(a) *Primordial materiality, the root of all, is not an effect.*

Primordial materiality, the root of the intellect, etc., produces variously (*prakaroti*). In the compound "primordial materiality" (*mūla-prakṛti*), the word "primordial" (*mūla*) means "root of the great principle, etc." The word "primordial," which is a part of the compounded word, cannot be attached to another word such as "of the great principle, etc,"[15] but interrelated words are always used together and they can be used in a complex formation (*vṛtti*). For example, the word "teacher," though requiring the word "of Devadatta" for completion of its sense, is used in a complex formation with the word "clan" in the expression "Devadatta's teacher-clan" (*Devadattasya gurukula*). Grammarians themselves have made such usages.[16]

It should not be said that the etymology of a technical term is irrelevant; it may be so with a conventional term but not with an etymologically meaningful word like "*saptaparṇa*" [(which has actually *sapta* (seven) *parṇa* (leaves)].

Primordial materiality, by implication, is known to be the cause and, therefore, it is not stated to be so.

Though mention of primordial materiality as such makes the specification "uncaused" superfluous, it has been provided to show that it is the final cause so as to avoid an infinite regress. Primordial materiality is uncaused, because it could only have either God or consciousness or the constituents as its cause. The existence of God shall be refuted later on. Consciousness is inactive. The effect means the attainment of some gross form by the subtle. Now, the constituents of materiality in the state of equilibrium apart from all modifications have no subtler form of which they could be said to be the effect. They are, therefore, uncaused.

(b) *The seven, beginning with intellect, etc., are both generative and generated.* Any one of them is a modification of the preceding one and the cause of the following.

Objection : Pañcaśikha mentions twenty-five elements, one of which (primordial materiality) is not caused, sixteen are only products and the sentient entity is neither the cause nor the effect. Hence, by process of elimination, the remaining seven are both the cause and the effect. There is no necessity of using the term "seven".

Answer : Patañjali (the Sāṃkhya teacher) holds that the principle of egoity is included in the intellect itself. It is to refute his view that the term "seven" is used.

Objection : The principle of egoity shall be separately spoken of in *Kārikā* 22.

Answer : These seven principles have various subvarieties. The purpose of saying "seven" is to show that an element remains only one in spite of the fact that it may have many varieties. This shall be elaborated later on.

(c) *Sixteen principles are transformations only.*

Five gross elements and eleven capacities constitute the group of sixteen.

By the word "only"—the word "*tu*" in Sanskrit, the use of which is discussed in some detail—the sense has been restricted in the sense that these (sixteen) are only generated and not generative. The body and other objects are not transformations of the gross elements, because they are not essentially different.

Objection : No effect, according to Sāṃkhya, is essentially different from the cause. Hence all the categories will be nongenerative in this way. The transformability of the five gross elements is perceptible also.

Answer : The difference between an object being transformable and its giving birth to a different principle has to be appreciated. Primordial materiality being the subtlest is the final cause; similarly this group of sixteen is only a modification and not generative.

(d) *Consciousness is neither generative nor generated.*

That it is not generative shall be explained in *Kārikā* 19. It cannot be a modification of another consciousness—a selfsame thing could not give birth to a selfsame thing. Moreover, consciousness, being all-pervasive and devoid of activity, cannot be a cause. The constituents of materiality, being of different genus, i.e., insentient (*acetana*), cannot give birth to consciousness, which is sentient (*cetana*).

II. The Instruments of Knowledge (E29-47)

(4) (E29-34) Intellect being one, the instruments of knowledge are also one, but they become manifold as perception or inference due to limiting adjuncts. Here, instruments of knowledge (*pramāṇa*) are spoken of as one, overlooking the difference of the limiting adjuncts. The word '*hi*" (=only) is used in the restrictive sense to indicate that the objects of knowledge are known "only through the instruments of knowledge." To say that "only the objects of knowledge" are known would be superfluous, as nonobjects of knowledge cannot be known at all. Regarding the innate knowledge of the seers, though it comes

directly without any instrument of knowledge (SK 43), yet it is an accomplished fact, and it does not require a means at all. Alternatively, the word "*hi*" (only) could be restrictive with reference to knowledge. To say that knowledge does not arise sometimes, even if its instruments are present, would be wrong, for the failure to know in such cases is due to the predominance of *tamas*—the inertia constituent of materiality. It does not affect the fact that the nature of an instrument of knowledge is to ascertain objects of knowledge.

The instruments of knowledge are said to be threefold, but these three kinds should not be thought of as three independent instruments of knowledge as, for example, in Nyāya. There is only one intellect that becomes differentiated due to the difference of instrument. Regarding the question as to how a single power can be differentiated, we have many examples in which one thing becomes differentiated. For example, the constituents of primordial materiality are differentiations within a single entity.

The instruments of knowledge are threefold "because all other means are included in this threefold instrument of knowledge." Or, alternatively, the expression could be explained as "the threefold instruments of knowledge are known in all the instruments of knowledge".[17]

The three kinds of instruments of knowledge are perception, inference, and verbal testimony. These three will be defined in *Kārikās* 5 and 6. As regards the instruments of knowledge accepted by other systems, let us take, first, comparison (*upamāna*), which is defined as "the knowledge of an object by means of its resemblance to something wellknown."[18] Others, however, define it as "the knowledge of the relation of a name and its denotation in the form that 'such and such an object is denoted by such and such a word' on the basis of a knowledge of similarity through the statement of an authority." In such a case it is not only similarity but the force of authority that leads to this knowledge. Likewise with tradition, which is accepted as a different instrument of knowledge by some.

Objection : The deciding factor in comparison is similarity, and not verbal testimony. If the use of words were to lead to the inclusion of comparison under verbal testimony, the same logic could be applied for including inference also under verbal testimony.

Answer : The similarity is only an aid. The speaker, finding it difficult to explain something, takes the help of a similarity. If this leads to the acceptance of mere similarity as an instrument of knowledge, then different gestures such as walking, etc., should also be accepted as an instrument of knowledge. The distinctive feature is not, therefore, similarity, but the authority of the speaker; otherwise, the sentence "*gavaya* (an animal resembling a cow) is like a horse" would also convey knowledge. The relationship of a word to the object it denotes is known not only through similarity but through the description of other qualities of the object also. So this is not a distinct feature of this so-called instrument of knowledge, comparison. Moreover, similarity is not always known through the teaching of someone else but could be known by oneself through his own observation.

Regarding presumption (*arthāpatti*), it is an instrument of knowledge that makes one aware of one thing, with which an invariable concomitance with something else is known, and this something else has been either heard or seen. For example, after seeing treacle or hearing its name, its sweetness is also known. There is another type of presumption where, after observing the invariable concomitance between two properties, there is the presumption of an association of their opposite properties also, e.g., knowing that a conjoined object is noneternal, one can imply that a nonconjoined object is eternal. An example of this type of presumption without exception is the case in which we know the defeat of the boar when we see the lion walking all alone stained with the blood of the boar. Yet this is really a case of inference. There is invariable concomitance between the victory of the lion and the defeat of the boar. So one of them can be inferred by another.

Inclusion (*sambhava*) is exemplified in calculating a half-measure when one is aware of the extent of a full measure of a *droṇa* (a measure of capacity). But this is a case of presumption and is not really different from inference.

Nonapprehension (*abhāva*) is the knowledge of the absence of fire through the absence of smoke. Now, this being a kind of presumption of an association between things of an opposite nature, it is, therefore, to be included in inference. The example quoted here has the exception of an ironball, where the absence of smoke cannot lead to the presumption of the absence of fire. This is, therefore, not an instrument of knowledge at all. In such cases as the presumption of eternality by noncreatedness, the awareness is valid, but it is included in inference. The knowledge of the existence of Devadatta outside the house from his absence in the house is, similarly, a presumption and, therefore, an inference.

Gestures (*ceṣṭā*) like that of a begging posture indicating hunger are only forms of inference. They do not form an independent instrument of knowledge.

Latent dispositions created by repeated experience lead to knowledge when certain words are uttered, even without the presence of the object. This is intuition (*pratibhā*), but this cannot be an independent instrument of knowledge, which is gained only through perception, etc. The knowledge of the supreme seer (Kapila) is already accomplished, and it does not stand in need of an instrument. Awareness inspired by desire and anger, etc., is not valid. Likewise, the awareness inspired by intuition is not valid. Hence there are only three types of instruments of knowledge.

(5) (E34-39) Perception has been differently defined as knowledge (a) "arising from sense-object contact (and which is) not caused by words, nonerroneous and is of a definite character" (*Nyāyasūtra* 1.1.4), (b) "which arises from the contact of the self, sense organ, internal organ, and the object" (*Vaiśeṣikasūtra* 3.1.18) and (c) "which arises due to the contact of a man's senses with something that is present" (*Mīmāṃsāsūtra* 1.1.4). The followers of Vārṣagaṇya define it as "the functioning of the ear and the rest." Others (Dignāga and other Buddhists) define it as "nonconceptual knowledge" or "knowledge devoid of constructions". (*kalpanāpoḍham*). In fact, perception is "reflective discerning of particular objects through contact with the senses." These objects are either specific (*viśiṣṭa*), like the earth, or nonspecific (*aviśiṣṭa*), like the subtle elements (SK 34). Intellect is ascertainment or reflective discerning (K 23). Perception is a pure form of *sattva* unmixed with *rajas* and *tamas* and this is the instrument; the result is that *sattva* illuminated by consciousness or sentience (*cetanāśakti* or *puruṣa*).

The instrument, being located in the intellect, is different from its result, which is located in consciousness, the existence of which will be proved in *Kārikā* 20.

The object known through perception is also known as "*pratyakṣa*' only figuratively. The object of perception bears upon the sense as the favoring thing and upon the determinative knowledge as the favored. So, both of them are denoted by the same term. The fire is known through inference, but nothing is inferred through fire. Hence inference and the object of inference are not denoted by the same term.

Obviously the term "reflective discerning" in the definition is necessary to indicate the instrument of knowledge, because the object itself is not the instrument of knowledge. Nor is the operation of the senses the instrument of knowledge. We know satisfactions, etc., from the efficient cause and its effect and not through the senses. The knowledge of Yogins is also suprasensuous. The inclusion of the term "reflective discerning" therefore serves many purposes.

The expression "through contact with the senses" is included to exclude the case of mirage from perception. The term "contact" signifies proximity of the senses with the object so as to exclude inference from the purview of perception. Memory is not an instrument of knowledge because it does not cognize anything new. Perception, in fact, includes objects that are known through the contact with the senses and includes also internal knowledge and the suprasensuous knowledge of Yogins.[19]

Inference is declared to be threefold—*a priori* (*pūrvavat*), *a posteriori* (*śeṣavat*), and based on general correlation (*sāmānyatodṛṣṭa*). *A priori* means having a cause, *a posteriori* means having an effect. In an *a priori* inference, one infers the effect from the cause, e.g., rain from the dark clouds. Of course, the possibility of an obstruction in the appearance of an effect has to be dealt with in some cases. An *a posteriori* inference is the inference of a cause from the effect, e.g., the inference of a sexual act by the parents from the existence of a boy, or of a seed from the sprout. When we infer the rains in the upper part of the river through the floods in the lower part, we have to be sure through exclusionary inference (*avīta*) that it is not due to some reason other than the rain, such as the melting of snow, etc. taking into account, in other words, time and place, etc. For example, if it is in South India, the flood cannot be caused by the melting of snow (there being no snow in South India).

Where, after once observing the invariable association of two objects, one comes to know the invariable association of the objects of the same groups at some other place and time, the inference is said to be based on general correlation.

Now, this is a common characteristic of all types of inferences and is not the truly unique feature in this kind of inference. In fact, this type of inference is meant for inferring things that are in principle imperceptible (SK 6). The inference of consciousness is not possible even through comparison because consciousness is unique and there is no object of the same kind. The distinguishing feature, therefore, is this, that we infer the coexistence of certain things on the basis of general correlation—for example, that a sound (*śabda*) is not eternal because it is produced.

Verbal testimony is reliable statement. Statements not made by human beings, i.e., the Veda, as well as statements made by detached persons like Manu are included under reliable authority.

(6-7) (E40-46) Objects directly in contact with the senses are known through perception, and those that are not directly in contact with the senses are known through inference. Objects that are in principle beyond perception can be known through inference based on general correlation.

Having realized the invariable concomitance between production and noneternality in the case of a pot, the same is inferred in the case of a sound also. Those who think that this type of inference is identical with *a posteriori* inference cannot account for the inference of consciousness that has no effect. The operations (*vṛtti*) of consciousness even if taken metaphorically to be its effect, do not lead to its inference, since the text (in SK 17) gives the nature of composite objects serving the purpose of some other object as the reason for the inference of consciousness.

This type of inference is positive (*vīta*) when the reason is employed in its own form; it is exclusionary (*avīta*) when some other object is implied.

The form of proof is twofold: general and particular. In the general form, the proof being coexistent with what is to be proved, indicates it. *Kārikā* 17, while giving the proofs of consciousness, uses the particular form of proof. An example of exclusionary inference might be the following: having excluded the possibility of atoms, the soul, God, action, fate, time, nature, or accident being the ultimate first cause, one infers that primordial materiality is that cause. When wishing to convey to others the manner in which an inference is to be made, the ten members of correct argumentation are employed. The conditions for an inference (*vyākhyāṅga*) are the desire to know (*jijñāsā*), doubt (*saṃśaya*), purpose (*prayojana*), conjecturing various possible alternatives (*śakyaprāpti*), and removal of doubts (*saṃśayavyudāsa*). The remaining members of an argument (*parapratipādanāṅga*) are thesis (*pratijñā*), reason (*hetu*), example (*dṛṣṭānta*), application (*upasaṃhāra*), and conclusion (*nigamana*).

Take, for example, the inference of the existence of consciousness: (a) there is a desire to know consciousness; (b) a doubt arises because consciousness is imperceptible; (c) the purpose is the realization of truth and thereby the attainment of liberation; (d) in the event that consciousness does not exist, the Buddhist's position of voidness might be acceptable; and (e) the removal of doubt leads to the ascertainment of the existence of consciousness.

Then the proof is formulated as follows: (a) a thesis is set forth that is the statement of what is to be proved, e.g., "consciousness exists"; (b) an appropriate reason is given, e.g., because things exist for another; (c) an example is offered, an illustration, e.g., like a couch—it may include a counter-example also, which is used in exclusionary inference; (d) bringing together what is to be proved and the example into one exposition, e.g., "as is this, so is that also," is the application; and (e) the conclusion is the repetition of the thesis. This connects the various components of the argument together in the form "therefore, consciousness exists."

Objection : The use of these members is unnecessary, because one knows objects for oneself without them and, therefore, their use for conveying knowledge to others is also unnecessary. When both parties are sure about their position, the question of doubt does not arise. They have no purpose for probing each other's doubt. The wise do not go after that which is meaningless or impossible. The mention of the purpose or of the possible alternatives is, therefore, unnecessary. The desire to know, etc., is hardly necessary. Similarly, if a thesis states what is to be proved, the proof and the example should also be stated. To say that the proof is the *hetu* is begging the question. Proof is of various types; to indicate all of them by one definition is wrong. The example is that of an object, which cannot be part of a sentence. The example and the application convey only invariable concomitance. The conclusion is just the thesis.

Answer : The tradition is meant for all and not the selected few. We have no objection if one can understand without these various members. They have been stated for those who need them. There are places where even the thesis is not mentioned. The rule is, therefore, that all these members become meaningful only when there is a necessity for them.

The nature of exclusionary inference is such that it should be used only after positive inference. If one uses exclusionary inference from the very beginning, one might end up eliminating everything including the unmanifest, and hence, end up proving nothing. If, however, the object is ascertained in its very nature, the conclusion that the manifest, being not a product of atoms, etc., is the product of the unmanifest, will be easily drawn.

Objection : There are reasons like excessive distance, etc. (SK 7), for the nonperception of an object. For example, a bird may soar out of sight, the light of a planet may be suppressed by the light of the sun, and so forth. How can these objects be known through inference based on general correlation? They have no general characteristics.

Answer : The farther away the bird, the greater the effort in perceiving it. It can be inferred by this that the bird can disappear also. So in other cases.

Objects like heaven, liberation, and the gods, which are neither perceived nor have any general characteristics, are known through the verbal testimony of the scriptures. Regarding the validity of verbal testimony, we accept the words of a seer who is detached, free from doubt, and has experienced supersensuous things. We do not accept the verbal testimony of just anybody. Verbal testimony is different from inference because it does not require a proof.

Objection : The meaning of a word is also understood through positive and negative examples. It is, therefore, not different from inference. We infer that if the words of Mr. X are authentic, so are those of Mr. Y.

Answer : This objection could be true of some words like "tree," etc., but not of words like "heaven," etc., whose meaning is ascertained only through scripture and not through inference. Moreover, inference does not depend upon the speaker for its validity, whereas verbal testimony does. The meaning of a word changes with time and place; this is not so with a *hetu* term. The *Mahābhāṣya* (1.1.1) speaks of words used in a particular sense in a particular country only. A *hetu*, moreover, has a natural relation to its *sādhya* (and not just a conventional one). Smoke cannot be drawn away from fire.

The *hetu* in an inference cannot be connected with anything whatever at the sweet will of the speaker. Inference can be with reference to objects having generality and not with reference to words that are only particular, like "moon" or "heaven," which, being unique, have no generality.

Objection : Statements that are verifiable by perception or inference can be valid, but that does not apply to statements about objects like heaven.

Answer : An object proved through one instrument of knowledge does not have to be verified by another. Otherwise, all veridical statements—and not only about heaven, etc.—will have to be questioned. After all, inference is also accepted as an instrument of knowledge under the same circumstances.

The only actual objects are those proved by the above instruments of knowledge.

(8) (E47) *Objection* : The unmanifest is free from all the conditions given in *Kārikā* 7 for nonperception of an object. It is still not perceived. It should, therefore, be presumed to be nonexistent, as, for example, a hare's horn.

Answer : The hare's horn has, obviously, no effect, and hence, it is a different case.

Objection : Having spoken of subtlety as a reason for nonperception of the unmanifest, speaking of its apprehension through its effects is superfluous.

Answer : The first part is meant to prove it through positive inference, whereas the second one is meant to prove it through exclusionary inference. The *hetu* "not due to nonexistence" is useful for both of these inferences. We, along with others, accept that both of the inferences prove the selfsame object.

III. The Notion of Preexistent Effect (E48-55)

(9) *Objection* : The effect should be examined. It should be discussed first whether the effect exists in the cause before its manifestation. Such a topic is not irrelevant, for the difference of opinion among teachers compells us to consider it. The followers of Kaṇāda and Gautama hold the nonexistence of the effect prior to its origination, whereas the Buddhists hold that it is both existent and nonexistent. There are still others who believe that the effect is neither existent nor nonexistent. Because of this diversity, the Sāṃkhyas should also clarify their position.

Answer : The effect does exist in the cause. If the effects, such as intellect, etc., would not exist in primordial materiality, they could not have come into existence, because the effect is only a particular arrangement of its cause. The three constituents serve as the ultimate cause of the universe. They are endowed with potencies. The particularly arranged form of them forms the effect. This position refutes the theory of origination from nonexistence.

Objection: The theory of the identity of cause and effect leading to the theory of the prior existence of the effect is unproved. On the other hand, the composite originates as different from the components. The following reasons also lead to the theory of the nonexistence of the effect prior to its origination. First, the effect is not perceived in the cause even though the conditions of its perception are fulfilled. It can also not be argued here that the nonperception is caused by some reason of the nonperception of an existent object, because reasons like extreme distance, etc., admitted by the Sāṃkhyas are not applicable here. Moreover, if cause and effect are located at the same place, the nonperception of an effect would imply the nonperception of a cause as well. Nor does the effect here come under the scope of inference that gives knowledge of nonperceptible objects, because there is no possibility of activity, property, or name of an effect that can serve as proof for its existence. Second, because the success of the agent in his efforts proves prior nonexistence of the effect, the Sāṃkhyas cannot argue here that the effort by the agent would be useful in bringing out the transformation; because transformation implies the introduction of some new qualities and the giving up of some old qualities, it would lead to the origination of a fresh object. Third, if the object is already existent, there would remain no criterion to stop or to begin the causal operation. Fourth, the theory of the prior existence of an effect implies the absurdity of the relation of the quality of origination prior to the causal operation in the way it is found after the causal operation. Fifth, if the existent object originates, origination and existence would be synonymous.

Answer : The composite cannot be produced as different from the components, because the former is not cognized to be different from the latter. If a cloth, for example, could be different from the threads serving as its components, it would be known as different from them as it is known to be different from some other piece of cloth or the heap of threads. It would not be logical to argue that the absence of cognition of the difference between the two is due to the relation of inference between them, which, unlike conjunction, does not allow cognition of distinction in relation. It is still to be proved that the composite is different from its components and that they are related through inference. Moreover, there is no example to support such a thesis. The objector may argue that the distinction between the two is not cognized because they are mutually pervasive. This argument also presupposes the causality and the relation of inference between them, both of which are still unestablished.

The objector may cite the example of loom and cloth to establish the distinction between cause and effect. Such as example would be unlike the present situation. The discussion is about the relation between material cause and effect whereas loom is the instrumental cause. In addition, the example would violate the rule of pervasion between cause and effect because loom and cloth are not mutually pervasive. Moreover, objects like threads and cloth, having different types of touch, activity, form, and weight, cannot be mutually pervasive.

The objector further cannot explain logically whether a composite exists in all the components collectively or separately in each component. The objector may again try to establish the difference between components and the composite on the ground that the effect is absent (prior to production and after destruction), whereas the cause is present. This argument also is inconclusive because the origination and destruction refer to the particular arrangement and not to the object, i.e., cloth. The first argument of the objector is based upon the wrong understanding of the Sāṃkhya theory. The effect does not exist in the cause in the way that the jujube fruit is in a bowl; rather, the effect is the cause itself. The cause is endowed with various potencies, and through the assisting potencies some of the potencies disappear and the others are manifested in the state of the effect. The potencies manifested are not perceived in the state of the cause.

The argument that there is no applicability of inference because of the absence of proof in the form of action, property, or name is also applicable to those who admit cause and effect to be different, but not to the Sāṃkhyas who accept the identity of the two. Moreover, here the Nyāya theory also suffers from the same defect. The Naiyāyikas hold that the objects exist in the first moment after origination without property, etc., and hence there remains no proof for their existence. The theory of the Sāṃkhyas is based upon the authority of Pañcaśikha, etc., who perceived the effect in the state of the cause.

The second argument is also wrong, because that which is nonexistent cannot be brought into existence. The effect may be related to the causal operation or not. In both the cases the theory of the nonexistence of the effect proves defective. The aforesaid relation may occur in the state of causal operation or the accomplished state of the effect.

Objection : The effect is related to the causal operation in the intermediary state.

Answer : There is no state of this kind. There can be either the state of existence or that of nonexistence but no third state called existence-cum-nonexistence.

The above defect does not apply to the Sāṃkhya theory, because of the relation of the cause (with the causal operation). Since cause and effect are identical, the effect is also related to the operation.

Objection : The effect should be distinct from the cause as is the case with the instrumental cause.

Answer : It is not so, because the effect is not different from its material cause. Moreover, everything is not possible everywhere. Without admitting the prior existence of the effect, the effect will be equally related to everything and would come out of everything. Moreover, in that case the effect would be distinct and of a different genus from cause just as it is from the instrumental cause. The selection of a particular cause proves the existence of the effect in that cause. Though coming together, manifestation, etc., are additional in the effect, yet it does not disturb the theory of the prior existence of the effect. These have nothing to do with the nature of the object. In fact, origination or destruction are only conventional notions, and in reality there is no production or destruction. Nor is it right to say that the word "production" proves prior nonexistence, because it is still to be considered whether production refers to nonexistent or existent objects. In conventional discourse "production" is used with an existent object also as "he makes a fist, or a knot, or an earring." The production from the nonexistent would prove the production of the horn of a hare also.

Here is another reason to prove the prior existence of effect. An efficient cause can produce an efficient effect only. It cannot be argued that the effect should not be considered existent in the material cause, since it is not existent in the efficient causes, which also have efficiency. If the assisting cause helps in producing by entering into the material cause, as water entering into a seed produces a sprout, the prior existence of the effect in it is still to be proved. Otherwise, the rule should be restricted to the material cause only.

Moreover, whatever does not contain the object cannot serve as a cause, just as a barren woman cannot give birth to a son. The object that does not contain the effect cannot be the cause, not to speak of the notion. The existing effect has a cause and vice versa. It should not again be argued that the consciousness, being existent, would also have to be considered as an effect. The above maxim applies to objects having particular arrangements.

The theory of the Buddhists involves many defects. They hold that there is neither conjunction (efficient cause) nor the composite as a distinct object, and hence, origination and destruction are all illusory. This is, however, strange in itself. By the force of the "and" in the *Kārikā*, the author refutes the view that the object is neither existent nor nonexistent, because it is already established that the effect exists in the cause.

IV. The Manifest and Unmanifest Aspects of Materiality (E55-60)

(10-11) Now we proceed to discuss the similarity and dissimilarity between the manifest and the unmanifest.

Objection : The similarity should be discussed first because it makes understanding easier.

Answer : No, it makes no difference, because both the similarity and dissimilarity are mutually dependent.

Objection : In this case it should be mentioned why dissimilarity is discussed first.

Answer : It is because similarity forms the present context. After knowing the similarity between the manifest and the unmanifest, the latter is known as a cause, then consciousness is known as an enjoyer, and the objects of creation as serving the means of enjoyment. Thus, dissimilarity that is not the main topic is discussed.

Objection : If it is so, what are the points of dissimilarity?

Answer : *Kārikā* 10 is quoted.

Objection : The property of having a cause (*hetu*) is common to all because even materiality and consciousness have causes.

Answer : Here, cause is understood in the narrow sense of a creating cause (*kāraka*).

Objection : The particular reason for such a restriction is not stated.

Answer : But it is implied by the context. Or, due to the association with the following word, "noneternal", it should be taken in the sense of having a cause that is invariably associated with noneternality. That cause is the creating cause.

Objection : In the case of noneternal objects also, both the creating (*kāraka*) and the revealing (*hetu*) causes are available.

Answer : To avoid absolutism some eternal entity must be accepted, and having a cause here excludes that eternal entity.

Objection : The idea of noneternity goes against the theory of the prior existence of an effect. The destruction would imply the production of a nonexistent object.

Answer : No, because we recognize the manifestation and disappearance of an object and not its absolute destruction. Disappearance or destruction means its becoming subtle. It is of two types—periodic world dissolution and dissolution for some time.

Objection : The above position is not final, because some philosophers, for example, Buddhists, believe in the momentariness of all the objects.

Answer : No, because there is no reason to support their theory.

Objection : The object is destructible because it meets destruction in the end.

Answer : Momentariness is still to be proved.

Objection : Here are the reasons to prove the momentariness of a flame. First, there is no addition in a flame when the flame continues burning with additional fuel. Second, due to the absence of a support, it is not always found. Third, because there would be a division in a flame when it is struck, if it were not momentary. A sound is also momentary, since, first, if it were not momentary, it would increase when a new sound is added. Second, it is directly perceived to be destructible every moment. Third, because, unlike eternal objects, it is heard at a place different from its production.

Answer : The first reason proves only the destructibility of flames and not their momentariness. The second reason is still to be proved. The third argument involves the undesirable consequence of the nonmomentariness of threads, etc., where such a division is seen. Similar arguments are also used to refute the momentariness of sounds.

Objections : Objects are momentary because there is no reason to prove nonmomentariness; otherwise objects would be immutable.

Answer : Latent dispositions (*saṃskāra*) serve as the cause for the subsistence of objects. Thus, there is no immutability of objects. Moreover, the theory would involve the undesirable result of the extirpation of the whole world. The objector may argue that the object produced earlier may serve as a cause for the production of what comes later. This will, however, be a deviation from the earlier argument. Nor should it be argued here that destruction is natural, because objects subsist for the purpose of consciousness and then they pass into nonmanifestation.

Moreover, the theory of momentariness involves the undesirable result of the absence of the perception of objects in the next moment. If their perception is supposed to be caused by the production of similar objects subsequently, it would also be wrong. First, because there is no material cause of objects. Second, there is no perception of sequence that is found in production. Third, because there are no instrumental causes at that time to produce the object. Fourth, there is no product of some other product. Fifth, with the production of some effect the causal form is destroyed and there remains nothing to produce anything from it. It would again involve causeless and continuous production. If it is argued that destruction of cause and origination of effect take place simultaneously, it would not leave a scope for causality between them. It would also not be right to argue that a particular change seen in objects proves momentariness, first, because it would imply production in the absence of an effect, and second, such a production is not perceived.

(The text of the further portion of the *Yuktidīpikā* up to the 12th *kārikā* is not available.)

V. The Three Constituents (E60-62)

(12-13) The word "only" (*eva*) is construed with the respective nature of each constituent. "Buoyancy" brings about the arising of effects and the efficient operation of the senses. "Illumination" causes the removal of darkness and the rise of knowledge in the senses. "Stimulation" and "mobility" refer to special effort and activity respectively. Activity causes change from an earlier state to another state, and there are two kinds of activity, namely, evolving or transforming (*pariṇāma*) and simple continuous motion (*praspanda*). The former is a basic change in characteristics (as, for example, when intellect becomes egoity, and so forth). The latter is simply motion without change or characteristics, as, for example, the motion or activity of the five breaths or the activities of the action capacities. "Heaviness" causes increasing density in an object and inertness in activities; "enveloping" causes concealment from sight in the case of objects, as also impurity in the senses. An object is composed of three constituents and the quality of a certain constituent dominates while the other constituents assist it. Their individual form and qualities are sometimes experienced also when they have not become subordinate.

Objection : There is no criterion to say that *sattva*, etc., becomes subordinate when experienced as intermixed with the other constituents.

Answer : If such distinctions cannot be made, then a husband would find his beautiful wife miserable just as the cowives find her. Hence, the dominance or subordinance of a certain constituent in a certain case must be admitted, and their individual form is not an intermixture of the said qualities.

It should also not be argued that the constituents, having mutually contradictory qualities, cannot coexist.

Just as the mutually contradictory components of a lamp such as the oil, wick, and flame work jointly for a single purpose of illuminating, the constituents work together for serving the purpose of consciousness. Although objects having equal powers cannot remain together, yet the principal and subordinate can remain together. The same rule holds good in the case of the constituents.

Objection : If the constituents are considered to be distinct in accordance with their qualities, a single constituent comes to be two because of its having two qualities. If the internal contradiction in the qualities of constituents is not admitted, it would be better to admit one constituent only, ignoring their differences. Their relation of subordinate and principal and the service rendered by the subordinate to the principal again implies that the constituents are either of one form or are of mixed form.

Answer : Admitting two qualities in each constituent does not amount to their being six. The constituents attain the state of principal and subordinate, which would not be possible if there were only one constituent. Moreover, it is not established that there are as many substances as qualities. Furthermore, the supposition implies that each object is unique. The latter argument is also wrong because the attainment of the state of principal and subordinate in the constituents is meant in a secondary sense. The above examples show that such a state is necessary in order to account for effects.

VI. The Inferences that Establish the Existence and Makeup of Primordial Materiality and Consciousness (E62-86)

(15) (E62-74) *Objection* : Due to the acceptance of similarity between effect and cause, primordial materiality, like its effects, is caused.

Answer : No, because the characteristics (see SK 10) that are opposed to the effect are the exception to the rule of similarity between cause and effect.

Objection : Objects are not known to be limited in magnitude in their past and future states.

Answer : There is no reason to deny their limited magnitude in those states also.

Objection : The nature of being specific is also not settled in the case of worldly objects.

Answer : The objects are distinct and specific and consequently limited in magnitude. This finite nature leads to inference of the existence of the unmanifest.

The common element in homogeneous objects exists as their essence or cause, like clay in a pot, etc. Similarly, all the objects have *sattva*, *rajas*, and *tamas* that should be understood as their cause.

Objection : How is it known that objects have pleasure, etc.?

Answer : It is because the objects give rise to these experiences.

Objection : Dissimilarity in cause and effect is observed and, hence, homogeneity is not established.

Answer : Our theory is that to whatever genus a particular effect belongs, that is the effect of that.

Objection : There is no proof for a particular causal efficacy (*śakti*). It is not observed before the origination of effect. If it is supposed to exist in the cause without giving rise to the effect, the efficacy would be incapable and hence would not be efficient. Therefore, causal efficacies arise because of the coming together of assisting factors. Moreover, their difference form or nondifference with primordial materiality cannot be logically explained.

Answer : It is not the case that there is no proof for a causal efficacy before the origination of an effect. Causal efficacy is the cause itself, which does exist before the effects. It does not deviate from its essential nature before producing an effect, because it exists in a potential form, just as a lamp, the light of which is obstructed by a wall, etc. Causal efficacy does not originate by assisting factors. On the contrary, such an argument proves the prior existence of causal efficacy, because objects capable of manifesting effects are selected by an agent. As regards the relation between the causal efficacies and primordial materiality, let it be nondifference. It will not give rise to the undesirable result of the plurality of primordial materialities or the oneness of causal efficacies, because number depends on knowledge or conceptualization. A single efficacy is manifested in many forms in the objects. The existence of causal efficacies is manifested in many forms in the objects. The existence of causal efficacies is proved through the inference based upon general correlation.

The relation between cause and effect is one of mutual interaction, and this is explained through the mutual subservience of the constituents.

Objection : The mutual subservience among the constituents is not in succession or in simultaneity. The constituents cannot function singly without requiring the activity of others before the existence of the other two. Those that are born simultaneously cannot be mutually subservient. Moreover, it cannot be explained whether illumination, etc., through which the constituents favor each other, exist prior to the activity of the constituents or come into existence afterward. The former alternative would lead to the single nature and the independent character of the constituents, whereas the latter goes against the prior existence of the effect.

Answer : The subservience among the constituents is simultaneous. Objects taking place simultaneously can be mutually subservient when acting for a single purpose. As regards illumination, etc., these are through mutual contact just as with the lame and the blind man. It does not involve the theory of causation because contact is not a substance. The potency of mutual subservience exists in the constituents and is manifested when they come into mutual interaction.

Objection : The theory of primordial materiality as the ultimate cause of the universe cannot be accepted unless other possibilities are excluded, including atoms (*paramāṇu*), consciousness (*puruṣa*), God (*īśvara*), action (*karman*), fate or destiny (*daiva*), inherent nature (*svabhāva*), time (*kāla*), chance (*yadṛcchā*), and negation (*abhāva*).

Answer : Atoms cannot be the cause because their existence is not proved. Their existence cannot be established on the basis of their homogeneity with worldly objects, because that homogeneity can be explained in other ways.

Objection : Let us accept the atoms in the form of the subtle elements ofthe Sāṃkhyas.

Answer : The subtle elements, being the cause of the gross elements, are greater than the latter, but this is not true of atoms. Even if the existence of atoms is accepted for the sake of argument, they cannot be the cause of the universe because they are products, whereas the ultimate cause must be unproduced. Otherwise, there will arise the defect of infinite regress. The caused nature of atoms must be accepted because of their finite magnitude, possessing form, heat, speed, etc., because of being located in space, because of interacting with one another in union, because of giving rise to other objects, and because of their being perceptible. Their subtlety cannot be taken as a cause for their being uncaused, since this would entail that the subtle baked atoms of earth are uncaused.

Consciousness cannot be the cause because it is not a causal principle. Because God is like pure consciousness in nature, God cannot be the cause of the universe.

Objection : The Pāśupatas and the Vaiśeṣikas accept God as different from pure consciousness, first because particular effects should be caused by some superior intellect, and second, because the union between conscious and unconscious is caused by some sentient entity.

Answer : It is still to be proved that objects are created by some superior intellect, because the intellect of God does not exist before the activity of primordial materiality, and there is no example to prove that God's intellect comes into being merely through His own will. Further, there is no God because there is no purpose for a God to fulfil. Moreover, objects such as trees, etc., are not caused by God's intellect, and there would be impropriety in God's creating objects that result in frustration. God is not needed for bringing about the contact between materiality and consciousness. Moreover, God's body must be accepted, first, because it is a requirement for the inference to His existence, and second, because His body is mentioned in the scripture. The Sāṃkhya equivalent to God is the "body of greatness" (*māhātmyaśarīra*). Thus, the Pāśupatas are wrong in accepting God as cause.

The following are the defects in the theory of the *Vaiśeṣikas*. They cannot logically explain whether God is included in the categories accepted by them or not. Hence, it is not accepted by Kaṇāda. Moreover, it is neither mentioned by Kaṇāda nor by any other old Vaiśeṣika teacher in their writings. The theory of the Pāśupatas about God is imposed on the *Vaiśeṣikasūtras*.

Because it has been explained that atoms are not the cause, so action or *karman* can also not be the cause.

Time can also not be the cause of the universe, because it does not exist as a separate entity. It is nothing but the continuing activity (*spandana*) of causes.

Accidence or chance is also not the cause of the universe, because it cannot account for the cause-effect relation found among objects in the world.

Negation also cannot be the cause, since it cannot account for the limited magnitude of worldly objects and the homogeneity of cause and effect. The universe is not caused by causal efficiency, because it has no independent existence. Favor (*upakāraka*) also is not the cause, for this would involve infinite regress. Disjunction (*vibhāga*) also is not the cause, because it is also not an independent entity.

(16) (E74-75) *Objection*: Because primordial materiality is single, it cannot give rise to differentiated objects.

Answer : At the time of creation the constituents mix together and bring about differentiation.

Objection : In the absence of activity, primordial materiality cannot give rise to creation. If it has activity, it will be like the manifest.

Answer : Primordial materiality, being subtle, has no activity of movement, but it has the activity of transformation. It creates the universe through transformation.

Objection : Transformation also should not be accepted in subtle objects like primordial materiality.

Answer : Though primordial materiality is subtle, yet its transformation is possible.

Objection : What is the transformation?

Answer: When the object without deviating from its essence acquires new qualities different from the earlier, that is called transformation.

Objection : What is the example here?

Answer : Just as an object made of *palāśa* wood without ceasing to be *palāśa* changes from black to yellow because of heat.

Objection : Why is it not considered that a new object is produced?

Answer : It is because we do not believe in momentariness.

Objection : The emergence of new qualities and the destruction of old qualities implies fresh emergence and destruction of an object, because you believe in the identity of cause and effect.

Answer : No, it can be explained on the analogy of an army and its parts.

Objection : The Sāṃkhyas do not have an adequate interpretation to explain the general (*sāmānya*) and specific (*viśeṣa*) features of an object.

Answer : Let the object (to be qualified) be understood as the general. It remains general until the knowledge of its cause (in the wider sense) becomes an issue. Or, the general (to be qualified) may be interpreted as the powers of *sattva*, *rajas*, and *tamas*.

Objection : But then there is no way to account for specific features.

Answer : The constituents attain differentiation through mutual combination, just as water gets many tastes and forms after coming into contact with various objects.

(17) (E75-82) *Objection* : The existence of consciousness needs to be established. Its existence is doubtful, first, because imperceptible objects are found to be existent as well as nonexistent, and, second, because no instrument of knowledge confirms its existence. Moreover, there is difference of opinion about its existence amongst the philosophers. The Buddhists deny its existence.

Answer : The existence of consciousness is established through the inference based on general correlation. The body, like a bed, etc., being composite in nature, is meant for something other, namely, consciousness.

Objection : Such an inference would simply lead to the existence of another composite object.

Answer : The discussion presupposes the noncomposite nature of consciousness, for its imperceptibility establishes its noncomposite nature.

Objection : One composite is meant for some other composite, just like the bed for Devadatta.

Answer : The other should be understood as the noncomposite. Moreover, there should be some entity under whose control the constituents give rise to manifest objects.

Objection : This would imply agency in pure consciousness.

Answer : No, here the purpose of consciousness is metaphorically spoken of as controller. The constituents depend on consciousness insofar as they serve his purpose.

Objection : The manifest and the unmanifest being of the nature of satisfaction, frustration and neutrality, require some enjoyer of them. What is then the enjoyment?

Answer : It is the capability of obtaining the objects.

Objection : It also implies no need of consciousness, because the purpose may be served by knowledge (or mind).

Answer : No, because knowledge, or mind, is the product of primordial materiality and hence unconscious in nature. Therefore, it cannot be an enjoyer.

Objection : If ordinary experience and consciousness are the same, you should accept only one of them.

Answer : No, the difference can be explained on the analogy of the difference between knowledge and the object of knowledge. In this way the relation between the object of enjoyment and the enjoyer can be established between intellect and consciousness.

Objection : If the mind is also considered an object, it would involve infinite regress because consciousness would again require some enjoyer.

Answer : The mind, being insentient in nature, requires an enjoyer, whereas consciousness, being sentient, does not. Therefore, there is no infinite regress.

Objection : The knowledge in this case would belong to consciousness and, thus, no scope for intellect is left.

Answer : Consciousness is free from the mixture of constituents and, hence, not an agent of knowledge. Otherwise, there would be knowledge even when the mind does not function, i.e., in the state of deep sleep, etc.

The activity of every object is purposeful. Primordial materiality's activity is meant for consciousness. Here, it cannot be argued that the existence of primordial materiality is also equally doubtful, because its existence is already proved. Nor should it be argued that, because of the controversy about it, consciousness does not exist, for this would imply the nonexistence of every object, as there is some controversy about every object. This disproves the argument that there is no reason to prove the existence of consciousness.

(18) (E82-83) *Objection* : Now it should be discussed whether consciousness is one or many.

Answer : Our assertion is that there are many consciousnesses. Birth and death being contradictory states of the body, they cannot be found in the case of a single consciousness simultaneously. The different capacities of the organs also lead to the same conclusion.

Primordial materiality's activity to produce bodies for the enjoyment of various consciousnesses is not simultaneous. If consciousness were single, it could enjoy all the bodies simultaneously.

The qualities of the three constituents and the like are in different proportion in many bodies. Consciousnesses, therefore, must be many.

(19) (E83-86) *Objection* : How are the witness-hood (*sākṣitva*), isolation (*kaivalya*), neutrality (*mādhyasthya*), subjectivity (*draṣṭṛtva*), and nonagency (*akartṛbhāva*) of consciousness established?

Answer : Through witnesshood the author suggests the dependence of the constituent's activities on the purpose of consciousness.

Objection : How does consciousness control the activities of the constituents?

Answer : The agent acts in accordance with the desire of the witness and not independently. The activity of primordial materiality is for the purpose of consciousness. Isolation negates consciousness' contact with the constituents. Neutrality implies the absence of increase or decrease in consciousness and, hence, the absence of extenuating interference or assistance. Subjectivity confirms consciousness' receiving the form of the objects merely through contact. Through nonagency the seven kinds of agency are negated. Witnesshood is proved through consciousness' being devoid of constituents.

Objections: Consciousness' nature of being devoid of the constituents is not proved, for it cannot be admitted by the one who admits that consciousness is endowed with satisfaction, frustration, etc., since the constituents are expressed and experienced as existing in consciousness as "I am happy," etc.

Answer : But this would imply the quality of being white, etc., also belonging to consciousness, because one says "I am white."

Objection : What type of dissociation from the constituents is intended here?

Answer : Dissociation here means the absence of a common purpose. In absence of a single purpose the constituents work separately. Consciousness is neutral because of its being the subject of experience.

Objection : Why is it so?

Answer : Because consciousness neither obstructs nor assists. Consciousness is a seer because of being conscious. It is inactive because of its being nonproductive. Therefore, it is devoid of activities. Moreover, consciousness is inactive due to its being conscious and of unmixed form, for activity is found in nonconscious objects and objects of mixed nature. It cannot be maintained that consciousness may be active because it is all-pervasive like primordial materiality, because the activity of primordial materiality is due to unconsciousness, which is not found in consciousness. Nor should it be argued here that consciousness created bodies merely through thinking, because the possibility of thinking or resolution is already refuted in the case of consciousness.

VII. The Association or Proximity of Primordial Materiality and Consciousness (E87-90)

(20-21) *Objection* : Why is consciousness transferred only to the intellect and not to a pot, etc., which also equally comes into contact with consciousness due to the all-pervasive nature of consciousness?

Answer : Consciousness is erroneously transferred to an object capable of receiving it. The intellect is capable, but the pot is not.

Objection : If consciousness is supposed to receive the form of the intellect, it would be modifiable.

Answer : Transference of form is meant metaphorically. The intellect's form is falsely attributed to consciousness because of their contact just as the attribution of victory and defeat of the servant is attributed to the king, or, just as impurity, to the sky, because of to its contact with clouds, etc.

Objection : How does Sāṃkhya account for contact?

Answer : The contact postulated just through proximity in general on account of the sameness of location, like that between space and a cow. It is a particular kind of contact postulated by the system for a certain purpose.

Objection : What is the purpose for which the above contact is postulated?

Answer : Since consciousness is conscious, it is so related to materiality. Or, it is meant for the experience of materiality by consciousness and comes to an end with the fulfilment of that purpose.

Puruṣa's power of consciousness becomes meaningful in the presence of primordial materiality, and materiality also becomes useful in the presence of consciousness. It is the contact through mutual expectancy called bondage of capability. This is like the contact of a blind man and a lame man, who function with mutual help for a single purpose.

Through such mutual expectancy the creation of elements, mental modes, and physical beings is brought about. Since consciousnesses are many, creation does not cease at any one time. Materiality keeps on functioning for the bound consciousnesses.

VIII. The Derivation of the Basic Principles (E91-92)

(22) There are varying views among teachers concerning the derivation and nature of the various basic principles, and the purpose of this verse is to set forth clearly the view of Īśvarakṛṣṇa. For example, some teachers assert that there is a separate, indescribable principle between primordial materiality and intellect/will. On the other hand, however, Patañjali (the Sāṃkhya teacher), Pañcādhikaraṇa, and the followers of Vārṣagaṇya assert that the intellect emerges directly out of primordial materiality. Still others assert the view that egoity has no separate status. Egoity is simply the notion of "I am" performed by the intellect. Yet again, some say that the subtle elements come from egoity, but Vindhyavāsin teaches that the five subtle elements and egoity all come directly out of the intellect. Similarly, all the teachers suggest that the sense capacities arise from egoity—except for Pañcādhikaraṇa, who teaches that the sense capacities are derived from the gross elements. Others suggest that each subtle element has only one generic form, but others suggest a theory of accumulation (that is to say, each subtle element in the series becomes increasingly complex). This latter view is that of Vārṣagaṇya. Some suggest that the sense capacities function together. Others suggest that they function separately. Vindhyavāsin suggests that the sense capacities are all-pervasive. Some suggest that the internal instrument is thirteenfold, but Vindhyavāsin suggests that it is only elevenfold. Again, some suggest that all experience occurs in the intellect, but Vindhyavāsin suggests that experience occurs in the mind. Some suggest that intentionality (*saṃkalpa*), self-awareness (*abhimāna*) and reflective discerning (*adhyavasāya*) are plural or separate functions, but Vindhyavāsin suggests that they are one. Similarly, Pañcādhikaraṇa argues that the sense capacities function only because of the power of primordial materiality and have no capacity in and of themselves, but others do not agree with this view. Vārṣagaṇya suggests that the organs act both within (subjectively) and without (objectively). Patañjali suggests that the activity in them is inherent. Pañcādhikaraṇa suggests that the activity in them depends upon external factors. Some argue

that the intellect is momentary, but others argue that it extends over time. Thus, there are numerous conflicting views among the teachers, and verse 22 sets forth the correct view of Īśvarakṛṣṇa, namely, that the intellect ("*buddhi*") (also called "great" or *mahat* because it occupies great space and time and has more magnitude) emerges from materiality, that egoity emerges from intellect, that the five sense-capacities, the five action capacities and the five subtle elements emerge from egoity; and that the five gross elements emerge from the subtle elements. Synonyms for "*buddhi*" include "*mahat*," "*mati*," "*brahmā*," "*khyāti*," "*īśvara*," etc. The term "*bhūta*" was used by some ancient teachers for subtle element and "*mahābhūta*" for gross element. The Mīmāṃsakas and Jains believe in the eternity of elements, but that is refuted here.

IX. The Functioning of the Thirteenfold Instrument (E92-117)

(23) The intellect is characterized by reflective discerning in the form of "this is a cow" or "this is a man." It is a transformation of materiality, and, hence, it is not momentary (as the Buddhists assert). When *sattva* is dominant in it, then the basic predispositions of meritorious behavior, knowledge, nonattachment, and power come into prominence. Meritorious behavior is of two varieties, namely, (a) those religious practices that lead to the enjoyment of bodies, organs, and objects in the realm of Brahmā, etc.; and (b) those religious practices of meditation including restraint, restriction, and so forth. Knowledge is also of two varieties, namely, (a) verbal or intellectual knowledge based on perception, inference, and verbal testimony; and (b) the ultimate discrimination of the difference between consciousness and the constituents (or, in other words, materiality). Nonattachment has four varieties of intensity, namely, (a) restrained apperception (*yatamānasaṃjñā*); (b) restricted apperception (*vyatireka-saṃjñā*); (c) concentrated apperception (*ekendriyasaṃjñā*) and (d) totally controlled apperception (*vaśikārasaṃjñā*). Power has eight varieties, or, in other words, the eight supernormal attainments, subtlety, greatness, etc. (see other commentaries for the standard listing). When *tamas* is dominant in the intellect, then the opposite tendencies (from the above) come into prominence.

(24) The notion of egoity is clearly distinguished from intellect, and both are transformations of materiality. Various technical terms for egoity are discussed, namely, "*vaikārika*," "*taijasa*," and "*bhūtādi*." These provide useful distinctions, for they specify the many effects of egoity.

(26-27) External organs are necessary, and they are different from the actual physical organs in the body. They are not derived from the gross elements. They are more than one in number. Otherwise, all things would be experienced simultaneously. The mind is both a sense capacity and an action capacity. Its function is intentionality.

(28) The term "sensing" (*ālocana*) refers to revealing and not to determining. The precise function of each sense capacity is described. The view of the Nyāya is refuted, namely, that the organs are derived from the elements. Rather, the sense capacities are derived from egoity.

(29) Reflective discerning, self-awareness and intentionality represent the particular or unique functions of the intellect, egoity, and mind respectively. Moreover, since intellect, egoity, and mind are extremely subtle, it is permissible to look to their specific functions as defining attributes (*svalakṣaṇa*). These three also have a general or common function, however, and that is the maintenance of the life of the organism both internally and externally. This common maintenance of life manifests itself in terms of the five life breaths, namely, *prāṇa* (the breath in the heart and mouth, which internally maintains respiration and externally maintains obedience), *apāna* (the breath of the lower limbs, which internally maintains the elimination of waste products and externally maintains a person's ability to change life style), *samāna* (the breath of the heart and stomach, which internally maintains digestion and externally maintains an organism's ability to relate socially), *udāna* (the breath of the body's fluids, which flows upward into the head and which internally maintains the ability to speak and externally maintains an organism's self-confidence), and *vyāna* (the breath diffused throughout the body, which internally maintains the homeostasis of the organism and externally maintains a sense of unity with all of nature). These five breaths together with the sense capacities, action capacities, and egoity make up what the ancient teachers called the "*prāṇāṣṭaka*," or a group of eight entities beginning with *prāṇa*. This eightfold vitality arises from the five sources of action, which reside in the intellect and have *rajas* as their dominant constituent.[20] These sources of action include the following:

(a) perseverance (*dhṛti*), a combination of *rajas* with *tamas*; (b) dutiful faith in conventional religious practice (*śraddhā*), a combination of *rajas* with *sattva*; (c) the desire for satisfaction (*sukha*), a combination of *sattva* and *tamas* wherein the activity component of *rajas* has been quieted; (d) the desire for wisdom (*vividiṣā*)), wherein the activity of *rajas* as the act of thinking is dominant; and (e) the desire for the cessation of the act of thinking (*avividiṣā*), wherein the reification of pure *tamas* becomes dominant. The first four sources of action can be productive for seeking truth. Even the fifth source (*avividiṣā*) can be productive if one interprets it to mean turning away from knowing trivial or counter-productive matters. Finally, the true seeker should come to be attracted to the purely *sāttvika* reflections of the world and should devote all of his activity to the attainment of discriminating knowledge.

(30) Although some of the older teachers argue that the functioning of intellect, egoity, mind, and a particular sense capacity may occur simultaneously, Īśvarakṛṣṇa teaches in this *kārikā* that they function sequentially. Recognition (*pratyabhijñā*) falls within the sphere of perception, and memory (*smṛti*) may arise even without a specific cause, that is to say, it may be accidental (*akasmāt*).

(31) Two explanations of "mutual coordination" (*parasparākūta*) are given, the first referring to the mutual impulsion of the organs, the second to the mutual influence of the objects. The organs are devoid of ideas (*pratyaya*) and are guided by the mind (*mānasādhiṣṭhita*). Several reasons are given for the assertion that everything functions "for the sake of the *puruṣa*" (*puruṣārtha*).

(32) The question of how many instruments there are is disputed in the tradition. The followers of Vārṣagaṇya assert that there are eleven instruments with intellect as the only internal organ. The Tāntrikas, Pañcādhikaraṇa, and so forth, assert that there are ten instruments, and Patañjali (the Sāṃkhya teacher) asserts that there are twelve instruments. The correct view is that there are thirteen instruments, namely, intellect, ego, mind, the five sense capacities and the five action capacities, and the commentary argues in favor of this view. The term "*karaṇa*" means the instrument of action. Seizing (*āharaṇa*) is accomplished by the action capacities. Holding (*dhāraṇa*) is accomplished by the sense capacities. Illuminating (*prakāśana*) is accomplished by the internal organ. Other teachers suggest that the action capacities accomplish seizing; mind and egoity accomplish holding; and intellect together with the sense capacities accomplish illuminating. The reference to the tenfold objects means the five specific objects (*viśeṣa*, i.e., the gross elements) and the five generic objects (*aviśeṣa*), i.e., the five subtle elements.

(33) The external sense capacities function through perception in present time only. The internal organ functions not only in perception but also through memory of the past and intentionality (or inference) with respect to the future. In other words, the internal organ functions in all three times. Reasons are given for the view that there are ten external organs even though the tenfold division of the external organs has already been referred to in verses 26 and 28.

(34) The sense capacities of gods and Yogis are able to experience generic objects, but ordinary mortals only experience specific objects. The action capacities relate to the activities of things having form. Speech grasps the vibrations of sounds alone. The other action capacities function with respect to the activities of all five kinds of objects. Organs cannot be regarded as having no objects of their own (*asadviṣaya*).

(35) The term "door" (*dvāra*) refers to a direct means of perception, as, for example, seeing a color. The term "possessing the door" (*dvārin*) refers to indirect or internal perception, as, for example, intellect, egoity, and mind. The latter can perceive a great variety of matters. The former is definitely restricted to certain specific kinds of perception.

(36) The term "*artha*" is taken in the sense of effect (*kārya*) in relation to specific and generic objects. The consciousness principle (*cetanāśakti*) becomes related to intellect when it determines something. Ordinary experience (*upabhoga*) begins with the apprehension of sound, etc., and reaches a conclusion when the difference between constituent and consciousness is attained.

(37) The activity of knowing is accomplished by the intellect as well as all decisions to act. Consciousness sees by means of the intellect and appears to act because of the intellect. When the intellect is confused (under the influence of *tamas*), a misconception occurs. When the intellect discriminates properly, however (under the influence of *sattva*), the misconception is removed. The intellect then realizes the difference between consciousness and the constituents.

X. The Subtle and Gross Elements (E117-121)

(38) The five subtle elements are produced from egoity. They are referred to as "generic." They are referred to as "subtle elements" because they represent general categories, e.g., the essence of audibility or the essence of visibility, and so forth. The gross elements are produced from the subtle elements. One subtle element produces only one gross element, that is to say, the subtle element of sound produces the sound-producing gross element or space; the subtle element of touch produces wind; the subtle element of form produces light; the subtle element of taste produces water; and the subtle element of smell produces earth. Space has only one quality, sound. Wind has two qualities, sound and touch. Light has three qualities, sound, touch, and form. Water has four qualities, sound, touch, form, and taste. Earth has five qualities, sound, touch form, taste, and smell. The elements are called "specific" because they are experienced as specific feelings that are comforting, discomforting, and confusing. Apart from the five qualities, namely, sound, etc., there are other qualities that are known as "one helping the other" (*parasparānugrāhaka*), and seven verses are quoted that enumerate these qualities. The subtle elements do not give rise to specific feelings, and, hence, they are called "generic." The specific features and qualities of each of the gross elements are given.

(39) The threefold specific bodies are as follows: (a) the subtle body (*prāṇāṣṭaka*, and see above under verse 29, made up of the five

breaths plus the sense capacities, the action capacities, and egoity), which depends on activity (*ceṣṭā*) and transmigrates from life to life; (b) bodies born of mother and father, which are of two types, namely, womb-born (*jarāyuja*) and egg-born (*aṇḍaja*), and which are wrapped in the sheaths (*kośa*) of hair, blood, and flesh (derived from the mother) and bone, tendon, and marrow (derived from the father); and (c) bodies born from the elements (*prabhūta*), which are also of two types, namely, seed-born or "coming out as a result of breaking through" (*udbhijja*) and sweat-born (*svedaja*). The gods and other transhuman personages have bodies that are womb-born, egg-born, seed-born, and sweat-born, depending on their functions. Of these various bodies, the subtle bodies are permanent and transmigrate from life to life. The other bodies cease at the moment of death.

Whereas the bodies born of mother and father and the bodies derived from the elements are simple enough to comprehend, the derivation of subtle bodies is not as clear. There is an old mythological tradition that describes the manner in which spiritual bodies are derived. This old tradition is that of the "six kinds of reproduction" (*ṣaṭsiddhi*). According to this tradition, in the time just prior to creation, spiritual entities simply willed or desired themselves into existence. This is the *manaḥsiddhi*. When this capacity became weakened, creatures reproduced themselves simply with amorous glances. This is the *cakṣuḥsiddhi*. When this became weakened, reproduction occurred simply by speaking or talking with one another. This is the *vāksiddhi*. When this weakened, reproduction took place simply by touching. This is the *hastasiddhi*. When this weakened, reproduction occurred through embracing. This is the *āśleṣasiddhi*. Finally, when even this weakened, reproduction occurred through sexual intercourse. This is the *dvandvasiddhi*, and it was at this point that the ordinary world of creation began to function with rebirth and transmigration. Only the last variety is our ordinary human level; the preceding varieties make up the hierarchy of supernatural beings.

The older Sāṃkhya teachers have interpreted the problem of the subtle body in various ways. Pañcādhikaraṇa, for example, referred to the subtle body as *vaivarta*, a moving body that serves as a carrier (*ātivāhika*) of consciousness. Patañjali (the Sāṃkhya teacher) accepted a subtle body that is propelled by merit and demerit. Vindhyavāsin, however, did not accept the notion of a subtle body, mainly because he believed that the sense capacities are all-pervasive. Hence, according to Vindhyavāsin, the notion of a subtle body was unnecessary.

XI. The Subtle Body (E121-123)

(40) The expression "*mahadādisūkṣmaparyanta*" means the eightfold

vitality or subtle body (*prāṇāṣṭaka*) that transmigrates from life to life. Vārṣagaṇya says that intellect is universal or general (*sādhāraṇa*), but here *mahadādi* refers to the eight *prāṇas* (*prāṇāṣṭaka*) (and cf. above under SK 29). There is no need to accept many subtle bodies for each consciousness. There is only one subtle body that accompanies a consciousness from life to life.

(41) The notion (of Vindhyavāsin) that the sense capacities are all-pervasive is wrong. If the sense capacities were all-pervasive, then one would know all things everywhere, which is not the case. There are lengthy discussions of the subtle body and the process of rebirth.

(42) Transmigration of the essential core (*liṅga*) is determined by the force of the basic predispositions, empowered by the constituents of materiality. When these causes are checked, then liberation results.

XII. The Basic Predispositions (E123-137)

(43) According to Īśvarakṛṣṇa, the basic predispositions (*bhāva*) are (a) innate (*sāṃsiddhika*), (b) natural (*prākṛtika*), or (c) acquired (*vaikṛta*). In sages such as Kapila knowledge is innate. In lesser sages it is natural and can be easily aroused. In ordinary mortals it is present as a possibility that can be acquired (*vaikṛta*) by proper study and instruction. Other Sāṃkhya teachers hold different views. Pañcādhikaraṇa, for example, asserts that knowledge is either natural or acquired. The former then breaks down into three varieties, namely, *tattvasamakāla* (knowledge that arises simultaneously with a basic principle), *sāṃsiddhika* (knowledge that can easily be aroused in a composite body), and *ābhiṣyandika* (potential knowledge that can be aroused but with more difficulty). The latter has two varieties; *svavaikṛta* (knowledge cultivated by oneself) and *paravaikṛta* (knowledge cultivated by means of others). Vindhyavāsin, on the other hand, does not accept *tattvasamakāla* or *sāṃsiddhika*, but he does accept the other varieties.

(44) The terms "upward" (*ūrdhva*) and "downward" (*adhastāt*) do not refer to physical regions (*bhūmiviśeṣa*) but simply higher and lower births. Only knowledge is a means to liberation.

(45) The basic cause of bondage is ignorance. When ignorance is conjoined with nonattachment, then dissolution in materiality results, which is known as *prakṛtibandha*. When ignorance is conjoined with pursuing various kinds of worldly power, then acquired bondage results, known as *vaikārikabandha*. When ignorance is conjoined with passionate attachment to seen and heard objects, then ordinary or worldly bondage results, known as *dakṣiṇābandha*. The term "nonattachment" in this context refers to improper nonattachment. The term "*rājasa*" indicates that passionate attachment toward objects is the cause of ordinary existence (*saṃsāra*).

(46-51) The term "*pratyaya*" is synonymous with "category" (*padārtha*) or "distinguishing characteristic" (*lakṣaṇa*). Hence, the expressions "*pratyayasarga*," "*padārthasarga*," and "*lakṣaṇasarga*" are roughly synonymous. On the other hand, one can also argue that the term "*pratyaya*" is synonymous with "*buddhi*," "*niścaya*," or "*adhyavasāya*," Hence, "*pratyayasarga*" means the intellectual creation as certainty and ascertainment. There is an old mythological tradition (here quoted) that describes the emergence of the intellectual creation as follows. The body of greatness (*māhātmyaśarīra*), at the beginning of creation, felt alone and wanted sons who would do his bidding. By an act of will (or inner contemplation) he produced five kinds of beings whose principal energy-streams (*mukhyasrotas*) became enveloped in immovable *tamas*. By another act of will (or thought) he produced twenty-eight kinds of beings whose energy-streams were more mobile but who were still largely dominated by *tamas* and were characterized as being *tiryaksrotas*. By yet another act of will (or thought) he produced nine kinds of beings whose energy-streams tended to flow upward and who were, thus, dominated by *sattva* and characterized as being *ūrdhvasrotas*. Finally, by an act of will (or thought) he produced eight kinds of beings whose energy-streams tended to flow downward and who were, thus, dominated by *rajas* and characterized as being *arvāksrotas*. Therefore, the intellectual creation has five misconceptions, twenty-eight dysfunctions, nine contentments, and eight attainments. The misconceptions and dysfunctions (dominated by *tamas*) are especially found among plants and animals (wherein there is a predominance of *mukhyasrotas* and *tiryaksrotas* respectively). The contentments are especially found among the gods (wherein there is a predominance of *ūrdhvasrotas*). The attainments are especially found in the human realm (wherein there is a predominance of *arvāksrotas*).

The five misconceptions break down into various subdivisions. There are eight varieties of *tamas* and eight varieties of confusion (see Gauḍapāda's *Bhāṣya* for an enumeration of both groups). There are ten varieties of great confusion, including problems related to the ten familial relationships, namely, those of mother, father, brother, sister, wife, son, daughter, teacher, friend, and personal assistant. There are eighteen varieties of gloom, made up of the ten problems related to familial relationships and eight varieties of power. Finally, there are also eighteen varieties of blind gloom made up of the fear of losing the ten familial relationships and the eight varieties of power. These five misconceptions are in a sequence of descending inferiority.

Reference in passing is also made to the eight generative principles indicating that each has fifteen subvarieties, based on five (*saṃhata*, *vivikta*, *pariṇata*, *vyasta*, and *samasta*) for each of the three constituents.

The twenty-eight dysfunctions are made up of the eleven injuries to the capacities (including mind, the five sense capacities, and the five action capacities) together with the seventeen kinds of injury to the intellect (see SK 49 and Gauḍapāda's *Bhāṣya* for an enumeration).

There are nine kinds of contentment and eight kinds of attainment. The nine kinds of contentment have the following ancient names: *ambhas* ("endless water"), *salila* ("absorbed along with endless water"), *ogha* ("carrying like a flood of water"), *vṛṣṭi* ("rain that pleases everything"), *sutāra* ("easily crossing"), *supāra* ("crossing to the other shore"), *sunetra* ("easily leading to liberation"), *sumārīca* ("the well-praised") and *uttamābhaya* ("the greatest fear"). Moreover, contentments are said overall to have two varieties, one for the wise (*vyutpanna*) and the other for the unwise (*avyutpanna*). Contentment is said to be relative as it relates to higher and lower objects. The eight kinds of attainments have the following ancient names: *tāraka* ("crossing the ocean of birth and rebirth"), *sutāra* ("crossing the difficulties of the ocean of rebirth"), *tārayanta* ("crossing now"), *pramoda* ("enjoying"), *pramudita* ("exceedingly joyous"), *modamāna* ("delighting"), *ramyaka* ("pleasure of good friends"), and *sadāpramudita* ("always delighted"). The differences between contentments and attainments are discussed, and reasons are given for not including destiny (*bhāgya*) in time (*kāla*)[21] (The basic meanings for the *tuṣṭis* and *siddhis* may be found in *Sāṃkhyakārikā* 50-51; and see the commentaries of Gauḍapāda, Vācaspati Miśra, and Paramārtha's Chinese version for variant listings of the ancient names. A precise characterization of each of these ancient lists is no longer available. The interpretations of the ancient terminology in each of the commentaries appear forced and fanciful.)

(52) (The effects of) merit and demerit are not the cause of creation. The ultimate cause is the unmanifest (or, in other words, primordial materiality), which fulfills its unique task (*adhikāra*).

XIII. The Empirical World (E137-141)

(55) Satisfaction is always associated with frustration, but birth is not considered one of the causes of frustration. Decay (*jarā*) operates even in the region of the gods. Decay and death (*jarāmaraṇa*) are said to be the fundamental causes of frustration.

(56) Three kinds of creation are described: of principles (*tattva*), elemental (*bhūta*) and predispositional (*bhāva*). The older Sāṃkhya view that each consciousness has its own primordial materiality (namely, the view of Paurika) is refuted. There is only one primordial materiality.

XIV. Similes Illustrating the Role and Function of Primordial Materiality (E141-142)

(57) The simile of milk (*kṣīra*) is discussed at length. Manifes-

tation is due to consciousness' purpose (viz, experience and liberation) and not to the "proximity of consciousness" (*puruṣasannidhi*).

XV. Liberation and Isolation (E143-144)

(62-63) (No commentary available)

(64) (Only a portion of the commentary is available, and it follows other standard commentaries)

(65-66) (No commentary available)

(68) Isolation (*kaivalya*) appears to be identified with the Buddhist *nirvāṇa*. In this state, called *brahman*, the properties of the constituents disappear.

(69) Various explanations of duration, origination, and absorption are given, and the use of the term "*bhūta*" is explained.

XVI. The Transmission of the Sāṁkhya Tradition (E145-146)

(70) Kapila out of compassion taught the truth to Āsuri. Āsuri taught the truth to Pañcaśikha, who expanded it and passed it on to many others. It is impossible to list all of the many teachers of Sāṃkhya, because it was set forth in the beginning by the blessed one (*bhagavat, Kapila*) and hence goes back hundreds and thousands of years (or one hundred thousand years).

(71) Other teachers after Pañcaśikha include Hārīta, Bāddhali, Kairāta, Paurika, Ṛṣabheśvara, Pañcādhikaraṇa, Patañjali, Vārṣagaṇya, Kauṇḍinya, Mūka, and so forth. Īśvarakṛṣṇa presents a balanced and useful account of Sāṃkhya. He is not biased toward anyone's interpretation, and he presents the system in a way that can be easily comprehended by students.

(72) Īśvarakṛṣṇa summarized the views of the vast tradition, leaving out many detailed disputations and focusing, rather, on the essence of the entire system.

JAYAMAṄGALĀ

The date and authorship of this commentary is unknown. It contains a good deal of material, however, from the commentaries already dealt with (namely, Paramārtha's Chinese version, the *Sāṃkhyavṛtti*, the *Sāṃkhyasaptativṛtti*, and Gauḍapāda's *Bhāṣya*). P. Chakravarti points out, furthermore, that it appears to know of certain views mentioned only in the *Yuktidīpikā* (that is, the discussion of seven types of action under SK 19 and the interpretation of the expression "*kāraṇakāryavibhāga*" under SK 15).[1] On the other hand, also according to Chakravarti, Vācaspati's *Tattvakaumudī* appears to presuppose the *Jayamaṅgalā*, for Vācaspati describes and rejects an interpretation of the eight attainments (under SK 51), an interpretation set forth only in *Jayamaṅgalā*[2]. All of this, of course, is very slim evidence, but overall it is perhaps not unreasonable to place *Jayamaṅgalā* some time between *Yuktidīpikā* and *Tattvakaumudī*, or, in other words, some time between about the seventh century and the ninth century.

Gopinath Kaviraj, in his introduction to the printed edition of *Jayamaṅgalā* by H. Sarma, suggests that the author of the *Jayamaṅgalā* may be the same as the author of two other texts (also called *Jayamaṅgalā*), namely, the *Kāmandakanītisāra* and the *Kāmasūtra*.[3] Moreover, on the basis of the benedictory verse of *Jayamaṅgalā*, which includes the expression "*lokottaravādināṃ praṇamya munim*," Kaviraj concludes that the author was a Buddhist. In a later article, however, entitled "Literary Gleanings, Jayamaṅgalā,"[4] Kaviraj offers yet another suggestion. He argues that the author of all of these commentaries called *Jayamaṅgalā* is a certain Śaṅkarārya of the Payyur family, who lived some time in the fourteenth century. The name Śaṅkarārya became somewhat garbled in the process of manuscript transmission and, therefore, comes to appear in the colophon of our extant version of the *Jayamaṅgalā* as Śaṅkarācārya (the great Vedāntin). Moreover, argues Kaviraj, this Śaṅkarārya of the fourteenth century is very possibly also the author of the *Yogasūtrabhāṣyavivaraṇa*, a text that is also wrongly attributed (according to Gopinath Kaviraj) to the great Śaṇkarācārya.

All of these are interesting speculations deserving of further exploration, but at the present time no firm conclusions are possible. The date and authorship of *Jayamaṅgalā* is simply an open question, although Chakravarti's claim that it precedes Vācaspati and comes after *Yuktidīpikā* appears to be the most likely avenue for further research.

The following summary is based on the edition of the text prepared by Haradutta Sarma (*Jayamaṅgalā*, Calcutta Sanskrit Series, No. 19, Calcutta: N.N. Law, 1926).

(*Summary by Ram Shankar Bhattacharya*)

I. Introductory Verses: The Scope and Task of the Sāṃkhya (E1-5)

In the benedictory verse there is a salutation to a certain *muni* who is said to be a "*lokottaravādin.*"[5] The object of composing the present work consisting of 70 verses is to help those who desire to comprehend the vast treatise called *Ṣaṣṭitantra.*

(1) The "three kinds of frustration" are said to be internal, external, and celestial. Internal frustration is said to arise in the body and the mind. Mental frustrations can be annihilated by the power of knowledge (*saṃkhyānabala*) or by experiencing satisfying objects. External frustrations are said to be caused by six factors: human beings (*mānuṣa*); domestic animals (*paśu*), e.g., cows; wild animals, (*mṛga*), e.g., lions; birds (*pakṣin*); reptiles (*sarīsṛpa*), e.g., snakes; and stationary beings (*sthāvara*), trees, posts, etc.[6] External frustrations can be annihilated by resorting to suitable places that are properly guarded. Celestial frustrations are caused by the influence of the planets; they arise in the body.

(2) The verse says that the method of understanding (*vijñāna*), i.e., knowledge of the principles is better than scriptural means to annihilate frustrations. Why? Because knowledge of the principles has pure results (*śuddhaphala*) owing to the forsaking of the body, undecaying results (*akṣayaphala*) owing to the forsaking of materiality, and unsurpassable results (*niratiśayaphala*) owing to its having nothing higher than it. "Understanding of what is manifested and unmanifested" is defined as correct cognition of the actual nature of things (*svarūpapariccheda*). It is remarked that the verses from 3 onward are to be understood as elucidations of the first 2 verses.

(3) The word "*prakṛti*" is analyzed to mean "that which is originated from *pradhāna*, i.e., the three *guṇas*" ("*prakriyate utpadyate pradhānāt asyāḥ*")[7]. "Ungenerated" is that which does not undergo any change. The five subtle elements produce the five gross elements respectively. The etymology of "*puruṣa*" is given as "*puraṃ śarīraṃ tasmin vasat*" (he who resides in the city, i.e., the body), with the remark that this

derivation is in accordance with the rules of the *Nirukta*[8]. Since consciousness is bereft of action (*niṣkriya*) nothing can come out of it. As consciousness has no beginning it is not generated[9].

II. The Instruments of Knowledge

(4) (E5-7) There is a long discussion on the inclusion of all instruments of knowledge in the accepted three, namely, (a) *dṛṣṭa*, explained as perception, (b) inference, that by which something is inferred, and (c) reliable authority, the statements of persons whose faults are completely destroyed. Intuition (*pratibhā*) falls under either perception or inference depending on the particular case. Comparison (*aupamya*, i.e., *upamāna*) is included in either reliable authority or in inference depending on the case. Tradition (*aitihya*) is the same as reliable authority. Nonapprehension (*abhāva*) comes under perception. Inclusion (*sambhava*) is included in inference, since there is a cause-effect relation between parts and whole. Presumption (*arthāpatti*) is the same as inference. An object to be known (*prameya*) can only be acquired or abandoned by use of an instrument of knowledge.

(5) (E5-7) "Ascertainment of (sense) contents" is explained as the awareness (*buddhi*) of sound, touch, etc., by the five (external) sense organs, viz., auditory, tactual, etc. In such an awareness, attention to what is particular (*viśeṣāvadhāraṇa*) predominates. Perception is an instrument of knowledge provided it is pure (*śuddha*), i.e., free from faults. That which is not an instrument of knowledge is of four kinds: (1) *savyapadeśya*, when one thinks someone approaching from far off is Devadatta because of resemblance; (2) *savikalpa*, when one in the same situation says, "this must be Devadatta," because it is doubtful; (3) *arthavyatirekin*, when one sees two moons because of some eye disease; (4) *indriyavyatirekin*, when one sees things in dreams when the organs are subdued by sleep. We are told that the three kinds of inference—*pūrvavat*, *śeṣavat*, and *sāmānyatodṛṣṭa*—were treated in the *ṣaṣṭitantra*. In the *pūrvavat* type, we infer a future occurrence; in *śeṣavat*, a previous occurrence; in *sāmānyatodṛṣṭa*, a present fact is inferred, e.g., the fact that the sun is moving is inferred from the change of position observed in both human beings and the sun.

"Depending on a mark and the bearer of that mark" is explained as (a) *liṅgapūrvaka*, inferring a mark-bearer, e.g., a cuckoo, from the perception of its mark, i.e., its coo; (b) *liṅgipūrvaka*, inferring the mark, e.g., the coo, from the mark-bearer, the cuckoo. The relation (which makes inference possible) between mark-bearer and mark is of seven kinds: (1) possessor-possessed relation (*svasvāmibhāva*), as between a king and his officers; (2) relation between stuff and its modification (*prakṛtivikāra*), as between barleycorn and fried flour made from it; (3) cause-effect relation (*kāryakāraṇa*), as between a cow and its calf; (4) utensil-user relation (*pātrapātrika*), as between an ascetic and his staff (*tridaṇḍa*); (5) constant association (*sāhàcarya*), as between male and female; (6) contrariety (*pratidvandin*), as between hot and cold; (7) efficient causality (*nimittanaimittika*), as between an eater and what he eats[10].

A reliable person is defined as a person bereft of attachment and hatred and in whom others have faith. Statements (*śruti*) of such reliable persons handed down through a tradition (*paramparā*) are called "reliable," and the cognition that arises after hearing these statements is called "reliable" authority. (*Śruti* may be taken in the sense of Veda also.) The particle "*ca*" at the end of the *kārikā* suggests that reliable authority is like inference in providing a basis for cognizing past and future, as well as present, object.

(6) (E9) Objects to be known (*prameya*) are either perceivable by the organs (*pratyakṣa*), beyond the field of perception (*atīndriya*), or absolutely beyond the field of perception (*atyantaparokṣa*). The last mentioned includes things like heaven and liberation, which can only be known through reliable authority.[11]

(7) (E9-10) Materiality and consciousness are absolutely beyond perception. Nonperception of existent things occurs owing to four kinds of factors: (1) defects in spatial position (*deśadoṣa*); (2) defects in the sense organs (*indriyadoṣa*); (3) defects in the contents of awareness (*viṣayadoṣa*); (4) defects due to other things (*arthāntaradoṣa*). The verse lists eight reasons for nonperception, which are brought under the above fourfold scheme. Being too far away or too close are cases of (1); injury of an organ is a case of (2), as is unsteadiness of the mind (because the mind is a sense organ); subtlety is a case of (3); and the rest come under (4). Though the mind is a sense organ, its unsteadiness is mentioned separately from defects in the other organs because of its prominence.

(8) (F19-11) "Nonexistence" here means the Nyāya's four kinds of absence.

III. The Notion of Preexistent Effect

(9) (E11-12) The Vaiśeṣikas hold that the effect is not existent in its cause, but the effect is existent there, according to Sāṃkhya, as causal efficacy (*śakti*). Illustrations explicate the five reasons offered in the verse. What does not exist does not get caused, e.g., a hare's horn cannot be produced, whereas a pot can be produced from a lump of clay. If oil or curd were not already existent in their respective material causes, viz., sesame seed and milk, we might well find them arising from sand, or water. If *asatkāryavāda* were true, anything might arise anywhere, at any time. If effects were not dependent on things having an appropriate causal efficiency, we might

find a sprout growing from a seed whose potentiality had been destroyed. The last reason—*kāraṇabhāva*—is explained alternatively as either the being or the nature of the cause: the nature of an effect is said to be the same as is found in the cause.

IV. The Manifest and Unmanifest Aspects of Materiality

(10) (E12-14) The manifested entities are those from the intellect to the gross elements. "Nonpervading" means that the manifested things occupy a particular region only, as contrasted with the *avyakta*, which pervades all the three worlds at all times. "Mobility" is said to mean transmigration (*saṃsāra*) here, because, if it means "activity" it would imply that unmanifested materiality has no activity, which would conflict with its being the agent of the universe. The manifested materiality is said to be "many," because it has twenty-three forms. It has a locus, namely, unmanifested materiality. It is a *liṅga*, because the unmanifested materiality is inferred through it—or the *kārikā* may mean that manifested materiality goes to dissolution (*layaṃ gacchati*), i.e., all of the forms of manifested materiality become dissolved in their respective material causes. Its "parts" are sound, etc. It is "dependent on another," and not self-dependent (*na svatantram*), because effects of the manifested materiality accord with the nature of its cause, namely, unmanifested materiality.

(11) (E14-16) "Undifferentiated" (*vivekin*) here means either nonsentient, having no power to discriminate, or else nonseparable from the constituents. "General" (*sāmānya*) means capable of being experienced by all consciousnesses. "Nonconscious" (*acetana*) means that the power of experiencing satisfaction, frustration, or confusion is lacking. The last part of the verse means that consciousness is opposite in nature to manifested materiality. It is, however, similar to unmanifested materiality in some respects: Consciousness is without a cause, owing to its having no beginning, and eternal for the same reason; it is pervasive when liberated from materiality, immobile because it is not an agent, without a locus because it has no cause, *aliṅga* (not being a mark of anything, or incapable of being dissolved), without parts, because it has no qualities such as sound, etc., and independent, not being originated from any cause.

It is pointed out that, although in verse 10 manifested materiality is called "many" (*aneka*), according to this verse, consciousness must be single. However consciousnesses are in fact shown to be many in *kārikā* 18; therefore it is not appropriate to call consciousness "single," and in this regard consciousness is dissimilar to unmanifested materiality, which is single.[12] Consciousness is without constituents (*nirguṇa*); the illuminator (*vivektṛ*) because of its power or illuminating (*cetanatva*); or owing to its being distinct from the constituents, contentless (*nirviṣaya*) owing to its being the enjoyer; not general (*asāmānya*) because of its contentlesseness; conscious (*cetana*) because it experiences pleasure, etc., and nonproductive (*aprasavadharmin*) since it lacks agency.

V. The Three Constituents

(12) (E16-18) The constituents are beyond the senses and must be inferred from the nature of satisfaction, frustration, and indifference. Illumination, etc., are the purpose (*prayojana*) of the constituents. The constituents are not themselves operations (*vṛtti*), as the verse might be thought to imply; rather, they cause operation, so the expression must be read in a secondary sense. "Mutual operations" ("*anyonya vṛtti*") shows that each constituent is the cause of the change in the other two, owing to which change, there arises satisfaction, etc.

(13) (E18-19) "Lightweightness" in *sattva* is responsible for the feeling of lightness in a body as well as in objects. It is because of the "shining" of *sattva* that the organs can illuminate objects, and external objects become devoid of impurity (*nirmala*) for this reason. "Enveloping" is a property owing to which the limbs become heavy, tired, or languid; the organs are subdued by weakness or stupor, and external objects become heavy and dirty (*anirmala*). The attributes of the constituents listed here are only illustrative; they have other attributes. "For the sake (of consciousness)" includes the functions of the constituents that lead to experience or liberation.[13]

VI. The Inferences that Establish the Existence and Makeup of Primordial Materiality and Consciousness

(14) (E19-20) Because an effect has the nature of its material cause, unmanifest materiality possesses properties such as being undifferentiated, etc., for these properties characterize the constituents.

(15) (E20-23) Because different things are limited, there must be something, the subject of the limiting relation, that is the cause of those things. "Because they share common characteristics" (*samanvayāt*) argues that effects possessing a single universal property (*jāti*) must have a cause exhibiting that property. In this case the property is having satisfaction, frustration, and confusion, a property that characterizes all internal and external entities, and so their cause must be something that also has that property, namely, unmanifest materiality. "Because of the disjunction between a cause and its effect" argues that, because an effect is that which is separated from its cause, the effects—twenty-three kinds—of manifested materiality must have been separated from a cause, which is unmanifested materiality. "Because of

the nondisjunction of the whole world" is explained in two ways: (1) owing to the absence of disjunction (*vibhāga*), and (2) owing to the occurrence of dissolution of the variegated world. The cause in which all effects become dissolved cannot be God, and this cause must be single in number.

(16) (E23-24) The unmanifest functions in two ways: (1) in the equilibrium state through the three constituents by virtue of the predominance of any one of them, which results in a state known as disequilibrium (*vaiṣamya*); (2) through transformation in which the world is the specific locus of the respective constituents just as a tree is a locus of the effects of its specific seed.

(17) (E24-26) "Because the aggregates exist for the sake of something else"—that which is aggregated or organized as a whole must be for others. The intellect, etc., that is, bodies, are "aggregates"; the "others" must be consciousness and nothing else. Because consciousness is entirely different from that which is undifferentiated, etc. (see *kārikā* 11), it cannot be identified with the intellect, etc. Every body has a controller (*adhiṣṭhātṛ*). This controller cannot be the internal organ, because it is nonconscious. Because the intellect, etc., are capable of being experienced, there must be some "enjoyer," someone who knows or experiences them and who is different from the nonconscious internal organ. This enjoyer is the self (*ātman*) in the body associated with other entities of a nature similar to it (e.g., the mind), because they are regulated in the same way with regards to rebirth, etc. "Because there is activity in order to gain isolation"—this activity consists in the intellect having cognitive awareness as one of its aspects. Had there been no consciousness, this would have been impossible. Thus, consciousness exists.

(18) (E26-27) Different views about the number of selves are alluded to—some say there is just one self in all bodies; others say there are different selves for each body; the "Vedāntins" hold that there is just one "ancient" (*purāṇa*) *puruṣa*, but from it are manifested (*āvirbhūta*) as sparks from fire, a consciousness for each body.[14] "Because births and deaths are regulated causally"—if there were only one consciousness, when one consciousness is (as it were) born, or dies, everyone would be born, or die. Actually, consciousnesses are not literally born nor do they die, since they are eternal.[15] "Because activity is not simultaneous"—again, if there were only one consciousness, then when merit and demerit, purpose and what is not one's purpose, satisfaction, and frustration operate, they should operate equally for everyone. "Because of opposition (in, or to) the three constituents" —because the controller (cf. commentary on SK 17) is made of the three constituents, consciousness, being associated with it, can be said to be of the nature of the three constituents. But if there were only consciousness and it was, say, *sāttvika*,

then all will be *sāttvika*. However, because the constituents are (mutually) opposed, consciousness must be held as many. If the various consciousnesses in each body came out of one "old" *puruṣa* like sparks out of fire (as the "Vedāntins" hold) the multiplicity of consciousnesses is nevertheless established: there will then be two views possible, differing in whether these consciousnesses are different or nondifferent from the one "ancient" *puruṣa*. I (the author of the *Jayamaṅgalā*) have discussed this at length in another work.[16]

(19) (E27-28) "Because of the opposition" (*viparyāsa*)—i.e., the opposition among the three constituents. The nonagency of consciousness is due to its not being productive. Because consciousness is nonagent, it is neutral (*udāsīna*), sitting apart unaffected by the activities of the constituents (cf. SK 02). This "neutrality" is of seven kinds.[17] Because consciousness is neutral, it is the witness (*sākṣin*) of the activities pertaining to materiality. The isolation of consciousness is due to its not being associated with anything, and its percipience is due to its being conscious. A verse (which is not quite intelligible) is quoted to explain how consciousness can be an experiencer (*bhoktṛ*) without being an agent,.

(20) (E28) The *liṅga* is defined as containing the fundamental principles beginning with intellect and ending with the subtle elements. As to how a nonconscious entity appears conscious, the illustration is offered of the hotness of a lump of gold owing to its contact with fire. Agency lies in the constituents and is falsely attributed to neutral consciousness, as fighting is attributed to the commander who does not directly fight.

(21) (E29) The connection between consciousness and materiality is like the connection between a fish and water or between a mosquito and the *udumbara* tree.[18] The illustration of the lame and the blind indicates that nonconscious materiality becomes conscious owing to consciousness' controllership. This illustration also shows that as two men leave each other after reaching their destination, so there arises disjunction between consciousness and materiality after achievement of consciousness' purposes. The connection is the cause of creation (*sarga*) of intellect, etc.

(22) (E30) Materiality is also called by such names as "great darkness" (*tamobahula*) and "unmanifest" (*avyākṛta*).[19] Intellect (*buddhi*) has other names, too—"*mahat*," "*pratyaya*," "*upalabdhi*." The subtle elements are also sometimes called "subtle" (*sūkṣma*), "unspecific" (*aviśeṣa*), and "small" (*aṇu*).[20] The five gross elements are space (*ākāśa*), air (*vāyu*), fire (*tejas*), water (*ap*), and earth (*pṛthivī*). They evolve from the five subtle elements according to the *ekottaravṛddhi* principle—i.e., each succeeding principle possesses the qualities it causes as well as its own quality. Thus, space has only one quality, sound, whereas earth has five qualities, viz.,

sound, touch, sight, taste, and smell. The gross elements are sometimes called "specific" (*viśeṣa*).

VII. The Functioning of the Thirteenfold Instrument

(23) (E31-32) "Reflective discerning" involves determination of a content as expressed in an assertion such as "this is a smell." Meritorious behavior is that kind of reflective discerning leading to the performance of restraints (*yama*) and restrictions (*niyama*) as described *Yogasūtra* II.30, 32, which are quoted here. Correct awareness is the determination (*avadhāraṇa*) of the twenty-five basic principles leading to awareness of the difference between consciousness and the constituents. Everything else is non-correct awareness. Nonattachment is turning away from the faults in the body, the senses, and their contents. Attachment is craving for these. Mastery is of eight kinds: (1) *Aṇiman* is the power of becoming very small. (2) *Laghiman* is the ability to become lighter than air. (3) *Mahiman* is the power to attain "greatness" (*mahattva*). (4) *Prāpti* is the power to attain what is desired. (5) *Prākāmya* is the power to satisfy various kinds of desires. (6) *Īśitva* is lordship. (7) *Vaśitva* is the power of independent action. (8) *Yatrakāmavasāyitva* is the power through which one can remain in the sky (*div*), atmosphere (*antarikṣa*), or earth according to one's will.

(24) (E32-33) "Self-awareness arises when one thinks, with respect to contents like color, etc., "I am characterized by them" or "they are mine." In the word "*tanmātra*," "*mātra*" signifies that though sound, etc., are possessed by both the gross and the subtle elements, they are distinct in the subtle elements.[21]

(25) (E33) The group of eleven organs evolving from egoity is *sāttvika*, because they grasp their own contents. Because these organs as well as the gross elements are characterized by both illumination (*prakāśa*) and inertia (*sthiti*) they require the help of the "fiery" form of egoity, which is characterized by action (*kriyā*).

(26) (E33-34) The sense organs are called "*buddhīndriya*" because they depend on the intellect for their activity. The order listed should have been auditory, tactual, visual, gustatory, and olfactory, because that is the order in which the respective contents grasped are listed. The action organs (*karmendriya*) are so-called because their business is to accomplish an action.[22]

(27) (E34-35) Mind has the nature of both kinds of organs. It is *saṃkalpaka*, i.e., its original nature is to form intentions. It is called an organ ("*indriya*)," because it is the mark of Indra (the self). The distinctive nature of the sense and action organs along with the mind (all being organs) are each based on the particular transformation of the constituents following their attributes,

namely, mutual suppression, etc. These particular transformations are the cause of the difference in location and function of organs as well as of their contents.

(28) (E35) The "mere" in "mere awareness" (*ālocana-mātra*), the function of the organs, means that the organs serve to illuminate their contents only, whereas belief (*niścaya*) (concerning name, species, etc.) is the business of the intellect. Really, according to Sāṃkhya, it is consciousness that causes those objects to be known (*cetayate*) which have already been grasped by the intellect. The function of the action organs is nothing but action. "Speaking" means the uttering of syllables (*varṇa*).

(29) (E35-36) The defining attributes of all the organs, including intellect, egoity, and mind, are also to be understood as their operations. According to the *Jayamaṅgalā*, each of the 13 organs (capacities)—and not the three internal organs along—has its own (*asāmānya*) function. The fourfold functions of the thirteen instruments is spoken of; they would seem to include the three functions of the three internal organs and one function of each of the external organs. Likewise, the "common operation" belongs to the thirteen organs, not to the three internal ones only. We are told that the *udāna* "breath" produces noise while flowing toward the head.

(30) (36-37) An example of the simultaneous functioning of the four is when one recognizes a cobra revealed by a flash of lightning. Here the visual organ provides the sensing (*ālocana*), the intellect provides reflective discernment (*adhyavasāya*), the ego relates it to the self, and the mind resolves to act (presumably by fleeing the vicinity). On the other hand, an example of progressive functioning occurs when, through increase of illumination, we first see an object indistinctly as a post or a man (a mental construction), then ascertain that it is a man, relate him to ourselves, and develop a resolution to act accordingly. The activities of the three internal organs must be preceded by the functioning of an external organ.

(31) (E37-38) The functioning of the three internal organs with any one of the external organs, whether simultaneous or successive, is prompted by "coordination" or mutual impulsion (*parasparasavyapekṣā*). "*Ākūta*" is the experience of one's own operating (*svavṛttibhoga*). It does not occur simultaneously in all of the organs. God cannot be held to be the agent, since He would also have to depend on materiality. The Sāṃkhya view is that consciousness only is the controller, since materiality is nonconscious.

(32) (E29) Seizing is the function of the action organs, holding, of the internal organs; and illuminating, of the sense organs. The ten effects of the functions of the sense organs, called *prakāśya*, are the five qualities—sound, etc.—each one having two subdivisions : (1) the

subtle, celestial elements and (2) the gross, noncelestial elements. The effects of the functions of the action organs are called *āhārya*. The effects of the functions of the internal organs are called *dhārya*, because they are capable of being determined (*avadhāryamāna*) through their own internal functions.

(33) (E40-41) The internal organ includes the intellect, ego, and mind. The ten "externals" of the verse are the sense and action organs, which are both the "gates" (*dvāra*) as well as the contents (*viṣaya*, i.e., things experienced, *bhogya*) of the internal organ(s). Time does not exist apart from contents, which are either past or future or present. So time is not a twenty-sixth principle.

(35) (E42) Sense contents are of two kinds: (1) the subtle elements known here as "nonspecific" (*aviśeṣa*) and (2) the gross elements, known here as "specific" (*viśeṣa*). Both kinds are capable of being perceived by the organs.[23]

(35) (E42) The term "every" refers to all contents whether past, present, or future.

(36) (E42-43) The thirteen organs, each having a distinct character, become manifested as a result of mutual suppression of the three constituents. They become associated with their contents with the help of their operations. Illuminating "everything", i.e., the gross as well as the subtle forms of sense contents: it is the consciousness that makes known those objects that have already been grasped by the intellect.

(37) (E43) Although the intellect is an organ, it is the chief of all the organs inasmuch as it accomplishes (*sampādayati*) fully all experience of the contents grasped by it while colored by *tamas*, and inasmuch as it furnishes discrimination between consciousness and materiality, a kind of awareness that is not empirical.

X. The Subtle and Gross Elements

(38) (E43-44) Because nothing is specified or particularized by the subtle elements, the subtle elements are called "nonspecific." The subtle elements are almost imperceptible. Each gross element possesses one quality more than its cause. For example, space has only one quality, sound, originating from the subtle sound element, whereas the gross element air has two qualities, namely, sound and touch. Similarly, the gross element earth has all of the five qualities, earth being a product of the gross element water, which has four qualities, namely, sound, touch, color, and taste. The gross elements are either comforting, uncomfortable, or confusing.

(39) Those subtle elements that have become the locus of body are known as "specific," though in reality, the subtle elements are nonspecific, as already mentioned. "Bodies born of mother and

father" have six components, namely, hair, blood, etc. The gross body, having six sheaths, is the product of these six "specifics." The external gross elements are called "*prabhūta*," meaning "eminent," because they are capable of (1) giving way (*avakāśa*), (2) arrangement, (3) causing cooking or burning,[24] (4) moistening, (5) sustaining (through their hardness or solidity) the gross body. The subtle body persists until the acquisition of discrimination, but the gross body perishes.

XI. The Subtle Body

(40) (E45) Each consciousness possesses a subtle body that is created by primordial materiality at the beginning of creation (*ādisarga*). The motion of this body cannot be obstructed by anything. It will persist until discrimination. It is composed of the principles beginning with intellect and ending with the subtle elements. Because it is devoid of the gross body, it is incapable of experiencing contents. It is called "*liṅga*" because it becomes dissolved at *pralaya*.[25]

(42) (E46-47) "Behaves like a player" refers to the taking on of various kinds of gross bodies belonging to gods, men, and animals. The plurality of subtle bodies is due to the power of their efficient causes (*nimitta*, i.e., merit and the like: cf. SK 44-45). It is the all-pervasiveness of materiality that is the sole cause of the play of the subtle body. Neither God nor a thing's own nature (*svabhāva*) are agents in its actions, which are influenced by the eight basic predispositions.

XII. The Basic Predispositions

(43) (E47) The predispositions are mentioned in *Kārikā* 23 and are of eight sorts, four *sāttvika* and four *tāmasa*. "Innate" predispositions are those that are found at birth in, for example, Kapila and others, who appeared at the beginning of creation. The "acquired" predispositions are those that are acquired through effort by persons after creation. Both these two kinds of predispositions reside either in the thirteen instruments or in the five kinds of effects.[26]

(44) (E47-48) The predispositions are called *nimittas*, and the moving upward, etc., are the results, the *naimittikas*. Meritorious behavior consists in respecting the restraints and restrictions. "Moving upward" means the attainment of the world of the gods, etc. Similarly, "moving downward" is the state of residing in animals. "Knowledge" here means discriminative awareness of the difference between materiality and consciousness. "Liberation" means the cessation (*nivṛtti*) of the subtle body. Misconception

(*viparyaya*) is the opposite of "(discriminative) awareness," i.e., it is *ajñāna* that is of the nature of bondage in *saṃsāra*. Bondage is of three kinds: (1) of those for whom materiality alone is the highest principle (*prakṛtibandha*) (2) of those *karmavādins* who think that human purposes are confined to the heavenly goals attainable by sacrifices, etc. (*dakṣiṇābandha*); (3) of those who take the modifications (*vikāra*: organs and gross elements) alone as the mark of the powers that constitute human purposes (*vikārabandha*). Between meritorious and nonmeritorious behavior, this author finds a third variety called "mixed" (*miśra*), which leads to rebirth among humans.

(45) (E48-49) A nonattached person who finds fault with sense-contents but is not desirous of discrimination becomes dissolved into any one of the eight generative principles (namely, the three internal organs and five subtle elements) at death but does not attain liberation, because at the time of creation (*sargakāla*) he is born again into *saṃsāra*.

(46) (E49-50) The group of sixteen comprising the efficient causes and their results (cf. SK 44) is known collectively as "intellectual creation" (*pratyayasarga*) ("*pratyaya*" is a synonym of "*buddhi*") and can be subdivided into four groups: (1) misconception; (2) dysfunction, or the inability to acquire discriminative knowledge in spite of one's desire to know; (3) contentment, aversion to the means of liberation; (4) attainment, i.e., acquisition of discriminative knowledge. Disequilibrium of the three constituents consists in the predominance of one (or two) constituents. Because the disturbance of each constituent may be of the form of increase or decrease, there must be six such varieties.[27]

(47) (E50) The five varieties of misconception, *tamas*, etc. (cf. the next verse), are equivalent to the Yoga system's five *kleśas* (cf. *Yogasūtra* II.3).

(47) (E50) The eight kinds of *tamas* correspond to the eight generative principles. The eight forms of confusion are associated with the eight kinds of Supernatural Powers (cf. SK 23). The ten forms of great confusion are associated with the five subtle elements (*divya*, yielding satisfaction) and the five gross elements (*adivya*, yielding satisfaction, frustration, and confusion). The eighteen forms of gloom (equals = *dveṣa*, hatred) are associated with the eight forms of Supernatural Power and the ten elements. The eighteen forms of blind gloom (equals = *abhiniveśa*, will to live) are associated with the same eighteen factors.

(49) (E51-52) Dysfunction is injury, due to defect or disease, of the eleven organs. As to why the defects of the organs are called "*pratyayasarga*," inasmuch as the organs cannot be regarded as *pratyaya* (equals = *buddhi*), it is replied that egoity being a modification of the intellect, at least the *ahaṃkārasarga* may rightly be called *pratyayasarga*,

and the creations of egoity are the organs. Or, "*pratyaya*" may be taken in the sense of property or attribute (*dharma*) and, as the organs are properties of the intellect, the defects in them may come under *pratyayasarga*.[28]

(50) (E52-54) The four internal contentments are also called *ambhas* (=*prakṛti*), *salila* (=*upādāna*), *ogha* (=*kāla*), and *vṛṣṭi* (= *bhāgya*). The word "internal" (*ādhyātmika*) shows that these contentments are to be experienced in one's own mind. The "mark" or "symbol" contentment (*upādāna tuṣṭi*) consists in thinking that an external means is enough to attain liberation. The five "turnings away from sense contents" (*viṣayoparāma*) come from observing the faults involved in acquisition (*arjana*), preservation (*rakṣaṇa*), destruction (*kṣaya*), enjoyment (*saṅga*), and injury (*hiṃsā*). The five external contentments are also called by the names "*sutāra*," "*supāra*," etc.[29] Contentment is a form of injury to the *buddhi* and as such it falls under dysfunction.[30]

(51) (E54-56) An attainment (*siddhi*) is explained as the acquisition of knowledge.[31] *Ūha*, etc., are also called by such names as "*tāra*," "*sutāra*," etc.[32] The contraries of the attainments (*asiddhi*) are injuries to the intellect and thus fall also under dysfunction.[33] The explanation of *ūha* is not clear. It seems to be a kind of reflection (*utprekṣā*) of the cause of bondage and liberation. "Oral instruction" is the hearing of Sāṃkhya treatises. "Study" is reading and reflection on Sāṃkhya works. Through these three one can attain knowledge that helps one to annihilate three kinds of frustration. Misconception, dysfunction, and contentment are like a hook (*aṅkuśa*), i.e., the curbing factors by which persons are compelled to remain in *saṃsāra*; thus they are obstacles to attainment. These fifty categories along with ten others form the sixty topics of Sāṃkhya called "*ṣaṣṭitantra*".[34]

XIII. The Empirical World

(52) (E56-57) *Sarga* is what is created and not creation.

(53) (E57-58) The eight kinds of divine creation are related to Brahmā, Prajāpati, Sūrya, Asura, Gandharvas, Yakṣas, Rakṣases, and Piśācas. The animal creation has five subdivisions: (1) *paśu*, beginning with cows and ending with donkeys; (2) *mṛga*, beginning with lions and ending with cats; (3) *pakṣin*, beginning with swans and ending with mosquitoes; (4) *sarpa*, beginning with worms and ending with snakes; and (5) *sthāvara*, beginning with trees and ending with other forms of life.[35] The human order has no variety, as there is only one human form. It is noted that beings can be grouped in a different way. There is a fourfold division based on the four sources, viz., the uterus (*jarāyu*), the egg (*aṇḍa*), sweat (*ūṣman*), etc., and plants (*udbhid*).[36]

(54) (E58) "Above" signifies the region of the gods (*devaloka*) where *sattva* exists in abundance. "Lower order" (*mūlataḥ sarga*) refers to the animals (cf. verse 53) where *tamas* predominates. "Middle" refers to the region of human beings. Owing to the predominance of *rajas* they are full of frustrations.

(55) (E58-59) Frustration has four kinds according to its four sources, viz., the womb (*garbha*), birth (*janman*), old age (*jarā*), and death (*maraṇa*). These form internal frustration. Consciousness continues to be the recipient of these until the cessation of the subtle body by attainment of discrimination. Although sometimes satisfaction is also achieved, not being a regular result, it is not mentioned. Frustration as a result of old age, etc., is regular, inevitable, and invariable'.

XIV. Similes Illustrating the Role and Function of Materiality

(56) (E59-60) There are three kinds of created things—subtle bodies (*liṅga*), predispositions, and elements. Neither God, consciousness, nor a thing's own nature are the cause of these three. Creation is nothing but the three constituents in essence. Created things cannot be held as self-produced (*svābhāvika*) as this will lead to an obvious contradiction, and the law of spatial association (*deśaniyama*) would be violated.[37] Elements comprise gross bodies as well as subtle and gross objects.[38]

(59) (E61-62) "Having illuminated itself" means having assumed the forms of gods and the like.

(60) (E62) The "various ways" are the seven forms of intellect of *Kārikā* 63, except knowledge. These are the accessories for awareness of the three kinds of objects.[39] Knowledge is, on the other hand, a means to isolation. Materiality is active because it possesses constituents; consciousness is inactive because it lacks them.[40]

(61) (E63) The unmanifested form of materiality is the same as the state of equilibrium (known as *parama rūpa*) of the constituents, and is incapable of being perceived. The perceptible aspect of the constituents should be known as *māyā* and unreal (*tuccha*).[41] *Sukumāra* ("reticent") is glossed as "subtle" (*sūkṣma*). The word "me" in the verse refers to *prakṛti*.

(62) (E63-64) The loci of materiality are of the forms of predispositions, subtle bodies, and elements.

XV. Liberation and Isolation

(63) (E64) The "self" (*ātman*) that becomes bound is the subtle body. Bondage is of three kinds (cf. commentary on vs. 44). It is dis-

criminative knowledge, a product of the unmanifested, which makes the unmanifested associated with a given consciousness cease. Merit, etc., are not properties of consciousness. "The sake of each consciousness" means here only isolation. "By means of one form" means by knowledge, one of the eight forms of intellect.

(64) (E64-65) "Concentration on fundamental principles" means repeated reflection on the real nature of the twenty-five categories. The expression "I am not" signifies that the self does not reside in the subtle or gross bodies. The expression "nothing belongs to me" shows that these bodies belong to materiality and not to the self. "There is no "I" suggests that the self is not materiality. Discriminative knowledge is complete in all respects, pure (*apariśeṣa*), being devoid of the blemishes involved in mundane existence. "Isolated" is explained as "single," which seems to mean that this knowledge remains of one form always.

(65) (E65) "Ceased producing" the two kinds of creation, namely, the *liṅgasarga* and the *bhāvasarga*: when materiality ceases from producing effects, it assumes unmanifested form. Consciousness perceives materiality whether it is engaged in creation or has ceased to be productive. "Spectator" indicates a state in which the self abides in itself.

(66) (E66) Objection: Because materiality is always connected with consciousness owing to its all-pervasiveness, why does creation come to an end? The verse answers this objection—there is no reason for it to begin again.

(67) (E66-67) "Correct awareness" means self-knowledge. "Noncausative state" is that of the burnt seed, having no power to produce effects. The latent dispositions are those that have been acquired in previous births.

(68) (E67) "Separation" is the separation of the subtle body from the (last) gross body.[42] "*Prakṛti*" here stands for its transformation, the subtle body, which ceases forever after the destruction of the (last) body. Isolation is certain and inevitable (*avaśyambhāvin*). It is final also, for, owing to the absence of purpose, the creation of intellect, etc., will cease forever.

XVI. The Transmission of the Sāṃkhya Tradition

(69) (E67-68) The "greatest sage" is Kapila.

(70) (E68) The doctrine is "pure," because it purifies, the three kinds of frustration. Its "excellence" (*agrya*) is analyzed as "*agre bhavatvāt*" i.e., "existing before all," and is explained as coming into existence before all the *bhedas*.[43] Āsuri was a great sacrificer who eventually became a *saṃnyāsin*.[44] The *Ṣaṣṭitantra* was composed by Pañcaśikha in sixty parts in which sixty topics are discussed.

(71) (E69) The names of two ancient teachers of Sāṃkhya are Gārga and Gautama. Īśvarakṛṣṇa is said to have been a wandering monk (*parivrājaka*).[45]

(72) (E69) The *Sāṃkhyakārikās* (or *Sāṃkhyasaptati*) is said to be "complete" in all respects, because it treats of all matters pertaining to bondage and liberation.

ŚAṂKARA

YOGASŪTRABHĀṢYAVIVARAṆA

If this commentary on Vyāsa's *Yogasūtrabhāṣya* should prove finally to be an authentic commentary of the great Śaṃkarācārya (the Vedāntin), the work will add a fascinating, though puzzling, chapter both to the early history of Vedānta and the early history of Sāṃkhya-Yoga. More than anything else, it will show that what we have been calling Pātañjala-Sāṃkhya was an important component in the formulation of Advaita Vedānta philosophy. It might also render more likely the possibility that the Gauḍapāda of the *Sāṃkhyakārikābhāṣya* is the same as the early Advaitin Gauḍapāda of the *Māṇḍūkyakārikā* in the sense that there may have been an interest among early Advaitins in the philosophy of Sāṃkhya and Yoga. We have already discussed the literature regarding the authenticity of this commentary (see note 36 Part One of the present volume) in which it was mentioned that Leggett, Hacker, Mayeda, and Nakamura are all in favor of the commentary's authenticity. At the same time, however, it should be remembered that Gopinath Kaviraj (see above entry under *Jayamaṅgalā*) attributes this commentary, as well as the *Jayamaṅgalā*, to a certain Śaṅkarārya of the fourteenth century.

Quite apart from the authenticity of the *Yogasūtrabhāṣyavivaraṇa*, it should also be noted that Śaṃkara's *Brahmasūtrabhāṣya* is itself an important, albeit highly critical, source for piecing together the history of Sāṃkhya philosophy. Sections I.1.5-11 and 18, I.4.1-28, II.1.1-11 and II.2.1-10 of Śaṃkara's *Brahmasūtrabhāṣya* are given over to a detailed treatment of Sāṃkhya philosophy (based largely on the *Sāṃkhyakārikā*). A full discussion of this material may be found in the epilogue to Gerald J. Larson's *Classical Sāṃkhya*.[1] If we accept Allen Thrasher's suggestion that Śaṃkara can be plausibly dated at about 700 or slightly earlier, Śaṃkara's presentation of Sāṃkhya clearly shows that the Kārikā-Sāṃkhya of Īśvarakṛṣṇa was evidently a potent rival in Brahmanical philosophical circles at the beginning of the eighth century.[2]

MĀṬHARAVṚTTI

As has already been discussed (see entries on the *Suvarṇasaptati*, *Sāṃkhyavṛtti*, *Sāṃkhyasaptativṛtti* and Gauḍapāda's *Bhāṣya*), our extant *Māṭharavṛtti* has a common core of content with four other early commentaries on the *Sāṃkhyakārikā*. Although for many years it was thought that the *Māṭharavṛtti* may have been the original upon which the other four were based, there is now a general consensus that our extant *Māṭharavṛtti* is the latest of the five commentaries and may be dated anywhere from the ninth century onward. The commentary contains quotations from the Purāṇas, appears to presuppose a much more sophisticated logic (based most likely on later Nyāya discussions), and presents overall a fuller and more systematic treatment of Sāṃkhya (strongly suggesting that it is a later expansion of the earlier and briefer discussions in the other related commentaries). E. A. Solomon has suggested that our extant *Māṭharavṛtti* closely follows her recently edited *Sāṃkhyasaptativṛtti*, and that the former may be an expanded version of the latter (with some borrowing also from the other three). She also suggests that *Sāṃkhyasaptativṛtti* may have been an original *Māṭharabhāṣya* by the ancient Sāṃkhya teacher Māṭhara, mentioned in the *Anuyogadvārasūtra* of the Jains, and that our extant *Māṭharavṛtti* may be the same as the commentary referred to by Guṇaratnasūri in his commentary (from the fifteenth century) on the *Ṣaḍdarśanasamuccaya* by the expression *māṭharaprānta* (the Māṭhara "corner" or school). She also speculates that the ancient Māṭhara may be the same as Mādhava (see entry above). These are all interesting suggestions worthy of further exploration. The dependence of the *Māṭharavṛtti* on the *Sāṃkhyasaptativṛtti* is sufficiently close that the latter may be considered an expansion of the former. Whether *Sāṃkhyasaptativṛtti* represents an original *Māṭharabhāṣya*, however or whether *Māṭharavṛtti* is to be identified with *māṭharaprānta*, or whether Māṭhara is the same as Mādhava, are all open questions and cannot be definitely determined by the present limited evidence.

For a full bibliography regarding the relationship of the *Māṭhara-*

vṛtti to the other four commentaries having common content, see above under the *Suvarṇasaptati* entry.

The edition used for the following summary is that of Vishnu Prasad Sharma, editor *Sāṃkhyakārikā of Śrīmad Īśvarakṛṣṇa with the Māṭhara-vṛtti of Māṭharācārya and the Jayamaṅgalā of Śrī Śaṅkara* (the latter edited by S. S. Vangiya) (Chowkhamba Sanskrit Series, Work No. 56, Varanasi, 1970).

(*Summary by Harsh Narain*)

I. Introductory Verses: The Scope and Task of the Sāṃkhya (E1-7)

(1) Kapila is a great seer (*maharṣi*) born of Svāyambhuva Manu's daughter Devahūti to Prajāpati Kardama, (and having the four constructive basic predispositions, namely, meritorious behaviour, discriminating knowledge, nonattachment, and power, see SK23). The end of Sāṃkhya is to abolish the three kinds of frustration. Of these the first, internal sort is of two kinds: physical and mental. The desire to eliminate the three kinds of frustration leads to their elimination—even though the desire is born of these—just as a crab kills its own mother.

(2) Heaven is perishable because it is limited. The knowledge of the manifest, the unmanifest, and the knower is absolute (*aikāntika*) because it necessarily bears fruit; final (*ātyantika*) because it is the knowledge of nature itself; pure because it is accompanied with the rules of restraint (*yama*) and restriction (*niyama*); and bearing maximum and inexhaustible fruit because it is exclusive and perfect.[1] (The commentary under this verse contains a number of quotations from the *Brāhmaṇa-* and *Śrauta-Sūtra*-texts as also one quotation from the *Bhāgavata* bearing upon the slaughter of animals in Vedic sacrifices.)

II. The Instruments of Knowledge (E8-12)

(4) The manifest, the unmanifest, and the knower are objects of knowledge that are established by the instruments of knowledge. The instruments of knowledge are three: perception, inference, and reliable testimony. Perception is caused by the sense capacities. Perception is the principal instrument of knowledge and is hence stated first. Where perception fails, inference comes into play. It takes the form of a three-membered or five-membered argument. It operates in the absence of perception and has to be free from the thirty-three faults (recounted in the next verse). What operates on the basis of, and follows upon a reason (*hetu*), is called inference. For example, fire is inferred on the basis of prior perception of smoke in the kitchen.

What cannot be established by inference is established by reliable testimony, as, for example, the propositions that there are nymphs in heaven, etc. Sanatkumāra and others are reliable persons being free from attachment and hatred. The Vedas also are reliable.

(5) The three members of the syllogism are subject (*pakṣa*), reason (*hetu*), and example (*dṛṣṭānta*). The subject is the enunciation of what is to be established. For instance, "this region is fiery." The reason has three forms: presence in the subject (*pakṣadharmatva*), presence in the positive example (*sapakṣe sattvam*), and absence from the negative example (*vipakṣe asattvam*). Fallacies of the *hetu* are fourteen. Examples are of two kinds, viz., by similarity and by dissimilarity (*sadharmyavaidharmya*). False examples are ten. So, inference has three members and has to be free from thirty-three fallacies. According to others, inference takes the form of a five-membered argument: thesis (*pratijñā*), reason (*apadeśa*), example (*nidarśana*) application (*anusandhāna*), and conclusion (*pratyāmnāya*). Inference is either for oneself, private (*svārtha*), or for others, public (*parārtha*). Inference for others is either *a priori* (*pūrvavat*), *a posteriori* (*śeṣavat*), or based on general correlation (*sāmānyatodṛṣṭa*). The *a priori* inference covers inference of both the past and the future on the basis of prior experience. Reliable testimony is twofold: reliable persons and the Vedas.[2]

(6) Because materiality is creative even though it is unconscious, there must be consciousness, which moves it just as a magnet moves a piece of iron.

(7) Nonapprehension of existents is eightfold, whereas absences are fourfold: prior absence (*prāgabhāva*), posterior absence (*pradhvaṃsābhāva*), mutual absence (*itaretarābhāva*), and absolute absence (*atyantābhāva*). Primordial materiality is subtle because it is not characterized by sound, etc., as are atoms, etc.

III. The Notion of Preexistent Effect (E12-13)

(9) The Vaiśeṣika philosophers say that an existent comes out of nonexistence. The Ājīvakas say that the existent is and is not in its cause before production. The Buddhists are also of the same view.

IV. The Manifest and Unmanifest Aspects of Materiality (E13-15)

(10) The specific feature of *Kārikā* 10 is that it speaks of two kinds of cause or reason (*hetu*): productive (*kāraka*) and informative (*jñāpaka*). Materiality, intellect, egoity, and the subtle elements are productive whereas misconception, dysfunction, contentment, attainment, and grace (*anugraha*) are informative. "Productive" refers to material cause; "informative" refers to the "intellectual creation" or *pratyaya* = *sarga* [see Introduction].

V. The Three Constituents (E15-18)

(12) The intelligibility constituent (*sattva*) is agreeable (*prīti*) and satisfying (*sukha*) as exemplified in simplicity, sweetness, truth, purity, intelligence, forbearance, compassion, knowledge, etc. The activity constituent (*rajas*) is of the nature of frustration exemplified by hate, animosity, jealousy, reproach, rigidity, anxiety, wickedness, deception, bondage, killing, cutting, etc. The inertia constituent (*tamas*) is of the nature of oppression (*viṣāda*) and confusion (*moha*), exemplified by ignorance, vanity, sloth, fear, misery, inactivity, infidelity, sorrowfulness, dream, etc. The suppression (*abhibhava*) of *rajas* and *tamas* gives rise to the peaceful tendency of meritorious behaviour (*dharma*), etc., belonging to *sattva*. The suppression of *sattva* and *tamas* gives rise to the violent tendency of demeritorious behavior (*adharma*), etc., belonging to *rajas*. The suppression of *sattva* and *rajas* gives rise to the delusive tendency of ignorance, etc., belonging to *tamas*.

Sattva, *rajas*, and *tamas* perform each other's functions. For example, the same woman possessing charm and chastity is an instance of *sattva*. She is a joy to her husband and relations but a pain and delusion to her cowives, thereby functioning as *sattva*, *rajas*, and *tamas* at the same time.

(13) The three constituents of materiality are different in kind for the simple reason that they have different properties.

VI. The Inferences that Establish the Existence and Make-up of Primordial Materiality and Consciousness (E18-25)

(14) The nondiscriminating character of the manifest and the unmanifest (postulated in SK 11) is established on the ground, inter alia, that both have the three constituents. What has the three constituents is undiscriminating, what is undiscriminating is objective, what is objective is general, what is general is unconscious, and what is unconscious is productive. Hence, lack of discrimination, etc., are established by the fact of having the three constituents. Another argument is that the cause, such as the yarn, is bound to be similar to the effect, and the unmanifest and the manifest are related by way of cause and effect. Nondiscrimination, etc., reside in the manifest and the unmanifest on account of the absence of the contraries of the three constituents therein. A Yogin perceives both the manifest and the unmanifest.

(16) Causation is twofold: transforming (*pariṇāmaka*) and non-transforming (*apariṇāmaka*). An example of the first is milk's becoming curd and that of the second, clay, etc. (becoming a pot, etc.).

(17) Consciousness is "*paramātman*" (the supreme self), and its presence impels materiality to act for liberation. The *Ṣaṣṭitantra* says,

"The creative nature acts under the guidance of consciousness" (*puruṣā-dhiṣṭhitaṃ pradhānaṃ pravartate*).

(18) Consciousnesses are many. Some are born in high families and some in low families. Hence, consciousnesses are many. Some interpret it like this. If there is only one consciousness, in the event of the birth or death of one, there will be the birth or death of all.

(19) There are two kinds of agents: user (*prayoktṛ*) and maker (*kartṛ*). Because consciousness is neutral (*udāsīna*) and free from the three constituents (*aguṇalakṣaṇa*), it is not an agent (of either kind) at all.[3]

(21) (E25-26) There are many kinds of conjunction (*saṃyoga*): unilateral (*anyatarakarmaja*), like that between a bare trunk and a falcon; bilateral (*sampātaja*), like that between two fingers; innate (*svābhāvika*), like that between fire and heat; due to special capacity (*śaktihetuka*), like that between fish and water; and accidental (*yadṛcchika*), like that between two birds. But the conjunction between materiality and consciousness is teleological (*arthahetuka*), as in the next *kārikā*.[4]

(22) (E26-28) *Mahat* (the great one), *buddhi* (intellect), *mati* (determination), *prajñā* (wisdom), *saṃvitti* (awareness), *khyāti* (discrimination), *citi* (understanding), *smṛti* (memory), *āsuri* (?), Hari (Viṣṇu), Hara (Śiva), and Hiraṇyagarbha (the Golden Egg, Brahmā) are synonyms. The synonyms for egoity (*ahaṃkāra*) are: *vaikṛta* (generated), *taijasa* (the bright one), *bhūtādi* (the first of the elements), *abhimāna* (self-awareness), and *asmitā* (I am-ness, egotism). *Ahaṃkāra* is so called because its base, "*aham*", represents all the sixty-four letters of the Sanskrit alphabet, which begins with "*a*" and ends with "*ha*," by way of grammatical comprehension (*pratyāhāra*), thereby standing for everything that is the object of language and thought. *Tāmasa*, *bhūtādi* egoity, gives rise to the subtle elements; hence, they are delusive. *Sāttvika*, generated egoity, gives rise to the eleven capacities. Hence, they are capable of sensing something (*kiñcij jananti*).[5] *Rājasa*, *taijasa* egoity gives rise to both subtle elements and capacities. Subtle elements give rise to gross elements: sound to the physical space (*ākāśa*), touch to air, color to fire, flavor to water, and odor to earth. Of these, each of the latter is a superaddition to the former. Kapila is called Bhagavat because "*bha*" stands for knowledge of creation and dissolution of things, "*ga*" for knowledge of the coming and going of things, "*va*" for *vidvat* (knower) or Yogin, and "*an*" for "*anati*" (moves). Combining all the letters, we have *Bhagavat*.

IX. The Functioning of the Thirteenfold Instrument (E28-40)

(23) "*Dharma*" means the general rules of conduct called "restraints": noninjury (*ahiṃsā*), truth (*satya*), nonstealing (*asteya*), chastity (*brahmacarya*), and nonpossession (*aparigraha*) (see *Yogasūtra* 2.30)—

and "restrictions" are purity (*śauca*), contentment (*santoṣa*), austerity (*tapas*), self-study (*svādhyāya*), meditation upon God (*iśvarapraṇidhāna*) (see *Yogasūtra* 2.32), prescribed for all the castes (*varṇa*) and stages of life (*āśrama*). Meritorious behaviour prevents people from falling into a bad condition. Chastity means detachment from enjoyment of sex in all its forms, even at the level of sound, touch vision, audition, and smell, experienced directly or remembered. Besides, semen is the germ of Brahmā, and one who does not part with it is a Brahmacārin (a chaste person). Again, "Brahmā" means the Vedas. One who follows them or one's teacher is a Brahmacārin. Lastly, one who bears a staff and an ascetic's water pot in imitation of Brahmā is a Brahmacārin.

(26) The word "*indriya*" contains "*in*" which means "object." *Indriyas* run after objects, hence, they are called *indriyas*. The reproductive organ is for reproduction as well as for pleasure.

(27) Diversity in the world is not due to God, consciousness, or self-nature (*svabhāva*), but due to the transformations of the constituents and diversity of the objects of knowledge. Capacities have also been planted in our body not by God, consciousness, or self-nature, but by the three constituents.

(23) "Mere awareness" is the capacity of the sense capacities to apprehend their own respective objects.

(29) Here, "*karaṇavṛtti*" means, not external, but internal organs.

(30) Simultaneous operation (*yugapadvṛtti*) means that the internal sense capacities appear to work simultaneously though, in fact, they work gradually. But the interval between them is too small to be apprehended. If we prick a needle into a bunch of betel leaves seemingly all at once, even then we in fact prick the first leaf first, then the second, then the third, and so on. So, eye, mind, egoity, and intellect seem to be working simultaneously in apprehending something, but they in fact work gradually.

(31) The constituents tend naturally and necessarily to fulfil the purpose of consciousness. The thirteen instruments move toward their objects automatically, without being moved by God or consciousness. And there is nothing like self-nature to impart motion to them.

(32) "Seizer" means capacities, "holder" means egoity, and "illuminator" means intellect.[6]

(34) The five subtle elements are nonspecific, because they have the character of causing only satisfaction to the gods, and neither frustration nor confusion. To human beings, they cause satisfaction, frustration, and confusion and are hence called specific.

(35) The intellect, ego, and mind are the gate keepers, and the ten capacities are the gates, for it is the intellect, egoity, and mind that apprehend things through capacities.

(36) Satisfaction, frustration, etc., residing in the intellect are experienced by consciousness.

(37) In Kapila's system, there is no duty that is binding. Knowledge of the twenty-five principles alone leads to liberation. Someone has said, "Laugh, drink, play, enjoy pleasures—do not hesitate. If you know Kapila's philosophy, then you are bound to attain liberation."[7]

X. The Subtle and Gross Elements (E40-42)

(39) There are [primary] subtle bodies (*sūkṣma*) made up of the five subtle elements. They produced the [secondary] subtle bodies (*sūkṣmaśarīra*) of the three worlds in the beginning of creation. The subtle body enters the mother's womb during the time favourable for conception. It lasts until the end of this world or until the discrimination between consciousness and materiality dawns, whichever is earlier.

XI. The Subtle Body (E42-44)

(40) The subtle body (*liṅga*) is so called because it merges with primordial materiality during the time of dissolution (*pralaya*). *Pradhāna* is so called because all is consigned to it.

(41) The subtle bodies emerging at the beginning of creation consist of thirteen subtle constituents: intellect, egoity, the five sense capacities, the five action capacities, and the mind. They cannot stand without the *liṅgaśarīras* (another name for the secondary subtle bodies) having the five subtle elements in addition.

XII. The Basic Predispositions (E44-51)

(43) The subtle body that enters the mother's womb is developed by the mother's blood and the father's semen.

(44) "Above" signifies the eight species of the gods: Brahmā, Prajāpati (the creative god), Indra, patriarchs, *gandharva*, *yakṣa*, *rākṣasa*, and *piśāca*. There, meritorious behaviour is the efficient cause (*nimitta*) and rising above is its effect (*naimittika*). "Below" means the five species of cattle, etc.: cattle, animals, birds, reptiles, and immovable species (trees, etc.). Here, demeritorious behaviour is the efficient cause, and sinking low is the effect. Knowledge of the twenty-five principles does away with the subtle body, followed by the liberation of consciousness (*paramātman*). Here, knowledge is the efficient cause, and liberation its effect. Ignorance (*ajñāna*) binds consciousness to the body. Hence, ignorance is the efficient cause and bondage its effect. Bondage is of three kinds: material bondage (*prakṛtibandha*), acquired bondage (*vaikārikabandha*), and personal bondage (*dakṣiṇābandha*).

Material bondage means identification of oneself with the eight generative principles (namely, *prakṛti*, *buddhi*, *ahaṁkāra*, and the five subtle elements). Acquired bondage means treating the *vikāras*, namely, *buddhi*, etc., as best. Personal bondage is caused by charity, sacrifice, etc.

(45) The basic predisposition called power (*aiśvarya*) leads to unobstructed fulfilment of desires, but not to liberation. Lack of power or impotence yields an opposite result, or, in other words, resulting in the nonfulfilment of desires. Merger with nature is called innate bondage; sacrifice, etc., are called personal bondage; and enjoyment caused by power, etc., is called acquired bondage.

(48) *Tamas* is what spoils something (*tad vastu malayatiti*).

(51) Knowledge arises through the teacher, scripture, and one's own self.

XIII. The Empirical World (E52-54)

(55) The subtle (*liṅga*) ceases to exist when knowledge dawns.

(56) Materiality serves two purposes of consciousness: knowledge of sound, etc., and knowledge of the distinction between the constituents and consciousness (the distinction is repeated under verses 42, 58, 60).

XIV. Similes Illustrating the Role and Function of Materiality (E54-56)

(59) When materiality operates, consciousness experiences the three kinds of frustration. When frustration is destroyed, consciousness is liberated.

(60) Materiality fulfils two purposes of consciousness—enjoyment of things and liberation—though consciousness does not return the good done to it.

(61) Because God is attributeless (*nirguṇa*), He cannot cause a world having the three constituents. Hence, the world is caused by materiality, not by God. Self-nature (*svabhāva*) is not an entity, hence it cannot be generative. Time also is not an entity, for Sāṃkhya postulates only three kinds of entities: the manifest, the unmanifest, and consciousness. And time is subsumed under them. Hence, creative nature alone is the cause of the world.

XV. Liberation and Isolation (E57-61)

(62) The subtle body of the five subtle elements having thirteen instruments alone transmigrates. When knowledge supervenes, the subtle body is liberated. "Subtle body," "the principal one" (*pradhāna*), "materiality" are synonymous.

(64) Knowledge means discrimination between the constituents and consciousness. Constant meditation on the twenty-five principles leads to the knowledge, "I am not the principles," "the principles are not mine," "I am not of the principles."

(65) Consciousness perceives materiality in its various modes by by dint of its innate knowledge (*ātmakṛtena jñānena*).

(66) Consciousness is single, isolated, pure. Materiality is also one and only one for the entire cosmos.

(67) Latent dispositions lead to meritorious and demeritorious behaviour, which is responsible for birth in different species.

(68) The enlightened one renders his actions incapable of fruition and is seedless. So, his actions do not cause another body. The past actions that have not yet begun to bear fruit are burnt up, though those that have begun to fructify have to be exhausted by reaping their consequences. When the past actions are destroyed, the body breaks up. Then the causal body called primordial materiality and composed of the subtle elements in the beginning of creation ceases to exist. Since the purpose of primordial materiality stands fulfilled, it does not start another body for the enlightened soul.

(69) Perseverance (*sthiti*) (of the world process) means presence of the gods, humans, subhumans in their respective abodes. Creation (*utpatti*) means emergence of intellect, etc., from primordial materiality. Dissolution (*laya*) means reduction of the gross elements into subtle ones, of the latter into the sense and action capacities, of these into ego, of this into intellect, and of it into primordial materiality.

XVI. The Transmission of the Sāṃkhya Tradition (E61-64)

(70) The knowledge of the twenty-five principles is supreme (*agrya*), because, being absolute and final, it is the highest.

(71) Liberation means the end of the causally determined body and nonreincarnation.

(72) *Ṣaṣṭitantra* means a system dealing with sixty topics: five misconceptions, twenty-eight dysfunctions, nine contentments, eight attainments, and the ten principal topics. The term "*tantra*" means where topics are dealt with (*tantryante*, *vyutpadyante*).[8]

VĀCASPATI MIŚRA

According to tradition, this famous interpreter of Indian philosophy was a Maithila Brahmin from the region of Bihar. He lived either in the middle of the ninth century (ca., 841) or toward the latter half of the tenth century (ca., 976). The reason for the discrepancy in date relates to a reference in one of Vācaspati's own writings, namely, the *Nyāyasūcinibandha*, in which Vācaspati reports that he composed the work in 898. If this latter date is calculated according to the Vikrama era (beginning in 58 B.C.E.), it becomes 841 of the Common Era. If the date is calculated according to the Śaka era (beginning in 78 C.E., it becomes 976 of the Common Era. Arguments have been given for preferring either of these dates, and the issue has yet to be resolved, although there appears to be a growing consensus in favor of the date 976.[1] For helpful discussions of both sides of the continuing debate, see S. A. Srinivasan.[2]

According to Umesha Mishra, the order of Vācaspati's writings are as follows: *Nyāyakaṇikā* (a commentary on Maṇḍana Miśra's *Vidhiviveka*), *Tattvasamīkṣā* (now lost), *Tattvabindu* (an original work on the theory of meaning in Pūrva Mīmāṃsā), *Nyāyasūcinibandha* (a work attempting to establish the number and order of the *Nyāyasūtra*), *Nyāyavārttikatātparyaṭīkā* (a commentary on Uddyotakara's *Nyāyavārttika*), *Tattvakaumudī* (on Īśvarakṛṣṇa's *Sāṃkhyakārikā*), *Tattvavaiśāradī* (a commentary on Patañjali's *Yogasūtra* and the *Bhāṣya* by Vyāsa), and *Bhāmatī* (on Śaṃkara's *Brahmasūtrabhāṣya*).[3]

TATTVAKAUMUDĪ

The *Tattvakaumudī* ("Moonlight on the Truth" of Sāṃkhya) was translated into German by Richard Garbe in 1891.[4] The text was critically edited (based on some 90 manuscripts) by S. A. Srinivasan in 1967.[5] An English translation was prepared by G. Jha in 1896, which was revised and re-edited by M. M. Patkar (along with an introduction and critical notes by Har Dutt Sharma) in 1965.[6] The following summary is based on this latter edition and translation of the text.

The *Tattvakaumudī* itself is a fairly simple and straightforward exposition of the *Sāṃkhyakārikā* and lacks the detailed analyses and incisive polemic so typical of some of the other works of Vācaspati (for example, the *Tattvavaiśāradī*, the *Nyāyavārttikatātparyaṭīkā*, and the *Bhāmatī*). One has the impression either that Sāṃkhya was no longer an important philosophical tradition in Vācaspati's time or that Vācaspati himself was not familiar with the details of the old Sāṃkhya system. The text has been historically very important, however, for it has inspired a long tradition of subcommentaries coming down to the present day. Moreover, it is fair to say that it is by far the best-known text of Sāṃkhya all over India.

(*Summary by Gerald J. Larson*)

I. Introductory Verses: The Scope and Task of the Sāṃkhya (ET1-16)

(1) The commentary begins with two poetic verses. The first verse pays homage to the feminine "unborn one" (*ajām ekām*) (namely, materiality), who is red, white, and black (*lohita*, *śukla*, and *kṛṣṇa*, corresponding to the three constituents *rajas*, *sattva*, and *tamas*) and who produces the many creatures of the manifest world, and to the many masculine "unborn ones" (that is, the many consciousnesses), who for a time enjoy the feminine "unborn one" but finally abandon her after having completed their enjoyment of her. The second verse pays homage to the tradition of Sāṃkhya teachers, including Kapila, Āsuri, Pañcaśikha, and Īśvarakṛṣṇa.[7]

The *Sāṃkhyakārikā* is a science (*śāstra*) whose subject matter is the attainment of a correct and complete understanding of the end or aim of man (*paramapuruṣārtha*). The science supplies the means to attain this highest goal, and, therefore, it is worthy to be studied by those who desire to attain ultimate philosophical understanding. The Sāṃkhya asserts (a) that there is frustration in the world; (b) that people desire to be free from it; (c) that its removal is possible; (d) that the Sāṃkhya science provides a necessary and sufficient means for removing it; and (e) that all worldly remedies for the removal of frustration (e.g., medicine, and so forth) are inadequate because such ordinary remedies are neither certain nor able to prevent the recurrence of frustration.

(2) The rejection of Vedic means for the ultimate removal of frustration refers only to the ritualistic portions of scripture. The philosophical portions of scripture (as, for example, in speculative Upaniṣads such as *Bṛhadāraṇyaka* and *Chāndogya*) are not rejected. Moreover, Vedic rituals are not being completely discarded by this verse. The point, rather, is the following: Vedic rituals are useful, but the way of

discriminative knowing is ultimately more useful. "We drank the Soma, and have become immortal," etc., and other scriptural passages reveal that the alleviation of frustration by ritualistic means is tainted with negative side effects (as, for example, the killing of sacrificial animals must be expiated, and so forth), leads to inequality of results, and provides an "immortality" that is really only a "long duration." The ancient Sāṃkhya teacher Pañcaśikha is quoted to the effect that Vedic rituals bring about negative side effects. A superior means for the certain and permanent alleviation of frustration is through the discriminative awareness of the manifest, the unmanifest, and the knower. The manifest is an effect, and by analyzing the effect, one discovers the unmanifest, which is its cause. By then realizing that the manifest and unmanifest must be construed together (namely, as effect and cause) and that these two exist together for the sake of another (*pārārthya*), one then infers the existence of a knower. One attains the ultimate discriminative awareness (*vijñāna*) by means of precise scientific reasoning (*śāstrayukti*) that is accompanied by patient meditation (*bhāvanā*).

II. The Instruments of Knowledge (ET16-42)

(4) The instruments of knowledge are the instruments for attaining the correct cognition (*pramā*) of objects (*prameya*). Sāṃkhya recognizes three instruments of knowledge: perception, inference, and reliable testimony. Other instruments such as comparison (*upamāna*) can be reduced to one of the three. Extraordinary or supernatural instruments of knowledge such as the intuition of Yogins are not discussed here because they have no relevance with respect to the awareness of ordinary people.

(5) Perception is the reflective discerning (*adhyavasāya*) that arises through the direct contact (*sannikarṣa*) between a sense capacity (*indriya*) and a knowable and real object (*prameya*) such as earth or pleasure, and so forth. Such reflective discerning, which is an operation of intellect, is one important kind of awareness, and this kind of awareness arises when the intellect is in its *sattva* modality and the *tamas* modality has been subverted. When there is such contact between a sense capacity and an object with the resulting awareness taking place in intellect, the condition is also known as an operation (*vṛtti*). Awareness, operation, and intellect, it should be noted, are manifestations of materiality and, thus, are devoid of consciousness. Nevertheless, the intellect casts a kind of shadow or, perhaps better, becomes a reflection (*pratibimba*) in the pure medium of consciousness so that it appears as if it were conscious. By the same token the images that manifest themselves in consciousness appear to characterize the nature of consciousness itself. Finally, it should be noted that the description of per-

ception as direct contact with a specific object excludes doubt, misconception, inference, and memory.

Inference depends upon perception and provides mediate knowledge based upon general conditions that invariably coincide in a knowing situation, as, for example, when the sight of smoke on a hill is present, even though the fire is not directly perceived. The *sādhya* or more inclusive term (namely, the fire or what is called the *liṅgin* or "that which bears or supports a mark") overlaps with the less inclusive term (namely, the smoke or what is called the *liṅga* or the "mark"), and the *liṅga* overlaps with the *pakṣa* (that is, the hill), which is the locus for the initial perception and the resulting inference. In formulating a correct inference, it is important to eliminate all distorting elements or "limiting adjuncts" (*upādhi*). There are three kinds of inference, namely, *a priori* (*pūrvavat*), *a posteriori* (*śeṣavat*), and inference based on general correlation (*sāmānyatodṛṣṭa*). These three can be classified into two types: (a) exclusionary inference (*avīta*), wherein knowledge arises based on that which remains or is left over after appropriate negations have been made; and (b) positive or affirmative inference (*vīta*), wherein knowledge arises based on an affirmative assertion of invariable concomitance. *A posteriori* inference is, thus, an exclusionary inference (and see under verse 9 for examples). *A priori* inference and inference based on general correlation are both positive inferences. "*A priori* inference" refers to the positive inference of the presence of a particular instance of the general notion of fire as a result of perceiving smoke on the hill. One is able to make such an inference because of previous perceptions of the concomitance of smoke with fire, as, for example, in a kitchen. Inference based on general correlation refers to the positive inference of the presence of a general notion for which no particular instance has been perceived, as, for example, when one infers the presence of a sense capacity as a requisite instrument in a knowing situation even though such a capacity cannot be directly perceived. (Vācaspati comments at this point that he has explained all of this much more fully in his *Nyāyavārttikatātparyaṭīkā*.)

Reliable testimony depends upon inference and involves the knowledge that arises as a result of the use of language. It depends upon inference inasmuch as one must infer that there is an invariable concomitance between certain verbalizations and certain objects or actions, but it is not itself an instance of inference. Reliable authority functions with verbal utterances that describe or relate objects and actions, but the verbal utterances (or sentences) are not inferential markers in the sense that smoke is an inferential mark for fire. Thus, reliable authority is different from inference. Also, the notion of creativity in the use of language shows clearly that verbalization is not simply inference. Whereas smoke is invariably and replicably concomitant with fire, a verbal utterance or sentence (e.g., of a poet) may express a meaning that is totally new or that has never been uttered in quite the same way. That which guarantees the validity of reliable authority (or trustworthy verbalization) is its ultimate source, and the only truly reliable source is the *Veda* or *śruti*, because it is free from human authorship and free from all defects. Other kinds of literature (e.g., *smṛti* and *itihāsa*) and certain respected teachers (e.g., Kapila) are also trustworthy inasmuch as their utterances are based on the Veda.

There are no other reliable instruments of knowledge in addition to perception, inference, and reliable testimony. What some schools call "comparison" (*upamāna*) is really a mixture of perception, inference, and reliable authority. "Presumption" (*arthāpatti*) is really an instance of inference. "Nonapprehension" (*abhāva*) is really a form of perception. "Inclusion" (*saṃbhava*) is only a case of inference, and "tradition" (*aitihya*)is only a form of reliable authority, and, in many instances, is only vague opinion (with no validity whatever).

(6) Imperceptible things (as, for example, materiality, consciousness, and so forth) can be known through inference based on general correlation and exclusionary or *a posteriori* inference (*śeṣavat*).

III. The Notion of Preexistent Effect (ET42-53)

(9) The Buddhist view that the cause is nonexistent but the effects are existent, the Vedānta view that the cause is existent (and unitary) but the effects are nonexistent, and the Nyāya-Vaiśeṣika view that the existent cause is completely different from the effect are all mistaken views inasmuch as they render the cause and effect relation unintelligible. Only the Sāṃkhya view is correct whereby the basic experiences (as effects) of satisfaction, frustration, and confusion are traced to their causal constituents *sattva*, *rajas*, and *tamas*, thus allowing for a valid inference that there is an ultimate root cause (namely, primordial materiality) that is constituted by the three constituents.

The arguments for the notion of *satkārya*, or the "existent effect," in this verse are directed primarily against the Nyāya-Vaiśeṣika notion of *asatkārya* or the "nonexistent effect" (or, in other words, the notion that the effect is not existent at the time of causal operation but only afterward). These arguments are as follows: (a) If one argues that what was nonexistent has been produced, one has to explain how something can come from nothing. The "nonexistent" must somehow be interpreted as being part of the causal process. Yet there is no intelligible way of speaking about causal operation vis-à-vis the "nonexistent". (b) If one argues that the effect is nonexistent at the time of causal operation, then one is denying that there is an existent relation between cause and effect. Hence, again, the very notion of causation becomes unintelligible. (c) Moreover, if one argues that the effect is nonexistent at the time of causal operation, then one cannot avoid the conclusion that any thing might come from anything. In other words, by denying an existent relation between an existent cause and an existent effect, one can no longer account for specific effects arising from specific causes. (d) Likewise, if one argues that the effect is nonexistent at the time of causal operation, one cannot account for a cause being able to accomplish that which it is capable of accomplishing. (e) Finally, if one argues that the effect is nonexistent at the time of causal operation, it is not possible to maintain any significant continuity in nature between cause and effect. In other words, everything becomes distinct and unrelated, and the whole notion of cause and effect becomes meaningless.

In addition to these arguments, which establish that the Nyāya-Vaiśeṣika notion of *asatkārya* is wrong, one can also set forth four exclusionary inferences (see above under verse 5) that prove that there is no difference between the cause and the effect. These are (a) A cloth (as an effect) subsists or is coextensive with its threads (as a cause), but two different things cannot subsist or be coextensive with one another—as, for example, a cow and a horse. Therefore, cause and effect are nondifferent. (b) The threads are the material constituents of a cloth, but two different things cannot be made up of the same material constituents—as, for example, a jar and a cloth. Therefore, cause and effect are nondifferent. (c) There can be no conjunction or separation between a cloth and its threads, but two different things can only relate to one another by means of conjunction and separation—as, for example, a well and a bucket. Therefore, cause and effect are nondifferent. (d) Finally, there can be no difference in weight between a cloth and its threads, but two different things almost always have at least a slightly different weight—as, for example, two bracelets. Therefore, cause and effect are nondifferent.

A cloth (the effect) is only a transformation or rearrangement of the threads (the cause) into a particular shape or form. Effects appear (*āvirbhāva*) and disappear (*tirobhāva*), but they are not different in essence from the cause. Effects may serve varying functions, but this does not change their basic identity with the cause. The relation of cause and effect can be compared to a turtle and its limbs. The limbs appear on some occasions and disappear on others. Or again, cause and effect can be compared to clay and a jar or gold and a crown. A jar is a particular appearance of clay, and a crown is a particular appearance of gold. Yet the jar is nondifferent in essence from the clay, and the crown is nondifferent in essence from the gold.

Finally, the Nyāya-Vaiśeṣikas might attempt to force the Sāṃkhya into the following problem: prior to the operation of a cause, is an effect as manifestation existent or nonexistent? If it is existent, then there is no need for a cause, for there is already an effect as manifestation. If it is nonexistent, then one must concede the Nyāya-Vaiśeṣika position of a nonexistent manifestation. One cannot argue that there is a manifestation of the manifestation without ending in an infinite regress. It is to be noted, however, that the Nyāya-Vaiśeṣika has the very same problem with its notions of "production" (*utpatti*), "inherence" (*samavāya*), and "existence" (*sattā*). If one argues for a "nonexistent effect," how can one possibly explain "production"? One cannot bring in notions like "inherence" or "existence," because these notions are eternal and cannot be used unequivocally in speaking about "production" or "destruction." Nor can one speak about the "production" of "production" without ending up in an infinite regress. Moreover, one cannot avoid these problems by speaking about the "form" (*rūpa*) of the effect and the "form" of the cause, because what is at issue is the problem of causal operation (*kriyā*).[8]

IV. The Manifest and Unmanifest Aspects of Materiality (ET53-60)

(10-11) "Being made up of parts" may also mean characterized by conjunction (*saṃyoga*), as, for example, the conjunction between earth and water, and so forth. Conjunction cannot occur, however, between primordial materiality and the intellect (and the other basic principles), because there is a fundamental identity (*tādātmya*) among the various principles of materiality. "Undiscriminated" may mean that the various principles cannot be distinguished from primordial materiality, or it may mean that the various principles cannot be separated—that is to say, they must cooperate with primordial materiality. "Objective" and "general" are included as characteristics of the manifest and unmanifest in order to distinguish Sāṃkhya from any idealist interpretation (whether Buddhist or Vedāntin). Primordial materiality and its related principles exist apart from consciousness. Finally, in some respects consciousness is similar to the unmanifest—for example, both are uncaused (see 10)—but in other respects it is different—for example, consciousness is not made up of the three constituents, etc.[9]

V. The Three Constituents (ET60-68)

(12-13) The term "operation" (*vṛtti*) applies to each member of the compound in 12, so that the compound means that the three constituents mutually dominate, support, activate, and interact with one another.

VI. The Inferences that Establish the Existence and Makeup of Primordial Materiality and Consciousness (ET68-92)

(14) One can infer (largely on the basis of exclusionary inference) that the three constituents are absent from consciousness inasmuch as they are present in all modalities of the satisfaction, frustration, and confusion of the manifest world of experience. In addition, one can infer that the three constituents are present in the unmanifest on the basis of the essential identity of cause and effect. In other words, satisfaction, frustration, and confusion must have a causal basis in materiality in the form of *sattva*, *rajas*, and *tamas*.

(15-16) The arguments in these verses are directed primarily against the atomism of Nyāya-Vaiśeṣika. Finite, manifest reality can only be intelligibly accounted for by positing an all-pervasive and all-powerful unmanifest whole within which (both analytically and synthetically) finite modalities subsist (occasionally appearing and occasionally disappearing).

(17-19) Verse 17 is directed against materialists who deny the separate existence of consciousness. Verse 18 is directed against the Vedāntins who think that consciousness is one. Verse 19 sets forth the essential characteristics of consciousness, for the understanding of these leads to ultimate discrimination and release.

(20) In ordinary awareness it appears to be the case that consciousness is active, but in fact only awareness (*antaḥkaraṇavṛtti*) is active. Consciousness only appears to be active. In fact, it is not. Similarly, the transformations of materiality appear to be conscious, but in fact they are not.

(21) Primordial materiality performs two functions vis-à-vis consciousness, namely, experience and release. Because consciousness is inactive it cannot perform these functions, and yet these functions are necessary if consciousness is to be discriminated.

(22) The gross elements emerge from the subtle elements in the following fashion: (a) the subtle element sound produces *ākāśa*, characterized by the quality of sound; (b) sound plus touch produces wind, characterized by the qualities of sound and touch; (c) sound, plus touch, plus form produces fire, characterized by the qualities of sound, touch and color; (d) sound, plus touch, plus form, plus taste produces water, characterized by the qualities of sound, touch, color and taste; and, finally ; (e) sound, plus touch, plus form, plus taste, plus smell produces earth, characterized by the qualities of sound, touch, color, taste and smell.

IX. The Function of the Thirteenfold Instruments (ET92-119)

(23) The notion of the intellect suggests reflective discerning as

well as its agent. There are four varieties or stages of nonattachment (*virāga*): (a) restrained apperception (*yatamānasaṃjñā*), in which one restrains emotional reactions to experience generally; (b) restricted apperception (*vyatirekasaṃjñā*), in which one restrains whatever other emotional reactions still remain after the "striving" stage (c) concentrated apperception (*ekendriyasaṃjñā*), in which one overcomes the yearning or longing for ordinary experience; and (d) totally controlled apperception (*vaśikārasaṃjñā*), in which one has no desire either for worldly or otherworldly attainments. Patañjali has described this latter stage in *Yogasutra* I.15.

(27) The sense capacities apprehend objects only in a way free from qualifying adjuncts (*nirvikalpa*). The mind performs the function of determining or explicating an object (*savikalpa*—that is to say, in terms of its general and specific properties. Kumārila's *Ślokavārttika* is quoted in explaining this construction-free/construction filled distinction. All differentiations of experience arise because of the particular modifications of the three basic constituents. Even the latent karmic residues (*adṛṣṭa*) are so constituted.

(29) The five vital breaths represent the common function of the internal organ.

(32) The action capacities have the function of "seizing"; the internal organ (made up of intellect, ego, and mind) has the function of "holding" by means of the vital breaths, and so forth; and the sense capacities have the function of "illuminating." The action capacities "seize" or extend to speaking, handling, walking, excreting, and sexual gratification, and these five spheres encompass both the celestial (*divya*) and noncelestial (*adivya*), thus being altogether tenfold. Similarly, the internal organ holds together the body made up of the five gross elements by means of the vital breaths, and it should be noted that the element earth is a composite of sound, touch, color, taste, and smell. Moreover, these elementary bodies are both celestial and noncelestial, and so again the aggregate is tenfold. Finally, the sense capacities illumine the five objects of sense, both celestial and noncelestial, thus again being tenfold.

(33) According to the Vaiśeṣikas time is one and indivisible. According to Sāṃkhya, however, the divisions of time are nothing more than heuristic distinctions or limiting adjuncts. There is no need to posit a distinct entity called "time."

(34) The term "specific" refers to gross elements. The term "nonspecific" refers to subtle elements. Ordinary mortals apprehend only specific or gross objects. Gods and sages can also apprehend nonspecific objects. Among the action capacities, speech apprehends sound alone. The other action capacities apprehend the whole range of manifest things made up of the gross elements.

(37) Consciousness comes to have satisfying or frustrating expe-

riences because of the presence of the intellect, which casts its shadow or reflects its image in consciousness. Likewise it is the intellect that provides the ultimate discriminative realization of the difference between consciousness and materiality. The intellect ultimately reveals that which has always been the case, namely, that there is a fundamental distinction between materiality and consciousness. Because of nondiscrimination this fundamental distinction has become blurred.

X. The Subtle and Gross Elements (ET119-122)

(38) The term "*mātra*" in the compound "*tanmātra*" suggests that the subte elements are devoid of that "specific" or gross dimension that would permit their apprehension as being comforting (*śānta*), uncomfortable (*ghora*), and confusing (*mūḍha*).

(39) Bodies born of paternal and maternal seed (*mātāpitṛja*) are made up of six sheaths, namely, hair, blood, and flesh from the mother and arteries, bones, and marrow from the father.

XI. The Subtle Body (ET122-127)

(40-41) The term "*liṅga*" in 40 encompasses intellect, egoity, mind, the five sense capacities, the five action capacities, and the five subtle elements, but the term "*liṅga*" in 41 encompasses only intellect, egoity, mind, the five sense capacities and the five action capacities. The five subtle elements in this latter verse are taken to be the subtle locus (*āśraya*) for the transmigrating instrument. The term "specific" in verse 41 refers to a specific, subtle body that is necessary for transmigration. A passage from the *Mahābhārata* is quoted, which refers to extracting consciousness from the body, and consciousness is said to have the size of a thumb (*aṅguṣṭhamātra*). The traditional (and fanciful) etymology of the word "*puruṣa*" is given, namely, that it "sleeps" (*śete*) in the city (*pur*), which is the gross body.

(42) As a dramatic actor assumes various parts, so the subtle body occupies various gross physical bodies.

XII. The Basic Predispositions (ET127-149)

(43) (It should be noted that Vācaspati accepts only two types of basic predispositions, namely innate (*prākṛtika*) and acquired (*vaikṛtika*), and not three as do Gauḍapāda and the Chinese commentary).

(44) Three kinds of bondage are enumerated: (a) *prākṛtika* or "*innate*" for those who abide in materiality; (b) *vaikṛtika* or "acquired" for those who abide in the products (*vikāra*) of materiality; and (c) *dākṣiṇaka* or "personal" for those who are intent on religious activities that lead to personal gain.

(47) The five kinds of misconception are the same as the five "afflictions" (*kleśa*) enumerated in the *Yogasūtra*.

(51) Two interpretations of the eight attainments are given, one following Gauḍapāda's exposition and the other apparently that of Paramartha's Chinese commentary. No preference is expressed for either interpretation. Removal of the three kinds of frustration is primary. The other five attainments are secondary.

XIV. Similes Illustrating the Role and Function of Materiality (ET154-168)

(57) Only materiality is the material and efficient cause of manifestation. God cannot be the cause. For God to be the cause it would have to be shown that He acts either out of self-interest (*svārtha*) or out of compassion (*kāruṇya*). Both motivations, however, are inappropriate for God. Hence, materiality is the only cause.

(58-61) Each of the similes in this series of *kārikās* (namely, 57-61) is designed to answer an objection to the Sāṃkhya philosophy. The simile of unconscious milk (57) answers the objections raised against the Sāṃkhya atheism. The simile of someone engaging in an action to fulfill a desire (58) answers the objection of the purposelessness of materiality. That is to say, materiality functions for the sake of consciousness. The simile of the dancing girl ceasing her dance (59) answers the objection that materiality will continue to act endlessly. The simile of the unselfish servant (60) answers the objection that materiality does not benefit from its interactions with consciousness.

XV. Liberation and Isolation (ET160-172)

(64) The expression "I am not..., etc." may be taken to mean the denial of productivity and possession in consciousness, or it may be taken to mean the denial of agency or activity. The term "truth" or "principle" (*tattva*) refers to the direct perception of truth (*tattva* = *sākṣātkara*).

(65) The final discrimination implies the complete overcoming of *rajas* and *tamas*, although a small amount of pure *sattva* remains. That is to say, all ordinary activity ceases.

XVI. The Transmission of the Sāṃkhya Tradition (ET172-174)

(72) The contents of the "sixty topics" (*ṣaṣṭitantra*) are enumerated as follows in the *Rājavārttika*:

(1) The existence of nature (*pradhānāstitva*);
(2) Singleness of nature (*ekatva*);

(3) Objectivity (*arthavattva*);
(4) Distinction of *puruṣa* (from *prakṛti*) (*anyatā*);
(5) Subservience (of *prakṛti* to *puruṣa*) (*pārārthya*);
(6) Plurality (of *puruṣas*) (*anaikya*)
(7) Disjunction (of *puruṣa* from *prakṛti*) (*viyoga*);
(8) Conjunction (of *puruṣa* and *prakṛti*) (*yoga*);
(9) Duration (*śeṣavṛtti*);
(10) Inactivity (*akartṛbhāva*).

These are the ten fundamental topics (*maulikārtha*). The remaining fifty are the five misconceptions, the nine contentments, the twenty-eight dysfunctions and the eight attainments.[10]

Among the fundamental (*maulikārtha*) topics, singleness, objectivity, and subservience characterize materiality; distinction, inactivity, and plurality characterize consciousness; existence, disjunction, and conjunction characterize both materiality and consciousness; and duration characterizes gross and subtle transformations.

TATTVAVAIŚĀRADĪ

This is a commentary on Patañjali's *Yogasūtra* and Vyāsa's *Yogasūtrabhāṣya*, probably written by Vācaspati Miśra at about the same time as or in tandem with the *Tattvakaumudī*. Unlike the *Tattvakaumudī*, the *Tattvavaiśāradī* is a detailed and technically proficient treatment of Pātañjala-Sāṃkhya. It will be summarized in detail in the forthcoming Yoga volume of the Encyclopedia. A complete translation of the entire text of the *Tattvavaiśāradī* may be found in J. H. Woods' translation. *The Yoga-System of Patañjali*.[11]

BHOJARĀJA

RĀJAMĀRTAṆḌA

Bhojarāja, or Bhojadeva, who was, according to Frauwallner,[1] the king of Malawa in the middle of the eleventh century, wrote a commentary on the *Yogasūtra* entitled *Rājamārtaṇḍa* (King-Sun" or "Sun among Kings"). It is a clear exposition of the old Yogā philosophy, which does not, however, go much beyond the views of Vyāsa's *Yogasūtrabhāṣya*. J. H. Woods points out, interestingly (in *The Yoga-System*, pp. xiii-xiv), that stanza 5 of the opening verses to this commentary contains the first reference in Sanskrit literature to the identity of the two Patañjalis, namely, the Patañjali of the *Mahābhāṣya* and the Patañjali of the *Yogasūtra*.

TATTVASAMĀSASŪTRA

Following the work of Vācaspati Miśra in the ninth or tenth century, there is a lacuna in the development of Sāṃkhya literature encompassing a period of several hundred years, i.e, from about 1000 through 1300 or 1400 of the Common Era. As Frauwallner has observed,[1] the creative period in the history of the Sāṃkhya had been in the first centuries of the Common Era with the work of Vārṣagaṇya, Vindhyavāsin, Mādhava, and so forth, and to some extent with the summary work of Īśvarakṛṣṇa. There had been vigorous polemics with Buddhists, Jains, and the followers of Nyāya-Vaiśeṣika as can be seen from references to Sāṃkhya in Dignāga's *Pramāṇasamuccaya*, Jinendrabuddhi's *Ṭikā* (on Dignāga's text), Mallavādin's *Dvādaśāranayacakra* with Siṃhasūri's commentary and Candramati's *Daśapadārthaśāstra*.[2] Moreover, from the evidence of the *Yuktidīpikā* there had also been wide-ranging debates within the Sāṃkhya tradition itself. Eventually, of course, Īśvarakṛṣṇa's *Sāṃkhyakārikā* was accepted as a normative summary formulation of the tradition, and the next several centuries—the sixth through the tenth century—represent for the most part attempts to explicate and consolidate Īśvarakṛṣṇa's interpretation of Sāṃkhya, with the *Yuktidīpikā* providing the best overall picture of the manner in which this explication and consolidation was accomplished. By the eighth century and onward Īśvarakṛṣṇa's formulation of Sāṃkhya had clearly won the day, and references to Sāṃkhya thereafter in the general philosophical literature uniformly reflect the Sāṃkhya of Īśvarakṛṣṇa. This is true, for example, in the dialectical criticisms of Sāṃkhya in the work of Śāntarakṣita (*Tattvasaṃgraha*) and Kamalaśīla (*Pañjikā*) of the eighth century.[3] This is also true, of course, in Śaṃkara's critique of Sāṃkhya in his *Brahmasūtrabhāṣya*. References to Sāṃkhya in Jain literature also reflect the Sāṃkhya of Īśvarakṛṣṇa. Haribhadrasūri's *Ṣaḍdarśanasamuccaya* of the eighth century (verses 33-44) summarizes the Sāṃkhya of Īśvarakṛṣṇa, as does the *Anyayogavyavacchedadvātriṃśikā* (verse 15) of Hemacandra (twelfth-century) with its commentary, *Syādvādamañjarī*, by Malliṣena (thirteenth century). Likewise, Rājaśekhara's *Saḍdarśanasamuccaya* (verses

42-59) of the fourteenth century follows Īśvarakṛṣṇa in its description of Sāṃkhya, and Guṇaratna's commentary (entitled *Tarkarahasyadīpikā*) on Haribhadra's *Ṣaḍdarśanasamuccaya* in its discussion of Sāṃkhya does not depart from Īśvarakṛṣṇa. The only additional information about Sāṃkhya from these later Jain summaries is that, according to Haribhadra, Rājaśekhara, and Guṇaratna, there were two groups of Sāṃkhya followers, one of which was theistic (followers of Nārāyaṇa, according to Rājaśekhara) and the other of which was atheistic. Also, according to Guṇaratna, some ancient Sāṃkhya teachers (*maulikya-sāṃkhya*) asserted a plurality of *prakṛtis* along with a plurality of *puruṣas*, obviously calling to mind Paurika or Mādhava (see above under appropriate entries). Alberuni's account of Sāṃkhya (see above under Gauḍapāda entry) from the eleventh century likewise follows that of the *Sāṃkhyakārikā*, and, finally, the *Sarvadarśanasaṃgraha* (chapter 14) of the Advaitin Mādhava, from the fourteenth century, also is simply a restatement of Īśvarakṛṣṇa's *Sāṃkhyakārikā*.

By the ninth or tenth century of the Common Era, then, it appears to be the case that the Kārikā-Sāṃkhya of Īśvarakṛṣṇa (as well as the Pātañjala-Sāṃkhya of Patañjali and Vyāsa) had about run its course. Its creative phase was definitely over, and its explication and consolidation phase never moved much further than the sorts of formulation found in the *Yuktidīpikā* and to a lesser extent in Vācaspati Miśra's *Tattvakaumudī*. Indian philosophy generally was moving into new areas (for example, the metaphysical debates among the developing Vedānta traditions, more sophisticated logical discussions among Nyāya, Jain, and Mīmāṃsā traditions, the philosophy of language, and so forth), and the older *bhakti* traditions were in the process of shaping themselves into impressive systematic theologies (for example, Śaiva Siddhānta, Kashmiri Śaivism, and the various Vaiṣṇava systems). Many of these new trends in Indian intellectual history obviously owed a profound debt to Sāṃkhya, especially perhaps the various Vedānta traditions and the developing systematic theologies, but it is clear enough that the old Sāṃkhya was not itself to be counted as a vital and active participant in these new trends. It is perhaps hardly an accident, therefore, that we find a *lacuna* in the history of Sāṃkhya literature after the tenth century.

Sāṃkhya philosophy reappears, however, sometime in the fourteenth or fifteenth century of the Common Era, and its reemergence (renaissance), both at that time and subsequently, appears to be linked with three distinct yet interrelated textual sources: (a) a cryptic little collection of *sūtras*, entitled *Tattvasamāsasūtra*, (b) a lengthy collection of *sūtras* (numbering 527, arranged in six books, according to the oldest version of *Aniruddha*), entitled *Sāṃkhyasūtra*, and (c) what might be called a subcommentarial tradition on Vācaspati Miśra's *Tattvakaumudī*. The *Tattvasamāsasūtra* and the *Sāṃkhyasūtra* are both attributed to Kapila (wrongly), and Vijñānabhikṣu (see below under appropriate entry) informs us in the introduction to his *Sāṃkhyapravacanabhāṣya* that the *Tattvasamāsa* is simply a shortened form of the larger *Sāṃkhyasūtra*. This latter comment of Vijñānabhikṣu is hardly likely, but there is no doubt that Vijñānabhikṣu wanted it to be so! In any case, Vijñānabhikṣu (latter half of the sixteenth century) is himself indebted to Aniruddha's edition (ca., latter part of the fifteenth century, see appropriate entry below) of the *Sāṃkhyasūtra*, for, as Garbe has shown in his critical edition of Aniruddha's *Sāṃkhyasūtravṛtti*,[4] Vijñānabhikṣu utilized Aniruddha's version of the *sūtras* as the basis for his own *Sāṃkhyapravacanabhāṣya*. Garbe has also shown[5] that Aniruddha in turn is dependent on Vācaspati Miśra's *Tattvakaumudī*, for Aniruddha borrows from Vācaspati in his comments at I.2, I.120, I.123, I.124, I.132, II.1 and V.94. Thus, there appears to be a close relationship between Aniruddha's *Sāṃkhyasūtravṛtti* and Vācaspati's *Tattvakaumudī*. It is also the case that Vijñānabhikṣu is aware of the *Tattvakaumudī*, for he disagrees with Vācaspati Miśra's interpretation of Sāṃkhya notions at several places in his *Sāṃkhyapravacanabhāṣya*. Finally, according to Vijñānabhikṣu, there is a purported relationship between the *Tattvasamāsasūtra* and the *Sāṃkhyasūtra*, in which the former is simply a summary version of the latter. These later Sāṃkhya traditions are, therefore, clearly interrelated, at least in the minds of the early commentators, but by the same token it is clear enough that three distinct traditions are operating—what we are calling in this volume Kārikā-Kaumudī-Sāṃkhya (later Sāṃkhya as read through Vācaspati's *Tattvakaumudī*), Samāsa-Sāṃkhya (later Sāṃkhya as read through the *Tattvasamāsasūtra*) and Sūtra-Sāṃkhya (later Sāṃkhya as read through the *Sāṃkhyasūtra*).

These later *sūtra* collections, that is, the *Tattvasamāsasūtra* and *Sāṃkhyasūtra*, are as it were, wild cards in the Sāṃkhya deck, since there is no way of determining their precise origin or authorship. They simply appear for the first time in the fourteenth or fifteenth century. They are neither mentioned in the older literature of Sāṃkhya nor are referred to in any of the summary accounts of Sāṃkhya up through and including Mādhava's *Sarvadarśanasaṃgraha* in the middle of the fourteenth century.

Regarding the *Sāṃkhyasūtra*, one might speculate that there were attempts in earlier centuries to put together various *sūtra* collections related to the old Sāṃkhya and that Aniruddha or someone like Aniruddha compiled these older collections into our extant *Sāṃkhyasūtra* perhaps some time in the fifteenth century. One might speculate further that the motivation for such a compilation might have been dissatisfaction with Vācaspati's less than detailed treatment of Sāṃkhya philosophy in his *Tattvakaumudī*. There is, unfortunately, no evidence one way or the other for such speculations. It is obvious, of course, even to a casual reader, that the first three books of the *Sāṃkhyasūtra* follow the order as well as the mode of expression of the *Sāṃkhyakārikā*, thereby suggesting that the *Sāṃkhyasūtra* is merely a restatement of the *Sāṃkhyakārikā* in *sūtra* style. It is also obvious that the polemics dealt with in the fifth book of the *Sāṃkhyasūtra* (on theory of error, *sphoṭa*-theory, and so forth) reflect a much later period in the history of Indian philosophy than the *Sāṃkhyakārikā* appears to reflect. Such observations do not prove, however, that all of the *sūtras* are later than the *Sāṃkhyakārikā*. Many may indeed be very old. There is simply no way of knowing.

Regarding the *Tattvasamāsasūtra*, the situation is equally murky, although there are a few hints here and there in the literature that would suggest that the *Tattvasamāsa* may be independent of the larger *Sāṃkhyasūtra* and possibly somewhat earlier. Max Müller suggested many years ago that the technical terminology in the cryptic *Tattvasamāsa* gives every appearance of being archaic and different from both Kārikā-Sāṃkhya and Sūtra-Sāṃkhya and that it may represent an extremely old collection that has been preserved by the *paṇḍita* communities in Varanasi.[6] Max Müller's suggestion was only a hypothesis when first put forth, but in more recent studies there has been some indication that at least some of the *sūtras* may be quite old. The *sūtra* "there are five kinds of ignorance" (*pañcaparvā avidyā*), for example which appears as the twelfth *sūtra* of the *Tattvasamāsa* (according to the *Kramadīpikā*, see appropriate entry below), is quoted by Vācaspati under SK47 of his *Tattvakaumudī* as an ancient utterance of the Sāṃkhya teacher Vārṣagaṇya. Also, the various groupings of "fives" (*sūtras* 8-11) followed by the enumeration of "fifty" (*sūtras* 12-15) reminds one of *Śvetāśvatara Upaniṣad* I.5. Even more significant, however, is the *sūtra* "there are five sources of action" (*pañcakarmayonayaḥ*), which appears as *sūtra* 9 in the *Tattvasamāsa* and is followed by "there are five breaths or winds" (*pañcavāyavaḥ*) or *sūtra* 10 of the *Tattvasamāsa* (according to *Kramadīpikā*). A comparable juxtaposition of the "five sources of action" and the "five breaths" (*vāyus* or *prāṇas*) is also discussed in the *Yuktidīpikā* (pp. 107-108), lending perhaps some support to the notion that such a sequence may go back to older Sāṃkhya traditions. In a similar vein, Chakravarti cites an old Jain text (perhaps from the eighth or ninth century), the *Bhagavadajjukīyam*, in which the *sūtras* "there are eight *prakṛtis*" (*aṣṭau prakṛtayaḥ*), "there are sixteen products" (*ṣoḍaśa vikārāḥ*), "there are five breaths or winds" (*pañcavāyavaḥ*), "the three constituents" (*traiguṇya*)), "manifestation" (*sañcaraḥ*), and "dissolution" (*pratisañcaraḥ*), or, in other words, *sūtras* 1, 2, 4, 5, 6, and 10 of the *Tattvasamāsa* (according to *Kramadīpikā*), all find their place.[7] None of this evidence proves, of course, that there was a *Tattvasamāsa* collection in the older period. It only establishes that there were certain old utterances circulating in the ancient period. It is quite possible, even likely, that old utterances such as this became the basis for putting together the later *sūtra* collections that we now know as *Tattvasamāsasūtra* and *Sāṃkhyasūtra*.

In any case, our extant *Tattvasamāsasūtra* is completely unintelligible apart from its related commentaries, and the commentaries, (to be summarized in the sequel) are all late with the possible exception of the *Kramadīpikā*. That there is no reference whatever to a *Tattvasamāsa* collection prior to the *Kramadīpikā*, however, is a strong indication that even it is not much earlier than the fourteenth century. Following is a complete listing of the *sūtras* of the *Tattvasamāsa* as set forth at the outset of the commentary *Kramadīpikā*. The edition used is that of V. P. Dvivedi, editor, *Sāṃkhyasaṅgraha* (Varanasi: Chowkhamba Sanskrit Series Office, 1969; Work No. 50), p. 74.

(1) (There are) eight generative principles (*aṣṭau prakṛtayaḥ*);
(2) (There are) sixteen generated products (*ṣoḍaśa vikārāḥ*);
(3) Consciousness (*puruṣa*);
(4) The three constituents (*traiguṇyam*);
(5) Emergence of the manifest world (*sañcaraḥ*);
(6) Periodic dissolution of the manifest world (*pratisañcaraḥ*);
(7) Pertaining to the internal (world), pertaining to the external (world) and pertaining to the celestial (world) (*adhyātmam adhibhūtam adhidaivataṃ ca*);
(8) Five functions pertaining to intellect/will (*pañca abhibuddhayaḥ*);
(9) Five sources of action (*pañca karmayonayaḥ*);
(10) Five breaths or winds (*pañca vāyavaḥ*);
(11) Five essences of action (*pañca karmātmānaḥ*);
(12) (There are) five varieties of ignorance (*pañcaparvā avidyā*);
(13) (There are) twenty-eight varieties of dysfunction (*aṣṭaviṃśatidhā aśaktiḥ*);
(14) (There are) nine varieties of contentment (*navadhā tuṣṭiḥ*);
(15) (There are) eight varieties of attainment (*aṣṭadhā siddhiḥ*);
(16) The fundamental principles are tenfold (*daśadhā mūlikārthaḥ*);
(17) (There is a) supporting creation (*anugrahasargaḥ*);
(18) (There is a) manifest (or gross) creation of fourteen levels (*caturdaśavidho bhūtasargaḥ*);
(19) (There is an) elemental creation that is threefold (*trividho dhātusargaḥ*);
(20) Bondage is threefold (*trividho bandhaḥ*);
(21) Liberation is threefold (*trividho mokṣaḥ*);
(22) Instruments of knowledge are threefold (*trividhaṃ pramāṇam*);
(23) Frustration is threefold (*trividhaṃ duḥkham*).

Following this listing of the *sūtras* the commentary *Kramadīpikā* comments as follows: "He who has properly understood this (doctrine or collection) in its proper sequence has nothing more to do and is no longer subjected to the threefold frustration' ("*etat paramparayā yāthātathyam etat saṃyag jñātvā, kṛtakṛtyaḥ syān na punas trividhena duḥkhena abhibhūyate*"). In Bhāvāgaṇeśa's reading of the *Tattvasamāsa*, however, this concluding comment is numbered as a separate *sūtra* of the *Tattvasamāsa*.

KRAMADĪPIKĀ, or TATTVASAMĀSASŪTRAVṚTTI

The date and authorship of this commentary on the *Tattvasamāsa* are unknown, but Chakravarti has argued, perhaps with some justification, that it is probably the oldest extant commentary on the *Tattvasamāsa* and that both it and the *Tattvasamāsa* are somewhat older than the *Sāṃkhyasūtra* and its commentaries.[1] The primary reason for suggesting an older date for the *Kramadīpikā* is that both Vijñānabhikṣu and Bhāvāgaṇeśa appear to know the text. Bhāvāgaṇeśa in his *Tattvayāthārthyadīpana* indicates in his introductory verses that he is following a gloss (*vyākhyā*) by Pañcaśikha, and in the course of his commentary he quotes three verses (see pp. 39, 46, and 52 of the *Tattvayāthārthyadīpana* in the Chowkhamba *Sāṃkhyasaṅgraha* edition), which he attributes to Pañcaśikha. It is interesting to note, however, that *Kramadīpikā* (see pp. 78, 82, and 87 of the Chowkhamba edition) quotes the same verses under the same *sūtras* but without attribution to Pañcaśikha. A reasonable explanation for this coincidence is that Bhāvāgaṇeśa was following *Kramadīpikā* and, in addition, thought that the author of *Kramadīpikā* was Pañcaśikha. Similarly, Bhāvāgaṇeśa's teacher, Vijñānabhikṣu, in his commentary on *Sāṃkhyasūtra* I.127 quotes a prose passage about the nature of the three *guṇas*, which he attributes to Pañcaśikha. The same passage (although with some additional words) appears in the *Kramadīpikā* (p. 81, *Sāṃkhyasaṅgraha* edition) as part of the main text. Taken together, then, there would appear to be a distinct possibility that Bhāvāgaṇeśa and Vijñānabhikṣu were both familiar with the *Kramadīpikā* and considered it to be a work of Pañcaśikha.

The *Kramadīpikā* quotes a number of old verses (for example, from the *Śvetāśvatara Upaniṣad*, the *Bhagavadgītā*, and so forth), and at one point it quotes an old verse about egoity that finds an interesting echo in the *Yuktidīpikā*. The verse in the *Kramadīpikā* is as follows:

ahaṃ śabde ahaṃ sparśe ahaṃ rūpe ahaṃ rase,
ahaṃ gandhe ahaṃ svāmī dhanavān aham īśvaraḥ.

("I am in sound; I am in touch; I am in form; I am in taste; I am in smell; I am the ruler; I am the wealthy lord.")

In the *Yuktidīpikā* (p. 97) one finds the following comment: "*yasya asmipratyayasya viśeṣagrahaṇaṃ bhavati—śabde 'haṃ sparśe 'haṃ rūpe 'haṃ rase 'haṃ gandhe 'ham iti*, which might be translated "when there is a sense of egoity, specific apprehensions occur as (in the old saying) ' I am in sound; I am in touch; I am in form; I am in taste; I am in smell."

That the *Kramadīpikā* contains a number of old verses does not at all mean, of course, that the text as a whole is old. It is perhaps reasonable enough, however, to accept with Chakravarti that it is probably somewhat older than the other commentaries on the *Tattvasamāsa*.

The following summary of the text is based on the Chowkhamba Sanskrit Series Office edition of *Sāmkhyasaṅgraha*, pp. 74-89, edited by V.P. Dvivedi (Varanasi, 1969; Work No. 50).

(*Summary by Anima Sen Gupta*)

(E74) The *Sāṃkhyasūtras*, forming the content of the *Tattvasamāsa*, will now be explained. A Brahmin, afflicted by the three kinds of frustration, approached the great teacher (*maharṣi*) of Sāṃkhya, Kapila, for refuge. He inquired of the great teacher about ultimate truth and what he must do to attain it. Kapila then recited the twenty-three *sūtras* (see the *sūtra* listing in the preceding entry).

Eight Generative Principles (E74-77)

The unmanifest, intellect, egoity, and the five subtle elements constitute the eight generative principles (*prakṛti*). The unmanifest is so designated because it is not manifested in the manner in which jars, clothes, etc., are manifested. In other words, the unmanifest is incapable of becoming known through the sense organs, such as the organ of hearing, etc.; and it is so because it has no beginning, middle, or end. The unmanifest is subtle, nonmergent, unconscious, beginningless, endless, productive, noncomposite, common, and one.

Intellect (*buddhi*) is reflective discerning (*adhyavasāya*). It is called that since it produces definite knowledge of objects, such as "it is that and not another"; "it is a cow and not a horse." The intellect possesses eight predispositions: merit, knowledge, nonattachment, and power, and their opposites.

Egoity is expressed in the feelings of "mine" and "I." "I am in sound," "I am in touch," etc., are the forms that the ego assumes. That which generates the idea of "I" is called egoity. The five subtle elements, linked with the ego, are (a) the subtle element of sound, (b) the subtle element of touch, (c) the subtle element of color, (d) the subtle element of taste, and (e) the subtle element of smell.

The old verse, "He who knows the twenty-five principles...is released...," is quoted.

Generated Products (E77-78)

The sixteen generated products are the five sense capacities, the five action capacities, mind, and the five gross elements.

Consciousness (E77-78)

Consciousness is beginningless, subtle, all-penetrating, conscious, devoid of the constituents, eternal, a seer, pure, the knower of the field (*kṣetrajña*), and nonproductive. Consciousness is called "*puruṣa*" because it is primeval, because it resides in the body, and because it is by nature the bestower of "fulfillment." It is beginningless because it has neither beginning, middle, nor end. It is subtle because it is partless and is beyond the range of sense perception. It is all-penetrating because it permeates everything and because it does not move toward anything. It is devoid of the three constituents. It is eternal because it is not a product, i.e., it has no origination. It is called a seer because the modifications of primordial materiality are revealed by it. It is an enjoyer because it is conscious and so satisfaction and frustration are experienced by it. It is a nondoer because it is neutral and because it is devoid of the constituents. It is called the knower of the field because it knows the characteristics of the field. It is pure because it is not the substratum of meritorious or demeritorious actions. It is nonproductive because it is devoid of seeds and so never produces anything.

Whereas activity belongs to the constituents, consciousness has been established as the nondoer. It is only the ignorant man who, being blinded and excited by the feelings of "me," "mine," and "I" considers himself as the doer, and thinks "I am the doer of all this and this is mine."

Because there are diversities in the experiences of satisfaction, frustration, and confusion and also in the sets of sense capacities, birth, and death, the plurality of consciousnesses is established. Differences in the stages of life and also of duties are other reasons to prove plurality. Had there been only one consciousness, then all would have been miserable with the misery of one, and all would have been happy with the happiness of one. With the birth of one, all would have been born; with the death of one, all would have died. The Vedānta teachers, however, speak of a single self. (Here a number of old Vedānta verses are quoted.)

Having Three Constituents (E80-81)

The three constituents are *sattva*, *rajas*, and *tamas*. Kindness, lightness, pleasantness, affection, contentment, endurance, satisfaction, etc., are the numerous effects of *sattva*. Misery, perspiration, anxiety, anger, vanity, etc. are the numerous effects of *rajas*. Veiling, covering, ugliness, poverty, extreme idleness, sleepiness, delusion, etc., are the numerous effects of *tamas*.

Emergence and Dissolution of the Manifest World (E81)

Emergence (*sañcara*) means the origination of objects. Dissolution (*pratisañcara*) means the mergence of objects. Origination means manifestation (as before) from the unmanifest, which, being watched over by consciousness (which is superior to it), produces intellect. From intellect arises egoity. Egoity is of three kinds, being dominated by each of the three constituents.

From the form of egoity in which *sattva* dominates originate the organs; from the form of egoity in which *tamas* dominates originate the five subtle elements. The form of egoity in which *rajas* dominates is operative in the production of both the organs and the five subtle elements. In the state of dissolution, the five gross elements disappear in the five subtle elements, the five subtle elements in egoity, egoity in intellect, intellect in the unmanifest. As the unmanifest is uncaused, it does not disappear in anything else.

Pertaining to the Internal, External and Celestial worlds (E81-82)

The thirteenfold capacities are the internal world. The objects of the capacities constitute the external world; for example, the external object of the intellect is the object to be apprehended by the intellect. The external object of egoity is the object to be owned by the ego. The external object of the mind is the object to be determined by the mind and so on. The presiding deities of the organs are the objects of the celestial world. For example, the presiding deity of the intellect is Brahmā. The presiding deity of the ego is Rudra, the presiding deity of the mind is the moon and so on.

Five Functions Pertaining to Intellect/Will (Abhibuddhi) (E82)

These are five in number: ascertainment (*vyavasāya*), expressed in the form "This should be done by me" is the function of the intellect and this is called determination (*vyavasāya*). The awareness of "I" or of "mine" (*abhimāna*), which produces the idea of self and not-self is called egoity, which is also a manifestation of the intellect (*buddhi-kriyā*). The wishes, desires, and intentions (*icchā*) of the mind are likewise activities of the intellect. The indeteminate sensing (*kartavyatā*), like hearing of the sound, etc., of the sense capacities are also functions of the intellect, and the activities (*kriyā*), like speaking, etc., performed by the action capacities, are the functions of the intellect. The five functions of the intellect, then, are *vyavasāya, abhimāna, icchā, kartavyatā* and *kriyā*.

Five Sources of Action (E82-83)

These are perseverance (*dhṛti*), faith (*śraddhā*), desire for satisfation (*sukha*), lack of desire to know (*avividiṣā*), and desire to know (*vividiṣā*). (Some verses are quoted that appear in a somewhat different reading in the *Yuktidīpikā* [p. 108].)

Five Breaths or Winds (E83)

Prāṇa, being seated in the mouth and the nose, keeps the body in a living condition. *Apāna* has its seat in the navel region and it removes the impure things through downward passages. *Samāna* has its seat in the heart. *Udāna* has its seat in the throat. It goes upward. *Vyāna* has its seat in the joints; it causes circulation of the blood.

Five Essences of Action Karmātman (E83)

The five essences of action pertain to the nature and functioning of egoity: (1) the doer of good works (*ahaṃkāra* or *vaikārika*); (2) the doer of bad works (*taijasa*); (3) the doer of deluded works (*bhūtādi*); (4) the doer of what is reasonable (*sānumāna*); and (5) the doer of what is nonreasonable (*niranumāna*).

Five Varieties of Ignorance

Twenty-Eight Varieties of Dysfunction

Nine Varieties of Contentment

Eight Varieties of Attainment (E84-86)

(The description of these fifty *padārthas* follows that of the *Kārikā*).

Ten Fundamental Topics (E86)

(The account of the ten fundamental topics follows that of the standard *Kārikā* summaries. See also Introduction to the present volume.)

Subtle Creation (E86)

This is the realm of the subtle elements, created by Brahmā.

Gross Creation of Fourteen Levels (E86)

(This is the same as the standard *Kārikā* accounts.)

Threefold Elemental Creation (E87)

(This refers to subtle bodies, gross bodies, and gross elements as outlined in SK 39).

Threefold Bondage (E87)

Bondage is said to be of three forms: (a) natural bondage (*prakṛti-bandha*), (b) acquired bondage (*vaikārikabandha*), and (c) personal bondage (*dakṣiṇābandha*).

Natural bondage is that of a person who views the eight generative principles as the highest principles. Such a person becomes merged in nature and this is called natural bondage.

There are other persons, who, having embraced the life of renunciation, are still not able to prevent their minds from getting interested in objects like sound, etc.; such persons who have not conquered their sense organs and are ignorant of true knowledge suffer from acquired bondage. Personal bondage is of those who perform actions such as sacrifices, charities, etc. having their minds influenced by personal desires, etc.

Threefold Liberation (E87)

Liberation is due to : (a) the awakening of knowledge, (b) the destruction of attachment through control of the sense capacities, and (c) the total eliminations of all impressions of merit and demerit.

Threefold Instrument of Knowledge (E87-88)

The three instruments of knowledge are perception, inference, and verbal testimony. (The text follows the standard *Kārikā* account.)

Threefold Frustration (E88-89)

(Standard *Kārikā* account.)

SĀṂKHYASŪTRA

As indicated in the earlier entry on the *Tattvasamāsasūtra*, nothing can be said about the *Sāṃkhyasūtra* apart from noting its traditional attribution to Kapila, which is obviously not the case, and that it first appears in the *Sāṃkhyasūtravṛtti* of Aniruddha some time in the fifteenth century. The only other reading of the *sūtras* themselves is to be found in Vijñānabhikṣu's *Sāṃkhyapravacanabhāṣya* from the latter half of the sixteenth century, and, as Garbe has clearly demonstrated (in his critical edition of *Sāṃkhyasūtravṛtti*), Vijñānabhikṣu is dependent throughout on both Aniruddha's reading and his interpretation of the *sūtra* collection.[1] There is no mention of, or reference to, this *sūtra* collection in the older Sāṃkhya literature, nor is any mention of it to be found in any of the standard summaries of Sāṃkhya by outsiders (Haribhadra, Rājaśekhara, Guṇaratna, and so forth, up through and including Mādhava's *Sarvadarśanasaṃgraha* of the fourteenth century). There can be hardly any doubt, therefore, that the *Sāṃkhyasūtra* is a late compilation, possibly put together by Aniruddha himself or an older contemporary in the fifteenth century. Possibly, of course, many of the *sūtras* may be very old, but there is no way of sorting out the newer from the older. As already mentioned (see *Tattvasamāsasūtra* entry), the *sūtras* of the first three books appear to follow the sequence and the language of the *Sāṃkhyakārikā* and are probably little more than a late recasting of the older *kārikās* in *sūtra*-style. Moreover, many of the references to other philosophical views in both the first and fifth books of the *Sāṃkhyasūtra* appear to reflect a much later period in the history of Indian philosophy than does the *Sāṃkhyakārikā*. Possibly, the *sūtras* in the fourth and sixth books have some claim to antiquity, but there is no way of establishing such a claim in the absence of additional evidence.

Since our reading of the *stūras* is totally dependent on Aniruddha's compilation (with some occasional variations proposed by *Vijñānabhikṣu*), the only reasonable approach to a summary of the content of the *sūtras* is to present them in tandem with the summary of Aniruddha's *Sāṃkhyasūtravṛtti* (see entry below) and with occasional reference to variations set forth by Vijñānabhikṣu. In the present context only a topic outline of the *sūtra* collection as a whole will be presented. The outline is based on Aniruddha's reading of the *sūtra* collection as critically edited by Richard Garbe (B3574; RB5524), pp. 1-300.

BOOK I: The Section on Topics (*viṣayādhyāya*) (roughly parallel to *Sāṃkhyakārikā* 1-21)

A. Introductory *sūtras*: On the Problem of the Scope and Task of the Sāṃkhya (1-6)

B. On the Problem of Bondage in Sāṃkhya (7-60)

1. Bondage and essential nature (*svabhāva*) (7-11)
2. Bondage and time (12)
3. Bondage and place (13)
4. Bondage and the body (14-15)
5. Bondage and action (16-17)
6. Bondage and materiality (18-19)
7. Bondage and ignorance (20-26)
8. Bondage and Buddhist theories of momentariness (27-41)
9. Bondage and Vijñānavāda Buddhist theories (42)
10. Bondage and Mādhyamika Buddhist theories (43-47)
11. Bondage and Jain views (48-54)
12. Summation of the discussion on bondage (55-60)

C. Derivation of the basic principles of Sāṃkhya (61-74)

D. Materiality as material cause and its relation to discrimination (75-86)

E. The instruments of knowledge in Sāṃkhya (87-107)

1. Three instruments of knowledge (87-88)
2. Perception (89)
3. Perception and yogic experience (90-91)
4. Perception and the existence of God (92-99)
5. Inference (100)
6. Verbal testimony (101)
7. Means of establishing the existence of primordial materiality and consciousness (102-107)

F. Materiality and the theory of cause and effect (108-123)

G. Manifest and unmanifest aspects of materiality (124-126)

H. The three constituents (127-128)

I. Inferences that establish the existence of primordial materiality and consciousness (128-164)

BOOK II: The Section on the Effects of Primordial Materiality (*pradhānakāryādhyāya*) (roughly parallel to *Sāṃkhyakārikā* 22-37)

The story of the she-frog (16)
The story of Indra and Virocana (17-19)
The story of Vāmadeva and others (20-22)
The story of the swan and the milk (23-24)
The case of Śuka and Vyāsa (25)
The case of a parrot bound by a cord (26)
The argument of ascetics like Kaṇva, and so forth (27-28)
The story of King Aja (29)
The illustration of the dirty mirror (30)
The illustration of the lotus (31)
The insufficiency of supernatural powers (32)

BOOK V: The Section on Arguments against Opponents (*parapakṣa-nirajayādhyāya*) Introduction: On the problem of an auspicious utterance (1)

A. On the problem of the existence of God (2-12)
B. On the problem of the notion of ignorance in Vedānta (13-19)
C. On the problem of the existence of meritorious behaviour (20-24)
D. On the problem of meritorious behaviour, qualities, inference, and so forth, in Nyāya-Vaiśeṣika (25-36)
E. On the problem of word and meaning (37-50)
F. On the problem of knowledge and error (51-56)
G. On the problem of the nature and meaning of words (57-60)
H. On the problem of nonduality in Vedānta (61-68)
I. On the problem of the mind and the internal organ (69-73)
J. On the problem of liberation (74-83)
K. On the problem of the derivation of the sense capacities (84)
L. On the problem of the categories and the theory of atomism in Nyāya-Vaiśeṣika (85-88)
M. On the problem of perception (89)
N. On the problem of dimension (90)
O. On the problem of generality (91-96)
P. On the problem of relation (97-100)
Q. On the problem of motion (101)
R. On the problem of the material cause of the body (102)
S. On the problem of the gross body and the subtle body (103)
T. On the problem of the scope of the sense capacities (104-110)
U. On the problem of the nature of bodies (111-115)
V. On the problem of the experience of liberation (116-120)
W. On the problem of types of beings (121-128)

X. On the problem of supernatural attainments (129)
Y. On the problem of consciousness and the elements (130)

BOOK VI: The Section on the Sixth or Summary Tantra (*ṣaṣṭhatantrādhyāya*)

A. On the nature of the Self and the discrimination of the Self (1-21)
B. On the means for attaining liberation (22-31)
C. On creative nature (32-44)
D. On the plurality of consciousnesses (45-51)
E. On the manifest world (52-66)
F. On consciousness and materiality being together as possessor and possessed (67-70)

ANIRUDDHA

In his critical edition to Aniruddha's *Sāṃkhyasūtravṛtti*, Garbe suggests that Aniruddha was evidently familiar with the *Sarvadarśana-saṃgraha* (from the middle of the fourteenth century) and clearly predated Vijñānabhikṣu (latter half of the sixteenth century). He, therefore, places Aniruddha about 1500 of the Common Era.[1] Garbe also calls attention to a report by R. G. Bhandarkar of a certain Aniruddha,[2] the son of Bhāvaśarman and grandson of Mahāsarman, born in 1464 of the Common Era and who composed at the age of thirty-one (or, in other words, in 1495) a commentary on the astronomical treatise *Bhāsvatīkaraṇa*, by Śatānanda. Garbe suspects that this Aniruddha of the astronomical commentary may be the same person as the Aniruddha of the *Sāṃkhyasūtravṛtti*, thereby confirming a fifteenth century date for Aniruddha.

As already indicated, Aniruddha's reading and interpretation of the *Sāṃkhyasūtra* is the oldest one available, and Vijñānabhikṣu's *Sāṃkhyapravacanabhāṣya* is dependent upon it. The following summary of the text is based on Richard Garbe's edition (E) and translation (T) of the text (*The Sāṃkhya Sūtra Vṛtti or Aniruddha's Commentary and the Original Parts of Vedāntin Mahādeva's Commentary to the Sāṃkhya Sūtras, edited with Indices,* Calcutta: J. W. Thomas, 1888 and 1891).

SĀṂKHYASŪTRAVṚTTI

(*Summary by Gerald J. Larson*)

Book I : Section on Topics

A. Introductory *sūtras*: *On the Problem of the Scope and Task of the Sāṃkhya* (TI. 1-6) (E1-8; T1-8)

(1) The complete or absolute cessation of internal, external, and celestial frustration (*trividhaduḥkha*) is the final or ultimate goal of Sāṃkhya. (2) Perceptible means for alleviating frustration (medicines, etc.) are ineffective because they are only temporary and, hence, leave open the possibility of subsequent frustration. (3-4) If someone

objects by suggesting that frustrations can be alleviated on a continuing, temporary basis just as a person overcomes the pain of hunger by eating every day, it is to be replied that this is to miss the point of our basic assertion. (Of course, frustrations can be eliminated occasionally be temporary means). What is at issue is that such means are not certain and permanent. Sometimes, for example, temporary remedies are not available. Moreover, even when remedies are available, the alleviation of frustration is not permanent. The issue, then, is one of determining the ultimate cause of frustration and its cessation. In other words, the issue is a philosophical matter. (5) In addition, it should be pointed out that temporary remedies admit of degrees of superiority (that is to say, this remedy is better than that one, etc.), whereas the ultimate cessation of frustration or the realization of liberation is, as it were, the presupposition for all remedies. Liberation, according to the Veda, is superior to all else, and in this sense, then, our philosophical quest for the ultimate cessation of frustration is fully in accordance with the Veda. (6) It should also be pointed out, however, that ordinary religious actions (sacrifices, etc.) are as ineffective as the temporary or perceptible remedies mentioned earlier.

(B) *On the Problem of Bondage in Sāṃkhya* (I.7-11) (E8-10; T8-10)

Bondage and Essential Nature (7-8) It is not correct to assert that consciousness is bound essentially (*svabhāvatas*), for this would render liberation from bondage impossible by definition. Hence, the injunctions to seek liberation would be pointless. Moreover, since the injunctions could not be carried out, the Veda would be unauthoritative (*aprāmāṇya*). (9) This obviously leads to the absurdity that the injunctions of the Veda are really not injunctions (that is to say, because the injunction cannot be followed, it cannot be considered as an injunction). (10-11) If someone objects by suggesting that the bondage of consciousness is essential although it can be altered, just as an essentially white cloth can be dyed or the productive power of a seed can be destroyed when the seed becomes a sprout, it is to be replied that both of these examples are inappropriate. In the case of the white cloth, whiteness is not destroyed—it is simply overpowered by another color. In the case of the seed, the sprouting capacity that is subdued can be revived. Therefore, with respect to both examples (that is to say, the white cloth and the seed), nothing impossible is being suggested, whereas the liberation of consciousness that is essentially bound is obviously an impossibility.

Bondage and Time (I.12) (E10; T10) It is also not correct to assert that consciousness is bound because of its connection with time, for consciousness is eternal and pervasive, and, hence, the issue of ordinary temporal bondage does not arise.

Bondage and Place (I.13) (E10; T10) Similarly, consciousness is not bound because of its connection with a place (*deśa*), for, again, consciousness as eternal and pervasive cannot be construed vis-à-vis ordinary spatial limitations.

Bondage and the Body (I.14-15) (E10-11; T10-11) Similarly, consciousness is not bound because of its connection with a bodily condition (*avasthā*). "Condition" is a quality or attribute of the body and does not apply to consciousness, which is declared to be "unattached" (*asaṅga*) (in the *Bṛhadāraṇyaka Upaniṣad* IV.3.16).

Bondage and Action (I.16-17) (E11-12; T11-12) It is also not correct to assert that consciousness is bound because of its connection with action, for action is an attribute of another (namely, materiality and the three constituents) and the attribution of the qualities of one thing to another thing is logically impermissible. Moreover, even if such attribution were permissible, one would be unable to explain the diversity in experience. (That is to say, if the qualities or attributes of one thing are relevant in explaining another thing, then, anything can be explained by anything, which is absurd.)

Bondage and Primordial Materiality (I.18-19) (E12-13; T12-13) Also, consciousness is not bound because of its connection with primordial materiality. Materiality is itself dependent on action and, hence, the preceding argument still applies. Bondage cannot arise other than through association with materiality; association occurs because of nondiscrimination between that which is eternal, pure, and intelligent, on the one hand (namely, consciousness) and that (which is characterized by the three constituents and action), on the other (namely, materiality).[3]

Bondage and Ignorance (I.20-26) (E13-16; T13-15) (20) Similarly, it is not correct to assert that consciousness is bound because of ignorance (*avidyā*)—that is to say, according to the theory of *avidyā* as put forth in Śaṃkara's Vedānta—because it is not possible for something that is by definition a nonentity (*avastu*) to be a genuine cause. (21-22) If it is claimed (by the Vedāntin) that somehow ignorance is an entity, then, obviously monism must be given up. If ignorance has a reality in any sense apart from the one thing that exists—namely, Brahman or *ātman*—then the monist position is no longer tenable, for there is then a duality of two different things—namely, Brahman and *avidyā*. (23-24) Moreover, if it is argued (by a Vedāntin) that ignorance is both real and not real, then one has simply a contradiction in terms or a situation that is rationally inconceivable (that is to say, such an argument simply places the issue in such a way that rational discourse can no longer deal with it). (25) Finally, since the Sāṃkhya position does not accept the categories of predication as set forth by the Vaiśeṣika (and Nyāya) schools, someone might object that the above argument rejecting ignorance as both real and not real cannot be sustained because the Sāṃkhya does not have an identifiable theory of predication on which to base its argumentation. (26) Such an objection, however, is ridiculous. Because the Sāṃkhya does not accept a definite number of possible predications (as does the Nyāya and Vaiśeṣika), it does not follow that Sāṃkhya does not accept any logic or any theory of predication. If the latter were the case, we would be reduced to the level of children or madmen.

Bondage and Buddhist Theories of Momentariness (I.27-41) (E16-22; T16-23) (27) Buddhists argue that bondage is brought about because of the beginningless influence of the contents of awareness (*viṣaya*) (that is to say, bondage is caused by *uparāgas* or "traces" that remain because of the influence of transient objects). (28) It is not the case, however, that there is a relation of the "influenced" and the "influencer" between the external and the internal, as the Buddhists suggest, just as there is no relation between the residents of Śrughna and Pāṭaliputra. (29) Moreover, even if such influence were possible, then there would be no way of distinguishing between the bound and released, for the influence would always be present. (30-31) If one wants to avoid this difficulty by arguing for the theory of the "unseen," or *adṛṣṭa* (that is to say, the influence of earlier actions imperceptibly influencing subsequent events), such an argument presupposes a continuity that the theory of momentariness does not allow. (32-33) For example, when ceremonies or rituals are performed for the sake of purification of the unborn son (that is to say, the *putreṣṭi* ceremony), the benefits to the son are only intelligible on the assumption that there is an abiding entity or self (*ātman*)—an assumption that cannot be allowed on the basis of the Buddhist position of momentariness. (34) The Buddhist also wants to argue that bondage is momentary along with everything else, because any kind of permanent entity cannot be proved. (35-36) This is not the case, however, because then there would be no way of explaining the fact of recognition, and such a view clearly is contradicted both by logic (*nyāya*) and Vedic authority (*śruti*). (37) Finally, and perhaps most important, the theory of momentariness cannot be framed into a valid inference having an example (*dṛṣṭānta*) (because everything is included in what is to be established and, hence, there is nothing left by means of which the principle could be illustrated).[4] (38-41) Furthermore, causation becomes unintelligible on the theory of momentariness, because there can obviously be no cause-effect relation between two things that arise simultaneously, or between two things that arise successively (that is to say, one preceding the other) because in both cases there can be no connection between the things on the theory of momentariness. Simple antecedence never establishes causal uniformity.

Bondage and Vijñānavāda Buddhist Theories (I.42) (E.22-24; T23-26) Other Buddhists (namely, Vijñānavādins) argue that all external objects are mere ideas (*vijñānamātra*) (and, hence, bondage is likewise a mere idea), but this is not the case because everyone has an incontrovertible conviction of some kind of external reality.

Bondage and Mādhyamika Buddhist Theories (I.43-47) (E24-27; T26-29) (43) Still other Buddhists (namely, Śūnyavādins) argue that if external objects do not exist, then by the same token even ideas cannot be shown to be real. Hence, there can only be a void (*śūnya*) (and, by implication, bondage is likewise a void). (44) "Reality is void," they assert; every entity is characterized by perishing. (45) But this sort of argumentation is little more than glib posturing by those who are not very intelligent. (46) The same arguments that we asserted earlier (in *sūtra* 35 against the adherents of momentariness and in *sūtra* 42 against the Vijñānavādins) are to be directed against the Śūnyavādins. (47) Moreover, apart from the logical difficulties of the theory of the void, there is the practical consideration that no one could possibly desire some such thing or state like the "void," whether such a void be considered a kind of nonexistence, or as something transcending both existence and nonexistence.

Bondage and Jain Views (I.45-54) (E25-30; T29-32) (48) Others (presumably various Jains) argue against the notion of the void on the basis of asserting that the soul is characterized by a kind of "wandering" or motion (*gati*), and that, therefore, the soul assumes the size of the particular body in which it resides. (49) But this idea (though more intelligible than the Buddhist view) is still wrong, because consciousness is incapable of activity and, hence, of any kind of motion. (50) If consciousness were material, then it would have the characteristics of material entities; but that is not the case even in your own (Jain) view. (51) Now, to be sure, in the Vedic literature the soul is sometimes described as "wandering" or in motion, but this is only a figure of speech. Consciousness, which is immutable and all-pervasive, appears to be characterized by the contexts in which it resides, but these are only limiting adjuncts or disguises, as it were, similar to the relationship between space and a jar. (That is to say, it appears to be the case that the space within a jar moves when the jar is moving, but such a "moving" of space is, of course, not the case. The appearance of movement is brought about because of space being cloaked or disguised by its relationship with the moving jar.) (52) By the same token it cannot be said that bondage is brought about by action, since action is not a property of consciousness (cf. I.16). (53) The Vedic literature clearly declares that consciousness is without all such characteristics, etc. (54) If one argues, then, that action is responsible for bondage, one comes upon the same difficulty that was discussed earlier (in I.16-17), for one is arguing in effect that the qualities of one thing determine the condition of something else (*anyadharma*).[5]

Summation of the Discussion of Bondage (I.55-60) (E30-34; T32-37) (55) To the extent that our previous arguments indicate that we accept the reality of such factors as action, merit, etc., and that, therefore, such factors are related to the problem of bondage, it might be argued by our opponents that in the final analysis our views about bondage amount to about the same position as theirs. In fact, however, this is not the case, because in our view nondiscrimination is the crucial, fundamental factor that determines bondage. (56) Moreover, just as the reality of darkness is dispelled only by the coming of the reality of light, so nondiscrimination is dispelled only by discrimination. (57) The fundamental nondiscrimination of the difference between materiality and consciousness is the basis for all other nondiscriminations and, hence, for all subsidiary bondages related to action, merit, etc. Therefore, if the fundamental nondiscrimination is removed, then all nondiscriminations and types of bondage are removed in principle. (58) Our view implies, furthermore, that it is, therefore, really only a matter of verbal convenience (*vāṅmātra*) to talk about the bondage of consciousness. Nondiscrimination belongs to materiality in its manifestation as ordinary awareness (*citta*), and hence, bondage is a function or reality of that manifestation. There is no nondiscrimination that adheres to consciousness *qua* consciousness. (59) It should be noted, however, that the realization of discrimination is not simply a matter of philosophical argument (*yukti*). It must also be realized in immediate awareness, just as one confused about direction must personally come to realize his error. (60) Finally, if one argues that our Sāṃkhya principles do not exist because they cannot be perceived, we reply that this objection would be valid if perception were the only reliable instrument of knowledge. In fact, however, fundamental principles, which transcend direct experience, can be apprehended by means of inference (as well as "verbal testimony)," and, hence a, our interpretation of discrimination and nondiscrimination can be argued and realized by means of philosophical reflection just as one infers the existence of fire from smoke.

(C) *The Derivation of the Fundamental Principles of Sāṃkhya* (I.61-74) (E34-39; T37-42)

(61) Materiality is a condition in which the intelligibility constituent (*sattva*), the activity constituent (*rajas*) and the inertia constituent (*tamas*) abide in equilibrium (*sāmya*). The "great one" (*mahat*, i.e., the intellect) arises from primordial materiality. Egoity arises from the great one or intellect. The five subtle elements arise from egoity. Then there are also the two kinds of capacities (sense capacities and action capacities) and the gross elements, and, finally, consciousness. Altogether, then, there is an aggregate (*gaṇa*) of twenty-five.

(62) The five subtle elements (are inferred) from the gross objects. (63) Egoity (is inferred) from the five subtle elements together with the various capacities (sense capacities and action capacities). (64) The internal organ (in its form as *buddhi*) (is inferred) from egoity.[6] (65) Primordial materiality (is inferred) from that. (66) Consciousness is neither a cause nor an effect, but it must be inferred to exist, since the various causal aggregates must function for the sake of something else (*saṃghātaparārthatva*) (cf. SK 17 and SS I.140). (67) Primordial materiality is the root (*mūla*) that itself does not have a root (*amūla*) (cf. SK 3). (68) In other words, it is a limiting notion, as it were a mere name (*saṃjñāmātra*), since the sequence of causes must be stopped somewhere in order to avoid an infinite regress. (69) In this sense it is like the ultimate atomic constituents or particles of the atomists.[7] (70) That our system is a rational system does not entail that all persons should achieve discrimination at once (upon learning of the inferential process), for it is a well-known fact that people have varying capacities for doing philosophy. There are at least three such types of persons (namely, the very bright, the mediocre, and the dull). (71) The first effect is called "the great one" (*mahat*). It is the thinking capacity (*manas*).[8] (72) The subsequent effect is egoity. (73) All of the other effects can be traced to egoity. (74) It is, therefore, the mediate first cause of all manifest awareness (both in terms of the experience of hearing, touching, etc., and in terms of the experience of what is heard, touched, etc.).

(D) *Materiality as Material Cause and Its Relation to Discrimination* (I.75-86) (E40-45; T42-48)

(75) Although consciousness and primordial materiality precede these effects, only materiality is the material cause, since we have already argued (see, for example, I.53 and elsewhere) that consciousness does not have this character (of being the cause of anything). (76) The theory of the atomists that atoms are the ultimate material cause is not as useful as our theory of primordial materiality as material cause, since such limited entities as atoms cannot account for all material causation. (77) Moreover, the Vedic tradition tends to support our theory of primordial materiality as the material cause. (78) Furthermore, it is not correct to argue that prior absence is the material cause (as, for example, is maintained by those who assert that the coming into being of a jar is caused by its prior absence, because something cannot come from nothing). (79) Moreover, it is not correct to argue that the world is unreal, for no convincing argument can be given to support its unreality, and more than that, it is not the case that there is faulty perception in our apprehension of the world.[9] (80) The notions of cause and effect are intelligible

only if the cause is existent; for if one argues for a nonexistent cause, there must by the same token be a nonexistent effect, which is absurd. (81) Then, too, it is also not correct to argue that action (*karman*) is the material cause, for action is not a material entity. (82) If one argues that action is a sufficient cause, because in the Veda it is said that ritual actions bring about results, it is to be replied that actions are always linked with repetition or returning (*āvṛtti*) and, thus, cannot be considered to bring about the realization of the ultimate freedom of consciousness. (83) Only one who has attained discrimination, according to the Veda, acquires nonrepetition or nonreturning—that is to say, ultimate liberation. (84) Action is always linked with some frustration, and hence if the realization of liberation were caused by action, liberation would entail frustration. One gains relief from cold by acquiring warmth, not by pouring water on oneself. (85) This is true even for "desireless" action (*akāmya*)—that is to say, this too is not the cause of liberation (because a desireless action like ordinary action is connected with repetition and with frustration—that is to say, is connected with the finite, temporal human condition). (Compare Aniruddha and Vijñānabhikṣu for differing interpretations of this *sūtra*.) (86) Finally, if one were to argue that discrimination is as perishable or finite as action and that, therefore, there is no difference between our two views, our reply is that this is simply not the case. For one attaining discrimination there is a complete destruction of bondage, and, hence, there can be no question of return or reversion or continuance as there always is with action.

(E) *The Instruments of Knowledge in Sāṃkhya* (I.87-88) (E46-47; T48-50)

Knowledge (*pramā*) has to do with a connection that takes place between a sense capacity and an object (namely, perception), or between an inferential mark and an object (namely, inference), or between an authoritative word and an object (namely, verbal testimony). It must now be determined what the best instruments of knowledge are. There are three instruments of knowing that encompass all other means of knowing (cf. SK 4).

Perception (I.89) (E49-50) ; T50-52) Perception (*pratyakṣa*) is the experience (*vijñāna*) that arises when a sense capacity comes into contact with an object and assumes its form.

Perception and Yogins (I.90-91) (E50-51; T52) This definition applies to ordinary external perception and does not, therefore, address the issue of yogic perception. But even from the point of view of yogic perception there is still contact with an object, as is true in ordinary perception, but, of course, the important difference is that the object cognized in yogic perception is of a special kind (namely, the object in its subtle form).

Perception and the Existence of God (I.92-99) (E50-54; T53-57) (92) Moreover, our definition of perception is not incorrect because it does not extend to the perception of God, for there is no adequate proof for the existence of God. (93-94) If God were existent, He would have to be connected with the world or not be connected with the world. If He were connected with the world, He could not be God, since connection with the world would entail limitation. If He were not connected with the world, He could also not be God, for He could not be the creator or an agent in any sense. (95) In the Veda when God is praised, this is just a verbal statement in praise of the liberated self (*muktātman*) or in praise of the accomplished Yogin (*siddha*). (96) Moreover, when we say that there is controllership, we do not mean this in the sense of God. Rather, we mean controllership in the sense of a crystal that assumes the reflection of a proximate object (thus leading to the wrong impression that the crystal possesses the characteristics of the object). (97) In fact, however, the empirical selves (*jīva*) are the agents *vis-à-vis* individual actions. (98) Discriminating knowledge, therefore, as well as agency, occur within materiality in its manifestation as the "internal organ." Hence, when in the Vedic literature one is taught to pursue knowledge, this means in effect that one should cultivate correct discrimination by means of the internal organ. (99) Consciousness provides the illumination (*ujjvalitatva*) that enables the internal organ to function as controller. Consciousness functions, then, like a magnet—that is to say, it brings about activity though in itsef it is inactive.[10]

Inference (I. 100) (E53-54; T57-58) Inference is knowledge derived from invariable concomitance by someone who knows the concomitance (that is to say, when someone perceives smoke, he knows by inference that there is fire, assuming that he also knows that wherever there is smoke, there is fire).

Reliable Authority (I.101) (E55; T58-59) Verbal testimony (*śabda*) is the authoritative teaching of the Veda (*āptopadeśa*).

Means of Knowing Materiality and Consciousness (I.102-107) (E56-58; T59-62) (102) Both primordial materiality and consciousness can be established by an instrument of knowledge, and that is why the Sāṃkhya teaches the existence of both. (103) Primordial materiality and consciousness are established by means of inference, and specifically that variety of inference known as inference based on general correlation. (104) When materiality in its manifestation as internal organ discriminates its difference from consciousness, then experience ends. (105) Experience, therefore, is for the sake of another (namely, consciousness), just as a cook prepares food for his master. (106) Or, putting the matter in a different way, because of nondiscrimination it appears to be the case that consciousness possesses the fruit of experience because it is the agent. (107) In fact, however, consciousness does not possess the fruit nor is consciousness the agent.

(F) *Materiality and the Theory of Preexistent Effect* (I.108-123) (E58-66; T62-69)

(108) On the one hand, an object is perceived when there is a direct contact a between the object and a sense capacity. On the other hand, something may not be perceived for a variety of reasons as, for example, excessive distance (*atidūra*), etc. (cf. SK 7). (109) Primordial materiality is imperceptible because of its subtlety (and not because of its nonexistence) (cf. SK 8). (110) The existence of primordial materiality can be inferred, however, because of its effects (cf. SK 8). (111-112) If someone objects that primordial materiality does not exist because this contradicts other teachers, our reply is that this begs the question. The issue is not what this or that teacher asserts. The issue, rather, is the validity of inferential reasoning. Our inferences are as follows : (113) In our ordinary apprehension of the world we experience satisfaction, frustration, and confusion, and this apprehension is most adequately accounted for by the positing of primordial materiality as material cause that is constituted by these three (*sattva*, *rajas*, and *tamas* as the very constituents of the ultimate material cause). If one denies the existence of primordial materiality in this sense or posits instead some other cause, this entails the contradiction of our ordinary apprehension. (114) Moreover, it cannot be argued that something can be produced from nothing, like a man's horn (and, therefore, it is necessary to infer that this ultimate cause does, in fact, exist). (115) Then, too, it is to be observed that there must be an appropriate material cause for every product. (116) Furthermore, since it is obvious that everything does not come forth from everywhere and always, there is, therefore, an intelligible sequence of causation. (117-118) Also, since it is observed that a thing produces only that which it is capable of producing, and that, likewise, it is observed that there is always a homogeneity between cause and effect (*kāraṇabhāva*) (we, therefore, conclude that creative nature is the ultimate material cause; that it, in fact, exists; that likewise all effects pre-exist in it prior to manifestation; that the process of causation is sequential, rational, and homogeneous; and that this explanation of cause and effect fully accounts for our ordinary experience of satisfaction, frustration, and confusion). (119-120) If someone objects that such a theory of causation (namely, *satkārya*) does not allow making temporal distinctions (in asserting, for example, that a jar will be, or a jar is, or a jar has been destroyed, etc.), our reply is that this is not the case. All such expressions are relative to a given manifestation and must

be dealt with contextually.[11] (121) Destruction is simply dissolution into the cause (as, for example, when a jar is broken, it becomes clay once again). (122) Moreover, our position does not entail a vicious regress, but, rather, describes an ongoing sequence of intelligible causal reciprocity, like that between a seed and a sprout (that is to say, that the seed becomes the sprout and the sprout produces a seed, is, admittedly, a regress, but it is not a logically vicious one). (123) Furthermore, it should be pointed out that our theory of existent effects has no more defects than our opponents theory of nonexistent effects (*asatkārya*).[12]

(G) *The Manifest and Unmanifest Aspects of Materiality* (I.124-126) (E67; T70-72)

(124) The manifest effects are caused (*hetumat*), transient (*anitya*), mobile (*sakriya*), complex and multiple (*aneka*), supported (*āśrita*), and mergent (*liṅga*) (cf. SK 10). (125) Although our manner of predication is different from the categorization or theory of predication of the Vaiśeṣikas, it is not correct to assume that we deny the relevant issues of predication (namely, quality, generality, etc.) as raised in the Vaiśeṣika system. Rather, we deal with these issues within the context of our twenty-five principles, or else these issues are dealt with within our notion of primordial materiality. (126) Both the manifest effects and the unmanifest cause are made up of the three constituents, are nonconscious, etc. (cf. SK 11).

(H) *The Three Constituents* (I.127-128) (E69-70; T72-73)

(127) The three constituents are differentiated respectively by agreeableness (*prīti*, a characteristic of the intelligibility constituent, or *sattva-guṇa*), disagreeableness (*aprīti*, a characteristic of the activity constituent, or *rajas*), and insensibility (*viṣāda*, a characteristic of the inertia constituent, or *tamas*), etc. (cf. SK 12). (128) By the distinguishing characteristics of being light (*laghu*), etc., the constituents function reciprocally (*sādharmya*) as well as differentially (*vaidharmya*) (cf. SK 12).

(I) *Inferences that Establish the Existence and Makeup of Primordial Materiality and Consciousness* (I.129-164) (E70-86; T73-88)

Primordial Materiality and its Effects (129) The "great one" (*mahat*) and all of the subsequent principles are different from consciousness and primordial materiality and, hence, are effects, like jars, etc. (cf. SK 8). (130-132) Moreover, they are finite (*parimāṇa*), uniform, or coherent (*samanvaya*) in being derivable from an ultimate material cause, and partake of the power (*śakti*) of the material cause (cf. SK 15 and 16). (133-134) Apart from these effects, there is only primordial materiality and one consciousness, and anything else (apart from these effects and apart from primordial materiality and consciousness) is simply nothing (*tucchatva*). (135) Cause is inferred from the effect because of the invariable concomitance between cause and effect. (136) The unmanifest can be inferred from the intellect, which is made up of the three constituents (cf. SK 14). (137) Hence, if the effects are established, the cause cannot be denied.

Consciousness (138) It should be noted, first of all, that because consciousness has no effects, its existence cannot be established in the same manner as primordial materiality is established. It should also be noted, however, that generally speaking, the existence of consciousness is not really disputed or questionable. Like the notion of merit, people generally assume its existence (that is to say, the existence of consciousness is to a large extent self-evident and incontrovertible). (139) Consciousness is distinct from the body and from the unmanifest cause (namely, primordial materiality) and all of the manifest effects (the intellect, etc.) (cf. SK 11). (140-144) Moreover, its existence is indicated (a) because aggregates exist for the sake of something else (*saṃghāta-parārthatva*); (b) because this "something else" is distinct from the three constituents; (c) because of the need for a controlling basis (*adhiṣṭhāna*); (d) because of the need for a ground or basis for subjective experience (*bhoktṛbhāva*); and (e) because there is an inclination in experience to seek freedom or isolation (*kaivalya*) (cf. SK 17 and SS I.66). (145) Furthermore,, since illumination cannot have its ground in what is nonconscious (*jaḍa*), it follows that illumination is the very essence of consciousness. (146) In other words, consciousness (*cit*) is not an attribute (of the soul) because it is attributeless (*nirguṇa*) (that is to say, *puruṣa* is consciousness). (147) Our view is supported by the Veda, whereas those who assert that the self has attributes are clearly in contradiction to the Veda (namely, the Nyāya and Vaiśeṣika systems, which assert that consciousness is only an attribute of the self). (148) Also, it should be noted that if consciousness were only an attribute of the self (as maintained in Nyāya and Vaiśeṣika) there would be no way of adequately accounting for the awareness in deep sleep, dream, etc. (149) In addition to the existence of consciousness, for which we have been arguing, it is also necessary to infer that consciousness is to be construed pluralistically because of the varieties of births, etc. (cf. SK 18). (150) Though consciousness is uniform in its essence (in the sense that it has no attributes and is only pure, contentless consciousness in and of itself), nevertheless, it is plural or multiple because one can only become aware of it by means of limiting adjuncts, just as one can only become aware of space by means of its location in jars, etc. (151-152) Moreover, the problem of nondiscrimination resides with these adjuncts, and, hence, nondiscrimination is a problem that must be discussed from the perspective of a plurality of consciousnesses. If one were to argue, as does the Vedāntin, that the adjuncts are plural but consciousness is one, one gets into the peculiar bind of attributing contradictory claims concerning the one consciousness (namely, that it is sometimes liberated and sometimes not). A problem like this can only be resolved by construing consciousness pluralistically. (153) This is not to suggest, however, that the limiting adjuncts actually constitute consciousness, for consciousness is absolutely simple and any imputation of the characteristics of the adjuncts onto consciousness is due to nondiscrimination. (154) It should be noted, furthermore, that a plurality of consciousnesses is not in conflict with the claim of the Veda that consciousness is nondual (*advaita*), because the reference to nonduality in the Veda has to do only with the generic essence (*jāti*) of consciousness. (155) Now, if one should argue that the notion of the plurality of consciousnesses leads to contradiction in the sense that something simple is sometimes bound and sometimes released, our reply is that this is not the case because neither bondage nor release resides in consciousness. For the one who has come to know the cause of bondage (namely, nondiscrimination), there is the realization by direct discrimination (*dṛṣṭi*) that consciousness is in fact absolutely simple (and always has been and always will be). (156) Then, too, because some are blind it does not at all follow that no one can see (but such a conclusion would follow as a result of arguing for the oneness of consciousness). (157) Similarly, when it is said in the sacred texts that "Vāmadeva has been released," it would necessarily follow on the argument for one consciousness that, therefore, all are liberated, which is obviously not the case. (158-159) Moreover, our view that there are some consciousnesses gradually attaining liberation does not imply that eventually all will be liberated. Such liberation has not happened thus far nor will it happen at any point in the future (that is to say, the plurality of consciousnesses rather than implying a final void, implies, to the contrary, that there will be no absolute cessation at any time.) (160) Finally, our notion of consciousness implies that it is not correct to attribute either bondage or liberation to it, for the very notion of consciousness (as we have described it) goes beyond such categorization. (161) Through the medium of the capacities, consciousness is the basis for there being a witness (*sākṣitva*). (162) Consciousness is the condition of being eternally free (*nityamuktatva*). (163) Consciousness is sheer neutrality (*audāsīnya*) (cf. SK 19-20). (164) The agency of consciousness is only an appearance, due to its proximity to creative nature (cf. SK 20).

BOOK II : Section on the Effects of Primordial Materiality

(A) *On the Activity of Materiality and Its Distinction from Consciousness* (II.1-9) (E87-92; T89-95)

(1) Primordial materiality functions ultimately for the sake of liberation. In a manner of speaking one can refer to materiality functioning for the sake of the release of the released (*vimukta* or consciousness), but it is perhaps more precise to suggest that creative nature functions for its own release (*svārtha*). (2) Only the one who has become completely nonattached attains liberation. (3) Such liberation cannot be quickly or easily attained because of the force (*paṭutva*) of beginningless latent dispositions (*vāsanā*). Hence, liberation is not accomplished by merely hearing about the notions of the Sāṃkhya. One must, rather, realize the notions and have an aptitude for overcoming the force of the latent dispositions. (4) The process of materiality is single, but it manifests endless differentiations on account of the proximity of the plurality of consciousnesses, just as a wealthy householder is associated with a variety of servants. (5) It is important to keep in mind, however, that activity for the sake of liberation is really only in materiality. Consciousness only appears (*adhyāsa*) to be involved in bondage and liberation. (6) That primordial materiality is, in fact, active is proved by inference from its effects and, hence, bondage belongs to materiality. (7) Nevertheless, this ongoing activity does not affect the one who has achieved the requisite discrimination, just as a thorn, though painful to some, is not painful to the one who knows it for what it is and avoids it. (8) Although consciousness is present in all experience, it is not the case that there is a real connection between consciousness, on the one hand, and bondage on the other. This can be illustrated with the example of the red-hot iron. It appears to be the case that iron burns, but iron is not intrinsically hot. Only the presence of fire makes the iron appear to be intrinsically hot. (9) Consciousness is related to nonattachment and leads to disciplined meditation (*yoga*). Materiality is related to passion (*rāga*) and leads to activity and the manifest world (*sṛṣṭi*).

(B) *Materiality and Its Effects* (II.10-11) (E93-94; 95-96)

(10) The effects of creative nature are inclusive of intellect through the five gross elements (that is to say, intellect, egoity, mind, and the five sense capacities, the five action capacities, the five subtle elements, and the five gross elements (cf. I.61 and SK 3 and 22). (11) All of these effects function for the sake of consciousness, but only as mediated through the activity of materiality (as was outlined in II.1-9 above).

(C) *Space and Time* (II.12) (E94; T96)

Space and time are not included among the enumerated effects; they are to be considered only on the gross, manifest level of *ākāśa*, etc.[13]

(D) *Intellect and the Basic Predispositions* (II.13-15) (E94-95; T96-97)

(13) Intellect is (possessed of) reflective discerning (cf. SK 23). (14) Its effects are the basic predispositions of meritorious behaviour, etc. (cf. SK 23). (15) Each positive basic predisposition also has its opposing correlate when counterproductive influences (*uparāga*) are present. (Compare SK 23 and 43-45.)

(E) *Ego and Capacities* (II.16-25) (E95-98; T97-100)

(16) Egoity is (possessed of) self-awareness (*abhimāna*) (cf. SK 24). (17) Its effects are the five sense capacities, the five action capacities, mind, and the five subtle elements. (18-19) The sense capacities, action capacities and mind arise from egoity in its mode called "generated" (*vaikṛta*) (cf. SK 25).[14] (20) These capacities are not derived from the gross elements; they arise solely from egoity. (21-22) Moreover, it is taught in the Veda that the elements dissolve into the deities—in other words, they dissolve into their causes. But the deities are not generative and, hence, do not produce the capacities. (23) Each capacity is itself imperceptible and, although a capacity resides in a given gross organ (e.g., the eye, etc.), it is a mistake to link the capacity with the gross organ either in terms of function or origin. (24) The various capacities perform distinct functions and, hence, cannot be reduced to one. (25) If someone objects that a plurality of capacities coming forth from one principle (namely, egoity) violates the rules of thought (*kalpanā*), it must be replied that rules of thought cannot be allowed to set aside what has been established by instruments of knowledge.

(F) *Mind as a Capacity* (II.26) (E99; T101)

Mind is both a sense capacity and an action capacity (cf. SK 27 and cf. above I.71).

(G) *The Capacities and Their Differentiation from Consciousness* (II.27-37) (E99-103; T101-105)

(27) The diversity among the capacities arising from ego can be accounted for because of the differentiations occasioned by the trans-

formations of the constituents, just as there are different conditions of a body in one lifetime (e.g., infancy, youth, etc.). (28) Each capacity relates to a specific content (e.g., seeing to visible form, etc.) (cf. SK 26). (29) The capacities taken together provide instrumentality (*karaṇatva*), whereas consciousness is the "seer" (*draṣṭṛtva*) etc. (30-31) Intellect, egoity, and mind, in addition to their unique and essential feature as already mentioned (in II.13, 16, 25-26), also have the common feature of the maintenance of life (*prāṇa*, etc.) (cf. SK 29). (32) The various capacities operate simultaneously and successively (cf. SK 30). (33) These operations are fivefold and are either hindering (*kliṣṭa*) or not hindering (*akliṣṭa*) (cf. *Yogasūtra*, I.5).

(34) When these functions subside (*nivṛtti*), consciousness, released from all influences (*uparāga*) appears as it is in itself (*svastha*) (that is to say, unattached and free). (35) This can be illustrated by the well-known example of the crystal and the rose. (That is to say, when the two are in proximity, the crystal appears to be red; but when the flower is removed, the crystal can be apprehended in its clarity and purity.) (36) The instrumental capacities (senses, etc.) derive their specific mode or function from the force of the "unseen" (*adṛṣṭa*) (which, in turn, is derived from meritorious behaviour or nonmeritorious behaviour, just as the cow spontaneously provides milk for the calf).

(H) *The Thirteenfold Instrument and Its Overall Functioning* (II.38-47) (E103-107; T106-109)

(38) Intellect, egoity, and mind together with the five sense capacities and the five action capacities make up the thirteenfold instrument (cf. SK. 32). (39) These taken together are the most effective means for accomplishing any act, just as an axe is the most effective means for cutting. (40) Among the capacities (namely, senses and actions), mind is the chief one, just as in everyday life a group of servants needs a leader. (41) Moreover, the mind's intellectual function is indispensable (*avyabhicāra*). (42-43) Furthermore, it is the abiding place (*ādhāra*) for latent dispositions (*saṃskāra*); and it is the basis for inference in that it provides the function of memory (which is essential in the inferential process and which cannot be explained as a function of the sense capacities). (44) Memory cannot be provided by consciousness, because it has already been pointed out that consciousness is without attributes (cf. I.146).

(45) Finally, it should be pointed out that the distinction between "primary" (*pradhāna*) and "secondary" (*guṇa*) among the various instruments is based on the different kinds of activities that they perform. (46) Various aggregations of actions accrue to each consciousness, just as in everyday life a servant fulfills the needs of his particular

master. (47) Overall, of course, the place of superiority (*pradhānya*) belongs to the intellect, just as in the world the governor of a state is superior to all lesser functionaries.[15]

BOOK III : Section on Nonattachment

(A) *The Specific and the Nonspecific* (III.1-6) (E105-110; T110-112)

(1) The specific or gross comes out of the nonspecific or subtle (cf. SK 38). (2) The gross body is made up of the specific. (3) The manifest world is, thus, produced from the gross elements. (4) This system of transformation continues to function until discrimination is attained. (5) In other words, for the one not having discrimination, ordinary experience continues. (6) Consciousness in and of itself, however, is free in fact from attachment both to the nonspecific and the specific (that is to say, free from the gross and the subtle); but it does become "embraced" (*pariṣvakta*) by the two in appearance.

(B) *The Gross Body and the Subtle Body* (III.7-19) (E110-117; T113-119)

(7) The gross body is produced from the father and mother; the subtle body is not so produced. (8) The subtle body, devoid of experience, is previously arisen (*pūrvotpanna*) or, in other words, is the causal presupposition of the gross (cf. SK 40). (9) The subtle body is made up of eighteen factors; intellect, egoity, mind, the five sense-capacities, the five action capacities, and the five subtle elements (cf. SK 40). (10) The varieties among individuals are to be explained by the different kinds of action (previously done). (11) The gross body and the subtle body function together. (12) Moreover, each body depends upon the other, just as a painting depends upon the canvas or frame (cf. SK 41). (13) Though conceptually one can speak about the subtle body separately, in its actual functioning it always operates with the gross, just as one can talk about the sun separately from that which it illuminates.[16] (14) The mind is of atomic magnitude (*aṇuparimāṇa*) because according to the Vedas it possesses activity. (15) Moreover, one also knows from the Veda that the subtle body is said to be nourished by food (*anna*), etc. (16) The subtle bodies transmigrate for the sake of consciousness, just as the cook prepares food for the king. (17-19) The gross body is made up of the five gross elements, although other traditions argue that it is made up of only four elements (excluding *ākāśa*) or only one element (namely, earth).[17]

(C) *The Gross and Subtle Bodies are not Made Up of Consciousness* (III.20-22) (E117-118; T120-121)

(20) Those (namely, *Cārvākas*) who maintain that consciousness

(*caitanya*) arises from the material components of the body are wrong, because it is obvious that consciousness is not present in any one of the material components. (21) Moreover, if consciousness were intrinsic to the material components, the disappearance of consciousness at death etc., would be unintelligible. (22) Nor can it be successfully argued that consciousness emerges because of the combination of the various material components, just as the capacity to intoxicate arises, not in any one thing but, rather, in a combination of contributing factors. For in the case of the power of intoxication, it can be demonstrated that there is an inherent capacity for intoxication in a given thing that can be made manifest under certain controlled conditions (in the winery or brewery), but the production of consciousness cannot be so demonstrated.

(D) *On Bondage and Release* (III.23-25) (E119-120; T122-123)

(23-24) Liberation is because of discrimination or knowledge; bondage is because of misconception. (25) These causes are such that they do not require the notions of "aggregation" (*samuccaya*) or "intermediacy" (*vikalpa*) (e.g., with action, etc.).[18]

(E) *Dreaming, Waking, and Yogic Awareness* (III.26-29) (E120-122; T123-125)

(26) Arguing that liberation can arise from a combination of knowledge and action is like arguing that an unreal dream object being combined with a real object of the waking state can produce some result or can fulfill some purpose. (27) The dream object is not totally false because, after all, it is constructed from latent dispositions left over from waking awareness, but at the same time, it is obvious that the dream object is not as real as the waking object. Indeed, if this were not the case—that is to say, if one were to maintain the position that waking and dream are equally real or equally unreal—then it would be impossible even to distinguish between a dream-object and a waking object. (28) In a similar way, even the intentional (*saṃkalpita*) constructions of accomplished Yogins are not conjured out of nothing.[19] (29) That is not to suggest, however, that the creativity of accomplished Yogins is not real or important. Indeed, the person whose awareness is purified as a result of continuing meditation (*bhāvanā*) develops extraordinary power on analogy with the power of materiality itself.

(F) *On the Nature of Meditation* (III.30-36) (E123-125; T125-127)

(30) Meditation (*dhyāna*) brings about the elimination of desire. (31) Meditation is accomplished by the cessation of the operations

of awareness (cf. *Yogasūtra* I.2). (32) One attains meditation by means of concentration or collectedness (*dhāraṇā*), prescribed posture (*āsana*), and appropriate kinds of action (*svakarma*) (33) Posture should be steady and comfortable. (34) The attainment of meditation is promoted by the controlled exhalation and retention of breath. (35) Appropriate kinds of action are those prescribed by the various religious stages of life (*āśrama*). (36) One also attains cessation of the operations of awareness by means of the cultivation of nonattachment (*vairāgya*) and ongoing practice (*abhyāsa*).

(G) *Misconception, Dysfunction, Contentment, and Attainment* (III.34-45) (III.37-45) (E126-135; T128-136)

(37) There are five kinds of misconception (cf. SK 47). (38) Dysfunctions are of twenty-eight varieties (cf. SK 49). (39) Contentments are of nine varieties (cf. SK 50). (40) Attainments (*siddhi*) have eight varieties (cf. SK 51). (41-42) The various subdivisions within these categories are well known from the older tradition. (43) "Contentment' has reference both to internal and external factors (cf. SK 50). (44) Attainment includes reasoning (*ūha*), etc. (cf. SK 51). (45) One cannot attain the benefits of the attainments until misconceptions, dysfunctions, and contentments have been overcome (cf. SK 51.)

(H) *The Manifest Universe* (III.46-53) (E135-138; T137-140)

(46) The manifest world is divided into subdivisions such as the divine, etc. (cf. SK 53). (47) From the world of Brahmā down to the lowest blade of grass, all functions for the sake of consciousness (cf. SK 54). (48-50) In the upper realm of the divine world, there is a predominance of the intelligibility constituent (*sattva*); in the lowest material world, there is a predominance of the inertia constituent (*tamas*); and in the middle, human world, there is a predominance of the activity constituent (*rajas*) (cf. SK 54). (51) As a born slave performs his various duties for his master, so materiality performs many diverse actions for consciousness. (52-53) Even on the highest levels of materiality (namely, the celestial level), rebirth (*āvṛtti*) occurs; hence, it also should be abandoned, for the frustrations occasioned by old age, death, etc., are equally present on these highest levels.

(I) *Role and Function of Materiality with Respect to Discrimination* (III. 54-62) (E138-144; T140-146)

(54) The final elimination of frustration is not accomplished even by dissolution into primordial materiality (that is to say, into the pure causal condition) because there is always a rising again (*utthāna*),

just as when a swimmer dives into a deep pool, he always rises again to the surface. (55) Though primordial materiality is itself not a product, it is nevertheless involved with bondage for it subserves or is under the influence of consciousness.[20] (56) Consciousness, being reflected in materiality, may manifest itself as omniscient (*sarvavid*) and omnipotent (*sarvakartṛ*). (57) The existence of such a God is accepted (in Sāṃkhya).[21] (58) What is created by materiality is for the sake of another. Materiality by itself is not capable of being an experiencer. Just as a camel carries the saffron for a merchant, so materiality functions for the sake of consciousness.[22] Even though materiality is, therefore, unconscious, this does not create a problem for our position. Materiality's functioning for another is just like unconscious milk serving as nourishment for the calf (cf. SK 59).[23] (60) Or, again, one can compare materiality's activity for another with the example of time, etc. (e.g., the farmer is served by time in the production of crops). (61) The activity of materiality arises from inherent capacity (*svabhāva*) and not from conscious motivation, just as a servant often functions for his master without being consciously motivated. (62) Or, again, it might be said that materiality functions because of the force of beginningless action.

(J) *Discrimination and Liberation* (III.63-75) (E144-152; T146-153)

(63) When discrimination takes place, then there is cessation of the manifestation of materiality, just as the cook stops working after the meal has been prepared. (64) Consciousness comes to be revealed as being distinct from materiality and its faults. (65) Liberation (*apavarga*) is the condition of neutrality, and this can verbally be expressed as the neutrality either of one or both (that is to say, of either consciousness or materiality). (66) Materiality ceases to function only for the consciousness that has been discriminated. For other consciousnesses it continues to function, just as the illusion of the snake in the rope disappears only for the one who realizes the illusion and not for the one who continues to be caught up in the illusion (cf. II.7). (67) Moreover, materiality continues to function for the undiscriminated because of the ongoing efficient causation of action. (68) Basically, however (cf. I.57 and III.24), nondiscrimination is the efficient cause operative in materiality. (69) After accomplishing the purpose of providing discrimination for consciousness, materiality ceases activity, just as a dancing girl ceases dancing after her performance (cf. SK 59 and 68). (70) Moreover, when materiality with all of her faults has been distinguished from consciousness (by the intellect) she no longer shows herself to consciousness, just as a woman of good family withdraws after having been seen in her nakedness (cf. SK 61). (71) The notions of bondage and liberation arise because

of nondiscrimination. In fact (that is to say, ontologically), consciousness is never in bondage or liberated. (72) Only materiality is bound, just as a beast is bound by a cord or rope (cf. K. 62). (73) Materiality brings about its own bondage because of the seven basic predispositions, like a silkworm; it becomes released by means of the basic predisposition toward knowledge (cf. SK 63). (74) Nondiscrimination is the cause of ordinary existence and its elimination by knowledge brings the fruit of liberation. There is no fault in this.[24] (75) Because of the continual meditation on the principles (*tattvābhyāsa*) and because of the systematic abandoning (*tyāga*) by realizing "not this," "not this" (*na iti na iti*), discrimination comes to be established (cf. SK 64).

(K) *The Liberated-While-Living* (*Jīvanmukta*) (III.76-84) (E152-157; T153-158)

(76) Discrimination becomes established in varying degrees because of the different capabilities of persons who practice the Sāṃkhya path (cf. I.70). (77) For those of highest capability, after discrimination, there is no further experience; but for those of middle-level capability some further experience occurs on account of the force of past action (cf. SK 67-68).[25] (78) The condition of being liberated-while-living (*jīvanmukta*) is an example of the middle-level capability. (79) It is this condition that allows for the teaching of the tradition, for the liberated-while-living by continuing to live is able to teach others. (80) This notion of the liberated-while-living is also supported in the Veda. (81) Moreover, if such a notion were not admitted, then the various traditions would be traditions of the blind leading the blind. (82) The liberated-while-living continues to function in the body for a time, just as the wheel of a potter turns for a while even after the potter has ceased from his work (cf. SK 67). (83) Some minimal latent dispositions continue to operate (cf. SK 67). (84) Finally, when frustrations have been completely removed through discrimination, the ultimate condition (*kṛtakṛtyatā*) is attained, and not through anything else.

Book IV: Section on Narrative Stories and Illustrations

The Story of the Prince (IV.1) (E158-178; T159)

The son of a king, because of inauspicious signs at his birth, is sent away and is brought up by a hunter. When the king dies, the ministers of state bring the son back to the palace, and, after suitable instructions, the prince is able to resume his true identity.

The Story of the Imp (IV.2) (T159-160)

A certain teacher is instructing his pupil in a lonely place, but the instruction is overheard by an imp (*piśāca*). The imp, by hearing the instruction, attains liberation.[26]

Frequent Instruction is Sometimes Needed (IV.3) (T160)

When persons are not very intelligent, sometimes frequent repetition of the teaching is required.

The Story of the Father and the Son (IV.4) (T160-161)

A poor priest must leave his pregnant wife in order to travel to another country for the sake of getting alms, etc. When he returns, after a long time, the son, who has in the meantime been born, does not know his father, nor does the father know the son. The wife, however, provides the necessary instructions, and father and son come to know each other. Thus there can be no knowledge of the principles without the help of a preceptor.

The Story of the Hawk (IV.5) (T161-162)

A man brings up a hawk from its early childhood, feeding and caring for it. When the hawk reaches his full growth, the man releases the hawk because he does not wish to keep the bird in bondage and frustration. The hawk is delighted to be free, but regrets his separation from the one who cared for him.

The Story of the Snake (IV.6) (T161)

A certain snake sheds its skin in due season but is so attached to it that he keeps it near the entrance of his hole. A snake charmer eventually captures the snake because he sees the abandoned skin and thereby finds the entrance to the dwelling of the snake.

The Story of the Amputated Hand (IV.7) (T163)

A certain ascetic enters the dwelling place of his brother to gather food. The brother accuses him of theft. Even though the ascetic's food gathering was not intended as theft, nevertheless the ascetic insists that his hand be amputated, for he feels as if he must make up for his inadvertent act.

The Story of King Bharata (IV.8) (T163-164)

King Bharata, though about ready to attain liberation, takes compassion on a small female deer whose mother had died, as a result of her birth. Bharata cares for and nourishes the deer and, hence becomes attached. At the moment of his own death, therefore, Bharata does not attain liberation.

One Should Avoid the Company of Others (IV.9-10) (T164)

Social contact hinders progress, and confusion results, just as many individual shells when tied together into a girl's bracelet, make a jingling sound. Even contact with one other may be a mistake.

The Story of Piṅgalā (IV.11) (T164-165)

A prostitute named Piṅgalā is waiting for her lover to come. When he does not arrive, she becomes despondent and is unable to sleep because her hope for love is frustrated. Only when she stops hoping for his arrival is she finally able to sleep peacefully.

The Case of the Serpent in Another's House (IV.12) (T165)

One can live quite happily without activity, just as a serpent finds a comfortable dwelling in a house built by a certain man.

One Should Take the Essence of the Various Sciences (Śāstras) Like a Bee (IV.13) (T165)

In the various intellectual traditions there is much quibbling and disagreement. A wise student should take only the essence of a given science, just as the bee only takes honey from the flower.

The Story of the Arrow Maker (IV.14) (T166)

A certain arrow maker is so engrossed in his work that he fails to take notice even when the king passes by.

One Should Follow the Prescribed Rules of Discipline (IV.15) (T166-167)

A student should not fail to observe all of the prescribed rules for his training in meditation, just as in the world a person who does not follow prescribed traditions of behaviour (in terms of contracts, commitments, etc.) is soon not trusted by anyone and is abandoned.

The Story of the She-Frog (IV.16) (T167-168)

A certain king falls in love with a maiden, who agrees to marry him so long as he promises never to show water to her. He agrees, and they are married. One day, when she becomes thirsty, she asks for water, and the king without thinking shows water to her. At once the lovely woman turns into a frog, for her true identity is that she is the daughter of the king of frogs. The king suffers grievously and is unable to find her again.

The Story of Indra and Virocana (IV.17-19) (T168-169)

Both Indra and Virocana go to the world of Brahmā and are instructed concerning the highest knowledge. Virocana returns to his home but fails to reflect further upon what he has learned. As a result, he does not gain release, whereas Indra, who does reflect further, gains release. Moreover, Indra does proper obeisance, observes student celibacy, and attends upon his teacher—all of which brings success in due time (cf. *Chāndogya Upaniṣad* VIII).

The Story of Vāmadeva and Others (IV. 20-22) (T169-172)

(20) One cannot predict the amount of time it will take to attain liberation. There is the story, for example, of Vāmadeva who attained liberation even when he was in the womb of his mother (cf. *Bṛhadāraṇyaka Upaniṣad* I.4.10 and see *Aitareya Upaniṣad* 2.1.5).

(21) Others, however, come to liberation gradually or mediately through the performance of appropriate sacrifices. (22) In all cases, however, liberation is attained, finally, only through discrimination. According to the Veda, all other means, including even the performance of the ritual of the five sacrificial fires, lead to rebirth.

The Story of the Swan and the Milk (IV.23-24) (T172-173)

Unlike the crow, a swan is able to separate milk, from water. The swan discards the water and uses only the milk. Similarly an accomplished teacher is able to separate important knowledge from trivial knowledge, and such a teacher should be sought.

The Story of Śuka and Vyāsa (IV.25) (T173)

Śuka, the son of Vyāsa, attains liberation because of his nonattachment. Vyāsa, on the other hand, does not attain liberation because he is still attached to some things.[27]

One Becomes Bound by a Cord Like the Parrot (IV.26) (T173-174)

Bondage arises because of connection with the three constituents, just as a parrot is bound by a cord (*guṇa*).

The Argument of Ascetics Like Kaṇva, Śaubhari, etc. (IV.27-28) (T174)

There are some ancient sages like Kaṇva, Śaubhari, etc., who argue that attachment to worldly desires may lead eventually to attachment to transcendental objects. They are wrong. One must avoid attachment both to the empirical self and to other worldly objects.

The Story of King Aja (IV.29) (T175)

King Aja is grieving over the loss of his beloved wife. Because of this, the teachings of Vasiṣṭha, which are presented to Aja during his grief, do not have any effect.

The Illustration of the Dirty Mirror (IV.30) (T175-176)

In a dirty mirror there can be no adequate reflection of a face.

The Illustration of the Lotus, etc. (IV.31) (T176)

Though a lotus emerges from the mud, it dwells in purity apart from its source.

Supernatural Powers are no Substitute for Discrimination (IV.32) (T176-177)

One does not attain the ultimate goal of discrimination by pursuing the attainment of supernatural powers.[28]

Book V: Section on Arguments Against Opponents

Introduction: On the Problem of an "Auspicious Utterance" (V. 1) (E179; T178-179)

A treatise should begin with an "auspicious utterance" (*maṅgalācaraṇa*) because this is a generally accepted custom (*śiṣṭācāra*), because it often leads to fruitful results (*phaladarśana*), and because a treatise so begun often becomes authoritative (*bhūti*). This practice need not be disputed, therefore.

(A) *On the Problem of the Existence of God* (V.2-12) (E179-184; T179-184)

(2) With respect to the problem of fruitful results, these grow out of action or work (*karman*). The notion of fruitful result does not imply the existence of God. (3) One cannot intelligibly assert that

God is responsible for this action or fruitful results because action is undertaken in everyday life for a specific personal reason or need, and God can have no such personal motive or need.[29] (4) To suggest that God has personal needs is to reduce Him to the status of a worldly ruler. (5) Or, again, if one argues that consciousness appears to be an agent when nondiscrimination makes materiality appear to be conscious, and in that sense it is legitimate to refer to consciousness at that stage as God (cf. III.57), that is permissible; but it is obvious that such a "God" is only a convenient verbal designation (*pāribhāṣika*) and nothing more. (6) In fact, however, there can be no action without desire or passion that is invariably associated with action; and God, of course, cannot be said to be characterized by desire or passion. (7) If He were so characterized, He could not be one who is permanently liberated. (8) If one argues that God acts through association with the activities of materiality, this also would entail an attachment on the part of God. (9) Moreover, if one argues that the mere existence of materiality's functioning is sufficient to make consciousness appear as God, then this entails that all consciousnesses are Gods. (10) The existence of an independent God cannot be established, since there is no adequate instrument for knowing such an existent entity. (11) Nor can the existence of God ever be established on the basis of inference because there would be no way of establishing an invariable concomitance.[30] (12) Even in the Veda the manifest world is spoken of as an effect of primordial materiality.[31]

(B) *On the Problem of the Notion of Ignorance* (*in Vedānta*) (V.13-19) (E184-188; T184-187)

(13) Because consciousness is without any contact with anything (*niḥsaṅga*), it is self-contradictory to assert that the self is somehow connected with the power of ignorance (*avidyāśakti*), as the Vedāntins wish to maintain. (14) Moreover, if one argues that there cannot be any creation without ignorance and that there cannot be any ignorance without creation, as the Vedāntin argues, then one gets caught in a vicious circle. (15) Similarly, one cannot maintain that these two are logically related as the seed and the sprout, because, one knows from the Veda that the manifest world has a beginning, that is to say, is temporal. (16) Also, if it is said that ignorance (*avidyā*) is that which is different from knowledge (*vidyā*), then Brahman, being different from knowledge (*vidyā*), would be identical with ignorance and so Brahman will be destroyed by knowledge. (17-19) There is also another difficulty in the Vedāntin notion of ignorance, which can be expressed as follows : is ignorance not disproved by knowledge or is it disproved? If ignorance is not disproved by knowledge, then obviously knowledge is useless, and more than that, a

meaningless term. If ignorance is disproved by knowledge, then the manifest world is likewise disproved, for the Vedāntin links ignorance and the manifest world together inseparably. This entails, however, that ignorance has a beginning in time or is temporal, since the manifest world is temporal. But the temporality of ignorance cannot be admitted by the Vedāntin without giving up his claim that ignorance is beginningless.

(C) *On the Problem of the Existence of Meritorious Behavior* (V.20-24) (E188-190; T187-189)

(20) Although primordial materiality is one and eternal, it nevertheless manifests a great variety of products. The notion of meritorious behavior (*dharma*) as the primary efficient cause is necessary in order to account for this diversity, and it is not correct to deny, this notion (of *dharma*), as the Cārvākas or materialists want to do, on the ground that things like merit are imperceptible. (21) This notion of merit is established both on the basis of verbal testimony (*śruti*) and on the basis of inference (*liṅga*), etc. (22-24) This, of course, is not to deny other efficient causes in addition to merit. It is only to suggest that meritorious behavior is the most important efficient cause. Other subsidiary causes are not ruled out, so long as they are established by reliable proofs.

(D) *On the Problem of Meritorious Behavior, Qualities, Inference, etc.* (in Nyāya and Vaiśeṣika) (V.25-36) (E190-196; T190-198)

(25) Having defended the notion of meritorious behavior, it must also be pointed out, however, that our view of its status differs from that of the Naiyāyikas. Whereas Nyāya asserts that merit is a quality of the self or consciousness, our view is that merit is a quality of the internal organ (that is to say, merit, etc., are aspects of materiality in its manifestation as intellect, ego, and mind). (26) Similarly, we differ from the Nyāya in our view of "quality" (*guṇa*), etc., although we do not completely deny the various kinds of predication dealt with in the Nyāya. All predication, however, in our view, is to be interpreted from within the context of materiality and the three constituents (cf. I.25-26 and I.125-126). (27) Regarding the problem of inference, our view is that the fivefold inference is the correct formulation of inference. This fivefold structure includes (a) thesis (*pratijñā*), (b) reason (*hetu*), (c) example (*dṛṣṭānta*), (d) application (*upanaya*), and (e) conclusion (*nigamana*). An inference can be easily and clearly established using these inferential components (and those Naiyāyikas who wish to reduce these five to two are misguided).[32] (28) The invariable concomitance that is the basis of inference is not established

because of one instance (*sakṛd grahaṇa*) of apprehension. (29) It is established only on the basis of constant or invariable association with a characteristic property (*niyata dharmasāhitya*), and may work two ways or only one.[33] (30) This invariable concomitance is not a new principle, it is simply a theoretical elaboration (*kalpanā*) of the relation between things. (31) The ancient teachers declare that invariable concomitance is grasped as an inherent capacity (*nijaśakti*) that exists in things—e.g., the "innate power" that exists in fire and smoke, which accounts for their being apprehended together. (32) The Sāṃkhya teacher Pañcaśikha, however, thought that invariable concomitance is a power (*śakti*) conferred or imposed upon two things by a person apprehending them. (33) Pañcaśikha's view has merit to the extent that it avoids the tautology (*punarvāda*) of saying that a thing has its own capacity, or simply is what it is. (34) To say that something is "powerful" in this latter sense would be completely superfluous. (In other words, all adjectives would become useless.) (35) Similarly, in various religious and magical rites, the "power" would reside inherently in the implements used—e.g., leaves, etc., used in certain rites—and the use of spells or *mantras* would become quite superfluous. (36) Perhaps the best interpretation, however, is to describe invariable concomitance in both senses—that is to say, to some extent it represents an "innate power" and to some extent it also requires that the person apprehending the concomitance be aware of the concomitance. Both these senses are, however, not basically different.

(E) *On the Problem of Word and Meaning* (V.37-50) (E197-205; T199-207)

(37) It is not correct to identify word (*śabda*) and meaning (*artha*), as some philosophers of language wish to do. A clear distinction must be made between the signifying (*vācaka* or *śabda*) and that which is signified (*vācya* or *artha*). (38) The relation between the signifying and the signified is established (a) by ostensive definition (for example, by someone pointing and saying, "This is a jar"); (b) by observing the behavior of someone who understands a word (for example, a child learning what "Bring a cow hither" means when he continually observes that someone brings a cow each time this utterance is spoken); and (c) by contextual usage (*padasāmānādhikaraṇya*) (for example, someone learning a new word by hearing it used in a context of familiar words). (39) Moreover, the distinction between word and meaning or signifying and signified is not to be restricted only to imperative statements, as the Mīmāṃsakas argue. Imperative statements, declaratory statements, hymns, etc., all involve the distinction between signifying and signified and, hence, are capable of being

meaningful utterances. (40) With respect to the contents of the Veda, which sometimes deals with matters that go beyond perception and inference, one is able to understand the relation between the signifying and signified on the basis of the analogy with secular words. In other words, one who knows ordinary usage is able to make an analogous connection with the special usage of the Veda. (41) The Veda was not composed by a person because (a) we have already shown (in I.92,99 and V.1-12) that there is no God who could have composed it; (b) certainly, no other person could possibly have composed it; and (c) even if for the sake of argument it is asserted that a person composed it, the Veda could not then be authoritative, because its contents would reflect the errors and limitations of the finite author. We know, however, that the content of the Veda deals with that which goes beyond perception, and, hence, it can have no human author. (42) It should be noted also that sacrifices, etc., as enjoined by the Veda are not to be understood mechanically or as providing automatic benefits. These acts are to be understood contextually and utilized properly by those who are fit to perform the sacrifices, etc. (43) One comes to understand the semantic significance (*nijaśakti*) of the Veda by means of the careful study of the meanings of the Vedic words. (44) Words lead to certain conceptions whether or not the objects talked about are immediately evident or not. (45-48) Because words are produced in time or are finite manifestations, it cannot be argued, therefore, that the Veda is eternal. To be sure, as already pointed out (in V.41), the Veda was not composed by a person—either one liberated or not liberated, but it does not follow from this that the Veda is eternal. Plants, etc., develop from seeds and plants have no human author, and yet no one would argue that because a plant has no human author, therefore, it is eternal. (49) If one wants to argue for some sort of invisible maker or author for plants, etc., there is no convincing inference to establish the argument. (50) One can argue convincingly for an unseen or invisible maker only for things that are obviously constructed like jars, etc. One cannot argue in a similar way for natural objects (like trees, etc.), for there is no appropriate inference to establish the contention.

(F) *On the Problem of Knowledge and Error* (V.51-56) (E205-209; T207-213)

(51) The validity of knowledge (based on perception, inference, or reliable authority) arises out of its own inherent capacity (*nijaśakti*). It is not correct to assert that the validity of knowledge depends upon some outside factor (that is to say, a factor other than that which gives rise to knowledge), as Naiyāyikas and others argue.[34]

(52) Regarding the problem of error, there are numerous theories

of error, some of the more important of which are (a) the theory of *asatkhyāti* (of the Buddhists); (b) the theory of *satkhyāti* (of the Mīmāṃsā of Prabhākara); (c) the theory of *anirvacanīya* (of the Vedāntins); (d) the theory of *anyathākhyāti* (of the Naiyāyikas); and (e) the theory of *sadasatkhyāti* (of our own Sāṃkhya tradition). (a) The Buddhist (presumably, Mādhyamika) theory of *asatkhyāti* (or the theory of the "apprehension of that which is nonexistent") (as, for example, when mother-of-pearl is taken for silver) is not convincing because this theory entails that nonexistence has the capacity to bring about a conception, but, of course, nonexistence *per se* has no such capacity. (53) (b) Similarly, the Mīmāṃsaka (Prabhākara) theory of *satkhyāti* (or the theory of the "apprehension of that which is existent") is faulty because it begs the question. According to this theory, when mother-of-pearl is taken for silver, the "this" of "this is silver" and the "silver" of "this is silver" are both correct apprehensions (the former being based on perception, and the latter on memory), but there is a failure to distinguish the two when the error occurs.[35] The problem with this theory is that it only isolates the correct cognition. The issue, however, is to account for the error. Hence, it begs the question. (54) (c) Likewise, the theory of *anirvacanīya* (or the theory of the "indescribable") is not convincing, because, again, the theory fails to account for error. To say that error neither is, nor is not, nor both, nor neither, or to say that error is "indescribable" is simply to say that there is no rational explanation for error. (55) (d) Finally, the Naiyāyika theory of *anyathākhyāti* (or the theory of the "apprehension of something under the guise of something else") is mistaken because the theory leads to self-contradiction. The theory entails that something nonexistent can be apprehended, but the Naiyāyika has already rejected such a notion in his criticism of the theory of *asatkhyāti*. (56) (e) The correct theory (as set forth in the Sāṃkhya tradition) is that of *sadasatkhyāti* (or the theory of the "apprehension of both what is existent and nonexistent"). According to our theory, an error involves both that which, in fact, is, and that which, in fact, is not. To some extent, there is a true perception when anyone mistakes one thing for another—that is to say, something, in fact, is perceived that cannot be denied. The problem, however, is that the thing perceived is mistaken to be something else. To this extent, therefore, something, in fact, is perceived as what it is not. The failure to distinguish between what is, in fact, the case and what is, in fact, *not* the case is the occasion for error. In other words, error involves both "what is" and "what is not" equally—hence, *sadasatkhyāti*.

(G) *On the Problem of the Nature and Meaning of Words* (V.57-60) (E210-212; T213-215)

(57) The meaning of a word (namely, its semantic significance)

is revealed by the word itself. There is no need to posit the existence of a "special disclosing capacity" (*sphoṭa*) as some philosophers of language (as well as Yoga philosophers) are inclined to argue. If a word, either in its constituent parts or as a whole, is incapable of disclosing meaning, then how can one account for an additional "special disclosing capacity"? Or again, if a word is able to disclose meaning, then what is the use of positing an additional "special disclosing capacity"? Either way, the notion of a "special disclosing capacity" is superfluous.

(58) Words convey meaning, and a word is revealed by a series of sounds. The sounds that make up a word are not eternal, as the Mīmāṃsakas suggest, because they are obviously products and anything that is produced cannot be eternal. (59-60) If one argues that sounds have a kind of permanence because they preexist prior to their actual manifestation in the same way that a jar preexists in an unmanifest condition in a dark room prior to lighting a lamp, we have no difficulty with such a claim, because that is quite in keeping with our own Sāṃkhya view of the "preexistent effect" (*satkārya*). We object only to the notion that sound *qua* sound is eternal.

(H) *On the Problem of Nonduality (in the Vedānta)* (V.61-68) (E212-218; T215-221)

(61) It is not correct to argue (as the Vedāntins do) that the self is one and nondual, because then it would be impossible to account adequately for the many differences that appear among people (e.g., in old age, youth, etc.) (cf. I.149-164). (62) Also, our immediate perception reveals that the self is not identical with the nonself. (63) Through perception, therefore, it becomes evident that there are many selves or consciousnesses, and that these selves are different from the nonself. (64) In the Veda, when nonduality is asserted, the reference is only to generic essence and does not imply numerical oneness (cf. I.154).

(65) Moreover, it is not correct to assert (as the Vedāntins do) that the self (*ātman*) or ignorance (*avidyā*) or both are responsible for material creation (*upādānakāraṇa*). The self is free from all relations or attachments (*niḥsaṅga*) and, hence, cannot be a material cause nor a locus for ignorance.

(66) Furthermore, it is not correct to argue, as do the Vedāntins, that the self is characterized by both bliss (*ānanda*) and consciousness. (*cit*). According to Vedānta, bliss and consciousness are two distinct things, but if that is the case then it is impossible to maintain that the self is free from all characterizations. (67-68) In fact, when the Veda refers to "bliss," that is just a verbal expression for the cessation of frustration, or, putting it another way, the term "bliss' is used to make liberation appear to be attractive to the unenlightened.

(I) *On the Problem of the Mind and the Internal Organ* (V.69-73) (218, 221; T222-224)

(69) The mind is not all-pervasive (as are materiality and consciousness) because the mind is a functioning instrument or a sense-capacity. It is an instrument (*karaṇa*) in the sense that an axe is an instrument; and it is a sense capacity (*indriya*) in the sense that seeing is a sense capacity. (70) From the Veda we know that the mind wanders (*gati*); and we also know that it is movable. (71) The mind is a finite entity having parts, like a jar—that is to say, it has extension in time and space as does a jar. (72) Only materiality and consciousness are eternal. (73) Materiality in and of itself—that is to say, taken as a whole—is not derived from any parts. The Veda teaches that it exists in and of itself.

(J) *On the Problem of Liberation* (V.74-83) (E221-226; T224-231)

(74) Liberation involves the realization of contentless consciousness, and hence the experience cannot be described as being blissful, as the Vedāntins want to describe it. (75) Nor is it correct to suggest (as Naiyāyikas do) that liberation involves the destruction of specific qualities (*viśeṣaguṇa*) because consciousness has no specific qualities. (76) For the same reason, one cannot describe liberation in terms of a specific kind of wandering (*viśeṣagati*), as the Jains describe it, for consciousness does not have the characteristic of wandering. (77) Nor is it correct to attribute liberation to the destruction or elimination of "forms" (*ākāra*), as some Buddhists suggest, because the Buddhist position denies the very existence of a permanent consciousness and, hence, there is nothing to be liberated. (78) Other Buddhists (possibly Vijñānavādins) suggest that liberation means the destruction of everything (*sarvocchitti*) (except consciousness), but such a view is absurd for a variety of reasons, the main one being that it is counterproductive to the purpose of consciousness. (79) For the same reason one must also reject the view of still other Buddhists (namely, Śūnyavādins) that everything is void—that is to say, it too is counterproductive to the purpose of consciousness.

(80) Furthermore, liberation cannot be equated with the attainment of any place or time, because all such attainments are limited or finite, and hence liberation would not be permanent. (81) One cannot argue that that which is without parts can be related to that which has parts, as the Vedāntin does when he argues that the individual selves become one with Brahman. (82) Nor can one argue that liberation is the attainment of supernatural powers as, for example, assuming very small size (*aṇiman*), etc., because all such attainments are not permanent and final. (83) Similarly, one cannot argue that libera-

tion is the attainment of the condition of a god like Indra, etc., for again, all such conditions are limited and subject to change. (cf. V.78-83 with I.7-60, and for the actual position of Śaṃkhya regarding bondage and liberation, see I.55-60).

(K) *On the Problem of the Derivation of the Sense Capacities* (V.84) (E227; T231-232)

It is not correct to derive the sense capacities from the gross elements, as the Nyāya school does, because the Veda teaches that the sense-capacities are derived from egoity.

(L) *On the Problem of the Nyāya-Vaiśeṣika Categories and Atomism* (V.85-88) (E227-232; T232-238)

(85) The reduction of philosophical categories to six (as set forth in the Vaiśeṣika) has no authoritative basis, and it is not correct to argue that liberation arises from the cognition of these six (namely, substance, quality, motion, universal, individuator, and inherence). (86) The same is true for the sixteen principles, etc., of Nyāya (namely, instrument of knowledge, object of knowledge, doubt, purpose, example, tenet, members of an inference, *tarka*, ascertainment, discussion, sophistry, cavil, fallacies of the reason, quibble, futile rejoinder, and way of losing an argument) (see *Nyāyasūtra* I.1.1.).

(87) The Veda teaches that everything is derived from materiality. Hence, even the atoms are products and, therefore, cannot be eternal. (88) Similarly, because they are products, they cannot be claimed to be without parts, because everything produced has parts.

(M) *On the Problem of Perception* (V.89) (E232; T238)

It cannot be argued that perception is only external and based on color or form (because space is perceived when one says "a bird is here" in the sky and because Yogins perceive many unusual entities in their contemplation). Hence, one cannot confine cognition only to external perception of form.

(O) *On the Problem of Universals* (V. 91-96) (E233-236; T239-243)

(91-92) It is true that only materiality and consciousness are eternal, but, nevertheless, the category of universal property (*sāmānya*) has a certain constancy. Therefore, we do not deny the existence of a more or less permanent universal property. We only deny that a universal property is eternal in the same sense that materiality and consciousness are eternal. (93) A universal, in our view, is a positive apprehension and is not an apprehension of exclusion, as some Naiyāyikas assert. (That is to say, when I apprehend "cowness," I apprehend something positive. I do not simply apprehend everything that is noncow.) (94) Moreover, the notion of similarity (*sādṛśya*) is a variety of universal and is not a separate principle as the Mīmāṃsakas of the Prābhākara school and some Buddhists assert. One apprehends similarity by perceiving sameness in a greater number of parts (between two things). (95) Or, putting the matter another way, similarity is the apprehension of an innate characteristic, which is the same in two things. (96) This apprehension of similarity is not necessarily dependent upon the relation between a thing and its name (*saṃjñāsaṃjñisambandha*), for sometimes a similarity is apprehended without recourse to language (as, for example, when perceiving two similar jars).

(P) *On the Problem of Relation* (V.97-100) (E236-239; T243-247)

(97) The relation (*sambandha*) between word and meaning (*śabdārtha*) is not eternal because both relata are noneternal. (98) Moreover, there are no beginningless relations, because perception and inference do not provide us with any reliable knowledge of such a beginningless relation. We apprehend relations through our apprehension of relata, and relata are never perceived as being beginningless. (99) Hence, the category of inherence (*samavāya*) that, according to Nyāya-Vaiśeṣika, is an eternal relation, cannot be proved. (100) The apprehension of constant connections between things (e.g., a "white cow" or "the horse runs") is to be explained by means of perception and inference, and there is no need to invoke a category of eternal relation, such as inherence.

(Q) *On the Problem of Motion* (V.101) (E239-240; T247-248)

Motion (*kriyā*) can be directly perceived by one who is standing near at hand and who observes the locus of the motion. There is no need, therefore, to hold that motion is inferable only.

(R) *On the Problem of the Material Cause of the Body* (V. 102) (E240; T248)

The body does not have five material causes (coinciding with the five gross elements). The gross body is derived only from earth. The other four gross elements are only auxiliary.

(S) *On the Problem of the Gross Body and the Subtle Body* (V. 103) (E241; T249-250)

There are two bodies. One is the gross, physical body, and the other is the transmigrating subtle body. The materialists, who accept only the gross body, are unable to give a full account of the human condition.

(T) *On the Problem of the Scope of the Sense Capacities* (V. 104-110) (242-246; T250-255)

(104) It is not correct to assert that the sense capacities can provide cognition for that which goes beyond their reach. If it were the case that they could, then one should be able to perceive the entire universe, which is absurd. The correct view is that the sense capacities have specific operations and limitations. (105) It is the operation of sight to see things even at a distance, but it does not follow, therefore, that this operation is the same as light, as the Naiyāyikas hold. (106) That there is such a special operation (*vṛtti*) of seeing is demonstrated when we cognize objects that are distant from us. (107) The special operation is neither a "part" (*bhāga*) nor a "quality" (*guṇa*); it is a different principle (*tattvāntara*) that moves (*sarpati*) in order to establish a relationship with an object (*sambandhārtha*). (108) *Qua* operation it is to be understood as being derived from egoity, and it is not restricted to substances. (109) Hence, seeing (together with the other sense capacities) originates and gets its function from the ego. Seeing is not a product of the material elements. (110) It is true, of course, that the gross elements are concomitant causes and that the sense capacities operate in the context of the gross elements. This is not to be denied. What we want to stress, however, is that the sense capacities originate and get their operations from egoity.

(U) *On the Problem of the Nature of Bodies* (V.111-115) (E246-249; T255-258)

(111) The conventional view that bodies are sweat-born, egg-born, embryo-born, seed-born, will-born and self-generated is too limited. One must keep an open mind in such matters, for bodies are produced in a variety of ways. (112) Bodies are mainly made up of earth with regard to their material cause, although one should keep in mind what was asserted above in *sūtra* 110. (113) Vital breath is not the origin of the body, because the vital breath subsists in the body in association with the sense capacities. (114) The body is enlivened because of the controllership of the experiencer (namely, consciousness). Without the presence of consciousness, decay takes place. (115) Consciousness does not control directly, but works, rather, through materiality, just as a master accomplishes his purposes through a servant.

(V) *On the Problem of the Experience of Liberation* (V.116-120) (E246-253; T258-261)

(116) Concentration (*samādhi*), deep sleep (*suṣupti*), and liberation (*mokṣa*) are analogous in the sense that they do not involve the experience of external objects. The content of these experiences is just the form of the Absolute (*brahmarūpatā*). (117) In concentration and deep sleep, however, some seeds that may lead to further ordinary experience, remain—that is to say, these experiences are not permanent and final states. They lead to regression—that is to say, to ordinary experience. Only liberation is the permanent and final experience in which all of the seeds are destroyed. (118) All three states exist (namely, concentration, deep sleep, and liberation) and are established by means of perception and inference. The first two, however, are secondary to the third. (119) Bondage is caused by faults like desire, etc., and also by latent dispositions that obstruct liberation. (120) A disposition possesses a certain speed or velocity, and one disposition is sufficient to account for one motion.

(W) *On the Problem of Types of Beings* (V. 121-128) (253-257; T261-265)

(121) Beings are of various types and cannot be restricted to the human condition alone. (122-123) Trees, bushes, and plants likewise are abodes of experience for an experiencer, for this is clearly taught in tradition and was referred to previously in V. 114. (124) This is not to suggest, of course, that trees and bushes engage in meritorious behavior as do people, for the Veda clearly indicates that meritorious behavior, etc., are characteristics of only certain bodily conditions. (125) With respect to types of bodies there are three varieties: (a) bodies that act (*karmadeha*); (b) bodies that experience (*bhogadeha*); and (c) bodies that act and experience (*ubhayadeha*). (126) The accomplished Yogin (*anuśayın*) is in a class by himself, and nothing whatever can be ascribed to him. (127-128) Understanding, knowledge, desire, and action are noneternal, and it cannot be argued that these reside in God, for we have already shown that God cannot be proved.

(X) *On the Problem of Supernatural Attainments* (V. 129) (E257-258; T266)

The supernatural attainments of Yoga praxis (*yogasıddhi*) are as real as are the effects of drugs, etc.

(Y) *On the Problem of Consciousness and the Elements* (V. 130) (E258-259; T266-267)

Consciousness is not a property of the gross elements either singly or in combination.

Book VI: Summary Section

(A) *On the Nature of the Self and the Discrimination of the Self* (VI.1-21) (E260-270; T268-277)

(1) The self exists because there is no adequate proof for its nonexistence (cf. I.138). (2) The self is distinct from the body and other material things, because if it were not distinct, then the qualities of the body, etc., would be ascribed to the self, the knower, which cannot be allowed logically. (3) Furthermore, one uses the genitive case when referring to the self, as when we say, for example, "my body"; hence, there is a clear distinction between the possessor and the possessed (namely, the self and the body). (4) If someone should object that the genitive case is also used in such expressions as "the body of the stone" (for grinding, etc.), that is to say, in an expression in which the "body" and the "stone" refer to the same thing—and that, therefore one need not maintain a distinction between the self and the body, our reply is that in such expressions the genitive case is being used only figuratively (whereas, in fact, there is an identity between "body" and "stone" by way of perception), but in our usage, we employ the use of the genitive case in its grammatically correct form (wherein there is a distinction between the possessor and the possessed). (5) The ultimate condition (*kṛtakṛtyatā*) is attained when frustration has been completely overcome (cf. III.84). (6) Frustration and satisfaction usually occur together—that is to say, there is no satisfaction without frustration and there is no frustration without satisfaction. (7) No one anywhere is completely satisfied—that is to say, there is no pure condition of satisfaction without some frustration. (8) Therefore, because pleasure is always linked with pain, the discriminating person considers even that satisfaction on the same level as frustration—that is to say, one who discriminates correctly does not seek satisfaction but seeks, rather, the nonexistence of frustration. (9) To seek satisfaction is to be motivated by a desire; but to seek the nonexistence of frustration is to be free from all desire; hence, the goal is twofold: frustration and the absence of frustration. (10) The self is devoid of all qualities, and in the Veda it is taught that nothing adheres to the self. (11) Owing to nondiscrimination, consciousness is said to attain heaven, etc., although such things are the transformations of materiality. In fact, consciousness is completely attribute-

less. (12) Nondiscrimination is without beginning. If one were to argue that nondiscrimination has a beginning then two insuperable difficulties would arise : either the liberated would have to become bound (at that moment when nondiscrimination arises), or activity to remove nondiscrimination would be pointless (because there would be prior absence of nondiscrimination). (13) To say that nondiscrimination is without beginning, however, is not to say that it is eternal like consciousness and materiality. If nondiscrimination were eternal, it could never be eliminated. Hence, nondiscrimination is without beginning, but it does have an end. (14-15) As darkness can be eliminated by light only, so nondiscrimination can be eliminated by discrimination only. (16) By implication, therefore, we must say that bondage is caused only by nondiscrimination. (17) Discrimination alone brings about liberation from bondage, and in the Veda it is taught that there is no renewal or returning (*āvṛtti*) after discrimination has occurred. (18) If a renewal or return could take place, then discrimination could not bring complete cessation of frustration, which is the ultimate goal or end of beings. (19) Also, there would be no intelligible distinction between the bound and the liberated, for both would be caught up in renewal or returning. (20) Liberation is not a state or condition; it is nothing other than the absolute elimination of all obstacles or hindrances that create distractions. (21) Even if one accepts that there must arise some state or condition in liberation, the view does not make any substantial change in the view of Sāṃkhya, for it is accepted that there is no return from the state of liberation.

(B) *On the Means of Attaining Discrimination* (VI.22-31) (E271-275; T277-281)

(22) There are three types of aspirants: the very bright, the mediocre, and the dull, and for each type there is an appropriate means for attaining discrimination (cf. I.70 and III.76). (23) (Hearing [*śravaṇa*] is sufficient for the very bright; hearing and thinking [*manana*] are sufficient for the mediocre); and hearing, thinking and meditation (*nididhyāsana*) are required for the dull. (24) Posture should be steady and comfortable, and there are a variety of useful postures (cf. III.33). (25) Meditation is a condition in which the mind is free from awareness of objects (cf. III.31). (26) In meditation one becomes free from all impulses or influences (*uparāga*). (In deep sleep, however, the influences continue to operate.) (cf. V.117). (27) Consciousness in and of itself, of course, is free from all influences; the appearance of influence is brought about by nondiscrimination. (28) The influence is like the case of the rose and the crystal (cf. II.35). There is no actual redness in the crystal; there is only the appearance of redness. Similarly, there is no real influence

in consciousness. (29) One attains the cessation of influence by means of meditation, concentration, constant practice, and nonattachment (cf. III. 30-36). (30) Liberation is attained by going beyond waking awareness and the state of deep sleep. (31) There is no special rule regarding the place for meditation. Any place is suitable so long as it is conducive to the goal, which is the cessation of worldly awareness (*cittaprasāda*).

(C) *Primordial Materiality* (VI.32-44) (E275-280; T281-287)

(32) Primordial materiality is the primal material cause, for we know from the Veda that all other things are of the nature of effects. (33) The self or consciousness cannot be the material cause because such a cause is unsuitable to consciousness (cf. I.66, I.75). (34) Anyone who ascribes causative agency to the self is in clear contradiction with the Veda. (35) Materiality operates as the basic material cause throughout all of the manifest world, although this primal causation operates mediately through the various effects. (36) Materiality is omnipresent as everything is its effect. (37) If one would argue that materiality is not omnipresent and that it is somehow a limited entity that moves from place to place, one then encounters the difficulty that the atomists have—that is to say, limited entities that move are really products and cannot be the final material cause (cf. I.76 and V.87). (38) Furthermore, if one asks whether materiality is one of the nine substances set forth in the Nyāya analysis of substance, our answer is no. Materiality is another kind of substance, for there is no need to restrict the number of substances to nine. (39) The three constituents are not attributes or properties of materiality. They are, rather, the actual constituents of materiality. (40) Materiality is devoid of experience in and of itself, but it functions for the sake of consciousness just as a camel carries saffron for a merchant (cf. III.58). (41) Although there is only one material cause, the manifoldness of creation is due to merit, demerit, etc., which are the results of action. (42) Materiality in its diversified condition is brought about when the constituents are out of equilibrium. Materiality in its quiescent condition is when the constituents abide in equilibrium (cf. I.61). (43) For the one who has become liberated, materiality no longer produces any diversified manifestations, just as in everyday life one ceases to work when a task has been accomplished. (44) Although materiality continues to be present, there is no inclination for further experience on the part of the one liberated, because nondiscrimination has been removed, or in other words, the occasion for further ordinary experience (has been removed).

(D) *On the Plurality of Consciousnesses* (VI.45-51) (E281-286; T287-294)

(45) As has already been argued, the plurality of consciousnesses follows from diversity (cf. I.149). (46-48) The limiting adjuncts or disguises, as it were, cannot by themselves account for diversity, as the Vedāntin wants to argue. If the adjuncts are real, then diversity is real, and the Vedāntin notion of monism must be given up. If, on the other hand, the adjuncts are unreal, they obviously cannot account for diversity, for something real cannot arise from something unreal. The only solution is to accept a plurality of consciousnesses in addition to the adjuncts, and to assert that the nonduality of selves has reference to their having a simple generic essence (cf. I.150-154). (49) Moreover, the Vedāntin position of nonduality has the difficulty that there is no way that it could be known. The self cannot be known by the nonself, since the nonself is unintelligent. By the same token, the self cannot know itself without committing the logical fallacy of claiming that the subject and object of an assertion are the same thing. (50) The self whose very nature is pure contentless consciousness illuminates that which is nonself. (51) When bliss or joy is ascribed to the self in the Veda, this is simply a figurative device for making liberation appear to be attractive for those affected by desires (cf. V.67-68).

(E) *On the Manifest World* (VI (VI.52-65) (E286-297; T294-306)

(52) The manifest world exists, as has already been argued. It is neither some sort of illusion, nor is there any adequate proof for its nonexistence (cf. I.79). (53) Because the manifest world could not have arisen from nonbeing, therefore it must be accepted that the manifest world has been derived from that which is eternally real (namely, materiality).

(54) Egoity, not consciousness, is the agent. (55) Experience ends when the realization of discrimination occurs, for experience is dependent on the activities of egoity (cf. I.104 and II.46). (56) Even the intense pleasure of the celestial realms (namely, the world of the moon, etc.) is not permanent, since renewal, or return, operates even there (because efficient causes continue to exist) (cf. III.52-53). (57) Liberation from the manifest world does not arise through instruction, as has been stated before in I.70 and VI.22, but rather through the practices prescribed for the various types of aspirants. (58) Hearing is said to be a means to liberation, though it is not the direct or immediate means. (59) When in the Veda consciousness, or the self, is referred to as "wandering" (*gati*), this is only a figurative expression and has relevance only with respect to the limiting adjuncts. In a

similar way, space sometimes appears to move because of its association with a jar, but, of course, space does not move (cf. I.51). (60) Consciousness is present during all stages of the formation of the embryo. When consciousness is not present, decay takes place (cf. V.114). (61) The body is not kept from decaying because of the "unseen" (*adṛṣṭa*) power of meritorious acts, etc., because the "unseen" is unconnected with the body. The body, therefore, is not an effect of the "unseen," just as a sprout is not the effect of water but, rather, the effect of a seed. (62) Such qualities as meritorious behavior, etc., belong to egoity and do not belong to consciousness, which is free from all qualities. (63) The empirical self having characteristics is known as the *jīva*, and the *jīva* is not consciousness, because consciousness is devoid of all characteristics. (64) All agency belongs to egoity; hence, all of the effects (of the manifest world) depend upon egoity. As has already been argued (in V.1-12 and I.92-99) there is no proof for an additional entity known as "God." (65) As the manifestation of *adṛṣṭa* is agentless, so egoity has no agent to produce it. (66) Everything arises from egoity except the "great one" or intellect (and this latter arises directly from primordial materiality.

(F) *On Consciousness and Creative Nature Being Together as Possessor and Possessed* (VI.67-70) (E298-300; T307-309)

(67) The relation of consciousness and materiality being together—that is to say, the relation of "possessor" and "possessed" (*svasvāmibhāva*—has been explained in various ways. Some have suggested that the relation is brought about by the beginningless instrumentality of action (within creative nature) like that between a seed and a sprout. (68) Others, like Pañcaśikha, have explained the relation as due to the instrumentality of nondiscrimination. (69) Still others, like Sanandana, have explained the relation as due to the instrumentality of the subtle body. (70) However one wishes to explain the relation, what is important to realize is that the ultimate end or goal of beings is only attained when this relation (namely, the *svasvāmibhāva*) is permanently and finally destroyed.

VIJÑĀNABHIKṢU

If it is legitimate to use the term "renaissance" with reference to these later Sāṃkhya traditions that focus on the *Tattvasamāsasūtra* and the *Sāṃkhyasūtra*, it is surely because of the work of Vijñānabhikṣu (and to a lesser extent his pupil, Bhāvāgaṇeśa). In the *Kramadipikā* and Aniruddha's *Sāṃkhyasūtravṛtti*, the interpretation of Sāṃkhya still very much followed along the older lines of the main tradition of the *Sāṃkhyakārikā* and its commentaries, even though the occasions for the *Kramadipikā* and *Sāṃkhyasūtravṛtti* were the emergence of the apparently recent *sūtra* collection. With Vijñanabhikṣu, however, new directions in the interpretation of the old Sāṃkhya are clearly evident. On one level, there is a much more synthetic attitude overall in which epic and Purāṇic themes, theistic devotional trends, and the developing themes of Vedānta philosophy (primarily of the *bhedābheda* or "identity and difference" variety) are being welded together into a grand metaphysical system. Sāṃkhya and Yoga, along with Nyāya, Vaiśeṣika, and Mīmāṃsā, are all assigned an appropriate place in this larger Vedānta synthesis. On a second level, however, the syncretism is hardly complete, for it is quite clear that Vijñanabhikṣu has very little patience with the *māyāvāda* or Advaita Vedānta of Śaṃkara and his followers, whom he unkindly characterizes as "crypto-Buddhists" (*pracchannaṃ bauddham*) in his remarks on I.22 of *Saṃkhyapravacanabhāṣya*. On this second level, one has the impression that Vijñānabhikṣu construes one part of his intellectual mission as one of rescuing Vedānta from the Advaitins, and some such motivation may well explain his predilection for Sāṃkhya, Yoga, and the older epic and Purāṇic materials. A discussion of the intramural polemics of later Vedānta is, of course, beyond the scope of the present volume except, perhaps, to point out that Vijñānabhikṣu's interest in Sāṃkhya and Yoga may have been occasioned by motives quite different from that of a faithful *bhāṣyakāra* trying to understand the old Sāṃkhya tradition. For a useful, general treatment of Vijñānabhikṣu's own Vedānta philosophy vis-à-vis other forms of Vedānta, see S. N. Dasgupta's chapter entitled "The Philosophy of Vijñāna Bhikṣu."[1]

The best estimate for the date of Vijñānabhikṣu is still the latter half of the sixteenth century as was argued long ago by Garbe[2] and accepted by Keith,[3] Winternitz,[4] and most others. Udayavīra Śāstrin, however, has argued for a fourteenth century date,[5] claiming that Vijñānabhikṣu knew the work of Sadānanda of the *Vedāntasāra* and must, therefore, be placed at the end of the fourteenth century. Chakravarti argues for a fifteenth century date based on a notation in a catalogue of manuscripts indicating that a manuscript of Vijñānabhikṣu had been copied in the fifteenth century.[6] These latter arguments appear to be based on rather limited evidence, and it is probably wise to retain the sixteenth century date in the absence of additional data.

Vijñānabhikṣu composed a number of works, and R. T. Rukmani in the Introduction to her new translation of the first part of Vijñānabhikṣu's *Yogavārttika* suggests that Vijñānabhikṣu's writings be placed in the following chronological order:[7] (a) *Upadeśaratnamālā* (a Vedānta work), (b) *Vijñānāmṛtabhāṣya* (his commentary on the *Brahmasūtra*), (c) a series of eight commentaries on various Upaniṣads, (d) *Īśvaragītābhāṣya*, (e) *Brahmādarśa* (a Vedānta work), (f) *Sāṃkhyapravacanabhāṣya* and *Yogavārttika* (both of which were written about the same time), (g) *Sāṃkhyasāra* and finally (h) *Yogasārasaṃgraha.*

SĀṂKHYAPRAVACANABHĀṢYA

(*Summary by Sangamlal Pandey*)

The following summary is based on the edition (E) of the text prepared by Ram Shankar Bhattacarya (Bharatiya Vidya Prakasana, Varanasi, 1966). The English translation (T) used is that of Nandalal Sinha in *The Sāṃkhya Philosophy* containing (1) *Sāṃkhya-Pravachana Sūtram*, with the *Vritti* of Aniruddha, and the *Bhāṣya* of Vijñāna Bhikṣu and extracts from the *Vritti-Sāra* of Mahādeva Vedāntin; (2) *Tatva Samāsa*; (3) *Sāṃkhya Kārikā*; (4) *Panchaśikha Sūtram* (New Delhi: Oriental Books Reprint Corporation, 1979; reprint of the 1915 Sacred Books of the Hindus edition).

Because Vijñānabhikṣu's commentary frequently repeats what Aniruddha has said, the reader is referred back to the Aniruddha summary for those portions of the *Bhāṣya* not covered in the following.

The *Sāṃkhyapravacanabhāṣya* literally means the "commentary on the exposition of Sāṃkhya." It is a full-length commentary on the *Sāṃkhyasūtra*. These aphorisms may be called the "Larger Sāṃkhya Aphorisms" and the other, that is, the *Tattvasamāsa*, the "Shorter Sāṃkhya Aphorisms." Vijñānabhikṣu was aware of both of the aphorisms and treated them as the detailed and the brief expositions of Kapila's formulation of the Sāṃkhya system respectively.

Book I

Introduction (El-7; T2-12)

The text begins with seven verses. (Verse 1) The author says that "one, without a second" (*Chāndogya* VI.11.1) means that there is an absence of difference in consciousnesses and not that the consciousness is nondual (*akhaṇḍa*). (Verse 2) He bows down to Kapila, the author of the Sāṃkhya, who is an incarnation of Nārāyaṇa and invented a complete system of arguments to clarify the meaning of Upaniṣadic passages. (Verse 3) He adores the universal consciousness that uniformly shines in all creatures under different limiting conditions. (Verse 4) There is one uniform consciousness, although the unenlightened perceive differences (divinity, nondivinity, etc.). (Verse 5) He promises to complete the Sāṃkhya system, which had been swallowed by the sun of time (*kālārka*) and has survived only in parts up to his time. (Verse 6) By writing this commentary, he will cut asunder the knot of consciousness and unconsciousness for his own benefit as well as for others. (Verse 7) Nondifference of all consciousnesses, declared by hundreds of scriptural passages, is the subject matter of this philosophy.

The nature of the self should be known from the study of the Upaniṣads. It should be thought about with the help of the Sāṃkhya system, which is the science of discrimination taught by Kapila consisting of six books, and it should be meditated upon with the help of the Yoga philosophy. There is no conflict among the six systems of Hindu philosophy.

It is true that the Nyāya and the Vaiśeṣika also prepare the ground for the discrimination of the self from the body. They are not the final or transcendental philosophy, however, since they take the self to be an agent. The *Bhagavadgītā* (III.29) rejects their view and establishes the Sāṃkhya view. The view is further proved by hundreds of Upaniṣadic texts such as the *Bṛhadāraṇyaka*, and hundreds of *smṛtis* such as the *Viṣṇu Purāṇa*. Thus the Nyāya and the Vaiśeṣika are contradicted at the transcendental level (*paramārthabhūmi*). They are not void of importance, however, since they have their own specific subject matter. The significance of a word (and also of a philosophy) is that to which it is directed. The significance of the Nyāya and the Vaiśeṣika is different from that of the Sāṃkhya. The Sāṃkhya does not contradict them, nor do they contradict it.

The Vedānta and Yoga, however, which accept an eternal God, seem to conflict with Sāṃkhya, which excludes God from its purview, but a little consideration will remove this conflict. Here too the relation of the empirical and the transcendental obtains. The exclusion of God in the Sāṃkhya is for practical purposes only; it is designed to produce indifference toward lordliness. Nowhere is there any condemnation of theism as such. There is no wisdom equal to, or greater than, the Sāṃkhya system of thought. The superiority of Sāṃkhya over other systems rests upon its focus on discrimination and not upon its rejection of God. Hence, cultured persons like Parāśara unanimously maintain that there is a God that is transcendentally real. The followers of the Vedas should give up those portions in the teachings of Akṣapāda, Kaṇāda, Sāṃkhya, and Yoga, which are in conflict with the Vedas. There is again no conflict between the system of Jaimini and the system of Vyāsa, since both of them make use of the Upaniṣads. The arguments of the Vedānta, the Nyāya, the Vaiśeṣika, the *Mokṣadharma* (*Mahābhārata*), and other systems that demonstrate the existence of God must be accepted as having greater validity than the Sāṃkhya rejection of God. The *Kūrma Purāṇa* declares that Sāṃkhya lacks in the knowledge of God. Moreover, the principal object of the Vedānta is God and if this object is contradicted then the Vedānta would be altogether void of its principal object—a case that is impossible according to the maxim that the significance of a word is that to which it is directed. The principal object of the Sāṃkhya is the discrimination between self and nonself.

Thus, Vedānta and Sāṃkhya are not in conflict with each other. Their spheres and purposes are different. The Sāṃkhya is certainly weak to the extent that it rejects God. Its rejection of God is simply a concession to current views (*abhyupagamavāda*) or simply a dogmatic assertion (*prauḍhivāda*). Such concessions and assertions are recorded in the *śāstras*. They can be safely ignored and it will then be found that the Sāṃkhya has no conflict with Vedānta and Yoga. Or for the purpose of impeding the knowledge of the sinful persons, even in theistic philosophies some portions that are opposed to the Vedas are included, although these portions are not authoritative. Hence Lord Siva condemns in the *Padmapurāṇa* (VI.263.66-75) the Pāśupata, the Vaiśeṣika, the Nyāya, the Sāṃkhya, the Mīmāṃsā, the Buddhist philosophy, and the Vedānta of Śaṃkara and says that he himself included some wrong doctrines in these systems in order to confuse some people.

Thus none of the orthodox systems is either unauthoritative or contradicted by another. Every one of them is authoritative in its own sphere and remains uncontradicted by other orthodox systems in that sphere.

Objection : Is not the doctrine of the plurality of consciousnesses in the Sāṃkhya a concession to current views (*abhyupagama*), for it contradicts the monism of the Vedānta?

Reply : No. There is no contradiction between Sāṃkhya and Vedānta, for the *Brahmasūtra* (2.3.43-50) itself establishes the plurality of *jīvas*. Although the plurality of consciousnesses is contradicted by the Vedānta doctrine of one universal consciousness, the Sāṃkhya is not invalidated thereby, for there is no contradiction in the doctrine of the plurality of empirical selves being useful in the discipline of liberation. Thus, the relation between the Sāṃkhya and the Vedānta is that between the practical view and the transcendental view. This has been discussed in greater detail by the author in the *Vijñānāmṛtabhāṣya*.

This *Sāmkhyasūtra* of Six Books is not a repetition of the *Tattvasamāsa* because the *Sāṃkhyasūtra* is an elaborate exposition of the Sāṃkhya, whereas the *Tattvasamāsa* is just a short description of it.

Now, the name "Sāṃkhya" is significant. This system discriminates the self correctly (*samyak viveka*); hence it is called "Sāṃkhya." Moreover, it enumerates the principles beginning with materiality; thus, it is called "Sāṃkhya" or the science of enumeration.

This philosophy is the science of liberation (*mokṣaśāstra*). Like medical science, it has four divisions (*vyūha*): i.e., what is to be avoided (*heya*), its avoidance (*hāna*), the cause of what is to be avoided (*heyahetu*), and the way of avoiding it (*hānopāya*). Frustration is threefold; its cause is nondiscrimination on the part of consciousness. The way for the elimination of frustration is the discrimination between consciousness and materiality. The absolute eradication of frustration is the goal or end of consciousness.

(A) *On the Problem of the Scope and Task of the Sāṃkhya*

(I.1) (E7-13); T12-26) Now, the complete cessation of the threefold suffering is the supreme end of consciousness.

The word "now" (*atha*) indicates auspiciousness, and it is used here as an introductory adverb to introduce the main theme. The conclusion of the theme will be the cessation of frustration (see VI.70). Thus the meaning of the aphorism is that the Sāṃkhya has been begun to determine the supreme end of consciousness.

Frustrations are threefold: (2) originating from the sufferer himself (*ādhyātmika*), (2) originating from created beings (*ādhibhautika*), and (3) originating from the gods (*ādhidaivika*). The first is of two kinds, physical and mental. Although all frustration is without exception mental, yet there is the distinction of the mental and nonmental since some frustrations are produced entirely by the mind, whereas other frustrations are not so produced. The complete cessation means the cessation of the threefold frustration without leaving any remainder (either gross or subtle). The frustration that is felt at the present moment ceases automatically in the second moment. Hence, it does not require knowledge for its cessation. Again, past frustration has already disappeared. Hence, it does not require any means of eradication. Only the frustration that is to come needs to be eradicated. That is why the *Yogasūtra* (II.16) states that the frustration that is avoidable is future frustration. Cessation does not mean destruction but a state that is over because posterior absence and prior absence are essentially the same as the past and the future states respectively. Absence is not admitted by the upholders of *satkāryavāda*.

Objection : Frustration that is not yet come is unreal, like a sky flower. So there is no need for any means to eradicate it.

Reply : Not so. For, it is well known in the philosophy of Patañjali that the power of things to produce their effects lasts so long as the things themselves endure. The existence of fire devoid of the power of burning is nowhere seen. This power lies in the form of those effects that are not yet come. This very power is called the capability of being the material cause of experience. Hence, the existence of future frustration is inferred so long as there is the existence of the cognitive faculty (*citta*). To remove it is the supreme end of consciousness. In the state of liberation-while-living (*jīvanmukti*) the seeds of all actions except those already begun (*prārabdha*) are burnt up, whereas in that of liberation from the body (*videhamukti*) they are destroyed together with the cognitive faculty. The burning up of seeds means only the destruction of the contributory cause of ignorance.

Objection : But still the cessation of frustration cannot be the supreme end of consciousness, because frustration is a quality of the cognitive faculty of consciousness and its cessation is not possible. Frustration is eternal like conciousness. If it is said that frustration arises from the foregetfulness of consciousness, then the discipline of meditation (*nididhyāsana*) that is enjoined after hearing and reasoning would remove the said forgetfulness. Moreover, the Veda, which has the power of removing all confusion, says that he who knows the self overcomes frustration. So the existence of frustration is established and it does not rest upon forgetfulness of consciousness.

Reply : No. This objection will be met by Aphorism I.19, namely, except for the relation with materiality there is no other bondage in consciousness, which is eternally pure, enlightened, and free. So, satisfaction and frustration exist in consciousness in the form of the intellect, but such a transformation is not possible in the case of the unchanging consciousness (*kūṭastha ātman*). Consciousness only receives the transformations of intellect in the form of an image.

Yogasūtra I.4 also supports this view. *Sāṃkhyasūtra* II.35 also holds that as the crystal gets the color of the China rose because of its proximity with it, so consciousness gets the influence of the intellect because of its proximity with it. Vedāntins (*Yogavāsiṣṭha* 5.91.133) also state that an object of knowledge is known only as it is superimposed upon, or reflected in, consciousness. This reflection means the transformation of the intellect in the form of the objects under their respective conditions. There the association with frustrations, called experience, exists in consciousness in the form of reflection. Hence the cessation of frustration in that very form becomes a proper object of the pursuit of consciousness.

The complete cessation of frustration is an intrinsic object of desire by itself.

(1.3) *Objection* : If wealth, etc., fail to give relief from frustration, then they are useless, like bathing an elephant. Why do people engage in such pursuits then?

Reply : Cessation of frustration, produced by worldly objects, is not the ultimate object of desires. To some extent, of course, it is certainly an object of desire. People seek the removal of frustrations by means of wealth, etc., and such activity is justified. The bathing of an elephant gives temporary relief from pain and so it is an object of desire, although of a lower kind.

(I.4) The cessation of frustration by ordinary means should ultimately be given up, since it is not possible to eradicate all frustration by such means. Even if it were possible, there would still necessarily exist some connection with the cause of frustration.

(I.5) The superiority of liberation to kingdom and other objects of desire is declared by the Vedas. Further, the objects of desire are the modifications of the constituents, which are the abodes of frustrations. No object can be found that is unmixed with frustration.

(I.6) The author here quotes *Sāṃkhyakārikā*, verse 2, to prove that the scriptural means are similar to ordinary means. The scriptural means, like the ordinary means, are also mixed with impurity or sin, because they enjoin the killing of animals.

Objection : Killing in a sacrifice is lawful, because it is enjoined by the scriptures. The significance of an injunction consists in its encouraging conduct (in accordance to it) that leads to the realization of a good that is not followed by a greater evil. If lawful killing will be productive of evil, it would not be possible.

Reply : Not so. The conduct related to an injunction is not productive of frustration in addition to the frustration immediately following the production of the good. Since the evil produced by lawful killing immediately follows the production of the good, the significance of the injunction remains intact. Some, however, hold that only killing other than lawful killing is productive of sin, but they are not right. Yudhiṣṭhira and others had to perform penances in order to condone the sin that they committed in killing their kinsmen in the great war of the *Mahābhārata*, although it was their *svadharma* to kill their enemies in battle. The author also quotes from the *Mārkaṇḍeya Purāṇa* (X.31) to prove that Vedic performances are mixed with demerit and hence resemble a fruit that is hard to digest. Scriptural texts such as *Chāndogya* (VIII.65.1) allow for certain kinds of lawful killing. They do not declare that lawful killing is unmixed with evil. More on this point is to be found in the author's *Yogavārttika*. Moreover the attainment of immortality by drinking the *soma* juice is only meant in a secondary sense. In the primary sense immortality can be gained only by renunciation (*tyāga*) and not by progeny, wealth, action, or sacrifices.

(B) *On the Problem of Bondage in Sāṃkhya*

(I.7-11) (E13-15; T26-31) Bondage is not natural to consciousness. Frustration is natural to the intellect only, and not to consciousness, because it is so constituted by three constituents. If bondage were natural to consciousness, there would be no liberation, and the teachings of the Veda for the attainment of liberation would become irrelevant.

Objection : Annihilation of even that which is natural is observed. So the annihilation of natural bondage in consciousness (in case it is admitted) is possible.

Reply : No. Removal of bondage involves a change of nature, which is impossible for consciousness.

(I.12) (E15-16; T31-32) The author now refutes the theory that bondage is related to time. If frustration, which is the mark of bondage, were occasional in consciousness, it would not be capable of being eradicated completely by knowledge and other means, inasmuch as subtle frustration in the form of the not-yet-come would remain so long as its substratum, consciousness, exists. Thus, because time, which is eternal, is connected with all consciousnesses, liberated or unliberated, and the determination of everything in time will entail the bondage of all consciousnesses at all times, liberation would be impossible on that hypothesis.

Objection : In the hypothesis that bondage is occasioned by time, gradation of consciousness as liberated and unliberated is possible, on account of the presence and absence of other secondary causes.

Reply : In that case bondage would be accidental only and so it can be accepted.

(I.17) (E17-18; T35-36) The consciousness' connection with frustrations is only apparent. The relation between the intellect and consciousness is like that of a servant and his master and is beginningless. This topic is discussed in detail in the *Yogabhāṣya*.

(I.18) (E18; T37) *Objection* : Does not the bondage of consciousness arise from materiality?

Reply : No, because materiality is dependent on consciousness. If bondage were possible without the particular relation of consciousness with materiality, then there would be bondage in the state of the dissolution of the world, too.

(I.19) (E18-22; T38-43) Vaiśeṣika philosophers hold that the relation of frustration to consciousness is real, but they are not correct. The relation of frustration to consciousness is only accidental (*aupādhika*) and is like the relation of redness in a crystal that is in relation to a rose.

Objection : Since Sāṃkhya is the science of reasoning (*mananaśāstra*), there must be reasons for the above nature of consciousness.

Reply : Yes. The principal clause in I.19 supplies the required reason. The internal organ (*antaḥkaraṇa*) is said to be the material cause of frustration and so forth, by the argument of concomitant agreement and variation, that is to say, where there is an internal organ, there is frustration and where there is no internal organ there is no frustration. Moreover, to regard both consciousness and the internal organ as the cause of frustration will be superfluous, for where one cause is sufficient it is superfluous to postulate another cause.

Objection : But experience such as "I am frustrated" proves that consciousness is the cause of frustration.

Reply : No; such experiences are mistaken, such as the experience that I am fair.

Objection : Like time, etc., the relation to materiality is common to all consciousnesses, free and bound. So how can relation become the cause of bondage?

Reply : No. The meaning of the word "relation" is technical. It is only by reason of the function of the intellect as limiting adjunct that a relation to frustration occurs in consciousness. Further, the relation of the internal organ to frustration is different from the relation of the intellect to frustration.

The author further refutes the opinion of some (e.g., Aniruddha) who believe that the relation of materiality with consciousness is, in fact, nondiscrimination, for then the experience of frustration would be entailed during the dissolution of the world also, as nondiscrimination exists in that state, too. Moreover, to hold that the relation consists of nondiscrimination in the form of false knowledge would involve the fallacy of arguing in a circle. Hence, relation is something more than nondiscrimination.

Objection : Is relation then transformation?

Reply : No. It is the cause of transformation.

Objection : How can a temporary relation of materiality with consciousness take place when both are eternal?

Reply : The relation of materiality with consciousness is possible by means of the limitation imposed by the manifested constituents.

Objection : Does not the relation of materiality with consciousness consist only of their respective fitness as the enjoyed and the enjoyer?

Reply : No. If fitness were eternal, it would be unreasonable to say that it could be terminated by knowledge, and if fitness were noneternal, then it would admit of transformation. Moreover, nowhere in the *sūtras* has it been declared that the relation consists of fitness as the enjoyer and the enjoyed. Such a view is not authoritative. Thus it follows that only a particular form of relation is the cause of bondage, namely, the relation with the intellect.

(I.20-22) (E22-23; T43-47) Now the author proceeds to examine the views of non-Vedic philosophers concerning the cause of bondage. First of all, he examines the view of the Buddhist idealists. Ignorance (*avidyā*) cannot be the cause of bondage, because ignorance is a nonentity and bondage is not unreal.

Objection : Why cannot ignorance be taken as real?

Reply : This entails the abandonment of the momentariness doctrine accepted by the Buddhists. There would be a second entity in addition to fleeting ideas, which cannot be allowed by the Buddhists.

Objection : Since ignorance is a kind of awareness, how can duality arise?

Reply : The ignorance that is a kind of awareness is subsequent to bondage, whereas the ignorance that is the cause of bondage is called "latent disposition."

Objection : Does this criticism apply to Advaita also?

Reply : No, because the *Brahmasūtra* nowhere says that ignorance is the cause of bondage, but our criticism perfectly applies to modern Vedāntists who are Buddhists in disguise (*pracchanna bauddha*). In our opinion ignorance lacks permanent being, but it has as much reality as a water pot.

(I.23-24) (E23-24; T47-48) *Objection* : Because ignorance is both real and unreal and as such it is different from the real as well as from the unreal, there is no defect in the theory of transcendental nondualism.

Reply : Not so, because such a thing is not observed. Moreover, if ignorance were the direct cause of bondage, then there would be no possibility of the experience of the action that has already begun (*prārabdha*).

(I.25-26) (E24-25; T49-51) *Objection* : We do not accept the Vaiśeṣika theory of six categories and the like. Hence a category that is both real and unreal, e.g., ignorance, may be admitted.

Reply : Even in that case something that is illogical cannot be accepted, otherwise we would be reduced to the level of children or madmen.

(I.27) (E25; T51) *Objection* from the Buddhist (*nāstika*): External objects of momentary duration exist, and in consequence of their influence the bondage of the embodied self takes place.

(I.28) (E25-26; T52-53) *Reply*: Not so. It is only where a relation exists that an adjacent tincture called "latent disposition" is observed as in the case of flower and crystal. But this relation is not possible in your theory of self, because you take self to be something limited and lying wholly within the body. Between the external and the internal there is no relation of the influenced and the influencer, because there is a spatial separation, as there is between the inhabitants of Śrughna and Pāṭaliputra.

(I.30-31) (E26; T54) *Objection* : Granting that a liberated soul and a bound soul are alike in respect of their coming into contact with objects, yet the reception of the influence may result from the force of the unseen (*adṛṣṭa*) residues on the soul.

Reply : It is impossible that there should be an influence of objects taking effect on someone occasioned by the unseen residues belonging to an agent, because, given the theory of momentariness, the agent and the one benefiting from an action do not exist at one and the same time.

(I.32-33) (E26-27; T55-58) *Objection* : As the works of a father benefit his son, so there may be an influence of objects.

Reply : In your theory there is no permanent soul of the son that is benefited by the works of his father. Thus, the illustration proves nothing. Moreover, in our theory it is possible that the benefit to the son should arise from the unseen merit deposited in the son's soul that is permanent.

(I.34-35) (E27-28; T56-58) *Objection*: Bondage is momentary, because it exists and everything that exists is momentary, like the apex of the lamp flame. As a momentary thing, bondage has no fixed cause at all.

Reply : No. Nothing is momentary. The absurdity of the doctrine of momentariness is proved by such experiences as recognition or memory.

(I.37) (E28; T59) The thesis of momentariness is illustrated by the lamp flame, but this illustration is unproven.

(I.39-41) (E29; T60-62) Further, the doctrine of momentariness asserts that the effect arises from the destruction of its cause. Hence the doctrine of causality is not possible on the hypothesis of universal momentariness. Although the antecedent exists, the consequence is incompatible, because the two are always separate. The relation of cause and effect is not possible in this theory. The cause is not merely an antecedent, because there are two types of cause, material and efficient. Antecedence constitutes no distinction between these two causes. Hence a causal phenomenon is not just a flux of events as the theory of universal momentariness argues.

(I.44-45) (E31-32 ; T66-68) *Objection* : Then accept the doctrine of the void.

Reply : No. This doctrine is foolish. The destruction of a thing is also something positive as nothing can exist without its own nature. There is no evidence for the void as the ultimate reality.

(I.50) (E34; T72-73) Moreover, if consciousness be material, like a jar, then it would consist of parts and would be perishable, but these traits of consciousness are contradicted by our system.

(I.52-52) (E35; T75) The bondage of consciousness is not caused by latent residues (*adṛṣṭa*) directly, because those residues are not the attributes of consciousness.

Objection : Even if latent residues are not attributes of consciousness, they may also bind it.

Reply : No. Then even the liberated ones would be bound.

(I.54) (E35; T76) Moreover, the alleged causes of the bondage of the soul are contradicted by the scriptures that declare that the soul is without qualities (*nirguṇa*).

(I.55) (E36-39; T77-82) The relation of consciousness and materiality is caused by nondiscrimination, which is not manifested in liberated consciousness. Hence the liberated are not in relation with materiality.

Objection : Nondiscrimination is either a prior absence of discrimination or a latent disposition. In either case it is not a characteristic of consciousness, but that of the intellect. So, if the quality of the intellect binds consciousness, it may bind both liberated and unliberated consciousness.

Reply : Not so. Nondiscrimination is only an object to consciousness. For the purpose of displaying its transformations materiality enters into relation, by the form of intellect, with consciousness.

Objection : Your reply presupposes a beginningless relation between materiality and consciousness in the form of the owned and its owner. Is not this very relation a sufficient explanation?

Reply : No, because by this relation the liberation of consciousness, which takes place only by means of knowledge, cannot be explained.

Objection : Why is action (*karman*) not the cause of the relation?

Reply : Because action is also dependent upon nondiscrimination. So in our theory it is nondiscrimination only that is the cause of relation in three ways, i.e, (1) immediately, (2) by the production of merit and demerit and (3) by means of visible influences such as desire, and so forth.

(I.56) (E39-40; T82-86) The older Vedāntins regarded action

as a subsidiary part of knowledge leading to liberation, but they did not mean that action is the direct cause of liberation.

(I.57) (E40-41; T86-88) The nondiscrimination of the intellect (from consciousness) is produced from the nondiscrimination of materiality from consciousness. The former is just an effect of the latter. So the former is also annihilated when the latter is annihilated.

(I.58) (E42; T89-90) The "bondage" of consciousness is merely verbal and not real because it belongs only to the intellect.

Objection : Then how is it that the removal of bondage is called the supreme value?

Reply : The apparent experiencing of consciousness consists in the mere reflection of frustrations. Hence, although frustrations are unreal, the removal thereof is a value because it is an object that is desired.

(I.59) (E43; T91-92) *Objection* : If bondage is a mere word, then let its removal take place by reasoning alone.

Reply : No. It cannot be removed with immediate cognition. Removal of bondage is nothing but the disappearance of the idea of bondage in consciousness, and not the immediate cognition of nonbeing. Like confusion about the points of the compass (*digbhrama*), nondiscrimination, which is the cause of bondage, is removed by direct or immediate cognition of the truth.

(I.60) (E43-44; T92-93) As fire that is not perceived is proved to exist by means of its smoke, so things that are not cognizable by senses are proved to exist by means of inference. The author here says that Sāṃkhya is preeminently the science of reasoning, so here only inference is mentioned as an instrument of knowledge although Sāṃkhya also accepts perception and verbal testimony as instruments of knowledge.

(C) *Derivation of the Basic Principles of Sāṃkhya*

(I.61) (E44-46; T94-98) Primordial materiality is the equilibrium of *sattva, rajas,* and *tamas*. From it evolves intellect; from intellect, egoity, from egoity, the five subtle elements and the two sets of capacities. From the subtle elements evolve the gross elements. Then, in addition to these principles, there is consciousness. Thus there are twenty-five principles. *Sattva, rajas,* and *tamas* are substances (*dravya*), and not qualities in the sense of Vaiśeṣika philosophy, because they admit of conjunction and disjunction and because they possess the properties of lightness, activity, and weight respectively. They are called "*guṇa*" (quality), because their existence is only subservient and not primary, and because they bind consciousness as a *guṇa* (which also means rope) binds a beast. The equilibrium of primordial materiality means a state of the constituents in which none of them is more or less than the other two. That is, that state is not developed, into that of an effect. In other words, materiality is the genus of the constituents. All the constituents are said to have the nature of materiality.

Over and above the twenty-five principles there is no category (*padārtha*). The six categories of the Vaiśeṣika philosophers are included in them. Those who have only one category (e.g., Advaita) and those who have six (Vaiśeṣika) or sixteen (Nyāya) categories are really only reinterpreting the twenty-five principles of Sāṃkhya in their own ways.

(I.62) (E46-48; T99-101) The inference to the existence of the five subtle elements from the gross elements goes as follows: gross elements must be produced from substances possessing their own distinctive attributes as a pot is produced from clay. The search for their causes must be stopped at some point in order to be intelligible. Such a stopping point is the subtlest material state of the cause, or in other words, the subtle elements. This inference is confirmed by the consideration that in absence of any counteracting agent, the production of the attributes of the effect in conformity with the attributes of the cause follows necessarily. Moreover, the Vedas and the Smṛtis also confirm the above inference. In the matter of the production of the subtle elements the process described in Vyāsa's commentary on the *Yogasūtra* should alone be accepted. Thus the subtle element of sound is produced from egoity, etc.

The inference to the existence of capacities is like that for *ākāśa*, that is to say, made by means of their functions; seeing, touching, and so forth.

(I.63) (E48-49; T102-103) Knowledge of the existence of egoity is derived by an inference from the external and internal sense capacities and from the subtle elements. The inference is this: the subtle elements and the capacities are made up of things consisting of egoity, because they are the products of egoity. Whatever is not so (i.e., made up of egoity) is not thus (i.e., a product of egoity), like the soul.

(I.64) (E49-51; T103-105) The knowledge of the existence of the intellect is derived by inference from egoity. Egoity has the intellect (whose function is determination or *niścaya*) as its material cause (*upādāna*).

Here the inference is based on the rule that the occurrence of an operation of the effect must result from the occurrence of the operation of the cause.

(I.65) (E51-52; T106-108) The knowledge of the existence of primordial materiality is derived by inference from the intellect. The inference is as follows: intellect, whose properties are satisfaction, frustration, and confusion, is produced from something that has these properties, because these properties, satisfaction, frustration, and confusion are products; and everything that occasions satisfaction, frustration, or confusion arises from something that is composed of these—like a lovely woman. The inference is based on the rule that the qualities of the effect must be in conformity with the qualities of the cause.

(I.66) (E52-53; T108-111) The existence of consciousness is inferred from the fact that the combination of the parts of materiality is for the sake of another (i.e., other than materiality). The inference in this case is this: primordial materiality and its products have an end, because they are composite, and every composite thing such as a couch or a seat is for another's use. Hence, consciousness, for whom materiality and its products are combined, exists.

(I.67-68) (E54; T111-112) A "root" (*mūla*) has no origin and so the original is without an origin. Here "root" means primordial materiality, the original substance of twenty-three principles. It is proved to be without an origin, for otherwise there would result an infinite regress.

Objection : Why not take consciousness as the cause of primordial materiality ? Consciousness is eternal and so it can avoid the infinite regress.

Reply : No. Where there is a succession of causes, the halt must be at a point in the same series of causes. "Primordial materiality" is merely a name that we give to the point in question. It is just a proper name of the root cause of all things.

(I.69) (E54-56; T112-115) *Objection* : Is ignorance (*avidyā*) not the primal cause of all things?

Reply : No. Ignorance, as declared in the *Yogasūtras*, is not a separate entity but a property of the mind. Moreover, the scriptures speak of the production of ignorance, too, since it is produced from the intellect.

(I.70) (E56; T116) *Objection* : If such were the inferences for the existence of primordial materiality and consciousness, then why does discrimination in the form of reflection not take place in all men?

Reply : There is no rule that all should equally grasp truth. Those who are qualified to meditate are of three kinds, dull, mediocre, and very bright. For the dull, Sāṃkhya arguments are set aside by the false arguments of Buddhists. For the mediocre, they are confronted with equally cogent contrary arguments. For the very bright, however, Sāṃkhya arguments are found to be genuine and true.

(I.71) (E57; T116-117) The first product of *prakṛti* is called "*mahat*." It is used synonymously with "*manas*," since its operation is reasoning (*manana*). "Reasoning" includes the operations of belief.

(I.74) Primordial materiality is the first cause of all products in and through the mediation of the intellect. This type of causality is also ascribed to atoms by Vaiśeṣikas.

(D) *Materiality as Material Cause and Its Relation to Discrimination*

(I.79) (E60-61; T123-124) The world is not unreal, because it is never contradicted and because it is not a result of false causes. The scriptural passages like *neti neti* (not this, not this) do not negate the existence of the world, but only give clues for discrimination.

(I.80) (E61; T124-125) An entity can have only an entity as its cause. How can a nonentity be the cause of an entity, since there is no union of the two?

(I.81) (E61; T125-126) Action is also not the material cause of the world. It is only the efficient cause of the world. Here action means ignorance also. So ignorance is not the material cause of the world.

(I.83) The word "*tatra*" in the *sūtra* is understood by Aniruddha as "in the context of materiality and consciousness." But Vijñānabhikṣu understands it as "in the highest heaven = *brahmaloka*." Vijñānabhikṣu contends that, even here, if one seeks liberation one has to attain final intuitive discrimination.

(I.84) (E63; T129) Those who resort to ritualism only get frustration after frustration, like the man suffering from being cold only gets pain from pouring water on himself.

(I.86) (E64; T131-132) *Objection* : Liberation is generated by knowledge. Hence, liberation is also perishable, because what is generated is perishable.

Reply : No. Knowledge generates only the removal of nondiscrimination. The soul itself is free by its very nature.

(E) *The Instruments of Knowledge in Sāṃkhya*

(I.87) The ascertainment of something, not previously known in the soul or the mind or in either of them, is knowledge (*pramā*), and that which produces right knowledge is an instrument of knowledge (*pramāṇa*).

(a) If knowledge is spoken of as located in consciousness, then an instrument of knowledge is an affection of the intellect. If it is spoken of as located in the intellect, then an instrument of knowledge is a relation between a sense capacity and its object. But if both consciousness' awareness and the operations of the intellect are spoken of, then both the operations of the intellect and the relation of a sense capacity with its object are instruments of knowledge.

(b) The process by which an instrument of knowledge works is this. First, the intellect assumes the form of an object as a result of a direct contact or through an inferential mark. Then, that form is reflected as an image in consciousness. Since consciousness cannot be modified, this reflection can only be an image.

(I.88) (E68; T137) Comparison (*upamāna*) is included under inference. Nonperception (*abhāva, anupalabdhi*) is included under perception.

(I.99) (E73-75; T149-152) Actual controllership belongs to the intellect illuminated by consciousness like fire in iron.

Objection : Then consciousness must be connected with the intellect.

Reply : No. The illumination of the intellect consists merely in its presence to consciousness. Hence only a reflection of consciousness is produced in the intellect through this copresence, which is the cause of the mutual reflection of the intellect and consciousness in each other.

The reflection of consciousness in the intellect is referred to as the falling of the shadow or superimposition of *puruṣa* or possession by consciousness, and the reflection of the intellect in consciousness is intended for the manifestation of the intellect together with the objects that have been apprehended by it. The theory of mutual reflection is found in (Vyāsa's) commentary on the *Yogasūtra* and in the author's *Yogavārttika*.

(F) *Materiality and the Theory of Preexistent Effect*

(I.111-112) (E80; T163 T165) *Objection*: If the effect were existent before its production, then the existence of primordial materiality can be established. But for those who do not accept *satkārya*, the inference of primordial materiality cannot be established.

Reply: Nevertheless the observation of an effect in your opinion proves the existence of its cause. So an eternal cause is certainly a possibility. From this changing cause is distinguished consciousness which is unchanging.

(I.113) (E80-81; T165-169) Moreover, all causes are past, present, and future. If an effect were not existent in its cause before its production, then this division of causes would be impossible.

(I.119-120) (E83-84; T171-173) *Objection*: If your view is accepted, then there is no possibility of a thing becoming another because the latter is already in the former.

Reply: No. It is not the case that what is cannot become. What is produced or not produced is a matter of manifestation or nonmanifestation.

(G) *The Manifest and Unmanifest Aspects of Materiality*

(I.125) (E88; T180-182) There are many arguments for the existence of an effect as something over and above its cause. It is proved, sometimes by perception itself, sometimes by inference based on correlation. The first cause is called the principal one (*pradhāna*), because all effects are sustained in it.

(H) *The Three Constituents*

(I.127) (E89-90; T183-185) The constituents differ among themselves in terms of satisfaction, frustration, confusion, and so forth. Pañcaśikha says that *sattva* means satisfaction, but it has innumerable variations such as happiness, lightness, affection, love, endurance, satisfaction, and the like. Similarly *rajas* and *tamas* have innumerable variations.

(I) *Inferences that Establish the Existence of Primordial Materiality and Consciousness*

(I.130-132) (E92-93; T188-190) Other reasons why there are effects are (a) because they are limited, (b) because they are components of *prakṛti*, and (c) because they are the instruments of the *puruṣa*.

(I.133-134) (E93; T190-191) If a thing is not an effect, then it is either primordial materiality or consciousness. Further, if it be neither of the two also, then it would be a nonentity (*tuccha*), like a hare's horn.

(I.138) (E 94-95; T193-195) The existence of consciousness, like that of merit, is by and large beyond dispute. Hence there is no need of proof for the existence of consciousness. If there were no consciousness, then the whole world would become blind. Certain aspects of consciousness, however, can be established by inference, namely, its being the basis of discrimination, its being eternal, and so forth.

(I.147) What is established by the scriptures cannot be denied. The scriptures declare that consciousness is free from all qualities. So the perception of qualities belonging to consciousness is contradicted by the scriptures.

(I.149-152) (E101-105; T207-213) The plurality of consciousnesses is proved by the fact of their separate births.

Objection: Let there be only one consciousness, for the so-called consciousnesses differ only in their limitations as pots do although they contain one and the same space. Limitations of consciousness are different and consciousness is not different from limitation to limitation.

Reply : Not so. It is not reasonable to introduce the simultaneous presence of contradictory properties in the form of birth, death, etc., in the case of one consciousness that is present everywhere. For, when Devadatta is born, Yajñādatta dies and it is contradictory to ascribe birth and death to the same soul at one time.[8]

(I.153) (E205-206; T213-216) As there is a well-regulated distribution of the properties of redness, blueness, etc., appearing in crystals, although these properties are only superimposed on them, so in the case of consciousness also, there is, according to the scriptures, a well-regulated distribution of the properties of the intellect and the body, although these properties are only superimposed on them. The distribution, like that of birth and death, cannot be explained on the theory of the unity of consciousness. The Advaita doctrines of limitation (*avacchedavāda*) and reflection (*pratibimbavāda*) are perverse, as has been shown in the author's commentary on the *Brahmasūtra*.

(I.154) (E106-109; T216-221) Moreover, there is no contradiction with the Upaniṣadic texts that assert that the soul is nondual, because these texts refer to the genus (*jāti*) of consciousness. The author says that he has discussed this noncontradiction in his commentary on the *Brahmasūtra* in detail.

(I.158-159) (E110-111; T225-227) *Objection*: The liberation of the sage Vāmadeva and others is not absolute, but relative only.

Reply : If until now absolute liberation has not been attained by anyone whatever, no absolute liberation will take place in the future.

(I.160) (E111; T226-227) *Objection*: Does the uniformity of consciousness arise at the moment of liberation? Or does it exist at all times?

Reply: The consciousness is, in fact, the same in the states of both bondage and freedom, because its uniformity is established by scripture, tradition, and reasoning.

(I.161) (E111; T227-228) *Objection*: As the character of being the witness is not permanent, how, then, can there be constant uniformity of consciousness?

Reply : The character of being a witness refers only to the notion of reflection. Consciousness is not at all involved in the transformations of materiality.

(I.164) (E112-113; T229-230) *Objection*: How can the scriptural texts that say that consciousness is an agent and the intellect is a knower be justified?

Reply: The agency attributed to consciousness arises from the influence of the intellect and the character of being a knower attributed to the intellect arises as a result of proximity to consciousness. This double reflection is the basis of nondiscrimination. Both the agency of consciousness and the consciousness in the intellect are unreal appearances.

Book II

(A) *On the Activity of Materiality and Its Distinction from Consciousness*
Introduction (E114; T231)

In the second Book the unchanging character of consciousness and the process of creation from primordial materiality will be discussed.

(II.1) (E114; T234) Materiality makes the world for the sake of removing the frustration that is really a shadow belonging to consciousness, or, that actually consists of itself. Although enjoyment is also a purpose of creation, liberation alone is mentioned in the *sūtra* because it is the principal purpose.

Objection: If creation were for the sake of liberation, then since liberation might take place through creation once for all, there would be no creation again and again.

(II.2) (E114-115; T234-235) *Reply*: Liberation does not take place through creation once for all. It occurs only in the case of one in whom complete dispassion arises.

(II.3) (E115; T235-236) Nonattachment is not established through the mere hearing of the scriptures, but through direct cognition, which, moreover, does not take place suddenly, but through the completion of concentration. There are many obstacles to concentration, and many rebirths are required before concentration, nonattachment, and liberation are realized.

(II.4) (E115; T236) There is another reason for the perpetual flow of creation. There are innumerable consciousnesses to be liberated. The creation has ceased to exist for him who is liberated but not for others. It takes place for their liberation.

(II.5) (E115-116; T237-238) *Objection*: Does consciousness not create?

Reply: Creativity belongs to materiality. The scriptures ascribe creativity to consciousness only by superimposition (*adhyāsa*).

(II.6) (E116; T238-239) *Objection*: According to this view, creation is real. But do the scriptures not declare that creation is like a dream?

Reply: The products of materiality are real because they produce latent dispositions and perform actions. So creation is real. When scriptures declare that creation is like a dream, they mean that its superimposition on consciousness is unreal.

(II.7) (E116-117; T239-240) Materiality does not cause frustration to the one who knows it. It causes frustration only to those who do not know it.

Objection: It is not proper to say that creativity is superimposed on consciousness, for, by reason of its relation to materiality, consciousness is also modified into the intellect, etc.

(II.8) (E117; T240-241) *Reply*: Although there is a relation of consciousness with materiality, creativity does not belong to consciousness immediately. As a piece of iron does not possess the power of burning directly but only in relation with wood, so consciousness does not have creativity directly, but only in relation with materiality.

(II.9) (E117-118; T242) Now passion is proved to be the principal efficient cause of creation by the argument of positive and negative instances; i.e., where there is passion, there is creation, and where there is no passion, there is no creation.

(C) *Space and Time*

(II.12) (E112-113; T245-246) Space and time, which are eternal, are of the nature of *ākāśa* and represent the functioning of the material constituents. Hence, space and time are all-pervasive. Empirical or limited space and time arise from *ākāśa* in terms of its limiting adjuncts.

(E) *Egoity, Sense Capacities, and Action Capacities*

(II.18) (E122-123; T251-252) The eleventh capacity is mind. It is produced from the *sattva* of egoity. The other ten capacities are produced from the *rajas* of egoity, and the five subtle elements are produced from the *tamas* of egoity.

(G) *The Capacities and Their Differentiation from Consciousness* (27-37)

(II.27) (E126; T258-259) As a man becomes a lover in the company of women, an ascetic in the company of ascetics and so on, so the mind assumes different roles in association with the different capacities.

(II.29) (E127-128; T259-261) As a king, though he does not fight, becomes a fighter through the instrumentality of his army, so consciousness, though inactive, becomes a seer, a speaker, a judge, and the like through the instrumentality of its capacities. Through its proximity consciousness motivates the organs just as the lodestone moves a piece of iron.

(II.30-31) (E128-129; T261-262) The functions of intellect, egoity, and mind are reflective discerning, self-awareness, and conceptualization respectively. The five vital airs are the common function of the threefold internal organ. The author does not agree with the Vaiśeṣikas who hold that the functions of the capacities take place only successively.

(II.32) (E130-131; T264-265) The sense capacities are capable of both construction filled (*savikalpaka*) and construction-free (*nirvikalpaka*) apprehension, and those who deny *savikalpaka* apprehension to the series (namely, Vācaspati) are wrong.

(II.33) (E131; T266-267) There are five operations (*vṛtti*) of awareness; knowledge (*pramāṇa*), error (*viparyaya*), conceptual construction (*vikalpa*), deep sleep (*nidrā*), and memory (*smṛti*), and these may be hindering (*kliṣṭa*) or not hindering (*akliṣṭa*). These are described in Patañjali's *Yogasūtra*. The only difference is that Vijñānabhikṣu takes "error" (*viparyaya*) as referring only to the failure to distinguish consciousness from materiality. Other kinds of misapprehension, wherein one takes one thing for another (usually called *anyathākhyāti*), are not to be included since Vijñānabikṣu rejects the notion of *anyathākhyāti* (see below).

(II.34-35) (E131-132; T267-268) On the cessation of these modifications, consciousness becomes quiet and free from all influences and abides in itself. The author quotes the *Yogasūtra* and the *Yogavāsiṣṭha* as documentation and explains the status of consciousness by the analogy of the crystal and the China rose.

Objection: As consciousness is motionless, and there is no God, by whose effort do the capacities come into operation?

(II.35-37) (E132-133; T268-270) *Reply* : As a cow secretes milk for the sake of its calf so the capacities arise for the sake of their Lord, consciousness.

(H) *The Thirteenfold Instrument and Its Overall Functioning*

(II.38-40) (E133-134; T270-272) In all there are thirteen organs: three internal organs, five sense capacities, and five action capacities. The intellect is the principal organ and the rest are secondary. Hence the function of the understanding is distributed among all the secondary capacities. The *sūtra* text here uses the term "*manas*" instead of "buddhi" for the principal organ. Vijñānabhikṣu solves the problem by asserting that *buddhi* is clearly meant and that the term *manas* is not the same as the *manas tattva*.

(II.41-44) (E134-135; T72-274) The intellect is the principal organ, because it pervades all the other capacities, because it is the receptacle for all of the fundamental predispositions, because it is capable of accomplishing inferences using memory, and because we infer its prominence by reason of awareness (*cintā*).

Objection: Is not awareness characteristic of consciousness;

Reply: No. Consciousness is immutable, whereas awareness is an activity.

(II.45-46) (E135-136; T274-276) *Objection*: If the intellect is the principal organ, how was it said before (see Aph. 26) that it is the mind (*manas*) that is both a sense capacity and action capacity?

Reply: The relation of principal and secondary organs is relative because of the difference of functions. In the operation of sight (vision), the mind is principal; in the operation of the mind, the ego is principal; and in the operation of the ego, the intellect is principal. As an axe is purchased for cutting for the man who purchases it, so the operation of a capacity is performed for its master, namely, consciousness. The author here refutes the view of Aniruddha, who holds that action belongs to consciousness as reflected in the intellect.

Book III

(A) *The Specific and the Nonspecific*

(III.2) (E138; T279) From the twenty-three principles, intellect, and so forth, two sorts of body are produced.

(III.3) (E138-139; T279) The twenty-three principles are the seed of the body that transmigrates from one life to another.

(III.4) (E139; T280) Transmigration continues until discrimination arises.

(III.5) (E139; T280-281) Transmigration occurs so that the *jīva* can experience the fruits of its own acts.

(B) *The Gross and Sutble Body*

(III.7) (E140; T282-283) The gross body usually arises from the parents, for there is no mention of a gross body not arising from the parents. The subtle body does not arise from the parents. It arises at the beginning of creation.

(III.8) (E149; T283-284) Satisfactions and frustrations are characteristic of the subtle body and not of the gross body.

(III.9) (E141; T284-286) The subtle body is twofold. In the beginning of creation it is one in the form of an aggregate. Later on, eleven capacities, five subtle elements, and the intellect—these seventeen principles constitute another subtle body. Egoity is here included in intellect and hence it is not separately counted as a factor of the subtle body. Five vital breaths are the functions of the internal organ and so they are also included in the subtle body.[9]

(III.10) (E142; T286-287) Although in the beginning of creation there was one subtle body in the shape of Hiraṇyagarbha, subsequently there becomes a division of it into many other *jīvas*, because of the diversity of actions (*karman*).[10]

(III.11) (E142-143; T287-288) The subtle body is the locus of experience. There is a subtle form of the five gross elements that provides a cover or wrap for the subtle body. Finally, there is also a gross body. Hence three kinds of body are established.[11]

(III.12) (E143-144; T288-290) As a shadow or a picture do not exist without a support, so the subtle body does not exist without its support, that is, the gross body. When a *jīva* gives up its gross body, it takes a substantive body to go to another world. This substantive body is called the eightfold city (*puryaṣṭaka*) because it consists of intellect, ego, mind, and the five subtle elements. The proponents of *māyāvāda* believe that there are five vital breaths in the eightfold city instead of the five subtle elements, but their belief is baseless.

(III.14-15) (E144-145; T291-293) The subtle body is very small, though not an atom, because it has parts.

(III.17-19) (E146; T294-295) Now the gross body is the modification of the intermingling of the five elements. There is another view also according to which it consists of four elements, because in this view *ākāśa* (space) does not enter into the production of anything. A third view describes the gross body as consisting of only one element. In the gross body of human beings there is predominance of earth, so it is said to be composed of earth only. The other elements are just its accessories.

(C) *Gross and Subtle Bodies Not Made up of Consciousness*

(III.20) (E146; T295-296) Since we do not find consciousness in the separate elements, consciousness is not natural to the body but is adventitious.

(E) *Dreaming, Waking, and Yogic Awareness*

(III.26-29) (E149-150; T201-304) As no value is attained from the combination of waking and dream objects, so liberation cannot be attained by the combination of knowledge and action. Action is unreal because it is impermanent and is the product of materiality; whereas consciousness is real because it is permanent and not the effect of materiality.

Objection: Can worship be combined with knowledge?

Reply: No. The object of worship is not completely real, because many categories are superimposed on it.

Objection: Wherein does the unreality of the object of worship consist?

Reply : It consists in that portion of the object meditated on which is imagined by the mind.

Objection: Then what is the result of worship?

Reply: Worship that is meditation makes the mind pure. Pure mind has all the powers of materiality.

(F) *On the Nature of Meditation*

(III.30) (E150-151; T304-305) Meditation is the cause of the removal of the passions of the mind. It involves concentration (*dhāraṇā*), pure, free-flowing awareness (*dhyāna*), and higher or altered states of awareness (*samādhi*).

(III.31) (E151; T305-306) Meditation detaches the mind from all objects other than the object of meditation.

(G) *Misconception, Dysfunction, Contentment, and Attainment*

(III.38-45) A standard account of the 50 "categories" of the intellectual creation is given. The only unique observation of Vijñānabhikṣu has to do with the meaning of the expression "threefold goad" (*aṅkuśa*) in SK 51. Vijñānabhikṣu argues that the "threefold *aṅkuśa*" refers to the first three attainments (*siddhis*) which encourage or attract the seeker to overcome the threefold frustrations.

(I) *Role and Function of Materiality with Respect to Discrimination*

(III.55) (E161; T329-330) *Objection*: Primordial materiality is self-subsistent, and so there should not be a rising of the individual who has absorbed himself into primordial materiality.

Reply: No. Materiality exists for the sake of consciousness. So he who is absorbed in it is again raised up by materiality for the sake of consciousness. The author cites the authority of the *Yogasūtra* in his favor.

(III.56) (E161-162; T330-331) He who is absorbed into materiality rises again for he becomes omniscient and omnipotent, that is, an individual who has attained absorption into materiality in his present birth becomes the omniscient and omnipotent God in his next birth.

(III.57) (E162-163; T332) The existence of God is a settled point. The dispute is, however, over the existence of an eternal God (as the Nyāya system asserts and Sāṃkhya denies).

(J) *Discrimination and Liberation*

(III.63-67) (E164-165; T337-338) When the aim of consciousness has been accomplished by means of nonattachment to all else through discriminative knowledge, materiality ceases to create, just as the labor of a cook ceases when cooking is completed.

Objection: Because materiality ceases to create when discriminative knowledge arises in the case of a single individual, would not all individuals then be liberated?

Reply: No. The creation of materiality ceases only for that individual who has discriminative knowledge and not for all others. (Note here that our author's reading of *sūtra* 64 is different from that of Aniruddha.)

(III.65-66) (E165-166; T339-341) The fruit of materiality's ceasing to act is the neutrality of both materiality and consciousness. It is liberation.

Objection: But then how could materiality engage itself in creation again for the sake of another consciousness?

Reply: Materiality, though ceasing to function for the liberated consciousness, does function for other consciousnesses; just as the snake in the rope-snake analogy does not produce fear in him who is aware of the reality of the rope, but does produce it in him who is ignorant of the reality of the rope. Some pseudo-Vedāntins have failed to understand the significance of the rope-snake analogy and maintained that materiality is an absolute nothing, or something merely imaginary. The analogy is not to be pushed too far. The reality of materiality is not to be denied, and the Vedas and the lawbooks should be understood according to Sāṃkhya philosophy and not the pseudo-Vedānta. (See the summary of Aniruddha's *Sāṁkhya-sūtrā-vṛtti* for the content of Book IV. Vijñānabhikṣu adds nothing new.)

Book V

Introduction: *On the Problem of an Auspicious Utterance*

(V.1) (E190; T388) Vijñānabhikṣu reads "*śruti*" instead of "*bhūti*." Hence the third reason for commencing a treatise with an auspicious utterance is "because it is commanded by scripture (*śruti*)."

(A) *On the Problem of the Existence of God*

(V.12) (E193; T396-397) Vijñānabhikṣu softens the denial of God by referring to his comments in the introduction, in which he argues that Sāṃkhya's denial of God is only a concession to current views and a dogmatic assertion that need not be taken seriously.

(D) *On the Problem of Meritorious Behavior, Qualities, Inference, etc. (in Nyāya-Vaiśeṣika)*

(V.25) (E198; T407) Merit, etc., are the properties of the internal organ.

Objection: What is the locus of merit and demerit at the time of the dissolution of the world, because then there is no internal organ?

Reply: The internal organ is not completely destroyed. It is causal as well as effectual. The causal internal organ dwells in primordial materiality and in it dwell merit, demerit, and other properties, even at the time of the dissolution of the world.

(V.26) (E198; T408-409) *Objection*: The existence of merit, etc., cannot be established by scripture and the inference based on the diversity of the products of materiality, because scripture asserts that materiality does not exist at all.

Reply: No. Scripture does not deny the existence of the constituents of materiality and its products like the intellect, etc. It only says that there is no intermixture of them with consciousness.

(V.27) (E198-199; T409-411) Although the *sūtra* mentions only satisfaction as an exemplification of inference, other aspects of materiality can also be established by inference. He gives a five-membered argument that consists of proposition, reason, example, application, and conclusion. The argument is this: (1) satisfaction exists, (2) because it produces a cognitive awareness that leads to action, (3) whatever produces cognitive awareness that leads to action exists—like the intellect, (4) satisfaction produces cognition leading to action as, for example, when one's hair stands on end because of an exhilarating experience, (5) therefore, it exists.

(F) *On the Problem of Knowledge and Error*

(V.51) (E206; T432-433) The validity of the Vedas is established intrinsically by the manifestation of their own natural power—like that of invocations and medical prescriptions. Because Vijñānabhikṣu limits his comment here only to the Vedas, he is construing this *sūtra* with the preceding rather than the following discussion. (No summary is provided of Book VI, because it simply repeats Aniruddha's *Vṛtti*.)

SĀṂKHYASĀRA

(*Summary by Ram Shankar Bhattacarya*)

This text presents a short overview of the Sāṃkhya system and was composed by Vijñānabhikṣu toward the end of his life. It has two sections, the first (called *pūrvabhāga*) containing three short prose chapters and the second (called *uttarabhāga*) containing seven chapters in verse.

The edition (E) for the following summary is that by Ram Shankar Bhattacharya (Varanasi: Bharatiya Vidya Prakasana, 1965).

(T) references are to the partial translation by Megumu Honda, which appears in *Indogaku Bukkyogaku Kenkyu* (*Journal of Indian and Buddhist Studies*), volume 19.1, 1970, 489-477 and volume 20.1, 1971, 488-474. The translation covers the first section only. References preceded by "Tl" refer to pages in the 1970 issue, "T2" to those in the 1971 issue.

Section I, Chapter I

(El; Tl.489) In these introductory verses the author pays obeisance to the self-born Viṣṇu, who is known as the *mahattattva*, and indicates that this little text is designed to give a brief overview of the author's larger work.

(El-2; Tl.489-487) It has been declared in *śruti* and *smṛti* that liberation (or the absolute cessation of the three kinds of frustration) is attained at the end of such actions as have already begun to bear fruit (*prārabdha*), owing to the absence of rebirth as a result of the annihilation of the fruits of action (*vipāka*). This cessation is caused by the eradication of the cooperating causes (ignorance, etc.) of the previous (i.e., stored) actions which (eradication) comes into existence in the absence of passion, aversion, etc., which are the effects of the erroneous notion that properties like agenthood, etc., really belong to the self. This erroneous thinking ceases when the difference between the self and the not-self is directly realized. Some scriptural passages are quoted to uphold this view.

(E2-3; Tl.487-485) Passion cooperates with actions in producing birth, span of life, and the experience of satisfaction and frustration. Although the five afflictions (*kleśas*), namely, ignorance, etc., are said to cooperate with action in producing birth, etc., yet passion is to be regarded as the chief cause. This character of passion is proved by its being the source of aversion and fear, and also by its mention in *Yogasūtra* II.3. It is said that knowledge not only nullifies actions but also eradicates them.

In fact, actions cease to produce their results when ignorance is destroyed by knowledge. Discriminative knowledge is the cause of the cessation of the afflictions. When, on account of the realization of discrimination the afflictions cease, the highest end (*paramapuruṣārtha*), i.e., the absolute negation of all kinds of frustration, is attained.

Chapter 2

(E3-4; Tl. 485-484) Ordinary perception shows that the self (*ātman*) is the experiencer of satisfaction and frustration, and the not-self comprises all inanimate objects, namely, materiality and the like. Self is immutable, indestructible, and without any attachment, wherea the not-self is mutable and capable of being forsaken. Materiality can be eschewed with the help of the knowledge of the fundamental principles. This knowledge consists in recognizing the difference between animate (*cetana*) and the inanimate (*acetana*) entities, beginning with the unmanifest materiality and ending with the five gross elements.

(E4; Tl.484-482) To recognize the difference between the self and the not-self is said to be the means to liberation.

Objection: How can discriminative knowledge of the difference between the self and the not-self eradicate ignorance, which is defined as the knowledge of the self in the not-self?

Reply: Discrimination can annihilate ignorance in an indirect way. Discrimination (in which the chief qualifier is the not-self) naturally gives rise to the knowledge that the not-self is different from the self, and, being opposite to ignorance (i.e., the recognition of the not-self as the self,) it is capable to eradicating *avidyā*.

The construction-free (*nirvikalpaka*) knowledge of the self derived through *yoga* is the indirect means (i.e., through discriminative knowledge) to liberation. Because from ignorance comes the knowledge that the self really possesses the qualities of the body and mind, it follows that the knowledge that the self is devoid of these qualities is capable of uprooting ignorance.

(E4-5; T1.482) The realization of the pure self through *yoga* shows that the self is devoid of properties like satisfaction, etc., which belong to the limiting adjuncts. This realization is the cause of the cessation of ignorance, etc.

The feeling of equality and the feeling that the self is all are to be taken as the helping factor or the means (*śeṣabhūta*, i.e., serving the purpose of another) to discriminative knowledge. According to the Brahmamīmāṃsā the true knowledge of the supreme self is the means to liberation, while according to Sāṃkhya the true knowledge that the self is different from the not-selves is the means.

(E5; T1.482-481) *Objection*: Discriminative knowledge cannot annihilate ignorance but can only obstruct it.

Reply: This contention is wrong, for the simple reason that mistaken perceptions are caused by some fault (*doṣa*) residing either in the objects or in the organ. Such faults are completely eradicated before the acquisition of the discriminative knowledge, and this is why there is no possibility of the rise of misconception in a person who has achieved discriminative knowledge.

(E5-7; T1.480-477) As the illuminator (e.g., light) is different from the illuminated (e.g., a jar), so the illuminator and perceiver self is different from the intellect, which is directly illuminated by it and also from the objects illuminated by the operations of awareness (*cittavṛtti*). It is to be noted that the self is not directly illuminated by the self; it, however, becomes its own object through the operations of awareness. As the operations are always known to their illuminator it is proved that the illuminator self is all-pervading, immutable, eternal, and of the nature of pure consciousness.

Because the intellect and the self are proved to be illuminated (perceived) and illuminator (perceiver) respectively, it follows that the self has attributes like all-pervasiveness, eternality, etc. The knowledge of the difference of the *sattva* (i.e., the intellect) and self (i.e., consciousness) has been regarded as the cause of liberation in Yoga philosophy. From the knowledge that self is different from the intellect it can be deduced that it is different from primordial materiality (the generative cause of the intellect, etc.), which is not perceived directly. The discriminative knowledge of the perceiver and the perceived has been declared to be the cause of the cessation of ignorance.

(EI.2; T1.477) The different forms of discriminative knowledge (viz., that the self is neither the body, nor the organs, and so on) are to be regarded as different aspects of the general discriminative knowledge (that the self is different from the not-self).

Chapter 3

(E7-8; T2.488-486) The entities from which consciousnesses are to be distinguished are 24 in number, namely, primordial materiality, intellect, egoity, five subtle elements, eleven capacities, and five gross elements. The entities like quality, universal property, etc., as accepted in other systems are included in these. Primordial materiality is the direct or indirect material (or generative) cause of all modifications. It consists of three constituents—*sattva*, *rajas*, and *tamas*—existing either in the state of equilibrium or in the state of unequal balance. In the state of equilibrium primordial materiality does not produce any effect (or more precisely, does not assume the form of any object). It must not be supposed to be a distinct entity possessing the constituents but, rather, an aggregate of the constituents. The three constituents may also be viewed as assuming the character of being an effect. Thus we get three more entities (i.e., the three "effect constituents"), and by adding them with the traditional twenty-five fundamental principles, we get an enumeration of twenty-eight principles—a view accepted by some ancient teachers. The words "*sattva*," etc., are found to be used in the Upaniṣads to refer to the state of disequilibrium. *Sattva*, etc., are to be known as substance (*dravya*), because they have no locus (*āśraya*) and because they possess modifications. These are called "*guṇa*", because they tie the selves ("*guṇa*" meaning a rope or a strand) and also because they are the accessories (*upakaraṇa*) of the self ("*guṇa*" usually meaning a subordinate part or a secondary object).

(E8-9; T2.486-484) Although the three constituents are the causes of satisfaction, frustration, and confusion respectively, yet they are figuratively stated to be identical with satisfaction, etc. Although *sattva* has more attributes than satisfaction, yet it is called one whose essence is satisfaction (*sukhātmaka*) on account of the predominance of satisfaction. Similar reasoning is to be applied with *rajas* and *tamas* in connection with their attributes, namely, frustration and confusion. These three attributes are the distinguishing characteristics of the three constituents. As *sattva* means the state of being *sat* (good, high, righteous, etc.), it is the highest accessory of consciousness (i.e., the *sattva-guṇa* is the best means of achieving the highest goal). As *rajas* signifies passion, it is the middling accessory. *Tamas*, being of veiling nature, is the lowest accessory. Each of these constituents has innumerable individualities (*vyakti*, i.e., self-existent, manifested entities), as is stated in *Sāṃkhyasūtra* 1.128, which clearly points to the plurality of each constituent. The innumerable manifoldness of the effects could not have been explained if the constituents were three entities only, for in this view the constituents, being all-pervasive, would be unable to produce innumerable manifoldness (*vaicitrya*). The varieties of the conjunction of the three constituents cannot be conceived as capable of producing innumerable manifoldness without the help of some determinant entity (*avacchedakībhūta dravyāntara*). As there is no such entity, each constituent must be regarded as having innumerable individuals. Each constituent is either of atomic or all-pervading magnitude as all their effects are either of limited or of unlimited magnitude. This two fold division of magnitude of the constituents is in accordance with the ever mutating nature of the *rajas guṇa*

(E9-10; T2.484-482) It is wrong to hold materiality to be identical with the atoms (of the Vaiśeṣika school), for materiality in its unmanifested form is devoid of the qualities like sound, touch, etc., whereas atoms possess such qualities. The existence of atomic qualities cannot properly be inferred in the primal cause, materiality.

Objection: Because materiality is an assemblage of innumerable individuals of atomic and all-pervading magnitude, it cannot be unlimited (*aparicchinna*), one, and devoid of activity.

Reply: "*Aparicchinna*" simply means being a causal substance (*kāraṇadravya*). Primordial materiality must be regarded as all-pervasive, for the evolving cause of *ākāśa* and the like must be all-pervasive. Because there is no difference of primordial materiality either in different creations or in its association with consciousness, it is one. "Being devoid of activity" must be taken to mean being bereft of reflective discerning, etc., and not having the sense of "inactive." Otherwise the phenomenon known as the agitation (*kṣobha*) of materiality as stated in scripture would be inexplicable. Since effects like intellect, etc., consist in satisfaction, frustration, and confusion, they must be inferred as originating from a cause of similar nature. As inference proves the thing inferred in a very general way, the particularities of primordial materiality are to be known from the *śāstras* or from yogic power. As to how the existence of satisfyingness, etc., in the external objects can be proved, it is to be noted that, because the internal organ is the cause of satisfaction, etc., they are proved to be existing in the external objects.

(E10-11; T2.482-480) The principle called "*buddhi*" (the intellect that underlies all forms of awareness), is produced from primordial materiality. It is called "*mahat*" (great), as it possesses merit, etc., which are its distinguishing characteristics. It pervades all. It has three aspects based on the three constituents, being the adjuncts of the three deities Brahmā, Viṣṇu, and Śiva. Sometimes it is regarded as identical with these deities. Although some scriptural statements say that the intellect itself is the same as the power of becoming small and other supernormal attainments, yet these are to be regarded as the attributes of the intellect. Sometimes the intellect is stated to be Viṣṇu himself because of the predominance of this deity. The intellect, being modified by the *rajas* and *tamas* constituents, is turned into a limited form characterized by demerit, etc. Its chief and distinguishing function is reflective discerning. It is the seed state of the internal organ. The producing of intellect by primordial materiality and of egoity by intellect is borne out by scripture alone. Inference cannot ascertain the order of the generated principles precisely.

(E11-12; T2.480-479) As a branch of a tree comes out from a sprout, so the ego comes out from the intellect. Its function as well as its distinguishing characteristic is self-awareness (*abhimāna*). Egoity has three aspects, characterized by the predominance of *sattva* (called *vaikārika*), of *rajas* (called *taijasa*), and of *tamas* (called *bhūtādi*). *Taijasa* is said to be the cause of capacities; *vaikārika*, of eleven gods; and *bhūtādi*, of the gross and the subtle elements.

(E12; T2.479-478) Egoity produces the mind before producing the external capacities, as they are said to be caused by the operations of awareness. Egoity, by its power of intentionality (*saṃkalpa*), produces both the ten capacities and the five subtle elements.

(E13; T2.478-476) The subtle body (*liṅgaśarīra*) consists of seventeen parts: the intellect (with egoity included in it). five subtle elements, and eleven organs. It is the place of the manifestation of the self. It comes into existence at the beginning of creation and lasts till the end of dissolution. The five vital breaths, being included in the functions of the intellect, are not separately mentioned. Five gross elements constitute the seat of the subtle body. Without this seat a subtle body is unable to move from one region to another. The subtle body is the adjunct of Svayambhū (the "self-born," viz., Hiraṇyagarbha, the creator). From this original subtle body proceed the subtle bodies of other individual selves.

(E13-14; T2.476-475) The gross body is the product of earth, which is covered by water, light, air, *ākāśa*, egoity, and intellect, one after another, each following having a ten times bigger magnitude in comparison to each preceding. The earth is transformed into the egg-shaped universe in which exists the gross body of Svayambhū consisting of fourteen regions. This first embodied Being is called Brahmā or Nārāyaṇa in authoritative texts. The Being is also called "one *ātman*" in scripture, as it is the source of origination and dissolution of individual beings (*vyaṣṭipuruṣa*). This Being creates Brahmā and makes him create other beings ending with the vegetable world.

(E14-16; T2.474) The twenty-four principles are constantly undergoing transformation. This is why all inanimate entities are called nonexistent from the transcendental standpoint. It is the absolutely real self that is to be realized for the eradication of frustration. One transcends the cycle of birth and death by correctly knowing the tree of *brahman* (consisting of the evolutes of primordial materiality with actions and results) but by cutting it with the sword of knowledge and by thereby attaining imperishableness (i.e., brahmanhood).

SECTION II, CHAPTER 1

(E17-19) The self (*ātman*) called "*puruṣa*" is to be known as distinct from primordial materiality and its evolutes. The experience "I know" proves the existence of the self in a very general way (i.e., it does not refer to the self as an absolute and immutable entity). As the intellect and other evolutes exist for the sake of the self, the enjoyer, being originated by the action of the self, the intellect is to be regarded as beginningless. Again, the beginninglessness of the intellect proves the beginninglessness of its enjoyer, the self. The beginningless relation of property and proprietor between the intellect and consciousness shows that the self, the enjoyer, is eternal. As the intellect contains the operations and latent dispositions enjoyed by consciousness, it is called a property (*sva*) of consciousness. The quality of being the proprietor (*svāmya*) is consciousness' illuminating the operation that give rise to latent impressions. When the intellect is free from these operations and dispositions of the self, it is eternal.

As the self is eternal, its illuminating power is not caused. Although the self is nothing but consciousness, yet it is regarded as a substance because of its similarity with substance. That is why the experience that "I am the locus or substratum of knowledge" is also accepted as valid. Being deluded by the beginningless erroneous awareness, an individual self considers himself to be identical with the body. Because of the self's association with the body it appears to possess knowledge.

Although knowledge is eternal, yet it seems to be noneternal because of its association with objects. Therefore it is perfectly reasonable to conclude that the eternal self is nothing but consciousness (*cit*). The apprehension of objects means the projecting of the reflections of objects on the self. It is the operations of awareness that cast their reflection on the self. An object is apprehended by the self through these operations.

As desire and the like are produced by operations of awareness, they exist not in the self but in the intellect. Thus it follows that all selves are immutable (*sama*), changelessly permanent. The self is pure, self-luminous, and eternally liberated.

It may be held that the self, like the *ākāśa*, is one in number. Someone's being satisfied and other's being frustrated cannot disprove the unity of self, because satisfaction and other qualities reside in the intellect. Because experiencing and absence of experiencing cannot be ascribed to one and the same person simultaneously it is justified to hold that the selves are innumerable.

Section II, Chapter 2

(E19-22) The nature of both self and not-self is to be known in order to comprehend their difference. The phenomenon of this mundane existence appears and disappears because of its proximity with the self. The self is said to be the material cause (*upādāna*) of this world because it is the abode (*ādhāra*) of all. The self is *paramārthasat* (a really existent entity) because it does not exist for others and because its existence is proved by one's own experience (i.e., it is self-luminous). As it is self-existent it is called "*sat*."

Materiality and all inanimate objects change constantly. This is why they are called "not self existent" (*asat*). Because an actual entity (*vastu*) is defined as an entity that undergoes no change, materiality and its evolutes must be regarded as nonactual (*avastu*). Moreover, because the existence of materiality depends upon another, and because it comes to be known being illuminated by another, materiality is called "not self-existent" (*asat*).

Consciousness is the essence of this world. It is the constant part, (*sthira aṃśa*) within mundane existence.

As the world is constantly changing it is wrong to hold it to be permanent. It exists only as transitory form. The self is true, all-pervading, calm, of inconceivable nature, pure awareness alone, taintless, and omnipotent. It apparently seems to assume the forms of the intellect. The world appears and disappears in the self like a mirage in the desert. The illusory world proceeds from the mind. The world is called "mind-made" (*manomaya*), as it is created by the creator by his mind. It appears to be existent to a deluded person who is ignorant of the self. As a man ignorant of gold cannot understand a bracelet as nothing but a piece of gold, so an unwise person cannot perceive the true nature of the world.

These statements show that the world is not absolutely nonexistent. Some other statements, however, show that existence has been ascribed to the evolutes of materiality. The world, being bereft of name and form, exists in materiality (also called "*māyā*" or "*aṇu*" by some teachers). In the self the world exists in a potential state.

Section II, Chapter 3

(E22-23) The difference of the self from the operations (*vṛtti*) of the intellect is now to be discussed. Illumination, because it is related to objects capable of being illuminated, becomes illuminator. The self becomes the seat of qualified knowledge when it is associated with cognizable objects. The connection of the self with the cognizable objects is not as real as its connection with the intellect. The reflection of images of the objects on the self occurs either directly or indirectly (i.e., through the operations).

In the absence of operations of the intellect the self remains in an unmanifest state. The operations of the intellect have forms similar to those of their objects. They are limited or conditioned and of momentary existence. These are inanimate, as they are illuminated by another entity (viz, the self). They are expressive of the objects, as they are capable of assuming the forms of all objects. It is the self that is the seer absolute. Objects coming in touch with the intellect are reflected in it. This reflection is seen by the self (and not by the intellect).

The difference of the self from the intellect, the body, etc., is well known. As there arises mutual reflection between the intellect and consciousness, the operations of the intellect look like consciousness. It is most difficult to distinguish pure consciousness from ordinary awareness. Some Bauddhas, not knowing this distinction, consider momentary awareness to be the same as the self of the Upaniṣads.

As an illuminator is always regarded as different from the things illuminated, the illuminator self must be different from the operations of awareness. Thus is shown the difference between the illuminatingness of the intellect and the illuminatingness of consciousness.

By the examples of dream, etc., as given in the Upaniṣads, it is proved that consciousness is different from the body, organs, and the like. While in the dream state the body, etc., is reflected in consciousness, in the waking state the external things also reflect in it. Because the dream contents are mental, they are the direct objects of consciousness. In the waking state the external things are the objects through the organs. In both these states all things are, however, equally illuminated by consciousness. In the dream state, cognition arises from latent dispositions (*vāsanā*), whereas in the waking state it arises from the instruments of knowledge. Dream cognition is to be regarded as the best example for understanding the self-vision. In the sleeping state the self abides in itself. The other two states are illusory, for in them the self is falsely identified with the intellect. The sleep of the intellect is its covering (*āvaraṇa*) by the *tamas* constituent. The sleeping state of the self is the state that is devoid of all operations of the intellect.

The changelessly eternal self illuminates the intellect only. Because the operations (which are objects to be seen) do not exist always, the self cannot be regarded as a perpetual seer. The self is (falsely) seen to assume the forms of the operations. The ignorant think that the self really undergoes change. It is the intellect residing in the body that is cause of all frustration. If the intellect is not properly distinguished through the help of discrimination, there is no hope for liberation. The mere renunciation of external things is no means to it. All selves, being nothing but consciousness, are alike. Because of its superimposition of agency on the attributeless self, the intellect falls into bondage.

Section II Chapter 4

(E26-28) The blissful nature of the self is now to be discussed. Real satisfaction is the absence of frustration as well as (worldly) satisfactions. As the nature of the self consists in the absence of frustration, it is called "satisfaction" (*sukha*). That the word "*sukha*" means absence of frustration is to be accepted. Consciousness is secondarily said to be identical with satisfaction in order to show that it is the dearest of all.

Love for a thing is always dependent on the self, but love for the self has no reference to any other thing. Incomparable satisfaction arising from the perception of the self is enjoyed by the liberated-while-living. Internal satisfaction concerning the self, which is enjoyed by the Yogins, is unattainable by persons desirous of external satisfactions.

Section II Chapter 5

(E28-32) Now the dissimilarity (*vaidharmya*) of the self and the not-self is to be discussed. Satisfaction and the like, being the effect of the operations of the intellect, are to be regarded as the attributes of the intellect. Because the effect and its cause belong to the same class (*sājātya*), primordial materiality, the material cause of the intellect, etc., is to be accepted as inanimate, devoid of consciousness. The self is nothing but consciousness. It is attributeless and changelessly permanent. All generated products belong to materiality. Because of contact with the objects there arises an influence (*uparāga*) in the intellect, which may be called "*lepa*" ("stain" or "defilement"). The connection causing *lepa* is to be known as *saṅga* (attachment). The self is bereft of all attachment or stain.

Because pure consciousness is the impelling factor (*preraka*) of the world, it is called "God." The whole inanimate world acts for its lord. The organs in the body deposit all enjoyable objects in the mind, which in turn present them to the intellect. Objects placed in the intellect are enjoyed by the witness self, which is the lord of the intellect. The self, being the supreme controller, is called "God" (*parameśvara*).

The self in the absolute state is called *paramātman*. It is called "individual self" (*jīva*) when associated with the internal organ. As the pervader with reference to the pervaded is called "*brahman*," primordial materiality and its generated products are called "*brahman*." Others, however, do not accept this view and state that consciousness is to be regarded as *brahman* because of its controllership (*adhyakṣatva*) and all-pervasiveness (*vyāpakatva*).

The self, which is the absolute seer and immutable consciousness, does not require any illuminator and is called self-luminous (*svapra-*

kāśa). Experience exists not in the self but in the intellect. The reflection of the operations of the intellect may be said to exist secondarily in the self, which, being the seer of the intellect, is known to be the witness of it. The quality of being a witness (*sākṣin*) is, however, not permanent or everlasting, because the influence caused by the noneternal objects is itself noneternal.

Because there is no dissimilarity among selves, the self is called immutable (*sama*).

Although the self in reality is bereft of association, yet it is called the lord and knower of all because it possesses the power of illuminating all. The self is called "nondual" (*advaita*) as all selves belong to the same class (i.e., they possess absolute similarity).

Section II, Chapter 6

(E32-37) Now the discussion on Rājayoga. One should take up Haṭhayoga, if one is unable to practice Rājayoga as has been advised by Vāsiṣtha and others. In Rājayoga the place of *jñāna* is predominant; in Hathayoga *prāṇāyama* and *āsana* (yogic posture) are the chief means.

(The remaining sections present a standard explanation of yogic praxis.)

Section II, Chapter 7

(E38-40) The characteristics of the liberated-while-living are now to be discussed.

One who perceives everything in the self transcends frustration and confusion. Spiritual insight (*prajñā*) becomes steady or firmly footed in him who neither rejoices nor hates. A wise man never fails to remember the existence of the transcending self. One liberated-while-living possesses an even and unshaken mind, and acts without any attachment. He is devoid of passion and aversion and has no attraction to the nonself. As all things are the transformations of the power of the self, he is not deluded by them. Even acting like an ordinary man he experiences the bliss of the self. He is introspective (*antarmukha*, i.e., having the group of organs turned away from the sense objects and directed toward the inner self). He, being free from duties, attains liberation. He is the same in honor and dishonor. In him lust, greed, anger, etc., have dwindled and erroneous awareness has come to an end forever. By crossing the cycle of birth and death he abides in the fourth (i.e., the liberated) state (the other three states being waking, dreaming, and dreamless sleep).

Liberation is manifested as soon as the mind is destroyed, owing to the dwindling of latent dispositions. One acquiring the state of liberation-while-living naturally attains the state called bodiless liberation (*adehamukti*, i.e., liberation acquired after death). When on account of the cessation of the reflections of objects the self becomes absolutely devoid of the operations of the intellect, then isolation becomes manifested. At that time the self abides in itself. The self is devoid of objects, decay, and death; it is eternal; it is neither void, nor seen, nor the act of seeking; it is *anākhya* (one that has no name or appellation).

YOGAVĀRTTIKA
YOGASĀRASAṂGRAHA

These two Yoga works of Vijñanabhikṣu parallel the two Sāṃkhya texts summarized above. The *Yogavārttika* is a complete explication of Patañjali's *Yogasūtra* and Vyāsa's *Yogasūtrabhāṣya*. The *Yogasārasaṃgraha* is a summary overview of Yoga philosophy and is evidently the last work that Vijñānabhiksu composed in his lifetime.

BHĀVĀGAṆEŚA

Bhāvāgaṇeśa or Gaṇeśa Dīkṣita was a direct disciple of Vijñānabhikṣu and can be dated, therefore, along with Vijñānabhikṣu in the latter half of the sixteenth century. His *Tīkā* on the *Tattvasamāsasūtra*, entitled *Tattvayāthārthyadīpana* ("Illuminating the Complete Meaning of the Truth"), is probably the oldest commentary on the *Tattvasamāsa* after *Kramadīpikā*.

The edition (E) used for the summary is that found in V.P. Dvivedi, editor *Sāṃkhyasangraha* (Varanasi: Chowkhamba Sanskrit Series, Work No. 50, pp. 50-92).

TATTVAYĀTHĀRTHYADĪPANA

(*Summary by Kapil Deo Pandey*)

It should be noted, first, that Bhāvāgaṇeśa reads the *sūtras* in a slightly different order than *Kramadīpikā*. *Sūtra* 7, "*adhyātmam adhibhūtam adhidaivataṃ ca*," is broken up into three separate parts (thus becoming 7, 8, and 9). *Sūtra* 19, "*trividho dhātusargaḥ*," is eliminated, and the concluding statement in the *Kramadīpikā* listing, namely, "He who has properly understood." etc., is counted as a separate *sūtra*, which is not the case in *Kramadīpikā*. Bhāvāganeśa, then, reads a total of 25 *sūtras* beginning with "eight generative principles" (*sūtra* 1) and ending with "he who has properly understood."... (*sūtra* 25). (See above entry under *Tattvasamāsasūtra* for a comparison with the *Kramadīpikā* ordering.)

(E50) The commentator opens his work with three verses of invocation, in the first of which he glorifies consciousness and materiality. In the second verse, he invokes Kapila, Āsuri, Pañcaśikha, and his teacher Vijñānabhikṣu. In the third, he proposes to write the commentary, depending on the *Samāsasūtras* and the gloss by Pañcaśikha.[1]

(1) (E50-54) The commentary starts with the etymology of "*prakṛti*" and a general definition of the eight generative principles (*prakṛti*) namely, the unmanifest, intellect, egoity, and the five subtle elements.

In defining the unmanifest, the term "*guṇa*" is used twice and in two senses: one as used in the Nyāya system and the other as used in the Sāṃkhya system. Including these three constituents, the number of principles becomes twenty-eight. Although they are substances, yet they are called "*guṇa*" on account of their being the accessories of consciousness. Limitedness, oneness, etc., of materiality (as accepted by Sāṃkhya) have been established by reason, and some contradictory arguments have been refuted with the remark that the Sāṃkhya views are in accordance with *śruti* and *smṛti*.

(E54-57) After a description of primordial materiality, intellect is defined in three ways. "*Manas*," "*mati*," "*mahat*," etc., as synonyms of the intellect, are enumerated and verses from the *Mahābhārata* are quoted to confirm the view. Intellect, because it possesses *rajas* and *tamas*, is said to be limited in size in the individual self. It is the adjunct of the creator. The same is called "*sūtrātman*," "*prajñā*," and "*īśvara*" in different states. In *Viṣṇupurāṇa*, its three types—*sāttvika*, *rājasa*, and *tāmasa*—have been described. Those who think of materiality as self attain the innate (*prākṛtika*) from of bondage and those who think of intellect, etc., as self attain the acquired (*vaikṛtika*) from of bondage.

(3) (E60-62) The essential nature of pure consciousness is described. By the knowledge of the twenty-five principles one becomes liberated and a verse ascribed to Pañcaśikha (possibly derived from *Kramadīpikā*) has been quoted to this effect. The multiplicity of consciousness is established on the evidence of *Sāṃkhyapravacanasūtra* 1.149, and it is remarked that if there were only one consciousness the whole universe would have been delighted or distressed with the delight or distress of one. All the Sāṃkhya preceptors (Kapila, Āsuri, Pañcaśikha, Patañjali, and others) and the followers of Nyāya-Vaiśeṣika systems propounded the plurality of consciousnesses. Others, such as the preceptors of the Upaniṣads, argue for the oneness of consciousness.

(5-6) (E63-71) These two *sūtras* are interpreted to justify mainly the Vedic sentences on *saguṇa* and *nirguṇa ātman*. At the beginning of creation, the primordial materiality is disturbed by itself and a contact with *nārāyaṇa* consciousness takes place. As a result of this contact, the intellect (*mahat*), made up of three material constituents, is manifested. When the intellect is produced, consciousness is manifested in it. Manifestation is sometimes called an effect.

The subtle body consists of the five subtle elements, ten organs, the mind, and the intellect (egoity is included in the intellect). The intellect, etc., cannot subsist without a subtle body. The distinction of individuals is proved by their distinct actions. *Manusmṛti* (1.16) is quoted to justify this view.

It is remarked that a thing is dissolved into another thing from which it has emerged. Transformations of the form of creation, preservation, and dissolution are gross and occur for the purpose of the discrimination of the immutable consciousness. Consciousness unchangeable and pure, is to be discriminated from materiality, etc. *Chāndogya Upaniṣad* 6.2.1. is quoted.

(7-9) (E71-73) "Pertaining to the internal" is the group of thirteen organs; "pertaining to the external," the group of objects; and "pertaining to the celestial," the group of governing deities of the organs.

(10) (E73) *Śvetāśvatara Upaniṣad* 1.5 is quoted as the source of *sūtras* 10-14. The five functions (*abhibuddhi*) are said to be as follows: intellectual functioning (*abhibuddhi*), self-awareness (*abhimāna*), desire (*icchā*), the functioning of the sense capacities (*kartavyatā*), and the functioning of the action capacities (*kriyā*). Intellectual functioning, self-awareness, and desire refer respectively to intellect, egoity, and mind. Identification and action are the functions of the sense capacities and action capacities respectively.

(11) (E73-74) The five sources of action, namely, perseverence, faith, satisfaction, the desire not to know, and the desire to know are explained. Four out of these lead to bondage, but the last is helpful in attaining liberation. Four verses, quoted in relation to this point, are found in the *Yuktidīpikā* (under SK 29, p. 108).

(12) (E74-75) Five vital breaths—*prāṇa*, *apāna*, *samāna*, *udāna*, and *vyāna*—with their respective seats and function are described as in *Kramadīpikā*. According to some exponents of Sāṃkhya, there are five more vital breaths known as *nāga*, *kūrma*, *kṛkala*, *devadatta*, and *dhanañjaya*.

(13) (E75) Five agents, namely, *vaikārika*, *taijasa*, *bhūtādi*, *sānumāna*, and *niranumāna* are defined as in *Kramadīpikā*.

(18) (E80) After propounding fifty components of the *sarga* (intellectual creation), a standard enumeration of the ten fundamental topics is given to show the appropriateness of the name "*Ṣaṣṭitantra*" for Sāṃkhya.

(19) (E80-81) The creation from the five subtle elements (as material cause) is called the supporting creation (*anugraha*). The creation of exalted beings in order to show favor or kindness to the devotees is also termed "supporting."

(20) (E81) There are fourteen types of gross or elemental creation. Out of these, eight are celestial, five are subhuman, and one is human.

(21-23) (E81-86) Bondage is threefold: innate (*prākṛtika*), acquired (*vaikṛtika*), and personal (*dākṣiṇa*). These are explained by quoting a verse ascribed to Pañcaśikha (and also found in the *Kramadīpikā*). Three types of liberation are discussed. The highest form of liberation is defined as the complete cessation of the three types of frustration, and *Nyāyasūtra* 1.1.2 is quoted.

It is remarked that as the objects of knowledge (*prameya*) cannot be established without the help of the instruments of knowledge; three instruments of knowledge—perception, inference, and reliable authority—are accepted (see *sūtra* 23).

(25) (E87-92) By following the order of these principles, one overcomes the threefold frustration. Extensive quotations from older popular texts (*Purāṇa*) are given.

In three benedictory verses, the commentator dedicates his work to competent persons and aspires for the favor of Hari (Śrī Kṛṣṇa) for the act of dedication.

MAHĀDEVA VEDĀNTIN

This commentator, also known as Mahādeva Sarasvatī or Vedāntin Mahādeva, lived in the latter part of the seventeenth century, according to Keith and others.[1] He was a disciple of Svayaṃprakāśa Tīrtha, according to a citation by F. E. Hall.[2] Although his commentary, entitled *Sāṃkhyasūtravṛttisāra,* purports to be based on Aniruddha, Garbe discovered that almost all of the first two books have been lifted from the *Sāṃkhyapravacanabhāṣya* of Vijñānabhikṣu.[3] The remainder is a paraphrase of Aniruddha. Garbe included a few extracts from Mahādeva Vedāntin's commentary in his critical edition of Aniruddha's *Sāṃkhyasūtravṛtti,* but there is nothing of importance in this that has not already been stated by Aniruddha or Vijñānabhikṣu from a philosophical point of view. Hence, a summary of these extracts need not be given.

SVAYAMPRAKĀŚAYATI

This author, also known as Svayaṃprakāśa Muni or Yatīndra, is listed in *A Descriptive Catalogue of Sanskrit Manuscripts* in the Adyar Library, IX, as having lived in the latter part of the seventeenth century and as having composed a number of works on Vedānta. He also wrote, evidently, a fifty-verse booklet on the functioning of the *guṇas*, entitled *Guṇatrayaviveka*. The author appears to have been a devotee of Rāma and to have been a pupil of Vāsudevendrayati

The following summary of the booklet is based on its publication by V. Krishnamacharya in the Adyar Library Bulletin 24 (1960): 175-181.

GUṆATRAYAVIVEKA

(*Summary by Ram Shankar Bhattacharya*)

The author has divided the transformations of the three constituents into three groups, the first giving rise to the second, and the second giving rise to the third, thus making a total of 39 kinds of transformations, each associated with a particular group of sentient beings. To be explicit: originally, there is a threefold transformation (based on the predominance of each of the three constituents), namely, *tāmasa*, *rājasa*, and *sāttvika*. (It should be noted here that the constituents, though distinct from one another, are incapable of being disjoined and remain combined producing transformations.) The *sthāvaras* (herbs, trees, plants, and the like, which are the immovable beings) come under the *tāmasa* transformation; the *jaṅgamas* (i.e., the living beings that can move) come under the *rājasa* transformation; the divinities such as Brahmā and others come under the *sāttvika* transformation.

The *tāmasa* transformation is again divided into three subdivisions according to the predominance of *tamas* (inertia constituent), *rajas* (activity constituent), and *sattva* (intelligibility constituent). The three subdivisions of the *sthāvaras*, comprising (1) soil, etc., (2) tree, etc., and (3) corn etc., come respectively under these three *tāmasa* transformations.

Similarly the *rājasa* transformation is again divided into three subdivisions according to the predominance of the inertia, activity, and intelligibility constituents. The three subdivisions of the moving beings, comprising (1) beings born of sweat, etc., (2) lion, etc., and (3) the Brahmins and other human beings, come under these three *rājasa* transformations respectively.

Similarly, the *sāttvika* transformation is divided into three subdivisions according to the predominance of *tamas*, *rajas*, and *sattva*. The subdivisions of the group comprising Brahmā and other gods, namely (1) the group of the Yakṣas and others, (2) the group of Devarṣis and others, and (3) the group of Virāj and others come under these three *sāttvika* transformations respectively.

The three *tāmasa* aspects predominated by the three constituents have been further divided into three divisions according to the predominance of the three constituents, and thus nine transformations come into existence. Similar is the case with the three *rājasa* and the three *sāttvika* aspects. Thus there arise 9+9+9=27 transformations. These 27 transformations are connected with the 27 kinds of groups of living beings, i.e., the tripartite group of the *sthāvara* (immovable) beings has been divided into 9 groups (each group having three subdivisions based on the three constituents); similar is the case with the category of movable beings and the category of beings forming the group of Brahmā and other gods. The author has clearly shown the twenty seven subdivisions of beings.

Thus the total number of the transformations of the constituents comes to 3+9+27=39. The equilibrium state (*sāmyāvasthā*) of the constituents is said to be connected with the witness (*sākṣin*, the attributeless immutable self).

NĀRĀYAṆATĪRTHA

Nārāyaṇa Tīrtha, the author of the *Sāṃkhyacandrikā* was well versed not only in the Sāṃkhya-Yoga philosophy but also in the philosophical systems of the Nyāya-Vaiśeṣika school and the Vedānta. He belonged to the last part of the seventeenth century. The following summary is based on the edition of *Sāṃkhyacandrikā* by Dundhiraja Sastri Nyaya-carya (Varanasi: Haridas Sankrit Series 132, 1977).

SĀṂKHYACANDRIKĀ

(*Summary by Anima Sen Gupta*)

(1-3) (E1-6) Life in this world is affected by the triad of frustrations, namely, (1) internal frustrations of one's own body and mind, (2) external frustrations caused by beings external to one's body and mind, and (3) celestial frustrations due to natural and supernatural causes.

The frustration of the present moment is destroyed naturally in the subsequent moment; past frustrations are already gone; so, it is future frustration that is to be alleviated. The Sāṃkhya, being the upholder of the theory of the existence of the effect in the cause prior to its production, does not believe in the prior absence or the posterior absence of any object. Cessation of anything, therefore, means getting merged in the subtle causal form and becoming incapable of appearing in a gross form, owing to subtlety.

The only means for the permanent removal of threefold frustration is discriminative knowledge; which is the correct knowledge of the manifested world of psychical principles and physical elements, the unmanifested primary cause, and the cognizer in the form of consciousness.

(4-8) (E6-12) Perception is that reflective discerning which is obtained through the relation between the sense organ and the object. On perceiving a cloud, we think of unperceived rain. This is a case of inferential knowledge. Inference is that process which depends on the knowledge of a universal relation between the *hetu* and the *sādhya* and also on the knowledge of the presence of the *hetu* in the *pakṣa*.

In other words, knowledge so produced, giving us the knowledge of the presence of the *hetu* in the *pakṣa* qualified by knowledge of the invariable relation between the *hetu* and the *sādhya*, is called knowledge by inference (*anumiti*); it is in the form of fire in the hill. Inference is of three kinds: (1) to infer the effect from the cause (*pūrvavat*), (2) to infer the cause from the effect (*śeṣavat*), and (3) inference due to the relation other than the cause and the effect ("*kārya-kāraṇa-anya-liṅgaka, sāmānyato dṛṣṭa*"). "*Āptavcana*" refers to the words of trustworthy persons. Statements are combinations of terms having expectancy (*ākāṃkṣā*), proximity (*āsatti*), and suitableness (*yogyatā*) and also referring to the intention of the speaker (*tātparya*). An *āpta* is a trustworthy person who possesses correct knowledge of the meaning of sentences.

The sense capacities are not the instrumental causes of knowledge. The instrumental cause is the operation of awareness (*vṛtti*) produced by the functioning of the sense capacities. Knowledge is the new and uncontradicted cognition of an object. When the reflective discernment of a specific object that is in contact with a sense capacity arises in the form of an awareness of the specific object, it is called perception (as for example, "it is a jar"). Inferential knowledge is that knowledge in which the operation of the intellect in the form of the inferred object (*sādhya*) takes place on the basis of the invariable relation between the *hetu* and the *sādhya* coupled with the knowledge of the presence of the *hetu* in the *pakṣa*. When there is the awareness of an object, signified by language uttered by a trustworthy person, then that is to be treated as a case of knowledge through testimony.

Those objects, which are capable of being related to organs of cognition, are proved to be existent by means of perception. Primordial materiality, which is supersensuous, is to be established by means of inference. *Apūrva* and similar things, which by issuing forth from the performance of sacrifices, etc., cause heavenly satisfactions, are to be known through scriptures, because of their supersensuous nature.

Primordial materiality cannot be perceived because of its very subtle nature. It is not nonexistent. Its existence is proved by means of the effects it brings into being. The intellect, egoity, the subtle elements, the gross elements, etc., are the effects that originate from materiality.

The effects that originate from materiality are of two kinds : similar and dissimilar.

The great principle (*mahattattva*), egoity, and the five subtle elements (seven in all) are similar to primordial materiality because these are characterized by the property of dividing themselves into further categories. Ether, air, etc. are dissimilar in the sense that these are not the originators of further categories.

(9) (E12-14) The effect is existent in the cause even before the causal operation. If we admit that a nonexistent effect can be produced, then we shall have to hold that even horns can issue forth from the head of a man. To produce curd, one always seeks milk, which is its inherence cause (*samavāyikāraṇa*). Had the effect been nonexistent in the cause prior to its production, one could have produced it from water as well. Again, if the effect is nonexistent in the cause prior to its production, then this prior absence of the effect being identical in all possible causes, every effect will arise from every cause. Scripture speaks of the identity between the cause and the effect even prior to the production of the effect. For this reason also, the effect cannot be regarded as nonexistent because in that case we shall have to admit the absurd identity between the existent and the nonexistent.

It cannot be urged that if the effect is always existent, then the operation of the causal factors for producing the effect becomes meaningless. The operation of the causal factors is necessary for the manifestation of the effect. Is the manifestation eternal or produced? If it is eternal, then there should always be the manifestation of effects. If it is produced, then one manifestation is to be produced by another manifestation, that by another, and so on. Thus, there arises the fallacy of infinite regress. There is no such fault, because, although the effect is existent, still it is not manifested on account of certain obstacles that prevent its manifestation. Being not manifested in the "effect form," it is not always practically useful. It is because of the presence of *sattva* in the effect that the effect is manifested by the operation of causal factors and becomes useful. Although the cause and the effect are identical, still, practical needs can be satisfied by the effect alone.

(10-11) (E15-18) The whole manifested world, consisting of principles beginning with the intellect and ending with the five gross elements, are caused, noneternal and nonpervasive. These are also active because intellect, egoity, etc., can pass from one body to another. Intellects, egoities, etc. are many in number, because these are differently associated with different consciousnesses. They are also many because creations too are many in number. On the basis of these effects, the existence of the unmanifest primary cause is inferred. These effects, which are the objects of enjoyment, also establish inferentially the existence of consiousness as the enjoyer. The manifest is the sign or reason (*liṅga = hetu*) to establish the existence of both primordial materiality and consciousness.

Primordial materiality is the objective basis of awareness, as all its effects become the contents (*viṣaya*) of awareness. They are not of the nature of awareness, as is held by the Yogācāra school. Had the content been of the form of awareness, then it could not have become the common content of enjoyment of many persons. Consciousness is devoid of the three constituents, is not a content (*nirviṣaya*), and hence not a common content of enjoyment. It is conscious and nonproductive. Like the unmanifest, consciousness is uncaused, eternal, etc., and like the manifest, consciousnesses are many in number.

(12-13) (E19-21) Satisfaction is the effect of *sattva*; straightforwardness, mildness, respect, forgiveness, knowledge, etc. are the different offshoots of satisfaction. Frustration is the effect of *rajas*; harted, envy, jealousy, disgrace, etc., are the distinctive features of frustration. Confusion is the effect of *tamas*; fear, crookedness, miserliness, ignorance, etc., are the distinctive features of confusion. *Sattva* and *tamas* produce effects being excited by *rajas*.

(14-19) (E22-30) It is because the intellect and other effects are formed of the three constituents that they are endowed with the properties of being undifferentiated, etc. That which is opposed to what possesses undifferentiatedness, etc., is consciousness; it is devoid of the three constituents. If we do not consider the intellect and the other principles as the products of some cause, then they will have to be regarded as eternal. In that case, consciousness will never be liberated. Hence, these principles are to be regarded as the products of some uncaused root cause. Because the effects are different from each other, they are to be regarded as specific and finite; because of multiplicity and differences, these products are also limited and nonpervasive. All these specific, limited, and finite products prove the existence of an eternal, infinite, and unlimited cause that is the primary cause.

Again the intellect and other effects are different from each other. Even then all of them are capable of producing satisfaction, frustration, and confusion. This common capacity, noticeable in all the products, proves that they have originated from a common cause. It is only primordial materiality that possesses such fitness. Again, it is the potency of the cause that brings about the effect. The potency to produce the great principle, etc., is possessed only by primordial materiality.

The effect emerges from causes and is differentiated from them. At the time of dissolution, all products get merged in a single cause. During creation, these are different, but in the state of dissolution, different effects are reduced to the same nature because of their origination from a single cause. Brahmā cannot be regarded as the cause because Brahmā can become the cause only (indirectly) by becoming the possessor of creative power, whereas the primary cause itself is the creative power and as such is the fit cause of the universe. Because the primary cause is of the nature of the three constituents, it can produce diversities of the world.

The *Sāṃkhyakārikā* proves the existence of consciousness by the following arguments:

All composite objects are created for the benefit of another, like the cot, etc. The benefit takes the form of the experiencing of satisfactions, frustrations, etc. Such experience is possible only in the case of consciousness and not in the case of anything that is unconscious.

The three constituents and their products are unconscious. An unconscious object can be made serviceable only by a conscious principle. The jar cannot, by itself, bring water. It can render this service only through the efforts of a conscious being. It is only in consciousness that the three constituents are absent. Consciousness, being the locus of the absence of the three constituents, is, therefore, necessary to make the unconscious products of the unconscious constituents serviceable. Just as an unconscious chariot can move in a systematic manner, being controlled by the charioteer, in the same manner, all these unconscious products do their respective functions, being watched over by consciousness. Consciousness, which is the seer and the illuminator of all objects, is, therefore, necessary. The wise people make sincere efforts to attain liberation. Liberation from satisfactions and frustrations can never be possible in the realm of materiality because satisfaction, frustration, and confusion are effects of the three constituents. Hence, there must be a consciousness.

Consciousnesses are many in number. Had there been only one consciousness then all would have been born simultaneously and all would have died simultaneously. Further, had there been one consciousness, then everyone would have been engaged in action simultaneously. We, however, find that, when one is engaged in religious activity, another engages himself in academic pursuits. So consciousnesses are many in number. Unequal aggregations of the three constituents are also noticed in this world. Some are satisfied, some frustrated and some suffer from confusion. It cannot be urged that such differences occur owing to the multiplicity of the internal organs, because the multiplicity of the internal organs proves the multiplicity of consciousnesses.

Consciousness gets seemingly involved in the worldly life because of materiality. In its true form, consciousness is wholly uninvolved and indifferent. It produces neither good nor evil. It is devoid of all good and bad qualities.

(20-21) (E30-32) Association is, indeed, the seed of illusion. The association is nothing but consciousness' capacity of being reflected in the intellect. Owing to such reflection of consciousness in the intellect, the unconscious intellect becomes permeated with consciousness, and it appears to have awareness in the form of "I am knowing." Agency is reflected in consciousness, resting on the intellect. As a result of reflection, the indifferent consciousness falsely appears as the doer of actions. The realization of the distinction of the intellect from consciousness is, however, not possible without the primary cause and its evolutes. So, consciousness needs the primary cause and there is the association of consciousness with the primary cause in the form of the relation of the enjoyer and the enjoyed. Creation, which may be regarded as the door to both enjoyment and liberation, is also due to this association.

It cannot be held that the five gross elements arise directly from egoity; this is because qualities like sound, etc., can never be produced from egoity as there is nonexistence of qualities like sound, etc., in it. There is no ground to hold that egoity possesses five qualities. The five qualities belong only to the five elements such as *ākāśa* and others.

(23-37) (E34-49) Reflective discerning, expressed in the form "This is to be done by me," is the function of the intellect. The intellect possesses merit, knowledge, nonattachment, and power when it is dominated by *sattva*. The intellect comes to possess demerit, ignorance, attachment, and impotence when it is dominated by *tamas*. The function of egoity is self-awareness, which is expressed in the form "I am knowing," "I am doing." Because there is nondifference between the cause and the effect, there is nondifference between egoity and the self-awareness of egoity. The intellect makes all its discernings, keeping harmony with egoity. Owing to nonrealization of the distinction, egoity (falsely) seems to reside in consciousness.

Sattva and *tamas* are by nature devoid of activity. They are moved to act by the active influence of *rajas*. The sense capacities, which are established as the causes of various sensations (color, etc.) are supersenuous: they remain in their respective seats.

The function of the mind is to apprehend as qualified or specific what is presented by the sense capacity in a general form. It gives us the knowledge of the "substance-attribute" form. In other words, the mind is generative of qualified knowledge. Some hold that although the mind assists the capacities, it itself is not a capacity. A thing cannot become a capacity merely by assisting the capacities. At the time of functioning, capacities are also assisted by a light of some kind. The light that assists the capacities should therefore be included in the group of capacities. This is wrong. The mind is regarded as a capacity because of its similarity with other capacities. Like other capacities, the mind, too, originates from that aspect of egoity in which *sattva* dominates.

The awareness that arises from the operation of the five external sense capacities is of a construction-free nature. The word "*mātra*" signifies that the eye possesses the potency of receiving color alone; the tongue can receive only taste; the nose only smell; the ear only sound; and the skin only touch. Speech, grasping, etc., are the functions of the action capacities. The five vital airs sustain life. So long as these vital powers remain operative, the living condition of a living being persists. Life flickers when the vital airs become completely inoperative.

The operation of the three internal capacities and one external capacity may be both simultaneous and successive (in the case of perception). In the case of inference and verbal testimony, the external capacities do not operate. In these two cases, therefore, there is no construction-free awareness, caused by the operation of an external capacity. The mind, here, is the capacity that operates first. Inference is dependent on perception because the universal relation between the *hetu* and the *sādhya* is established through it. In the case of verbal testimony, the potency inherent in language is to be inferred, and inference is dependent on perception.

(38-39) (E50-51) The five subtle elements are nonspecific in nature as these are not fit to be endowed with specific qualities. From these five subtle elements emerge the five gross elements, namely, ether, etc. These gross elements, being fit for the possession of specific characteristics of calmness, turbulence, and delusiveness, are specific.

(40-42) (E51-53) According to some, *kārikā* 41 speaks of the need of a gross body. The subtle body consisting of the principles such as the intellect, etc., cannot exist without a specific gross body.

(43-52) (E54-64) Dispositions like merit, etc., are innate. The "acquired" dispositions are brought about by personal efforts. The instrumental cause of virtue, etc., is the intellect. Merit enables a man to attain a higher plane, whereas vice leads him to hell. Discriminative knowledge alone enables a man to attain the highest good (i.e., liberation).

Misconceptions, dysfunctions, contentments, and attainments are the creations of the intellect (*pratyayasarga*). Being included in the intellect, these do not create any new category, owing to nondifference between the cause and the effect.

(54-56) (E65-68) According to Sāṃkhya-Yoga, the whole creation (from the intellect down to the five gross elements) emanates from materiality. God is not the creator; nor does creation depend on merits and demerits. If God creates (depending on merits and demerits), then merits and demerits may very well be regarded as the cause of creation. Why should we then admit the existence of a controller God in addition to merits and demerits? If God does not create in accordance with merits and demerits, then, there will be no diversity in the world. Further, an immutable principle can never become the cause of the world (because of its immutable nature). Materiality also, being unconscious, cannot act for its own personal benefit; its creation, therefore, is for the benefit of each consciousness. So, even if one consciousness is liberated, creation will not come to an end.

(57-61) (E69-72) In practical life we find that unconscious milk flows from the udders of a cow for the nourishment of her calf. Activity, here, is controlled, not by a conscious principle, but by the matured merits and demerits of *adṛṣṭa*. Hence, there is nothing to prevent us from holding that even an unconscious materiality can act for the liberation of consciousness. The flow of milk is not controlled by God because there is no proof for the existence of God as a controller. Even if evidence in favor of God as a controller is available, still He cannot be regarded as an active and working God; because He has no unfulfilled desire of His own that can be fulfilled by creation. Nor can God be supposed to create, being inspired by the feeling of compassion for frustrated beings; because before creation, there cannot be any form of frustration. So, a desire for removal of the frustration of living beings, prior to creation, is also impossible. Hence, it is proper to admit that materiality, though unconscious, can be engaged in creative activity for the benefit of consciousness, like unconscious milk.

Just as man acts with the thought, "This should be enjoyed by me," in the same manner materiality acts, being driven by the urge that its activity should serve the purposes of consciousness. Thus, by serving the purposes of consciousness, materiality, too, is satisfying its own urge. So there is no fault.

(62-69) (E73-79) Materiality keeps the embodied soul involved in worldly life by means of the seven predispositions of the intellect. It releases consciousness from worldly life by means of knowledge alone. This proves that, even in the absence of nonattachment, etc., discriminative knowledge can become the means of liberation. The liberated person, being the possessor of discriminative knowledge, perceives materiality in a disinterested manner with the help of his pure intellect, which abounds in *sattva*. Consciousness no longer regards as its integral parts the satisfying, frustrating, and confusing transformations of nature, owing to the arousal of discriminative awareness. The body of the wise, however, continues for some time on account of the impulse supplied by dispositions, the fruition of which has already commenced and which can be annihilated only through enjoyment with the body (which is their effect).

When, through enjoyment, previous fruit-bearing impressions are completely destroyed, then the body also comes to an end. Thus, when the two purposes of enjoyment and liberation have been served by the intellect, etc., consciousness attains self-fulfillment, and materiality ceases its activity in relation to it. Consciousness thus attains the inevitable and absolute freedom from frustration.

NĀGOJĪ BHAṬṬA, or NĀGEŚA

Nāgojī Bhaṭṭa, or Nāgeśa, lived in the first part of the eighteenth century, according to Keith[1] and others, and worked in the areas of philosophy of language, Nyāya-Vaiśeṣika, Vedānta, Yoga, and Sāṃkhya (see Potter, *Bibliography of Indian Philosophies*, 2d Rev. ed. [Delhi; Motilal Banarsidass, 1983], pp. 327-328, for citations to his work).[2] His *Laghusāṃkhyavṛtti* on the *Sāṃkhyasūtra* is rightly characterized by Keith as a "mere imitation" of Vijñānabhikṣu's *Sāṃkhyapravacanabhāṣya*[3]. Because it contains nothing original, the text will not be summarized in this volume.

VAMŚĪDHARA MIŚRA

Because this author refers to the views of Mahādeva Punataṃkara who is likely to have flourished in 1710, it may be presumed that he composed his commentary after 1750.[1] Nothing else is known about him. In the six benedictory verses we find no information either about him or his teacher.

The edition (E) used for this summary was prepared by Rama Sastri Bhandari and was published as Chowkhamba Sanskrit Series 54, Varanasi 1921.

TATTVAVIBHĀKARA

(*Summary by Kedaranatha Tripathi and Ram Shankar Bhattacharya*)

This is the most extensive commentary on Vācaspati's *Tattvakaumudī*. It deals with the views and statements of Vācaspati in a manner found in the later works on Nyāya, and thus it is not very useful in understanding Sāṃkhya notions in their original forms. It is similar in essence to other commentaries on *Tattvakaumudī* of traditional Sanskrit scholars. Its criticisms and refutations are, however, often characterized by an incisiveness (using the terminology of Navyanyāya) that is seldom found in other commentaries. In addition, its elaborate treatment of the theories of error (*khyāti*) is highly polemical and deserves to be studied by serious students of Indian philosophy.[2]

I. Introductory Verses: The Scope and Task of the Sāṃkhya (E1-117)

Vācaspati is said to have composed the first invocative verse by changing a few letters of the *Śvetāśvatara Upaniṣad mantra* (4.5), to indicate that the Sāṃkhyan materiality is not non-Vedic.

Although no scriptural statement is available to prove that invocation (*maṅgala*) is the cause of the completion of a literary composition, yet such a statement should be inferred. In ancient times such scriptural statements existed, but because of various kinds of unfavorable conditions Vedic study was neglected and consequently Vedic statements enjoining invocations came to be forgotten.

Now the commentator tries to show the significance of some of the words in this initial verse. The word "one" (in "unborn one") shows that the Nyāya-Vaiśeṣika theory that the atoms are the (material) cause of the world is untenable.

The words "red, white, and black" refer to the three constituents, viz., *rajas*, *sattva*, and *tamas* respectively, through secondary significance (*gauṇī vṛtti*). These constituents have, respectively, the functions of coloring (*rañjana*), illuminating (*prakāśa*), and concealing (*āvaraṇa*). "Red" has been placed first to indicate that *rajas*, being dynamic, is the most powerful factor in the act of creation.

Who "produces"—it is remarked that Vācaspati, instead of using "*sṛjati*," used the word "*sṛjamāna*" to indicate that materiality is an everchanging entity. The use of the term "unborn ones" in the plural indicates the plurality of consciousnesses. That is why the use of the singular word "unborn" in the original verse of the *Śvetāśvatara Upaniṣad* is to be taken as indicating consciousness in general (*puruṣasāmānya*, the property common to all consciousnesses).

Materiality is described as one that has been enjoyed (*bhuktabhogā*). Although experience of satisfaction and frustration belongs to consciousness, it is caused by materiality. Because experience is a transformation, it cannot arise in the immutable consciousness. Satisfaction, etc., which are operations of the intellect, get reflected in consciousness and this reflection is what is known as the experiencing of consciousness. When this experiencing ceases, consciousness is liberated from materiality.

Materiality is capable of being avoided (*heya*), because connection with frustration is prompted by it. A proper means is to be adopted for disjoining consciousness from materiality; this means is awareness of the difference between the intellect and consciousness.

A question may be raised as to how association, the source of bondage, is possible between two unlimited (*aparicchinna*) and all-pervading (*vibhu*) entities, because, if such an association is admitted it will create bondage in liberated consciousnesses also. The commentator comes to the conclusion that consciousness becomes associated, not with materiality, but with the intellect, a transformation of materiality. As the intellect is limited, its association with consciousness cannot be eternal and thus the aforesaid problem does not arise at all. This association has its own peculiarities: e.g., in deep sleep, although there is association, there is no experience of frustration.

The association is caused by nondiscrimination and so cannot be eternal. As it does not exist in liberated consciousnesses, these consciousnesses cannot be associated with bondage again. It should be noted in this connection that consciousness does not become mutable or attached because of its association with the intellect.

Objection: Because nondiscrimination is a kind of latent disposition (*vāsanā*), it is an attribute of the intellect. If association caused by an attribute of the intellect (viz., nondiscrimination) can exist in consciousness in the bondage state, it can exist in a liberated consciousness also.

Reply: Nondiscrimination is attributed to consciousness through its reflection in the intellect. Because nondiscrimination has been annihilated in a liberated consciousness, its reflection cannot arise in that consciousness. And, as a liberated consciousness cannot be in association with the intellect, bondage does not take place again. Nondiscrimination causes bondage, not directly, but through association.

(1) *Objection*: The Veda is the only means to self-realization leading to liberation, and so no one will be interested in studying Sāṃkhya.

Reply: Because hearing, reasoning, and meditation are prescribed in the Vedas as the means for realizing the self, there will naturally arise a desire to study Sāṃkhya, for without a study of Sāṃkhya, reasoning is not possible. Although reasoning has been treated in Nyāya and Vaiśeṣika also, yet the study of Sāṃkhya is necessary, for Nyāya-Vaiśeṣika regards the self as the substrate of satisfaction, frustration, etc., a view that is not in accordance with the Veda.

The Sāṃkhya atheism is not anti-Vedic, for, in refuting the existence of God, Sāṃkhya simply follows the worldly point of view, which does not accept the existence of God. The purpose of this refutation is to lay stress on practising nonattachment. Since Sāṃkhya does not enjoin that the mind is to be fixed on the eternal God in order to acquire discriminative wisdom, Sāṃkhya must be regarded as a system that does not accept the existence of God.[3]

Because Sāṃkhya asserts that frustration is a modification of *rajas*, it is evidence that Sāṃkhya does not follow the originationism (*ārambhavāda*) of the Vaiśeṣikas or the manifestationism (*vivartavāda*) of the Advaita Vedantins. Although it is the absolute cessation of frustration, and not satisfaction, that is called the ultimate human goal (*puruṣārtha*), yet satisfaction is sometimes called an ultimate human goal, because at the time of experiencing satisfaction cessation of frustration occurs.

The commentator criticizes the Vedāntic view that the attainment of eternal bliss is liberation. He remarks that so long as a consciousness is not liberated, absolute cessation of all frustrations is not possible, and that so long as a consciousness is in the state of bondage, there cannot arise absolute cessation of all frustrations.

(2) *Objection*: There is no contradiction between the Vedic statements (a) "no living thing should be killed" and (b) "a goat is to be killed in the Agniṣṭoma sacrifice."

Reply: No, (a) is a general rule, and (b) a specific one that limits, and so vitiates it. Violence of all kinds invariably gives rise to ill results to the person concerned. That is why the victorious Kṣatriya heroes of the *Mahābhārata* had to perform expiatory rites (*prayaścitta*) for their killing in the war, though such killing is enjoined for Kṣatriyas. The statement made in *Chāndogya Upaniṣad* 8.15 says that if one ceases from committing violence which is not sanctioned he will achieve the desired result.

The cavity (*gūha*) in which the self is said to dwell (in scripture) is the body or, according to some, the heart. One who has attained the Brahmaloka returns to the world if he has not acquired knowledge of the fundamental principles (of *Sāṃkhya*).

(3) The word "*gūṇa*" in Sāṃkhya signifies that it is the accessory (*upakāraṇa*) of consciousness. Or it may mean a strand (*rajju*) that binds consciousness through the strand's transformations, viz., intellect, etc.

The categories of Vaiśeṣika are said to be included within the twenty-five principles of Sāṃkhya. It is remarked that spatial direction (*diś*) and time (*kāla*) are all-pervading, and that the entities known as limited (*khaṇḍa*) direction and time arise from *ākāśa* as limited by adjuncts.

In contrast to the Nyāya-Vaiśeṣika way of treating properties and their possessors as always distinct, it is more logical to accept non-difference between properties and their possessors. Vaṃśīdhara remarks that the doctrines of inherence and of universal properties, as found in the Nyāya-Vaiśeṣika system, are untenable.

II. The Instruments of Knowledge

(6) (E182-184) Materiality, consciousness, and their association can only be known through inference, not perception.

(8) (E186-188) The word "subtlety" (*saukṣmya*) in this *kārikā* must not be taken in the sense of small dimension (*aṇutva*), since both materiality and consciousness are all-pervading. Rather, the sense of this term is to refer to the state of having no component parts.

III. The Notion of Preexistent Effect

(9) (E187-200) In the course of discussion of the first argument Vācaspati remarks "As long as there is no sublator of nonexistence, it is not possible to cognize the empirical world as false" (*prapañcapratyayaścāsati bādhake na śakyo mithyeti viditum iti*). While explaining this comment, Vaṃśīdhara says that, instead of saying "since there is no sublating factor" (*bādhakābhāve*), Vācaspati deliberately uses the expression "*asati bādhake*" with a view to intimating the fact that there does exist a sublator, viz., the scriptural statement "*neha nānāsti kiñcana*" (*Bṛhadāraṇyaka Upaniṣad* IV.4.19). As Vācaspati was commenting on a Sāṃkhya text, he simply presents the view of a Sāṃkhya teacher.

Vaṃśīdhara further says that the passage "*avyākṛtam āsīt*" (*Bṛhadāraṇyaka Upaniṣad* I.4.7) shows that all effects (intellect and the rest) remain in an unmanifested state during dissolution and come out of this state at the time of creation. In the Sāṃkhya doctrine of *satkārya*, prior absence and posterior absence of the Nyāya-Vaiśeṣika are regarded as the future and past states of an effect respectively, and a creating cause (*kāraka*) is regarded as necessary for rendering the future state of an effect to be manifested. Although the future state is manifested because of such a creating cause, once that state is destroyed (i.e., gone to the past state), the effect cannot reappear.[4]

At the end of this section the commentator refers to the Vedāntic view that, because it is impossible to determine whether the manifestation of an effect is caused or not, it is proper to regard the origination of effects as inexplicable (*anirvacanīya*).[5]

IV. The Manifest and Unmanifest Aspects of Materiality

(10) (E201-207) "Cause" (*hetu*) in this verse is to be taken in the sense of a cause for manifestation or emergence (*āvirbhāva*). The commentator elaborately discusses the nature of transformation and describes its three varieties, viz., *dharma*, *lakṣaṇa*, and *avasthā*.[6]

Although some scriptural statements say that materiality is innumerable (*asāṃkhyeya*), such statements should be taken to mean that although materiality is single in reality it becomes diversified in different creations.

(11) (E207-213) When it is said that the essential nature of the *sattva* constituent is satisfaction, "satisfaction" stands for tranquillity (*prasāda*), lightness, contentment, and the like. Similarly "frustration" (the essential nature of *rajas*) stands for grief, etc., and "confusion" (the essential nature of *tamas*), for sleep, etc. Pañcaśikha is quoted to uphold this view.

While elucidating Vijñanavāda the commentator at first establishes that objects are different from awareness of them and then explains idealism on the basis of the reason of the co-arising of the two (*sahopalambha*). While refuting this idealism in detail Vaṃśīdhara remarks that one and the same entity cannot be both grasped and the instrument of grasping, and that if all objects are regarded as the forms of awareness then the blue form would be nondifferent from the yellow form, both being not different from awareness, and that offering co-arising as a reason for idealism is faulty, for it presupposes the difference between an object and its awareness.

V. The Three Constituents

(12) (E213-220) A constituent is said to obstruct other constituents

when it becomes manifest (*udbhūta*), being incited by *adṛṣṭa*, which is the cause of the attainment of human goals (i.e., experience and liberation). Because the constituents are all-pervading, a constituent cannot exist without being associated with the other two constituents. It is remarked that there is no logical fault in holding that there is association between beginningless entities.

(13) (E220-227) As in the Vaiśeṣika view there exists the common property of earthiness in both earth atoms and the things made up these atoms, so lightness (*laghutva*), etc. are the common properties of the innumerable individuals (*vyakti*) of *sattva*, etc. When a large number of individuals of a constituent get united, the constituent becomes increased; similarly when they become disunited decrease occurs in the constituent. Although *sattva*, *rajas*, and *tamas* have innumerable individuals, they are not the same as the atoms of the Vaiśeṣikas, for the constituents are devoid of sound, touch, etc.

Although *sattva* is the same as satisfaction, lightness, and illumination, yet they are not to be regarded as three distinct aspects of *sattva*, for there is no opposition in them. A similar view applies to *rajas* and *tamas*. That is why materiality is said to consist of three constituents only, and not nine.

The Vedāntin's criticism that in the Sāṃkhya view a thing would be experienced in a uniform way at all times by all experiencing beings is refuted, and it is established that the nature of experience depends on many facts, namely, time, state, etc., and a change in these necessarily brings about change in experience.

VI. The Inferences that Establish the Existence of Materiality and Consciousness

(14) (E227-229) It is shown that there arises the fault of overcomplexity (*gaurava*) in the Mīmāsā view that causal efficacy (*śakti*) is a distinct category, and that it is correct to hold that causal efficacy is the same as the unmanifested state of an effect.

(17) (E252-264) Vaṃśīdhara affords a corroborative argument (*anukūla tarka*) to prove that all aggregates act for others, and refutes an argument given by Śaṃkarācārya at *Brahmasūtrabhāṣya* II.2.39 that materiality cannot be held to be capable of being ruled, because it is devoid of color, etc.

Consciousness, being of the nature of eternal illumination, does not require any helping factor to illuminate objects. It becomes associated with objects through the operations of the intellect. Materiality cannot be regarded as experiencing satisfaction, etc. for such experiencing would involve the fault of the contradition of agent with its action (*karmakartṛvirodha*).

Because unmanifest materiality is not conscious, it is under the control of some conscious being. To be "under the control" means "to be connected in such a way as to become the occasion of activities" (*pravṛttiprayojaka*). This is a special kind of contact (*vilakṣaṇasaṃyoga*). That there exists contacts between eternal entities is a proved fact.

It is time that gives rise to the disturbance (*kṣobha*) in the constituents. Then the aforesaid contact comes into existence because of action. This contact in turn gives rise to the transformation, viz., intellect, egoity, etc. Thus it follows that there is no effort or activity in consciousness to activate materiality and it is this association that causes materiality to transform.

(18) (E264-271) There is an elaboration of the Vedāntic view about the unity of consciousness (the self) with such reasons as are usually given by Vedāntists, and refuting the plurality of consciousnesses.[7]

(19) (E271-273) Because consciousness perceives objects immediately, it is called a witness (*sākṣin*). These objects are the intellect and its operations. Because consciousness' connection with objects other than these is through the intellect, it (the intellect) is called a "seer" (*draṣṭṛ*).

It is remarked that neutrality (*mādhyasthya, audāsīnya*) is different from nonagency (*akartṛtva*). Because the word "neutral" is used for those persons who, though without attachment or passion, act to maintain their bodies—a fact that shows that they possess agency—the word "nonagency" has been used to indicate that consciousness is absolutely bereft of agency.

(21) (E274-279) Dependence (*āpekṣā*), which is necessary for affecting association between two separate entities, is defined as acting as an accessory in order to produce effects.

Explaining the simile of the union of a blind and a lame man, Vaṃśīdhara remarks that as these two leave each other when the purpose of the union (i.e., reaching the destination) is fully served, so materiality ceases from its activities when consciousness is liberated and consciousness gets rid of materiality as soon as it attains isolation.

(22) (E279-301) Creatorship really belongs to materiality, as is proved by *Svetāśvatara Upaniṣad* 4.5.

Vaṃśīdhara offers a long discussion showing that all Sāṃkhya principles are mentioned in the Upaniṣads. He also shows that, although in some scriptural passages the Sāṃkhya process of transformation has not been stated in full, yet such nonmention is no fault, for in other scriptural passages the unmentioned principles are found to be mentioned.

IX. The Functioning of the Thirteenfold Instrument

(23) (E301-336) Because the intellect pervades its effects and

because it possesses power, it is called "*mahat.*" Hiraṇyagarbha is also called "*mahat,*" as he takes the intellect as his empirical self (*buddhy-abhimānin*).

Because the intellect receives the reflection of consciousness, its character is different from that of objects like a jar, etc. Although consciousness is without color, yet there is no logical fault in its reflecting on the intellect.

(24) (E336-342) Reasons are adduced to prove the nonelemental character of the capacities and to refute the Nyāya view (propounded here in detail) that the capacities are elemental. Vaṃśīdhara further establishes that the capacities are transformations of egoity and not to be confused with their vehicles, which are bodily regions called "*golaka.*"

Vaṃśīdhara is in favor of the view that the mind is the only transformation of the acquired (*vaikṛta*), i.e., *sāttvika* aspect of egoity, whereas the capacities are the transformations of the *taijasa*, i.e., the *rājasa* aspect of egoity. The view of some exponent that the acquired aspect of egoity gives rise to the superintending deities of the capacities, a doctrine not stated in the *Sāṃkhyakārikā*, is regarded as secondary for the deities are not in reality created by the acquired aspect of egoity.

(27) (E352-395) The mind is regarded as of the nature of both the sense and action capacities, for the functions of these two kinds of capacities depend on it. It cannot be urged that since the mind is a single entity, awareness (*jñāna*), which is a transformation of the mind, cannot be of various kinds. As the same body becomes fat or thin through the use or nonuse of food, similarly awareness assumes various forms through its relation with different capacities, auditory, etc.

The Nyāya view that the sense organs are *prāpyakārin* (coming into actual contact with their objects) is elucidated and refuted. It is established that construction-free (*nirvikalpaka*) awareness is caused first by the sense capacities and then construction-filled (*savikalpaka*) awareness is caused by the mind.

(30) (E399-405) In the simultaneous rise of the operating of four organs (three internal organs and any one of the external capacities), all four give rise to many operations separately. Since cross-connection of universals (*saṃkārya*) is not recognized as a defect, there is no logical fault in holding that many organs give rise to one operation at a time. The use of plural number in the verb (*prādur bhavanti*) predicated of operation(s) is not wrong; it is used to show manifoldness in one and the same operation. If the operation is not accepted as single, the use of the singular number in the word *vṛtti* in this verse would be wrong.

In imperceptible objects there arises simultaneously only one operation of the three internal organs. But if the operations arise gradually, they will be many. In the gradual rise of operations there arise many operations whether the object is perceptible or not.

(31) (E405-407) Consciousness, being immutable, cannot be an instigator (*pravārtaka*). Instigating cannot be attributed to God, either, for His existence is refuted in Sāṃkhya. Even if God is accepted, He cannot be an instigator of organs of all embodied selves. That is why the cause for the activity of the organs is said to be the ends of man, namely, experience and liberation.[8]

If the organs were regarded as impelled by an agent (and not by the ends of man as accepted in Sāṃkhya) then there would arise the fault of self-dependence (*ātmāśraya*). To be explicit: awareness, desire, and effort constitute agency (*kartṛtva*), and awareness, being an effect, is dependent on agency. Agency is not always necessary for activity; for example, there is no function of any agent in the act of waking after dreamless sleep.

(32) (E407-415) "Instrument" (*karaṇa*) must not be taken in the technical sense of the Nyāya i.e., as a nongeneric (*asādhāraṇa*) cause possessing operation (*vyāpāra*) but in the sense of a particular kind of creating cause (*kāraka*). The commentary provides an elaborate discussion on the nature of *karaṇa*, the sense of verbal terminations (*tiṅ*), the meaning of the mood and tense indicators (*lākara*), etc.

The subtle body is not the material cause of the gross body. It resides within it. The subtle body is an aggregate of seventeen factors—eleven organs, five subtle elements, and the intellect, egoity included in the intellect.

In reality, experience (*bhoga*) belongs to the subtle body and not to the gross body. There is no experiencing of objects in a dead body. The gross body is called a body only in a secondary sense, because it is the seat of the subtle body.

(35) (E418-419) It is remarked that the internal organs are the chief instruments (*karaṇa*), whereas the external capacities are regarded as instruments only in a secondary sense. Such a division of instruments is an established fact; that is, in the act of cutting it is the striking (*prahāra*) that is the actual instrument, whereas the axe is regarded as an indirect (*paraṃparā*) instrument.

(37) (E420-422) The experiencing of satisfaction, etc., which are operations of the intellect in association with consciousness, is a reflection (*pratibimba*). Consciousness perceives images through its own reflection existing in the intellect. It is the intellect that, because it has taken on the reflection of consciousness, helps it experience satisfaction, etc. Consciousness' experience of satisfaction, etc., is dependent on the question of the intellect, which acts not for itself but for another's purpose.

X. The Subtle and Gross Elements

(39) (E424-426) The subtle body is "persistent" (*niyata*), because it remains until liberation is attained.

Vaṃśīdhara expressly states that the "subtles" of this verse are not the same as the subtle body of verse 40 and that they are the effects of the subtle elements. These bodies (*sūkṣmadeha*) are subtle in comparison to the bodies born of parents. The bodies are the seats of the subtle bodies, i.e., of the *liṅgaśarīras*. Vaṃsīdhara says that this view does not contradict Vācaspati's view about the subtle body.

XI. The Subtle Body

(40) (E426-428) The subtle body is not a whole (*avayavin*) but an aggregate of intellect, etc. Trees, creepers, and the like possess gross bodies in spite of the fact that they don't have limbs (hands, feet, etc.). Merit, etc., give rise to satisfaction in an embodied self with the help of appropriate contributory causes (*sahakārikāraṇa*), which are also produced by merit, etc. Because the subtle body is a product of materiality and because it gets dissolved in primordial materiality, it may be regarded as the inferential mark for the proof of primordial materiality.

XII. The Basic Predispositions

(46) (E435-437) The inclusion of the predispositions among the four aspects of the intellectual creation is discussed here. It is stated that demerit and ignorance are included among the misconceptions; impotence and attachment among the dysfunctions; merit, power, and nonattachment within contentment. Some are said to hold that misconception is included in ignorance, dysfunction in demerit, contentment in merit, and attainment in knowledge.

XIII. The Empirical World

(53) (E451-452) *Objection*: Because trees, etc., are embodied and conscious, the predispositions such as merit, etc., should arise in them.

Reply: No, for it is said that only the bodies of Brahmins, etc., are capable of that. Such bodies are of four kinds: (1) those capable of performing actions (*karmadeha*), belonging to the great sages (*paramarṣi*); (2) those capable of experiencing only the results of actions (the gods such as Indra); (3) those capable of both acting and experiencing the results of actions (sagacious kings (*rajarṣi*); and (4) the kind that belongs to nonattached persons such as Dattātreya and others.

There is no requirement that bodies have to be born only from one of the four sources mentioned—the womb, the egg, sweat, or seed—for there are bodies that are produced by intentionality (*saṃkalpa*), etc.[9]

(55) (E453-486) Vaṃśīdhara provides an elaborate discussion of the theories of error of the Sautrāntika Buddhists (*ātmakhyāti*), the Vaibhāṣikas (*asatkhyāti*), the Naiyāyikas (*anyathākhyāti*), and the Advaitins (*anirvacanīyakhyāti*). After criticizing these, he argues that it is *akhyāti*, i.e., nonapprehension of difference (*bhedāgraha*), that is the logically sound position and that of Sāṃkhya. He says that although there are some merits in the *anyathākhyāti* and *anirvacanīyakhyāti* theories, on closer examination they are found to have logical faults.

XIV. Similes Illustrating the Role of Materiality

(57) (E488-492) A few verses are quoted from Kumārila's *Ślokavārttika* to show that because of the absence of purpose the existence of an intelligent creator cannot be logically proved.

The view of Śaṃkarācārya (cf. *Brahmasūtrabhāṣya* II.2.3) that the activity of a nonintelligent entity is due to the existence of an intelligent agent is faulty. There is Purāṇic authority for the doctrine of creation not preceded by awareness (*abuddhipūrvakasarga*).

The controllership of consciousness is said to be secondary since it is of the nature of association or proximity. In fact it is the internal organ reflecting consciousness that possesses controllership.

(59) (E493-495) Cessation (*nivṛtti*) of materiality means its disjunction from consciousness. Since the association of consciousness with materiality is caused by nondiscrimination, a liberated self, because he is without nondiscrimination, does not fall again into bondage.

(60) (E495-496) *Objection*: Because materiality is nonconscious there can be no regularity in its activities.

Reply: No. The activities of materiality are like those of a born slave, not random but fully regulated by natural tendencies. In the activities of materiality *adṛṣṭa* has its own play, as has been propounded by Vijñānabhikṣu in his *Sāṃkhyasūtrabhāṣya*.

(61) (E496-497) The word "*prakṛti*" (in this verse) stands for the intellect (along with the organs), which seems to be conscious because of its association with consciousness. Because nondiscrimination, which causes the association, is repressed by discriminative enlightenment, the activities of materiality come to a close forever.

(62) (E497-499) "*Prakṛti*" again stands here for the intellect. It is said to be "the locus of many" (*nānāśraya*), as it is endowed with eight predispositions.

(63) (E499-500) Materiality binds consciousness, not directly, but through the intellect. Knowledge, i.e., discrimination, is the only

means for liberation. In the word "*ekarūpa*" in the verse referring to knowledge, "*eka*" means "principal." Here the Vedāntic view is quoted to the effect that the result of nonattachment is not liberation but indifference to the enjoyment of objects; similarly the result of the cessation of the intellect is not liberation but nonapprehension of duality.

(64) (E500-506) Vaṃśīdhara remarks that although faultless knowledge of the principles (*tattvajñāna*) has a beginning, yet it is not contradicted or sublated by the beginningless misconception. The knowledge that leads to liberation is the discernment of the difference between materiality and consciousness. If this discernment is acquired, misconceptions of all kinds are uprooted.

ṢIMĀNANDA, or KṢEMENDRA

A commentary on the *Tattvasamāsasūtra*, called *Sāṃkhyatattvavivecana*, is published in the Chowkhamba Sanskrit Series No. 50, *Sāṃkhyasaṅgraha*, edited by V.P. Dvivedi, pp. 1-49. Its author's name is Ṣimānanda, or Kṣemendra, and he was a Brahmin from Kānyakubja. About his date, we know nothing. Because Kṣemendra follows Vijñānabhikṣu's views on Sāṃkhya, he probably wrote after Vijñānabhikṣu. As a rough estimate we place this commentary somewhere in the eighteenth or nineteenth century, anywhere, in other words, between 1700 and 1900. In the following summary (based on the *Sāṃkhyasaṅgraha* edition), attention is given primarily to the ordering of the *sūtras* and the manner in which the commentary explains the meaning of the *sūtras*, so that readers can compare this commentary with the two earlier commentaries on the *Tattvasamāsasūtra* already summarized, namely, the *Kramadīpikā* and *Tattvayāthārthyadīpana*.

"E" references are to the *Sāṃkhyasaṅgraha* edition.

SĀṂKHYATATTVAVIVECANA

(*Summary by Anima Sen Gupta*)

(1) (E2-9) Eight generative principles;
(2) (E9-10) Sixteen generated products;
(3) (E10-14) Consciousness;
(4) (E14-15) Having three constituents;
(5) (E15) Emergence of the manifest world;
(6) (E15) Periodic dissolution of the manifest world;
(7) (E15-16) Pertaining to the internal, external, and celestial (worlds);
(8) (E17) Five functions pertaining to the intellect;
(9) (E17-18) Five sources of action (*karmayoni*), explained here as perseverence (*dhṛti*), faith (*śraddhā*), satisfaction (*sukha*), desire (*icchā*), and the desire to know (*vividiṣā*);

(10)	(E18)	Five breaths or winds;
(11)	(E18)	Five essences of action;
(12)	(E18-19)	Five varieties of ignorance;
(13)	(E19-20)	Twenty-eight varieties of dysfunction;
(14)	(E21)	Nine varieties of contentment;
(15)	(E21-22)	Eight varieties of attainments;
(16)	(E22-23)	Ten principal topics;
(17)	(E23)	Supporting creation (*anugrahasarga*);
(18)	(E23)	Elemental creation (*bhūtasarga*);
(19)	(E24)	Threefold bondage;
(20)	(E24)	Threefold liberation, explained as increase of knowledge, destruction of merit and demerit, and passing on to total extinction in *kaivalya*;
(21)	(E24)	Threefold instrument of knowledge;
(22)	(E25)	Threefold frustration;
(23)	(E25)	This is the correct sequence for proper understanding ("*etat paramparayā yāthātathyam*");
(24)	(E25)	For one who understands all of this, everything has been done that needs to be done ("*etat sarvaṃ jñatvā kṛtakṛtyaḥ syāt*");
(25)	(E25)	Moreover, one is no longer overcome by the threefold frustration ("*na punas trividhena duḥkhena abhibhūyate*").

Ṣimānanda explains each of the *sūtras* in a series of verses (pp. 1-25). His explanations follow those of the *Kramadīpikā* and *Tattvayāthārthyadipana*, except for a few instances, as mentioned in the preceding list of *sūtras*. The latter portion of his commentary is in prose (pp. 25-49), in which he simply paraphrases the meaning of the Sāṃkhya system as found in Vijñānabhikṣu's *Sāṃkhyapravacanabhāṣya* and *Sāṃkhyasāra*.

SARVOPAKĀRIṆĪṬĪKĀ

This work appears in *Sāṃkhyasaṅgraha*, pp. 93-104. Nothing is known about its author.

(*Summary by Kapil Deo Pandey*)

(1) (E94) Eight generative principles;
(2) (E94) Sixteen generated products;
(3) (E94) Consciousness;
(4) (E95) Emergence of the three constituents (*traiguṇyasañcāra* [reading *sañcāra* instead of *sañcara*, and combining *sañcāra* with *traiguṇya* represents a deviation from all the other commentaries on *Tattvasamāsa*]);
(5) (E95-96) Dissolution (but reading *pratisañcāra* instead of *pratisañcara*);
(6) (E96) Pertaining to the internal;
(7) (E96) Pertaining to the external;
(8) (E96) Pertaining to the celestial—and interpreting (6-8) as describing the three ways in which frustrations arise;
(9) (E96) Five functions pertaining to the *buddhi*—described here as the five sense capacities, hearing, touching, seeing, and so forth;
(10) (E97) Five sources of action—explained here as the five action capacities, speaking, grasping, walking, and so forth;
(11) (E97) Five breaths or winds;
(12) (E97) Five essences of action (the commentary is corrupt at this point and cannot be read intelligibly);
(13) (E97-98) Five varieties of ignorance;
(14) (E98) Twenty-eight varieties of dysfunction;
(15) (E98-99) Nine varieties of contentment;
(16) (E99-100) Eight varieties of attainment;
(17) (E100-101) Ten principal topics. The commentary quotes a passage from the *Rājavārttika* setting forth the ten

principal topics that is identical to the passage quoted by Vācaspati Miśra in his *Tattvakaumudī* (under SK 72) and that appears also in the introductory verses of the *Yuktidīpikā*—the commentator is probably following Vācaspati Miśra here;

(18) (E101) "Creation of help or kindness" (*anugrahasarga*)—instead of taking *anugrahasarga* as the creation of the subtle elements as the other commentaries do, the author of this commentary refers to the help or kindness of materiality in allowing creation, indicating that in Sāṃkhya, materiality takes the place of God;

(19) (E101-102) Gross creation of fourteen varieties;

(20) (E102) Threefold bondage;

(21) (E102-103) Threefold liberation;

(22) (E103-104) Threefold instrument of knowledge.

This commentary does not read "threefold frustration" (*trividhaṃ duḥkham*) as a separate *sūtra*, because in the commentator's view, it is already presupposed in his interpretation of *sūtras* 6-8. Throughout the commentary the author appears to be following the *Sāṃkhyakārikā* closely, and his interpretation of the *abhibuddhis* and the *karmayonis* appears clearly designed to bring these technical notions into line with the old Sāṃkhya of Īśvarakṛṣṇa.

SĀṂKHYASŪTRAVIVARAṆA

This commentary is published in the *Sāṃkhyasaṅgraha* pp. 105-116. It does not number the various *sūtras*, but they appear in the text in the following order:

(*Summary by Anima Sen Gupta*)

(1)	(E105)	Eight generative principles;
(2)	(E105-106)	Sixteen generated products;
(3)	(E106)	Consciousness;
(4)	(E106)	Having three constituents;
(5)	(E106-107)	Emergence;
(6)	(E106-107)	Dissolution;
(7-9)	(E107-108)	Pertaining to the internal, pertaining to the external; and pertaining to the celestial (worlds);
(10)	(E108-109)	Five functions pertaining to the intellect—listed here as intellect itself (*buddhi*), self-awareness (*abhimānā*), desire or intention (*icchā*), activities of the five senses (*kartavya*), and actions of the five action capacities (*kriyā*);
(11)	(E109)	Five sources of action—listed as perseverence (*dhṛti*), faith (*śraddhā*), satisfaction (*sukha*), the desire not to know (*avividiṣā*), and the desire to know (*vividiṣā*), the first four conducing to bondage and the last one to release;
(12)	(E109-110)	Five breaths or winds;
(13)	(E110)	Five essences of action—same as in the *Kramadīpikā* and *Tattvayāthārthyadīpana*;
(14)	(E110-111)	Five varieties of ignorance ;
(15)	(E111)	Twenty-eight varieties of dysfunction;
(16)	(E111-112)	Nine varieties of contentment;
(17)	(E112)	Eight varieties of attainment;
(18)	(E112-113)	Ten principal topics (quoting the same verse as does the *Sarvopakāriṇī* that is, from the *Rājavārttika* and probably following Vācaspati's citation

		of the same but without citing the source);
(19)	(E113)	Supporting creation (*anugrahasarga*);
(20)	(E113)	Elemental creation (*bhūtasarga*);
(21)	(E113-114)	Threefold bondage;
(22)	(E114)	Threefold liberation;
(23)	(E114-115)	Threefold means of knowledge.

The commentary does not read "threefold frustration" (*trividhaṃ duḥkham*) as a separate *sūtra*, probably because it presupposes its discussion from *sūtras* 7-9, although the commentator makes no comment about this.

KAVIRĀJA YATI

Nothing is known about this author beyond his name and the fact that he wrote a little text entitled *Sāṃkhyatattvapradīpa*, probably some time in the eighteenth or nineteenth century. The text is not a commentary. It is an independent manual that provides an overview of the Sāṃkhya based on the *Sāṃkhyakārikā* as interpreted by Vācaspati Miśra in his *Tattvakaumudī*. It contains nothing original and, hence, will not be summarized. It does provide, however, a short and accurate account of the *Sāṃkhyakārikā* and the *Tattvakaumudī* and was probably used as a textbook by beginning students. It is published in the Chowkhamba anthology *Sāṃkhyasaṃgraha*, pp. 151-178.

MUDUMBA NARASIṂHASVĀMIN

The manuscript of Muḍumba Narasiṃhasvāmin's *Sāṃkhyataru-vasanta*, a commentary on the *Sāṃkhyakārikā*, is preserved in the Adyar Library, Madras (Descriptive Catalogues Vol. 8; s. no. 10E). The author has shown remarkable originality in explaining some of the expressions of the *Sāṃkhyakārikā*. He does not seem to follow any of the commentators of the *SK*, though in a few places he appears to regard the views of Vijñānabhikṣu as highly authoritative. At the beginning we find the expression "*Nṛsiṃhakārikābhāṣyam*," which simply means "a *bhāṣya* on the *Sāṃkhyakārikā* composed by one who is known as nṛsiṃha." The word "nṛsiṃha" undoubtedly refers to the author (see the expression "narasiṃha" in the name of the author). The author seems to be a devotee of Narasiṃha (an incarnation of Viṣṇu) as is proved by the passage "*anena bhagavān prīṇātu varāhanarasiṃhaḥ*" in the colophon. No other work of the author is known to us. As he has quoted Vijñāna-bhikṣu, he may be placed some time in the eighteenth or nineteenth century.

Because the commentary has not been published, we have not prepared a regular summary, but a summary of most of the important views held by the commentator. In a very few places we have only alluded to the views instead of stating them fully.

SĀṂKHYATARUVASANTA

(*Summary by Ram Shankar Bhattacharya*)

Introductory verses: The Scope and Task of the Sāṃkhya

(1) *Jijñāsā* (inquiry) is explained as discussion or deliberation (*vicāraṇā*); reason has been afforded for the nonemployment of the word "*jijñāsā*" in the first aphorism of the *Sāṃkhyasūtra*, which is regarded as a work by Kapila (*Kapilaprokta tantra*) by the commentator.

(2) *Puruṣārtha* (the purposes of consciousness) is said to be of two kinds: secular (*dṛṣṭa*) or scriptural (*ānuśravika*). It is remarked that

liberation is attainable by means of the discriminative knowledge of the difference between consciousness and materiality.

(3) Significance of the term "primordial" (*mūla*) in the term "*mūlaprakṛti*"; reasons for not regarding the earth, etc., as materiality; comparison of the Sāṃkhyan views expressed in *Sāṃkhyasūtra* 1.61 with the Vedāntic views; Kapila's doctrines regarded as not contradictory to the views of Vedānta.

II. The Instruments of Knowledge

(4) Meaning of the word "inference" (*anumāna*) and its nature; nature of instrument of knowledge called verbal testimony (*āptavacana*); the varieties to be included in the three Sāṃkhya instruments of knowledge are named as *upamāna* (comparison), *arthāpatti* (presumption), *ākṣepa* (also called *pratibhā*, intuition, which is of two kinds), *aitihya* (tradition), *sambhava* (possibility), and *abhāva* (nonperception); comparison and verbal testimony as indirect (*parokṣa*) instruments of knowledge.

(5) All objects are said to be revealed through the instrument called perception; perception is said to be of six kinds: five external and one internal, i.e., mental; the three forms of inference, namely, a *priori*, *a posteriori*, and based on general correlation are said to have their objects existing in the past, future, and present times; verbal testimony is the hearing of valid statements.

(6) The process of applying the form of inference based on general correlation to prove the existence of the elements, etc.; inability of inference to prove an anti-Vedic entity or view; inference is said to to be applied to prove a thing already known through the Vedas.

(8) A nonexistent thing is said to be either absolutely nonexistent like the horn of a man or illusorily perceived like water in a mirage; an effect cannot be nonexistent, because it is the cause of other effects; an effect is a transformation of a substance and is as existent as its cause.

IV. The Manifest and Unmanifest Aspects of Materiality

(10) The manifested is said to be manifold, because it possesses subdivision and to be mergent (*liṅga*), because it gets dissolved in its material cause.

(11) Both the manifest and the unmanifest are called undifferentiated, because they are the locus of nondifferentiation.

V. The Three Constituents

(12-13) Illumination (*prakāśa*), activity (*pravṛtti*), and restraint (*nivartana*) are said to be the effects of the three constituents, *sattva*, *rajas*, and *tamas* respectively. The rise of *sattva* is to be inferred from buoyance or lightness (*lāghava*) and illumination; of *rajas*, from the power to go upward by subduing inertia (*śaithilya*) and from mobility; of *tamas*, from heaviness (*durbharatva*) of the limbs. "Operation" (*vṛtti*) is explained to mean "illumination of objects" and is defined in accordance with the *Sāṃkhyasūtra* 5.107 with the remark that, according to the Sāṃkhyan tradition, an operation is a transformation of the organs.

VI. Inferences for Materiality and Consciousness

(14) The unmanifest, which is the generative cause of the intellect, is none other than the three constituents. In the *samānatantra* (sister system, i.e., the Yoga philosophy) it is held that one object (substance) has three sorts of transformations, namely, (1) transformation of essential attributes (*dharmapariṇāma*), (2) transformation of temporal characters (*lakṣaṇapariṇāma*), and (3) transformation of state (*avasthā-pariṇāma*). See *Yogasūtra* 3.13.

(15-16) The unmanifest, which is the inferred cause of the manifest, is said to be all-productive, all-pervasive, and one in number.

(17) An aggregate (*saṃghāta*) is defined as an assemblage of many component parts that produces a result. By its function an aggregate serves the purpose of its controller, who must be regarded as a conscious entity possessing desire and effort that is aware of its egoity (*ahaṃpratyayaviṣaya*). Had there been no conscious entity, no Yogin would have strived for acquiring discriminative discernment (*prasaṃkhyāna*).

(18) Had there been only one enjoyer (i.e., one consciousness) in all the embodied beings, one being would have been associated with the birth, death, and organic faculties of other beings and would also have maintained the bodies of others as his bodies. The variation in the constituents as found in different beings would not have come into existence had there been only one consciousness.

(19) In reality the constituents are the agents, and consciousness is the witness of the transformations of the constituents. Consciousness' perceiving of the transformations of the constituents is what is known as *vṛttisārūpya* (assuming the forms of the operations of awareness). See *Yogasūtra* 1.4. Consciousness is called seer as it is the seat of experience. The superimposition of materiality's agency on consciousness is called bondage.

(20) Although the subtle body (composed of the intellect and the rest, see SK 40) is perceived by consciousness, yet because it is affected by beginningless ignorance, consciousness (*caitanya*) seems to exist

in a subordinate state in it. As consciousness is covered by the subtle body, it is not known as distinct from it.

(21) The conjunction (*saṃyoga*) of consciousness and materiality is for experience as well as for the liberation of consciousness. Consciousness becomes associated with materiality as a result of forgetting its own nature, and consequently it experiences the fruits of its deeds. The embodied self acquires discriminative knowledge being properly instructed by a teacher and gradually it transcends transitory existence.

IX. Functioning of the Thirteenfold Instrument

(23) Reflective discerning is awareness free from doubting. It is the characteristic of the intellect and continues to exist (*anuvartate*) in egoity and its transformations.

(25) The view of the *Bhāgavata Purāṇa* that the motor organs proceed from egoity dominated by *rajas* is quoted here.

(27) The mind possesses both the powers of perceiving and action. It possesses similarity with egoity also. The purpose of diverse modifications of the constituents is to serve the various purposes of consciousness.

(28) *Ālocana* (perception in general, *jñaptimātra*) exists in all the five particular external perceptions. Similarly, all the motor organs have a common function known as acting (*kriyā*). *Sāṃkhyasūtra* 5.107 ("*Bhāgaguṇābhyām.*") has been quoted and explained. The word "*vṛtti*" (operation of the two kinds of organs) is derived from the root "*vṛt*" and it is defined as the transformation of an organ assuming a form similar to its objects.

(29) Although the operations, namely, reflective discerning, etc. (see verses 23, 24, and 27), are suspended in sleep, yet the vital breath, the general operation of the internal organs, does not cease to act. The internal organ, because of its proximity to consciousness, actuates or incites the vital air to act, and this action is regarded as the operation of the internal organs. The *Praśna Upaniṣad*, passage 6.4, speaks of the vital breath described in this verse.

(30) Simultaneous cognition of many objects is accepted in Sāṃkhya. The Nyāya view about the gradual operation of the organs is refuted and the Sāṃkhyan view of the simultaneous operating of all the organs is established here. It is remarked that the operation of an external capacity may be ascribed to the intellect, egoity, and mind.

(31) An organ is found to be helped by other organs at the time of discharging its functions. It is the nature of the nonconscious materiality to act for consciousness. Consciousness' power to make materiality act is said to be its agency.

(32) The operation of the action capacities is seizing (*āharaṇa*)

and holding (*vidhāraṇa*), whereas that of the sense capacities and the internal organs is illuminating or disclosing (*prakāśa*). The ten operations of the external capacities are regarded as the operations of the internal organs also.

(33) The assertion that the ten external capacities are the contents of the internal organs means they are capable of being perceived by the internal organs.

(34) The sense capacities are capable of perceiving a thing as distinguished from others. The organ speech (*vāc*) can produce sounds of the nature of *dhvani* and *varṇa* (inarticulate and articulate sounds) and the letters become the object of the ear. This organ can imitate the sounds uttered by other persons. *Yogasūtra* 2.19 has been quoted and explained here with the remark that the general form (*sāmānya-ākāra*) of the constituents is eternal and the specific forms are transitory. The views of some teachers that tie subtle elements, egoity, intellect, and materiality serve as the bodies of gods, exalted persons, and others, and that *nirguṇa* brahman has no body, have been quoted here.

(35) Awareness of external objects arises in the mind when the objects are in connection with their respective capacities.

(36) The expression "*kṛtsna puruṣārtha*" means "all things capable of being enjoyed."

X. The Subtle and Gross Elements

(38) The organs of the gods are said to be capable of perceiving the subtle elements. It is remarked that the Yoga philosophy uses the word "*aṇu*" for "subtle element" (the author is in favor of using the word "*tanmātrā*," ending in long *ā*, which is not in accordance with the use of ancient teachers).

(39) The word "*sūkṣma*" is explained to mean "of atomic size," i.e., invisible to the eyes of ordinary beings.

XI. The Subtle Body

(40) The doctrine that the subtle body is composed of $17+1=18$ entities (as stated in *Sāṃkhyasūtra* 3.9) is in consonance with this verse. The word "*saptadaśaika*" in *Sāṃkhyasūtra* 3.9 means "one (i.e., intellect) in which exist 17 other entities," namely, five subtle elements, ten capacities, mind, and egoity.

(41) The author is in favor of reading "*viśeṣaiḥ*" (and not "*aviśeṣaiḥ*" as has been read by Gauḍapāda and others) and he shows two faults, namely, *aprāmāṇika* (admission of an absurd position) and *ātmāśraya* (self-dependence) if the reading "*aviśeṣaiḥ*" is accepted.

(42) The word "*nimitta*" stands for "merit, demerit, ignorance,

desire, and action"; "*naimittika*" stands for "birth, span of life, and experience." See *Yogasūtra* 2.13. The commentator says that the exposition of this verse by Gauḍapāda may also be taken as valid.

XII. The Basic Predispositions

(43) Innate predispositions are caused by the eight generative principles. The acquired predispositions are caused by the sixteen generated principles.

The *sattva* constituent predominates in the former predispositions, which exist in God, in His incarnations, and in sages like Kapila. The latter predispositions exist in ordinary persons who are required to be instructed by teachers. The commentator seems to hold the view that the acquired predispositions (and not the innate ones) are to be found in ordinary persons and they exist in the thirteen organs only.

(45) The *prakṛtilīna*(s) (persons subsisting in elemental constituents through nonattachment) are said to remain in a state that is almost similar to the state of liberation.

(48) Confusion is said to be of ten kinds (and not of eight kinds as held by Vācaspati and others) because of egoism's attachment to five kinds of celestial and five kinds of worldly objects, namely, sound, etc. Extreme confusion is said to be of eighteen kinds (and not of ten kinds as held by Vācaspati and others). The commentator shows alternative explanations while dealing with the nature of extreme delusion, gloom, and utter darkness.

(50) The author has quoted *Sāṃkhyasūtra* 3.37-40 with reference to misconceptions, dysfunctions, contentments, and attainments and has remarked that the five contentments are called external inasmuch as they are based on nonattachment to the five external objects, namely, sound, etc.

(51) The eight attainments are said to produce knowledge that leads to liberation. The use of the expression "goad" (*aṅkuśa*) suggests that ignorance, etc., are obstacles to knowledge.

(52) The subtle body has seventeen component parts (ten capacities, the mind, egoity, and the five subtle elements). It exists in a seat made up of the subtle forms of the five elements. It is affected by the eight predispositions and by ignorance, etc. (see SK 46). Both subtle bodies and consciousnesses are innumerable.

XIII. The Empirical World

(53) *Kṛmi* (worms in general) are regarded as forming the fifth subdivision of the subhuman beings—a view not found in other commentaries.

(55) One cannot get rid of frustration even after attaining the region of Brahmā, the creator, who has a definite span of life and who is said to attain liberation as a result of acquiring discriminative discernment.

XIV. Similes Illustrating the Role of Materiality

(57) Materiality being inspired by the human goal called liberation produces discriminative knowledge, which leads to liberation. Giving reasons to support the Sāṃkhyan view embodied in this verse, the commentator informs us that God, the great teacher, appeared as Kapila in order to impart divine knowledge. *Sāṃkhyasūtra* 1.92 and 3.57 have been quoted to show the theistic nature of the Sāṃkhya philosophy.

(58) The factor that causes materiality to function is the idea that consciousness is to be released.

(59) The beginningless union of consciousness with materiality is the source of nondiscriminative awareness, which is uprooted by discriminative knowledge.

(61) The doctrine of materiality being perceived by consciousness is explained in two ways: (1) "materiality is perceived so far as it is perceivable," and (2) "the faults of materiality are perceived at the time of the rise of discriminative knowledge."

XV. Liberation and Isolation

(62) The three activities of materiality mentioned here are said to serve the purpose of consciousness.

(63) Although bondage and liberation are connected with materiality, yet they are realized by consciousness. So long as consciousness is in bondage, experience is to be taken as a goal of consciousness. When bondage (i.e., consciousness' association with materiality) is about to be destroyed because of the rise of discriminative knowledge, consciousness becomes delighted (*ullasati*). As this state is desired by consciousness, it is rightly called *puruṣārtha* (the goal of consciousness).

(64) Fundamental principle is explained to mean the twenty-five entities or principles as enumerated in *Sāṃkhyasūtra* 1.61. (*Sāṃkhyasūtra* 3.73 and 3.75 are also quoted.) *Kevala jñāna* is the realization of consciousness as distinct from materiality. The three expressions "*nāsmi*," "*na me*," and "*nāham*" negate the three ideas (1) that "I" am included either in materiality or in its generated products, (2) "I" possess materiality, and (3) "I" am identical with the body respectively.

(67) It is the latent dispositions of action that have begun to

work themselves out (and not the newly performed acts) that sustain or maintain the living organism.

(68) The commentary reads "*abhaya*" (fearless) in the place of "*ubhaya*" and remarks that isolation is free from fear.

(69) The commentator thinks that the extant *Sāṃkhyasūtra* (in six chapters) called "*Tantra*" was taught by Kapila.

RAGHUNĀTHA TARKAVĀGĪŚA

The *Sāṃkhyatattvavilāsa* (also known as the *Sāṃkhyavṛttiprakāśa*) by Raghunātha Tarkavāgīśa, son of Śivarāma Cakravartin, is purportedly a commentary on the *Sāṃkhyakārikā*, but only the introductory (*upodghāta*) portion of this commentary has been published (with a Sanskrit subcommentary by Rāmesacandra Tarkatīrtha) (Calcutta: Metropolitan Publishing House, 1935; Calcutta Sanskrit Series No. 15). It was possibly composed some time in the nineteenth century. For the manuscripts of this text, see the Catalogue of Sanskrit Manuscripts in the Asiatic Society, Calcutta, and the Catalogue of Sanskrit Manuscripts of Calcutta Sanskrit College. The text has been referred to in the "Index to the Bibliography" by F. E. Hall (p. 6).

The introductory (*upodghāta*) portion is a short statement of the *Tattvasamāsasūtra*, giving twenty-five *sūtras*. While commenting on the twenty-third *sūtra*, the author remarks that there will be "further elucidation. . . . in the *Vṛtti*." The word "*Vṛtti*" probably stands for the commentary on the *Sāṃkhyakārikā* by Raghunātha Tarkavāgīśa. It appears that the author referred to the *Tattvasamāsasūtra* at the beginning of his commentary to show the original teaching of the Sāṃkhya *śāstra* that was later enlarged upon by Īśvarakṛṣṇa.

His comments on the *Tattvasamāsasūtra* show no originality and, hence, no further summarization is needed.

DEVATĪRTHA SVĀMIN

Devatīrtha Svāmin, also known as Kaṣṭhajihva Svāmin, was a disciple of Vidyāraṇyatīrtha. He was patronized by the Mahārāja of Kāśī during his scholarly career. He died in 1852 at the age of eighty. His text, the *Sāṃkhyataraṅga*, is a booklet containing a collection of the important *sūtras* of the *Sāṃkhyasūtra* with occasional brief observations of the author. In the introductory part there is a discussion of the word "*atha*." Curiously enough, the author gives the meaning of its two component parts (letters), namely, "*a*" and "*tha*" as "*puruṣa*" and "*prakṛti*" respectively. Some verses from the *Garbha Upaniṣad* have been quoted to show the reason for following the path of Sāṃkhya-Yoga. The word "Śāṃkhya" has been derived from *saṃkhyā*, meaning "a methodical or ordered reflection or investigation" ("*kramapūrvā vicāraṇā*"). There is a short note on frustration and the means for its eradication. It is remarked that Sāṃkhya was originally declared by Kapila to his mother, Devahūti.

After these introductory remarks the author sums up serially the views propounded in the six chapters of the *Sāṃkhyasūtra* either by quoting the *sūtras* in full or in part, or by using expressions similar to the *sūtras*. There is a short note on the meaning of the word "*atyanta*" used in the first *sūtra*. Some verses from the *Saurarahasya* (an *Upapurāṇa*) have been quoted to show the divine character of the sun. In these verses, *prakṛti* has been compared with the sun. It is remarked that the word "*mātra*" in the word "*tanmātra*' means "*avadhāraṇa*" (limitation of the sense of a word).

TĀRĀNĀTHA TARKAVĀCASPATI

Tārānātha Tarkavācaspati worked in the middle of the nineteenth century. In addition to his *Upodghāta* on Vācaspati's *Tattvakaumudī*, he published works on Nyāya and Vedānta.

The *Upodghāta*, as the title clearly indicates, is not a full commentary. It is only a series of introductory notes about the *Tattvakaumudī*, possibly composed for the author's students. It was first published in Varanasi in 1868; a second edition was issued in Jīvānanda Vidyāsāgara in 1895.

Ram Shankar Bhattacharya did not prepare a full summary of the work but, instead, calls attention to the following checklist of topics covered in the text:

UPODGHĀTA

(*Summary by Ram Shankar Bhattacharya*)

(1-5) Discussions of the terms "*lohita*," "*tyāga*," and the *anugraha* of *cetanā-śakti*;

(6-8) Lengthy discussions of inference, both *vīta* and *avīta*, and *svataḥ prāmāṇya*;

(9) Elaborate notes on *asatkāryavāda* and *vivartavāda*;

(11) Notes on Buddhist *vijñānavāda*;

(23) Explanation of the word "*kāmāvasāyitva*";

(26) Useful discussions of *buddhīndriya* and *karmendriya*;

(32) Discussion of the reason for calling *buddhi*, "*puruṣa-rūpa iva*" ("as if it were in the form of *puruṣa*")

(50-51) Attempts to explain the names of the various *tuṣṭis* and *siddhis*;

(56) Reasons showing that God cannot control *prakṛti*; and

(64) Useful notations regarding the meaning of doubt (*saṃśaya*).

NARENDRANĀTHA TATTVANIDHI

Narendranātha Tattvanidhi composed his commentary on the *Tattvasamāsasūtra* toward the end of the nineteenth century. It is included in *The Sāṃkhya Philosophy*, volume 11 of the Sacred Books of the Hindus, translated by Nandalal Sinha (Panini Office, 1915 but recently reprinted by the Oriental Books Reprint Corporation, New Delhi, 1979).

As has been the case in the preceding summaries of the *Tattvasamāsa-sūtra* commentaries, attention will be given primarily to the ordering of the *sūtras* and the manner in which Narendra explains them differently from the others.

(1) Now, hence, a summary regarding the truth ("*atha atas tattve samāsaḥ*")—no other commentary reads this *sūtra*;

(2) I declare eight generative principles ("*kathayāmi aṣṭau prakṛtayaḥ*")—the expression "I declare" appears as "I shall now declare" ("*kathayiṣyāmi*)" in the *Kramadīpikā*, as spoken by Kapila, but the *Kramadīpikā* does not consider the expression part of the *sūtra*;

(3) Sixteen generated products;

(4) Consciousness;

(5) Having three constituents;

(6) Emergence (and) dissolution;

(7) Frustration is threefold: internal, external, and celestial;

(8) Five functions pertaining to the intellect (*pañcābhibuddhi*)—listed here as *adhyavasāya*, *abhimāna*, *saṃkalpa* (pertaining respectively to *buddhi*, *ahaṃkāra*, and *manas*), *kartavya* (pertaining to the activities of the sense capacities), and *kriyā* (pertaining to the actions of the five action capacities);

(9) Five sources of action—listed here, interestingly, as instrument of knowledge (*pramāṇa*), misconception (*viparyaya*), constructed or verbal knowledge (*vikalpa*), sleep (*nidrā*), and memory (*smṛti*) or, in other words, the *citta vṛttis* of *Yogasūtra* 1.6;

(10) Five vital breaths;

(11) Five essences of action—listed here, interestingly, as restraint

(*yama*), yogic practice (*abhyāsa*), nonattachment (*vairāgya*), concentration (*samādhi*), and insight or wisdom (*prajñā*);

(12) Five varieties of ignorance—listed here as ignorance, egoity, passion, hatred, and love of life or, in other words, the five afflictions of Yoga philosophy;

(13) Twenty-eight varieties of dysfunction;

(14) Nine varieties of contentment;

(15) Eight varieties of attainment;

(16) Ten principal topics—again reference is made to the old verse quoted in *Yuktidīpikā*, *Tattvakaumudī*, and so forth, but in this commentary the verse is said to have been derived from *Bhojavārttika*;

(17) Supporting creation—said here to relate to the subtle elements and the latent dispositions;

(18) Gross creation of fourteen varieties;

(19) Threefold bondage;

(20) Threefold liberation;

(21) Threefold instrument of knowledge;

(22) By knowing this properly, everything that needs to be done will have been done and one will no longer come under the control of the threefold frustration ("*etat samyak jñātvā kṛtakṛtyaḥ syāt na punas trividhena duḥkhena anubhūyate.*

Narendra does not read "threefold frustration" (*trividhaṃ duḥkham*) as a separate *sūtra*, because he obviously believes that it is included in *sūtra* 7. Also, he is keen throughout to include Yoga notions in his interpretation of the *Tattvasamāsa*, very much in the manner of Vijñānabhikṣu's approach in the *Sāṃkhyapravacanasūtra*.

BHĀRATĪ YATI

Śrī Bhāratī Yati, a disciple of Śrī Bodhāraṇya Yati, wrote his *Tattvakaumudīvyākhyā*, a commentary on the *Sāṃkhyatattvakaumudī* of Vācaspati, in 1889. It was printed at the Jaina Prabhakara Press, Varanasi, in 1889 and published by Babu Kaulesvarasimha Bookseller, Varanasi, the same year.

TATTVAKAUMUDĪVYĀKHYĀ

(*Summary By Esther A. Solomon*)

I. Introductory Verses: The Scope and Task of the Sāṃkhya

(1) Frustration is something not desired. Frustration being of the nature of *rajas*, which is eternal, cannot be completely destroyed, but it can certainly be subdued and hence the relevance of this science. A point raised by Vācaspati is clarified. In the verse "Because of the onslaught of the threefold frustration, there is the desire to know the cause of its removal," "onslaught" is the principal term, "the threefold frustration" being its qualifier or epithet, so "it" in "its" should refer to onslaught and not to the threefold frustration as Vācaspati maintains. The explanation given in Vācaspati is that the threefold frustration is uppermost in the thought of the inquirer and so "it" refers to this threefold frustration. Bhāratī Yati adds that what Vācaspati intends to say is that the mention of onslaught would become meaningful only if the threefold frustration is taken as meant. Vācaspati explains that, although it is true that in the beginning of a scientific treatise something auspicious should be mentioned, and frustration is not auspicious, yet the removal of frustration is certainly auspicious and it is but proper that it is mentioned in the beginning. In the Vedic expression "we have drunk *soma* and become immortal" immortality is mentioned but not inexhaustibility, so Vācaspati clarifies that inexhaustibility can be taken as established by presumption (*arthāpatti*), because immortality could not be possible without inexhaustibility.

(2) Summing up Vācaspati's argument, Bhāratī Yati says that the two statements "One should not kill or injure any creature" and "One should slaughter the *agniṣomīya* animal" refer to two different subjects—one says that injury or killing is the cause of evil and the other says that slaughter of the *agniṣomīya* animal contributes to the sacrifice—so there is no conflict between the two. Moreover, their contents also are not contradictory to each other and so one cannot sublate the other. The slaughter that is meant for the sacrifice will bring about demerit for the man and at the same time contribute to the success of the sacrifice. It can do both without entailing any contradiction. It is said that what is mentioned in the Veda is associated with destruction and excess (*atiśaya*). Actually, the destruction and excess pertain to the fruit of the sacrifice, etc. Then, how are they referred to as pertaining to the Vedic rites? Vācaspati answers this by saying that the cause and the effect are secondarily regarded as nondifferent and hence such a statement is made.

Again, it may be argued that even the destruction of frustration should be noneternal (it cannot be eternal) because it is something brought about, like heaven, etc. But this is not so; for the rule that what is brought about is noneternal applies only to positively existent things. That which, being positive, is brought about is noneternal, whereas destruction of frustration is the reverse of this. And another frustration will also not arise, for the cause of frustration is the nondiscrimination of materiality and consciousness, and this latter no longer being present, the effect, frustration, will not arise. This cause can function only until the discriminative knowledge arises.

At the end of the commentary on (2), Bhāratī Yati clarifies that manifest, unmanifest, and knower constitute the subject of this scientific treatise; the treatise propounds the subject and the subject is propounded—there is the relation of propounder-propounded between the treatise and its subject matter. Isolation is the purpose (*prayojana*), and one who is disenchanted or detached from the seen objects and Vedic rites is the one qualified for this treatise.

(3) We cannot infinitely go on searching for the cause of the cause of the cause..., for whatever cause of materiality we may hypostatize, we will have to show something special and different about it, otherwise the relation of cause-effect will not be there. And if the difference is said to consist in the fact that it is hypostatized as sentient and devoid of constituents and so on, even then it cannot be the cause, for it could not undergo transformation. If it is regarded as of the nature of causal efficacy, then this is how materiality also is conceived, and the difference of opinion would be only in regard to the terminology.

II. Instruments of Knowledge

(4) Commenting on this verse, Vācaspati himself says that he has not followed the order of mention in the text, but rather he followed the order of relevance of the topics (*arthakrama*). He explains "*pramāṇa*" first and then mentions their number. Justifying this, Bhāratī Yati says that when words are related by expectancy (*ākāṃkṣā*), fitness (*yogyatā*), and contiguity (*saṃnidhi*), they convey some meaning.

(5) Here, Bhāratī Yati justifies particular expressions used by Vācaspati. For instance, Vācaspati describes determination as "*tadāśrita*," "supported by or dependent on it (the sense organ, which is in contact with the object) "—in order to answer the objection that "reflective discerning" is a transformation of the intellect and not an attribute of the sense capacity; and he defines "reflective discerning" as an awareness that is an operation of the intellect in order to show its nature and rise. Bhāratī Yati explains by means of syllogistic reasoning why Vācaspati believes that even the Lokāyatika will have to admit inference as an instrument of knowledge in order to infer the ignorance or doubt or the like of the person he is speaking to. While explaining Vācaspati's exposition of "less inclusive" and more inclusive" terms, Bhārati Yati explains what a limiting adjunct (*upādhi*) is and its types, giving quotations from Udayana and Kumārila. "*Mukhena*" in "*anvayamukhena*" and ' *vyatirekamukhena*" is meant to prevent the definition from applying to the rule of positive-negative concomitance, in which both positive concomitance and negative concomitance are equally prominent. Bhāratī Yati clarifies the concept of "*sāmānyaviśeṣa*," generality-cum-particularity. A doubt may arise that in the definition we find the term "*adṛṣṭa*," "not seen" in "*adṛṣṭasvalakṣaṇasya*," whereas what is to be defined is "*sāmānyatodṛṣṭa*." To answer this objection, Vācaspati explains that "*dṛṣṭa*" in "*sāmānyatodṛṣṭa*" signifies "*darśana*," a seeing or perceiving of a generality-cum-particularity the particular individual substratum of which has not been perceived.

The commentary explains, mostly on the lines of the Pūrvamīmāṃsā, how Vedic language is intrinsically valid. The term "*Śākya*" in Vācaspti's commentary signifies Buddhists; "*Bhikṣu*" signifies the Avadhuṭas; "*Nirgrantha*," the Jainas; and "*Saṃsāramocaka*," those who believe that when the body is torn apart, the self in its interior is released. "Etc." (*ādi*) comprehends the Cārvākas. The statements of all these are *āgamābhāsa*, semblances of verbal testimony, and to exclude them the term "*āpta*" is used. Their invalidity can be known from their mutual contradictions. The commentary asserts that, although the Mīmāṃsaka holds that the relation of language and meaning is eternal, it is language alone, along with the knowledge of its relation derived from the usage of elders, that enables us to know. The meaning of a sentence is based on the meaning of the words, so the sentence does not stand in expectancy of the knowledge of relation in order to convey its meaning.

III. The Notion of Preexistent Effect

(9) Bhāratī Yati says that Vācaspati has refuted here the other theories of causality and established that the effect is existent even before as well as after the operation of the cause. The commentary is very brief, connecting each statement in Vācaspati's commentary with the words in the verse. It also explains some difficult words in the commentary. To explain that the effect and the cause are nondifferent even though they are differently designated, Vācaspati gives the example of "cloth in the threads" and "*tilaka* (trees) in the forest." Bhāratī Yati remarks that the forest is just an aggregate of *tilaka* trees, the forest is nondifferent from it; still the two are mentioned differently. If their nondifference is what is meant to be conveyed, the example should be worded differently—"forest in the *tilaka* trees" corresponding to "cloth in the threads."

IV. Manifest and Unmanifest Aspects of Materiality

(10) Noneternal (*anitya*) is explained as perishing (*vināśin*). But previously it was stated that origination signifies emergence or manifestation, and destruction signifies being hidden or merging. So Vācaspati mentions another synonym—*anityavināśin* = *tirobhāvin* (merging, disappearing). "*Prakṛtyā pūra*" signifies the addition made by materiality, help received from materiality.

(11) Bhāratī Yati explains that Vācaspati is referring to the view of the Vaiśeṣikas when he speaks of others who hold that satisfaction, etc., are qualities of the self.

V. The Three Constituents

(12) Someone objects that, because the constituents are beginningless and devoid of a cause, they cannot be said to be mutually creative. Vācaspati answers by saying that creation signifies transformation, which is homogeneous in the case of the constituents. Hence they are causeless because there is no other entity that is their cause; neither are they noneternal for they are not dissolved in a distinct principle.

IX. The Functioning of the Thirteenfold Instrument

(33) When we speak of Yudhiṣṭhira having existed in the past or Kalkin as existing in the future, speech operates on things that are

not present. To answer such an objection Vācaspati says that the near past and the near future are also included in the present and so speech can be said to operate in respect of objects in the present. One may doubt that the Sāṃkhya accepts time as an independent principle, for then the principles would be more than twenty-five. To avert such a doubt, Vācaspati explains that the Sāṃkhya does not accept time as a distinct independent principle.

XI. The Subtle Body

(40) It may be urged that, because the subtle elements are said to be nonspecific, the subtle body could not be said to be specific. Vācaspati explains that the subtle body is said to be specific because it is associated with the capacities that are comforting, discomforting, and confusing. The subtle body transmigrates, being influenced by the predispositions (merit, etc.). Bhāratī Yati says that this amounts to saying that the subtle body transmigrates in the company of the intellect, because these predispositions are associated with the intellect.

XIV. Similes Illustrating the Role of Materiality

(57-59) The commentary explains why, according to Vācaspati, God cannot be regarded as controlling and provoking materiality to activity. There is no logical fault in regarding materiality as active, although it is unconscious.

XV. Liberation and Isolation

(64) From persistent efforts, knowledge free from doubt, and so on, arises and leads to realization of the truth. The intellect has a partiality for truth. Even the Buddhists who do not admit the authority of the Veda accept this. "Knowledge of the nature of reality, which is free from faults, cannot be sublated by false knowledge even if one makes no effort, for the intellect has a partiality for truth," say the Buddhists. Bhāratī Yati discusses different readings of this stanza from a Buddhist work.

Vācaspati has with the help of grammar explained "*nāsmi*" as negating action in general with respect to the self. Consequently all particular actions like determining, arrogating to oneself, conceiving, perceiving, and all external actions are negated of the self. He gives another explanation of this expression, construing it as "*nā asmi*" —"*na*" being the nominative singular of "*nṛ*," man, *puruṣa* (I am the noncreative *puruṣa* [and am not creative].) The *puruṣa* realizes that no action pertains to him; because he is not the doer, lordship does not belong to him.

PRAMATHANĀTHA TARKABHŪṢAṆA

Pramathanātha Tarkabhūṣaṇa (1865-1941), son of Tārācaraṇatarkaratna, was a versatile scholar of very high rank. Equally proficient in literature, religious and social study (*Smṛti*), neo-Nyāya, Sāṃkhya, Mīmāṃsā, and Vedānta, he was, perhaps, most learned in Mīmāṃsā and Vedānta. He learned *Smṛti* under Vireśvarasmṛtitīrtha, neo-Nyāya under Śivacandrasārvabhauma, Sāṃkhya under Hṛṣikeśaśāstrī, and Mīmāṃā and Vedānta under Svāmi Viśuddhānanda—all outstanding teachers. Pramathanātha Tarkabhūṣaṇa taught *smṛti* and Indian philosophy at, among other institutions, Calcutta Sanskrit College, the University of Calcutta, and Banaras Hindu University. He retired from Banaras Hindu University in 1922 as Principal, College of Oriental Learning. In recognition of his superb scholarship he was awarded the title "Mahāmahopādhyāya" by the British Indian Government and the honorary degree of Doctor of Letters by Banaras Hindu University.

The subcommentary *Amalā* on Aniruddha's *Vṛtti* was written, it appears, as an elementary textbook, clarifying not so much the Sāṃkhya principles (*tattva*) as studing Sāṃkhya arguments vis-à-vis parallel counterarguments in non Sāṃkhya systems of philosophy and, at important places, the ways in which some Sāṃkhya thinkers other than Aniruddha interpreted some of the *Sāṃkhyasūtras*. Unlike other subcommentaries of his day, *Amalā* is a refreshing study, free of unnecessary neo-Nyāya techniques.

The significant new points stated in this subcommentary may be summarized as follows:

AMALĀ ON SĀṂKHYASŪTRAVṚTTI

(*Summary By Kalidas Bhattacharya*)

The subcommentary begins with a preface in which Pramathanātha tries to fix Aniruddha in a particular century. He argues as follows:

Of the three commentaries on the *Sāṃkhya* (*pravacana*) *sūtra*, that is, *Aniruddhavṛtti*, *Sāṃkhyapravacanabhāṣya*, and the one by Vedāntimahādeva, the first must be the earliest, for not only Vedāntimahādeva has himself admitted this in the introductory verse in his commentary, but there are at least seven texts in the *Sāṃkhyapravacanabhāṣya* (which Pramathanātha summarizes in the preface), strongly suggesting that Vijñanabhikṣu must have read the *Aniruddhavṛtti*. If Aniruddha is thus earlier than Vijñānabhikṣu, certain passages in the *Aniruddhavṛtti* itself (which too Pramathanātha summarizes in the preface), as verbatim reproductions of what (the elder) Vācaspati Miśra and Sāyanamādhavācārya have said in their *Tattvakaumudī* and *Sarvadarśanasaṃgraha*, prove that Aniruddha must have lived after them. It may not be hazardous, therefore, to fix him some time in the fifteenth century. To which part of India he belonged is not known.

Pramathanātha says that he is not quite sure which of the three theories, *pariṇāmavāda* (holding that effects are only transformations of their constitutive causes), *vivartavāda* (holding that effects are but false appearances of their constitutive causes), and *ārambhavāda* (holding that effects are novel events), Aniruddha really subscribes to. For, although he appears generally to subscribe to the first theory, there are passages in the *Aniruddhavṛtti* in which some Sāṃkhya concepts are interpreted in the language of the other two theories (see *Sūtras* I.9, 10, and 11). Pramathanātha writes that he has, for this reason, tried to reconcile these three theories as far as is practicable.

The points worth noting in the subcommentary are as follows:

Aniruddha's Introduction

1. Aniruddha says that it is nonattachment that puts a man on the path to liberation. Pramathanātha adds that to be on this path involves as much the reading of authoritative texts as acting upon them.

2. Aniruddha distinguishes two kinds of nonattachment—one born of frustration and the other resulting from the exhaustion of Karmic potentials (traces and dispositions) accumulated through previous life cycles. Pramathanātha states the point more precisely, saying that the Karmic potentials in question must not include those that are responsible for the present life cycle and its experiences (these potentials, forming a lump, are called *prārabdha*). Only other potentials (called *sañcita*) must be so exhausted, The *prārabdha* can be exhausted only through experiencing whatever has to be experienced in the present life because of it. The *sañcita* potentials, particularly those for which we may *suffer* in some subsequent life cycle,

can be exhausted through expiation, visiting holy places, worshiping God, etc. The second type of nonattachment, mentioned above, is again of two varieties—proximate and ultimate. It is only the proximate variety (traced by Aniruddha to the Jābāla scripture) that is a necessary condition for entry onto the path of liberation. The underlying idea is that proximate nona ttachment is necessary for "purification of awareness" (*cittaśuddhi*), and, unless that is achieved, the discriminating intuition of the metaphysical separateness of pure consciousness and primordial materiality does not arise.

Book I:

(A) *Introductory Sutras: On the Problem of the Scope and Task of Sāṃkhya*

(*Sūtra*) (I.1) (a) Aniruddha writes that every satisfaction or frustration lasts for "two or three" moments. Pramathanātha corrects the statement, saying:

As a matter of fact, it lasts for two moments only. Indeed, in some, texts the reading actually runs as "lasts for two moments." The addition "or three" is a slip.

(b) "Absolute cessation of frustration" means that in the self in question there is not merely no frustration now but also no prior absence of any suffering (that is, no frustration in the offing, either). In case older Sāṃkhyans object that Sāṃkhya cannot admit absence (*abhāva*), the whole thing might be rewritten as that in the self in question all frustrations are ever in the past. Modern Sāṃkhyans do not see any reason why Sāṃkhya should not admit absence; its principles are, indeed, all positive, but outside of these one may well admit absence.

(c) When Aniruddha writes that liberation is *nitya* and *prakāśarūpa*, "*nitya*" means sui generis, not simply eternal, and "*prakāśarūpa*" means that freedom is of the very nature of (pure) consciousness.

(I.2-4) "Absolute cessation of the origination" (*utpattinivṛtti*) of frustration "means that it is kept ever as future, never allowed to occur at any present moment of time. I.3 is an objection from the Cārvākas, who hold that the main objective of life is to get rid of frustration every time it occurs (and also to prevent frustrations as far as possible, through "natural" means). Pramathanātha interpretation of I.4 differs from Aniruddha's. It is as follows:

By the application of ordinary "natural" means one cannot get rid of all the frustrations that occur to him, and, in case such removal occurs by chance, even then there is no assurance that no further frustration is in store for him.

(B) *On the Problem of Bondage in Sāṃkhya*

(I.7) (a) According to Vaiśeṣika and kindred systems, frustration' like many other qualities, really belongs to the self and, therefore, bondage is one of its real features. But the problem for Sāṃkhya is precisely whether it is so.

(b) The term "*svabhāvataḥ*" in the *sūtra* means "*svarūpataḥ*," "*svarūpa*" meaning essential character.

(I.9) If Aniruddha here anticipates an objection, it is only to show that in some sense bondage, too, really belongs to the self and can be removed exactly as, according to *satkāryavāda*, cause can be removed (really, suppressed) to make room for its effect. (Pramathanātha believes that Aniruddha is here describing bondage and salvation in the language of *satkāryavāda* and *vivartavāda* simultaneously. He referred to this anomaly in his preface).[1]

(I.19) Aniruddha interprets "*tadyogāt*" as *prakṛtiyogāt.* Pramathanātha interprets it as *avivekayogāt* and says that nondiscrimination is to be understood not merely as the absence of discrimination but positively, as the false owner-owned relation. That relation, really a mode of intellect, is reflected on (pure) consciousness, which, therefore, only appears to be bound by it.

(I.20) This *sūtra* and the next three are against the Advaita Vedānta theory that ignorance (*avidyā*) is the principle that binds. The refutation of that theory would be as follows: "Ignorance" is either the prior or posterior absence of knowledge and either way, sheer negation, unless characterized by the counterpositive of the absence. But, first, sheer negation is just nothing and cannot by itself bind; and, second, as necessarily characterized by the counterpositive, how possibly can it bind another, when it is itself bound by the counterpositive? That which cannot stand on its own cannot influence another.

(I.22-28) Should ignorance be regarded as something positive and yet not of the nature of consciousness, it would be different, entiatively, not only from that consciousness but also from the things of the phenomenal world, as the latter are, unlike ignorance, not eternal; and then Vedānta would only be doubly dualistic, never monistic (*advaita*).[2]

"Influence" in I.27, means *vāsanā*, i.e., latent attitudinal disposition left by what is past. The same word, however, in the introduction to I.28 has meant relation of contact and, again, as implied by the expression "*uparañjyoparañjakabhāva*" in the body of the *sūtra*, knower-known relation.[3]

(I.34-38) Pramathanātha interprets the Buddhist notion of *arthakriyākāritva* in an unorthodox way and offers some details of the traditional Buddhist argument for universal momentariness. In I.35 he elaborates an argument, which Aniruddha has just noted in passing, for the Buddhist theory of universal momentariness. Pramathanātha elaborates as follows on I.38 and Aniruddha's commentary on it: Everybody admits that the constituent material (*upādāna*) of every effect is synchronous with it (at least at the moment the effect emerges) and yet that it is its cause (material cause—*upādānakāraṇa*). If, now, this (material) cause is taken, as by the Buddhists, to be momentary, i.e., real only for that moment, there would be no ground (for the Buddhists) to call it cause (because the effect in question does not arise after the cause is destroyed). This proves that at least no material cause is momentary.[4]

(I.40) The difficulty for the advocate of universal momentariness is that he cannot prove the cause-effect relation; for momentariness implies that when the cause is gone (i.e., absent) the effect is there and when the cause is there the effect has not arisen (i.e., is absent).[5]

Some Buddhists might still contend that whatever be the real situation there is at least the linguistic (or phenomenal) use of cause-effect relation. One would, however, reply that, in that case, anything in the world that immediately precedes the effect would be called its cause and anything that occurs after whatever is called cause would be called its effect.

(I.41) After explaining Aniruddha's points against the Buddhists Pramathanātha concludes that, according to the Sāṃkhya theory of transformation, a just-preceding phenomenon is called cause only insofar as it continues nonmanifestly (or half manifestly?) in the form of functional intermediary, called the operation (*vyāpāra*).

(I.42) When the Vijñānavāda Buddhist contends that things are not outside awareness, this does not amount to total negation of such things. They need not be outside awareness. But the very proposition that they are not outside logically implies that they are at least other than knowledge. How, otherwise, could one have asserted this proposition at all? If there are no such things at all, one would only be denying what is not there. In order, therefore, that the Vijñānavādin's contention be of any worth at all his proposition has first to be stated more precisely. Aniruddha states it precisely and then refutes it.

(I.43) Whereas Aniruddha interprets the *sūtra* in a simple manner, saying that were there no object there would be no awareness either and that, in that case, *vijñānavāda* would reduce itself to *śūnyavāda*, Pramathanātha interprets the *sūtra* as follows: If even while seeing an object as other than awareness the Vijñānavādin could deny it, he should, on the same ground, deny awareness also, for it too is seen as an object, and, to that extent, an "other," in self-consciousness, not as that seeing itself. The Vijñānavādin cannot take consciousness to be self-illuminating. That would amount to a sort of contradiction: what is subject cannot itself be its object.

(I.44-45) Pramathanātha interprets Aniruddha's commentary on the two *sūtras* differently. His interpretation is as follows:

If positive entities could cease of their own nature, then frustration too, as a positive entity, would cease of itself, which means that liberation would be automatic, needing no effort whatsoever. This position, however, is refuted by the Sāṃkhya thesis that there is no absence (*abhāva*) other than that which is said to be its locus. To speak of it as other is only a language habit mistaken as knowledge.

Pramathanātha next seeks to present all the forms of absence in the Sāṃkhya language of nonmanifestness.

If Aniruddha has, in the context of *sūtra* 45, admitted absence as other than its locus, this admission is from the point of view of modern Sāṃkhyists.

(I.48) In the context of I.48, Pramathanātha gives a short but fairly complete account of Jaina metaphysics and, in connection with I.58, regarding whether darkness is only absence of light or something positive, he supports Aniruddha's point that it is positive.

(C) *The Derivation of the Basic Principles of Sāṃkhya*

(I.61) By themselves, the three constituents—intelligibility (*sattva*), activity (*rajas*), and inertia (*tamas*)—are each a substance (*dravya*). They are called *guṇas* (qualifying characters) only insofar as they are used as means to bondage or release of (pure) consciousness. Primarily, materiality is nothing but these substantives *sattva*, *rajas*, and *tamas*, not their receptacle.

(E) *The Instruments of Knowledge in Sāṃkhya*

(I.87) Aniruddha is apparently content with claiming that knowledge (*pramā*) has for its object something that is not already known (*anadhigata*). Pramathanātha supplements this, saying that it must also be one that is not contradicted (*abādhita*), the object of which, in other words, is not sublated. Pramathanātha quotes in full Vijñānabhikṣu's commentary on the *sūtra*.

(I.92) Aniruddha writes that whichever of the two alternatives—God has a body; God has no body—is taken, He cannot be the agent cause of the world. Pramathanātha adds that if He has a body He is in bondage, like any ordinary man; and if He has no body He is one of the liberated consciousnesses, entirely disinterested whether there be a world or not.[6]

Those to whom Aniruddha is referring by the name "*viśeṣavādin*" are the Sāṃkhyists.

The word "*ābhāsa*" in "*kāryatvābhāsa*" in Aniruddha's commentary means a fallacy regarding the ground of the inference (*hetvābhāsa*).

(I.103) (From the statement "All compounds are for the purpose of something else, and materiality is a compound", one can infer consciousness in very general terms only, not immediately the consciousness of Sāṃkhya with whatever it further implies. That could be inferred through a series of other such inferences based on general correlation supplementing the most general one.

(F) *Materiality and the Theory of Preexistent Effect*

(I.108) Aniruddha interprets I.108 in one way. Pramathanātha accepts it but points out at the same time that others have interpreted it differently (he does not say, however, who these others are). The interpretation to which he refers is as follows: Distant things can or cannot be objects for the senses (i.e., perceived), according as they are accepted or avoided by the senses (exactly as near things are), because of the presence or absence of attractive features in them. (Pramathanātha probably intends here to include the case of "*yogaja* and other extraordinary (*alaukika*) types of perception" of Nyāya-Vaiśeṣika).

(I.148) There are two stages of dreamless sleep. In one, even though it is very deep, the depth is yet not at its maximum; in the other it is so. As one awakes from the former one's memory is of the form "I slept a pleasant sleep," but when awakened from the latter it is of the form "I knew nothing."

(I.149) Birth (*janman*) is the connection of consciousness with a body-mind complex such as has never been experienced before, and death its separation from that.

BOOK II: On the Effects of Materiality

(A) *On the Activity of Materiality and Its Distinction from Consciousness*

(II.1) (a) Aniruddha mentions only four kinds of nonattachment. Pramathanātha gives a fuller account, reproducing verbatim what Vācaspati Miśra has said in his *Tattvakaumudī* on *Sāṃkhyakārikā*.

(b) Even existing satisfactions are a form of frustration, not only because they contain some frustration, however little (there is no pleasure with which no pain is intertwined), but also because the very attachment to this satisfaction brings in its trail other items conducing to frustration.

(c) Literally, *avidyā* is actual wrong knowledge. But, secondarily, it also means the disposition to have such wrong knowledge.

(d) Not to allow something (e.g., frustration) to emerge into being is to keep it even in a state of prior absence, that is, even in the state of potentiality, by keeping ever at a distance whatever tends to end that antecedent absence.

(e) If Aniruddha here speaks of God as an ultimate consciousness, this is in deference to that school of Sāṃkhya which admits

God. For, he has already said that there is no evidence whatsoever for God.

(II.3) Aniruddha's commentary on II.3 is not at all clear. Indeed, it is positively confusing. For this reason Pramathanātha writes something else in its stead and passes that off as Aniruddha's real intention. Pramathanātha writes:

For the removal of defective dispositions accumulated through previous life cycles, one will, in the present life, have to listen to scriptures unceasingly and also to practice meditation. Only if one had already done these things in the just-preceding life cycle can he attain liberation quickly, that is, without going through the entire process once again.

(II.7) Pramathanātha offers an alternative interpretation that, he says, has been given by others but that, it appears, does not differ substantially from Aniruddha's interpretation.

(II.9) According to Pramathanātha the word "*yoga*" in the *sūtra* has to be connected with the word "*virāga*," and "*sṛṣṭi*" with "*rāga*."

"*Yoga*" here, he holds, means liberation as the true character of consciousness.[7]

(C) *Space and Time*

(II.12) Aniruddha writes that the ablative case ending in "*ākāśebhyaḥ*" should here, more desirably, be a locative case ending and that the word "*ādi*" ("etc.") suffixed to "*ākāśa*" is redundant. Pramathanātha however, finds some justification for both in the *sūtra*. He says that "*ādi*" here means "other limiting adjuncts," the idea being that one can only speak of space (in the sense of "direction") and time of *ākāśa* is considered as somehow limited by these adjuncts. And, because *ākāśa* as so limited is, in each case, the result of (generated by) *ākāśa* and the relevant adjunct, the ablative case ending, implying generation from out of some thing or things, has not been improper.

(D) *Intellect and the Basic Pre-dispositions*

(II.13) Aniruddha writes that "reflective discerning" means the objective assurance that a thing is such and such. Pramathanātha adds that objective assurance need not be theoretical only, it includes objective assurance even of what one ought to do.

(G) *The Capacities and Their Differentiation from Consciousness*

(II.29) Consciousness is spoken of as "seer," that is, one who owns awareness (*draṣṭā*). Pramathanātha says that this so-called ownership is because of the intervention of intellect, modes of which are reflected on consciousness.

(II.32) The Nyāya philosophers will never agree that external senses and mind (in Sāṃkhya, all psychic capacities, including egoity and intellect) can ever function simultaneously. That sort of cross-operation would, according to them, be as illogical as cross-division. But Sāṃkhya has no such scruple : it abides by facts as they are found to be (unless contradicted). Although this is the correct Sāṃkhya position, Aniruddha has missed it and holds (almost apologetically) that these different capacities cannot operate simultaneously (on a given object); it is only because of very rapid succession that one fails to detect their sequence.

As a matter of fact, "construction-filled perception" (*savikalpapratyakṣa*), where, undoubtedly, mental capacities have functioned, occurs at the level of the external senses. This proves that the different capacities have functioned simultaneously. This has been clearly stated not only in the oft-quoted passage "*Asti hyālocanaṃ jñānam*. . ." but also in Vyāsa's *Yogabhāṣya*.

(II.33) Aniruddha describes *vikalpa* as "touching both." Pramathanātha understands by "both" two alternatives, as in doubt, and so identifies *vikalpa* as doubt (*saṃśaya*). Naturally, he argues that this notion of *vikalpa* is different from Vyāsa's in his *Yogabhāṣya* and from Vijñānabhikṣu's (in his commentary thereon.")[8]

Book III: Section of Nonattachment

(A) *The Specific and the Nonspecific*

(III.1) Gross materials (*sthūlabhūtāni*) are called "specific" (*viśeṣa*) (perceptively distinguishable in themselves and from one another) because they differ in being more or less comforting, uncomfortable, and confusing.

(III.2) According to Pramathanātha the literal meaning of III.2 is that the subtle and the gross material bodies rise out of the twenty-five metaphysical principles.[9]

(B) *The Gross Body and the Subtle Body*

(III.14) The "atomic" (*aṇu*) size (which otherwise means the size that is infinitesimal) of mind here means only finite size. In contrast, "*vyāpaka* size," in Aniruddha's commentary, means the size that is limitlessly infinite.[10]

(F) *On the Nature of Meditation*

(III.30) By "*vṛttinirodha*" (prevention of a mode of intellect from emerging) is meant prevention of all modes of intellect except those that refer to objects concentrated on.

(G) *Misconception, Dysfunction, Contentment, Attainment*

(III.37) The difference is not so much regarding the objects of attachment, aversion, and fear (of death) as of the corresponding cognitive states.

(III.38) Aniruddha does not detail the twenty-eight types of dysfunction (*aśakti*); Pramathanātha collects them from the *Sāṃkhyakārikā*.

(I) *Role of Materiality in Discrimination*

(III.56) According to Aniruddha, the word "*saḥ*" (he) in III.56 means consciousness. Some others mean by it "materiality," holding that it is materiality, rather than consciousness, that is omniscient and omnipotent. Vijñānabhikṣu understands by the term "*saḥ*" one who, having practiced all regular spiritual exercises, has ultimately merged in the unmanifest materiality. Vijñānabhikṣu's interpretation of the *sūtra* is that, when such a person re-emerges at the beginning of the next cycle of creation he reemerges as omniscient and omnipotent God, the first to emerge as a person.

(J) *Discrimination and Liberation*

(III.64) For "*itarajjahāti*" there is an alternative reading, "*itaravajjahāti*." According to this latter reading, the meaning of the *sūtra* would be: with mere listening to scriptures, even the wise one (i.e., one who apparently knows the separateness of materiality and consciousness) would, like other fools, miss liberation, because mere listening is not enough and has to be followed by spiritual practices.

(K) *The Liberated-While-Living*

(III.83) The last lingering traces (*adṛṣṭa*), in the case of a *jīvanmukta*, operate only as his apparent attachment, aversion, etc.—"apparent" in the sense of being without sting.

Book V: Arguments Against Opponents

(B) *On the Notion of Ignorance*

(V.15) In support of his thesis that the world has a beginning, Aniruddha quotes a scriptural passage that asserts this. The passage asserts equally, however, that the world comes from God. Aniruddha would never go so far. Pramathanātha defends Aniruddha, arguing that the term "God" here stands for materiality as it evolves in the form of "collective intellect" called "*mahat*."

(D) *Merit, Qualities, Inference*

(V.28) The judgment "wherever there is M there is P" is arrived at neither through perceiving a single case of P going with M nor through perceiving a number of such cases, but only through the supplementation of such perceived agreement-in-presence by the perception of agreement-in-absence of the form "wherever there is no P there is no M." Pramathanātha holds that this conclusion is what Aniruddha intends. (But how Pramathanātha could gather this is difficult to see.)

(V.29) "*Kṛtaka*" in Aniruddha's commentary should mean that which, being a positive entity, emerges at a point of time, not, like destruction, a negation that originates at a point of time. Similarly, "*anitya*" in Aniruddha's commentary should mean that which, being a positive entity, is liable to get destroyed at a point of time, not the prior absence of a thing that gets destroyed when that thing gets into being.

(V.31, 36) Because, in Sāṃkhya, power is not understood as anything wholly different from that which possesses it, therefore, power need not be considered as belonging to a separate category. This is more clearly stated in V.36 where it is said that between power and the holder of power there is identity-in-difference (*bhedaghaṭitābheda*).

(E) *Word and Meaning*

(V.39) Aniruddha refutes the Mīmāṃsā doctrine that the meaning of a sentence uttered by a speaker consists in some act to be done by the hearer—all sentences being imperative in import directly or indirectly—and that the constitutive words, therefore, are to be understood as having meanings only in the context of such an act, nor as meaning independent objects standing on their own right. According to the Mīmāṃsakas all sentences are imperative, none indicative, and meaning is always act-orientedly holistic. They interpret scriptural sentences, particularly, from this point of view. Obviously, however, this doctrine cannot be accepted by those who believe that knowledge is an autonomous affair.

(V.42, 43) The question of the validity of scriptural injunctions (such as those concerning performance of rites) has relevance only so far as supernatural (supersensuous) elements and their functions are concerned, not so far as visible "natural" things are concerned. In other words, it is relevant primarily for those who know these supernatural elements and their functions. For those, however, who just see the results occurring, the validity of these injunctions is only secondarily relevant. (That is why these rites have to be performed directly by those who know.)

(V.44) According to Sāṃkhya, all awareness is intrinsically valid. When it becomes invalid, it is because of some defect in the way it is derived. This is true as much of the awareness of supernatural scriptural truths as of any cognition of ordinary affairs of the world. The only difference is that in the former case no such defect can possibly be pointed out there; for the way in which that awareness is derived is itself also supernatural and has nothing to do with the defects that vitiate perception and inference.

(V.50) The word "*nijaśakti*" in Aniruddha's commentary means "intrinsic" and is used there as an adjective of "*jñānajanakasāmagri*," meaning that the validity of the awareness in question is due to that awareness itself. Other important points in Aniruddha's commentary on this *sūtra* are that (1) the word "*autsargiki*" means "not depending on any merit of the factors that make one aware of the knowledge" and (2) the word "*tat*" and "*abhivyakti*" in "*tadabhivyakti*," both in the *sūtra* and the commentary, mean "object" and "the manifestation of object," respectively, the latter in its turn meaning knowledge that refers to that object.

(F) *Knowledge and Error*

(V.53-54) Under 53, Pramathanātha gives a short account of the Prābhākara theory of illusion and, in connection with 54, he gives a short introductory note on the Advaita Vedāntic theory of illusion as it could be developed in contrast to the Vaiśeṣika theory. Pramathanātha notes also that the purport of the last three sentences in Aniruddha's commentary on 54 is that because the illusory rope-snake is after all described as "It is a snake," it cannot be indescribable as the Advaita Vedāntin holds.

(V.56) Pramathanātha gives a short introductory account of the grammarian's concept of *sphoṭa*.

(H) *On Nonduality*

(V.66) Aniruddha writes that ignorance is nothing positive that could conceal consciousness from our view. Pramathanātha adds that this refutes the Advaita Vedāntic theory that it is positive wrong knowledge, or a positive disposition that way.

Pramathanātha interprets the last three sentences in Aniruddha's commentary as follows: Just as the self-luminosity of consciousness through the three stages—waking, dreaming, and dreamless sleep—cannot by itself prove eternal existence of the self, because these three stages all somehow hang on to one's body, so is the case with (pure) satisfaction in the meditation stage called *samādhi*, in which with the removal of all operations of the intellect one is said to experience that (pure) satisfaction. Here Aniruddha uses the term "*samādhi*" thrice—twice in connection with the self-luminosity of consciousness and once in connection with the removal of the operations of the intellect. In the first two cases it means "proving" (*samādhāna*), but in the third it refers to the final stage of meditation.[11] (But was this interpretation, with the same word taken to be used so differently in two successive sentences, at all necessary?)

(V.68) Aniruddha interprets the word "*manda*" in V.68 as "growing out of the inertia constituent" (*tāmasa*). Pramathanātha notes that, by implication, one has to include also "growing out of the activity constituent" (*rājasa*).

(I) *Mind and Internal Organ*

(V.71) Two important points regarding Aniruddha's commentary are:

(a) That mind is not partless is evident from the fact that its constituent cause, egoity, is not itself so. Egoity is directly apprehended in the form "I" by the intellect, but nothing that is partless could ever be so apprehended.

(b) Pramathanatha says that some others interpret the *sūtra* differently. They understand the word "*bhāga*" in the *sūtra*" to mean "cause" and take the *sūtra* to mean that mind cannot be uncaused, because egoity is known to be its cause.

(J) *Liberation*

(V.74) This *sūtra* is meant for refuting the Bhāṭṭa Mīmāṃsā view that liberation is but the manifestation of eternal satisfaction.

(V.78) "Cessation of everything" (*sarvocchitti*), in V.78, should mean cessation of everything other than self (or itself).[12]

(V.80) The view rejected in this *sūtra* is that of the Mīmāṃsakas.

(V.82) Although Aniruddha gives a fairly long account of the Naiyāyika's sixteen types of entities (*ṣoḍaśapadārtha*), Pramathanātha elaborates the account to a greater length.

(P) *Relations*

V.100) "*Ubhayatra*" ("in both cases") is interpreted by Pramathanātha as "as much in the case of property as in that of what possesses the property."[13]

(V) *The Experience of Liberation*

(V.119) Pramathanātha understands "*vāsanā*" as that through which one becomes aware of beauty (*saundarya*) and ugliness (*asaundarya*). The term "*anarthakhyāpana*" means, according to him, this awareness.[14]

(W) *Types of Beings*

(V.127) The purport of this *sūtra* is to refute the Nyāya view that God's intellect (*buddhi*—in Nyāya, cognition) is all uncaused: none of his cognitions either originate or ever cease to be.

KṚṢṆANĀTHA NYĀYAPAÑCĀNANA

This subcommentary was written in 1902 by M. M. Kṛṣṇanātha Nyāyapañcānana. He was a famous Bengali scholar, versed in various branches of learning, particularly in Nyāya, for which he earned the degrees Nyāyapañcānana, Nyāyaratna, and others, and the honorary title Mahāmahopādhyāya. He belonged to a village named Pūrvasthalī near Navadvīpa, in an area then noted as a great seat of learning.

The subcommentary was a textbook for beginners in Sāṃkhya philosophy. Sāṃkhya at that time was understood to include only Iśvarakṛṣṇa's *kārikās* with Vācaspati Miśra's commentary, and perhaps Gauḍapāda's commentary in addition. Vijñānabhikṣu's *Sāṃkhyapravacanabhāṣya* (on the *Sāṃkhyasūtra*) and *Yogavārttika* (on the *Yogasūtra*) were not unknown, but orthodox scholars seldom attached importance to them. Texts like Aniruddha's *Vṛtti* and the *Māṭharavṛtti* were probably unknown, and acquaintance with the *Yuktidīpikā* was obviously out of the question. Thus despite his scholarship, Nyāyapañcānana could not go beyond *Tattvakaumudī*, or at most Gauḍapāda's commentary. If, in the interest of clarification he has referred to, or quoted passages from, other texts, these are, as was usual in those days, either some Upaniṣads or Purāṇas or Patañjali's *Yogasūtra* with Vyāsa's *Bhāṣya* and Vācaspati Miśra's *Tattvavaiśāradī* on the *Bhāṣya*. He has also referred to other Indian systems of philosophy such as Mīmāṃsā, Buddhism and (Advaita) Vedānta for comparison and contrast. His task was nothing more, and nothing less, than elucidating for beginners Vācaspati Miśra's *Tattvakaumudī*.

Indeed, he has wherever possible rewritten Vācaspati Miśra's sentences more precisely according to the Nyāya technique, and the commentator's implicit and explicit arguments too in clear Nyāya forms—a style that, even to this date, is very much in fashion with oriental scholars. But generally speaking, he has added very little that is substantially new. If his *Āvaraṇavariṇī* is widely read even to this day, it is because the book is a brilliant introductory text written in excellent lucid Sanskrit.

His significant recasting of Vācaspati Miśra's sentences, and the new points he has added, are stated below.

ĀVARAṆAVARIṆĪ ON TATTVAKAUMUDĪ

(*Summary by Kalidas Bhattacharya*)

I. Introductory Verses: Scope and Task of Sāṃkhya

(1) In the *Tattvakaumudī* Vācaspati Miśra writes that, because frustration is felt as antagonistic to the self-awareness of pure consciousness, it is taken as "hitting" it (from outside), and that this very antagonism is the reason why one spontaneously seeks to get rid of frustration. Kṛṣṇanātha Nyāyapañcānana explains this as follows: Because frustration is felt as (so) antagonistic, it follows that it is not eternal (i.e., not coeternal with pure consciousness). Were it so, there could be no question of antagonism at all. Nor of any nonantagonism either.

(2) In the course of explaining Vācaspati Miśra's point that the slaughter of animals, even though done in performing a rite, generates some sin (demerit), although subordinate to the central merit generated by that rite, Kṛṣṇanātha Nyāyapañcānana writes: Although the final Mīmāṃsā theory is that by the time one has got the appropriate satisfaction as the final result of the rite performed, the sin (demerit) accumulated is over, yet this (according to Pañcaśikha, not according to Mīmāṃsā) does not nullify the force of that sin altogether. (What Kṛṣṇanātha Nyāyapañcānana means is that all the time the potential sin was doing its appropriate job, it was pressing the agent for expiation; and where through inadvertence the agent does not expiate, it goes on generating in him, in the meantime, a sort of calm endurance of all the "implicit" frustration that ensues.)

The Mīmāṃsakas permit slaughter of animals where that is necessary for the performance of certain rites. They permit it on the following simple ground: If a discourse starts with a general prohibition but if in the same discourse the prohibition is explicitly suspended (and even the opposite course of action is recommended) for certain specific cases, the suspension of the prohibition stands justified if only because the specific cases are of stronger import. Vācaspati Miśra writes he would concede this logic if only there were some contradiction (of whatever sort) between the prohibition and its suspension (or the corresponding recommendation). He maintains, however, there is no contradiction here between the general prohibition of slaughter and its recommendation in the context of certain rites. What, according to him, is meant in such cases is that, whereas slaughter in general produces demerit in the agent (and is, therefore, prohibited), specific cases of slaughter are recommended explicitly as necessary means to the performance of the rites in question and nothing is said so far as to whether any demerit accrues here or not. In course of further clarification of this position, Kṛṣṇanātha Nyāyapañcānana writes that an opponent might still argue that unless the means injunction is also understood as producing some merit (or, at least, the absence of the demerit of general slaughter) the agent would not feel inclined to abide by it; and this means that there is some awareness of some contradiction—the contradiction, say, between not slaughtering and slaughtering, or between generation and nongeneration of demerit.

Some Sāṃkhyans, Kṛṣṇanātha Nyāyapañcānana imagines, might reply that even then there is no contradiction: all that is to be inquired into is whether here the frustration that the agent would undergo because of the slaughter is just sufficient for or exceeds the satisfaction that would result from the performance of the rite. These Sāṃkhyans, Kṛṣṇanātha Nyāyapañcānana claims, would hold that it is just sufficient and does not exceed, which means that there is no question of contradiction so far.

Kṛṣṇanātha Nyāyapañcānana rejects this claim of the hypothetical opponent on another ground, however. He holds that the agent's frustration that results from slaughter of animals is not like the frustration caused by fast, huge expenditure, physical exertion, etc., required for the performance of a rite. The latter type of frustration ends with the performance of that rite and pales into insignificance when compared with the total merit gained and the total satisfaction to be gained. On the other hand, the demerit caused by slaughter continues even after the rite is over and produces appropriate frustration at the appropriate time (maybe, in hell). That way, therefore, there is still some contradiction involved—contradiction (i.e., trial of strength) between the merit of the rite (and the consequent satisfaction) and the palpable (i.e., not "implicit") frustration caused by slaughter.

Kṛṣṇanātha Nyāyapañcānana concludes, however, that the relation that truly obtains here is between greater satisfaction and lesser frustration, and that that relation is not contradiction. One who performs a rite through slaughter of animals earns greater satisfaction, though with some frustration (because of slaughter), and, decidedly, the frustration is less in magnitude.

But even then Kṛṣṇanātha Nyāyapañcānana anticipates a further objection: if only that act that produces greater frustration must be desisted from (i.e., more frustration and lesser satisfaction), why then should Sāṃkhya find fault at all with the slaughter, which is necessary for the performance of rites and which the Mīmāṃsakas in so many words recommend? Kṛṣṇanātha Nyāyapañcānana's reply is twofold: Even as a necessary means slaughter is unjustified, first, because there is the general prohibition against (any) slaughter (whatever), and, second, because frustration in hell (i.e., after the merit gained through the rite has produced appropriate mundane satisfaction) is greater in magnitude (particularly, in intensity) than any mundane satisfaction.

II. The Instruments of Knowledge

(4) In connection with the three instruments of knowledge that are recognized in Sāṃkhya, Kṛṣṇanātha Nyāyapañcānana writes: The Lokāyatas recognize only one instrument, perception; the Vaiśeṣikas two, perception and inference; Nyāya, four, perception, inference, comparison, and verbal testimony; the Prābhākaras add a fifth, presumption; the (Bhāṭṭa) Mīmāṃsakas add another, (appropriate) nonperception; and the Paurāṇikas two more, inclusion and tradition.

(5) In connection with the definition of perception Vācaspati Miśra explains "reflective discerning" as belief (*niścaya*), as opposed to doubt and vacillation. Kṛṣṇanātha Nyāyapañcānana, however, understands it as judgment of the form "This is such and such" (without underscoring "is"). Of course, a few lines later he accepts Vācaspati Miśra's interpretation almost in toto: he calls it "belief" (*niścaya*) in the sense that there is no vacillation between unassured alternatives.

In connection with the analysis of the concepts "having wider denotation" (*vyāpaka*) and "having narrower denotation" (*vyāpya*), in the context of inference (*anumāna*), Vācaspati Miśra only insists that for a legitimate inference there must not be any other limiting adjunct (*upādhi*) involved, assured, or suspected. Kṛṣṇanātha Nyāyapañcānana elaborates this notion of *upādhi* further in the line of neo-Nyāya. He writes: If from a case of M one seeks to infer P, one has first to see that there is no adjunct *x* (*upādhi*) involved such that the class of *x*-s includes the class of P-s (i.e., wherever there is P, there is *x*, or negatively, there is no P without *x*) and also that it is not true that the class of *x*-s includes the class of M-s (i.e., wherever there is M, there is *x*). The relation between M and P will be unconditional (*svābhāvika*) if only such *x*, assured or suspected, is known to be absent.

The presence of *x* is "assured" when it is either perceived or correctly inferred (of course, this would be an additional inference); it is "suspected" when it is neither perceived nor (correctly) inferred but just believed to be there on some ground, say, on some testimony.

Kṛṣṇanātha Nyāyapañcānana refers, in this connection, to the Vaiśeṣika doctrine that the relation between M and P is unconditional (*svābhāvika*) if only M is the effect of, or the cause of, or in contact with, or opposed to P, or where P inheres in M. But he does not elaborate it further.

In connection with the type of inference called positive (*vīta*) Kṛṣṇanātha Nyāyapañcānana adds that this is a type of inference that is based on a merely affirmative universal proposition, or two universal propositions, one of which is affirmative and the other negative. "*Vīta*," in other words, stands both for only-positive (*kevalānvayī*) and positive-negative (*anvayavyatirekī*) inference. Exclusionary (*avīta*) is that type of inference which is based on a mere negative universal proposition. It is what is otherwise called only-negative (*kevalavyatirekī*) inference.

In connection with exclusionary inference he, by way of clarification, adds the following further point: The traditional example of exclusionary inference is: "Earth (soil) is other than water, fire, air, and *ākāśa*, because it has the quality of smell." The corresponding general proposition is spelled out as: whatever material is not other than water, fire, air, and *ākāśa* has no smell. Obviously, it cannot be "whatever material has smell is other than water, fire, air, and *ākāśa*," for that precisely is what has to be established, given that earth is the only example of the material (we have so far) that has smell and is other than water, fire, air, and *ākāśa*. Kṛṣṇanātha Nyāyapañcānana describes the inferential process that is involved here as follows: Finding that in water there is otherness neither from water nor smell; in fire, otherness neither from fire nor smell; and so on in air and ether, one is assured (provided he is assured also that these are *all the cases* of "being other than whatever is not earth") that wherever there is absence of anything other than earth there is absence of smell. All these other materials being thus exluded, it follows, reductio ad absurdum, that what has that smell (viz., earth) is other than all other materials. This is why this type of inference is also called "inference by elimination" (*pariśeṣa anumāna*).

"Other than earth" cannot here mean anything other than earth. For, whenever we relevantly compare two or more entities we compare them on the ground of their proximate generic features, not on the ground of any of their distant generic features; or better, a proximate generic feature being available, no relevant comparison should proceed on the ground of a more distant generic feature. In the present context, the proximate generic feature is their "being materials" (*bhūtatva*). So, their "being just things" (*dravyatva*) is an irrelevant, consideration here.

In connection with knowledge from verbal testimony, i.e., knowledge of an object acquired through hearing someone speak of it, Kṛṣṇanātha Nyāyapañcānana writes: When somebody is speaking about an object that the hearer happens also to perceive (i.e., where both testimony and perception are available as methods of acquiring knowledge), the resulting knowledge comes through perception, not through hearing (except that we then have awareness of certain sounds). Perception takes the upper hand and testimony ceases to function as a method. This is certified by whatever introspection we have into the resulting cognition: the introspection in such cases, is invariably of the form "I perceive this," not of the form" I learn it through testimony."

In connection with Vācaspati Miśra's thesis (common practically to all systems of Indian philosophy) that awareness derived through hearing (or reading) Vedic statements is intrinsically valid (*svataḥ pramāṇa*) Kṛṣṇanātha Nyāyapañcānana adds a short note on intrinsic and extrinsic validity of awareness. An awareness is intrinsically valid if only the very factors that make us take it as an awareness also guarantee its validity, i.e., when for its validation, or for the awareness of its validity, other factors or other confirming awarenesses are required. Such is the case with awareness of things derived from hearing (or reading) Vedic statements that are about them. These statements as eternal, i.e., as not spoken by any person, are free from all limitations of time and personality and, therefore, cannot be false. Hence, knowledge derived through hearing (or reading) them does not require extrinsic validation. It is intrinsically valid.

Another point that Kṛṣṇanātha Nyāyapañcānana discusses in this connection is worth noting: That sentences have the general capacity for indicating (meaning) particular states of affair is indeed inferred from the (perceptual) awareness that different states of affairs emerge consequent upon the utterance of different particular sentences. That the constituent words also have similar general capacity for indicating constituent items or relations is equally a matter of inference. Yet, however, for a definite particular sentence or word to mean a definite particular type of state of affair, item, or relation (where the state of affairs, etc., are known through our hearing that sentence, etc.) is not necessarily a case of inference (though sometimes it is so). According to Vācaspati Miśra and Kṛṣṇanātha Nyāyapañcānana, it is a case of immediate knowledge, and this immediate knowledge—obviously, not perception—is precisely what is called "knowledge through testimony" (*śābda jñāna*).

Vācaspati Miśra reduces comparison partly to testimony, partly to inference, and partly to perception. In connection with its partial reduction to perception he claims that the perceived similarity and the remembered similarity are entitatively one and the same. Obviously, by "comparison" here he understands the *upamāna* of the Naiyāyikas. Kṛṣṇanātha Nyāyapañcānana adds that Vācaspati Miśra's statement with regard to the identity of the two similarities applies equally against the Mīmāṃsā notion of *upamāna*.

In connection with the reduction of (appropriate) nonperception, Kṛṣṇanātha Nyayapañcānana writes that there is not only no separate instrument of knowledge called nonperception, for Sāṃkhya there is also no object (of knowledge) called absence (*abhāva*). Kṛṣṇanātha Nyāyapañcānana believes that Vācaspati Miśra has hinted at this when he named the instrument in question as "*abhāva*" and not "*anupalabdhi.*"

In connection with Vācaspati Miśra's reduction of the Paurāṇika's inclusion (*sambhava*) to inference, Kṛṣṇanātha Nyāyapañcānana gives, as examples of this instrument of knowledge, the passing from the knowledge of a thousand rupees to that of a hundred rupees and from the knowledge of the Brahminhood of a man to that of his being learned, etc.[1]

III. The Notion of Preexistent Effect

(9) By way of introducing this *kārikā*, Vācaspati Miśra states four different views. They are (1) Being arises from nonbeing; (2) everything whatsoever that arises from one primal Being is, insofar as it arises, nonbeing; (3) nonbeing arises from Being; and (4) Being arises from Being. Kṛṣṇanātha Nyāyapañcānana further specifies these views as follows: View (1) is of the Buddhists—*a* can arise from *b* only after *b* has ceased to be. View (2) is of the (Advaita) Vedāntin. (A little later, in the *Āvaraṇavarṇī* the Advaita theory of *Vivarta* has been explained). View (3) is of Nyāya and Vaiśeṣika—the effect that was not there, that, in other words, was so long nonbeing, arises out of the cause that was there. (Atoms are the ultimate causes.) View (4) is of Sāṃkhya.

Vācaspati Miśra writes that this verse is addressed to the Naiyāyikas and Vaiśeṣikas, not to the Buddhists or (Advaita) Vedāntists. Kṛṣṇanātha Nyayapañcānana explains why it is addressed to Nyāya-Vaiśeṣika only. In the course of this explanation he gives a short account of the five-membered inference for others (*parārthānumāna*) and repeats Vācaspati Miśra's contention that the arguments in this verse are not relevant against Buddhism or (Advaita) Vedānta.

IV. Manifest and Unmanifest Aspects of Materiality

(10) Vācaspati Miśra holds that the manifest aspects of materiality —from intellect downward—are noneternal because some time or other they get destroyed (cease to be). Kṛṣṇanātha Nyāyapañcānana, unhappy over the expression "get destroyed" (or 'cease to be'), puts Vācaspati Miśra's view a little differently, as follows: These manifest principles cannot be said to have originated, for that would go against the Sāṃkhya theory of preexistent effect. But then the theory of preexistent effect is equally against destruction (something ceasing to be). So by "destruction" Vācaspati Miśra must have meant getting latent again in the (material) cause, quite as much as "originational" should mean just getting patent.

(11) Kṛṣṇanātha Nyāyapañcānana explains why the three consti-

tuents are named by Vācaspati Miśra (and also by the author of the *Kārikā*) as (1) agreeableness (*prīti*=*sukha*), (2) disagreeableness (*aprīti*=*duḥkha*), and (3) lethargy, apathy, sluggishness, and, in the extreme case, dumbfoundedness (all represented by the Sanskrit term "*viṣāda*" or "*moha*"), and why they have not been named here, as is the usual practice elsewhere, as intelligibility (*sattva*), activity (*rajas*), and inertia (*tamas*). The reason, as Kṛṣṇanātha Nyāyapañcānana states it, is that up till now no verse has stated these under the latter names, nor has it till now been established that the manifest and the unmanifest possess them (under such names). Kṛṣṇanātha Nyāyapañcānana holds that this is a broad enough hint that *sattva*, *rajas*, and *tamas* are inferred as causes that produce satisfaction, frustration, and confusion respectively.

Further, these three constituents belong, according to Sāṃkhya, to the manifest and the unmanifest, not to self that is pure consciousness.

In connection with Vācaspati Miśra's contention that neither the unmanifest nor any of the manifest principles can transform itself alone, i.e., merely through its own effort, Kṛṣṇanātha Nyāyapañcānana writes, by way of clarification, that none of these can be transformed without the help of merit or demerit (good or bad *adṛṣṭa*) acquired through acts done in the prior life.

In introducing the Sāṃkhya view that the manifest principles and the unmanifest are all objects (not modes of pure consciousness), Vācaspati Miśra says that this view is posited against the opposite view of the Vijñānavāda Buddhist; Kṛṣṇanātha Nyāyapañcānana, by way of elucidation, adds a short but on the whole adequate account of this Buddhist view along with the arguments that are usually offered in its behalf.

VI. Inferences for Existence of Primordial Materiality and Consciousness

(17) Vācaspati Miśra, after explaining how self that is pure consciousness is to be inferred from "*bhoktṛbhāva*" (hedonic experience of satisfaction, frustration, etc.), gives an alternative interpretation of the term. He says that some others mean by it (i.e., by "*bhoktṛbhāva*") "*draṣṭṛbhāva*" (cognitive experience of objects). But he does not criticize this other interpretation. Kṛṣṇanātha Nyāyapañcānana, however, declares openly that this alternative interpretation is definitely less acceptable, because the Sanskrit root "*bhuj*" cannot mean cognitive experience, except secondarily.

(18) Vācaspati Miśra defines "birth" as the first-instant relation of a self (pure consciousness) with a unique complex of the subtle and gross (physical) body.

Kṛṣṇanātha Nyāyapañcānana adds that this definition successfully excludes the possibility of several other relations being (wrongly) called birth. At the very beginning of creation, for example, when subtle bodies were created (creation of subtle bodies corresponds to that which in other religions is called creation of selves), one for each single self, the self (pure consciousness) in question, which is eternal, came to be related to the subtle body appointed for it. But this was no case of birth, because no gross body was there at that time. And, similarly with regard to the transitional "life" between one death and the next birth (the theory of transmigration of the subtle body being assumed). Again, though from one birth to the next death the self remains in close relation with one and the same complex of subtle and gross body, this is not to be understood as continuous birth (or a series of births), for it is no first-instant relation (except at the first instant). The gross body in that particular life, no doubt, changes from moment to moment, but its continuant identity is experienced at every two successive segments of time, whether by the agent himself or by observers from outside. The gross body is one that is initially contributed by parents, though in consonance with the merits and demerits acquired by the agent in his prior life.

(20) In this verse, and in Vācaspati Miśra's commentary on it, it is stated that the nonconscious subtle body appears (wrongly) as with conscious. Kṛṣṇanātha Nyāyapañcānana clarifies this statement the help of a traditional analogy: a white crystal appearing (falsely) as red when adjacent to it there is a red flower.

Similarly, for the second thesis of the verse—that due to the nearness of the subtle body, which is truly the agent of all action, the self (as pure consciousness) appears (falsely) as an agent—Kṛṣṇanātha Nyāyapañcānana offers another traditional analogy. It is that of a red-hot iron ball (falsely) said to burn whatever comes in contact with it, because of some fire being in its maximum vicinity (i.e., penetrating it through and through).

IX. The Functioning of the Thirteenfold Instrument

(29) Vācaspati Miśra identifies each of the five airs (*vāyu*) by the places they occupy in the body. Kṛṣṇanātha Nyāyapañcānana does not elucidate this further. Rather, he collects from earlier literature (Upaniṣads, *Yogasūtra*, and medical literature) various bits of edifying information regarding this.

(30) Vācaspati Miśra explains the appropriate functions of the instruments, intellect, egoity, and the different capacities (mind as the internal organ and the sense and action capacities), all teleologically. Kṛṣṇanātha Nyāyapañcānana adds that teleology here is only

another name for merits and demerits (acquired through actions done in the prior life) now functioning (i.e., maturing).

(35) In connection with the distinction between the functions of external capacities and internal organs Vācaspati Miśra writes, following the *kārikā*, that, although the former have to be in relation with objects that are copresent with them, the latter may have for their objects things and events that are past or future too. But he adds that in the case of sound as the object of the action capacity called speech its presentness means "immediate past," which is contiguous with the present. Kṛṣṇanātha Nyāyapañcānana explains this as follows: According to Sāṃkhya, as opposed to the view of the Mīmaṃsakas, sound is not eternal. It is generated by contact of things—here, in the case of speech, by some contact in the throat and the cavity of the mouth (*kaṇṭhatālusaṃyoga*)—and, therefore, occurs after this contact has taken place. Yet, as that future occurrence is immediately after the contact it is taken, in common parlance, as copresent with it, much as when intending that I shall come immediately I often say "I am coming."

(34) Vācaspati Miśra, in identifying the nonspecific (*aviśeṣa*) as subtle elements (*tanmātra*), writes that the word "*mātra*" (*tanmātra*= *tat*+*mātra*="that only"), suffixed to the word "*tat*," shows that *tanmātras* are not elements (*bhūta*). Kṛṣṇanātha Nyāyapañcānana adds, in the interest of precision, that "*bhūta*" here stands for the gross elements (*mahābhūta*) only, for *tanmātras* are, after all, subtle elements.

(37) After explaining whatever Vācaspati Miśra has said, Kṛṣṇanātha Nyāyapañcānana adds: Although liberation cannot be sought by consciousness, because liberation constitutes the very essence of consciousness that is, its being other than materiality, which is the source of all frustration, yet as we have started our life with the confusion of the two (precisely because of which we are frustrated), consciousness' true essence (as being other than materiality) remains hidden so far from our view. It is only against this background that one can intelligibly seek recovery from the confusion—seek, in other words, to intuit this otherness of consciousness from materiality. And, that comes to the same thing as seeking absolute cessation of frustration.

X. Subtle and Gross Elements

(39) Vācaspati Miśra writes that the existence of the subtle body constituted by intellect, egoity, mind, and the five subtle elements is (only) inferred, never known directly (except by Yogis and superhuman beings). Vācaspati Miśra, however, does not give any hint as to how it can be inferred. Kṛṣṇanātha Nyāyapañcānana adds that it is to be inferred on the ground that in its absence there cannot be any experience of satisfaction, frustration, or confusion, or even of dumbfoundedness.[2]

At this point he diverts the discussion by bringing in a quite different consideration, that is, whether there could be any such experience in the absence of the gross physical body. He replies that there can be because, otherwise, no transmigrating self, during the period between one death and the next birth, could experience pleasures of heaven or sufferings of hell. It follows, he concludes, that the subtle body is the minimum that is required (as a medium) for experiencing satisfaction, frustration, etc., whether in this earthly life or elsewhere. The gross body, in addition, is required for earthly satisfactions and frustrations.

Vācaspati Miśra holds that from the mother's side one gets his hairs (*loman*), blood, and flesh. Kṛṣṇanātha Nyāyapañcānana adds that by "hairs" he must have meant skin, for that is what is stated in the scripture. Kṛṣṇanatha Nyāyapañcānana holds that Vācaspati Miśra does not use the word "skin" (*tvak*) lest readers confuse it with the sense-capacity 'touch'.

XI. The Subtle Body

(40) Kṛṣṇanātha Nyāyapañcānana refers to a different reading of the verse in which, in place of "*asakta*" there is the word "*aśakta*" which means "than which there is nothing more powerful," in short, "that which is capable of doing everything."

Kṛṣṇanātha Nyāyapañcānana holds that where in (38) it has been said that the gross elements are specific as distinct from the subtle elements, which are nonspecific, what has really been meant is that the gross elements are so because they are either comforting or uncomfortable or confusing. This further means, Kṛṣṇanatha Nyāyāpañcānana holds, that whatever is comforting or uncomfortable or confusing is a specific. Now, sense and action capacities, egoity, and intellect are immediately experienced that way,[3] which means further that whatever else involve them are of that nature. This is why in Sāṃkhya, Kṛṣṇanātha Nyāyapañcānana holds, the subtle body is taken as a specific. But on all counts subtle elements are excluded.

XII. The Basic Predispositions

(45) In connection with the distinction between the innate predispositions of the intellect and those predispositions that are modalized by other factors, that is, by good or bad deeds (Sāṃkhya calls these acquired predispositions) (*asāṃsiddhika* = *vaikṛta*), Kṛṣṇanātha Nyāyapañcānana writes that this distinction is valid with regard to the right (as opposed to "wrong") states only,[4] that is, to meritorious behavior, knowledge, nonattachment, and supernormal powers, not with regard to the corresponding wrong states, demeritorious

behavior, ignorance, attachment, and loss or lack of supernormal powers. These latter are all acquired through bad deeds. What Kṛṣṇanātha Nyāyapañcānana means is that right predispositions of intellect are either intrinsic to it—and are thus innate predispositions—or acquired by good deeds, and are, therefore, partly extrinsic. All wrong predispositions, on the other hand, are distorted—and thus extrinsic—modes effected through bad deeds.

II. Although Vācaspati Miśra has never said anything about whether the different predispositions of the gross physical body can also be grouped as either innate or acquired, Kṛṣṇanātha Nyāyapañcānana does. He says that the different predispositions in the development of the fetus are all innate in it, and all other states of the physical body (obviously, states after one is born), that is, childhood, puberty, youth, and decrepitude, are acquired from outside. Vācaspati Miśra has only said that there are four crucial fetal states and four crucial postnatal states.

Kṛṣṇanātha Nyāyapañcānana, in support of his point, has quoted medical and semimedical passages from ancient literature.

(48) In connection with sixty-two varieties of misconception Kṛṣṇanātha Nyāyapañcānana shows in detail how every variety of confusion, attachment, aversion, and fear involves error through chain implication.

(50) To Vācaspati Miśra's commentary Kṛṣṇanātha Nyāyapañcānana adds that every second form of *ādhyātmika tuṣṭi* (deeper contentment) points, by implication, to the invalidity of the just preceding form. He shows it very clearly in the case of the fourth form (called *sopādāna* or *salila*). Madālasa's (a mythical princess) children could intuit the separateness of pure consciousness and materiality apparently without any spiritual exercise, only because they had gone through it all in their prior life. The spiritual exercise in question is listening to scriptural truths (*śravaṇa*), justifying them by analysis and arguments (*manana*), and concentrating on them in meditation (*nididhyāsana*). Those complacent people who, finding that even children who, apparently, had not undergone these exercises could intuit the final truth, conclude that these exercises are, therefore, not necessary prerequisites are wrong in that they do not know that those children practiced them in their previous life, as the full story testifies.[5]

(51) After offering his account of eight attainments, Vācaspati Miśra puts forward another interpretation. He writes "*vinopadeśādinā jñānī jñānaṃ prayacchati*" and simply ends with the remark that the merits and defects of this interpretation are to be judged by wise scholars. He himself does not examine it.

Kṛṣṇanātha Nyāyapañcānana, however, examines it and exposes its defects one by one. (Vācaspati Miśra, he says, did not care to examine it, because its defects were evident.) The defects as Kṛṣṇanātha Nyāyapañcānana finds them are as follows:

(1) In spite of all spiritual practice in the prior life, what is absolutely needed in the present life is the expert teacher's advice (imparting the final truth through the medium of language).

(2) If it were possible to intuit the separateness of consciousness and materiality just through hearing others reading Sāṃkhya one could as well intuit it through just reading Sāṃkhya himself. Why not, then, add this last as a ninth accomplishment? And this so-called ninth is certainly not identical with ratiocination (*ūha*).

(3) Further, again, if it were possible to intuit the separateness of consciousness and materiality just through hearing others reading Sāṃkhya, then even "learning the scripture under the tutelage of a teacher" (*adhyayana*) would be redundant, because that teacher is as much an "other person" as anybody else.

(4) As for getting in touch with another spiritual practitioner (*suhṛtprāpti*), this could be of use only if that experienced practitioner imparts advice (*upadeśa*) through speech; and similarly with the fee paid to him (*dāna*), for learned men, properly paid, will after all impart advice. So such cases would only be repetitious.

Toward the end of his commentary Kṛṣṇanātha Nyāyapañcānana refers to another "modern" interpretation of the text "*siddheḥ pūrvo'ṅkuśas trividhaḥ*" in the *Kārikā* without, however, naming this "modern" interpreter. He, of course, exposes the errors of this interpretation.

XIII. The Empirical World

(52) Kṛṣṇanātha Nyāyapañcānana holds that body as the medium through which one is to have experience (with hedonic tone) is primarily the subtle body and, through that only, the gross physical body secondarily.

(56) Kṛṣṇanātha Nyāyapañcānana explains Vācaspati Miśra's "*akāraṇatve atyantābhāvaḥ* etc." as follows: The world is not without some cause. It has a cause because, being composite in structure and having a shape, it must have emerged at a point of time (and must get destroyed too at some other point of time). That which has no cause can neither emerge nor disappear at a point of time.

XIV. Similes Illustrating Materiality

(57) Where Vācaspati Miśra writes that all actions of an agent are determined by desire for some satisfaction (or removal of some frustration) of his own or of others (as in the case of benevolence), Kṛṣṇanātha Nyāyapañcānana adds that the satisfaction (or the removal

of frustration) of others is never a direct determinant. The direct determinant is always some satisfaction (or removal of frustration) of one's own.

XV. Liberation and Isolation

(64) Kṛṣṇanātha Nyāyapañcānana writes that what has to be practiced with care, etc., is not the intuition of the separateness of consciousness and materiality—for obviously that cannot be practiced—but the corresponding conceptual knowledge derived from the teacher.

HARIPRASĀDA

Hariprasāda's commentary on the *Sāṃkhyasūtras* is based on the *Bhāṣya* of Vijñānabhikṣu and also quotes, in one or two places, Aniruddha's *Vṛtti*. Views summarized here are those either not found in the *Bhāṣya* or those especially held by the author in adducing arguments. The author is the disciple of a teacher named Ātmarāma who belonged to the order of the Udāsīna sect. The commentary was published in 1905 towards the end of the author's l'Fetime.

SĀṂKHYASŪTRAVṚTTI

(*Summary by Ram Shankar Bhattacharya*)

Book I:

(A) *Introductory Verses: The Scope and Task of Sāṃkhya*

(I.1) Among the two human goals, that is, experience of objects and liberation, experience of objects cannot be regarded as final as it is capable of being annihilated. As absolute cessation of frustration has no end; it can reasonably be regarded as the supreme goal. Frustration is superimposed on consciousness.

(I.5) Liberation is regarded as the highest goal; the goal to be attained by secular means is regarded as forsakable (*heya*).

(B) *Bondage*

(I.7) Bondage is nothing but connection with frustration.

(I.10) As a seed's natural power of producing sprouts can be destroyed so the natural bondage of consciousness can be eradicated by the means prescribed by the scripture.

(I.26) It is remarked that some of the views of Śaṃkarācārya (e.g., that ignorance is inexplicable [*anirvacanīya*]) are similar to those of the Yogācāra school.

(I.95) The purpose of the scriptural passages on God is either to glorify liberated souls or to prescribe devout meditation for perfect beings.

(I.96) Because of His association with consciousness and materiality, God becomes their controller.

(I.104-105) Although experience of objects is a kind of modification of the intellect, yet it does not ultimately reside in the intellect, which is inert. That is why it cannot be regarded as enjoyer. Consciousness, although devoid of agency, is enjoyer because it is awareness. Experience becomes reflected in the modifications of the intellect, which is influenced by objects. Consciousness enjoys the fruits of actions performed by the intellect.

(I.107) Both agency and enjoyership cease if the essential nature of consciousness and materiality is realized.

(F) *Materiality and the Theory of Preexistent Effect*

(I.108) The word "*hāna*" in the *sūtra* means injury to the organs and "*upādāna*" means nonsteadiness of the mind.

(I.113) The three kinds of opposition mean contradiction with the Vedas, smṛtis, and ratiocination (*nyāya*).

(H) *Three Constituents*

(I.128) The similarities in the constituents are to be understood in respect of human goals, etc., and the divergences in respect of their characteristics such as lightness, etc.

(I) *Inferences Establishing Primordial Materiality and Consciousness*

(I.130-132) The three arguments stated in these two *sūtras* show that the intellect, etc., are of the nature of effect.

(I.142) Although it is God, and not the embodied self (*jiva*), who is the controller of materiality, yet an embodied self is said to be the controller as he is regarded as the enjoyer. In fact an embodied self is the controller of his own intellect.

(I.145) Consciousness is nothing but awareness (*jñāna*) that is divine (*aprākṛta*, of the nature of anti-*guṇa*).

(I.146) Awareness cannot be regarded as a property of consciousness, for consciousness is not a substrate of properties or qualities (*guṇa*).

(I.160-162) God is different from consciousness and materiality. He is a particular kind of consciousness who is not touched or affected by afflictions, etc. He is the witness of all and is eternally liberated.

(I.164) The agency of God is due to His association with materiality, and it is of the nature of prompting or instigating (*prayojaka*-

kartṛtva). In reality proper agency belongs to materiality because of its association with God.

Book II: Effects of Materiality

(A) *Activity of Materiality and the Distinction from Consciousness*

(II.8) The power of creation found in the divine consciousness (*puruṣeśvara*) is dependent on His association with materiality.

(II.9) The association of materiality (called *rāga* in this *sūtra*) and the divine consciousness (called *virāga* in this *sūtra*) is the cause of creation (the word "creation," [*sṛṣṭi*] stands for the cause of creation).

(B) *Materiality and Its Effects*

(II.11) The creation done by materiality is for itself as well as for others. Creation done by intellect, etc., is not for themselves but for others only.

(C) *Space and Time*

(II.12) In this *sūtra*, "*ākāśa*" means "*ākāśa* characterized by different limiting adjuncts " (*tattadupādhiviśiṣṭākāśa*).

(E) *Ego and Capacities*

(II.18) The word "*ekādaśaka*" means the eleven organs (according to Bhikṣu, the word means "eleventh," i.e , the organ of mind).

(G) *Capacities and Their Differences from Consciousness*

(II.31) Vital breath is the general function of the internal as well as the external capacities. The author has refuted the view of Bālarāma Udāsīna that breath is the operation of the three internal organs only. Here he has referred to his commentary, *Cittaprasādinī* on the *Sāṃkhyakārikā*.

(H) *The Thirteenfold Instrument*

(II.39) An instrument (*karaṇa*) is an uncommon (*asādhāraṇa*) cause possessing operation (*vyāpāra*).

(II.43) The existence of latent dispositions is inferred through the existence of memory caused by past experience.

(II.44) Without the help of external organs the intellect cannot apprehend exernal objects.

Book III: Nonattachment

(A) *Specific and Nonspecific*

(III.2-4) The gross body is the product of the five gross elements; the subtle body, which is made up of seventeen factors, is the seed (*bīja*) of the gross body; the intellect, etc., create the body.

(B) *Gross and Subtle Body*

(III.8-10) It is the subtle and not the gross body that is the seat (*āyatana*) of experience. Each subtle body is associated with one consciousness and the difference in the subtle bodies is due to the difference of actions.

(III.11-14) Properly speaking, the word "body" (*śarīra*) means subtle body (*liṅgaśarīra*); it means the gross body in a secondary sense only. The subtle body has a form (*mūrta*); it is of medium magnitude; it affords experience to consciousness, when it becomes associated with a gross body. Intellect cannot exist without it.

(E) *Dreaming, Waking, and Yogic Awareness*

(III.27-28) The results of the threefold actions, namely, *nitya* (obligatory), *naimittika* (obligatory on special occasion), and *kāmya* (to be performed with a view to attaining a desired object) cannot be everlasting (*ātyantika*).

(III.29) Knowledge dawns in a purified heart as a result of practicing the higher forms of meditation by suppressing attachment to objects.

(I) *Materiality and Discrimination*

(III.55-57) The all-producing materiality is under the control of God, who is omniscient and omnipotent and whose existence is proved by the Vedas only. An individual self comes again and again to this world, a product of materiality, in accordance with the divine law.

(J) *Discrimination and Liberation*

(III.74) It is nondiscrimination that is the cause of bondage.

Book V : Arguments Against Opponents

(A) *On the Existence of God*

(V.10-12) Divine nature cannot be attributed to all embodied or individual selves (*jīva*). The powers of the selves are the products of materiality.

(B) *Notion of Ignorance*

(V.13-14) Brahman, which is beyond all attachment, is called "God" when it becomes associated with the power called ignorance. This association with ignorance cannot be proved to be false.

(V.19) If the transitory world (*jagat*) is essentially the same as nescience then the latter must have a beginning.

(C) *The Existence of Meritorious Behavior*

(V.21) Because the experience of satisfaction is a form of experience it must have a cause, as is found in the case of frustration. This cause is called "*adṛṣṭa*" (unseen), i.e., merit. Yogic perception is also a proof for the existence of merit.

(D) *Merit, Qualities, Inference*

(V.26-27) The word "*guṇādi*" (in *sūtra* 26) means merit and the rest (see V.25), whose existence can easily be proved through inference.

(V.30-36) Pervasion (*vyāpti*) is nothing but invariable coexistence, which is manifested by the natural power of things. What is pervaded has natural concomitance with its pervader. The word "*ādheyaśakti*" (in V.32) signifies the relation between pervaded and pervader. It is remarked that the view of the sage Pañcaśikha on pervasion is not identical with the generally accepted view of Sāṃkhya teachers.

(E) *Word and Meaning*

(V.46-51) "*Pauruṣeya*" means "not composed by the embodied or individual self (*jīva*)" (and not "not composed by God" as is explained by some commentators). Although the Vedas are not composed by an embodied self, yet they are not eternal. The Vedas are self evident, as they are not based on any other means of knowledge.

(F) *Knowledge and Error*

(V.53-56) This *sūtra* is explained as refuting the illusion theory of the Vijñānavādins saying that had silver (apprehended in a mother of pearl) been identical with its consciousness (*vijñāna*) it would not have been sublated. It is remarked that (1) the theory of *anyathākhyāti* (taking one thing for another) is not in accordance with the Nyāya theory declaring correspondence between cognition and its content and that (2) in reality erroneous knowledge is nondiscrimination of two cognitions (such nondiscrimination arises in every case of erroneous knowledge, as we find in the case of the erroneous knowledge of silver in mother of pearl).

(H) *Nonduality*

(V.65) God is existence-consciousness-bliss, whereas the individual self is existence-consciousness. The essential nature of an embodied self consists in consciousness only and not in consciousness and bliss, for there is no feeling of bliss at the time of experiencing frustration.

(V.68) It is the ignorant who hold the anti-Vedic doctrine that in the state of release the individual self becomes full of bliss.

(I) *Mind and Internal Organ*

(V.73) Both the individual self and materiality have no parts—a view sanctioned by the Vedas.

(L) *Nyāya-Vaiśeṣika Categories and Atomism*

(V.87) The word "*aṇu*" means *trasareṇu* (triad, an aggregate of three dyads), which are the products of the five subtle elements.

(*O*) *Universals*

(V.91-92) A universal is a property inhering in many things; it is neither materiality nor consciousness, and it is noneternal. Recognition (*pratyabhijñā*) is based on it.

(V.96) The knowledge of the relation between a name (*saṃjñā*) and the named (*saṃjñin*) is not based on similarity. This relation is to be known through the statements of trustworthy persons (*āptopadeśa*).

(P) *Relations*

(V.98) The contact or association between noneternal things must be noneternal. All contacts are invariably preceded by disjunctions.

(V.99) The relation called inherence in the Nyāya-Vaiśeṣika system is known as a self-linking connector (*svarūpasambandha*) in Sāṃkhya-Yoga and as identity (*tādātmya*) in Vedānta.

(U) *Bodies*

(V.113) The vital breath is originated from a particular power of the capacities.

(V.115) The body, being the seat of the embodied self, is said to be the seat of God, as the former is under the control of the latter. The former is similar to and not identical with the latter. Properties like the absence of frustration and the like are common to both the embodied and the Supreme Self.

(W) *Types of Beings*

(V.127) Awareness, etc., being the properties of intellect (and not of the individual self) cannot be eternal.

Book VI : Summary

(A) *Nature and Discrimination of the Self*

(VI.9) Although according to Sāṃkhya, absolute absence of all frustration is liberation, yet it is held that an embodied self attains Brahman's bliss in the state of liberation. This attainment of bliss is, however, not the result of any effort but is manifested naturally. That is why the supreme goal is said to be one only.

(VI.20) Liberation is nothing but the eradication of nondiscrimination.

(B) *On the Means of Attaining Discrimination*

(VI.25) When the mind becomes engrossed in *ātman* (and not in any other object), then the state is called meditation (*dhyāna*).

(VI.30) Latent dispositions (*vāsanā*) come to an end if all the five kinds of operations of awareness (see YS 1.5-6) are repressed by means of meditations, etc.

(C) *Primordial Materiality*

(VI.37) Although materiality acts in accordance with the will of God yet there is no wrong in holding that it is the primal (*ādya*) cause of the world.

(D) *Plurality of Consciousnesses*

(VI.48) Advaitins support their theory of the unity of self (*ātman*) by taking the divergence of birth, etc., of embodied beings as associated with the limiting adjuncts only and not with self. This, however, is untenable and there is no proof to prove the unity of selves.

(VI.50) Consciousness is not the substrate (*āśraya*) of awareness (*prakāśa*, illumination) but is awareness only; it is the all-witnessing entity.

(E) *The Manifest World*

(VI.55) Consciousness is associated with action through the ego; this is why it is regarded as the doer. Agentship and enjoyership cannot be attributed to consciousness, as both of them are in essence of the same nature. Consciousness is regarded as enjoyer, for egoity, being inert, cannot be an enjoyer.

(VI. 59) According to Sāṃkhya, consciousness is of atomic magnitude and is devoid of motion.

(VI.63) Consciousness is called embodied self (*jīva*) when it becomes associated with egoity. An embodied self is independent, not in experiencing satisfaction and frustration, but in performing actions.

BĀLARĀMA UDĀSĪNA

Bālarāma Udāsīna, born in 1855, was a follower of the Udāsīna sect and studied Vedānta with Rāmamiśra Śāstrin. He went to Bengal to study Nyāya and lived, for last part of his life, in Varanasi. He composed a short Sanskrit commentary on the *Vyāsabhāsya-Tattvavaiśāradī*, a Hindi commentary on the *Yogasūtras*, and a few works on religious matters also (*Śrautasarvasva*, etc.).

The *Vidvattoṣiṇī* on Vācaspati's *Tattvakaumudī* was composed by the commentator up to verse 33. The remaining part of the commentary (along with the last four paragraphs of the commentary on the 33rd verse)—which is obviously very brief—was composed by Pandit Rāmāvatāra Śarman, one of his disciples.

The summary is prepared from the edition published by Ātmasvarūpa Udāsīna in Varanasi in 1930.

VIDVATTOṢIṆĪ ON TATTVAKAUMUDĪ

(*Summary by R. S. Bhattacharya*)

I. Introductory Verses: Scope and Task of Sāṃkhya

The creativity of the unmanifest materiality (the three constituents in their unmanifested form) in some śāstric passages means assuming the state of nonequilibrium of the constituents, which immediately gives rise to the evolutes. Similarly, the dissolution of the unmanifest in consciousness (as stated in some authoritative texts) means the unmanifested state of the constituents.

It is further remarked that śāstric statements showing origination and dissolution of consciousness are to be regarded as secondary—that is, the origination of consciousness is its enjoyership because of limiting adjuncts; dissolution is consciousness' abiding in its own immutable form. Vijñānabhikṣu, however, thinks that association and disjunction of consciousness and materiality are called their origination and dissolution respectively. Materiality is regarded as one, because there is no other entity that is of the same kind (*sajātīyadvitīyarahita*).

The three colors (red, white, and black) of the three constituents (as stated in the relevant stanza of the *Śvetāśvatara Upaniṣad*) are not real; they are used in a figurative sense. For example the *sattva* constituent is called white, for as white water cleans everything so *sattva* cleans the mind through knowledge. Materiality in the state of equilibrium is called "*lohitaśuklakṛṣṇa*" (red-white-black), for materiality is nothing but a whole composed of three parts, i.e., the three constituents.

(1) Internal frustration—which is of two kinds, bodily and mental—is said to be amenable to internal remedies. It may be asked: although mental frustration is of this nature, yet can bodily frustration (disease) be called so, for the medicines are not internal? The reply is: because medicines become effective if they are taken in, there arises no logical fault in holding that bodily frustration is also amenable to internal remedies. The commentator is in favor of taking the word "*sādhya*" in the expression "*āntaropāyasādhya*" (amenable to internal remedies) in the sense of "*janya*" (to be produced). Because bodily and mental frustrations happen in the body and the mind they are regarded as internal.

As to the question that since a subtle entity existing in the future state may appear in a gross from because of causal operation, why cannot an entity acquiring the past state appear again in a gross form, it is replied that because experience does not attest that fact, we hold that a past entity is incapable of appearing again in a gross form. This is in accordance with the *Vyāsabhāṣya* on *Yogasūtra* 3.14.

(2) Bālarāma remarks that besides meaning "satisfaction unattached with frustration" the word "*svarga*" means a place connected with some asterism (*nakṣatradeśa*) or *merupṛṣṭha* (the summit of the mountain Meru).

Bālarāma considers the question of violence in sacrificial acts (especially in killing animals in sacrifices) in various ways, quoting the views of some Vedāntins, Mīmāṃsakas, and Vijñānabhikṣu and concludes with cogent reasons that in reality violence in sacrificial acts is prohibited.

(3) While explaining vicious infinite regress (*anavasthā*) Bālarāma gives reasons why materiality can not possibly have a cause.

Question: The word "*avikṛti*" (in "*mūlaprakṛtiravikṛtiḥ*") can legitimately suggest the idea that materiality is also the primordial (or "root") cause, and thus it is pointless to use the word "primordial" in the term "primordial materiality."

Reply: Because "*prakṛti*" simply means the generative cause of a fundamental principle (that is why intellect, etc., are rightly regarded as *prakṛtis*), it is necessary to use the word "primordial" (*mūla*") in order to indicate that there is a generative cause that is not the product of any other principle. Here *Sāṃkhyasūtras* I.67-68 are quoted and explained.

The commentary has quoted the definitions of materiality as given in the Purāṇas and an attempt is made to show the validity of the definition of *prakṛti* (*tattvāntaropādānatvam prakṛtitvam*) as given in the *Tattvakaumudī*. The expression "*tattvāntara*" in the definition has been explained elaborately, and it is shown that this view is based on *Vyāsabhāṣya* 2.19.

II. Instruments of Knowledge

(4) The commentary thinks that the Vaiśeṣika *sūtra* is anterior to the *Sāṃkhyakārikā*.

"*Pramāṇa*" in the verse is to be taken as two words; whereas the first "*pramāṇa*" is the thing to be defined (*lakṣya*), the second "*pramāṇa*" is the definition (*lakṣaṇa*), i.e., "the instrument of knowledge." Knowledge is regarded as *anadhigata* (not known previously), *aviparīta* (not erroneous; error includes mental construction (*vikalpa*) or vague conception also; see YS 1.8) and *asandigdha* (not doubtful). An instrument of knowledge is a kind of operation of the intellect.

Knowledge is twofold: secondary and primary. Secondary (*gauṇa*) knowledge is caused by the contact of organs. Primary (*mukhya*) knowledge is the result of the operations of awareness. It is called *pauruṣeya* (existing in consciousness). This twofold knowledge has been elaborately discussed by quoting *Sāṃkhyasūtra* I.81 and *Vyāsabhāṣya* 1.7, and it is remarked that in reality consciousness is not knower (*pramātṛ*, the seat of *pramā*) and so knowledge, which is regarded as residing in consciousness, is only to be ascribed to consciousness in a figurative sense.

An instrument of knowledge is also said to be of two kinds. The organs are the secondary instruments of knowledge, having contact (*sannikarṣa*) as their operation (*vyāpāra*), whereas awareness is the chief instrument of knowledge. The former is the instrument of the secondary knowledge, the latter, of knowledge residing in consciousness.

It is remarked that the knowledge of Yogins is a kind of perception and so it has not been separately stated in the *Kārikās*. Similarly *siddhadarśana* (perception caused by the application of various kinds of medicinal preparations, [collyrium, etc.]) is also included in perception. The commentary quotes *Sāṃkhyasūtra* I.88 and *Manusmṛti* 12.105 to uphold the Sāṃkhya view of the threefold instrument of knowledge; it quotes Nārāyaṇatīrtha's explanation of the expression "*sarvapramāṇasiddha*," which is different from that of Vācaspati.

(5) It is remarked that a defining attribute (*lakṣaṇa*) may be taken as a reason based on negative concomitance (*vyatirekihetu*). For example, smell is the defining attribute of earth and it can be taken as a reason to prove that earth is different from all similar and dissimilar things.

Although the literal meaning of the word "*prativiṣaya*" "*viṣayaṃ viṣayaṃ prati vartate*" may suggest that the organs reach the place of their respective objects, yet this meaning is not applicable. The operation of the organs is to be known as association (*sannikarṣa*). The relation, which is also called "operation" (*vyāpāra*) is favorable to producing effects; e.g., the particular association is the function of threads in producing a cloth.

Reflective discerning is not the property of the sense capacities; in reality it belongs to the intellect. That is why reflective discerning or awareness is regarded as the operation (*vṛtti*) of the intellect. The intellect becomes connected with the objects through the capacities and gets modified in the forms of objects. This intellect (also called "*citta*") is composite or conjunct (*sāvayava*) and so must be taken as possessing middling dimension (*madhyama parimāṇa*).

Knowledge and its instruments have been exemplified as follows: The reflective discerning that "this is a jar" is an instrument of knowledge, whereas the experience "I am aware of the jar" (which arises afterward) is knowledge. An instrument of knowledge (a kind of intellectual operation) exists in the intellect. Knowledge, though called "connected with consciousness," in reality arises in the intellect and not in the unattached consciousness. Because consciousness and intellect are not discriminated, knowledge (though existing in the intellect) is regarded as belonging to *puruṣa*.

Here Bālarāma has referred to the view of the Naiyāyikas that awareness, satisfaction, etc., are the attributes of the self and has remarked that the view is anti-Vedic. He has also referred to Vijñānabhikṣu's criticism of Vācaspati's view about the existence of knowledge in the intellect and has refuted the criticism by showing that it is against the view of *Vyāsabhāṣya* and Pañcaśikha. There is a discussion here on the nature of consciousness' reflection in the intellect. It is further remarked that there is no necessity to accept two kinds of knowledge (as shown above); it is quite sufficient to accept awareness based in consciousness as knowledge.

The word "*lokāyata*" is explained to mean "*pratyakṣapramāṇa*" (perception as an instrument of knowledge) and it is said that this very word means the Cārvāka system in a secondary sense. The arguments given to refute the view of this school denying the validity or truth of inference have been elucidated by quoting relevant passages from *Bhāmatī*, etc.

The commentary contains elaborate discussion on (1) limiting adjunct (*upādhi*), (2) exclusionary inference, (3) different interpretations of *pūrvavat*, *śeṣavat*, *and sāmānyatodṛṣṭa*, (4) authoritativeness and eternity of the Vedas, (5) authoritativeness of the *smṛti* works, (6) criticism of omniscience by the Mīmāṃsakas, and (7) the nature of comparison, presumption, inclusion, and nonperception, with quotations from authoritative texts upholding them as independent instruments of knowledge.

While commenting on the *Tattvakaumudī* passages refuting the independent position of the aforesaid instruments, Bālarāma sometimes indicates views of other schools also; for example, he says that although Sāṃkhya includes nonperception in perception, yet most of the followers of the Nyāya-Vaiśeṣika system include it in inference.

(6) Strictly speaking it is unmanifest materiality and pure consciousness that are the proper objects of knowledge for Sāṃkhya and that are capable of being known by general correlation. This is in accordance with *Sāṃkhyasūtra* I.103. Entities like subtle elements, etc., may be known through the *a posteriori* form of inference.

III. The Notion of Preexistent Effect

(9) Bālarāma quotes *Nyāyasūtra* 4.1.14 to elucidate the Buddhist view that nonexistence (*abhāva*) is the cause of existent things. It defines the relation of identity (*tādātmya*) as "nondifference existing with the notion of difference not considered properly" (*avicāritabhedapratītisahakṛtabheda*). The Vedāntic view of causal relations has been propounded by quoting Śaṃkara's comment on *Brahmasūtra* 2.1.14 "*tadananyatvam*. . . ." as "it is understood that in reality the effect is nondifferent from the cause and it has no existence apart from the cause." The argument given in *Bhāmatī* 2.2.36 against the Buddhist doctrine of the causality of nonexistence has been quoted here.

The *śruti* passage "*vācārambhaṇaṃ vikāro nāmadheyam mṛttikety eva satyam*" (*Chāndogya Upaniṣad* 6.1.4) usually quoted to prove the falsity of the world is interpreted to justify the Sāṃkhyan view. It is explained to mean that in order to accomplish the functions of fetching water, etc., clay is arranged in a jar form, this is why a jar is essentially nothing but clay only. It is remarked that this *śruti* passage establishes that the effect is essentially the same as its cause and not that an effect is illusory.

A slightly different interpretation of two arguments "*upādānagrahaṇa*" and "*sarvasambhavābhāva*" is given here.

In elucidating the argument "*śaktasya śakyakaraṇāt*" Bālarāma has discussed the nature of causal efficacy (*śakti*) according to the view of Sāṃkhya, and it is shown that the view has been accepted by Śaṃkara (see his comments on *Brahmasūtra* 2.1.18).

The view of the logicians that "it is its prior absence that is the cause of the effect" is refuted and it is remarked that it is impossible for a logician to answer the question "what is the locus of the prior absence of a cloth when the threads have not come into existence." Moreover, the perceptual knowledge of future effects as found in Yogis would be impossible if it is not accepted that effects exist in their causes (in subtle forms).

While elucidating the argument of "*gurutvāntarakāryagrahaṇa*" (not making any difference in weight) Bālarāma says that weight is supersensible and refutes the view of the *Nyāyakandalī* about the fall of a body because of its weight.

Bālarāma Udāsīna has shown that some of the arguments given by Vācaspati to prove real difference between the (material) cause and its effect were originally given by Uddyotakara (in *Nyāyavārttika* 2.1.36). He quotes a new argument given in *Bhāmatī* (1.2.15) refuting the view that practical efficiency (*arthakriyā*) proves the difference between cause and effect. Incidentally he discusses (1) the nature of a self-linking connection (*svarūpasambandha*) and (2) the causes of erroneous perception, etc. He indicates that arguments in favor of *satkāryavāda* are to be found in *Śrībhāṣya* (of Rāmānuja) 2.1.15, *Vijñānāmṛtabhāṣya* (of Vijñānabhikṣu) 2.1.21 and *Vyāsabhāṣya* 3.13. Some *Sāṃkhyasūtras* and a few scriptural passages have been quoted to support the views propounded in the *Tattvakaumudī* and the *Sāṃkhyakārikās*.

IV. Manifest and Unmanifest Materiality

(10) Destruction (*vināśa*) is explained as disappearance (*tirobhava*), for destruction, according to Sāṃkhya is "the existence of the effect in its (material) cause in a subtle form." Vijñānabhikṣu's finding fault in Vācaspati's explanation of "*sakriya*" (possessed of activity) and his own explanation of this term are criticized by Bālarāma, and the validity of Vācaspati's view is shown. Vijñānabhikṣu's explanation of the plurality of the manifest is shown to be untenable. An alternative explanation of "*liṅga*" has been given as "that which gets dissolved in its own material cause."

Both the unmanifest and consciousness are said to possess opposite characteristics to manifest materiality (e.g., both are causeless). Although the unmanifest is not many yet oneness is not to be attributed to consciousness, as the plurality of consciousnesses is an established doctrine of Sāṃkhya.

(11) *Sattva*, *rajas*, and *tamas* possessing satisfaction, frustration, and confusion as their characteristic properties are called constituents because they resemble strands (*guṇa*, i.e., *rajju* meaning" a strand") in binding the consciousnesses. Sometimes satisfaction, frustration, and confusion are called "*guṇa*" in a secondary sense (by taking an attribute as identical with its substrate).

It is remarked that although some authoritative texts aver that the subtle elements are devoid of satisfaction, etc., yet such statements should be taken to mean that the subtle elements are incapable of producing satisfaction, etc., in sentient beings like us. In fact the subtle elements, being products of the constituents, possess satisfaction, etc., and are also capable of producing satisfaction, etc., but the power of producing the effects varies. Had the subtle elements been devoid of satisfaction, etc., their transformations (i.e., the gross elements and objects) would not possess satisfaction, etc.

Vijñānabhikṣu's view that the subtle elements are devoid of satisfaction, etc., has been criticized by Bālarāma, and it is shown that Vijñānabhikṣu contradicts himself, for he adds that the subtle elements afford satisfaction to the gods. Incidentally it is remarked that the Nyāya view declaring that statisfaction, etc., are the attributes of the self is anti-Vedic.

While explaining the Vijñānavāda (idealism) of the Yogācāra Buddhists Bālarāma adduces the well-known reason of '*sahopalambhaniyama*'' of the Buddhist teachers. It is shown that no meaning of the word "*saha*" is applicable in the present context and that the rule of *sahopalambha* is incapable of proving identily of an object with its awareness. Arguments given in the *Vyāsabhāṣya* and in other works to refute Buddhist idealism have also been quoted.

V. The Three Constituents

(12) Bālarāma has shown that it would be wrong to interpret the expression "*prītyaprītiviṣādātmakāḥ*" in the verse as meaning "each of the three *guṇas* possesses agreeableness, disagreeableness, and oppressiveness." The intended meaning is: the essential characteristic of *sattva* is satisfaction; of *rajas*, frustration; and of *tamas*, confusion. According to Sāṃkhya an attribute is identical with its substrate. In the expression "*prītyaprītiviṣāda*," "agreeableness," etc., are to be taken as indicators (*upalakṣaṇa*) of other attributes, for example, "agreeableness' stands for lightness (*lāghava*), etc., as has been stated by ancient teachers. *Sāṃkhyasūtra* I.127 has been quoted to uphold this view. Bālarāma provides a discussion on the similar and dissimilar transformations of materiality.

(13) Arguments are given for proving lightness as an independent quality like heaviness. As to why Vācaspati has given another example to illustrate "mutul opposition of the three constituents," although the verse has only one example, the lamp, the commentary remarks that as the three things (wick, oil, and fire) making a lamp are not fully opposite in character, the second example of wind-bile-phlegm (*vātapittakapha*) has been given, for they are fully opposite to one another according to the teachers of Āyurveda.

It is said that, as there are appropriate efficient causes (*nimitta*) for the rise of *sattva, rajas,* and *tamas,* so there are contributory causes (*sahakārin*), namely, species, time, etc. Owing to the absence of appropriate contributory cause, thorns are not pleasurable to human beings though they are pleasurable to camels.

There is an alternative interpretation of the passage "*atra ca sukha-duḥkhamohāḥ*. . . ." According to this interpretation, satisfaction, etc., are said to exist in awareness (*citta*) and their appearance is said to be due to the efficient causes like satisfaction, etc., existing in the objects.

VI. Inferences to Primordial Materiality and Consciousness

(15-16) Bālarāma's comment at the beginning contains a clear account of the process of creation according to the Vaiśeṣika system. It quotes *Bṛhadāraṇyaka Upaniṣad* 1.4.7 and *Bhagavadgītā* 2.28 to prove the existence of the unmanifest. It is remarked that although "*parimāṇa*" signifies limitation because of space, time, etc., yet such a sense is not applicable here; here "*parimāṇa*" must be taken to mean "the state of not being all-pervasive." A passage from *Vyāsabhāṣya* 2.18 is quoted here to show that the three constituents are mutually pervasive. This mutual pervasion exists even in the state of dissolution. Bālarāma has here criticized *Bhāmatī* for holding that the three constituents are not mutually pervasive.

Bālarāma quotes a passage from Śaṃkara's commentary on *Brahmasūtra* 2.2.1 saying that the Sāṃkhyan argument of homogeneity (*samanvaya*) (see *SK* 15) is incapable of proving the existence of the unmanifest and remarks that Śaṃkara's view is against *Bhagavadgītā* 18.40. There is a discussion on the two states of materiality on the basis of *Sāṃkhya sūtra* VI.42 and of Pañcaśikha's statement quoted in *Vyāsabhāṣya* 2.23.

Acting in collaboration (*saṃhatyakāritva*) is said to exist in both the constituents and their transformations. These transformations are dependent on the filling in of the evolving cause (*prakṛtyāpūra*) (see *Yogasūtra* 4.2) while functioning. *Yogasūtra* 4.24, along with Vyāsa's *bhāṣya* thereon, has been quoted to elucidate the argument that aggregations serve a purpose of some being other than themselves (*saṃhataparārthatva*).

It is remarked that the controllership of the inactive consciousness is not of the nature of activity. It is nothing but proximity (*sannidhimātra*), as has been stated in *Sāṃkhyasūtra* I.96. A passage from the *Ṣaṣṭitantra* has been quoted to the effect that primordial materiality's activity is due to the controlling of consciousness.

Vācaspati has offered two explanations of enjoyership (*bhoktṛbhāva*). The first explanation is said to be faulty, for it takes the unattached consciousness as an enjoyer. Bālarāma at the end remarks that, because subjectivity and enjoyership depend upon the limiting adjunct of intellect, etc., the first explanation may also be taken as valid.

(18) While explaining the respective restrictions of the instruments (*karaṇapratiniyama*) the commentator remarks that though

blindness, etc., are the attributes of organs, yet they are attributed to consciousness, for it is the superintendent of the aggregate (*saṃghāta*) made up of the organs.

Incidentally, Bālarāma has refuted the view of the logicians that a whole (*avayavin*) is destroyed as soon as one of its parts is destroyed and a new whole is originated as soon as a new component part comes into existence, for this view fails to explain recognition. Moreover it compels the logicians to run on the path of the Buddhists—their opponents.

Bālarāma quotes *Sāṃkhyasūtras* I.149-151 to justify the Sāṃkhyan view of the plurality of consciousness and quotes the view of Vācaspati (*Tattvavaiśāradī* on *Yogasūtra* 2.22) that the scriptural passages declaring oneness of consciousness are to be taken as secondary, i.e., they propound that there is no distinction in *puruṣa* because of space or time. According to Vijñānabhikṣu nondifference (*abheda*) in *ātman* means "nondivergence in *ātmans*".

(19) Consciousness is witness in connection with the intellect only; he may be regarded as subject of awareness so far as the other organs are concerned.

(20). It is remarked that the erroneous notion that one and the same entity is both subject of awareness and agent is caused by the affliction called egoism (*asmitā*) (*Yogasūtra* 2.6). Because intellect and consciousness are not distinguished, the properties of one are attributed to the other.

(21) It is remarked that the simile of a lame man and a blind one suggests that (1) primordial materiality depends upon the superintending consciousness in creating transformations like intellect, etc., and that (2) consciousness (in the bondage state) attains liberation with the help of materiality.

(22) It is remarked that the view of the *Vyāsabhāṣya* that the subtle elements are the products of the intellect is to be taken in the sense that egoity, the modification of intellect, is the direct material cause of the subtle elements. The *Vyāsabhāṣya* on *Yogasūtra* 1.45 expressly states that egoity is the cause of the subtle elements—a view that is supported by the *Gopālatāpanī Upaniṣad* and the *Sāṃkhyasūtra* (V.61) as well. It is further remarked that the inference given by Vācaspati (*Tattvavaiśāradī* on *Yogasūtra* 2.19) proving that the subtle elements are the effects of the intellect is wrong, because it contradicts authoritative texts. Bālarāma here quotes the *Vyāsabhāṣya* on *Yogasūtra* 2.19 about the nature and origination of the five subtle elements.

IX. The Functioning of the Thirteenfold Instrument

(25) Bālarāma refutes the view of Vijñānabhikṣu (see his *Bhāṣya* on *Sāṃkhyasūtra* II.18) that from *sāttvika* egoity come the gods (i.e.,

the superintending deities of the capacities) and the mind; from *rājasa* egoity come the sense and action capacities, and from *tāmasa* egoity come the subtle elements. He establishes the view propounded in this verse with the remarks that the view of the *Sāṃkhyakārikās* is in consonance with *Sāṃkhyasūtra* II.18-19.

(26) A scriptural passage has been quoted in which the word Indra has been used in the sense of *ātman*.

(27) After clearly explaining the two verses (quoted from ancient works) on the twofold perception, Bālarāma criticizes Vijñānabhikṣu's view on twofold perception and holds that not only general but also specific characteristics are apprehended by the capacities, as has been clearly stated in *Vyāsabhāṣya* 3.47. It further says that Kumārila's view on the construction-free form of perception is in consonance with the *Vyāsabhāṣya*.

Bālārāma refutes Uddyotakara's view that if only one entity is regarded as the material cause of the organs (as is accepted by Sāṃkhya) then either all organs would apprehend all kinds of objects or each of the organs would apprehend all objects, and asserts that it is the *adṛṣta* (merit and demerit) that regulates the power of organs.

(29) The five vital breaths are called "air" (*vāyu*), as their movements are similar to that of air. Bālarāma is of the opinion that in the *Vyāsabhāṣya* passage on the vital breath (on *Yogasūtra* 2.39), the expression "*samaṣṭendriya*" must be taken to mean the three internal capacities only and not the external capacities also. It is further stated that the vital breaths are not the operations of the external capacities, because in dreamless sleep vital breaths continue to function although the external capacities cease to act. Bālarāma takes the views of Vācaspati and Vijñānabhikṣu on the nature of the vital breaths as untenable.

Because the operations of the external capacities are said to be simultaneous also, there may arise five kinds of knowledge in the five sense capacities simultaneously. Although this is against the Nyāya view, yet there is no logical fault in the Sāṃkhya doctrine, for, according to Sāṃkhya, the mind possessing middling dimension can be associated with all the five sense capacities at the same time.

(31) While elucidating the view that human purpose (i.e., experience and liberation) is the instigator of all the capacities, Bālarāma remarks that although consciousness is the controller and knower (*abhijña*), yet because, it is unattached and immutable, consciousness cannot be regarded as the instigator of the capacities.

(32) It is remarked that, although the physical body is made up of the five gross elements, yet it may be called earthy, watery, etc., because earth, water, etc., predominate.

(33) Bālarāma quotes the *Vyāsabhāṣya* passage (on *Yogasūtra* 3.52) on time and establishes the view that in reality time is nothing but

moment only. It refutes the Vaiśeṣika view that time is one and eternal, saying that there is no proof of this view.

(34) It is remarked that one and the same egoity predominated by *sattva* gives rise to the sense capacities; and predominated by *rajas*, to the action capacities. It produces the mind when it possesses the operation of self-awareness only. All of these are called "specific. In the five subtle elements (sound, touch, color, taste, and smell) each one following contains the attributes of the preceding one in the list as well as of its own, for the simple reason that the following subtle element is the effect of the preceding element or elements.

X. Subtle and Gross Elements

(38) It should be noted that among the five gross elements (*ākāśa*, air, fire, water, and earth) the following gross element is the effect of the preceding subtle element, that is, *ākāśa* is the effect of the sound *tanmātra*, air is the effect of both the sound and touch subtle elements, and earth is effect of all the five subtle elements.

XI. The Subtle Body

(41) Bālarāma quotes *Brahmasūtra* 2.3.25 to justify the measure of a thumb in connection with "*puruṣa*" (i.e., the subtle body).

XII. The Basic Predispositions

(K. 44) *Prakṛtilayas*, i.e., those who are engrossed in *prakṛti* are those beings who take their bodies as identical with the self. These are said to be the followers of the Cārvāka school. *Vaikṛtikas*, i.e., who regard the elements, organs, egoity, and intellect as identical with the self, are also said to be the followers of the same school.

(50-51) Bālarāma shows the significance of the alternative names of the contentments (*salila* etc.) and the attainments (*tāra* etc.).

XIII. The Empirical World

(54) It is remarked that the words "*mūla*" and "*madhya*" in the *Sāmkhyakārikā* do not signify direction (*diś*); the former signifies *tamas*, the latter, *rajas*.

XIV. Similes for Materiality

(57) Bālarāma holds that in the act of transforming grass into milk there is no effort of either the cow or the calf and further states

that Śaṃkarācārya's criticism of the Sāṃkhyan view about the function of unknowing milk for the nourishment of the calf (*Bhāṣya* on *Brahmasūtra* 2.2.4) is untenable. Incidentally he remarks that according to some exponents, self-interest (*svārtha*) and compassion (*karuṇya*) are not the two separate causes of activity (*pravṛtti*) of the wise, for compassion is found to be based on self-interest.

XV. Liberation and Isolation

(64) It is remarked that, according to the Naiyāyikas, a beginningless thing may be destroyed by a thing having a beginning, for example, the beginningless prior absence (*prāgabhāva*) is destroyed by posterior absence (*dhvaṃsa*), which has a beginning.

(69) The commentator is of the opinion that Kapila instructed Āsuri orally; he did not compose any formal treatise on Sāṃkhya.

PAÑCĀNANA TARKARATNA

Pañcānanatarkaratna, son of Nandalālakavi of Bhatpara, West Bengal, was born in 1865. A brilliant student of Śivacandrasārvabhauma and famous since his youth for his extraordinary erudition and native intelligence, he soon won recognition as a scholar of a very high order. He worked as a professor in a Bhatpara *catuṣpāṭhī* and later at Bangabasi College, Calcutta, and was for some time the Dean of the Faculty of Religious Learning at Banaras Hindu University. He was awarded the honorary title "*Mahāmahopādhyāya*" by the then British Indian Government. He died in 1940. He published a number of books, translated into Bengali the *Śrīmad-Bhāgavata* and about thirty major and minor Purāṇas, and edited a number of the Purāṇas.

His *Pūrṇimā*, published in 1919, is a subcommentary on Vācaspati Miśra's *Tattvakaumudī* on *Sāṃkhyakārikā*. He understood, in accordance with the practice in those days, particularly in Bengal, that his task was to be largely a restatement of Vācaspati Miśra's points in precise neo-Nyāya language, as clearly presented as possible, and with all the paraphernalia of neo-Nyāya techniques, the implied or explicit arguments in Vācaspati Miśra's text, and the anticipation and refutation of all possible objections. Occasionally, he has referred to different Sāṃkhya views on particular topics and refuted, wherever possible, the views of Vijñānabhikṣu that are opposed to Vācaspati Miśra's views. Like the vast majority of scholars in those days, he refused to recognize the *Sāṃkhyasūtra* and Vijñānabhikṣu's *Pravacanabhāṣya* as authentic Sāṃkhya texts.

The salient points of the subcommentary *Pūrṇimā* are noted below:

PŪRṆIMĀ ON TATTVAKAUMUDĪ

(*Summary by Kalidas Bhattacharya*)

I. Introductory Verses; Scope and Task of Sāṃkhya

Vācaspati Miśra begins with the *mantra* "*Ajāmekām*, etc." Pañcānanatarkaratna in course of elucidating the term "*ajā*", writes that although its etymological meaning is "that which has never originated" it equally means "eternal," i.e., "that which not only does not originate but also does not cease to be." He adds that to be without cessation follows from "being without origination", for, except prior absence, i.e., the absence of anything prior to its origination, nothing that ends is ever found without a beginning, and Pañcānanatarkaratna reminds the reader that Sāṃkhya does not recognize prior absence.

Even for those who recognize prior absence, Sāṃkhya would only state the corresponding premise more correctly as "whatever positive entity is without a beginning is without an end " (and, therefore, eternal)." That materiality is a positive entity is clear from its characterization (in the *mantra*) as red, white, and black.

In reply to an anticipated objection that the (Advaita) Vedāntin's "ignorance" (*avidyā*) is both positive and without beginning and yet ends, Pañcānanatarkaratna writes that this ignorance of the (Advaita) Vedāntin being itself conceptually inadmissible, the question does not arise. That concept of ignorance is inadmissible inasmuch as it has been illegitimately characterized as neither existent nor nonexistent. (Every entity in the world is either existent or nonexistent.)

Ignorance, being after all illusion (basic illusion, though), has to originate as all other illusions do and cannot, therefore, be beginningless. (Hence, this ignorance could not have been meant in the *mantra*.)

Pañcānanatarkaratna goes further and argues that because the same adjective "*aja*" (or its feminine form "*ajā*") has been used in the *mantra* to characterize both materiality and consciousness, it must have one and the same meaning in both the cases, for where ambiguity could be avoided, no scripture would indulge in that. Now, in the case of consciousness it, assuredly, means "without cessation", that is, eternal. Hence, the other thing, too, materiality, to which this adjective has been applied, must also be as much without end as without beginning.

Materiality is not only eternal, it is also "one without a second." This one "without a second" may mean either (a) one without a second of the same sort or (b) whatever, being the constituent (cause) of everything else, and having nothing beyond itself as its own constituent (cause), has no plurality within itself (i.e., is not breakable into parts). The former, (a), is the definition of "one without a second" given by the advocates of the theory of *asatkhyāti*, who mean to say that any such "second of the same sort," though a conceptual possibility, is after all negated, the possibility being no more than that of a negatum. The latter, (b), is the definition given by others (those who were not the advocates of the theory of *asatkhyāti*). Obviously, this definition excludes the possibility that atoms are the last constituents.

Vijñānabhikṣu who admits (intrinsic) plurality of materiality would understand its (so-called) unity (*ekatva*) to be no more than belonging to one and the same class (*sāmānya*). He would not also understand "class" in the Nyāya sense of (a really existent) property called "universal"; it is what is just meant as covering all the instances in question.

In the *mantra*, materiality is represented as red, white, and black, i.e., (balanced copresence of) *sattva*, *rajas*, and *tamas*. (Materiality *is* the three constituents; these three are not the constituents of materiality.) This is a clear indication, (at least) according to this scriptural *mantra*, that the ultimate constituent of the manifest world is not the (Advaitin's) featureless Brahman. The ultimate constituent, as the *mantra* understands it, has three constituents.

Materiality is not only the ultimate constituent of the manifest world, it is also the agent that creates that world. This is evident from the word "*sṛjamānām*" in the *mantra*. There is nothing incongrous here, for the precise Sāṃkhya doctrine is that all activity, involving attachment or detachment, belongs to materiality only, not to consciousness. This disposes of the theory (held by others) that the manifest world is created by God.

Pañcānanatarkaratna here anticipates an objection and answers it. The objection is this: Undoubtedly from the *mantra* under study it follows that materiality is the agent that creates the world; but where is there any indication (in the *mantra*) that it is the ultimate *constituent* of the world? Pañcānanatarkaratna admits that as Vācaspati Miśra quotes the *mantra* there is no such indication anywhere. The real *mantra*, however, as it occurs in the *Śvetāśvatara Upaniṣad*, contains the word "*sarūpāh*" meaning similar to "itself" (see *bahvīḥ prajāḥ sṛjamānāṃ sarūpāḥ*". This word suggests that materiality is the ultimate constituent: effects could be similar to their cause if only the cause were their constituent, that is, material (cause).

If Vācaspati Miśra begins his *Tattvakaumudī* with the *mantra*, it is only to show that Sāṃkhya philosophy is approved by the scripture, and not heterodox. Vācaspati Miśra, however, has not quoted the *mantra* exactly as it occurs in the *Śvetāśvatara Upaniṣad*. The *mantra* there is

ajāmekām lohitaśuklakṛṣṇāṃ
bahvīḥ prajāḥ sṛjamānāṃ sarūpāḥ
ajo hyeko juṣamāno' 'nuśete
jahātyenāṃ bhuktabhogāmajo'nyaḥ.

"*Eko*" in the third line means one "class of", that is, those *puruṣas* who are still in bondage, and "*anyaḥ*" in the fourth line means "another class of," that is, those *puruṣas* who have attained liberation.[1]

As for the second invocatory verse, the important points Pañcānanatarkaratna adds are:

(1) There is no reason to hold that Kapila, author of Sāṃkhya philosophy, is other than the Kapila mentioned in the Vedas.

(2) Sāṃkhya, therefore, is not a heterodox system. If scripture and traditional texts do not refer to it with as much regard as they pay to other orthodox systems, that is because it is meant for the superior few who are past the stages of detachment, etc., recommended in those orthodox scriptures and traditional texts.

(3) Kapila, Āsuri, and Pañcaśikha were three immediately successive Sāṃkhya philosophers, each one being the teacher of the next. It is only between Pañcaśikha and Iśvarakṛṣṇa that there was a long gap. Pañcānanatarkaratna says that this is unerringly suggested by the word "*tathā*" in the verse. ("*Tathā*" here means "and".)

(1) The author of the *Sāṃkhyakārikā*, and Vācaspati Miśra, too, says that no ordinary means can remove frustration necessarily, that is, there is no ordinary means about which one can say that it *must* remove the frustration in question. In Indian philosophy, under the influence of Nyāya, such necessities are stated through double negation. Following this tradition Pañcānanatarkaratna writes the whole thing as follows: There is no means that does not have some exception. "Having exception" = *anaikāntika*. Hence, "*ekānta*" means "not having any exception."

Absolute cessation of frustration (*ātyantikaduḥkhavināśa*) is also stated more analytically by Pañcānanatarkaratna, in a subtle neo-Nyāya phraseology in terms of prior absence, alternatively to another Sāṃkhya way of putting it.[2]

(2) To Vācaspati Miśra's criticism of the Mīmāṃsā doctrine of legitimate slaughter, Pañcānanatarkaratna adds a long discussion purported to represent the central idea of Vācaspati Miśra's criticism. The idea, he says, is this.

When a means is enjoined (in the case of a Vedic injunction), it is either because something desired will be attained thereby or because something greatly undesirable will be avoided. The two motives do not operate jointly. Had that been the case, the Vedas would never enjoin the "*Śyena* rite," which eventually brings in great frustration (greater than that which is positively gained as satisfaction).

It cannot be said that in such cases there is no greater demerit, just as there is none such, according to Manu, in the case of killing outright an enemy who is about to kill one. The parallelism is wrong; for, injunctions such as "Kill outright the enemy who is about to kill you" is only sociopolitical, meaning that neither the society nor the body politic to which you belong will punish you for this act. Manu never meant that this act will not generate any great spiritual demerit.

So, as one acts according to a Vedic injunction, only one of the two principles—(1) leading to the realization of what is desired and (2) not generating a great demerit—not both of them, operates as the occasion demands. When, for example, an animal has to be slaughtered for the performance of a rite, it is only the first principle that operates, whereas cases of prohibition like "Do not kill any animal" are governed by the second principle only.

It would be no use (for a defector) arguing that prohibitions are after all negative injunctions and, therefore, like all positive prescriptions, understood as leading to the attainment of something that is desired (here just the absence of great frustration). Such argument would be of no avail if only because avoidance as a mode of action is here more directly and centrally operative (and a more parsimonious objective) than the attainment of the absence of an undesirable end. Attainment of what is desired and avoidance of great frustration being thus two different interests altogether, there is, equally, no clash between the two.

It follows that there is no clash also between slaughter of animals as a means to the performance of a rite and the undesirable frustration that results from that slaughter, quite as much as there is none between eating a sumptuous dinner and the languor that ensues.

Even granting that the two principles—attainment of a desired and avoidance of great frustration—are disparate and, therefore, nonclashing, might not one still ask whether "prescription" (*vidhi*) and "prohibition" (*niṣedha*) are not after all each "injunction" and so far indistinguishable from the other and, therefore, governed by the two principles, either indiscriminately or together. Pañcānanatarkaratna replies that the distinction is clear enough. Prescriptions are unerringly understood as urging one to do something positive and and their guiding principle is, obviously, to attain something desired; whereas prohibitions are clearly understood as urging one not to do certain things in order that certain undesirable consequences (ultimately some great frustration) may not occur. That prescriptions are for realizing certain positive ends is a self-complete proposition, and should one seek to add that they are for avoiding undesirable consequences too, that would only be an additional different proposition not needed for defining prescription. Similarly, prohibitions are for avoiding undesirable consequences. This is what Vācaspati Miśra has in mind when he uses the term "*vākyabheda*": he means to say that there are two sentences, not one, meaning two different situations.

Pañcānanatarkaratna then indulges in certain niceties of gramatical and linguistic analysis and, after that, discusses in some greater details the Mīmāṃsā theory of injunction, particularly in relation to slaughter, and its refutation by Sāṃkhya.[3]

Vācaspati Miśra holds that even the (perfect) bliss of heaven (indeed, heaven = bliss) has to undergo decay and infers this character of decaying on the ground that as a positive being (as distinct from absence, which is negative) it has emerged (i.e., come into being at a moment of time). Pañcānanatarkaratna adds: Although for the Sāṃkhyan himself the first half of the ground (viz., positive being) is unnecessary, because Sāṃkhya would never admit anything that is not a positive existent, this half has yet been stated in so many words in order only to convince others who do recognize that even (effected) destruction (*dhvaṃsa*) is a sort of being. What Pañcānanatarkaratna means is that if the decay of heavenly bliss were sought to be inferred from "that bliss merely coming into being (i.e., getting effected)," then even destruction would also have to be taken as decaying, which, in the face of it, is absurd.

Pañcānanatarkaratna adds that "modern Sāṃkhyans" still insist on this first half of the ground.[4] They hold that decay is not what Vācaspati Miśra has literally meant: according to them, he meant by that term nothing but "becoming latent" (*tirobhāva*). and, in paralled fashion, by the term "coming into being" becoming patent (*āvirbhāva*). They hold that, had the fact of something becoming latent been inferred merely" on the ground of its once having become patent, then even the very fact of becoming latent would have to undergo a second latency, which is absurd. So, just in order to exclude this possibility a second ground like "because it is not *tirobhāva* itself" has to be added. And this gound is, from the Sāṃkhya point of view, the same thing as "it is a positive being."

Decaying (*kṣayın*) = not everlasting = (some time) ceasing to be = (in Sāṃkhya language) capable of becoming latent. X as becoming latent (*tirobhāva* of X) is for that X to remain thenceforward as only future X, that is as any X that will, in future, emerge into being (will be manifest = patent). A latent X to become latent again is normally inconceivable, unless it means (quite in another interest and context) the process of step-by-step retrogression ultimately into primordial materiality.

(3) As elsewhere, here too Pañcānanatarkaratna indulges in analytical niceties in the style of neo-Nyāya. A few specimens:

(a) In connection with Vācaspati Miśra's statement, "Some (Sāṃkhya) 'essence'(s) is (are) not-both" (*kaścidanubhayarūpaḥ*), he writes that "not-both" here does not literally mean not "both" (i.e., either); it means "neither."

(b) In clarification of Vācaspati Miśra's sentence "Primordial materiality is the three constituents in the state of equilibrium" ("*prakṛtiḥ pradhānaṃ sattvarajastamasāṃ sāmyāvasthā*"), he writes: What is intended is that materiality is capable of (characterizable as) being in such equilibrium. This explains why, even at the time of creation, when it modifies itself into intellect, etc., it is still characterizable as materiality. The state of complete dissolution (*pralaya*), however, is an actual state of equilibrium.

(c) Vācaspati Miśra writes that individual cows, pots, etc., are not "metaphysically different" (*tattvāntara*) from the "essences" called gross elements (soil, water, fire, etc.) because they are as much gross (i.e., productive of satisfaction, frustration, and confusion) and possess as much sensory qualities as those gross elements themselves. Pañcānanatarkaratna adds: That these are not metaphysically different from the gross elements is not inferred on the ground of that similarity. The ground here is either their grossness (*sthūlatā*) or their possessing sensuous qualities (*indriyagrāhyatā*), the similarity spoken of being only to exclude the fallacies of *svarūpasiddhi* and *dṛṣṭāntasiddhi* (the fallacies, viz., (1) that the *pakṣa* that has to be proved in the *sādhya*—on the ground of the *hetu*—is not already known to be obtaining anywhere in the world and (2) there is no known instance whatsoever of a thing that, possessing *h*, also possesses *p*. The similarity in question forms no part of the ground.

(d) He then puts the whole inference in the typical Nyāya form, taking all precautions, and shows how it excludes all that ought to be excluded and includes whatever ought to be included. In that connection he further shows: Even atoms of gross elements are not excluded, for they too possess the grossness and the sensuous qualities in question; or, probably, Vācaspati Miśra and Iśvarakṛṣṇa would, as does (the Naiyāyika) Raghunātha, deny atoms and replace them by minimal perceptibles (*trasareṇu*). In the latter case, the gross elements would also be gross (*sthūla*) in another commonly accepted sense, that is, being of finite size.

Other metaphysical entities (fundamental principles = categories)[5] recognized in other systems of philosophy are all reducible to the twenty five Sāṃkhya principles.[6] The Nyāya-Vaiśeṣika's "attributes" (*guṇa*), that is, color, taste, etc., are nondifferent from substances (*dravya*), and so it is with their motions (*karma*) and "universals" (*jāti*): these latter are but substances in different forms and functions. Different distinct substances, too, are but the three Sāṃkhya constituents (*sattva*, *rajas*, and *tamas*) in different unbalanced forms of combined manifestation. As for inherence (*samavāya*), it too is, in a way, nondifferent from that which the inherent inheres in (or, maybe, from the inherent itself). Absence (*abhāva*) of A is nothing except that which is said to be the locus of that absence; posterior absence and prior absence are just the latency respectively of what has been and what will be patent. As for time (*kāla*), Sāṃkhya does not recognize its reality, and similarly with space (*diś*).

II. Instruments of Knowledge

(4) In the neo-Nyāya style Pañcānanatarkaratna offers a complete and yet concise definition of instrument of knowledge and shows how noninstruments like doubt, error, and memory, are excluded.

As instruments, instruments of knowledge are but transformations of intellect, which, in Sāṃkhya, is nonconscious. Knowledge is the corresponding awareness, that is, awareness *as* that mode (it being presupposed that awareness by itself, i.e., pure consciousness, is a separate metaphysical principle that is only reflected in that mode). Knowledge, thus, is the mode of intellect only insofar as it has been enlightened (manifested) by the light of pure consciousness. Not that here the means and what it is a means of are one and the same. It is an instrument of knowledge only so far as it is an operation of intellect, other than doubt, error, and memory; but it is the result (knowledge) only insofar as consciousness has enlightened (manifested) it. Again, it cannot be said that the operation has continued for a certain period of time (however small) and then become enlightened. Without being in contact with pure consciousness no such operation can continue even for a moment, and they are in contact from the beginning, which shows that, though synchronous, the operation by itself and the same operation as enlightened (manifested) are not wholly identical. It follows that all operations of intellect are, insofar as they are in themselves and are not enlightened by pure consciousness, instruments of knowledge, and such enlightened operations in general are called true awarenesses (*pramā*). Knowledgehood (*pramātva*) of an intellectual operation is thus, in whatever way, effected by its contact with (the reflection of) pure consciousness.

So far there is a distinction between (a) the operation of intellect according to the thing (object) perceived[7] and (b) knowledge of this this (*ghaṭajñāna* = enlightened *ghaṭākāra vṛtti*). This enlightened operation stands necessarily revealed as enlightened to after-cognition (*anuvyavasāya*) of the form "I know this pot (*ghaṭa*)," though this introspection does not enlighten the enlightenedness of the operation in question (i.e., enlightened modes in general). It, too, is just another operation of intellect, as much enlightened as any other operation; only it is a necessary prerequisite for any operation to become enlightened. Enlightenedness of an operation of intellect requires no further enlightenment: it is self-enlightening (*svaprakāśa*).

Or, as some others hold, no intervention of after-cognition is needed for, if other operations have to be enlightened through some intervention of after-cognition, this after-cognition, being itself an intellectual operation, has in its turn to require another after-cognition (and that, too, as an intellectual operation) to intervene in order that the first after-cognition may become enlightened, which means fruitless infinite regress. According to this second view, even an unreflective (unintrospected) operation becomes directly enlightened, and that unreflective enlightenedness is self-enlightening.[8]

(5) Vācaspati Miśra states three reasons why, of all the instruments of knowledge, perception has to be considered first. They are

(1) perception occurs in time before the other instruments (such as inference, etc.), (2) the other instruments of knowledge depend on perception, and (3) every system of philosophy accords the first place to perception. Pañcānanatarkaratna. explains this as follows: In this beginningless world (of human speculation), where perception and other instruments of knowledge (inferences, etc.) precede one another in a beginningless chain, who will determine which instrument has really preceded, and how? This is why Vācaspati Miśra has added the second reason stated above. But, even then, because in performing rites it is inference, rather than perception, that primarily guides us and makes perception depend so far on it, Vācaspati Miśra adds the third reason as the last resort.[9]

As Pañcānanatarkaratna understands the *Sāṃkhyakārikā* and *Tattvakaumudī*, perception as an instrument of knowledge is either a sense capacity insofar as it is connected with the object (to be known) *or* intellect operating on an operation of that sense capacity (i.e., on the sense capacity itself that has taken shape, as it were, of the object), the operation in question being effected by its relation with the object.[10]

In either case, the relation of the sense capacity to the object may be of various kinds according as the capacities, those objects, and other factors differ in different cases; and the relations may in some cases be even understood (in the Nyāya fashion) as extraordinary (*alaukika*). Only Sāṃkhya, Pañcānanatarkaratna claims, cannot recognize *jñānalakṣaṇapratyakṣa* (a nonperceptual idea becoming fused with other presented data in such a manner that it is turned thereby into a veritable presentation).

Vācaspati Miśra and others speak often of "the favor" (*anugraha*) of pure consciousness conferred on intellect (*buddhi*). Pañcānanatarkaratna analyses it etymologically as intellect accepts (acceptance = *grahaṇa*) the excellence or similarity of consciousness. The prefix "*anu*" suggests this.

The operation of intellect on an operation of a sense capacity is to be understood as such an operation of intellect according to the object (which is said to be known), which is also, at the same time, of the nature of belief (*niścaya*). In other words, the said operation of intellect is but belief of the form "*I know* that this is such and such."[11] In contrast, the operation of a sense capacity—especially of mind (*manas*)—is only of the form "This is such and such."

One may, therefore, legitimately ask whether the mere operations of sense capacities are not to be excluded from the category of knowledge until the operation of intellect has supervened. Some might reply that they are to be excluded on the ground that they are not necessarily of the form of the belief "*I know* that, etc." (whereas modalizations of intellect are always of that form). Pañcānanatarkaratna, however, would not accept this reply. He argues that the reply misfires inasmuch as Vācaspati Miśra himself has claimed elsewhere that the function of mind is intentional (*saṃkalpa*). Yet (he would claim that) no operation of mind is ever by itself an instrument of knowledge.[12] It would be an instrument of knowledge only insofar as it forms part of the operation of intellect. In fact, the operation of intellect consists of three distinct operations, though functioning jointly. One of these is the operation of mind, through which intellect relates itself to the object, shaping itself, according to the form of the object, in to the form "This *is* such and such" ("is" underscored, indicating that there is belief). The second operation is that of egoity, through which intellect relates itself to consciousness, shaping itself into the form "*I* am such and such" or "Things are in such and such ways relevant to me," underscoring the way the "I" feeling evolves. The third operation is that of intellect exclusively, which, according to Vācaspati Miśra is of the form of belief as to what "I have *to do*."[13] Pañcānanatarkaratna's point is that it is only when all these three operations function that intellect, shaping itself according to the form of object, is entitled to the name "instrument of knowledge." What is meant here by "three operations of the intellect" is that each such operation, though not depending for its exercise on the other two, yet exercises itself only in the context of the other two operating jointly with itself. The second operation stated above is, qua independent, precisely the autonomous operation of ego, and the first, similarly, of sense capacity (particularly, of mind).

Or, as Pañcānanatarkaratna contends, "intellect with three operations" means just the three fundamental principles, each with its specific operation, functioning successively—mind just presenting the object, egoity presenting the same object to consciousness, and intellect deciding (involving belief or objectivity) what to do with it.

Vijñānabhikṣu holds that intellect and consciousness must each get reflected on the other, because there is nothing here to determine that one specifically is capable of receiving reflection and the other not. This view, according to Pañcānanatarkaratna is wrong, because there are such determinants. Intellect as *sāttvika* (i.e., made of *sattva*= intelligibility constituent) is, like a mirror, capable of taking in reflection (image of other things); and consciousness, as it is made of nothing, is incapable of that. Vijñānabhikṣu's view is unacceptable for another reason also. If intellect and consciousness were like two mirrors facing each other, then there being a single object between them to be reflected in one of the mirrors, there would be an infinite number of such reflections (images) in each mirror.

Pañcānanatarkaratna has, in this connection, very thoroughly examined Vijñānabhikṣu's theory of mutual reflection by raising some other crushing objections against him. He has also studied the relevance of the well-known citation "*tasmiṃściddarpaṇe sphāre* . . ." to Sāṃkhya philosophy and shown also that the term *pratisaṃvedin*" in "*buddheḥ pratisaṃvedī puruṣaḥ*" (*Vyāsabhāṣya*) does not in any way connote anything like reflection (imaging = copying). Even an echo, according to him, is not, at least obviously, reflectionlike.

Pañcānanatarkaratna has also, in this connection, analyzed the concept of doubt, distinguishing between two kinds of indefinitude (awareness of the indefinite)—one, of a thing being apprehended simultaneously as X and not X and the other, of a thing being simultaneously apprehended as X, Y, etc.

Vācaspati Miśra has shown why inference has to be studied after perception. Pañcānanatarkaratna adds that "after" here means immediately after and states the whole problem in a very precise (neo-Nyāya) form and, he, as usual shows in detail the relevance of every word of the statement—shows, in other words, why no type of instrument of knowledge that is not inference should be considered immediately after perception and why no type of inference should be excluded by this rule.

Pañcānanatarkaratna also offers another simpler interpretation of Vācaspati Miśra's claim that inference has to be considered after perception. In this interpretation he ceases to insist on "immediately after," understanding the expression "*pratyakṣakāryatvāt*" not as "inference is somehow *effected* by perception" but as "the consideration of inference, as a *work* to be done, comes naturally after the consideration of perception as a *work*." The work in question is the work of consideration.

Pañcānanatarkaratna discusses in detail (1) the Nyāya concept of *upādhi* (limiting condition that vitiates inference), (2) its two forms, suspected and assured *upādhi*, (3) the entire mechanism of inference in neo-Nyāya fashion, (4) the Sāṃkhya view of universal (*jāti*) as distinguished from the Nyāya view, (5) how Vācaspati Miśra's definition of inference distinguishes it adequately from all other instruments of knowledge and (6) how in exclusionary inference the negative predicate ("other than what is other than X") really points to something being X, without X being shown as a predicate in the knowledge content (*jñānākāra*). (It is, however, only the object of that knowledge.) For example, in the inference "Earth is other than whatever is not earth, because it has smell" the predicate is indeed negative (a negation of negations — not-water, not-fire, not-air and not-ether), but what is meant is that it is *earth*, which, however, does not figure here as a predicate, earthness here being the very identity of the soil. This exclusionary inference is, in this point, different from what the Naiyāyikas call "only-negative inference" (*kevalavyatirekyanumāna*) which, according to them, is no form of Vācaspati Miśra's *a posteriori* inference, though Vācaspati Miśra's exclusionary inference is exactly that. In Sāṃkhya, the final result of exclusionary inference is the inferential knowledge of what remains over after all the other alternatives are negated. According to Nyāya, this knowledge of what remains over is only an *ad hoc* mental intuition (*mānasapratyakṣa*) that follows.

As usual, Pañcānanatarkaratna formulates Vacaspati Miśra's account of verbal testimony (both as an instrument and as knowledge) in precise neo-Nyāya style and shows the relevance of every term of that formula.

In connection with the instrument of verbal testimony, Pañcānanatarkaratna clarifies the notions of self-validation and extrinsic validation.

Knowledge is validated either intrinsically, that is, independently of any extrinsic consideration, or on extrinsic grounds. Perceptual and inferential knowledge and knowledge of X derived from hearing somebody speaking of X have all got to be extrinsically validated (by conditions other than those that cause such knowledge). Why? Because in such cases there is alwasys the possibility of some defect. But scriptural knowledge, which looks like knowledge derived from hearing somebody speaking out those truths, is yet intrinsically valid because, as a matter of fact, these truths are not originally spoken by anybody and are, therefore, free of all defects that might belong to a speaker. (This is what orthodox thinkers mean by "original scripture"). That which, on the other hand, is *spoken by some person* can be taken as true (1) if, and so far as, it is derived directly from the original scripture (as in the case of ethico-social studies called *smṛti*, *itihāsa*, *purāṇa*, etc.) or (2) if it is a literal reproduction of the original scripture every time the world is created anew after total dissolution.[14] Kapila's Sāṃkhya refers to the latter.

Some scholars hold that in Sāṃkhya all awarenesses (even perceptual and inferential ones) are self-validating. Pañcānanatarkaratna rejects that view on the ground that ordinarily at least verbal testimonies are often found to be invalid. Further, the word "*tat*" ("that"), in Vācaspati Miśra's commentary "*tat ca svataḥ pramāṇam*" "and that is self-validating") does not, in the context where it occurs, refer to ordinary testimonies (but only to scriptural testimony); and, *a fortiori*, it does not refer to other instruments of knowledge such as perception and inference.

Some Sāṃkhyans, again, have understood "self-validating" (*svataḥpramāṇa*) as "self-illuminating" (*svataḥprakāśa*) and held, on this assumption, that all knowledge (and, therefore, all instruments of knowledge) is self-validating because knowledge as manifestness, i.e., as in the context of consciousness, is always self-manifesting. According to Pañcānanatarkaratna this assumption is unwarranted and, further, even if on this assumption all knowledge insofar as it is in the context of consciousness self-manifesting, none of the corresponding modes of intellect, which alone are called instruments of knowledge, are definitely of that character.

In connection with Vācaspati Miśra's reduction of comparison (*upamāna*) to inference, Pañcānanatarkaratna adds: What is meant by the word "*gavaya*"[15] is, according to some, the universal *gavaya*hood (*gavayatva*) and, according to others, particular *gavayas* insofar as they are instantiations of the universal *gavaya*hood (*gavayatvāvacchinnagavaya*). Pañcānanatarkaratna admits both.

Some hold that the word "*gavaya*" means as much the universal *gavaya*hood as also the *similarity* of the animal in question to the cow, and that, whereas the former is known through comparison, the latter is known through inference. But Pañcānanatarkaratna would reply that where both the similarity and the universal *gavayahood* (both as possible designata of the word "*gavaya*") are perceptually present, it would be more parsimonious to take the universal *gavayahood* as the designatum than alternating between the two. (The mere similarity cannot be taken as the designatum because (1) the universal is equally present to perception[16] and (2) whereas the presented similarity can be understood in terms of the universal, the reverse is not possible.)

That in the case under consideration the word "*gavaya*" signifies the universal *gavayahood* (or any animal as an instantiation of *gavaya*hood) is, as a matter of fact, inferred on the ground of the major premise "When elders use a word for me to have an attitude to something present to my perception they *mean* that thing by that word." (In the case under consideration they have used the word "*gavaya*" for me to understand that the animal called *gavaya* is like a cow.) But this major premise itself could not be unless, through a new instrument of knowledge, one had taken a particular animal present before him as bearing the name "*gavaya*." This latter is possible, in the case under consideration, through the perception of the similarity of the animal to what is called "cow." In case, on the other hand, an elder asks me to bring an animal that is present before us both by saying "Bring that *gavaya*," I would know that the animal is called "*gavaya*" merely on the strength of the testimony of that elder.

Where Vācaspati Miśra simply writes that it is one and the same similarity whether it is the similarity of cow with a *gavaya* or of a *gavaya* with a cow, Pañcānanatarkaratna adds: To say in this case that the cow perceived in the past and now only remembered is similar to the *gavaya* now perceived would indeed pose a difficulty. As the *gavaya* is perceived, its similarity with any cow (whether that cow is now perceived or not) is also perceived, for the similarity in question is after all the presence (in the *gavaya*) of quite a good number of perceivable features of any cow. In the case, on the other hand, of the similarity of a remembered (not now perceived) cow—when the *gavaya* stands perceived—with that *gavaya*, one might object that it (i.e., the similarity) cannot be perceived, because that cow itself is not then perceived. This objection can, however, be met (Pañcānanatarkaratna holds) through the Nyāya theory of *jñānalakṣaṇapratyakṣa*, the theory that the remembered object becomes so fused (complicated) with the perceived object as to be itself also presented to perception (as in the case of a block of ice *looking* cold).[17]

While explaining Vācaspati Miśra's notes on the instrument of knowledge called presumption, Pañcānanatarkaratna adds the following: According to the Mīmāṃsakas presumption as an instrument of knowing is to be understood in two ways—either explaining an enigmatic situation by imagining (i.e., with the hypothesis of) something without which it cannot be explained (the enigmatic situation, for example, that somebody is known to be living and is yet not found in his residence, cannot be explained except by postulating that he is outside his residence) or by defining the situation so precisely that no contradiction remains (the contradiction, for example, between his remaining elsewhere—for he is still living—and not remaining in his house—the house being after all one of the "anywhere(s)"—is removed by defining "anywhere" as anywhere else).

Again, according to the Mīmāṃsakas, presumption, could look like inference if only it were of the exclusionary type in which the major premise merely shows that the absence of the *sādhya* has (so far) been found to be concomitant with the absence of the *hetu*. But they hold at the same time that this type of argument is no inference at all; it is precisely what they call presumption. Pañcānanatarkaratna adds that it is just in order to counter this challenge that Vācaspati Miśra has reduced presumption to a positive (*vīta*) form of inference.

Regarding nonapprehension as an instrument of knowledge, Pañcānanatarkaratna adds: According to the Bhāṭṭa Mīmāṃsaka, when I assert (know) the absence of an object X, this is not possible except through the absence of my knowledge of X (though other conditions are also required). This absence of the knowledge of X is the instrument called nonapprehension (*abhāva* = *anupalabdhi*). In Sāṃkhya language, it ought to be the absence of the operation relating to X. But (as Pañcānanatarkaratna claims) this absence is itself an operation after all, though of the form "absence of the operation (*vṛtti*) of X." According to Sāṃkhya, absence of X in Y is nothing but that mere Y, that is, Y as even uncharacterized in any manner by that absence. Hence, the absence of an operation, which absence must be taken as another operation, has to be nothing but that other operation uncharacterized even by that absence.

Pañcānanatarkaratna next explains this identity of the absence of X in Y with mere Y with reference to different types of absence and also with reference to the two broad categories of counterpositives, that is, the counterpositive that occupies a part of the locus and one that occupies the whole of it.

One might object (as Pañcānanatarkaratna imagines it) that if the absence of X in Y is the same thing as Y itself, there could not be an expression like "the absence of X *in* Y." But the reply (as Pañcānanatarkaratna offers it) is that as much as in the case of seawater and waves here too there is some difference (in spite of identity), which would guarantee the use of the said expression and all that is like it. Pañcānanatarkaratna next raises some subtle points and disposes of them in the neo-Nyāya fashion.

(6) Intellect and egoity are inferred exactly in the same way as unmanifest materiality is inferred, that is, by passing from relative limitedness to relative "beyond that limit."

Pañcānanatarkaratna next shows that subtle elements are inferred on the ground that every gross entity must have for its causal basis what is subtler than it. The well-known process of inferring sense capacities is stated over again here.

All such inferences are of the general correlation (*sāmanyatodṛṣṭa*) type.

Vācaspati Miśra holds that neither the *a posteriori* (*śeṣavat*) nor general correlation type of inference applies in the case of the order of sequence of the fundamental principles from intellect to gross elements. But Vijñānabhikṣu has actually applied the *a posteriori* type of inference here. Pañcānanatarkaratna states these inferences and has gone so far as even to refute a relevant objection against Vijñānabhikṣu's venture. Yet he explodes these inferences on the ground that exactly in the same manner counter conclusions could be arrived at in all these cases.

Pañcānanatarkaratna next quotes a large number of passages from different scriptures in support of the Sāṃkhya order of the emergence of the fundamental principles and shows how some apparently different statements can be reconciled.[18]

III. The Notion of Preexistent Effect

(9) By way of introducing the theory of preexistent effect Vācaspati Miśra refers to three other theories and states them very briefly. Pañcānanatarkaratna elaborates and identifies these theories as follows:

The first is the Buddhist theory, according to which beings come out of nonbeing: An effect arises just after its (material) cause has ceased to be. Just before a seed sprouts it has ceased to be a seed, and from this we may infer that this is the rule of causation everywhere—even where, as in the case of a cloth arising out of threads, this cessation of being is not visible. Pañcānanatarkaratna here raises a relevant objection:

but, then, like the burning of the cloth following upon the burning of its constituent threads, would not the cessation of the being of the threads lead to the cessation of the being of the cloth itself? Pañcānanatarkaratna replies on behalf of the Buddhists: the threads having already ceased to be cannot now burn; what is commonly called "burning of threads" is really the burning of the cloth itself.

The second is the (Advaita) Vedānta theory. It is that from Being (ultimate Being = Brahman) *appears* the world as constituted by ignorance but wholly to be rejected by knowledge proper and, therefore, as not ultimately real. In this respect the world is like the false snake that appears in the locus of a real rope except that this rope too is not ultimately real. There are, in effect, three types of reality = being: (1) ultimate reality (*pāramārthikasattā*), (2) worldly reality = useful reality (*vyāvahārikasattā*), and (3) apparent reality (*prātibhāsikasattā*).

The third view is that of the Vaiśeṣika and Nyāya thinkers. By "real," in this view, is meant the eternal = permanent, and by "not real" the noneternal = impermanent. All impermanent beings come out of permanent beings, like atoms.

All these three views are exploded immediately, for it is shown that all impermanent worldly things are made of satisfaction-yielding, frustration-yielding, and confusion-yielding constituents and that there is a relation of identity of the (material) cause and its effect. This is precisely what Sāṃkhya proposes to show. That the gross elements are so is perceptually evident. That subtle elements are so is inferred on the basis of (material-) cause-effect identity, and that the further subtler essences are so can be inferred in the same manner step-by-step retrogressively. Even primordial materiality is so, though only in chain relation to the other essences, not in its intrinsic status.

(11) (Vācaspati Miśra in the *Tattvakaumudī* writes "*naiyāyikanayairudbhāvanīyam.*" Pañcānanatarkaratna points out that there is another alternative reading. It is "*naiyāyikatanayaiḥ.*" He rejects this alternative reading as childish and practically out of context.)

All the arguments for the theory of *satkārya*, stated in the *Sāṃkhyakārikā* and elaborated in the *Tattvakaumudī*, are reformulated by Pañcānanatarkaratna in precise neo-Nyāya forms and defended against possible objections.

Because the effect and its (material) cause are substantively identical, it follows that qualities (*guṇa*), in the Nyāya-Vaiśeṣika sense, motions (*karman*), and universals (*jāti*) are identical with the corresponding (individual) substances.[19]

V. The Three Constituents

(13) In verse 12 it has been stated that the constituents are *for* (i.e., aids to) enlightenment = manifestation (*prakāśa*), activity (*pravṛtti*),

and regulation (*niyama*). The present verse, 13, shows that these belong to the very nature of the three constituents respectively.

Or, in the previous verse the functions of the three constituents have been stated in lump, without any attempt at showing which one is to be connected with which. This has been done in the present verse.

Vācaspati Miśra writes that the constituent *rajas* drives the constituents to behave as they do. Pañcānanatarkaratna adds: There is nothing paradoxical here. It is not that one and the same *rajas* is here as much the wielder as the object that is wielded, at one and the same point of time. As in the case of a tree obtaining in a group of trees, called forest, or a tenth man in a group counting himself as the tenth, there is here some difference somewhere involved in spite of all identity, a difference that we have to postulate. This is how some Sāṃkhyists understand the situation. Some modern Sāṃkhyists, however, are bold enough to assert that, even about the agent and the object of his act being identical, there is nothing that is wrong, for how, otherwise, could one explain the phenomenon that one knows *himself*? What is required here, they claim, is only a clear analysis of the apparently paradoxical situation. Pañcānanatarkaratna offers that analysis here in correct neo-Nyāya language.

That satisfaction (*sattva*), frustration (*rajas*), and confusion (*tamas*) must belong to the objects that appear to produce these is to be inferred from cases such as the following: Through the senses one can perceive color, taste, etc., of an object only if that object already possesses color, taste, etc. Again, just as one can perceive color only through his eyes, not through his tongue, so, we contend, the same object produces satisfaction in one person, not in another, only because of the differing constitutions (temporary though they may be) of these different persons (*sattva* dominating in one and *rajas* and *tamas* dominating in others).

It should not be said that the object is always neutral but that it produces satisfaction, frustration, etc., in different minds according as these minds have different constitutions. For, then, the same thing could be said about the color sensation, taste sensation, etc., noted above.

Nor should one argue that the object outside is only an efficient cause of the satisfaction, frustration, etc., in the mind, much as rods, wheels, etc., are of the pots that are made, and as these efficient causes do not contain the pots, so with the object that produces satisfaction, frustration, etc. As for the said production of satisfaction, frustration, etc., this would only be an unnecessarily complicated (i.e., involving the defect called complexity (*gaurava*)) account, however true it may be of the production of pots. A simpler account would be that the object itself contains (and is, therefore, of the nature of) satisfaction, frustration, and confusion.[20]

VI. Inferences to Primordial Materiality and Consciousness

(16) The word "*samudaya*" (in "*samudayāt*") in the *Sāṃkhyakārikā* is sought to be rendered clearly by Vācaspati Miśra by means of the word "*samavāya*." Pañcānanatarkaratna writes: The word "*samavāya*" used by Vācaspati Miśra means the state of being just on the point of a (material) cause changing itself into an effect.

(17) Vācaspati Miśra writes: Whatever is composed of the three constituents is a composite entity, where the denotation of the term "composite entity" is wider than that of the term "composed of the three constituents." It follows that the denial of the latter (i.e., of the composite character of pure consciousness) would necessarily entail denial of the former (i.e., of pure consciousness being composed of the three constituents).

So far so good, but immediately after this he writes something that seems to contradict what he has just written. He writes that, by denying the three constituents, etc., of pure consciousness (i.e., by means of the premise that pure consciousness is not composed of the three constituents, etc.), the author of the *Sāṃkhyakārikā* seeks as it were to deny the composite character of it (i.e., that it has a composite character).

This looks illogical, but Pañcānanatarkaratna removes the anomaly. We must not forget that Vācaspati Miśra has added an "etc." after "three constituents." This means that Īśvarakṛṣṇa has taken into consideration, not merely the three constituents, but along with these, and in the same act of denial, all other coordinate characters of pure consciousness (except its being a composite entity). "To be composed of the three constituents, etc., provided it is a composite entity" is not of narrower denotation than "to be a composite entity."

"Whatever is a composite entity is designed to serve some other's interest"—this is no statement of the *ground* of the inference in question. (In other words, "to be a composite entity" is not the *hetu* here. For, whereas in every inference the *hetu* has to be found in the locus of the *sādhya*, this is not the case here.) To be a composite entity is only an instigating factor (*prayojaka*) of the inference in question. This point must be kept in view in all the different inferences leading to the establishment of (pure) consciousness.

Vācaspati Miśra writes—and this is what everybody would admit—that satisfaction is that which, in effect, is appreciated as favorable to oneself, and frustration is that which, in effect, is appreciated as inimical. But satisfaction and frustration are, after all, operations of the intellect. Hence, the one that appreciates must be other than the intellect. Were it not so, the situation would be a contradictory one of the form "X (as subject) knowing itself (as object)"—one and the same act having an identical entity as the agent and the object. Pañcānanatarkaratna asks, in this context, the question whether the injunction "Know thyself" would then be a self-contradictory and shows in various ways that it is not.[21]

(18) Birth is to be understood as the (first-moment) relation (of a self) with a novel (*apūrva*) body, etc., not the relation (with the same body) that continues.

The relation that explains birth is called by Vācaspati Miśra *abhısambandha*. Pañcānanatarkaratna explains it as follows: This relation (contextually, at the first moment, but equally so at all subsequent moments of the same life) is called "*abhisambandha*," because it is no genuinely real relation. It is a relation that is superimposed, taken as though it is a relation (*āropitasambandha*).

Vācaspati Miśra says that birth is the (superimposed) relation (of a self) with a particular system of novel body, sense capacities, egoity, intellect, and native dispositions (*adṛṣṭa*) for particular satisfactions and frustrations (to be reaped in the life to begin). Pañcānanatarka ratna explains why, over and above body, these other entities are required: If, over and above novel body, there must be in birth these other novel entities, that is, novel sense capacities, novel egoity, novel intellect, and novel dispositions for particular satisfactions and frustrations, this is only to exclude the *self-created* body system of the Yogin, in which, though the body so created (sometimes several such bodies simultaneously), along with the necessary sense capacities, etc., is novel, the dispositions for satisfactions and frustrations are not so (they being exactly those for the speedy exhaustion of which the *yogin* creates that body system).

But what inadequacy, it may be asked, would be there if novel sense capacities, novel ego, and novel intellect were not required? The reply is that without them the body system would not have its full uniqueness. Equally again, intellect alone (though along with body and dispositions, i.e., without egoity and sense capacities) would not be sufficient, for, as a matter of necessity, a unique egoity and a unique set of sense capacities always accompany a unique intellect.

In different stages of life, such as childhood, youth, and decrepitude we do not, in spite of substantial changes otherwise, have (with each stage) a novel body (those changes being but changes in the same body).

(21) Pañcānanatarkaratna speaks of a kind of nonmanifest feeling-toned experience before the world of any particular creative cycle comes into being (manifestation). It is exactly what is otherwise called not-yet-maturing-into-actual-feeling-toned experience and to-mature-that-way-later disposition (*adṛṣṭa*).

(22) Pañcānanatarkaratna shows in his own way why all the twenty-five fundamental principles (*tattva*) have to be admitted and confirms what he says by reference to what a great teacher has already said.[22] He proceeds as follows: To start with, at least two principles

have to be admitted, consciousness and objects (both gross and subtle), all objects together being called materiality. But, certainly, over and above these two we must admit some relation of the objects to that consciousness, for without this there could not be any experience. Now, does this relation belong to the nature of consciousness or does it belong to the nature of materiality, or to that of the objects themselves, or to something else? The first two alternatives are unacceptable, for had we accepted them there could be no liberation. Nor does the relation belong merely to the nature of the objects, for then the distinction between direct (perceptual) and indirect (nonperceptual) experience would go unexplained. In order that this distinction is explained we have to admit something else, that is, sense capacities, without the operation of which there could not be perceptual experience. But still all difficulties are not over. Even though an object stands in relation to a sense capacity, it sometimes goes unnoticed, which means that yet another principle is required to make a sense capacity help experiencing object. That other principle is exactly what we have called mind. Other phenomena, for the explanation of which three other principles, egoity, intellect, and unmanifest materiality, have to be admitted are (1) dream experience, (2) experience in dreamless sleep, and (3) the difficulty that if intellect is a permanent principle then there would be no liberation (which implies that intellect, before it comes into being (manifestation) and after it ceases to be (manifest), remains unmanifest (as unmanifest materiality).[23])

IX. Functioning of the Thirteenfold Instrument

(23) Reflective discerning = belief = rational objectivity is as much operative in will as in cognition. Objectivity in willing is the awareness of what I *ought to do*, and that in cognition, the awareness of what *ought to be*.

Supernormal powers, called *aiśvarya*, form also a kind of willing. (Rational objectivity here is the awareness of attaining the maximum in the line.) As forms of willing they should not be taken as states (or attitudes) of the *body*.

Meritorious behavior, knowledge, nonattachment, and power (*aiśvarya*) are composed of *sattva* constituents, and demeritorious behavior, ignorance, attachment, and impotence are composed of *tamas* constituents. But *rajas* is required in both cases, for without *rajas* nothing can be exercised into operation. Thus all the three constituents are required—*sattva* and *tamas* as constitutive, and *rajas*, helping both to get into operation.

In connection with the notion of eightfold *yoga*, Pañcānanatarkaratna gives a short account of the entire Yoga discipline according to Patañjali.

All the types of nonattachment that Vācaspati Miśra mentions are only provisional (*aparā*). The ultimate (*parā*) nonattachment is disinterestedness even in the direct intuition of the difference of (pure) consciousness and materiality. Although Vācaspati Miśra has not mentioned it as a predisposition of intellect it is one (Pañcānanatarkaratna says), as held by Patañjali who calls it a "lingering cognitive tone" or, as it has sometimes been understood, "knowledge at its excellence" (*jñānaprasāda*).

Demeritorious behavior, ignorance, attachment, and impotence are not mere absences of their opposites, meritorious behavior, etc. They are positive counterstates (or counterattitudes).

From the account of merit, knowledge, etc., and satisfaction, frustration, etc., given in this *kārikā*, it follows that they belong to intellect and not to consciousness.

(24) Pañcānanatarkaratna collects a good number of passages from the Upaniṣads and Purāṇas and reconciles their differences. Further, he contends that when we awake from deep (dreamless) sleep we pass through stages where the order of the Sāṃkhya principles is rehearsed in that context, and in the reverse order when from the waking stage we lapse into deep (dreamless) sleep.

(29) If the five vital breaths are called air (*vāyu*) of different types, this must not be understood literally. They are called air of different types merely on the ground of the similarity of function.

(31) At the time one instrument of knowledge and/or action is activated to perform its own function other instruments of knowledge and/or action (of the same individual)are activated. The former, so far, is the occasioning cause of the latter, both meeting at the same point of time. Yet this is neither a matter of accidental coincidence nor due to the agency of any conscious being. The coincidence is all determined teleologically, in the interest (experience or liberation) of the individual whose instruments they are. The interest in question is the maturation of dispositions that, among other things, constitute the individuality of that individual.

What Īśvarakṛṣṇa and Vācaspati Miśra call "*ākūta*" (to be on the point of starting an operation) is but the activation of the *sāttvika* and *tāmasika* dispositions by the *rājasika* constituents. Or, it is nothing but the dispositions themselves just insofar as all impediments to their maturation into actuality are gone. It may also be said that the dispositions and their operations (in effect, the operative=maturing dispositions) are entitatively identical (the only point to be noted being that the operations in question are constitutionally end oriented).

What is denied here is only pure consciousness as agent, not pure consciousness as itself.

(32) "Seizing" is a wide term comprehending creation of sound

(in speech), acceptance of things, reaching up to things, ejection and enjoyment.

According to Sāṃkhya, a substance, say, earth, and the corresponding attribute, say, smell, are entitatively identical.

(33) Just as in the case of speech, the sound that is created comes after the exercise of the instrument of speech, so is the case with every satisfaction and like phenomena, which, according to some, last for two successive moments. In all these cases, the present (*vartamāna*) time may cover adjacent moments.[24]

(39) Where Vācaspati Miśra writes that the gross physical body (*ṣāṭkauṣikadeha*) is made of such and such strands he does not mention semen, which, following the tradition on this line, ought to have been included. Pañcānanatarkaratna writes that it has, in effect, been included, because it is at the back of all the rest.

"Hairs" (*loman*) here means skin. Pañcānanatarkaratna shows elaborately why it should mean that.

XII. The Basic Predispositions

(46) Vācaspati Miśra writes that within the four intellectual creations are to be included the eight predispositions of the intellect, each as it fits in with one or another of them. He says that seven of these predispositions, i.e., all of them except knowledge, are to be included in the first three intellectual creations, and knowledge in the last one called attainment. Pañcānanatarkaratna takes up the problem in all seriousness and discusses in this connection how certain difficulties that arise can be removed and what alternative views there are regarding this.

(50) Contentment is a kind of satisfaction resulting either from following wrong paths (wrongly prescribed or understood) for intuiting the otherness of (pure) consciousness from materiality or from wrongly understanding materiality, at any of its transformational stages, to be the real "I", that is, pure consciousness. Vācaspati Miśra has distinguished four kinds of the former type of contentment and five kinds of the latter. Pañcānanatarkaratna has, in this connection, and in reference to *kārikā* 49, discussed, in addition, the kinds of dysfunction, "to attain contentment" and says that, as contentment is of nine kinds so is this dysfunction, called *tuṣṭiviparyaya*. Alternatively, too, he understands *tuṣṭiviparyaya* as just not getting the contentment in question, though he makes it clear at the same time that this "not getting the contentment in question" (*tuṣṭyabhāva*) is not, therefore, what is called attainment (that which is direcly conducive to the intuition of the otherness of pure consciousness from materiality), and that way he refutes Vijñānabhikṣu's charge that all forms of *tuṣṭiviparyaya* ought not to have been included in dysfunction.

Pañcānanatarkaratna explains, too, the relevance of the five technical names—*ambhas, salila,* etc.—for the five kinds of the first type of contentment. Similarly, with the five names—*pāra, supāra,* etc.[25]

(51) Vācasapati Miśra after he has explained the eight kinds of attainment in one way, explains them in another alternative way. He begins this alternative interpretation saying, "Others, however, . . ."

Pañcānanatarkaratna says that by "others" Vācaspati Miśra means Gauḍapāda and his followers.

Vijñānabhikṣu understands by the term "*aṅkuśa*" "that which attracts." He holds that *ūha, śabda,* and *adhyayana,*[26] as attracting what is called intuition of the otherness of consciousness from materiality, are *aṅkuśas* that way. From this he concludes that these three alone constitute the main means to this realization and the other two only secondary (indirect) means. But (Pañcānanatarkaratna holds that) such interpretation is unacceptable, because the *Sāṃkhyakārıkā* never distinguishes that way between main and subordinate means.

XIII. The Empirical World

(53) The word "*paśu*" stands for a creature possessing a hairy tail, and the word "*mṛga*" for a quadruped that does not possess a hairy tail.

(54) "*Loka*" here means not regions but residents of the regions.

(56) The three views that Vācaspati Miśra rejects one by one, *viz.,* (1) the world is not caused (i.e., no transformation of any ulterior substance), (2) it is a transformation of consciousness and (3) God (a pure consciousness freely possessing infinite capacities) changes the ultimate substance into the world, are the views, respectively, of the Sarvāstivāda Buddhists, (Advaita) Vedāntins, and the Yoga system of Patañjali.[27]

XIV. Similes for Materiality

(57) The urge, the active force, behind the (initial and all later) movement of materiality is but "a form of (intrinsic) transformation" (*rajaḥparıṇāmabheda*), and it always requires "a third contributory factor" (*vyāpāra*), for which reason such urge cannot belong to consciousness. The idea is that no transformation of materiality can ever be ("efficiently" or "materially") caused by consciousness.

XV. Liberation and Isolation

(66) The "contact" (*saṃyoga*) of materiality and consciousness, because of which creation takes place, is actual contact (*sannidhāna*) caused (in its turn) by the prenatal disposition complex (*adṛṣṭa*)

of the worldly person (*jīva*). Over and above this, however, there is an eternal contact that is only the capability (*yogyatā*) of consciousness to experience materiality and of materiality to be experienced by consciousness. This capability is far removed from "actual contact." Vācaspati Miśra therefore, never understood by "contact that generates experience" the mere capability (*yogyatā*) for contact, for, then, he could not have called the contact in question "occasioned" (*naimittika*) and "many" (*nānā*). Vijñānabhikṣu did not follow this distinction and was, therefore, wrong and only wrongly believed that by "contact" Vācaspati Miśra had always meant capability for contact.

KUÑJAVIHĀRĪ TARKASIDDHĀNTA

Kuñjavihārī Tarkasiddhānta (Bhaṭṭācārya), the second son of Rūpacandra Bhaṭṭācārya and Śāradā Devī, was born in Medinimandala, Dacca (now in Bangladesh). He studied Vyākaraṇa, Nyāya, and Sāṃkhya from eminent scholars such as Gaṅgānārāyaṇa Cakravartī, Durgācaraṇa Sāṃkhyavedāntatīrtha, Rāsamohāna Sārvabhauma, Kailāśacandra Śiromaṇi, and Vāmācaraṇa Bhaṭṭācārya. Having taught at different seminaries, he joined Government Sanskrit College, Calcutta, as a teacher of Nyāya and trained a number of eminent Naiyāyikas, of whom special mention may be made of Anantakumāra Nyāyatarkatīrtha and Heramba Tarkatīrtha. In 1933, the then British Indian Government conferred on him the honorary title "*Mahāmahopadhyāya*".

Among the numerous literary and scholarly works of Kuñjavihārī Tarkasiddhānta, we may mention here the *Tattvabodhinī* (a commentary on Aniruddha's *Sāṃkhyasūtravṛtti*), *Pratibhā* (a literary work), and annotated editions of the *Siddhāntamuktāvalī*, *Mālatīmadhavam* and Piṅgala's *Chandaḥsūtra* with Halāyudha's commentary. For some time, Kuñjavihārī Tarkasiddhānta also edited the journal *Āryaprabhā*.

"E" references are to the edition of *Tattvabodhinī*, published from Berobeltora, Manbhum, 1919.

TATTVABODHINĪ

(*Summary by Prabal Kumar Sen*)

As has been stated above, the *Tattvabodhinī* is a commentary on Aniruddha's *Sāṃkhyasūtravṛtti*. Although the *Sāṃkhyasūtravṛtti* is not a profound work, certain portions of it are difficult to understand, and according to Tarkasiddhānta, the *Tattvabodhinī* was written primarily for elucidating these portions (E3-4). Most of these difficulties are due to incorrect readings, and Tarkasiddhānta tried to correct them by collating three earlier editions of the *Sāṃkhyasūtravṛtti*.

As an exposition of the *Sāṃkhyasūtravṛtti*, the *Tattvabodhinī* is useful and comprehensive, though mostly conventional in character. On some points, the *Tattvabodhinī* has explained the *Sāṃkhyasūtra* in ways that have not been adequately explained in the *Saṃkhyasūtravṛtti*. It also provides novel explanations of some words in the two texts. Occasionally, however, Tarkasiddhānta's predilection for Nyāya-Vaiśeṣika doctrines have made him ascribe to Sāṃkhya views that are totally alien to it.

Book I: On Topics

(A) *Introductory Sūtras: Scope and Task of Sāṃkhya*

(I.1) (E4) The *Sāṃkhyasūtravṛtti* maintains that the word "*atha*" in *sūtra* 1 stands for "auspiciousness." The *Tattvabodhinī* points out on cogent grounds that in this case, *atha* does not stand for auspiciousness, though its utterance ensures an auspicious beginning. It may be noted that on this point, Tarkasiddhānta has followed Vijñānabhikṣu.

(E7) The *Sāṃkhyasūtravṛtti* adduces reasons for maintaining that *dharma*, *artha*, and *kāma* cannot be regarded as summum bonum. The reasons are (1) they are subject to destruction (*kṣayitvāt*) and (2) they are satisfactions generated by desired contents (*viṣayajasukhatvāt vā*). It is to be noted that the second reason adduced here is an alternative one (as suggested by the particle "*vā*"). The *Sāṃkhyasūtravṛtti* does not explain the necessity for adducing an alternative reason. The *Tattvabodhinī* points out that, because the possibility of destruction is not admitted in Sāṃkhya metaphysics, the first reason is not acceptable and is, therefore, rejected in favor of the second one.

(B) *On Bondage*

(I.11) Aniruddha has not explained the word "*aśakya*" in "*śaktyudbhavābhyāṃ nāśakyopadeśaḥ*." The *Tattvabodhinī* maintains that *aśakya* means, in this context, "natural" or "intrinsic" (*svābhāvika*) It is further suggested that the word "*upadeśaḥ*" should be understood to be followed by the word "*sambhavati*," as otherwise the sentence would remain incomplete.

(I.12-13) According to the *Tattvabodhinī*, the word "*kālayogataḥ*" in (12) and the word "*deśayogataḥ*" in (13) should be understood to be followed by the word "*bandhaḥ*." These two aphorisms would then apparently mean that bondage is not caused by space and time, because on that assumption consciousness, being eternal and ubiquitous, would always be in bondage. But they really mean that space and time are not the specific instrumental factors of bondage. As a matter of fact, space and time are general instrumental factors of bondage.

(I.15) (E19) The word "*iti*" *asaṅgo'yaṃ puruṣa iti*), left unexplained in the *Sāṃkhyasūtrāvṛtti*, indicates that the different stages of life, e.g., childhood, youth, etc., cannot belong to consciousness.

(I.59) (E68) This *sūtra* (*yuktito'pi na bādhyate diṅmūḍhavadaparokṣādṛte*) has not been fully explained in the *Sāṃkhyasūtravṛtti*. The *Tattvabodhinī* suggests that "*yukti*" stands for reasoning (*manana*), and "*api*" suggests the association (*samuccaya*) of scriptural knowledge (*śravana*). Moreover, "*bādhyate*" should be understood to be followed by "*aviveka*." The aphorism thus means that, in the absence of immediate knowledge of consciousness, nondiscrimination cannot be sublated by scripture or reasoning, which are accredited sources of mediate knowledge alone.

(C) *Derivation of the Fundamental Principles*

(I.61) (E71) The *Tattvabodhinī* maintains that although *sattva*, *rajas*, and *tamas* are called "*guṇa*" in the Sāṃkhya system, the word "*guṇa*" should not be understood in the sense in which it is used in the Vaiśeṣika system. These three constituents should be regarded as substances (*dravya*), because they are characterized by features like movement, etc.

(E) *Instruments of Knowledge*

(I.89) (E95) The *Tattvabodhinī* gives an interesting explanation of (89). It appears at first sight that the expression "*yatsambandhasiddham*" is a single compounded word. But this is not tenable, for in that case the *sūtra* would mean, inter alia, that the operation of the intellect, produced by sense-object contact and assuming the form of the object, is regarded as the causal condition par excellence of the perceptual knowledge of that object. But such an interpretation is inconsistent with *Sāṃkhyasūtra* V.107, which specifically states that the intellectual operation concerned is not produced by sense object contact. Hence, the word "*yat*" should be associated with the word "*vijñānam*." Moreover, "*sambandhasiddham*" should be treated as a word formed by *caturthī tatpuruṣa* compound, the word "*siddham*" being treated as a synonym of *prasiddham*. Thus construed, the *sūtra* would mean that the intellectual operation that assumes the form of an object and establishes a relation with the latter, should be regarded as the causal condition par excellence of the perceptual knowledge of that object.

(H) *The Three Constituents*

(I.127) (E130-131) The dissimilarity of the three constituents is stated in (127). The *Sāṃkhyasūtravṛtti* maintains that the word "*ādi*" in this *sūtra* means that *sattva* is light and revealing, *rajas* is mobile and exciting, whereas *tamas* is heavy and enveloping. Nevertheless, it is stated in (128) that features like lightness, etc., constitute the similarity and dissimilarity of the constituents. The *Tattvabodhinī* following Vijñānabhikṣu, points out that the mention of dissimilarity in this *sūtra* serves no specific purpose, since it has been already mentioned in the foregoing *sūtra*.

Book III: Nonattachment

(B) *Gross and Subtle Bodies*

(III.15) (E192) The *sūtra* maintains that since the internal sense organ is material (*annamaya*), it cannot be identified with consciousness. The *Sāṃkhyasūtravṛtti* is somewhat clumsy and confusing on this point. According to it, the internal sense organ is material, and being material, it is lunar in nature. In support of this, it quotes a scriptural passage to the effect that the vital breath is material in nature ("*annaṃ vai prāṇāḥ*"). It is difficult to give a coherent explanation of these lines. The *Tattvabodhinī* has tried to clear up the difficulty by drawing our attention to *Chāndogya Upaniṣad*, 6.5.4, which maintains that the internal sense organ is material and "*somya*" (*annamayaṃ hi somya manaḥ*). The *Tattvabodhinī* points out that, according to the *Sāṃkhyasūtravṛtti*, the word "*somya*" occurring in this passage should not be taken in its usual sense of address, but as an adjective of the internal sense organ. Thus, the relevant part of the *Sāṃkhyasūtravṛtti* means that the internal sense organ is both material and lunar in character, and, because consciousness is not identical with the moon, it cannot be identical with the internal sense organ that is lunar in nature. Although this succeeds to some extent in setting the matter straight, one feels nevertheless that this portion of the *Sāṃkhyasūtravṛtti* is unnecessarily complicated and obtuse. It seems that the *Tattvabodhinī*, being primarily expository in character, has tried to defend the *Sāṃkhyasūtravṛtti* as much as possible.

Book V: Arguments Against Opponents

(D) *Merit, Qualities, Inference, etc.*

(V. 30) (E264) Aniruddha has not explained the word "*vastukalpanā*." The *Tattvabodhinī* explains the *sūtra* to mean that pervasion need not be considered as an entity over and above the nondeviation (*avyabhicāra*) obtaining between the pervaded and the pervader.

(U) *The Nature of Bodies*

(V 114) (E329) Apart from some introductory remarks, Aniruddha does not provide any explanation of this *sūtra*. Accordinng to the *Tattvabodhinī*, the *sūtra* means that a body is formed only when it is connected with the enjoyer, i.e., the conscious principle. Otherwise, like the dead body, the body unconnected with consciousness would have putrefied

KṚṢṆAVALLABHĀCĀRYA

This subcommentary was composed in Varanasi by Kṛṣṇavallabhācārya, a teacher of the Svāmi Nārāyaṇa sect, in 1926. It is a running commentary on the *Tattvakaumudī* and explains the expressions of the text in a very elaborate but lucid manner. The important views of the commentator are noted below.

KIRAṆĀVALĪ ON TATTVAKAUMUDĪ

(*Summary by Ram Shankar Bhattacharya*)

I. Introductory Verses: Scope and Task of Sāṃkhya

Second benedictory verse. The sage Kapila is said to have been mentioned in *Śvetāśvatara Upaniṣad* 5.2., and in the chapter on one thousand names of Viṣṇu (*Mahābhārata*, *Anuśāsana Parvan* 149.70). Pañcaśikha was so called because he had five tufts, or locks, of hair (*śikhas*) on his head.

(1) The word "*abhighāta*" is said to mean "conjunction that produces sound," according to Nyāya, and "conjunction that creates bondage," according to Sāṃkhya. Frustration is said to arise because of its reflection existing in the intellect.

(3) As to why the grossness and the capability of being perceived by the organs of a jar and the like are said to be equal to those of the earth, this is answered by saying that both the jar and the earth possess all the five qualities (sound, touch, color, taste, and smell) and that both are the objects of all the five sense organs.

II. Instruments of Knowledge

(4) Gesture (*ceṣṭā*) is said to be the ninth instrument of knowledge according to the rhetoricians; the word "*ūrdhvasrotas*" is explained as meaning those persons who possess the awareness of supersensuous objects.

(5) Kṛṣṇavallabha discusses the significance of defining the defining attribute (*lakṣaṇa*) as that which distinguishes the *lakṣya* (definiendum) from both the things of the same kind and things of a different kind (*samānāsamānajātīyavyavaccheda*). He gives a clear elucidation of "*pauruṣeya bodha.*" The word "*lokāyata*" is explained as meaning "secular perception." There is an elucidation of *upādhi* (limiting adjunct) and of the three varieties of inference, and an explanation of the expression "*vahnitvasāmānyaviśeṣa.*" Inference by general correlation is explained as having for its object a universal of which a specific individual has not been perceived. Two kinds of *apauruṣeyatva* (the character of not having an author) of the Vedas are distinguished, based on the viewpoints of the theist and the atheist. The sect called *saṃsāramocaka* is identified with the followers of Cārvāka. The Vaiśeṣika view that the proof called verbal testimony is included in inference is explained.

(7) There is a clear explanation of the nonperception of objects capable of being perceived (*yogyapratyakṣanivṛtti*).

III. Preexistent Effect

(9) Elucidation is provided of the view of the Māyāvādins about the nature of the transitory existence and its relation to *Brahman*. *Brahmasūtra* II.1.14 is said to establish, not identity (*abheda*) of the objects with *Brahman*, but the absence of their separate existence from *Brahman*. There is an elaborate explanation of the sentence "*kriyānirodhabuddhi* . . . ." taking it as speaking of either five or three reasons and also showing a variant reading that speaks of one additional reason called *vyavasthā*. *Sāṃkhyasūtras* I.122-23 are quoted and explained.

VI. Inferences to Primordial Materiality and Consciousness

(15-16) Homogeneity consisting in the similarity of different objects (*samanvaya*) is explained by quoting the explanations of others. One constituent's being more powerful than the other two is dependent on relative suppressiveness (*upamardyaupamaradkabhāva*) otherwise known as relative subjugation. Agitation (*kṣobha*) is said to appear in materiality because of the agency of the purposes of consciousness. The agitated materiality gives rise to the principles, namely, the intellect and the rest, and this process is said to be called the tendency to action (*gatirūpā pravṛtti*).

(18) Derivation of the word "*puruṣa.*" Not all creatures possess all the ten sense and action capacities. The word "*kūṭastha*" suggests the sense of "an everlasting entity having only one form" (*ekarūpatayā kālavyāpin*).

(21) Creation is said to be of three kinds, namely, creation of the principles such as the intellect and the rest; creation of the eight basic

predispositions (merit, demerit, etc.) and creation of the elements, (the earth, etc.).

IX. Functioning of the Thirteenfold Instrument

(23) In the group of attainments, *gariman* (the power to become extremely heavy) is enumerated and "*kāmāvasāyitva*" is taken to be another name of the attainment called lordship (*iśitva*). Ignorance is explained as nonapprehension of difference (*vivekāgraha*); and misconception, conceptual construction (*vikalpa*), etc., are said to be varieties of ignorance.

(25) The view of some teachers, that the mind (the eleventh organ) is an effect of egoity dominated by *sattva* and that both of the two kinds of organs are the effects of egoity dominated by *rajas*, is set forth.

(27) Explanation of the term "*pravṛttinimitta*" (the reason for using a word in a particular sense).[1]

(28) The purpose of using the word "*mātra*" in the expression *ālocanamātra* is said to exclude the attributes, that is, in the perception called "*ālocana*," an object is perceived being devoid of the relation of substance and attribute. (It is, however, to be noted that in *ālocana* perception, characteristics or attributes are perceived, but they are not perceived as the features of the object. The object would thus be a simple entity and not anything complex.)

(29) Vital breath and its varieties, namely, *apāna*, etc., which are nothing but air, are said to disappear in the absence of the internal organs. Life (*jīvana*) consists in maintaining the body, which is a joint function of all the three internal organs. Nāga, Kūrma, and the rest are also accepted as forms of air.

(30) Svāmi Nārāyaṇa is mentioned as the supreme *Brahman* and other gods or deities are regarded as His incarnations.

(31) Traditional reasons are given for not holding consciousness (which is regarded as the controller) as the directive agency or instigator (*pravartaka*).

(33) A precise description of the function of speech is given.

XI. The Subtle Body

(44) The subtle body, according to the school of Svāmi Nārāyaṇa, is said to consist of 19 principles, namely, the ten capacities, five vital breaths, and four internal organs—mind, intellect, egoity, and the awareness faculty (*manas*, *buddhi*, *ahaṃkāra*, and *citta*, respectively).

XII. Basic Predispositions

(45) The word "*prakṛti*" in the expression "*prakṛtilaya*" is explai-

ned as referring to primordial materiality, intellect, egoity, the subtle and gross elements, and the ten capacities.

(46) Relative strength and weakness of the three constituents is shown to be of 36 kinds (each of the two aspects having 18 subdivisions).

XIII. The Empirical World

(53) *Paśu* is said to be an animal having hoofs and four feet, whereas *mṛga* is said to be an animal having many legs but no hoof.

XIV. Similes for Materiality

(61) The word "*me*" (of mine) is explained as referring to the author of the *Sāṃkhyakārikā* (some, however, take it as referring to consciousness).

XV. Liberation

(65) The epithet "inactive" (*niṣkriya*) applied to consciousness is explained as meaning "devoid of all actions other than the act of seeing."

(67) It is remarked that the expressions like "intelligence of consciousness" (*puruṣasya caitanyam*) and "inertness of materiality" (*prakṛter jaḍatvam*) are to be taken in a secondary sense, for in reality intelligence and inertness are not the attributes of consciousness and materiality respectively, but are their essential nature.

XVI. Transmission of Sāṃkhya Tradition

(72) A verse has been quoted about the ten principal topics that enumerates them in a way different from the way shown in the *Tattvakaumudī*; the ten topics, accorhing the this enumeration, are: (1) consciousness, (2) primordial materiality, (3) intellect, (4) egoity, (5-7) the three constituents, (8) subtle elements, (9) capacities, and (10) gross elements.

SĀṂKHYAKĀRIKĀBHĀṢYA

(*Summary by Anima Sen Gupta*)

In addition to *Kiraṇāvalī*, Kṛṣṇavallabhācārya also composed an independent commentary on the *Kārikā*. It was published in Varanasi in 1933 by the Jyotish Prakash Press. It closely follows Vācaspati's interpretation of the *Sāṃkhyakārikā* throughout the text.

The following summary, therefore, calls attention only to a few passages that are somewhat different from the standard viewpoint of Vācaspati.

Introductory passages. For those who argue that Sāṃkhya is non-Vedic because it does not explicate the teachings of the Veda, the commentator remarks that "non-Vedic" means only that a school does not accept the authority of the Veda. The Sāṃkhya, which does accept the authority of the Veda, is not, therefore, non-Vedic. Moreover, the absence of a discussion of God is not necessarily a defect. The Sāṃkhya discussion of *puruṣa* clearly indicates its commitment to a concern for a highest spiritual principle. The explicit nontreatment of God in this tradition, therefore, does not at all prove that the author is a nonbeliever. A *nāstika* or "nonbeliever" is one who admits neither the authority of the Veda nor the existence of God.

(1-3) To the critic who argues that frustration applies only to *buddhi*, because *puruṣa* is always pure and free, and that, therefore, it is absurd to speak about the cessation of frustration as the supreme end or purpose of *puruṣa* (*paramapuruṣārtha*), it can be pointed out to such a critic that *puruṣa*, though pure in itself, does become reflected in the *buddhi* or internal organ. *Puruṣa* then appears to be characterized by the various intellectual modifications, and both *buddhi* and *puruṣa* appear to have the same nature of frustration. In other words, there is an apparent transfer of frustration to *puruṣa*, even though, in actual fact, *puruṣa* cannot be frustrated.

Puruṣa is neutral in character. It is neither the cause nor the effect. It is not a cause because it does not become the material cause of an effect of a different order. It is not an effect because it does not possess the characteristic of being produced. *Buddhi*, on the other hand, is mutable because it sometimes knows an object and sometimes not. *Puruṣa*, however, is always the seer or revealer, and as such it is different from the intellect (*buddhi*).

The commentator then provides an elaborate description and refutation of the Buddhist Vijñānavāda discussion of consciousness. Naiyāyika and Jaina views are also refuted.

(4-8) Knowledge is discussed in terms of the five "cognitive conditions" (*vṛtti*) of the *citta* as formulated in Pātañjala-Sāṃkhya, and thereafter follows a long discussion of Sāṃkhya epistemology along the lines of Vācaspati's interpretation.

(9) A standard discussion of *satkāryavāda* is given. If one asks "What is the proof that the effect is always existent?" it is suggested that the existence of the effect in the past as well as in the future can be proved on the basis of the extrasensory perception of Yogins. Events taking place in different temporal periods can be perceived by Yogins through powers (*siddhis*) born of yogic concentration and meditation.

(11-16) A standard discussion of *triguṇa* is given. The primary cause (*pradhāna*) undergoes modifications even when the various "evolutes" remain in an unmanifested condition, because the primary cause is actually constituted by the three constituents. In the state of dissolution, the three constituents give up the method of functioning in a heterogeneous manner (that is to say, in a mixing or blending way) and engage only in homogeneous transformation (with each *guṇa* functioning totally in terms of itself).

(17-20) The supposition of a single consciousness principle is incapable of providing a satisfactory explanation of the various forms of experience among differing creatures.

(30-37) The purposes of the *puruṣa* are directly accomplished by the *buddhi*. The *buddhi*, therefore, is the supreme evolute. Its supremacy is due to the following five factors: (a) it accomplishes the purposes of the *puruṣa* directly; (b) it is the common substratum for the latent impressions and the contents of cognition received through the various sense and action capacities; (c) it exists as the locus of impressions even when the mind and egoity become dissolved as a result of discriminative realization (*viveka-khyāti*); (d) it is also the substratum for the reflection of *puruṣa*; and (e) it is the substratum for the highest mode of awareness (*vṛtti*) that occurs in meditation (*dhyāna*) and concentration (*samādhi*). The *buddhi*, first, provides experience for *puruṣa*; finally, it becomes the vehicle for ultimate release.

(40-42) At the beginning of the process of manifestation (evolution), the fitst item to appear was the subtle body, one for each *puruṣa*. During the state of dissolution, *puruṣa* remains merged along with the subtle body to which it is inseparably related. It is manifested again at the time of creation. This association continues until the time of liberation.

(64-68) One might argue that *prakṛti* will continue its ordinary activities even after the attainment of liberation because of the contact between *puruṣa* and *prakṛti* (that is to say, because *puruṣa* and *prakṛti* are always present to one another). This, however, is not the case, for the sort of contact or presence that brings about ordinary experience is always qualified by the absence of discriminative discernment (*aviveka*). By developing the presence of discrimination, though *prakṛti* and *puruṣa* continue to be present to one another, the condition for the recycling of frustrating experience is no longer the case. In other words, ordinary (frustrating) experience will no longer manifest itself.

Actions are of two kinds: the accumulated action (*karman*) from past lives, the fruition of which has not yet started (*sañcita*); and the accumulated action of the past, which has begun to bear fruit (*prārabdha*). The first is destroyed by discriminative realization (*viveka-khyāti*), whereas the second is exhausted within the context of ordinary experience (*upabhoga*). So long as the second is not completely exhausted, the body remains associated with the *puruṣa*.

According to the commentator, the second form, too, namely, *prārabdha*, can be destroyed through devotion to God. After the destruction of *prārabdha karman*, the liberated soul continues to live in the body according to its own will, with the sole motive of helping others.

RĀJEŚVARA ŚĀSTRIN DRĀVIḌA

Rājeśvara Śāstrin Drāviḍa, son of the well-known Vedāntic scholar, M.M. Lakṣmaṇa Śāstrin Drāviḍa, was a renowned traditional scholar of Nyāya, Vedānta, and ancient Indian political science as well. Associated with many learned institutions, notably the Saṅga Veda Mahāvidyālaya and the All-India Kashiraj Trust of Varanasi, he was a professor in the Sanskrit University at Varanasi for a few years in the later part of his life. As well as the Sāṃkhya commentary summarized below, he also composed a few works on Nyāya and Vedānta.

R.S. Drāviḍa's commentary on the *Tattvakaumudī* of Vācaspati was published in the Haridas Sanskrit Series in 1932. It is not a running commentary, but rather a series of notes. The commentator's purpose seems to be to explain the difficult expressions and to elucidate only the most important doctrines. Most of his views are to be found as well in other commentaries on the *Tattvakaumudī*. Sections are identified by the numbers of the *kārikās* commented on.

NOTES ON TATTVAKAUMUDĪ

(*Summary by Ram Shankar Bhattacharya*)

(2) In the expression "*sāhasrasaṃvatsara*" (one thousand years) used in connection with the time to be taken in performing the *jyotiṣṭoma* and other sacrifices, the word "*saṃvatsara*" is said to mean "a day", as has been established in Pūrvamīmāṃsā. The impure Vedic means are said to be the sacrificial acts that are the sources of frustration.

(3) The gradations of subtlety in earth, water, fire, air, and *ākāśa* consist in each possessing a lesser number of qualities, so that earth possesses all five qualities (smell, taste, color, touch, and sound); water, the last four; fire, the last three; air, the last two; and *ākāśa*, the last, that is, sound alone. Moreover, the earth can be apprehended by five sense capacities, water by four, and so forth, in a corresponding fashion. The writer here refers to a passage in the *Bhāmatī* (II.2.16),

which contains a discussion on the gradation in subtlety of the elements.

(4) The definition of perception as "one whose object has not been apprehended before" (*anadhigata*) is not vitiated by that type of perception called "continuous" for the awareness in each moment is different from the awareness occurring in the moment preceding. Here the writer reviews the Sāṃkhya view on time and has shown elaborately that the awareness in each succesive moment must vary.

Knowledge (*pramā*) may be taken as an operation of the intellect qualified by a reflection of consciousness (*caitanyapratibimbaviśiṣṭabuddhivṛtti*) or as consciousness reflected in the intellect. The sense capacities, being the instruments of the instruments of knowledge, are sometimes called instruments of knowledge in a secondary sense.

Knowledge and the instruments of knowledge are of two kinds. When the capacities are taken as instruments, the operations of the intellect are called knowledge; when the operations of the intellect are considered to be the instruments, then it is the resulting cognition (*pauruṣeya bodha*) that is called knowledge.

The writer is in favor of the view that consciousness is reflected in the intellect. This is the reason that satisfaction, frustration, etc., existing in the intellect are superimposed on consciousness, and that the unchanging awareness (*caitanya*) found in consciousness is thought to exist in the intellect. Sentences such as "*tasmiṃś ciddarpaṇe*," which identify consciousness as the mirror in which the intellect is reflected, are to be interpreted as showing that the reflection of consciousness (*citpratibimba*), and not consciousness itself, is the mirror.

Memory cannot be veridical, for at the time of the rise of memory the thing remembered no longer exists in the same state in which it was cognized.

(5) Inference by exclusion (*pariśeṣa, śeṣavat*) as discussed, e.g., by Vātsyāyana in the *Nyāyabhāṣya*, is not the same as the only-negative form of inference. Vācaspati here follows his own view on inference by exclusion, which he also propounds in his *Nyāyavārttikatātparyaṭīkā*.

The author offers elaborate discussion concerning the inclusion of verbal testimony in inference, comparison in inference, and nonapprehension in perception.

(9) Explanations are provided of the following: (1) the views of the Śūnyavādins and the Vedāntins on causal relations; (2) the difference proving the existence of primordial materiality; (3) the reasons advanced by Vedāntins for not regarding primordial materiality as the material cause of the world; (4) the argument, given in the *Tattvakaumudī*, from the absence of difference between the weight of an effect and of its material cause (*gurutvāntarakāryagrahaṇa*).

(10) Elucidation of the argument, adduced by the Yogācāra

school, intended to prove that objects are nothing but forms of awareness.

(12) The constituents are not related as container and contained (*ādhārādheyabhāva*), because they are all-pervading. There is a fundamental difference between each constituent and the others, even though they are eternally united.

(16) Although an effect and its material cause are identical, yet there arises the notion that this is an effect and that is its cause (*bheda-buddhi*) having an apparent, not a real, difference as its content. That is why nothing can be regarded as a newly produced thing.

(23) Because *rajas* acts as the helping factor in the rise of the two aspects of the intellect as characterized by the predominance of *sattva* or *tamas*, it is not necessary to speak of aspects dominated by *rajas*. Both *sāttvika* and *tāmasa* aspects can be regarded as *rājasa* aspects.

(30) The *Sāṃkhyakārikā* refutes the Vaiśeṣika view that there cannot be simultaneously arising awarenesses.

(47) The afflictions are called misconceptions in a figurative sense.

(51) Vijñānabhikṣu's explanation (*regarding Sāṃkhyasūtra* 3.44) of the word "*aṅkuśa*" (goad) as "*ākarṣaka*" (one that attracts or draws, i.e., that helps something rise or appear) is wrong. He is trying to make out that the first three attainments (*ūha*, *śabda*, and *adhyayana*) are the chief ones, because they are the most powerful means for eradicating the threefold frustration.

RĀMEŚACANDRA TARKATĪRTHA

Rāmeśacandra Tarkatīrtha was born in 1881 in the village of Suhilapura, adjacent to Tripura in the eastern part of Bengal. His father was Candrakumāra and mother Guṇamayī, and he named the subcommentary in memory of his mother. In his student life he specialized in different branches of Indian philosophy and obtained highest degrees in Sāṃkhya, Vedānta, and Mīmāṃsā. We learn from the subcommentary that Rāmeśacandra's teacher's name was Raghunātha Tarkavāgīśa. S. N. Dasgupta was one of his students. The title Mahāmahopādhyāya was conferred on him in 1944. He died in 1960.

The subcommentary was published in 1935 while Rāmeśacandra was Professor of Sāṃkhya at the Sanskrit College, Rajsahi and was meant as a lucid textbook for beginners in Sāṃkhya philosophy. The author's purpose was to clarify Vācaspati Miśra's *Tattvakaumudī*, and, as was usual in those days in Bengal, clarification meant, first, stating over again the points of the original commentary in terms of the Sāṃkhya that was prevalent at the time and, second, reformulating Vācaspati Miśra's sentences, wherever possible, in precise neo-Nyāya language. The *fundamental* obscurities of Sāṃkhya remained, therefore, as they were in the *Tattvakaumudī*.

In the present summary, we note only the special features of *Guṇamayī* and whatever points of special worth Rāmeśacandra added.

GUṆAMAYĪ ON TATTVAKAUMUDĪ

(*Summary by Kalidas Bhattacharya*)

Two striking features of the *Guṇamayī* are the author's long excellent preface, very unusual with oriental scholars and the inclusion, by way of beginning the subcommentary, of an entire monograph—named *Sāṃkhyatattvavilāsīya* and written by Rāmeśacandra's teacher Raghunātha Tarkavāgīsa. This monograph, in its turn, is a commentary on twenty-five (supposed) Sāṃkhya aphorisms (having nothing to do with the aphorisms collected under the title *Sāṃkhyapravacanasūtram*). In the present article we shall omit the monograph altogether.

There are at least ten points in the preface worth noting. They are:

(i) What man seeks *primarily* is the cessation of frustration, not so much the attainment of satisfaction. Whether the latter follows by implication or not is irrelevant to Sāṃkhya pursuit.[1]

(ii) A modern Indological attempt is made at identifying Kapila, Āsuri, Pañcaśikha, Vārṣagaṇya, Paramārtha, Vindhyavāsin, and a few others. Rāmeśacandra has supported his arguments by means of texts collected from ancient Sanskrit literature and has not hesitated to rely also on tradition.

(iii) A study is made of the influence of Sāṃkhya on different Indian literatures of the past—different systems of Indian philosophy (including Tantra), Indian medicine, mythology (*purāṇa*), and history (*itihāsa*).

(iv) A short biography of Vācaspati Miśra is given and what is more important, a full list of available Sāṃkhya works in print or otherwise, written in Sanskrit.

(v) A short, yet full, account of the philosophy of Sāṃkhya as propounded by Vācaspati Miśra in his *Tattvakaumudī* on the *Sāṃkhyakārikā*.

(vi), (vii), and (viii) New interpretations are given of three famous similes used by Īśvarakṛṣṇa (a) the cooperation of the lame man and the blind man, (b) materiality as a dancing girl and (c) spontaneous flow of milk to the mother cow's udder for the benefit of the calf.

(ix) There is a short discussion of "theistic" (*seśvara*) and "atheistic" (*nirīśvara*) Sāṃkhya and also a discussion, in this connection, on the role of God in Yoga.

(x) A list is given of the different views regarding the exact number of the couplets in the *Sāṃkhyakārikā*. In the *Tattvakaumudī* and in the commentary of Nārāyaṇatīrtha, it is 72; in Gauḍapāda's commentary, 71; in Māṭhara, 70; and Īśvarakṛṣṇa himself, 70. In different Chinese editions of the *Sāṃkhyakārikā*, we again find other numbers. Some scholars have added even a seventy-third, which runs as:

> *kāraṇam īśvarameke bruvate kālaṃ pare svabhāvaṃ vā*
> *prajāḥ kathaṃ nirguṇataḥ vyaktaḥ kālaḥ svabhāvaś ca.*

But, evidently, this is a gross interpolation, for in *sāṃkhyakārikā* 56 it has been clearly stated that all this (world) is created by materiality (*ityeṣaḥ prakṛtikṛtaḥ*).

And let it be borne in mind that, whatever the number of the couplets, the main Sāṃkhya doctrine has been stated in *seventy* couplets only.

II. Instruments of Knowledge

(4) Knowledge as effected by its instruments is but the enlightenment (*prakāśa*) of the operation of awareness by (pure) consciousness

and is (necessarily) of the form "*I am knowing* (perceiving) this pot," "*I am inferring* fire on the hill," etc.

Vācaspati Miśra writes, "This excludes the *pramāṇas* that lead to doubt, error, and remembering (*Eteṣu saṃśayaviparyayasmṛtisādhāraṇeṣu pramāṇeṣu na prasaṅgaḥ.*" Rāmeśacandra adds: Instead of "*pramāṇa*" Vācaspati Miśra ought to have called these three "*apramāṇa*" (non-*pramāṇa*).

Vācaspati Miśra calls the supernormal cognitions of Yogins "*vijñāna.*" Rāmeśacandra adds: "*Vijñāna*" is a technical name given to such operations (*vṛtti*).[3]

(5) While clarifying the definition of perception as an instrument of knowledge Vācaspati uses the word "*viṣayin,*" meaning awareness. Rāmeśacandra clarifies this further by saying: "Awareness" here means the operation (*vṛtti*) (of awareness).

The term "direct contact" (*sannikarṣa*) used by Vācaspati as indicating the relation between sense capacity and object means the operation of the sense capacity according to the form (*ākāra* = distinctive feature) of the object. This necessity for sense capacity to operate that way automatically excludes the possibility of perceiving subtle elements. Subtle elements have no definite forms (*ākāra*, here *viśeṣa* = specific feature).[4]

Vācaspati Miśra writes that even in the case of perception reflective discerning is a function of intellect. Rāmeśacandra corrects him, saying: Reflective discerning here is really a function of mind. (See Vācaspati Miśra's own commentary on *kārikā* 30). Or, if "intellect" (here) is understood as composed of three parts (some modern Sāṃkhyists understand it that way), that is, of intellect (*buddhi* proper), egoity, and mind, then reflective discerning is a function of intellect just insofar as it is mind. Vācaspati Miśra has used the term "operation of the intellect" indiscriminately elsewhere, too, in his *Tattvakaumudī*. In every such case the function has to be properly understood.

Older Sāṃkhyists (like Vācaspati Miśra) do not, while accounting for knowledge (perception, in particular), follow the way of the later Naiyāyika by recognizing additional necessary factors (called *vyāpāra*)[5] between the instrument (i.e., the stated = direct cause) and its effect, on the ground that this would unnecessarily complicate the issue.

Knowledge that results from an operation of awareness is called by Vācaspati a "favor" (*anugraha*) of consciousness. This "favor" can be understood in various ways. (1) It may be understood as just the relation of the operation to (pure) consciousness. (2) (Pure) consciousness, being only reflected on (i.e., not bodily present in) the awareness, may be understood as incorporating that awareness. This is evident in the awareness of the form "*I know* it (the object)." According to this meaning, the same operation of awareness stands as either so incorporated (another name of which is "enlightened") or not so incorporated (enlightened). According to this view, the operation insofar as it is unenlightened is the instrument of knowledge and the same state *as enlightened* is that knowledge itself. (3) A third view is that, because of the reflection of consciousness on intellect, egoity appropriates the operation reflexively. (4) A fourth view is that the operation also is reflected, in its turn, on consciousness. Vijñānabhikṣu holds this fourth view. Rameśacandra confesses that he is unable to decide which view is correct.

The pervasion "All cases of A are cases of B" is said to be the natural (*svābhāvika*) relation of A to B. "Natural" here means "not depending on any other extrinsic factor (called *upādhi*)."

In other systems of philosophy pervasion has been defined in other different ways. But the Sāṃkhya definition stated above is by far the best, because it is simple and covers all those other definitions. Rāmeśacandra then discusses the notion of "*upādhi*" in the Nyāya fashion.

Vācaspati Miśra's "*samāropitopādhi*" is nothing but assured *upādhi* as distinct from suspected *upādhi*.

Natural relation of A to B is not merely the universal concomitance of A and B but also that of not-B and not-A. Both these types of concomitance have to be kept in view except when the former is constitutionally unavailable. In such cases exclusionary inference as stated above is the only recourse; and by a secondary process we arrive at whatever is left over when the already asserted cases of those that are characterized as A because of the *hetu* in question are excluded one by one. The remaining one stands as the object of the secondary knowledge.

Vācaspati Miśra clarifies the notion of *svalakṣaṇasāmānya* as follows: The object that is inferred when one concludes "There is fire on the hill" (because smoke is found there) is only an instantiation of the universal firehood, i.e., a particular fire (*svalakṣaṇa*) like the one found in the kitchen from the perception of which one could arrive at the corresponding universal concomitance. Rāmeśacandra adds: This is only the older Nyāya way of understanding the term "*svalakṣaṇa-sāmānya*." There is, however, another way. The term may be understood as "*svalakṣaṇa*-and-*sāmānya*," meaning "definite particular fire and universal firehood," not *sāmānya* of *svalakṣaṇa* (better, *svalakṣaṇa* understood just in the light of the corresponding *sāmānya*). The idea is that, in order that there be inference, both these have to be perceived; and further also, even though that which is inferred may be a definite particular fire, in the same awareness there is equally the awareness of firehood; quite as much as in perceiving a definite particular fire, one also perceives firehood.

Regarding the inference by general correlation like "(Perceptual) knowledge of color, etc., must be effected by some instrumental agency (viz., sense capacity) quite as much as the separation of a branch from a tree is effected by an axe," Rāmeśacandra says the following: Normally, this inference is possible only if different other supposed agencies are eliminated one by one according to their impossibility of acceptance. This is how the Naiyāyikas understand the *sāmānyatodṛṣṭa* inference in question. Yet, however, the simple way in which Vācaspati Miśra has put forward this inference is not wrong, for he has taken for granted (started with the assumption) that (perceptual) knowledge is an *act* (like the act of separating the branch).[6]

In connection with *testimony*, and in elaboration of what Vācaspati Miśra has said, Rāmeśacandra offers a short full account, right on Nyāya lines, of the entire process involved in the knowledge derived from testimony.

The part "*āpta*" in the expression "*āptaśruti*" is to be paraphrased as obtained through preceptor-disciple tradition, meaning that the words and sentences concerned have not been spoken (and, therefore, caused) by some person.

Vācaspati Miśra holds that knowledge derived on the testimony of scripture has to be self-validating. Rāmeśacandra adds that, by implication, other cases of knowledge are not self-validating.

That knowledge is self-valid, the validity of which is derived from the very factors that produce the knowledge. This applies only to the case of knowledge obtained on the testimony of scriptural sentences (i.e., through hearing them), and not to other cases of knowledge such as perception, inference, etc. In these other cases of knowledge validity is known (inferred) from their pragmatic success or when we somehow come to know that they contain no defect.

Scripture (Vedas) (according to Sāṃkhya) is noneternal, because, according to Sāṃkhya the only eternal things are consciousness and primordial materiality. How possibly could, then, the noneternal scripture be uncreated (unspoken) by some person? Rāmeśacandra believes that Sāṃkhya can avoid this difficulty by holding that the scripture emerges *of itself* from materiality.

Vācaspati Miśra has shown why knowledge derived from testimony cannot be a case of inference. Rāmeśacandra adds another ground. He shows how in another way an opponent might try to reduce such knowledge (*śābdajñāna*) to inference and then refutes that. If the designata of different words have after all to be related with one another into a complete fact—for that is what is meant by a whole sentence—this has to be inferred from the remembered relations between the different words. This exactly (Rāmeśacandra contends) has been refuted by Vācaspati Miśra when he writes that a sentence to mean a complete fact need not always presuppose knowledge of the relations between constituent words.

Rāmeśacandra then refers to the Nyāya-Vaiśeṣika thinker Viśvanātha Nyāyapañcānana, who holds that the memory of the relations between constituent words is *immediately* followed by the knowledge of the complete fact without intermediation by any awareness of pervasion coupled with that which has to possess the inferred character (*pakṣadharmatā*). (As such, it is no case of inference.)

Against this contention of Viśvanātha, however, an opponent might hold that it is only an undeveloped logical mind that misses the gap between remembering the relations of the words (on the one hand) and the knowledge of the complete fact (said to be meant on the other), and that it would be more logical (economical) to admit such a gap and lessen the number of instruments of knowledge "by reducing knowledge from testimony" to inference. It is this objection (against Viśvanātha) that (Rāmeśacandra holds) is refuted by Vācaspati Miśra when he refers to the case of poetic sentences.

In the passage in which Vācaspati Miśra shows that comparison is not a separate instrument of knowing, the first part deals with the refutation of the Nyāya view of comparison and the second part, with that of the Mīmāṃsā view.

The Naiyāyikas reduce presumption to inference of the only-negative (*vyatirekin*) type, but Vācaspati Miśra reduces it to inference of the only-positive (*anvayin*) type.

In the last few lines of Vācaspti Miśra's reduction of presumption to inference, presumption is understood as the reconciliation of two apparently contradictory cognitions arrived at through different instruments of knowledge (i.e., in two different ways). This is different from presumption as the postulation of a valid hypothesis to explain a difficulty (not necessarily a contradiction) arising out of a knowledge situation—that hypothesis, that is, without which the difficulty could not be overcome.

In connection with Vācaspati Miśra's reduction of nonapprehension to inference, Rāmeśacandra offers a succinct account of this instrument of knowledge as developed in Mīmāṃsā against the Naiyāyikas who hold that what is said to be known through this instrument, that is, absence of a content, is primarily perceived.

Vācaspati Miśra has reduced five kinds of so-called "instruments of knowledge" to the Sāṃkhyist's three. Rāmeśacandra adds: The Sāṃkhyist would reduce that way all other imaginable (so-called) "instruments of knowledge"—mystical or otherwise.

(6) Rāmeśacandra shows in brief how exactly the fundamental principles, from subtle elements up to primordial materiality and consciousness, are inferred. Each subtler principle in inferred as the material cause of each grosser principle. And conscionsness is inferred on a ground of teleology. All these inferences (Rāmeśacandra says) will be taken up in detail later.[7]

Vacaspati holds that the order of the sequence of the emergence of the fundamental principles, and entities like heaven and hell, are to be known from the scriptures only. Rāmeśacandra quotes some such scriptural passages.

III. Pre-existent Effect

(9) Vācaspati Miśra refers to three types of non-Sāṃkhya theories of the relation between material cause and effect. Rāmeśacandra gives a somewhat more elaborate account.

The Vaināśika Buddhists hold that every effect is immediately preceded by the destruction of its so-called constitutive cause. Hence it really comes from *absence*. Hence, too, the world must have come from a great void. Rāmeśacandra quotes scriptural passages in support.

The (Advaita) Vedānta view is that the world with everything in it arises from (the absolute) Being and that in relation to that Being the world is false, i.e., not ultimately real (in effect, neither being nor nonbeing). Rāmeśacandra quotes scriptural passages in support.

Nyāya-Vaiśeṣika thinkers hold that from *what is* arises *what is not*—from the constitutive cause arises what was not in that cause. Dyads, which were not there (before production), arise from (eternally existing) atoms, and similarly, minimal perceptibilia from dyads, and so on.

Sāṃkhya, which is older than all these philosophies, holds an altogether different view.

Rāmeśacandra taking a cue from Vācaspati Miśra's use of the words "thesis" (*pratijñā*) and "reason" (*hetu*) understands his (Vācaspati's) first argument for preexistent effect (the theory that what is comes from *what is*) as arranged (almost) neatly in the Nyāya order of five membered inference. Rāmeśacandra first explains this five-membered order and then points it out in Vācaspati's argument. Similarly, in the other four inferences.

IV. Manifest and Unmanifest Materiality

(11)The Vaiśeṣikas hold that satisfaction, frustration, and confusion are features of the self (and not of outer objects). Rāmeśacandra adds: They are felt equally as in the relation of (predicative) identity with things of the world (outer objects), as when we say such and such things (sandalpaste, girls, etc.) are satisfactions (and similarly, with regard to frustration = pain and bewildement = confusion). It would be more parsimonious to understand predicative identity as constitutive identity than to interpret it otherwise and satisfaction (happiness), frustration (unhappiness), and confusion (bewilderment) can be so understood.

In the course of elaborating Vācaspati's refutation of Yogācāra idealism, Rāmeśacandra offers a short account of its central features.

When Vācaspati Miśra says that primordial materiality, intellect, etc., are nonconscious (*acetana*), Rāmeśacandra adds: They are nonconscious just in the sense that they are other than consciousness, not in the (Advaita) Vedāntic sense that they are not self-enlightened (revealed) by something else (here, by pure consciousness). The reason he offers is that even consciousness itself is also first revealed by some thing other than itself, that is, by some operation of awareness that is a state of intellect containing reflection of pure consciousness.

V. The Three Constituents

(12) In Sāṃkhya, when intelligibility (*sattva*), activity (*rajas*), and inertia (*tamas*) are called "*guṇa*," the term "*guṇa*" means what is conducive to others' interests. Rāmeśacandra says this is just what distinguishes Sāṃkhya "*guṇa*" from the Vaiśeṣika's "*guṇa*."

The passage that Vācaspati Miśra quotes toward the beginning of his commentary on the verse is a saying of Pañcaśikha. According to Rāmeśacandra "*moha*" = (confusion) stands for erroneous cognition.

Each constituent, when it emerges into prominence, suppresses the other two. Here (according to Rāmeśacandra) "emergence into prominence" means that it begins to produce effect, and "suppression" means that the constituent that is said to be suppressed has not, first, begun to produce effect and, second, as in that state, it (somehow) helps the constituent that has emerged into prominence.

(13) According to Sāṃkhya, if constituents emerge into activity and join with one another, it is only in the interest of consciousness. Commentators have generally understood this interest to be either the mundane experience of consciousness as *jiva* or the attainment of its absolute liberation. Rāmeśacandra adds a third alternative: Pure consciousness's interest is, alternatively, its experience as it is effected by traces and dispositions acquired from the preceding cycle of life (*adṛṣṭa*).

Rāmeśacandra puts Vācaspati Miśra's statements in Nyāya forms of arguments. Modern commentators consider it almost as a sacred duty to do so.

VI. Inferences to Primordial Materiality and Consciousness

(15) If Vācaspati Miśra has, through the arguments stated in this verse, established unmanifest materiality as the ultimate source of the world, this, by implication, refutes the (Advaita Vedānta) thesis that the ultimate source is pure consciousness.

(16) As it is of the very nature of the three constituents to be dynamic (always in some form of transformation), evidently for this intrinsic dynamism no consciousness need be postulated. However, for all their heterogeneous dynamism (= manifest activity), that is, for these constituents to change into entities like intellect, egoity, etc., consciousness has to be postulated, because all these changes are teleologically in the interest of consciousness, that is, either for mundane experience or for attainment of complete freedom.

(17) Vācaspati Miśra's first argument for proving that there is consciousness is not of an ordinary type. How much could be proved by any ordinary type of inference is that, (as) materiality at any of its stages (is complex, it) must be meant for some other entity. But that is not what precisely is sought to be proved here. What is sought to be proved is (the existence of) pure consciousness. And yet with this desired *sādhya* one cannot associate the *hetu* complexity in structure. Nor is it easy to decide whether even the unmanifest materiality is of any complex structure. It is because of these difficulties that Vācaspati Miśra (in the opinion of Rāmeśacandra) rewrites the argument as he does.

"Meant for some other entity" is to be understood as "to be experienced (with affective fringe) by some other entity," and, obviously, no nonconscious entity can in that way experience anything. Once nonconscious entities are thus excluded what remains over is consciousness.

As for unmanifest materiality, (Rāmeśacandra holds that) it, too, is of complex structure. It is complex in the sense that it is made of three constituents. Some Sāṃkhyists, again, have understood by "complexity" a situation in which several entities act in cooperation. This definition applies to unmanifest materiality also.

One of the arguments for establishing consciousness is "because there has to be some control" (*adhiṣṭhānāt*). The idea is: whatever is constituted by the three constituents must depend on some control (*adhiṣṭhāna*), that is, must be informed by a certain other principle, in order that it may operate. Rāmeśacandra says that consciousness is the controller or the informing principle here, though only as reflected on it.

Similarly with the notion of experiencership (*bhoktṛtva*) in the argument "*bhoktṛbhāvāt*" ("because there is experience"). Satisfaction, frustration, etc., as psychic states are operations of the intellect. What, however, this really means is that they are certain psychic attitudes (at the level of intellect) toward objects that are known (experienced). Without implying such awareness of objects, there are satisfactions, frustrations, etc. This awareness, on the other hand, belongs to consciousness through its reflection on intellect. Hence, the expressions "object to be *experienced* with" (i) "a favoring attitude," (ii) "a disfavoring attitude," etc., to it (*anukūlavedanīya*, *pratikūlavedanīya*, etc.).

Vācaspati Miśra holds that the activities of all scriptures and all sages are for the attainment of complete cessation of frustration. Rāmeśacandra explains this as follows: Activities of scriptures consists in establishment of truth, and when sages exercise themselves it means their actual effort for attaining (realizing) the truth. Truth here is the complete cessation of frustration, that is, liberation.

(18) Vācaspati Miśra defines birth as a novel relation of self (pure consciousness) with body, sense capacities, mind, ego, intellect, and the "traces and dispositions" (*saṃskāra*) derived from the prior cycle of life. Obviously, by "body" here is meant the gross (physical) body, and by the rest, the subtle body. Mention of "traces and dispositions" is designed to exclude the Yogin's direct assumption of self-created (gross) body.

(19) The distinction between consciousness as witness (*sākṣin*) and consciousness as knower (*draṣṭṛ*) is this: As witness, (pure) consciousness knows (incorporates through enlightenment) the intellect and its operations directly, whereas as knower, it knows (incorporates through enlightenment—also through the intermediation of intellect) the objects of (i.e., the objects that are referred to by) these models—that is pots, linens, etc.

(20) Vācaspati Miśra, after saying that the false identification of consciousness with intellect is due to their contact, immediately replaces the word "contact" by "contiguity" (*sannidhāna*), the latter implying that consciousness is reflected on intellect. Rāmeśacandra adds: This replacement is justified by the fact that, whereas all cases of contact are not false, all cases of (the type of) contiguity (mentioned above) are false—for example, the case of a red rose (contiguous to a crystal column) being reflected on (the) crystal column and making it appear red.

(21) Vācaspati Miśra does not explain the analogy of a lame man and a blind man cooperating with each other. Rāmeśacandra explains it, saying: Each takes the help of the other to reach their common goal and then separate, each in the state of separation doing his own job. Just in the same way, materiality and consciousness cooperate for their common mundane life at all stages (up to the stage of knowing the separateness of each) and then separate, each, after the separation, pursuing its own course (consciousness remaining absolutely in itself and materiality continuing in its intrinsic status as the three constituents in equiposise).

IX. Functioning of the Thirteenfold Instrument

(23) Vācaspati Miśra writes that in this verse Iśvarakṛṣṇa dis-

tinguishes intellect from whatever looks similar and whatever looks dissimilar to it. Rāmeśacandra adds: The principles that are similar to intellect are egoity and mind; and those that are dissimilar are the sense capacities.

Rāmeśacandra introduces a whole reflection of his own (much on the line of Nyāya) as to why intellect has to be admitted over and above sense capacities and ego. It is as follows: Mere sense contact (with objects) is not sufficient for awareness, for many things in contact with the senses are cognitively igonored. Hence, mind as the principle of attention (according to Nyāya, of infinitesimal size) has to be admitted; and, further too, it has to be admitted that the senses come into contact with it. But even then all things do not get explained. What, for example, is the principle that determines the behavior of a man in dreamless sleep, a man whose senses and mind (as understood by the Naiyāyika) have stopped functioning? A third principle has, therefore, to be admitted, and that is intellect. Such behavior is not of the (gross) body only, for it is not found in corpses; neither is it of the mind, for the mind (in Nyāya, "internal organ", not very different from the ego of Sāṃkhya), left to itself, has the function of intentionality (*saṃkalpa*), whose function is absent here. It will not do to object here that, after all, senses and mind are kept here in forced suppression and are, therefore, unable to discharge their functions, for that would be a more complicated account than the simpler one admitting a third principle, intellect, operating alone at this stage. But why then (it may be asked) is it that this sleeping man is not aware of the function of intellect? The reply is twofold: first, mind that was to aid such awareness is not functioning and, second, pure consciousness, left to itself, cannot account for the behaviors of such a sleeping man.

(24) In contrast with the deep-sleeping man, Rāmeśacandra considers the case of a dreaming man to show that in this latter case the only operating principle other than senses and mind is egoity. The I-sense in dream, fully explicit in examples such as "I am a tiger" and less explicit in other cases, cannot be due to the function of mind.

X. Subtle and Gross Elements

(39) *Loman* (literally, hairs) here means skin. *Māṃsa* (literally, flesh) means flesh (muscles, etc.) with fat. Similarly, *majjan* (humors) include semen.

XI. The Subtle Body

(40) Vācaspati Miśra writes that the subtle body continues up to the time of the major dissolution of the world. Rāmeśacandra adds: To say that the subtle body continues until the major dissolution of

the world would only be intelligible if one looks at the whole thing from a collective point of view, that is if all such bodies are considered together. Otherwise, a single subtle body continues much further, until the attainment of liberation.

XII. The Basic Predispositions

(44) Īśvarakṛṣṇa in this verse says that knowledge as a predisposition leads to the realization of liberation. Rāmeśacandra holds that by liberation he (Īśvarakṛṣṇa) must have meant both liberation-while-living (*jīvanmukti*) and liberation after the present cycle of life is over, that is, after death (*videhamukti*).

(45) Īśvarakṛṣṇa writes that practice of nonattachment leads to final absorption in materiality. This he calls "*prakṛtilaya.*" Vācaspati Miśra puts the case more precisely by adding a "mere" before the word "detachment." Rāmeśacandra clarifies the idea further by adding: Practice of nonattachment *along with knowledge of the separateness (in metaphysical status)* of the materiality and consciousness leads to the attainment of liberation.

(47) In connection with Vācaspati Miśra's reference to the afflictions, Rāmeśacandra quotes their definitions as found in the Yoga system of philosophy.

Vācaspati Miśra says that these five are called five kinds of misconception, because the last four, egoism, passion, hatred, and love of life, are all traceable to ignorance, which is misconception par excellence. However, immediately after saying this, he offers another explanation. Rāmeśacandra holds that this second explanation could only be suggested because the first one was not considered happy by Vācaspati Miśra.

(51) Because frustration are of three kinds, that is (1) those for which the person himself is (mainly) responsible (called "internal"), (2) those that are caused by other persons (and living beings) (called "external"), and (3) natural evil (called "celestial")—because that way there are three kinds of frustration, therefore, cessation of frustration must also be of three (corresponding) kinds.

"Attainment" means success in catering to one's needs. Cessation of frustration is everybody's most primary need, not subservient to any other need. Hence, success in catering to this need is the central success (and, as just shown, of three kinds).

XIII. The Empirical World

(53) The word "*mṛga*" stands for all kinds of quadrupeds, whereas the word "*paśu*" stands for particular kinds of quadrupeds, such as

rats, having tails and hairs of a different kind. The word "*pakṣin*" stands not only for birds but also for winged insects.

VIVEKAPRADĪPA

Rāmeśacandra Tarkatīrtha is also credited with a running commentary on the *Sāṃkhyasāra* of Vijñānabhikṣu. Its title is *Vivekapradīpa* and it was published in 1922 by Rajkumar Roy at the Pasupati Press. (Calcutta). It simply paraphrases the *Sāṃkhyasāra* and, hence, need not be summarized.

KĀLĪPADA TARKĀCĀRYA

Kālīpada Tarkācārya was one of the most erudite traditional Sanskrit scholars in modern times. He specialized primarily in Nyāya, especially Navyanyāya. He composed several works (texts, commentaries, and learned papers) on different systems of Indian philosophy. He was also known for his work in poetry. He served as Professor of Nyāya for many years in the Government Sanskrit College, Calcutta, and the honorary title "Mahāmahopādhyāya" was conferred on him by the Government of India. He died about ten years ago.

The *Sāraprabhā*, a commentary composed by Kālīpada Tarkācārya on Vijñānabhikṣu's *Sāṃkhysāra*, was published by Chhatra Pustakalaya, Calcutta, in 1930.

It is to be noted that in the first part of the work (in prose) the numbers of the sections are given by the commentator and not by the original author. The second part (in verse) follows the numbering of the original author, namely Vijñānabhikṣu.

SĀRAPRABHĀ

(*Summary by Ram Shankar Bhattacharya*)

PŪRVABHĀGA (Part I), Chapter 1

Introductory comments: Because Kapila's Sāṃkhya does not accept an entity like the eternal God (*nityeśvara*), God in this system must be taken to mean the aggregate of the *mahat-tattvas*. Such a God has not been repudiated in *Sāṃkhyasūtra* I.92. This *mahat-tattva* has three aspects, namely, Brahmā, Viṣṇu, and Śiva. Because its appearance is not dependent on any other factor it is called self-existent (*svayambhū*). Whereas Sāṃkhya chiefly deals with creation, *seśvara*-Sāṃkhya (that is to say, Yoga philosophy or theistic Sāṃkhya) chiefly deals with those means that are conducive to the attainment of emancipation.

(Section 5) That form of action which is usually called "*sañcita*" (accumulated) is called here "*pūrvotpanna*," and that form of action which is usually called "*prārabdha*" (past actions already bearing fruit) is called here "*ārabdha*."

(14) Actions called *prārabdha* are worked out within the course of ordinary experience (*bhoga*).

Part I, Chapter 2

(4) The verse has been explained in two ways: (a) knowledge of difference between all the modifications of *avyakta* (that is to say, the twenty-three nonsentient principles) and the sentient self (*cetana ātman*) is called discriminative knowledge (*jñāna*); and (b) knowledge of difference between all the twenty-four principles along with the gross modifications of the *bhūtas* and the sentient self is called *jñāna*.

(8) The knowledge that the self is different from what is not the self is the means of emancipation, because this realization uproots ignorance.

(10) Direct perception of the absolute self is explained in two ways: (a) perception of *ātman* associated with pleasure, etc.; and (b) perception of *ātman* devoid of all kinds of qualifications.

Part I, Chapter 3

(2) Because qualities (*guṇa*), actions (*karman*), etc., are never apprehended without the *guṇin* or substratum, they are to be taken as identical with the substratum.

(3) *Sattva*, *rajas*, and *tamas* are not to be regarded as attributes (*dharma*) of *prakṛti*; rather, they are identical with *prakṛti*. *Sattva*, etc., are neither the effects of *prakṛti* nor are they to be regarded as existing in *prakṛti* as air exists in the sky.

(5) *Guṇas* are to be regarded as "instrument" or "implement" (*upakaraṇa*) of pure consciousness (*puruṣa*).

UTTARABHĀGA, (Part II)

Part II, Chapter 3

(6) When *buddhi* becomes bereft of all latent impressions (*saṃskāras*), there arises no reflection of *buddhi* in the self; consequently *ātman* abides in itself.

(7) A beginningless positive entity cannot be destroyed, although a beginningless negative entity (for example, prior absence) can be destroyed.

(25-26) *Bhoga* or experience is not the experience of pleasure and pain; in fact, *bhoga* is of the nature of reflection (*pratibimba*) of pleasure and pain (both of which are modifications of *buddhi*) on the transparent self.

(27) The world is compared to a cloud to indicate that it has momentary destruction. The simile of a cloud's existing in the sky suggests that although the world is originated in the self, the self neither becomes attached to the world nor becomes modified.

(36) The word "*mātra*" in "*sva-sva-dhī-mātra-dṛk*" suggests that the *ātman* perceives its own *buddhi* and not the *buddhis* associated with other *ātmans*.

Part II, Chapter 6

(2) According to the Vedāntins, the essential character of the self is pleasure (*sukhātmaka*), which is not the absence of pain but a positive entity.

(31) Omnipotence and other powers (*siddhis*) are to be understood as existing in the self so long as it is associated with *prakṛti*.

(36) The expression "*pumān ekaḥ*" (*puruṣa* is one) is to be taken in the sense of "*ekarūpa*" (of one form, that is to say, without change, immutable).

(37) Sāṃkhya appears to argue that the world, which is of the nature of reflection (*pratibimba-rūpa*), is different from the external world and that, whereas the former is unreal, the latter is real.

(59) Yogins can realize that the objects and their cognition are different from each other (though they seem to be inseparable) and that this is the reason that Yogins can apprehend cognition separately, dissociating it from the objects.

(62-63) *Buddhi* being transformed into the forms of objects is reflected on the transparent self because of proximity and the self possessing this reflection transmigrates.

HARIHARĀNANDA ĀRANYA

Swāmi Hariharānanda Āraṇya, a Bengali *saṃnyāsin*, lived from 1869 to 1947. He is the founder of Kapila Maṭha, located in Bihar, a monastic community claiming to maintain the tradition of Sāṃkhya and Yoga in modern India. Hariharānanda was a disciple of Swami Triloki Āraṇya, but nothing is known of this teacher or his tradition.

Hariharānanda wrote a number of works on *Sāṃkhyayoga* in Bengali and Sanskrit. His best-known work in Bengali is the *Kapilāśramīya-pātañjalayogadarśana*, which has been partly rendered into English by P.N. Mukerji under the title, *The Yoga Philosophy of Patañjali* (Calcutta: University of Calcutta, 1963) with a foreword by Dharmamegha Āraṇya, the current head of Kapila Maṭha. His Sanskrit commentary *Bhāsvatī* on *Vyāsa-bhāṣya* has also been published.

Hariharānanda also composed a work, entitled *Sāṃkhyatattvāloka* and edited by J. Ghosh, with a foreword by Gopi Nath Kaviraj (Princess of Wales Saraswati Bhavana Texts, No. 59, Varanasi), Hitchintak Press, 1936). It is a composite Sāmkhya-Yoga work in seventy-two paragraphs and gives a good overview of Hariharānanda's thought. "E" references below are to this edition.

SĀṂKHYATATTVĀLOKA

(*Summary by Ram Shankar Bhattacharya*)

(E1) In six benedictory verses there is a salutation to Kapila (1-2), praise of Sāṃkhya (3) and a statement regarding the precise character of the work (4-6).

I. Sec. 1-8: Consciousness (E1-5)

(1) Awareness (*prakāśa*) is twofold, absolute or unconditioned awareness (*svaprakāśa*) and awareness caused by some illuminator (*vaiṣayika prakāśa*). The awareness by itself is the indicatory mark of absolute awareness (i.e., pure consciousness). Its object is constantly

cognized because it is the illuminator of the intellect. The objects of awareness caused by some illuminator become known only when they color the intellect.

(2) Proper revelation of absolute awareness is impossible in the state of distraction (*vyutthāna*). In this state consciousness is indirectly realized with the help of the functions of the empirical self. It is realized in the state called the "concentration of cessation" (*nirodhasamādhi*).

(3) Transformation is either *aupadānika* (in which there is plurality of material causes) or *lākṣaṇika*. The latter consists in the difference in position of space or time. It is nothing but the change of form and the like (without any change in the material cause itself).

(4) Absolute consciousness (*svacaitanya*) existing in every sentient being, not being a composite element and having no limit, cannot be affected by transformation. No temporal or spatial relation can be attributed to consciousness. It is devoid of parts and as such the act of pervading cannot be applied to it. It is wrong to hold that consciousness is one in number and is common to all beings.

(5) The objection that consciousnesses would lose their propery of limitlessness if they are said to be many in number is untenable as the argument cannot be applied to entities that have no spatial dimension.

(6) It is reasonable to hold that consciousnesses are many (innumerable) in number and they are equal in all respects, as is stated in *Śvetāśvatara Upaniṣad* 4.5.

(7) The word "*eka*" in propositions like "*ekam eva advitīyam*" shows that consciousnesses belong to the one and the same species or that there is absence of dualistic apprehension in consciousnesses. Texts like "*eko vyāpi*," etc., do not refer to the nature of pure consciousness but to the character of God. Consciousnesses are devoid of all attributes found in objects of awareness.

(8) Consciousness remains immutable though awareness remains in a distracted or inhibited state. All stimulations after reaching the intellect are transformed into awareness. (The process is technically known as *prākāśya paryavasāna*). Consciousness remains unaffected by these stimulations. It is said to be the immutable perceiver. The intellect with its objects becomes object of consciousness and is wrongly identified with consciousness.

II. 9–13: Materiality and the Three Constituents (E5–9)

(9) Through the concentration of cessation, awareness and the capacities attain an absolutely unmanifested state. This state is known as primordial materiality, the ultimate form of the three constituents, and it is regarded as the material cause of *citta* (mind) and the capacities. It is positive and real, although said to be unreal owing to its

perceptual unmanifestedness to a person who attains liberation. The word "*avyakta*" in *Kaṭha Upaniṣad* I.3.11 refers to this primordial materiality, which is also referred to by the word "*tamas.*"

(10) In fluctuating states the experiencer is to be taken as the transforming seer (consciousness). It is the same as the ego.

(11) Egoity has three aspects, characterized by *prakāśa* (capacity for expression), *kriyā* (capacity for mutation; it is the cause of transformations), and *sthiti* (capacity for remaining in a latent state), respectively called *sattva, rajas,* and *tamas.* There arises equilibrium in these three constituents when the internal organ dissolves primordial materiality.

(12) The state known as disequilibrium found in *citta* (mind) and the capacities consists in the predominance of one constituent and the subordination of the other two. All pervading constituents are inseparable and they help one another act. All phenomenal forms are but particular collocations of the constituents. A thing is named after a particular constituent (as *sāttvika,* etc.) because of its predominance.

(13) There are two fundamental goals of consciousness, experience (*bhoga*) of satisfaction and experience of frustration; consciousness is defined as the realization of the beneficial and injurious forms of the constituents and liberation, realization of the true nature of consciousness. The absolute illuminator consciousness and the unmanifested state of the three constituents are respectively the efficient and the material cause of the phenomenal state. From these two opposite causes proceed three aspects in the manifested entities, namely, *prakāśa* (resembling *puruṣa*), *sthiti* (resembling *avyakta*), and *kriyā* (concerning the mutual relation of these two and possessing the nature of transitoriness or unsteadiness), respectively known as *sāttvika, tāmasa,* and *rājasa.*

III. 14-22: The Three Internal Organs and Their Functions (E9-12)

(14) The first evolute, intellect, also called experiencer (*grahītṛ*), is the I-sense, which dissolves in the state of liberation. It can be realized through the concentration with egoity (*sāsmitā samādhi*). Its illumination is mutable, and cognitions, etc., are completed with reference to it.

(15) Intellect is atomic (*aṇumātra,* i.e., *sūkṣma,* subtle).

(16) Being in close proximity to consciousness, intellect is possessed of the highest illumination. That is why consciousness is described as one whose dwelling place is *sattva,* or the intellect.

(17) Egoity is the dynamic aspect of the intellect, through which a not-self becomes related to the self. It is *rājasa* and the source of "me" and "mine" feelings (*mamatā, ahaṃtā*).

(18) The heart (*hṛdaya*), also called "mind" (*manas*), is that aspect of the internal organ by which nonselves become attached to the self. It is *tāmasa* and has the preponderance of *sthiti*.

(19) Intellect, egoity, and mind are called the internal organ (*antaḥkaraṇa*) because they exist between consciousness and the external capacities.

(20) Awareness (*prakhyā* or *jñāna*) is of the nature of illumination, and it arises when the intellect becomes affected or excited by external stimuli. The modifications of awareness caused by a stimulus are related to the I-self by egoity.

(21) Because the internal organ is a product of the three constituents, the transformation of any of its parts involves the transformation of the other two.

(22) The character of awareness, activity, and inertia shows that they possess the preponderance of *sattva*, *rajas*, and *tamas* respectively.

IV. 23-26: Awareness and Egoity (E12-14)

(23) I-awareness (*asmitā*) is the internal organ transformed into awareness and capacities. It is I-awareness through which feelings like "I am the hearer" and the like come into existence.

(24) I-awareness has two kinds of transformation, which are also the cause of transformation into a different species (*jātyantarapariṇāma*). The first is the knowledge transformation (*vidyāpariṇāma*); it is *sāttvika* as it flows toward illumination or knowledge; the second is the ignorance transformation (*avidyāpariṇāma*), which flows toward concealment and which has a greater relation to what is different from the self.

(25) Three kinds of external organs arise from the internal organ because of its contact with external objects. They are five sense capacities, five action capacities, and five vital breaths, in which there is predominance of *prakāśa*, *kriyā*, and *sthiti* respectively.

(26) Awareness (*citta*) is the aggregate of the operations of the internal organ that arise from the contact of the internal organ with objects through the external capacities. It has two kinds of operations, the *śakti* operations, by which thinking and the like are performed, and the *avasthā* operations, the states of awareness that are invariably associated with cognition, conation, and retention. The internal organ has two kinds of properties, *pratyayas* (cognitions and conations) and *saṃskāras* (latent dispositions, the objects of *hṛdaya*).

V. 27-35: The Operations of Awareness (E14-20)

(27) Cognition (*prakhyā*) has five operations, instrument of knowledge (*pramāṇa*), memory (*smṛti*), cognition of activities (*pravṛttivijñāna*), conceptual constructions (vague notions based on verbal cogni-

tion) (*vikalpa*), and misconception (*viparyaya*). Similarly, activity *pravṛtti*) has five subdivisions, intentionality (*saṃkalpa*), imagination (*kalpanā*), effort employed in voluntary activity (*kṛti*), wandering of mind caused by doubt and hesitation (*vikalpanā*), and futile effort as in dream and the like (*viparyāsta*). Similarly, inertia (*sthiti*), the property of *hṛdaya*, has five kinds of latent dispositions concerning the five operations of cognition as its objects.

The two opposite aspects (*sattva* and *tamas*) in the tripartite internal organ give rise to a fivefold subdivision of the external capacities and also of the power residing in awareness. Thus, three of the subdivisions have the predominance of the three constituents. The fourth subdivision is predominated by the properties of both *sattva* and *rajas*, and the fifth, by the properties of both *rajas* and *tamas*.

(28) *Vijñāna* is the cognition pertaining to the field of *cetas* and it is accomplished with the help of the capacities. *Pramāṇa* is the instrument of knowledge (*pramā*), the correct cognition of that which was not known before. Perception (an instrument of knowledge) is the awareness through the channels of the sense capacities. The sense capacities give rise to sensation (*ālocanajñāna*) only, which is devoid of the notion of species (*jāti*), etc. After sensation there arises perception, which is characterized by species, etc.

(29) Inference depends upon the invariable concomitance, which is either positive (*sahabhāvin*) or negative (*asahabhāvin*).

Verbal testimony arises in a person's awareness after hearing a sentence pronounced by a trustworthy person who is able to convey his ideas to his audience (*āpta*). It is different from ascertainment through reading. The presence of the speaker and hearer is an indispensable condition in verbal testimony.

(30) Whereas inference and verbal testimony give knowledge of general properties, perception gives knowledge of particulars, which consists in peculiar properties and forms.

(31) Memory is the experience of that object only which exists in the form of latent dispositions. It is *sāttvikarājasa* and has three subdivisions concerning *vijñāna*, *pravṛtti*, and inhibited states like sleep etc.

(32) *Pravṛtti vijñāna* is the consciousness of voluntary activities efforts also of the involuntary activities of the five vital breaths. It *rājasa*.

(33) Conceptual construction (*vikalpa*) is based on the verb cognition with respect to a thing that does not exist. It is of three kind (1) *vastuvikalpa* is that in which one and the same thing is taken more than one; (2) *kriyāvikalpa* is that in which a nonagent is tak as if it were an agent; and (3) *abhāvavikalpa* arises when the *ci* thinks with the help of words denoting nonexistence. Place and ti are regarded as arising from conceptual construction. In reality th

is no place absolutely devoid of color and the other four qualities. Although place and time have no reality, yet they have their use. This operation of awareness falls under the class *rājasa-tāmasa*.

(34) Misconception is mistaken awareness. It is based on a thing as other than what it is. It is *tāmasa*. To understand the not-self as self is the fundamental misconception.

(35) Intentionality (*saṃkalpa*), the first activity (of awareness), is the application of the I-awareness in conscious activities. The resolve in such statements as "I shall go" is to be known as intentionality. It is *sāttvika*. Imagination (*kalpanā*), the second activity, is that activity which superimposes previously known objects one on the other. It consists in joining names, species, etc. It is *sāttvikarājasa*. Effort (*kṛti*), the third activity, follows desire. It helps the organs to poduce the desired results. Wandering of mind (*vikalpanā*), the fourth activity, arises at the time of doubt or while a man employs the entities (like time, etc.) known through the conceptual construction (see 33). Futile effort (*viparyāsta*) is the effort that follows misconception; the mental effort in dream is an example of this activity. Activity comes to the action capacities from within.

The "inertias" (*sthiti*) or latent dispositions are also of five kinds. The traces of knowledge, memory, activity, conceptual construction, and misconception have respectively the predominance of *sattva*, *sattvarajas*, *rajas*, *rajastamas*, and *tamas*.

VI. 36-40: THE STATIC OPERATIONS (AVASTHĀ VṚTTI) (E20-23)

(36) Satisfaction, etc., are the nine static operations that arise in awareness while it performs its functions. Cognitions and other functions of the *citta* are not caused by these operations.

(37) Satisfaction, frustration, and confusion are the three static operations related to cognition. Satisfaction and frustration are due to stimulation by things that are beneficial and injurious respectively. Confusion arises from the excessive experience of satisfaction and frustration.

(38) Craving the types of satisfactions already enjoyed (*rāga*), aversion to frustrations of a sort already suffered (*dveṣa*), and love of life (*abhiniveśa*) are the three static operations related to effort. Love of life is instinctive dread in general and not the fear for death only. It springs naturally from the latent dispositions.

(39) Waking state (*jāgrat*), dreaming state (*svapna*), and dreamless sleep (*suṣupti*) are the three static operations related to the body, that is, they are psycho-physical states, in which there is predominance of *sattva*, *rajas*, and *tamas* respectively. In the first the seats of awareness and capacities remain active; in the second the sense and action capacities become inactive though the mind remains active; in the

third all these capacities become inactive. In nightmare (*utsvapna*) the seats of the action capacities become active.

(40) Determination, the conjoint action of the faculties belonging to awareness (*vyavasāya*), is threefold. *Sadvyavasāya* is direct perception, *anuvyavasāya* is reflection, and *paridṛṣṭa vyavasāya* is the undistinguished activity that causes mutation in sleep or sustains the latent dispositions and other subconscious characteristics.

VIII. 41-52: External Capacities and Their Functions (E20-30)

(41) The ear, etc., are the five sense organs, which are the channels of the modification called perception. Egoity, the essence of the capacities, becomes excited by contact with external objects. This excitation in the ego is received by the grasper (*grahītṛ*), and the objects become illuminated. This illumination is called sensory perception (*indriyajñāna*). Sense capacities or the cognitive senses receive external impressions that are converted into sensations.

(42) The ear receives sound. The skin receives thermal sensations (heat and cold) only. Pressure, weight, and hardness are known through the activity of the action organs and the vital breaths. The eye receives color, the tongue taste and the nose smell only. In these five there is the predominance of *sattva*, *sattvarajas*, *rajas*, *rajastamas*, and *tamas* respectively. The objects of sense organs are called cognizables (*prakāśya*).

(43) Speech, grasping, locomotion, excretion, and sex are the action capacities whose common function is voluntary employment (*svecchācālana*). These are employed in speech, manipulation, locomotion, excretion, and reproduction respectively.

(44) The five vital breaths, whose chief function is to sustain the body, are also to be known as external capacities.

(45) The chief function of *prāṇa* is to sustain the living organism.

(46) The chief function of *udāna* is to sustain the tissues (*dhātu*).

(47) The chief function of *vyāna* is to sustain the power of voluntary actions.

(48) The chief function of *apāna* is to sustain those organs of the body that separate excreta (*mala*) from different parts of the body.

(49) The chief function of *samāna* is to sustain digestion.

(50) A body is the aggregate of the five vital breaths.

(51) The vital breaths proceed from egoity. In other words, it is the internal organ that gives rise to the vital breaths.

(52) Because of the predominance of illumination, of activity, and of inertia, the sense capacities, the action capacities and the vital breaths are to be known as *sāttvika*, *rājasa*, and *tāmasa* respectively.

VIII. 53-59: The External Objects of the Capacities (E30-36)

(53) The contents of the instruments reside in the objects grasped (*grāhya*). They are the results of the interaction of the *grahaṇa* (internal and external capacities) and objects. Because contents are the results of the said interaction it is practically impossible to perceive directly the ultimate material cause of the external objects. Yogins, however, can perceive the subtle forms of objects through particular yogic concentrations, but the reality behind the objects cannot be perceived. The nature of this reality can be indirectly known through inference.

(54) There are three original properties in external objects, perceptibility (*bodhyatva*), mutability (*kriyātva*), and inertness (*jaḍya*).

(55) Some varieties of these three kinds of properties reside in all the external substances called elemental (*bhautika*).

(56) *Ākāśa*, an element, is that inanimate and mutable thing which has sound as the only property. Similarly the elements air, fire, water, and earth possess temperature, color, taste, and smell as their only properties respectively.

(57) It is the Yogins who directly perceive the elements as having only one of the five illuminating properties.

(58) An analysis of the illuminating properties reveals that there is a predominance of *sattva*, *sattvarajas*, *rajas*, *rajastamas*, and *tamas* in sound, temperature, color, taste, and smell respectively.

(59) Sound, etc., possess differentiation (*viśeṣa*). When sound, etc., attain such subtlety that these differentiations disappear, then the substrata in which such sound, etc., inhere are called subtle elements. The five subtle elements are the causes of the five gross elements respectively. Because they are devoid of all differentiations they are called generic (*aviśeṣa*). They do not give rise to the feeling of satisfaction, frustration, and confusion. The subtle elements are directly perceived through yogic concentration.

IX. 60-64: The Material Cause of the Subtle Elements (E36-39)

(60) The material cause of the subtle elements cannot be perceived externally, but is to be inferred only. Because this substance excites our mind through the organs, it must be of the nature of mind. Again, because this substance is devoid of sound, etc., its action must be without any spatial dimension. Such an action must belong to the mind only. Thus the source of the external objects is proved to be mental in nature.

(61) Because external qualities like color, etc., cannot be attributed to the source of external objects, it is reasonable to ascribe internal qualities to it as we have no knowledge of a thing that is neither external nor internal.

(62) The being whose mind is the source of external objects is

called *Virāṭ puruṣa*. The manifestation and dissolution of the universe are the result of his awakening and sleeping states.

(63) The doctrine of some schools that the will of God is the only cause of the universe points to the aforesaid viewpoint, because will is a transformation of the internal organ. The mind, which is the source of all objects, is called *bhūtādi*. The three functions of the internal organ are transformed into cognizability, mutability, and inertia in the field of the cognizable objects. Time is the locus of mental process (*grahaṇabhāva*), whereas space is the container of grasped things (*grāhyabhāva*).

(64) A gross external element is not a principle; it is an aggregate of the three kinds of attributes as stated above.

A living organism is an assemblage (*saṃghāta*) made up of these three properties.

X. 65-71: Creation and Dissolution of the Brahmāṇḍa (E39-44)

(65) Primordial materiality and consciousness are said to be, respectively, the ultimate material and efficient cause of the beginningless capacities (*karaṇa*). These associated with the subtle elements are called "subtle bodies," which are innumerable in number, a fact that establishes the plurality of consciousnesses. The capacities, being products of the three constituents, possess infinite varieties. This is why the subtle bodies, either with dissolved organs or with manifested organs, lead their lives in various realms.

(66) The subtle bodies become dissolved either through Yoga or through the dissolution of objects. Such subtle bodies appear again when the objects become manifested.

(67) When the *vairāja abhimāna* (the mind of the *virāṭ*, the Prajāpati) sinks into quiescence, objects become dissolved. This is the sleeping state of Prajāpati.

(68) When Prajāpati remains in the sleeping state the external existence assumes a motionless, immovable, and undistinguishable state. Creation, which in reality is the imagination of Prajāpati, takes place in the intermediate state between waking and deep sleep. Prajāpati's imagination of subtle forms of the gross elements gives rise to the creation of subtle elements.

(69) The creation of subtle elements, being associated with the mental procss of other Virāṭ consciousnesses, becomes more and more gross and consequently there appears the manifestation of the gross elements (elemental creation), which consists of properties like solidity, fluidity, etc.

XI. 70-72: The Created Brahmāṇḍa and Other Sentient Beings (E44-46)

(71) A *brahmāṇḍa* is said to comprise seven realms (*loka*). The first, called *bhūrloka*, is visible. The realms from *bhuvar* to *satya* are invisible to ordinary persons. All the realms are established in the *satyaloka*, which is established in the *mahadātman* of the *virāṭ puruṣa*. This realm is the center of the cosmos as the *mahat* principle is the center of all mental activities.

(72) After the manifestation of the *bhūtādi* there appeared *Hiraṇyagarbha* the creator, endowed with omniscience and omnipotence. Because he acquired lordship in the previous cycle he, through the power of his will, created this *brahmāṇḍa* inhabited by beings.

HARIRĀMA ŚUKLA

Harirāma Śukla was a professor of Saṃpūrṇānanda Sanskrit University, Varanasi, and was well known for his erudition in the field of Nyāya, which he studied with Rajeśvara Śāstrin Drāviḍa, the renowned scholar of Nyāya and Advaita Vedānta in modern times. He died in about 1975.

The commentary chiefly explains the expressions of the *Tattvakaumudī* and discusses difficult points in detail. It has very little new to say. In a few places it criticizes the views of other commentators.

The summary is prepared from the edition published in the Kashi Sanskrit Series no. 123 from the Chowkhamba Sanskrit Series Office, Varanasi in 1937.

SUṢAMĀ

(*Summary by Ram Shankar Bhattacharya*)

I. Introductory: Scope and Task of Sāṃkhya

First benedictory stanza. Although there are systematic statements showing the origination and destruction of materiality and consciousness, yet because of being directly contradicted by the express statement of *Śvetāśvatara Upaniṣad* 4.5, "*prakṛti*" and "*puruṣa*" are to be taken in a restricted sense, "*prakṛti*" in the sense of the power of creation and "*puruṣa*" in the sense of consciousness' reflection in the intellect. According to Vijñānabhikṣu (whose view has been quoted by the commentator) "the origination of materiality" means its conjunction with consciousness and "the destruction of materiality" means its disjunction from consciousness.

Some are of the opinion that although materiality is established in the Vedas, yet it may be inferred from its effects, which are stated in the *Śvetāśvatara* passage "*bahvīḥ prajāḥ sṛjamānāṃ sarūpāḥ*" (4.5). This view is not accepted by the commentator. According to him "that entity is established in the Vedas which cannot be proved by inference" (See *Saṃkhyakārikā* 6). Because materiality can be proved by inference, it cannot be regarded as capable of being established by the Vedas.

The word "*eka*" in the *Śvetāśvatara* passage means "devoid of a second thing of a similar nature" (*sajātīyadvitīyarahita*). It cannot be urged that because some statements of the system speak of "a plurality of *māyās*" materiality cannot be accepted as one, for in those statements "*māyā*" is to be taken in the sense of the three constituents, and so the use of the plural number in the word "*māyā*" becomes justified. In the statements of the system mentioning eight *prakṛtis* the word "*prakṛti*" is to be taken in the sense of "the material cause of a *tattva*" (*tattvāntaropādāna*), that is, in these statements "*prakṛti*" would mean eight entities, namely, the unmanifest, intellect, egoity, and the five subtle elements. The commentary shows the significance of the order of the words in the expression "red-white-black" (*lohitaśuklakṛṣṇam*); the word "*lohita*" (representing the *rajas guṇa*) has been mentioned first because *rajas* is the inciting factor (*pravārtaka*) in creation.

(1) Vācaspati refers to two kinds of persons: ordinary persons (*laukika*) and specialists or experts (*parīkṣaka*). Harirāma remarks that the ordinary persons are those who do not take the Vedas and the systems dependent on them as authoritative whereas the specialists are those who accept the Vedas, etc., as authoritative.

Because frustration is mental (i.e., it is an attribute of the mind), the division of frustrations into mental and bodily seems to be illogical. This difficulty can be avoided by taking the word "mental" in the sense of "caused by the mind only". Thus bodily frustration does not fall under mental frustration, because it is caused by both the body and the mind. Some, however, think that "mental" means "caused by those factors that exist in the mind."

The word "*āntaropāyasādhya*" (used to refer to internal frustration) may mean either "caused by internal means" or "removed by internal means," that is frustration is called mental either because it is caused by internal factors or because it is removed by internal factors.

(2) While elucidating the relation between a *sāmānya śāstra* (a generic rule) and a *viśeṣa śāstra* (a specific rule) (as stated in *Tattvakaumudī*), Harirāma quotes the view of some teacher that because Vedic *hiṃsā* (sanctioned violence as is found in sacrificial acts) yields much more satisfaction than frustration, people are naturally attracted to sacrificial acts associated with violence. There is an elaborate exposition of *kratvartha* (subserving the purposes of sacrifices) and *puruṣārtha* (subserving the purposes of men)—the two Mīmāṃsā terms.

On the authority of statements in the system, Vācaspati concludes that sacrificial acts invariably lead to death (i.e., frustration). Thus it follows that heaven, being the result of sacrificial acts, must be associated with frustration, and so to define it as "not mixed with frustration" (see the verse" *yan na duḥkhena,*" etc., quoted by Vācaspati) becomes faulty. To avoid this difficulty, some think that in the expression" not mixed with frustration" frustration is to be taken in the sense of "bodily frustration" only. As has been stated in some authoritative texts, beings residing in heaven are devoid of such frustration although they face death. The commentator thinks that the aforesaid verse " (*yan na duḥkhena,*" etc.) is a supplemental text (*arthavāda*) and so simply glorifies heaven.

II. Instruments of Knowledge

(6) It is the unmanifest and consciousness that are chiefly discussed in Sāṃkhya, and the main purpose of Sāṃkhya is to prove their existence. Harirāma refers to the view of another commentator who says that the indeclinable "*tu*" suggests the exclusion of perception and that the expression "*sāmānyatodṛṣṭa*" suggests exclusion of the *pūrvavat* form of inference. A few passages of the system on the evolution of the intellect, etc., on heaven, and on *apūrva* (the invisible potency leading to certain results) have been quoted.

III. Preexistent Effect

(9) It is remarked that, when a material cause is inferred from its effects, it is assumed that the cause possesses the same qualities (*guṇa*) as the effects.

Harirāma says that Vācaspati accepted, not the absolute existence, but conventional or empirical existence of the world (*jagat*). According to Vedānta, the world, which is superimposed on *brahman*, is not different from *brahman* (i.e., it has no independent existence), although it is not identical with *Brahman*. *Brahmasūtra* 2.1.14 (*tadananyatvam...*) has been quoted to show the Vedāntic view on the cause-effect relation.

While explaining the *Tattvakaumudī* passages refuting the view of the Buddhists, the commentator says that so long as a seed remains intact, there arises no sprout from it. This is why destruction of the seed is also a condition for the genesis of a sprout. It may be reasonably held that a seed in an intact state is an obstacle (*pratibandhaka*) for the genesis of a sprout. Thus it follows that the destruction of a seed must be regarded as the absence of obstacle, which also falls under the causes of an effect. The following argument (from *Bhāmatī* 2.2.26) has also been adduced in this connection: because jar, etc., are not homogeneous (*anvita*) with nonexistence, they cannot be regarded as the effects of nonexistence.

While refuting the Vedāntic view Harirāma quotes the scriptural passage "*vācārambhaṇaṃ...satyam*" (*Chāndogya Upaniṣad* 6.1.4) that is usually cited by the Vedāntins to prove the unreality or illusoriness of the effects. He interprets it to mean that the effect is nothing but a special combination (*saṃsthānaviśeṣa*) of its (material) cause; as for example a jar is essentially nothing but clay in a new arrangement—it is as real as clay. Thus, it is clear that the aforequoted scriptural passage shows nondifference between the cause and its effect. It is incidentally remarked that the Sāṃkhya process of inference has five members and not three, like the Vedāntic process of inference.

Commenting on Vācaspati's passage stating that the statement "this cloth is in these threads" is similar to "there are *tilaka* trees in this forest" and so there is no difference between a cloth and the threads (as there is no difference between the trees and the forest), *Suṣamā* remarks that it may be objected that there is no real difference between the trees and the forest, because the statement "there are *tilaka* trees in the forest" lays stress on the relation of the container and the contained between the forest and the trees and so this statement (i.e., "there are tilaka trees in the forest") is secondary, whereas in the statement "this cloth is in these threads" the notion of difference is real and so it is not similar to the former illustration. In reply to this Harirāma says that because the *Chāndogya* passage (*vācārambhaṇaṃ*, etc.) expressly shows nondifference between a cause and its effects, the notion of difference in the statement "this cloth is in these threads" must be taken as metaphorical.

Harirāma quotes *Sāṃkhyasūtra* I. 122-123 while refuting the Nyāya view criticizing the Sāṃkhya theory of manifestation (*abhivyakti*). He quotes a passage from the *Sāṃkhyacandrikā* (by Nārāyaṇatīrtha) that justifies the Sāṃkhya view and shows why a cause is needed in giving rise to the manifestation of an effect. Manifestation being *sāttvika* (chiefly caused by *sattva*) is sometimes obstructed by *tamas* and so some factor is needed to give rise to it.

(10) It is remarked that, because the manifest has a cause, the mind has also a cause and consequently it is to be regarded as noneternal—a view that is opposed to the Nyāya view. Harirāma argues that the word "*kriyā*" (activity, mobility) is to be taken in the sense of vibration (*parispanda*) and not in the sense of transformation, for mutation exists in materiality also, whereas vibration does not, as materiality is all-pervasive. The word "*aneka*" (an epithet of the manifest) does not means "not-one" but "associated with things of similar kind."

(11) Although the word "*guṇa*" usually refers to *sattva*, *rajas*, and *tamas*, yet in the expression "*triguṇam*", *guṇa* means satisfaction, frustration, and confusion, which are the properties of the constituents. (According to Sāṃkhya, there is no difference between a *dharmin*, substrate, and its characteristics, properties).

While refuting the argument of *sahopalambhaniyama* given by the

Buddhists to prove idealism (*vijñānavāda*), Harirāma remarks that none of the meanings of the word "saha" (in "*sahopalambha*") is applicable here.

V. The Three Constituents

(12) While elucidating *tantrayukti* Harirāma says that because in *Bhagavadgītā* 14.5 we find the order of *sattva-rajas-tamas* in the enumeration of the three constituents, the same order is to be followed in this verse also. This is why the agreeableness, disagreeableness, and oppressiveness referred to in this verse are to be connected with *sattva*, *rajas*, and *tamas* respectively.

Harirāma remarks that the word "*anyonyāśrayavṛtti*" suggests that a constituent takes the help of the other two constituents in producing the effect of the nature of dissimilar transformation (*virūpapariṇāma*), whereas "*anyonyajananavṛtti*" suggests that a constituent takes the help of others in producing the effect of the nature of similar transformation (*svarūpapariṇāma*). Because in similar transformation no new principle is produced, this transformation is said to be "devoid of cause." In the proposition "the manifest has a cause" (verse 10), the cause is a principle. In the similar transformation, because *sattva* is caused, not by anything other than *sattva*, but by *sattva* itself, this transformation is rightly regarded as causeless.

(13) Like weight, lightness is also an inferable quality. Although lightness is the cause of going upward, it cannot be taken to be the cause of going downward, both the motions being of opposite nature. (Two opposite things cannot be produced by the same cause).

Although the constituents possess the characteristic of mutual opposition, yet in their transformations the constituents exist in the principal—subordinate relation, that is, while one constituent becomes principal, the other two remain subordinate to it.

VI. Inference to Primordial Materiality and Consciousness

(17) Commenting on Vācaspati's definition of satisfaction as that which is experienced as desirable (*anukūlavedanīya*), Harirāma adds that it should not be subservient to any other desire. Similarly he says that although frustration is defined as that which is experieneed as undesirable, yet this dislike must not be subservient to any other dislike.

The argument from enjoyership (*bhoktṛbhāva*) has been interpreted in two ways in *Tattvakaumudī*. The commentator remarks that the first interpretation is not basically different from the second. It is remarked that although in reality the intellect is a knowable object, yet because of its association with the self, it appears to be the knower.

IX. The Thirteenfold Instrument

(23) As to how reflective discerning, which is a form of awareness, can be attributed to the nonintelligent intellect, it is replied that because the intellect is associated with the intelligent self, reflective discerning can be taken to be an attribute of the intellect.

Nonattachment is not the absence of attachment but a positive entity, that is, an anti-attachment entity. Similarly ignorance is not the mere absence of knowledge, but its opposite, a positive entity.

(26) The Vaiśeṣika view that the four sense organs (the ear being excluded) are elemental has been discussed in detail, and it is shown that the arguments as adduced by the Vaiśeṣika teachers contain fallacies of *asādhāraṇa*.[1] It is further stated that because the four capacities (excluding the auditory) are nonelemental, the remaining capacity, ear, the auditory one, must also be nonelemental.

Harirāma has provided a few new arguments to prove that the capacities are nonelemental. Consequently they must be regarded as the transformations of egoity.

(27) The reason for accepting construction-free awareness as found in Nyāya treatises is given here. It is said to be the cause of construction-filled awareness.

(29) The vital breath, which is of the nature of a capacity, cannot be the same as air, which is a substance.

(31) Harirāma argues that, the embodied self cannot be regarded as the controller of the capacities because of its inability to perceive directly the supersenuous things like the intellect, etc., and since the existence of God is denied in Sāṃkhya, the Sāṃkhya teachers regard the goals of consciousness, experience, and liberation as the reason for capacities.

XI. Subtle Body

(40) It is remarked that, because the subtle body is nothing but an aggregate of 18 entities, namely, intellect, etc., it is not regarded as a distinct entity different from the 25 principles.

XIV. Similes for Materiality

(57) Harirāma quotes Śaṃkara's commentary on *Brahmasūtra* 2.2.3 criticizing the Sāṃkhyan view of the activity of a nonintelligent entity and also establishing the view that because it is inspired by an intelligent being, nonintelligent milk functions for the nourishment of the calf. (This suggests that materiality being incited by God is the cause of creation). It then establishes the view that, because there can be no invariable rule that nonintelligent entities act, being inspired by

intelligent beings, Śaṃkara's criticism of the Sāṃkhyan view is untenable. Statements of the system declaring that nonintelligent things act, being incited by intelligent beings, refer to the secondary creation. The primary creation (*ādisarga*) is not preceded by any thought (*abuddhipūrvaka*).

(62) The word "*prakṛti*" in this verse means the intellect, for it is the intellect (and not primordial materiality) that is directly connected with worldly existence. Two authoritative passages are quoted to show that in reality bondage, liberation, and transmigration do not belong to consciousness.

(69) It is remarked that *Śvetāśvatara Upaniṣad* 5. 2 "(*ṛṣiṃ prasūtaṃ kapilaṃ*)" refers to the sage Kapila.

XVI. Transmission of Sāṃkhya Traditions

(72) While commenting on the verses of the *Rājavārttika*, Harirāma explains duration (*śeṣavṛtti*) twice and exemplifies it by the two verses (60 and 67) of the *Sāṃkhyakārikā*.

ŚIVANĀRĀYAṆA ŚĀSTRIN

Pandit Śivanārāyaṇa Sāstrin wrote this commentary on Vācaspati Miśra's *Tattvakaumudī* in the early decades of the twentieth century. It was published in 1940 in Bombay at the Nirnaya Sagar Press by Pandurang Jawaji. "E" refers to the edition.

SĀRABODHINĪ

(*Summary by Anima Sen Gupta*)

I. Introductory: Scope and Task of Sāṃkhya

(1-3) (E8-11) Both experience in the world and liberation from it are goals of consciousness. Primordial materiality acts in order to achieve these two goals. Experience, being caused, cannot be final. Because this goal is not the final goal, no scriptural inquiry is to be undertaken to realize it. The scriptural instruction is necessary to bring about absolute cessation of frustration but had there not been an opposing force in the form of frustration in this world, people would not have been interested in the scriptural study, which shows the way of removing misery. Further, nobody is going to make a scriptural inquiry if he is convinced that frustration cannot be removed even though its removal is desirable.

(E11-12) Further, even if it is possible to remove frustration by having recourse to suitable means, still in the absense of adequate scriptural knowledge regarding the means, the subject matter of the scripture will not be inquired into. Again, if easier means are available elsewhere, then also the scriptural inquiry will not be undertaken by anybody.

(E17) Granted that there is a desire to remove frustration. According to the Sāṃkhya school, which upholds the theory of preexistent effect, the nonexistent cannot be produced and the existent cannot be destroyed. It can be stated here that, even though frustration cannot be absolutely uprooted, still it can be reduced to its calm and inactive form with the result that it becomes incapable of making its appearance again.

(E83) Mere hearing (*śravaṇa*) about manifested objects will not enable a man to understand correctly their true character. Realization of truth regarding manifested objects needs constant meditation, which alone is the producer of true knowledge.

(E90-94) Materiality is defined as that which can serve as the material cause of an effect of a different order. This definition of materiality enables the intellect, egoity, etc. (which are both causes and effects), to be called materiality. In fact, this is a definition that is neither too wide nor too narrow, and it permits the application of the word "materiality" to all the generated principles (from intellect down to the earth). The definition of materiality as the state of equilibrium of the three constituents is, however, applicable to the root cause only. It is not applicable either to the intellect, etc., or to the lump of clay and the like, which are mere material causes.

II. Instruments of Knowledge

(4-5) (E95) The fundamental principles have been enumerated. These will be established by the instruments of knowledge. One instrument of knowledge cannot establish all the principles. So, there must be more than one instrument.

Perception, inference, and verbal testimony are the three instruments that have to be admitted. Because the twenty-five principles are to be proved by these instruments, they are to be examined. Some principles are established by perception, some by inference and some by verbal testimony. All other instruments are included in these three.

(E96-97) Knowledge is a mental operation that is different from doubtful cognition, erroneous cognition, vague cognition, and memory. Knowledge, in its primary form, refers to an apprehension by the experiencing subject of an object as a result of an operation of the awareness. *Sāṃkhyasūtra* I.43 has spoken of two forms of knowledge (1) the intellectual mode (through which consciousness is reflected) and (2) apprehension of the object by an experiencing agent.

(E98) There are some things that are only instruments of knowledge and not themselves knowledge. The visual capacity is called an instrument of knowledge because it produces valid intellectual cognition in the form of "This is a jar." There are other objects that can take the form of knowledge and are also instruments of knowledge. The operation of awareness is called knowledge when it is regarded as a product of the operation of sense capacities. Because this operation of awareness is the instrument that results in the arousal of cognition in the cognizer, it is also called an instrument of knowledge. Apprehension by the experiencing agent is mere knowledge as it never serves as an instrument for any other cognition. Further, there is an object in the form of consciousness that is reflected in the intellect; it is only the experiencer. There is also an object that is only the witness. It is pure consciousness that falls in the snare of the intellect through reflection.

(E99) If apprehension by the experiencing agent implies that the consciousness is the substratum of awareness of contents, then such an attribution does not seem to be suitable for it; because consciousness, being the possessor of characteristics like knowerness, etc., will then become mutable in nature. There is, however, no ground for such apprehension. The awareness of contents is really of the nature of an intellectual operation and so it is not an attribute of consciousness. It is because the intellect and consciousness are not differentiated that awareness of content is falsely attributed to consciousness. Consciousness is not the substratum of such awareness.

(E103-105) Three instruments of knowledge have been mentioned because objects of the world become known to ordinary persons (who are not Yogins) through these three instruments. The things that can be known by Yogins cannot be known by ordinary persons. Although the supernormal cognition of Yogins is admitted, still this has not been mentioned here as such supernormal cognition is not used in practical life. Moreover, this supernormal cognition is a form of perceptual cognition produced by yogic power; so it is included in perception.

(E108) Here the word "*dṛṣṭa*" (which is synonymous with perception) means that which is defined, and the remaining portion of the definition differentiates perception from the instruments of knowledge of the same class as well as from doubt, error, memory, etc. (which are different from the instruments of valid knowledge). The definition must be free from the defects of being too wide or too narrow.

(E111) Objects like jars, etc., color awareness with their own forms through sense contact. The word "object" should be taken to mean not only the gross objects but also the subtle objects like the subtle elements, etc., which are perceptible by Yogins alone.

The definition of perception indicates that the sense capacities must come in contact with the object; but it does not mean that the sense capacities should leave their own places to meet the objects. Had this been the case, there would have been blindness, etc. (because of the absence of the sense organs in their respective places in the body). The word "operation" (*vṛtti*) means contact. It does not mean that a sense capacity goes to the object leaving its own place.

(E114) Although reflective discerning has been declared to be dependent on the sense capacities, still it is not a disposition of an external sense capacity. It subsists in the intellect, depending on the sense capacities. It is called an intellectual operation. The external sense capacities, no doubt, assume the forms of the objects to which they become related but reflective discerning stands for the excess flow of the thought constituent, or *sattvaguṇa*, that results from the suppression of the covering of the intellect formed of *tamas*. The word "operation" really refers to the arousal of the (excess) flow of the *sattva* as a result of the overpowering of *tamas*. Therefore, the word "operation" is not to be understood to refer to sense contact, etc., even though such things cause arousal of the operation by stopping the operation of the *sattva* constituent. Hence the word "operation" is easily applicable to cases of inference and verbal testimony as well, and the definition of operation does not suffer from the defects of under and overextension. An operation becomes the revealer of an object of knowledge because of the subdued condition of *tamas*. The intellect, no doubt, is capable of revealing all objects but because it is obstructed by the activity of *tamas* it cannot, by itself, manifest objects. In the case of perception, the *tamas* is overpowered by sense contact and the intellect, therefore, reaches the object through the operation of the sense capacities and assumes the form of the object. Perception is, thus, the definite cognition of the object through the contact of the sense organs. It is groundless to urge that awareness, being partless, should be regarded as immutable like consciousness. This is because (according to Sāṃkhya) partlessness does not imply immutability. Had this been so, the primary cause, being partless, would have been treated as immutable.

(E120) Knowledge, which is the outcome of the operation of the instruments of knowledge, arises in the intellect and not in the self. The self, being absolutely nonattached, cannot be the substratum of knowledge.

(E125) Perception cannot give us knowledge of all objects. Moreover, ignorance, etc., of another person cannot be known through perception. So, inference has to be admitted even by a materialist.

Inference is to be ascertained after perception because inference depends on repeated observations.

(E136) Inferential knowledge is not possible merely on the basis of the universal relation between pervaded (*hetu*) and the pervader (*sādhya*). The knowledge of the existence of the *hetu* in the *pakṣa* is also required for arriving at inferential cognition. These two (taken together) lead to the arousal of the inferential operation in the form of the inferred object. The operation of the intellect in the form of the inferred object is known as its functioning (*vyāpāra*), and the knowledge in the form of inferential cognition arises as a result of this functioning. That functioning operation therefore is the instrument of inferential knowledge.

Inference is divided into two forms : positive and exclusionary. The positive form of inference is again of two kinds : *pūrvavat* and *sāmānyatodṛṣṭa*. Exclusionary inference is called *śeṣavat* and it is of one form only.

(E 152-153) Verbal testimony as an instrument of knowledge is to be considered after inference, because the inexperienced person understands the relation between the word and its meaning by means of inference. Valid assertion (*āptavacana*) refers to cognition of the meaning of a sentence (*vākyārthajñāna*), and right revelation (*āptaśruti*) stands for correct knowledge of a sentence that is produced by the sentence.

(E 155) Knowledge that is produced by a sentence may be intrinsically valid or its validity may be externally caused. When the meaning of a sentence can be cognized correctly without the help of any other instrument of knowledge, that verbal cognition is valid intrinsically (as, for example, knowledge derived from the Vedas). If the help of other instruments is necessary to understand the correct meaning of some sentences, then the knowledge derived from these sentences is not self-sufficient in authority (as for example, sentences of the traditional texts, which depend on the Vedas for authority).

(E 159) Here the scriptures have been enumerated and defined. "*Smṛti*," for instance, stands for that scripture which is a recollection of the Vedas. *Itihāsa* records past happenings, whereas the Purāṇas deal with creation, dissolution, '*manvantara*,' dynasty, and character of the hereditary rulers. *Vedāṅgas* are six in number and *upāṅgas* include Purāṇas, Nyāya, Mīmāṃsā, and *dharmaśāstra*.

III. Preexistent Effect

(9) (E 218-223) Buddhists hold that an entity can arise from a nonentity. Curd is produced from the destruction of milk. All positive effects are caused by nonentities.

Others hold that Brahman is the only Reality without a second; but it appears in the form of a multicolored universe due to ignorance which is a limiting adjunct of Brahman. The visible object is not metaphysically real : Brahman, which is devoid of worldly display (*prapañca*) displays itself as the phenomenal world because of superimposition and refutation of a wrong imputation (*apavāda*). Superimposition (*adhyāropa*) stands for laying of a nonreal object on a real object. Refutation of a wrong imputation means retaining the real after negating the unreal.

(According to Kaṇāda and Akṣapāda) the previously nonexistent things, such as dyads, arise from the atoms, etc. The effect is nonexistent in the cause prior to its production. Owing to the operation of the causal factors, it comes into being. The effect is metaphysically real.

(The Kapila view) : It is the cause that is changed into the form of the effect. So there is nondifference between the cause and the effect and both of them are real.

Of these four views, the first three are incapable of establishing that type of the primary cause, the knowledge of which can be derived from the knowledge of its effect. The knowable effect (in which satisfaction, frustration, etc., are inherent) can establish only that type of cause which possesses satisfaction, frustration, etc., as its inherent ingredients. The first three views cannot prove the existence of such a cause.

(E225) That which is the cause of satisfaction, etc., must be capable of producing satisfaction, etc., because the demand of the causal rule is that there must be identity between the cause and the effect from the point of view of the material stuff. The nonexistent cause is not capable of serving this purpose and no identity is possible between an entity and a nonentity.

(E230-232) The world appearance is not false because it is perceived. In the case of silver in the conch shell there is the sublating knowledge (this is conch shell and not silver) but there is no such sublating knowledge so far as the perception of the world (in the empirical life) is concerned. So, how can the world be regarded as false ? The world is real because it is not produced by any defective cause, and because there is no empirical knowledge to negate it. The scriptural passage "*vācārambhana*" (*Chāndogya Upaniṣad* VI. I.4) also proves that the effect is of the same nature as the cause. It does not prove its nonreality. Again, nobody resolves to produce an illusory object. The world has been brought into being through divine resolution. Hence, the world is not illusory. If the whole world, except Brahman, is regarded as false, then the Vedas, too, being of this world, should be treated as false. Had the Vedas been false, Brahman, that has been spoken of in the Vedas, would have been equally false. If this be so, then the Vedāntins, too, will be regarded as the upholders of voidness (*śūnyavāda*). Hence the scriptural texts that seem to speak of the falsity (*mithyātva*) of the world, really speak of the noneternal nature of the phenomenal world.

(E237) Although prior to production, the effect exists in its causal form; still, in its effect form, it is nonexistent. This view does not favor the view of the nonexistence of the effect. Causal operation, too, becomes necessary. It does not, however, produce anything that is entirely new, because it does not possess this ability.

(E256) Because the theory of preexistence is free from all defects, it is valid and superior to all other views.

IV-VI. (11-16) (E262) Here, if the word "*guṇa*" is to be understood to refer to the three constituents (*sattva, rajas,* and *tamas*), then we are to hold that these three constituents form the substratum of the manifest and the unmanifest. The three constituents are, no doubt, the substratum of the manifest but these cannot be regarded as the substratum of primordial materiality, which is of the nature of these constituents. *Sāṃkhyasūtra* VI.39 too has stated that materiality cannot be understood to form a characteristic of the three constituents because these constituents themselves are of the nature of materiality. The word "*guṇa*" is to be interpreted here in the sense of satisfaction, frustration, and confusion. In this sense only, the word "*guṇa*" can be applied here to materiality as it is the substratum of satisfaction, frustration, etc., which are the effects of the constituents. As there is no difference between quality and the possessor of quality, the word "*guṇa*" has been used here to mean satisfaction, etc., and not the intellect, etc. Egoity, which is endowed with satisfactions, etc., is the cause of the five subtle elements. Because the effect is of the same nature as the cause, the five subtle elements, too, possess satisfactions, etc. Like egoity and as such, they continue to be of the nature of the three constituents.

(E263-264) The Nyāya view that qualities like desire, aversion, effort, satisfaction, frustration, and knowledge are the indicators of the substance self is not correct. In fact, satisfactions, etc., are the qualities of the manifest and the unmanifest, and are other than the self. Scripture, too, has described the self as nonattached, witness, alone and qualityless. If the Nyāya view is accepted, and satisfactions, etc., are regarded as qualities of the self, then this will go against scripture. Phenomena like sound, touch, etc., are only awarenesses according to Vijñānavādins. (In their opinion) consciousness alone is real. The external object as something other than consciousness cannot be admitted as real. We can refute this view by asserting that the knowable external object—because it is knowable—must be different from awareness of it. Nobody is capable of establishing the oneness of awareness and its objects. It is because the jar is accepted as the content of awareness and awareness as the entertaining of content that these two are clearly perceived as different. The jar that is cognizable is one thing and quite different from it is the cognition that becomes its receiver. It is because the external object is different from cognition that it can become a common object of awareness. Because the knowable remains the same, although knowers are different, the knowable object is regarded as different from the knower. The Vijñānavādins cannot prove how a particular object can become the common object of cognition (of many persons). Just as the cognition of one person cannot be directly known by another person, in the same manner the object of knowledge of one person cannot be apprehended by another person.

(E276-277) The three constituents form a state of equilibrium that is called primordial materiality. This may be regarded as the first transformation of the three constituents.

Now, if primordial materiality is regarded as the "homogeneous transformation" of the three constituents, then it becomes a caused principle (*hetumat*). This is not so. The homogeneous transformation does not make it a caused entity. Where an object of a different order originates from a particular entity, there the heterogeneous transformation of principles gives rise to the character of being caused. Primordial materiality is none other than the three constituents, and so there is no transformation from one order to a different order in the case of primordial materiality.

Neither can we regard primordial materiality as noneternal on the ground that the state of equilibrium is destroyed at the time of creation. At that time, primordial materiality is merged in the constituents, and the disappearance of the equilibrium in the constituents does not mean the origination of a different entity.

(E296) Primordial materiality possesses the tendency of acting in two different ways. One kind of activity results in creation and another in dissolution. At the time of creation, the three constituents act in unison (some becoming primary and some remaining in a subdued condition).

(E302) That which is active becomes a cause. An inactive principle like consciousness cannot serve as a cause.

(17-19) (E312) Scripture has declared that consciousness is nonattached. That which is nonattached cannot become an enjoyer.

Others, however, interpret the word "*bhoktṛbhāva*" (the characteristic of being an enjoyer) in the sense of *draṣṭṛbhāva* (the characteristic of being a seer). The enjoyer is the seer, and the seer is to be inferred from the object of sight. The intellect and the rest, being objects of sight, lead to the supposition of a seer. The nonattached consciousness, however, cannot be a seer in the true sense. Its visibility is to be understood only by admitting the intellect as its limiting adjunct. The characteristic of being a seer and an enjoyer is ascribable to consciousness only when it is conditioned by the intellect.

(E314) According to Vedānta, the self is one, eternal, all-pervading, immutable, and devoid of all defects. One reality appears as many due to the power of the principle of illusion (*māyā*), and not by its own inherent nature.

(E317-318) The adjustment of birth, etc., cannot be explained by attributing it to a single self as differently conditioned by contact with different bodies, etc., because this will create another difficulty of admitting birth, etc., of the soul in connection with hands and other limbs as well. Further, *ākāśa* limited by a particular jar may become liberated if the jar is destroyed; but it can be associated with a different jar, thereby becoming conditioned again. Similarly, the single self, being dissociated from one limiting adjunct, may be conditioned by another. Because of this conditioning, embodiment and liberation cannot be properly explained.

(20-23) (E326-336) It has already been established that consciousness and activity are differently located. So, the feeling that I am doing this as a consciousness principle is wrong. In other words, the feeling that consciousness and activity belong to one and the same locus is wrong. The seed of this illusory feeling is association. The apparent activity of the self is due to its being in (seeming) union with the intellect and the apparent conscious nature of the intellect is due to its being intelligized by the self through association.

Why should the consciousness principle depend on primordial materiality? Without primordial materiality, discriminative discernment is not possible. It is the primary cause that changes into the form of the intelleet and the discriminative knowledge is produced by the intellect. Because the yogic discipline is practiced disinterestedly, it is not to be reckoned as a form of white action. Again being devoid of an external and (to be achieved by external means) yogic discipline, aiming simply at a steady and waveless awareness, does not assume the form of black action, either. Hence this discipline and the excellences arising therefrom are neither black nor white.

IX. Thirteenfold instrument

(30-37) (E365-366) According to the thinkers of the Sāṃkhya school, the functions of awareness are both simultaneous and gradual in the case of perception. Perception, however, is not possible unless there is the operation of an external sense capacity along with the three internal organs.

According to Nyāya-Vaiśeṣika, the mind is one and atomic and so it cannot supervise simultaneously the different sense capacities located in different places. Just as a piece of iron, if moved rapidly, does not produce an awareness of succession even though succession is present, in the same manner, because of the quick succession of different bits of knowledge, gradualness is not felt. Hence in the opinion of the Nyāya-Vaiśeṣika, the feeling of simultaneity is illusory. This is not the view of the Sāṃkhya school. According to this school, the mind, being middle-sized, can supervise the actions of many sense capacities simultaneously. In the case of indirect knowledge such as inference, etc., the external sense capacities do not operate.

(E375) The statement that the internal organs act at all the three points of time should not be wrongly interpreted to mean that Sāṁkhya admits time as a distinct principle in addition to twenty-five principles (already admitted by them). According to Vaiśeṣika, time is one, indivisible and eternal. The expression "time that is yet to be" cannot be applied to one eternal time. Neither can the Vaiśeṣikas hold that although time is one, divisions as past, present, and future can be attributed to the limiting adjuncts of time because the Sāṃkhyans believe that the limiting adjuncts themselves form the basis of the three divisions of time. The activities (like the solar activity, etc.) themselves are to be regarded as time. There is no need for imagining a separate principle in the form of time.

(E 384) The various experiences of consciousness in the forms of sound and the rest are brought about by the intellect. The intellect also produces the apprehension of the subtle difference between materiality and consciousness.

XI. Subtle body

(40-42) (E393) The word "*liṅga*" here stands for the subtle body, In the very beginning of transformation, primordial materiality produced one subtle body for each consciousness. The subtle body cannot be obstructed, and so it can enter even a solid piece of stone. It continues to exist until the time of the final dissolution. It is a collection of eighteen principles. The subtle body is incapable of experiencing objects without the help of the gross body. The comfortable, uncomfortable, and confusing nature of the sense capacities can be experienced even by ordinary persons, and so these are specific.

(E395) The subtle body, being composed of capacities that are specific, should be regarded as specific. Again, the five subtle elements are nonspecific and being composed of them, the subtle body should become nonspecific. The subtle body is, however, regarded as specific because the number of specific principles of which it is composed is larger than the number of its nonspecific ingredients.

(E397) One may pose a question: Why should not the subtle body, like primordial materiality, continue to exist even after the final dissolution ? The subtle body, being a product, cannot be permanent (like primordial materiality). That which is caused is sure to be merged into its own cause. On the basis of this universal principle, all effects of primordial materiality should be supposed to lose their identity (either directly or indirectly) in that materiality. Hence, the subtle body too is lost in its cause in final dissolution.

(E398-399) The word "*liṅga*" stands for the intellect and the rest because they are the instruments of knowing primordial materiality. During the period intervening between death and rebirth, the intellect and the rest must have a support until they are associated with a gross body.

To prove the existence of the subtle body, we can refer to the scriptural text that speaks of a thumb-sized body that was extracted from the body of Satyavat (by Yama). Consciousness is not limited by space and time and so it does not have any prior entrance into the body or any posterior extraction. Hence it is the subtle body that performs the activities of going up or going out.

The subtle body transmigrates in order to serve the purposes of consciousness. It becomes connected with causes in the form of virtue, vice, etc. Being associated with the gross body, it again becomes interested in meritorious and demeritorious actions. The transmigration of the subtle body does not stop because of nondiscrimination. The *Purāṇas* and *Itihāsas*, however, speak of persons who have appeared in gross bodies even after attenuation of their actions by means of true knowledge because of divine will.

XII. Basic Predispositions

(43-52) (E410) The dispassion that is coupled with knowledge does not lead to mergence into materiality, but mere dispassion unaccompanied by a quest for the knowledge of consciousness becomes the cause of such mergence. The word "*mātra*" ("mere") in "*vairāgyamātra*") ("mere dispassion") excludes the quest for the knowledge of the consciousness.

(E416-418) The Yoga philosophy speaks of five afflictions, which are ignorance, ego sense, attachment, hatred, and fear of death: these are the five limbs of misconception.

XIV. Similes for Materiality

(57-62) (E463) Those things that are insentient and that are not actively controlled by consciousness cannot act for the benefit of others. On the basis of this universal principle, primordial materiality should be regarded as being actively controlled by consciousness because it acts for the benefit of another.

(E473) *Puruṣa* is mere consciousness : it is immutable and ever free. Enjoyment in the form of going through worldly satisfactions and frustrations belongs to the mutable intellect. Because the transformations of the intellect are reflected in consciousness, the latter seems to be one with the intellect and its enjoyment is nothing but apprehension of this nondiscrimination. Therefore, the characteristic of being the enjoyer is attributed to consciousness through nondiscrimination. Consciousness in its true nature is subject neither to embodiment nor to liberation.

XV. Liberation

(62-69) (E479) If the practice of knowledge is not done with meditation, then even if it is carried on for a long period of time, it will not bear fruits. Further, if practice of knowledge is done for a short while only, then also it will not bear fruit. In the course of practice, knowledge of the distinction between the intellect and consciousness does not arise directly. It arises because of meditation in the form of constant thinking of the distinction between the intellect and consciousness as taught by the preceptor, and such uninterrupted and constant thinking produces a direct awareness of the distinction between the intellect and consciousness.

(E480) According to another view, the term "absence of error" does not remove doubt and how can doubtful knowledge be pure? So it is said that steadiness is the sign of truth and that there is no scope for doubt in steadiness. Doubt arises whenever a steady object is apprehended in an indefinite and unsteady manner. That also is a form of erroneous knowledge in which an object is apprehended in a form that it does not possess.

(pp. 484-486): "I am not" (*nāsmi*) denies any action on the part of consciousness. It is equivalent to "I am not active." Because consciousness is not active, it is also devoid of the characteristics of being an agent. "Nothing is mine" means that consciousness does not own anything. As it is not an agent, it is also not an owner. Awareness in the form of "it is mine" causes embodiment, whereas awareness in the form of "it is not mine" liberates. "Not I" shows that even such expressions as "I know" etc., are not to be used in relation to consciousness.

When pure knowledge is directly apprehended, materiality ceases to be productive (in relation to the liberated consciousness) and turns back from the seven forms of transformation.

NARAHARINĀTHA

Naraharinātha's *Sāṃkhyavasanta* was published by the Yogapracāriṇī Sabhā in 1950, and it was composed, according to the last verse in the text, in 1946. The author appears to be a follower of the Nātha school of Yoga. He was a disciple of Kṣipranātha (according to verse 74). The work is nothing but a version in the *vasantatilaka* meter of the *Sāṃkhyakārikā*. The text has six benedictory verses, and thereafter each verse of the *Sāṃkhyakārikā* is restated in a separate verse. Interestingly, Naraharinātha includes in his rendering of the text the so-called missing *kārikā* suggested by B. G. Tilak (reconstructed from verse 61 of the Gauḍapāda *Bhāṣya* [see above under Īśvarakṛṣṇa]).

SĪTĀRĀMA ŚĀSTRĪ

The text called *Abhinavarājalakṣmī* purports to be a commentary on the *Sāṃkhyakārikā* but is really an expanded paraphrase of Vācaspati Miśra's *Tattvakaumudī*. The work was first written by Guruprasāda Śāstri and then revised for publication by Sītārāma Śāstrī. The text was published in Varanasi in 1953 along with a Hindi commentary called *Bhāṣāṭikā*. The work is only a paraphrase of Vācaspati.

BRAHMAMUNI

The text called *Sāṃkhyasūtrabhāṣya*, published by Brahmamuni himself in 1955 from the Vedānusandhānasādhana, Haridvāra, is little more than a restatement of the view of Aniruddha and Vijñānabhikṣu on the *Sāṃkhyasūtra*. The author is evidently a follower of Swami Dayānanda Sarasvatī.

KEŚAVA

KṚṢṆA MIŚRA

SĀṂKHYAPARIBHĀṢĀ

These short independent works are included in the collection *Sāṃkhyasaṅgraha*, Varanasi : Chowkhamba Sanskrit Series Office, 1969, on pages 90-95, 114-124, 125-144 respectively. Although the authors' names are known for the first two, nothing more can be said about them. Nothing at all is known about the date or authorship of the *Sāṃkhyaparibhāṣā*.

The *Sāṃkhyatattvapradīpikā* of Keśava is a simple summary presentation of the Sāṃkhya system along the lines of Vijñānabhikṣu.

The *Tattvamīmāṃsā* of Kṛṣṇa Miśra provides a short resumé of the *Saṃkhyakārikā*. It stresses that everyone naturally searches for satisfaction, and in order to find satisfaction, one must remove the cause of frustration. The text also suggests that *prakṛti* is really the same as *māyā* or *avidyā* in other systems, the author thereby betraying his Vedānta bias.

The *Sāṃkhyaparibhāṣā* may not be a Sāṃkhya work at all. The word "*sāṁkhya*" in the title seems to be used in the general sense of knowledge and not in the sense of the Sāṃkhya system. The editor of the text, V. P. Dvivedi, indicates that the work appears to be incomplete and full of mistakes. Generally speaking, the text is a collection of quotations from the Upaniṣads and the *Gītā* and has a clear Advaitin bias.

M. V. UPĀDHYĀYA

The *Sāṃkhyasiddhāntaparāmarśa* is a booklet containing 253 verses in Āryā meter with occasional notes by its author, M. V. Upādhyāya. Upādhyāya has also composed a commentary in verse on the *Brahmasūtra*, arguing that Sāṃkhya is in full harmony with the Vedas. The text was published in 1972 by the Superintendent, Avadhūta-vidvanmaṇḍala, Baroda.

ŚRĪ RĀMA PĀṆḌEYA

The author is currently professor of Sanskrit at Sampūrṇānanda Sanskrit University, Varanasi. His text, *Sāṃkhyarahasya*, was published in Varanasi in 1966. It contains 102 verses interspersed with an autocommentary (*svopajña*) entitled "*Prakāsa*." The text follows the order of the *Sāṃkhyakārikā* and on all important points follows the interpretation of Vācaspati Miśra's *Tattvakaumudī*.

NOTES

(References given with "B" followed by a number are to Volume I of the *Encyclopedia*, the *Bibliography of Indian Philosophies* 1st. Ed. (Delhi: Motilal Banarsidass, 1970). References beginning "RB" are to the second revised edition of the *Bibliography*, (Delhi: Motilal Banarsidass, 1983). Complete citations are provided with the first reference to a publication. "B" and "RB" citations appear thereafter.) All notes not otherwise attributed are by G.J. Larson.

The History and Literature of Sāṃkhya

1. For a detailed discussion of, and bibliography for, early Sāṃkhya references and for a full treatment of the history of the secondary literature on Sāṃkhya, see Gerald J. Larson (RB1378), *Classical Sāṃkhya: An Interpretation of Its History and Meaning*, 2nd ed. rev. (Delhi: Motilal Banarsidass, 1979).

2. "*. . . sāṃkhyaṃ yogo lokāyataṃ ca iti ānvīkṣikī. . . .*" *Arthaśāstra* I.2., pp.16ff. in N.S. Venkatanathacharya, ed., *Kauṭalīyārthaśāstra of Śrī Viṣṇugupta*, Oriental Research Institute, Sanskrit Series 103 (Mysore: Oriental Research Institute, 1960).

3. "*. . . hetubhir ānvīkṣamāna. . .* ," ibid. Compare also the discussion by Paul Hacker (B8877; BR12428) "Ānvīkṣikī," *Wiener Zeitschrift für die Kunde Süd- und Ostasiens* 2 (1958): 54-83.

4. Paul Hacker, B8877; RB12428, 54-83; and Erich Frauwallner (B6431A; RB9627), "Die Erkenntnislehre des Klassischen Sāṃkhya-Systems," *Wiener Zeitschrift für die Kunde Süd- und Ostasiens* 2 (1958): 84-139.

5. For a recent discussion of *tantrayuktis*, see W.K. Lele, *The Doctrine of the Tantrayuktis* (Varanasi: Chaukhamba Surabharati Prakashan, 1981).

6. Richard Garbe (B6227; RB9527), *Die Sāṃkhya Philosophie* (Leipzig: H. Haessel 1917), 5ff.

7. Franklin Edgerton, "The Meaning of *Sāṃkhya* and *Yoga*," *American Journal of Philology* 45, 50, No. 177 (1924): 16.

8. Ibid., 32.

9. *Mahābhārata* (Critical Edition) XII.239, XII.267.28.

10. *Mahābhārata* XII.267.30.

11. *Mahābhārata* XII.306.

12. *Mahābhārata* XII.298.

13. J.A.B. Van Buitenen (B6423; RB9620), "Studies in Sāṃkhya (II)," *Journal of the American Oriental Society* 77 (1957): 101-102.

14. For a discussion of the fragments of Pañcaśikha, see Larson, RB1378, 139-140, and R. Garbe (B278; BR536), "Pañcaśikha Fragmente", *Festgruss an Rudolph von Roth* (edited by E.W.A. Kuhn, Stuttgart, 1893), 77-80.

15. Richard Garbe, B6227; RB9527, 52-65; and Hermann Oldenberg (B6275; RB9540), "Zur Geschichte der Sāṃkhya Philosophie," *Nachrichten von der königlichen*

Gesellschaft der Wissenschaften zu Göttingen, Philologische-historische Klasse aus dem Jahre 1917 (Berlin: Weidmannsche Buchhandlung, 1918), 218-253.

16. Larson RB1378, 122-124.

17. Edgerton, "The Meaning of Sāṃkhya and Yoga," 34.

18. P. Chakravarti, ed. (B1046A; RB2207), *Yuktidīpikā*, Calcutta Sanskrit Series 23, (Calcutta: Metropolitan Printing and Publishing House, 1938); R.C. Pandeya, ed. (RB1370), *Yuktidīpikā* (Delhi: Motilal Banarsidass, 1967); Albrecht Wezler (RB2213), "Some Observations on the Yuktidīpikā," *Deutscher Orientalistentag* (*Wiesbaden*), Supplement II.XVIII (1974), 434-455; P. Chakravarti (B6381; RB9596), *Origin and Development of the Sāṃkhya System of Thought* (Calcutta: Metropolitan Printing and Publishing House, 1951).

19. Erich Frauwallner, B6431A; RB9627, 84-139.

20. Paul Hacker (B6456; RB9646), "The Sāṃkhyization of the Emanation Doctrine shown in a Critical Analysis of Texts," *Wiener Zeitschrift für die Kunde Süd- und Ostasiens* 5 (1961): 75-112.

21. According to Chakravarti, the correct name of the Sāṃkhya teacher is "Vārṣagaṇya" (meaning a descendent of Vṛṣagaṇa). Moreover, such a name formulation usually indicates a later descendent beginning with the grandson. According to Frauwallner the correct name of the Sāṃkhya teacher is "Vṛṣagaṇa" and the name "Vārṣagaṇya" refers to the followers of Vṛṣagaṇa. It would appear, however, that Chakravarti is correct, for in the *Yuktidīpikā* the "followers of Vārṣagaṇya" are referred to as "*vārṣagaṇāḥ*." In other words, the Sāṃkhya teacher was known as "Vārṣagaṇya, the grandson or later descendent of Vṛṣagaṇa" (who presumably was *not* a Sāṃkhya teacher), and his followers (including probably Vindhyavāsin, Īśvarakṛṣṇa and others) were called "*vārṣagaṇāḥ*."

22. Frauwallner B6431A; RB9627, 84-139.

23. Hacker B6456; RB9646, 75-112.

24. For a full discussion of the variant accounts of the debate see Larson RB1378, 141ff.

25. Masaaki Hattori, trans. (RB1791), *Dignāga, On Perception*. Harvard Oriental Series 47 (Cambridge: Harvard University Press, 1968). For a good discussion of the other references to Mādhava see Esther A. Solomon (RB1387), *The Commentaries of the Sāṃkhya Kārikā* (Ahmedabad: Gujarat University, 1974), 153-163.

26. Erich Frauwallner (B8590; RB12160), *Geschichte der indischen Philosophie*, (Salzburg: Otto Müller Verlag, 1953), Vol. 1, 408ff, and Chakravarti B6381; B9596, 138ff.

27. A never ending problem in Sāṃkhya studies has to do with the content and authorship of the so-called *ṣaṣṭitantra*, "Sixty Topics." In my book *Classical Sāṃkhya* (RB1378), 135-138, I summarized the range of the debate and assumed a skeptical posture regarding both content and authorship. I now think, however, that more can be said. The evidence in the Sāṃkhya philosophical literature proper is overwhelming in terms of the content of *ṣaṣṭitantra*, namely, the ten *mūlikārthas* ("principal topics") and fifty *padārthas* ("categories"). The enumeration of ten plus fifty is implied in the *Kārikā* itself and is explicitly spelled out in Paramārtha, the *Sāṃkhyavṛtti*, *Sāṃkhyasaptativṛtti*, *Jayamaṅgalā*, *Yuktidīpikā*, *Tattvakaumudī*, and *Māṭharavṛtti*. It appears, furthermore, in the *Tattvasamāsa* and its commentaries, and in the *Sāṃkhyasūtra* and its commentaries. There can be little doubt, therefore, of the content of *ṣaṣṭitantra* in the extant Sāṃkhya philosophical literature. There are some variant items in the various listings (as E.A. Solomon has helpfully summarized in RB1387, 182-185), but that the "sixty topics" are the ten *mūlikārthas* and the fifty *padārthas* is firmly fixed in the tradition. F.O. Schrader's variant listing of *ṣaṣṭitantra* from the Pāñcarātra (*Ahirbudhnyasaṃhitā*) can only be construed as an eccentric, non-Sāṃkhya fluke, a classic example of an exception proving the rule!

Regarding authorship of the *ṣaṣṭitantra*, three names appear repeatedly, Kapila, Pañcaśikha, and Vārṣagaṇya. According to the *Yuktidīpikā*, Kapila revealed the *ṣaṣṭitantra*. Moreover, Bhāskara in his commentary on *Brahmasūtra* II.1.1 ascribes authorship to Kapila. But Kapila's authorship can hardly be taken seriously except to say that there may have been a format for discussing old Sāṃkhya ideas that centered on "sixty topics," and that this format may have been attribute to the founder of the system. There is some support for the authorship of Pañcaśikha, for both Paramārtha and *Jayamaṅgalā* refer to him as author. There is also support for Vārṣagaṇya, with references by Vācaspati Miśra seeming to imply that Vārṣagaṇya was the author of *ṣaṣṭitantra*. Chakravarti and Frauwallner solve the problem of multiple authorship by suggesting that there was an old *ṣaṣṭitantra* that underwent several revisions. For further discussion see Larson RB1378, 135-138, and Chakravarti B6381; RB9596, 116-127. My own suspicion is that in the ancient period "*ṣaṣṭitantra*" may not have referred primarily to a literary work but may rather have been an old proper name for the Sāṃkhya system itself, that is the *tantra* of "sixty" (*ṣaṣṭi*) enumerations. If such were the case, then there could have developed various ways for arranging the enumerated contents. Moreover, a number of works could eventually have been composed having to do with *ṣaṣṭitantra* or, in other words, the Sāṃkhya *śāstra* (that of Pañcaśikha, Vārṣagaṇya, and so forth), one important summary of which has come down to us as Īśvarakṛṣṇa's *Sāṃkhyakārikā*.

28. An issue that deserves some mention but has only been obliquely treated thus far is the relation between early Sāṃkhya philosophy and Buddhist thought. Richard Garbe was the first to emphasize affinities between Sāṃkhya and Buddhism (in B6227; RB9527, 3-5), and in his edition and translation of *Sāṃkhyasūtravṛtti* (B3574; RB5524) (Calcutta: J.W. Thomas, 1888), v-xiv. H. Oldenberg, (B6275; RB9540, 240-245), disagreed with Garbe and argued, instead, that Sāṃkhya arose directly out of the old Upaniṣads and is more dissimilar than similar to Buddhist thought. H. Jacobi compared the twelvefold chain of dependent origination with the Sāṃkhya theory of *guṇas* in his article (B5452; RB8317) "Über das Verhältnis der buddhistischen Philosophie zu Sāṃkhya-Yoga und die Bedeutung der Nidānas," *Zeitschrift der Deutschen Morgenländischen Gesellschaft* 10.2 (Leipzig, 1898), 1-15; and Th. Stcherbatsky offered an interesting comparison between "The '*dharmas*' of the Buddhists and the '*guṇas*' of the Sāṃkhyas" (B5039; RB7950), *Indian Historical Quarterly* (Calcutta, 1934): 737-760. More recently Alex Wayman has returned to these old debates in his (RB1218) "Buddhist dependent origination and the Sāṃkhya *guṇas*," *Ethnos* 1962, 14-22. A useful discussion of other secondary literature on the issue may be found in M. Eliade (B6395; RB9805), *Yoga, Immortality and Freedom* (London, 1958), 377-381. Erich Frauwallner follows Oldenberg's approach to the problem both in his older essay (B6293; RB9549) "Untersuchungen zum Mokṣadharma, III: Das Verhältnis zum Buddhismus", *Wiener Zeitschrift für die Kunde des Morgenlandes* 33 (1926): 57-68, and more recently in B8590; RB12160, Vol. I, 477.

My own view is that the Oldenberg/Frauwallner readings of the ancient literature are undoubtedly correct, namely, that Sāṃkhya and Buddhist thought have some general affinities insofar as they emerge from the common intellectual heritage of post-Upaniṣadic thought but that they are really much more dissimilar than similar on a deeper level. Regarding ontology, epistemology, psychology, theory of causation, and theory of consciousness, the two traditions are notably divergent. There are some similarities in the areas of theory of values and yogic *praxis*, but such similarities likewise abound in almost all ancient Indian speculative traditions. The truly interesting point of contact between Sāṃkhya and Buddhism is not regarding origins but relates, rather, to the polemical debates occurring between the two traditions in the early centuries of the Common Era, long after each had reached maturity and had numerous subvarieties. Moreover, what is remarkable are the striking *differences* between the two styles of philosophizing—Sāṃkhya with its bold, constructive and speculative system-building in contrast with the Buddhist fear of systematic thought and its predilection for critical, dialectical, and skeptical debunking.

29. For a useful summary of the varying views regarding the date of Vācaspati Miśra, see Karl H. Potter, ed. (RB9446), *Nyāya-Vaiśeṣika up to Gaṅgeśa: Encyclopedia of Indian Philosophies*, Vol. 2 (Delhi: Motilal Banarsidass, 1977; Princeton University Press, 1978), 453-455.

30. S.K. Belvalkar (B1285; RB2153A), "Māṭharavṛtti and the date of Īśvarakṛṣṇa," *Bhandarkar Commemorative Essays* (Poona, 1917), 171-184.

31. A.B. Keith (B1286; RB2153B), "The Māṭharavṛtti," *Bulletin of the School of Oriental Studies* 3.3 (1924): 551-554; S.S. Suryanarayana Sastri (B1289), "Māṭhara and Paramārtha," *Journal of the Royal Asiatic Society*, 1931, 623-639; Umesh Mishra (B1288; RB2153D), "Gauḍapādabhāṣya and Maṭharavṛtti", Allahabad University Series 7 (1931): 371-386.

32. E.A. Solomon, ed. (RB1585), *Sāṃkhyasaptativṛtti* (Ahmedabad: Gujarat University, 1973); E.A. Solomon, ed. (RB1818), *Sāṃkhyavṛtti* (Ahmedabad: Gujarat University, 1973); and Solomon RB1387.

33. Solomon RB1387.

34. Chakravarti B6381; RB9596, 164-168.

35. M.R. Kavi (B2541; RB3823), "Literary gleanings—Jayamaṅgalā," *Quarterly* Journal of the Andhra Historical Research Society, 1927, 133-136, cited in Chakravarti B6381; RB9596, 165.

36. Trevor Leggett in the "Technical Introduction" to his useful translations of the first two parts of the *Yogasūtrabhāṣyavivaraṇa*, entitled *Śaṅkara on the Yogasūtras* (*vol.* 1: *Samādhi pāda*) (*vol.* 2: *Sādhana-pāda*): *The Vivaraṇa Subcommentary to Vyāsabhāṣya on the Yogasūtras of Patañjali* (London: Routledge and Kegan Paul, 1981 and 1983), xviii-xix (vol. 1), cites P. Hacker, H. Nakamura, and S. Mayeda as generally supporting the view that the *Vivaraṇa* is a genuine work of Śaṃkara. Leggett himself also subscribes to the text's authenticity, although he admits that the matter is still open. The arguments for the text's authenticity include (a) the use of technical terms (for example, *adhyāsa, adhyāropa, parivijṛmbhita*, and so forth), (b) overall stylistic tendencies, and (c) ideological content. Regarding technical terminology a plausible case appears to ha· ɜ been made. The same cannot be said, however, regarding matters of style and ideology. On the face of it, the Sanskrit style of the *Vivaraṇa* is dramatically different from the other so-called "authentic" works of Śaṃkara. The matter of ideology is even murkier. Not only is Śaṃkara's own position in the so-called "authentic" works unclear, but more than that the tenets of Yoga Philosophy in these early centuries is far from adequately understood. At the present moment there is nothing in the evidence that would prevent one from arguing that the author of the *Vivaraṇa* was one of Śaṃkara's later followers. In other words, the text may be much later than the time of Śaṃkara. Gopinath Kaviraj has suggestively argued, for example, that the *Vivaraṇa* is a fourteenth-century work by a certain Śankarārya (in "Literary Gleanings, Jayamaṅgalā," Quarterly Journal of the Andhra Historical Research Society (Oct. 1927): 133-136). It should be noted, finally, that Albrecht Wezler of Hamburg, Germany, is currently working on a critical edition of the text. When completed, there will be much additional information upon which to base a discussion of the text's authenticity.

Regarding the current discussion, in addition to Leggett's discussion already mentioned, see also Paul Hacker (RB3313), "Śaṅkara der Yogin und Śaṅkara der Advaitin: Einige Beobachtungen," *Wiener Zeitschrift für die Kunde Süd- und Ostasiens* 12-13 (1968-69): 120-148; Hajime Nakamura, three articles in Japanese in *Indogaku Bukkyogaku Kenkyu* for 1972; and Sengaku Mayeda, "Śaṃkara" in *Encyclopedia Britannica*, 15th ed. vol. 16 (Macropaedia), pp. 222-223.

37. For discussions of the dating of the Yoga literature see the following: J. H. Woods, trans., (B340; RB1121), *The Yoga-System of Patañjali*, Harvard Oriental Series 17 (Cambridge: Harvard University Press, 1914), xvii-xxiii; Frauwallner B8590; RB12160, vol. 1 408ff. and 482ff.; and Eliade B6345; RB9805, 370-372.

38. Vyāsa in *Yogasūtrabhāṣya* III.13 illustrates the three modalities in the following manner: a lump of clay is made into a water jar, thus undergoing a change in "external property" (*dharma*); while in its present condition as water jar, it is able to hold water (its *lakṣaṇa*); finally, the jar gradually becomes "old," thus undergoing "stages of development" (*avasthā*).

39. For discussions of early Vedānta up through Śaṃkara see the following: S. L. Pandey, *Pre-Śaṃkara Advaita Philosophy* (Allahabad: Darshan Peeth, 1974); E. Deutsch and J. A. B. Van Buitenen, *A Source Book of Advaita Vedānta* (Honolulu: The University of Hawaii Press, 1971); and Karl H. Potter, ed., *Advaita Vedānta up to Śaṃkara and His Pupils: Encyclopedia of Indian Philosophies*, Vol. 3 Delhi: Motilal Banarsidass and (Princeton: Princeton University Press, 1981.

40. For a detailed discussion of the difference between Śaṃkara and Sāṃkhya, see the new epilogue to the second edition of Larson RB1378, 209-235. It should be noted, moreover, that there is some evidence that Śaṃkara himself may have originally been a follower of Yoga philosophy. See the interesting discussion of Paul Hacker in RB3313, 120-148. For the relation of this issue to the matter of Śaṃkara's authorship of the *Vivaraṇa* see note 36 above.

41. George Thibaut, trans. (B1610; RB243), *The Vedānta Sūtras of Bādarāyaṇa with the Commentary by Śaṃkara*, Sacred Books of the East (New York: Dover, 1962), vol. 34, 289.

42. Even the expression "cryptic little text" is an exaggeration. The *Tattvasamāsa* is not a philosophical text in any sense. It is only a "checklist" of Sāṃkhya enumerations.

43. F. Max Müller (B7625; RB1286), *The Six Systems of Indian Philosophy* (London: Longmans, Green, 1919); Frauwallner, B8590; RB12160, vol. 1 251ff.

44. For useful treatments of Vijñānabhikṣu's views see the following: S. N. Dasgupta (B7653; RB11305), *A History of Indian Philosophy* (Cambridge: Cambridge University Press, 1922; Delhi: Motilal Banarsidass, 1975), vol. 3, 445-495; and T. S. Rukmani, trans., *Yogavārttika of Vijñānabhikṣu*, vol.1 (Delhi: Munshiram Manoharlal, 1981).

The Philosophy of Sāṃkhya

1. K. C. Bhattacharya, *Studies in Philosophy*, edited by Gopinath Bhattacharya (Calcutta: Progressive Publishers, 1956), vol. 1, 127.

2. Garbe B6227; RB9527, passim; Dasgupta B7653; RB11305, vol. 1, 208-273; Frauwallner B8590;; RB12160, vol. 1, 275-450; and K. C. Bhattacharya, "Studies in Sāṃkhya Philosophy" in *Studies in Philosophy*, vol. 1, 127-211.

3. Garbe B6227; RB9527, iv.

4. Dasgupta B7653; RB11305, vol. 1, 221 and 223.

5. Frauwallner B8590; RB12160, vol. I, 298ff. Cf. also Frauwallner B6431A; RB9627, 84-137 and especially 130-137.

6. K. C. Bhattacharya, *Studies in Philosophy*, vol. 1, 127.

7. For Wittgenstein's own laconic discussion of a "complete system of human communication," "form of life," or "language game," see L. Wittgenstein, *The Blue and Brown Books* (New York: Harper Colophon Books, 1965), 165 ff. For a useful interpretive expansion of Wittgenstein's insights see Norman Malcolm, *Thought and Knowledge* (Ithaca, New York: Cornell University Press, 1977), 191-216.

8. The ancient texts are unanimous in considering Kapila as the first teacher or "founder" of the Sāṃkhya tradition, and Kapila is referred to variously as the "supreme seer" (*paramarṣi*) (*Yuktidīpikā, maṅgala*, vs. 2), the "great seer" (*maharṣi*) (*Māṭharavṛtti* on SK 1), the "primal knower" (*ādividvān*) (*Yogasūtra* (YS) I.25), the "son of Brahmā" (*brahmasuta*) (*Gauḍapādabhāṣya* on SK 1) and an "incarnation of Viṣṇu"

(*viṣṇor avatāraviśeṣaḥ*, *Tattvavaiśāradī* on Y.S I.25). In epic and Purāṇic texts his name is directly linked with Agni, Sūrya, Śiva, Nārāyaṇa, Svāyambhuva, and Hiraṇyagarbha. He is a "mind-born" (*mānasaputra*) "son of Brahmā," who appears at the beginning of each cycle of creation perfectly equipped from the moment of birth with the fundamental predispositions of knowledge (*jñāna*), merit (*dharma*), nonattachment (*vairāgya*), and power (*aiśvarya*), and capable of assuming an appropriate apparitional form (*nirmāṇacitta*, YS I.25) so that he can transmit his knowledge of Sāṃkhya to Āsuri and thereby initiate the *guruparamparā* in each cycle of manifestation. Vācaspati Miśra in the *Tattvavaiśāradī* goes so far as to call Kapila "God of all the descendents of Svayambhū" (*svayambhuvānām... Īśvara iti bhāvaḥ*, on YS I.25). For an interesting (discussion of Kapila as the "God of Sāṃkhya," see Albrect Wezler's intriguing article (RB3984), "Der Gott des Sāṃkhya: Zu *Nyāyakusumāñjali* 1.3", *Indo-Iranian Journal*, 12 no. 4 (1970): 255-262.

9. Throughout this section on "Sāṃkhya as Enumeration," the various Sāṃkhya components are being set forth as quantifiable "sets" with little or no attention to the philosophical issues involved. Detailed discussions of the philosophical meaning of the "sets" are to be found in the sequel, namely, in the sections entitled "Sāṃkhya as Process Materialism," "Sāṃkhya as Contentless Consciousness," and "Sāṃkhya as Rational Reflection."

10. See for example, K. C. Bhattacharya's discussion of the *tanmātras* and *mahābhūtas* in *Studies in Philosophy*. vol. 1, 176-177. Compare also Richard Robinson's discussion of "universals and particulars" (and the predilection of Indian philosophies not to be concerned about such matters) in his "Classical Indian Philosophy" in J. W. Elder, ed., *Chapters in Indian Civilization*, vol. 1 (Dubuque, Iowa: Kendall/Hunt, 1970), 189-191.

11. For a useful discussion of the Sāṃkhya emanation scheme vis-à-vis the Upaniṣadic, early Buddhist, Vaiśeṣika, and later Sarvāstivāda Buddhist emanation schemes, see Richard Robinson, "Classical Indian Philosophy," 161-177. Robinson provides a series of comparative charts that reveal at a glance how the various emanation schemes relate to one another.

12. S. S. Suryanarayana Sastri, trans. (B742; RB1322) *The Sāṅkhyakārikā of Īśvara Kṛṣṇa* (Madras: University of Madras, 1948), xxvi-xxviii, presents three comparative charts of Sāṃkhya emanation schemes: (a) that of the *Sāṃkhyakārikā* itself; (b) that of the Chinese commentary on the *Kārikā*, translated by Paramārtha; and (c) that of the Śaiva Siddhānta. Robinson, "Classical Indian Philosophy," p. 174, also provides a chart of the emanation scheme in the Chinese commentary of Paramārtha.

13. These East Asian (Chinese) variants may be found in Taisho 25, 546c 17-29 (Ta-chih-tu-lun) and Taisho 30, 170c 13 (Pai-lun), both of which are charted and discussed in Robinson, "Classical Indian Philosophy," 171-174. Robinson became aware of these variants from the following: Ryusho Hikata, *Suvikrāntavikrāmiparipṛcchā Prajñāpāramitāsūtra* (Fukooka, Japan: published by the Committee of Commemoration Program for Dr. Hikata, 1958), lxv.

14. As the chart indicates, Sāṃkhya philosophy appears to intend that the various pentadic sequences correlate, recapitulate, or are cognate with one another, so that, for example, hearing correlates with speaking, sound, and space, or again, touching correlates with grasping, touch, and wind, and so forth. A possible problem arises, however, regarding the last two components of the *karmendriya* series, namely, excreting and procreating. It is not immediately apparent how excreting correlates with tasting, taste, and water, and how procreating correlates with smelling, smell, and earth. One possible solution is to suggest that excreting is linked with taste and water in the sense that the motor capacity of excreting has to do with the digestion and assimilation of food, and that procreating is linked with smell and earth in the sense that the motor capacity of sexual functioning has to do with characteristic animal sexual odors that generate mutual attraction. Moreover, for complete reproduction it is perhaps reason-

able to assume that the process would encompass all five *mahābhūtas*, thereby necessitating linkage of procreating with the earth element. Another, perhaps somewhat better solution, is to reverse the order of the last two *karmendriyas*, so that the sequence is speaking, grasping, walking, procreating, and excreting. The motor capacity of sexual functioning then correlates with taste and water in the sense of the ejaculation of semen, menstrual periods, and so forth. The motor capacity of excretion then correlates with the expulsion of material waste from the body. This latter solution is preferable mainly because there is textual evidence for it. In *Manusmṛti* 2.90, *Ahirbudhnyasaṃhitā* 7, *Matsyapurāṇa* III.20, and *Aśvamedhaparvan* 21.2 of the *Mahābhārata*, such a reversal of the last two components of the series is specifically mentioned. The *Matsyapurāṇa* sequence, for example, is *ālāpa*, *ādāna*, *gati*, *ānanda*, and *utsarga*. In the epic passage the sequence is *vākya*, *kriyā*, *gati*, *retas* and *utsarga*. The only problem with this latter solution is that it violates the order of the *indriyas* as set forth in *Kārikās* 26 and 28. This is not a crucial problem, however, for the order set forth in the *Kārikās* itself appears to reflect the dictates of the *ārya* meter more than it does a specific philosophical meaning. The same is true for the sequence of the sense capacities in *Kārikās* 26 and 28. Gauḍapāda, for example, reads *Kārikā* 26 as giving the sequence seeing, hearing smelling, tasting, and touching, as does Vācaspati Miśra. The *Māṭharavṛtti* and *Yuktidīpika*, however, read *Kārikā* 26 with the correct philosophical sequence of hearing, touching, seeing, tasting, and smelling. Regarding *Kārikā* 28, the matter becomes even murkier. The *Māṭharavṛtti* and *Yuktidīpikā*, which had maintained the correct philosophical order of senses in *Kārikā* 26, proceed to read *Kārikā* 28 as beginning "*rūpādiṣu* . . . ." instead of "*śabdādiṣu* . . . ." which latter would have been the obvious reading given their reading of *Kārikā* 26. By the same token, Gauḍapāda and Vācaspati read *Kārikā* 28 as beginning "*śabdādiṣu* . . . ." instead of "*rūpādiṣu* . . . ." which latter would have been the obvious reading given their reading of *Kārikā* 26. Herein, of course, is an interesting problem for a critical text editor. The relevant issue in this discussion, however, is that the order of the *indriyas* in the *Kārikā* itself cannot be considered determinative in interpreting the philosophical meaning of the *indriyas* within the overall Sāṃkhya system.

15. This interpretation of *āharaṇa*, *dhāraṇa*, and *prakāśakara* follows that of the *Yuktidīpikā* (RB1370, 113). It is to be noted, however, that other interpretations are also possible. The *Yuktidīpikā* itself (RB 1370, 113) refers to an alternate interpretation wherein *āharaṇa* refers to the *karmendriyas*, *dhāraṇa* to *manas* and *ahaṃkāra*, and *prakāśakara* to the *buddhīndriyas* and *buddhi*. Vācaspati assigns *āharaṇa* to the *karmendriyas* *dhāraṇa* to the *antaḥkaraṇa*, and *prakāśa* to the *buddhīndriyas*. *Māṭharavṛtti* assigns *āharaṇa* to all the *indriyas*, *dhāraṇa* to *ahaṃkāra*, and *prakāśākara* to *buddhi*. Gauḍapāda assigns both *āharaṇa* and *dhāraṇa* to the *karmendriyas*, and *prakāśakara* to the *buddhīndriyas*. There is also disagreement as to the term "tenfold" in *Kārikā* 32, with some commentaries (for example, Vācaspati, the *Candrikā*, the *Yuktidīpikā*) arguing that "tenfold" refers to objects apprehended either in terms of "human" (*adivya*) and "divine" (*divya*) or in terms of "specific" (*viśeṣa* or gross) or "nonspecific" (*aviśeṣa* or subtle), and with other commentaries (Gauḍapāda, the *Māṭharavṛtti*, the *Jayamaṅgalā*) arguing that "tenfold" simply refers to the functions of the five sense capacities and the five action capacities in the aggregate. The variety of views seems to indicate clearly that such epistemological issues were very much at issue within the Sāṃkhya tradition itself.

16. It might be noted here, however, that Vijñānabhikṣu argues in his *Sāṃkhyapravacanabhāṣya* on *sūtra* III.9 that the "subtle body" (*liṅgaśarīra*) is "seventeenfold" or a 'set of 17." The *sūtra* itself reads as follows: *saptadaśaikaṃ liṅgam*. According to Vijñānabhikṣu, the *sūtra* is to be construed to mean "the seventeen *as* one (makes up) the subtle body," and the seventeen are the eleven capacities, the five subtle elements, and *buddhi* (with *ahaṃkāra* to be included within the *buddhi*). Aniruddha in his *Sāṃkhyasūtravṛtti* construes the same *sūtra* in a different manner, namely, "the seventeen plus one (make up) the subtle body," indicating, in other words, that the subtle body

is eighteenfold, which, of course, is the standard view of Īśvarakṛṣṇa and his commentators. Aniruddha's interpretation is undoubtedly correct, but it must be admitted that Vijñānabhikṣu's view may well preserve a pre-*Kārikā* view of the matter. Reference has already been made to pre-Īśvarakṛṣṇa forms of Sāṃkhya in which the makeup of the subtle body was at issue (see, for example, the discussion of the views of Paurika, Pañcādhikaraṇa, and Vindhyavāsin in the preceding chapter). It should be remembered also that Pātañjala-Sāṃkhya reduces the threefold internal organ to the notion of *citta* and does away with the notion of subtle body by arguing that the *citta* is all pervasive, a view that appears to come close to Vindhyavāsin's position (and has led Frauwallner and Chakravarti to suggest that Pātañjala-Sāṃkhya may represent an extension of the older Vārṣagaṇya-Vindhyavāsin interpretation of the Sāṃkhya system). We also know that Vindhyavāsin argued that the standard Sāṃkhya "thirteenfold instrument" (namely, the ten capacities, *manas*, *ahaṃkāra*, and *buddhi*) should be reduced to an elevenfold instrument (namely, the ten capacities plus *manas*, with *ahaṃkāra* and *buddhi* functions being encompassed by the *manas*). Traces of this view appear to be present in the *Sāṃkhyasūtra*, for in *sūtras* I.71, II.40 and VI.25 the term *manas* is clearly used in the sense of *buddhi* or *citta*. It would appear, then, that there were a variety of views within Sāṃkhya regarding the structure of internal cognition and, corollary to that, the precise makeup of the subtle body. One view (on the evidence of Vijñānabhikṣu's interpretation of *sūtra* III.9) evidently reduced *ahaṃkāra* to a dimension of *buddhi*. Another view (on the evidence of references to Vindhyavāsin in the *Yuktidīpikā* together with the use of the term *manas* at I.71, II.40 and VI.25 of the *Sāṃkhyasūtra*) evidently reduced both *buddhi* and *ahaṃkāra* to *manas*. Yet another view (on the evidence of Pātañjala-Sāṃkhya) introduced the notion of *citta*, which encompasses the functions of *manas*, *ahaṃkāra*, and *buddhi*. Īśvarakṛṣṇa's own view, of course, is that *buddhi*, *ahaṃkāra*, and *mcnas* each perform distinct internal functions (SK 29) but together perform the common function of maintaining life (the circulation of *prāṇa*, and so forth), either by themselves (if one follows the interpretation of Vācaspati and Vijñānabhikṣu) or in concert with the other ten capacities (if one follows the interpretation of Gauḍapāda and *Jayamaṅgalā*). Regarding the corollary issue of the subtle body, if one follows the interpretation of Vijñānabhikṣu in *sūtra* III.9, the subtle body is seventeenfold. If one follows Īśvarakṛṣṇa's own view, the subtle body is eighteenfold (namely, the thirteenfold instrument together with the five subtle elements). If one follows the view of Vindhyavāsin or Pātañjala-Sāṃkhya, there is no need for a subtle body for transmigration. For Vindhyavāsin, *manas* is central and the sense capacities are all-pervasive; hence, a subtle body is unnecessary. For Pātañjala-Sāṃkhya, *citta* is all-pervasive; hence, a subtle body is unnecessary. There are yet other views concerning the problem—e.g., the so called *prāṇāṣṭaka* or eightfold medium made up of the five breaths, *manas*, *pur*, and *vāc*, and the *vaivarta-śarīra*, presumably made up of the five subtle elements plus *buddhi*, *ahaṃkāra*, and *manas*—all of which are conveniently discussed by P. Chakravarti (B6381; RB9596, 269-270 288-298).

At the risk of complicating matters even further, attention might also be drawn to an early Vedāntin reference, namely, the *Māṇḍūkya Upaniṣad*, verses 3 and 4, in which the "waking" and "dreaming" quarters of Oṃ, Brahman, and *ātman* are described as having "seven limbs" and "nineteen mouths." According to Śaṃkara's *Bhāṣya*, the "seven limbs" refer to heaven (*dyuloka*), the sun, space, air, fire, water, and earth. The "nineteen mouths" are called by Śaṃkara the "doors of perception" (*upalabdhi-dvārāṇī*) and are made up of the five sense capacities (*buddhīndriya*), the five motor capacities (*karmendriyas*), the five breaths (*vāyu*, *prāṇa*, and so forth), plus *manas*, *buddhi*, *ahaṃkāra*, and *citta*. In this formulation, instead of reducing the internal cognitive functions to one another (with *manas* or *buddhi* or *citta* encompassing the others), all four internal functions stand as distinct components.

17. See the preceding note.

18. For a fuller discussion of the *karmayonis* in prephilosophical and non-Sāṃkhya texts, see P. Chakravarti, B6381; RB9596, 270-277.

19. The correlation of the five *viparyayas* of Sāṃkhya with the five *kleśas* of Pātañjala-Yoga is specifically made by Vācaspati Miśra in his *Tattvakaumudī* on *Kārikā* 47. The correlation is also made by Vijñānabhikṣu in his discussion of *viparyaya* in *Yogavārttika*, under *Yogasūtra* I.8. For the full discussion of the *kleśas* in Yoga philosophy, see *Yogasūtra* I.5, I.8, and II.2-9 together with the comments of Vyāsa, the so-called Śaṃkara (of the *Vivaraṇa*), Vācaspati Miśra's *Tattvavaiśāradī*, and Vijñānabhikṣu's *Yogavārttika*.

20. It must be admitted that the set of 50 *padārthas* represents one of the most obscure problems in Sāṃkhya studies. The origin, role, and function of the set within the Sāṃkhya system as a whole have puzzled not only modern scholars but the native commentarial tradition as well. Especially vexing are the peculiar technical names that have been given to the "contentments" (*tuṣṭi*) and the authentic "spiritual attainments" (*siddhi*). The names of the five "misconceptions" (*viparyaya*), namely, *tamas*, *moha*, *mahāmoha*, *tāmisra*, and *andhatāmisra*, though obviously difficult in terms of the words themselves, are nevertheless reasonably intelligible in terms of content because of the testimony of the Yoga tradition that they are archaic names for the well-known five *kleśas*, namely, *avidyā*, *asmitā*, *rāga*, *dveṣa*, and *abhiniveśa*. By the same token, the first eleven of the twenty-eight "dysfunctions" (*aśakti*) are reasonably intelligible in terms of content, since they refer to the inadequate functioning of the eleven capacities, that is, the five sense capacities, the five motor capacities, and mind. The remaining seventeen "dysfunctions" are not as clear, however, since they are only characterized as being the opposities of the nine contentments and the eight spiritual attainments. According to the *Kārikā* (along with *Tattvakaumudī* and *Yuktidīpikā*), the manifest names of the *tuṣṭis* are *prakṛti*, *upādāna*, *kāla*, *bhāgya* (internal) and *arjana*, *rakṣaṇa*, *kṣaya*, *bhoga*, and *hiṃsā* (external, according to *Yuktidīpikā*). The manifest names of the *siddhis* are *ūha*, *śabda*, *adhyayana*, *duḥkhavighātās trayaḥ* (the "triad" of ways for overcoming the threefold frustration), *suhṛtprāpti*, and *dāna*. All of the commentaries to the *Sāṃkhyakārikā*, however, then proceed to offer archaic technical names for these *tuṣṭis* and *siddhis*. Unfortunately, however, there are a number of variants, the more important of which are charted on p. 632.

A century ago Richard Garbe (in the introduction to B3574; RB5524, xiv-xv) offered the following interesting observations regarding the problem:

> I have already .... pointed out the peculiar figurative way in which the different stages of acquiescence (*tuṣṭi*) are named, viz., water, wave, flood, rain, excellent water, most excellent water, crossing, happy crossing, perfect crossing (*pāra*, *supāra*, *pārapāra*). Add to this the synonymous denominations of the first three perfections (*siddhi*): *tāra*, *sutāra*, *tāratāra*. All Sāṃkhya commentaries have preserved these strange denominations ...., beginning with Gauḍapāda who has found them in "another compendium" (*śāstrāntara*). Wilson ....does not know what to do with these expressions which, in his opinion, have quite different meaning than they usually bear, in this connection; he regards them as "slang or mystical nomenclature" and ends his remarks on them with these words: "No explanation of the words is anywhere given, nor is any reason assigned for their adoption." Thus all commentators of the *Kārikās* as well as of the *Sūtras* find themselves here before a riddle which they do not even try to explain, while they believe they are able to expound everything else. This speaks in favour of the assumption that these obscure words represent a very old tradition which has become totally unintelligible. I have no doubt that these denominations are based on the same metaphor which is current in Buddhism, viz., on that of passing over the ocean of mundane existence into the harbour of liberation. The "acquiescences" (*tuṣṭi*) of the Sāṃkhya system are, as preliminary stages of liberation, compared with smooth waters which facilitate the passage of those who have reached them.

tuṣṭis	*GB*	*YD*	*STK*	*M*	*J*
1. *prakṛti*	*ambhas*	*ambhas*	*ambhas*	*ambhas*	*ambhas*
2. *upādāna*	*salila*	*salila*	*salila*	*salila*	*salila*
3. *kāla*	*ogha*	*ogha*	*ogha* (*megha*)	*ogha*	*ogha*
4. *bhāgya*	*vṛṣṭi*	*vṛṣṭi*	*vṛṣṭi*	*vṛṣṭi*	*vṛṣṭi*
5. *arjana*	*sutamas*	*sutāra*	*pāra*	*tāra*	*sutāra*
6. *rakṣaṇa*	*pāra*	*supāra*	*supāra*	*sutāra*	*supāra*
7. *kṣaya*	*sunetra*	*sunetra*	*pārāpāra*	*sunetra*	(?)
8. *bhoga*	*nārīka*	*sumarīca*	*anuttama-ambhas*	*sumarīca*	*anuttama-ambhas*
9. *hiṃsā*	*anuttama-ambhasika*	*uttamābhaya*	*uttama-ambhas*	*uttama-ambhasika*	*uttama-ambhas*
siddhis					
1. *ūha*	*tāra*	*tāraka*	*tāra*	*tāra*	*tāra*
2. *śabda*	*sutāra*	*sutāra*	*sutāra*	*sutāra*	*sutāra*
3. *adhyayana*	*tāratāra*	*tārayanta*	*tāratāra*	*tāratāra*	*tāravi* (?)
4. *duḥkhavighāta I*	*pramoda*	*pramoda*	*pramoda*	*pramoda*	*pramoda*
5. *duḥkhavighāta II*	*pramudita*	*pramudita*	*mudita*	*pramudita*	*pramudita*
6. *duḥkhavighāta III*	*pramodamāna*	*modamāna*	*modamāna*	*mohana* (*modamāna* ?)	*modana*
7. *suhṛtprāpti*	*ramyaka*	*ramyaka*	*ramyaka*	*ramyaka*	*ramyaka*
8. *dāna*	*sadāpramudita*	*sadāpramudita*	*sadāmudita*	*sadāpramudita*	*sadāpramudita*

A. B. Keith in (B6291; RB9548) *The Sāṃkhya System* (Calcutta: YMCA Publishing House, 1949), 104-105, exercising his characteristic Anglo-Saxon common sense, dismisses the whole problem as "hopeless" and suggests that verses 46 to 51 of the *Kārikā* (or that portion of the text dealing with the 50 *padārthas*) are a later interpolation. Erich Frauwallner, B8590; RB12160, vol. 1 319ff., argues that the 50 *padārthas* were added to the Sāṃkhya system by Vārṣagaṇya and his followers after the time of Pañcaśikha, which latter figure first formulated, according to Frauwallner, the basic evolutionary theory of Sāṃkhya (that is to say, the theory of *prakṛti*, *triguṇa*, and *satkārya*). Frauwallner argues further that the 50 *padārthas* represent an innovation regarding the psychology of the Sāṃkhya system and have very little philosophical significance. Īśvarakṛṣṇa's own doctrine of eight *bhāvas*, according to Frauwallner, is a great improvement over the older formulation of 50 *padārthas*, but Īśvarakṛṣṇa allowed the older set of 50 *padārthas* to remain in his summary, since it had become authoritative in the tradition and could not be deleted. Frauwallner's treatment (as he himself readily admits) is highly speculative. There is no clear evidence that Vārṣagaṇya and his followers were responsible for the set of 50 *padārthas*, and there is no evidence whatever that Īśvarakṛṣṇa's doctrine of 8 *bhāvas* was meant in any sense as an improvement over the set of 50 *padārthas*. Quite the contrary, the *Yuktidīpikā* clearly indicates that the 8 *bhāvas* refer to a realm (the *pravṛtti* realm) that is clearly distinguished from the realm of the 50 *padārthas* (the *phala* realm). Frauwallner's treatment, therefore, cannot be taken seriously. Most recently, Gerhard Oberhammer in (RB9925) *Strukturen yogischer Meditation: Untersuchungen zur Spiritualität des Yoga* (Vienna: Osterreichische Akademie der Wissenschaften, Nos. 13, 1977) has discussed the 50 *padārthas* in an intriguing chapter entitled "Die sāṃkhyistische Struktur der Meditation" (pp. 17-56), in which he argues, largely on the basis of references in the *Yuktidīpikā*, that the scheme of 50 *padārthas* represents an archaic method of meditation that focused mainly on the first three *siddhis* (namely *ūha*, *śabda*, and *adhyayana*), or, in other words, meditation as rational reflection, while relegating nonattachment (*vairāgya*) to the lower status of "contentment" (*tuṣṭi*). Fortunately, Oberhammer refrains from speculating whether this ancient system of meditation was originally Sāṃkhya or whether it can be attributed to Vārṣagaṇya, and so forth, and thereby avoids the implausible excesses of Frauwallner. Indeed, Oberhammer's treatment tends to bring the discussion back to Garbe's observations of almost a century earlier (as quoted above).

My own view regarding the interpretation of the 50 *padārthas* comes through very clearly in my introductory essay in the main text on the Philosophy of Sāṃkhya. Far from being an embarrassment, I tend to see the *pratyayasarga* as a fundamental structure of the full Sāṃkhya system. I would agree with Oberhammer that it does function as a system of meditation, but I would go much further as well. The *pratyayasarga*, in my view, represents the Sāṃkhya interpretation of the phenomenal, empirical world of ordinary life that is clearly to be distinguished from the "noumenal" or "causal" realm of the *tattvas*. The *pratyayasarga* is, therefore, important for the epistemology as well as for the ethics of Sāṃkhya, making Sāṃkhya a critical realism instead of a naive realism or a confused idealism. Finally, regarding the peculiar technical names for the *tuṣṭis* and *siddhis*, I am inclined to agree with Garbe and Wilson that there is a "slang or mystical nomenclature" operating here that uses a metaphor that is fundamental in early Buddhist literature. By the same token, however, comparable metaphors are common in the older Vedic literature. For example, V.S. Agrawala in his *Sparks from the Vedic Fire: A New Approach to Vedic Symbolism* (Varanasi: Chowkhamba, 1962) sets forth a symbolic network of terms relating to the notion of *soma* (including *ṛta*, *āpas*, *asura*, *ambhas*, *salila*, *samudra*, *tamas*, *rātri*, and so forth, which he contrasts with another network relating to *agni* (Indra) (including *sūrya*, *manu*, *deva*, *jyotis*, *hiraṇyagarbha*, *ahar*, and so forth). "Crossing" in such a symbolic environment may refer not only to crossing a body of water but also to the sun and moon crossing the heavens, the sequence of day and night, and the symbolic boundaries of life and death. It is my suspicion that if the ancient Sāṃkhya terms can ever be deciphered, it will be in some such symbolic network of "crossing,".

21. Somewhat analogous conceptions of creation or manifestation by progressive deteriorization may be found in Udayana's *Nyāyakusumāñjali* II.3 and in *Vāyupurāṇa* VIII. 72-88, both of which are mentioned briefly in Chakravarti B6381; RB9596, 287-288. Similar notions are also present in Buddhist literature. See Alex Wayman's chapter entitled "Buddhist Genesis and the Tantric Tradition" in his *The Buddhist Tantras: Light on Indo Tibetan Esotericism* (New York: Samuel Weiser, 1973), 24-29, for a good general discussion of possible Buddhist parallels. Buddhist references, however, appear to link deteriorization with the ingestion of progressively coarser food. The ancient Sāṃkhya a sequence focusses, rather, on progressively different activities thereby linking the deteriorization with the unfolding of the *karmendriyas*.

22. *Tattvasamāsasūtravṛtti* (also called *Kramadīpikā*) in V. P. Dvivedi, ed. (B3714; (RB1862), *Sāṃkhyasaṃgraha* (Varanasi: Chowkhamba Sanskrit Series, 1969), 81-82.

23. The correlations here and following are only speculative suggestions. The linkage of Brahmā, Prajāpati, and Indra with such *tattvas* as *prakṛti, buddhi, ahaṃkāra,* and *manas* is plausible enough in view of comparable linkages prevalent in the cosmological portions of the *Purāṇas,* and so forth. I am not as sure about the correlations of *tanmātras* and *bhūtas* with *pitṛs, gandharvas,* and so forth.

24. Ibid.

25. Ibid.

26. But see above, note 16, in which the seventeenfold set is linked with the subtle body.

27. I am using the terms "*adhidaiva,*" "*adhyātma*" and "*adhibhūta*" in the *Kramadīpikā* sense and not in the *Kārikā* sense of the three kinds of *duḥkha,* although I am inclined to think that the two senses are clearly cognate.

28. The Sanskrit is as follows (*Yuktidīpikā,* p. 21): *tatra rūpapravṛttiphalalakṣaṇaṃ vyaktam. rūpaṃ punaḥ mahān ahaṃkāraḥ pañca tanmātrāṇi ekādaśendriyāṇi pañca mahābhūtāni. sāmānyataḥ pravṛttir dvividhā: hitakāmaprayojanā ca, ahitapratiṣedhaprayojanā ca. viśeṣataḥ pañca karmayonayo vṛttyādyāḥ prāṇādyaś ca pañca vāyavah. phalaṃ dvividham: dṛṣṭaṃ adṛṣṭaṃ ca. tatra dṛṣṭaṃ siddhituṣṭyaśaktiviparyayalakṣaṇam; adṛṣṭaṃ brahmādau stambaparyante saṃsāre śarīrapratilambha ity etad vyaktam.*

29. The Sanskrit is as follows (*Yuktidīpikā,* p. 140): *tattvākhyo mahadādir bhāvākhyo dharmādir bhūtākhyo vyomādiḥ.*

30. *Bhagavadgītā* III.28. The Sāṃkhya conceptualization of *mūlaprakṛti* as *triguṇa* and *guṇapariṇāma* obviates the need for separate treatments of such traditional philosophical notions as time, space, or God. Put another way, these latter categories have no place in the Sāṃkhya philosophical analysis, since *mūlaprakṛti* as *triguṇa* represents the functional equivalent. Space and time are derived correlates of a beginningless process of combination (*saṃghāta*) and change (*pariṇāma*). The measurable space and time of ordinary experience, therefore, are not *tattvas,* but only phenomenal appearances, presumably generated by the projections (*pravṛtti*) of the *buddhi* that bring about the "consequent" (*phala*) realm of the *pratyayasarga* and the *bhautikasarga.* Moreover, because both *prakṛti* and *puruṣa* are beginningless and all pervasive, there could never be a "time," therefore, when *puruṣa* is not in proximity to *prakṛti* (in any given cycle of manifestation). It would appear to be the case, then, that the emergence of the causal *tattvas* is not a temporal process in the sense of measurable time. Putting the matter another way, the process of combination and change has neither a beginning nor an end. The notions of "beginning" and "end" are relative constructs within the combination and change of manifestation occasioned by *aviveka* or nondiscrimination. Regarding the problem of God, Sāṃkhya argues that *prakṛti* as *triguṇa* is both the material (*upādāna*) and efficient (*nimitta*) cause of the manifest world; hence, there is no rational need for a doctrine of God (*īśvara*). To be sure, one might conceive of *buddhi* as Hiraṇyagarbha, Brahmā, and so forth, or one might assign a crucial revelatory (or

teaching) role to sages such as Kapila or Āsuri, but all such formulations are derivative of *mūlaprakṛti* in its *buddhisattva* modality (or, in terms of Yoga philosophy, *īśvara* as *puruṣaviśeṣa*). The older Sāṃkhya literature does not directly mention space, time, or God. The notions are mentioned in the later *Sāṃkhyasūtra,* at II.12, I.92-99 and V.1-12. See also the discussion of "Time, Space and Causality" in K. C. Bhattacharya, *Studies in Philosophy,* 165-172.

31. By "reductive materialism" is meant a philosophical view that construes or "reduces" mind, thought, ideas, feelings, and so forth, in terms of some sort of material stuff or energy or force. The expression "reductive materialism" has been used in recent philosophical writing, especially in the area of philosophy of mind—for example, in the work of Kai Nielsen, J.J.C. Smart, and others. For an older but still useful collection of discussions, see V. C. Chappell, ed., *The Philosophy of Mind* (Englewood Cliffs, New Jersey: Prentice-Hall, 1962). For a popular and entertaining approach to the issues in a recent collection, see D. R. Hofstadter and D. C. Dennett, eds., *The Mind's I: Fantasies and Reflections on Self and Soul* (New York: Bantam Books, 1982). See especially the useful bibliography in "Further Reading," pp. 465-482.

32. K. C. Bhattacharya, *Studies in Philosophy,* vol. 1, 158-164.

33. It is generally the case in Indian philosophy that a sharp distinction is not drawn between analytic and synthetic statements or between *a priori* and *a posteriori.* The Sāṃkhya treatment of *triguṇa,* therefore, is not at all anomalous in its context.

34. K. C. Bhattacharya, *Studies in Philosophy,* vol. 1, 182.

35. In the preface to *The Phenomenology of Mind* (in the J. B. Baillie translation, London, George Allen & Unwin, 1931, p. 80) Hegel comments, "In my view—a view which the developed exposition of the system itself can alone justify—everything depends on grasping and expressing the ultimate truth not as Substance but as Subject as well."

Or, again, near the end of *The Phenomenology of Mind* (p. 790), Hegel comments: "Consciousness . . . must have taken up a relation to the object in all its aspects and phases, and have grasped its meaning from the point of view of each of them. This totality of its determinate characteristics makes the object *per se* or inherently a spiritual reality; and it becomes so in truth for consciousness, when the latter apprehends every individual one of them as self, i.e., when it takes up towards them the spiritual relationship . . . ."

36. K.C. Bhattacharya, *Studies in Philosophy,* vol. 1, 162ff. and 187ff.

37. . . . .*calatā, kriyā; sā ca dividhā pariṇāmalakṣaṇā praspandalakṣaṇā ca. tatra pariṇāmalakṣaṇayā sahakāribhāvāntarānugṛhitasya dharmiṇaḥ pūrvadharmāt pracyutiḥ. praspandalakṣaṇā prāṇādayaḥ karmendriyavṛttayaś ca vacanādyāh.* Pandeya, RB1370, 60.

38. Again, it should be noted that I am using *adhidaiva, adhyātma,* and *adhibhūta* in the *Kramadīpikā* sense.

39. Cf. G. J. Larson RB1378, 115ff. and 167ff.

40. Cf. Richard Robinson, "Classical Indian Philosophy," 167-177.

41. Cf. G. J. Larson RB1378, 167ff.

42. By "ghost in the machine" I am, of course, referring to Gilbert Ryle's famous essay, *The Concept of Mind* (New York: Barnes and Noble, 1949), in which he debunks the notion of a separate or distinct "self" or "soul."

43. E. S. Haldane and G.R.T. Ross, trans., *The Philosophical Works of Descartes,* vol. 1, 240.

44. Ibid., 190.

45. Kai Nielsen, *Reason and Practice* (New York: Harper and Row, 1971), 333.

46. See above, note 31.

47. As has been noted since the time of Deussen, there is a striking similarity between *Kārikā* 3 and the opening passage of Johannes Scottus Eriugena's *Periphyseon* (*De Divisione Naturae*), which reads: "It is my opinion that the division of Nature by means of four differences results in four species, (being divided) first into that which

creates and is not created, secondly into that which is created and also creates, thirdly into that which is created and does not create, while the fourth neither creates nor is created." (critical ed.: I. P. Sheldon-Williams and L. Bieler, eds. and trans., *Periphyseon,* De Divisione Naturae, Book I, opening passage; Dublin: Scriptores Latine Hiberniae, vii, 1968).

48. Some of the commentaries on the *Kārikā* explain the terms in the sequence variously. For example, there is divergence of views regarding the interpretation of *eka* and *aneka.* Vācaspati passes over the problem (perhaps thereby suggesting that the terms can be taken to mean simply "simple" and "complex"), but Gauḍapāda, the Chinese commentary, the *Jayamaṅgalā,* and the *Māṭharavṛtti* take the terms as meaning "one" and "many." If *eka* means "one" in this context, however, then it is not correct to apply the term to both *prakṛti* and *puruṣa.* The commentaries handle the difficulty by arguing (somewhat lamely) that this one component in the sequence is not to be applied to both *prakṛti* and *puruṣa.*

49. Unfortunately, a portion of *Kārikā* 10 and all of *Kārikā* 11 are missing from the extant manuscripts of the *Yuktidīpikā.* This is very much to be regretted, because it is the *Yuktidīpikā* that most often offers the most cogent interpretations of the kinds of technical terms that one finds in these verses.

50. I should hasten to add that this is my own view of the matter, and there is no textual support for my view other than Vijñānabhikṣu's comments under *Sāṃkhyasūtra* I.154, which, alas, is not much supporting evidence. All of the commentaries on the *Kārikā* do imply that *puruṣas* are somehow countable entities. If such is the case, then it must be conceded that the ancient Sāṃkhya *ācāryas* allowed themselves to fall into an insuperable difficulty. In my view, however, such elementary errors are not at all characteristic of the Sāṃkhya system. In almost every instance of the so-called weaknesses of the Sāṃkhya system, the weakness is traceable to later misunderstandings and distortions by subsequent interpreters (both in the commentarial tradition itself and in modern scholarship). This is why I agree so often with K. C. Bhattacharya who has argued that Sāṃkhya is a bold speculative philosophy the original arguments for which have been largely lost and must, therefore, be reconstructed from what remains. From a methodological point of view, this means some thing like the following: when one finds a glaring discrepancy in any given presentation of Sāṃkhya, one strong possibility is that the given issue has not been carefully thought through by the later transmitters of the system. Instead of pouncing on the discrepancy as polemical ammunition for showing that Sāṃkhya is a hopeless "bundle of contradictions" (per Śaṃkara in the native tradition, or per A. B. Keith in modern scholarship), a better approach might be to ask if possibly the discrepancy represents a misunderstanding or distortion of what the ancient Sāṃkhya thinkers intended. This approach presupposes that the ancient teachers were not stupid and were fully as capable of apprehending contradictions as their later opponents. It also presupposes that an ancient system of thought may be as sophisticated within its contextual framework as other later systems are within theirs. In any case, returning to the issue at hand, my suspicion is that the "plurality of *puruṣas*" (*puruṣabahutva*) has not yet been properly understood by interpreters of Sāṃkhya (in the extant native textual tradition and in modern scholarship). One possible way of thinking through the problem is to approach the issue as having to do with the epistemology of the *buddhi* rather than the ontology of the *puruṣas.*

51. See the preceding chapter for a fuller discussion of the differences between Vācaspati Miśra and Vijñānabhikṣu.

52. It should be noted that the metaphors and similes in the Sāṃkhya literature are by and large not technical inferential *dṛṣṭāntas.* They are closer in intention to the sorts of figurative language one finds in Plato—for example, in the *Timaeus.* The old creation myths in the *Yuktidīpikā* are to be construed in a similar manner, in my view.

53. Frauwallner puts the matter as follows:

> Das Sāṃkhya hat also eine doppelte Bedeutung. Es wirkte bahnbrechend in der Entwicklung der klassichen Philosophie Indiens und hat wesentlich dazu beigetragen, diese Philosophie auf ihre Höhe zu führen. Ferner hat es durch seine enge Verbindung mit brahmanischen Kreisen das gesamte indische Geistesleben ungewöhnlich weit durchdrungen und hat bis in die neueste Zeit sein Bild in wesentlichen Zügen mitbestimmt. Wenn also seine rein philosophische Bedeutung auch geringer ist als die mancher anderer Systeme, so ist seine historische Bedeutung um so grösser. Und man kann mit Recht behaupten, dass ohne Kenntnis der Sāṃkhya-Philosophie ein volles Verständnis der indischen Geistesentwicklung nicht möglich ist. (B8590; RB12160, vol. 1, 450.)

54. Chakravarti, for example, B6381; RB9596, 123, quotes xii.29 of the *Ahirbudhnyasaṃhitā* as evidence that there were many versions or variants for the *ṣaṣṭitantra*, namely, "*. . . .ṣaṣṭitantrāṇy atha ekaikam esāṃ nānāvidhaṃ . . . .*"

55. See, for example, the following: E. Frauwallner B6431A; RB9627, 84-139; G. Oberhammer, "On the 'śāstra' Quotations of the *Yuktidīpikā*," *Adyar Library Bulletin* 25 (1961): 131-172; G. Oberhammer (B1046D; RB2210), "The Authorship of the *Ṣaṣṭitantra*," *Wiener Zeitschrift für des Kunde Süd- und Ostasiens* 4 (1960): 71-91; N. Nakada (RB2212), "Word and Inference in the *Yuktidīpikā*", pts. 1, 2, 3, in *Indogaku Bukkyogaku Kenkyu*, 18.2 (1970): 36, 41-45; 19.2 (1971): 38, 25-31; 21.1 (1972): 41, 19-22; A. Wezler (RB2213), "Some Observations on the Yuktidīpikā," *Deutscher Orientalistentag*, suppl. 2 (Wiesbaden), 434-455. See also A. Wezler, "Studien zum Dvādaśāranayacakra des Śvetāmbara Mallavādin: I. Der *sarvasarvātmakatvavāda*," in *Studien zum Jainismus und Buddhismus*: Gedenkschrift für Ludwig Alsdorf, edited by K. Bruhn and A. Wezler (Wiesbaden: Franz Steiner, n.d.). It should also be noted that Dr. E. Harzer, of the University of Washington, Seattle, has recently completed a dissertation having to do with the epistemology of Sāṃkhya with special reference to the *Yuktidīpikā*. I might add, finally, that I am indebted to Dr. Harzer for drawing my attention to the above-cited work of N. Nakada on Sāṃkhya epistemology.

56. Frauwallner B6431A; RB9627, 84-139.

57. I should like to make clear that my comments through this section on "philosophical methodology" and "Sāṃkhya numbers" are entirely my own and admittedly highly speculative. They represent a variety of intuitions that I have reached over many years of pondering what could possibly be a deeper rationality in the Sāṃkhya predilection for enumerations. Since, to my knowledge, no one has ever attempted to explain the significance of Sāṃkhya numbers, there has been no way to proceed other than by way of my own intuitions regarding the problem. I fully recognize that I may well be wrong and that the Sāṃkhya numbers may not have any rational significance whatever. By the same token, however, I also recognize that I may well be right, but naively so. That is to say, my own lack of knowledge of the history of ancient mathematics, music, and astronomy may be preventing me from understanding a great many mathematical and astronomical allusions in the Sāṃkhya literature. In any case, I invite those with greater expertise in such matters to respond to my groping intuitions.

58. I first noticed the Sāṃkhya predilection for prime numbers when working with the *Tattvasamāsasūtra* and its commentaries, and I published some of my preliminary findings in an article entitled "The format of technical philosophical writing in ancient India: inadequacies of conventional translations" (*Philosophy East and West* 30, no. 3 (July 1980): 375-380). Then, in April of 1981 I attended a Conference on Sāṃkhya-Yoga, sponsored by the Institute for Advanced Studies of World Religions in Stony Brook, New York. I read a paper at the conference entitled "An Eccentric Ghost in the Machine: Formal and Quantitative Aspects of the Sāṃkhya-Yoga

Dualisim," (published in *Philosophy East and West* 33, no. 3 (July 1983): 219-233 and available in typescript through the Proceedings of the Conference, prepared by the IASWR), and the respondent to the paper was Ernest McClain, Professor Emeritus of Music at Brooklyn College of the CUNY and author of *The Myth of Invariance* (New York: Nicholas Hays, 1976), *The Pythagorean Plato* (New York: Nicholas Hays, 1978), and so forth. McClain suggested that my intuitions concerning Sāṃkhya enumerations were probably more on target than I suspected, and he directed me to read R. S. Brumbaugh's *Plato's Mathematical Imagination* (New York: Kraus Reprint, 1954) and O. Neugebauer's *The Exact Sciences in Antiquity* (New York: Dover, 1957/69). He suggested, furthermore, that I might well find that the first three prime numbers were especially important in Sāṃkhya since these numbers are especially important in Pythagorean tuning theory. Moreover, it appeared to him that the Sāṃkhya numbers probably bear some relation with the sexagesimal system of counting (as opposed to the decimal system). My own subsequent work confirmed that, indeed, the numbers 2, 3 and 5 (the first three prime numbers) are especially prominent in the Sāṃkhya system. I have also been struck by the possible parallel between the sexagesimal system of counting and the old Sāṃkhya term, *ṣaṣṭitantra* ("the system of 60"). In any case, for those interested in mathematical allegorizing among the Babylonians, Sumerians, Pythagoreans, Hindus, and so forth an issue of the *Journal for Social and Biological Structures*, 1982, no. 5 (London Academic Press) has been given over to publishing a symposium on the topic, the lead paper of which is Ernest G. McClain's "Structure in the Ancient Wisdom Literature: The Holy Mountain" (pp. 233-248). My own contribution to the symposium appeared in the next issue of the journal, entitled "McClain's Mathematical Acoustics and Classical Sāṃkhya Philosophy."

59. See the earlier exposition of the 50 *padārthas* in the present chapter, and see also note 20, supra.

60. For useful and brief summaries of Indian views concerning astronomy and the calendar, see A. L. Basham, *The Wonder That was India* (New York: Evergreen 1959), 489-495. For more detailed treatments, see O. Neugebauer, *The Exact Sciences in Antiquity*; and A. Pannekoek, *A History of Astronomy* (New York: Interscience Publishers, Inc., 1961).

61. The best discussion of the sexagesimal system is to be found in O. Neugebauer, *The Exact Sciences in Antiquity*.

62. Ernest McClain, *The Myth of Invariance*, 13.

63. Ibid., 12-17.

64. Ibid., 13.

65. Ibid., 33-42.

66. Ibid., 73-93.

67. Cf. Gerald J. Larson, "A Possible Mystical Interpretation of Ahaṃkāra and the Tanmātras in the Sāṃkhyas" in *Sri Aurobindo: A Garland of Tributes*, edited by Arabinda Basu (Pondicherry: Sri Aurobindo Research Academy, 1972), 79-87.

68. Parallels between ancient Indian philosophy and ancient Greek philosophy have been noted and debated for well over a century, and A. B. Keith's comments (in *A History of Sanskrit literature*, London: Oxford University Press, 1920, 500) are still very much to the point, namely:

> Parallels between Indian and Greek philosophy are well worth drawing, but it may be doubted whether it is wise thence to proceed to deduce borrowing on either side. The parallelism of Vedānta and the Eleatics and Plato is worth notice, but it is no more than that, and the claim that Pythagoras learned his philosophic ideas from India though widely accepted rests on extremely weak foundations. The attempt to prove a wide influence of the Sāṃkhya on Greece depends in part in the belief in the very early date of the Sāṃkhya, and if, as

> we have seen, this is dubious, it is impossible to assert that the possibility of influence on Herakleitos, Empedokles, Anaxagoras, Demokritos, and Epikuros is undeniable. But what is certain is that there is no such convincing similarity in any detail as to raise these speculations beyond the region of mere guesswork. An influence of Indian thought on the Gnostics and Neoplatonists may be held to be more likely, and it would be unjust to rule it out of court.

There is evidence, of course, for historical contacts between ancient Greeks and Indians, some of which were extensive and involved considerable detail, as Jean Filiozat has shown (in his *La doctrine classique de la medicine indienne*, Paris, 1949, and in other writings). Moreover, such contacts may well have occurred already in the fifth and fourth century B.C.E. in the Persian courts, and increasingly thereafter. Furthermore, there is little doubt that there was some awareness among the Greeks and Indians concerning the philosophical and religious views of one another. In almost every instance, however, whether it be Pythagoras, Pyrrho, Plotinus, and so forth, on the Greek side, or the Buddhists, Sāṃkhya, Vedānta, and so forth, on the Indian side, the views of a given thinker or system can be most satisfactorily dealt with in their own specific historical contexts. Regarding specifics, after the fifth century B.C.E. there is neither sufficient evidence nor, even more than that, a pressing need to posit any kind of external borrowing. If such is the case, then the question naturally arises: how are the parallels to be explained? One avenue of approach would be to push the matter further back, to the research of Georges Dumézil and his followers and to look for a common proto-Indo-European ideology from which the later Greeks, Iranians, Indians, and so on derived many of the basic categories and notions concerning corporate life. This is still basically a historical approach but a much more sophisticated one (albeit fraught with the problem of even less evidence!). Another approach would be along the lines of what social scientists have called "independent invention" (whether in terms of Jungian "archetypes" or one or another form of structuralism). Yet another approach, which interestingly combines both historical perspectives and "independent invention" perspectives, is that represented currently in the work of Ernest McClain who wishes to argue that certain principles of ratio theory, mathematical acoustics, astronomy, and music were widely known in the ancient Near East, the Mediterranean world, South Asia, and Central Asia (and extending even into China) and that these principles formed the basis of much ancient ritual and myth and remain as latent residues in many later cultural productions (for example, Pythagorean speculations about numbers and things, number references in Plato, the numerical relations between the *kalpas* in Purāṇic texts, and so forth). McClain hypothesizes, in other words, that there was a sophisticated "structure of ancient wisdom" (related to mathematics, music, and astronomy), that, if cogently reconstructed, would go a long way toward explaining the striking "parallels" that one finds in ancient thought.

Returning now to Sāṃkhya philosophy, my own inclination is to argue along the latter lines (namely, the approaches of Dumézil, structuralism, or an archaic tradition of mathematical allegorizing) by way of explaining parallels, rather than the former (namely, some kind of historical borrowing between India and Greece). Put another way, my own view is that the Sāṃkhya in ancient India is an interesting and context-specific variant of the kind of thing one finds in Pythagoreanism as a context-specific variant in Greek thought. Both provide intriguing glimpses of the birth of philosophy in their respective contexts, and both proved to be profoundly influential for the subsequent development of their respective intellectual traditions.

69. Paul Hacker B8877; RB12428, 54-83; Frauwallner B6431A; RB9627, 84-37.

70. Variant listings of the ten *mūlikārthas* are conveniently summarized by E. A. Solomon RB1387, 182-185.

71. A useful and brief discussion of these attributions may be found in the *Krama-dīpikā*, 86.

72. Frauwallner B6431A; RB9627, 84-137.

73. Ibid., 131.

74. Ibid., 126-130. Here and following I am providing an English paraphrase of Frauwallner's German translation of the reconstructed fragments.

75. Ibid., 126-127.

76. Ibid., 128-129.

77. *Yuktidīpikā*, pp. 40-41.

78. The expression "*puruṣārtha*" in the Sāṃkhya literature always refers to ordinary "experience" (*bhoga* or *upabhoga*) and the extraordinary "experience of release" (*apavarga*). The usual translation "for the sake of the *puruṣa*" (*puruṣārtha*), therefore, simply refers to the inherent teleology of *prakṛti*.

79. See especially Vācaspati's treatment of *Kārikā* 23, 24, and 27.

80. See above, note 35.

81. For an interesting discussion of Sāṃkhya as critical realism, see M. Hiriyanna (B6316; RB9566), "The Sāṃkhya View of Error," *Philosophical Quarterly* (Amalner, 1929): 99-105.

82. The comparisons and contrasts with Kant have been nicely formulated by S. K. Maitra (B6416; RB9617), "Sāṃkhya Realism: A Comparative and Critical Study", in *Recent Indian Philosophy*, edited by Kalidas Bhattacharya (Calcutta: Progressive Publishers, 1963), 130-143. Some passages of Maitra's analysis are worth quoting in this context:

> Sāṃkhya realism stands on a different plane in this respect and must be distinguished both from Prabhākara and Nyāya realism. Both the Naiyāyika and the Prābhākara appeal to introspective evidence, to the immediate deliverance of consciousness. Sāṃkhya however arrives at realism on the way of transcendental analysis and criticism. The Sāṃkhya method in this respect has a close family likeness to Kant's transcendental method. Both start from experience, but both alike resolve experience into its noumenal antecedents, its transcendental presuppositions. But these noumenal antecedents, according to Sāṃkhya, are themselves objects of a metapsychological intuition, of transcendental Yogika vision. This is not admitted by Kant and here Sāṃkhya Transcendentalism parts company with Kantian Phenomenalism. We have no faculty of nonsensuous intuition, says Kant. Therefore we have no more than a negative knowledge of the noumenal principles. We are capable of a metaempirical nonrelational intuition in Yogika vision, says Sāṃkhya. We have thus a positive knowledge of the noumenal principles and no more negative consciousness of them as limiting principles. The metapsychology of Sāṃkhya is, therefore, to be distinguished alike from the psychological realism of Nyāya and Mīmāṃsā and the critical Phenomenalism of Kant. (133-134)

83. Ibid., 135-137. Again, Maitra's comments are worth quoting at some length, for they nicely "locate" the Sāṃkhya epistemological position within the framework of cross-cultural philosophy:

> The conception of a realistic transcendental background that is not constituted but only manifested by consciousness is common both to the Kantian and the Sāṃkhya theories of knowledge. Common to both also is the distinction between consciousness as the transcendental presupposition of experience and consciousness as a temporal mental event. But the analogy breaks down when we come to Kant's dualism of phenomena and noumena. Kant will not allow an extension of the forms of experience beyond the domain of phenomena. The categories, according to Kant, cannot be employed except in relation to sense-intuited data. Hence the subject of our empirical judgments is not the noumenal reality but only the phenomenal world which is ontologically discontinuous with its generative antecedent. We have

thus no more than a negative knowledge of the noumenal principles, a positive knowledge of them requiring a faculty of nonsensuous intuition which we lack. To none of these positions does Sāṃkhya subscribe. The manifested Prakṛti, according to Sāṃkhya, is not ontologically discontinuous with its nonmanifest background. It is continuous with the latter or rather one with it. Hence the subject of our causal, spatial and temporal world is the manifested Prakṛti as consubstantial with its nonmanifest background. The world evolves in Prakṛti and is Prakṛti itself. Phenomenalism either in the Kantian meaning of the term or the Vedāntic sense of an unreal projection of consciousness is not admitted by the Sāṃkhya realist. The world is a real determination of a realistic Prakṛti, no "no man's land" which is neither a qualification of consciousness nor a determination of the things-in-themselves. Neither is it an unreal projection of consciousness, a self-alienation of the pure Intelligence as the Śaṃkara-Vedāntist contends. On the contrary it is one with its noumenal background and held within the bosom of the latter. Further the noumenal Prakṛti is not an unknowable reality which we cannot know except only as a negative limit. We can realize it positively in nonrelational Yogic intuition though we may not know it in the relational consciousness of the empirical life.

The Sāṃkhya theory of experience thus answers more nearly to the Aristotelian theory of a monistic becoming of an original primal matter than to the Kantian dualism of appearance and unknowable things-in-themselves. The world is a transformation of Prakṛti, a transition from potentiality to actuality of form. The transition presupposes a *materia prima*, a formless primal matter, viz., Prakṛti which comes to form in the process. But the temporal unfolding presupposes an unmoved mover, an unchanging Intelligence as its final cause. Puruṣa is this unmoved mover, the final cause that imparts meaning to the process. The parallelism here with the Aristotelian metaphysics is too obvious to deserve special mention. But the Sāṃkhya regards this temporal unfolding from the dual standpoint of epistemology and metaphysics. The successive stages of the unfolding are the stages not merely of a world coming into being but also of our experience of the world. The Sāṃkhya theory here overreaches both Kant's purely epistemological standpoint and that of Aristotle's metaphysics and may be said to be a sort of synthesis of the two.

One final comment. Although I have referred to Kant and Hegel in passing throughout my presentation of the Philosophy of Sāṃkhya, I have done so only for heuristic reasons. That is to say, there appear to be what might be called "selective affinities" in the general history of philosophy, and there is some value in highlighting these when attempting to explain one or another aspect of a given Indian system. Overall, however, I would not subscribe to the views of those (for example, T.R.V. Murti in his discussion of Kant and Hegel vis-à-vis Mādhyamika Buddhist thought) who would claim that such affinities are symptomatic of an identity of purpose or fundamental content between a Western or Indian system of thought. Regarding the Kantian philosophy, for example, the matter has been well put by Edward Conze (in his article, "Spurious Parallels to Buddhist Philosophy" (RB9016), in *Thirty Years of Buddhist Studies*, London, Bruno Cassirer, 1967, 231-232) :

... we must first of all bear in mind that it is the whole purpose of Kant's philosophy to show that morality and religion, as understood by the German Protestantism of East Prussia, can survive, even though Newtonian physics be true and Hume's skepticism significant....

Kant's great specific contribution to philosophy stems from his insight into the problems posed by the tension between traditional values and the implications of natural science, and in his having found a solution acceptable to many for a long time. This tension was quite unknown in India. Since he answers a question no pre-Macaulayan Indian could ever ask, his answer can have no real correspondences in Indian thought, which never underwent the onslaught of the "mechanical" method.

By the same token, however, the force of Conze's remarks goes the other way as well, which Conze to some extent recognizes with his eulogizing of the "perennial philosophy." By this I mean that there are certain issues in Indian philosophy that no "pre-Macaulayan" Westerner could ever have asked, one of the more interesting of which concerns the possibility of a nonrelational (nonintentional), metaempirical (or metapsychological) consciousness (*puruṣa*), the presence of which may be achieved in a nonsensuous intuition of intellect/will (*buddhi*). Sāṃkhya philosophy argues that this is a possibility. Sāṃkhya argues furthermore that this is a possibility from the perspective of a critical realism that fully affirms the presence of a natural, material world. If the purpose of the Kantian philosophy were the survival of the German Protestantism of East Prussia, then one might formulate the purpose of Sāṃkhya-Yoga philosophy as the survival of a transcendent point of reference for freedom (*kaivalya*) within an elitist social and material reality (that was oppressively real) in which the sanctions and consolations of conventional ritual and mythology had become utterly meaningless. Although we may have grown beyond the problematic of Kantian philosophy, it is in my mind an open question whether we have yet faced up to the sort of problem that the ancient Sāṃkhya teachers addressed.

NOTES TO SUMMARIES

1. Kapila

1. Wezler RB3984, 255-262, and see note 8 above under Philosophy of Sāṃkhya.

3. Pañcaśikha

1. V. M. Bedekar, Introduction to *The Śāntiparvan*, vol. 16 of the *Mahābhārata* (critical edition), pp. ccv-ccxlvii.
2. Franklin Edgerton, *The Beginnings of Indian Philosophy* (Cambridge: Harvard University Press, 1965), 256-334.
3. Dasgupta B7653; RB11305, vol. 1, 213-222.
4. E. H. Johnston (B6346; RB9587), *Early Sāṃkhya* (London, 1937).
5. Aśvaghoṣa, *Buddhacarita*, translated by E. H. Johnston (Calcutta, 1936), 166-187.
6. Frauwallner B6293; RB9549, 179-206.
7. Van Buitenen B6423; RB9620, Pt. 1, 153-157.
8. V. M. Bedekar (B285; RB543), "Pañcaśikha and Caraka," *Annals of the Bhandarkar Oriental Research Institute* 38 (1958): 140-147; V. M. Bedekar (B286; RB544), "The teachings of Pañcaśikha in the Mahābhārata," *Annals of the Bhandarkar Oriental Research Institute* 38 (1958): 233-234.
9. Larson RB1378, 36-57.
10. Bedekar, Introduction to *The Śāntiparvan*, ccxi and ccxxxvi.
11. Woods B340; RB1121, *passim*.
12. N. L. Simha (B281; RB539), *The Sāṃkhya Philosophy*. Sacred Books of the Hindus 11 (1915), 415.
13. Ibid., 571.
14. Ibid., 184.
15. Translation of Gauḍapāda's *Bhāṣya* on *Kārikā* 1 by T. G. Mainkar (RB1363), *The Sāṃkhyakārikā of Īśvarakṛṣṇa*. Poona Oriental Series 9, (1964), 3.
16. Bedekar, Introduction to *The Śāntiparvan*, ccxliii.
17. Chakravarti B6381; RB9596, 115-116.
18. Frauwallner B6431A; RB9627, 84-139.
19. Frauwallner B8590; RB12160, vol. 1, 408-411, 476-477.

4. Ṣaṣṭitantra

1. In F. Otto Schrader (B280; RB538), "Das Ṣaṣṭitantra," *Zeitschrift der Deut-*

sche Morgenländische Gesellschaft 68 (1914): 101-110, and his *Introduction to the Pāñcarātra and the Ahirbudhnya Saṃhitā* (Madras: Adyar Library, 1916), 109-111.

2. A Berriedale Keith (B6291; RB9548), *The Sāṃkhya System* (Calcutta, 1924), 1949, 73-76.

3. Dasgupta B7653; RB11305, 219-221.

4. Frauwallner B6431A; RB9627, 84ff.

5. Chakravarti B6381; RB9596, 126-127.

8. Vārṣagaṇya

1. M. J. Takakusu (B742; RB1322), "La Sāṃkhyakārikā étudiée à la lumiére de sa versione chinoise," *Bulletin de l'École Française d'Extrème-Orient* 1 and 2 (1904), 2, 40-41.

2. Ibid., 2, 38.

3. Ibid., 1, 1-65; 2, 978-1064.

4. Frauwallner B6431A; RB9627, 84-137.

5. Chakravarti L6381; RB9596, 115.

6. Woods B340; RB1121, 291.

7. Ibid., 317.

8. Th. Stcherbatsky (B504; RB1400), *The Central Conception of Buddhism* (Calcutta, 1956), 75.

9. Cited in Chakravarti B6381; RB9596, 140.

9. Vindhyavāsin

1. Cited in Chakravarti B6381; RB9596, 145, note 4.

2. Cited in Chakravarti, ibid., 142-143.

3. Ibid., 144.

4. Ibid., 141.

5. Ibid., 188.

6. Ibid., 138 ff.

7. Frauwallner B8590; RB12160, vol. 1, 482, footnote 212.

8. Chakravarti B6381; RB9596, 138ff.

10. Mādhava

1. Frauwallner B8590; RB12160, vol. 1, 408.

2. Hattori RB1791, 6.

3. Translated and annotated in detail by Hattori, ibid., 52-62 and 148-160.

4. Frauwallner B8590; RB12160, vol. 1, 408.

5. Solomon RB1387, 153-169.

6. Solomon RB1818.

11. Īśvarakṛṣṇa

1. In *Sanskrit Research* 1, 107-117, cited in Chakravarti B6381; RB9596, 156-157.

2. S. Suryanarayana Sastri B742; RB1322.

3. Pandeya RB1370, 146-153.

4. Solomon RB1387, 194-207.

5. The term "*vaikṛta*" is evidently an ancient technical term. There is insufficient evidence from available sources to determine its precise significance.

6. In both cases, however (that is to say, whether in knowing what is perceptible of what is beyond perception), intellect/will, egoity, and mind function only when preceded by perception of an external object.

7. The term "*dvārin*" here signifies "principal" whereas "*dvāra*" signifies "subordinate."

8. That is to say, just as a dramatic actor is capable of assuming a variety of roles, so also *prakṛti* by its inherent power is capable of producing any number of bodies.

9. To "come upon frustration" (*duḥkhaṃ prāpnoti*) is, of course, meant here only figuratively. Indeed, consciousness (*puruṣa*) cannot do anything. It is completely inactive.

10. This verse does not appear in the Chinese translation.

11. Verses 72 and 73 are probably later interpolations.

12. Verse 73 is read only by *Māṭharavṛtti* and *Sāṃkhyasaptativṛtti.*

12. Patañjali

1. Yoga entries will be treated in greater detail in the Yoga volume of the *Encyclopedia* (in preparation).

2. Woods B340; RB1121, 13ff.

3. Dasgupta B7653; RB11305, vol. 1, 230ff.

4. J. W. Hauer (B6322A; RB9775), *Der Yoga im Licht der Psychotherapie* (Leipzig, 1930), 239-258.

5. Frauwallner B8590; RB12160, 287-288.

6. Chakravarti B6381; RB9596, 138ff.

7. Woods B340; RB1121, xx.

13. Suvarṇasaptati

1. M. J. Takakusu B742; RB1322.

2. Belvalkar B1285; RB2153A.

3. A. B. Keith B1286; RB2153B.

4. Suryanarayana Sastri B1289; RB2153E.

5. S. S. Suryanarayana Sastri (B742; RB1322), *The Sāṃkhya Kārikā Studied in the Light of Its Chinese Version* (Madras, 1933).

6. Umesh Mishra B1288; RB2153D.

7. N. Aiyasvami Sastri, ed. (B775; RB1352), *Suvarṇasaptati Śāstra.* Sri Venkatesvara Oriental Series 7 (Tirupati 1944).

8. Ibid., xxxvii.

9. Solomon RB1585 and RB1818.

10. Solomon RB1387.

11. Frauwallner B8590; RB12160, vol. 1, 478.

12. It is to be noted that here at *kārikā* 3 and again later in the commentary on *kārikās* 8, 10, 26 and 56 the present commentator derives the sense capacities as well as the gross elements from the five subtle elements, even though this clearly contradicts the *Sāṃkhyakārikā* itself (cf. verses 24, 25 and 38). Possibly the explanation of derivation here and again under *kārikā* 26 reflects an older, pre-Īśvarakṛṣṇa account of the system. In any case it strongly suggests that the author of the *Suvarṇasaptati* is not the same as the author of the *Sāṃkhyakārikās.*

13. Suryanarayana Sastri thinks that the Chinese text may have read "*vyāpini*" or "*vyāpti*" instead of "*khyāti,*" which usually means "discrimination."

14. For purposes of symmetry, one would have expected form (*rūpa*) to give rise to the organ of seeing and to be related to the gross element fire, but the commentator instead relates form to all five gross objects. In N. A. Sastri's Sanskrit reconstruction from the original Chinese, however, the text is reconstructed to relate *rūpa* (form), *cakṣus* (eye), and *tejas* (fire or light). The reconstruction is undoubtedly correct.

15. There is an obvious anomaly here. In *kārikā* 25 the subtle elements are said to be endowed with *tamas,* but here they are said to be characterized by *sattva.* Possibly

the commentator holds a view that includes two sets of subtle elements, one pertaining to a very subtle (and largely sattvic and divine) set of essences from which the sense capacities, action capacities, mind, and the gross elements are all derived, and another less subtle (and largely tamasic and human) set of essences from which the gross human world is derived. There is little evidence in other texts, however, for postulating two sets of subtle essences, although it must be admitted that the various commentaries appear to be confused regarding the interpretation of the notions *viśeṣa* and *aviśeṣa* in the *Sāṃkhyakārikā*. It could be the case, of course, that in classical times issues such as this had not been definitively settled one way or the other.

16. It is to be noted that Paramārtha differs here from the other commentaries. According to Paramārtha, the subtle body has seven components: intellect, ego, and the five subtle elements. According to Gauḍapāda, the subtle body has eight components: intellect, ego, mind, and the five subtle elements. According to most commentators (e.g., Vācaspati Miśra) the subtle body is made up of intellect, ego, the five subtle elements, and the eleven capacities.

17. It should be noted that the *Suvarṇasaptati* reads *mohanatāra* for the sixth *siddhi*, but this is probably an error in transmission. *Mohana* means "deluded" or "confused," whereas this *siddhi* appears to describe a joyous state in which the three kinds of frustration have been overcome. It is perhaps justified then to read *modana* instead of *mohana*, or possibly to follow Gauḍapāda who reads *pramodamāna*.

18. Note that Gauḍapāda lists *saumya* (*soma*) instead of *asura*. Vācaspati Miśra lists *pitṛ* instead of *soma* or *asura*. *Yuktidīpikā* lists *nāga* instead of *yakṣa*.

19. *Kārikā* 63 does not appear in Paramārtha's Chinese version, suggesting perhaps that this verse is a later interpolation after the period of Paramārtha (who dates from around the middle of the 6th century).

20. In three Chinese editions the name "Vindhyavāsin" appears, but in the Korean text Vindhyavāsin is not mentioned.

21. The same quotation appears with minor variations both in *Māṭharavṛtti* and in *Jayamaṅgalā*.

22. According to Paramārtha, this final verse is not original to the *Sāṃkhyakārikā* but is a later addition by an intelligent follower of the Sāṃkhya school.

23. It is to be noted that this listing of the ten important subjects is different from the list as set forth in the *Tattvakaumudī* and the *Yuktidīpikā*. See the Introduction for a full discussion of the principal topics (*mūlikārtha*).

14. Sāṃkhyavṛtti

1. *Sāṃkhyavṛtti*, edited by E. A. Solomon, RB1585.
2. The commentary does not refer to the problem of plurality of *puruṣas*.
3. An old verse enumerating the ten basic topics (*mūlikārtha*) is given here:

> *astitvam ekatvam atha arthavattvaṃ*
> *pārārthyam anyatvam atha nivṛttiḥ;*
> *yogo viyogo bahavaḥ pumaṃśaḥ*
> *sthitiḥ śarīrasya ca śeṣavṛttiḥ,*
> *evam ete mūlikārthāḥ.*

See Introduction, p. 82, for translation. The *Sāṃkhyasaptativṛtti*, *Māṭharavṛtti*, *Jayamaṅgalā* and *Tattvakaumudī* cite this verse in their explanations of *kārikā* 72. The *Yuktidīpikā* cites a variant of the verse in its introductory verses. Yet another variant is cited in *Suvarṇasaptati* under *kārikā* 71.

4. It should be noted that this commentary, like the *Sāṃkhyasaptativṛtti* and Paramārtha's commentary, does not quote or follow the *Yogasūtra*.
5. The text of verse 27 here is the same as in the *Yuktidīpikā*:

> *saṃkalpakam atra manaḥ tac ca indriyam ubhayathā samākhyātam;*
> *antas trikālaviṣayaṃ tasmād ubhayapracaraṃ tat.*

6. The commentator says that "*ete*" in verse 36 should not be construed with "*gunaviśeṣāḥ*." "*Etāni*" referring to the above-mentioned "*indriyāṇi*" would have been better.

7. According to Paramārtha, his family name was Kauśika.

15. Sāṃkhyasaptativṛtti

1. *Sāṃkhyasaptativṛtti*, edited by Esther A. Solomon RB1818.

2. For a useful discussion of this problem, see E. A. Solomon RB1387, 153ff.

3. The last part of the first *kārikā* has a different reading: "*naikāntātyantatobhāvāt*."

4. The second line of this *kārikā* as read here is different from the well-known one: it reads "*prakṛtijño vikārajñaḥ sarvair duḥkhair vimucyate*."

5. The first line of verse 56 is differently read here than in most of the versions. Here it is "*Ity eṣa prakṛtivikṛtaḥ pravartate vaikṛtaḥ prajāsargaḥ*."

16. Gauḍapāda

1. E. A. Solomon RB1387, passim.

2. For a useful discussion of the Vedāntin Gauḍapāda, his life, and works, see Karl H. Potter, ed., *Advaita Vedānta up to Śaṃkara and his Pupils*, 103-105. For discussions pro and con about the identity of the two Gauḍapādas, see the following: A. B. Keith B6291; RB9548, 85; Umesh Mishra B1288; RB2153D, 371-386; Amar Nath Ray (B1250; RB1917), "The Māṇḍūkya Upaniṣad and the *Kārikās* of Gauḍapāda," *Indian Historical Quarterly* 14, (1938); 564-569; B. N. Krishnamurti Sarma (B1236; RB1901), "New light on the Gauḍapādakārikās," *Review of Philosophy and Religion* (Poona) 2, no. 1 (1931), 35-56; Vidhusekhara Bhattacharya (B1254; RB1922), The *Āgamaśāstra of Gauḍapāda*, lxxxix ff.; R. D. Karmarkar (B1264; RB1933), trans., *Gauḍapādakārikā* (Poona 1953), v.ff; E. A. Solomon RB1387, 171-175.

3. See E. Sachau, trans., *Alberuni's India*, 1 (London: Kegan Paul, 1910), 266-267.

4. It should be noted that the nature of inference is not discussed at this point in the commentary.

5. It should be noted that Jaimini and the Mīmāṃsakas do not mention these six in any available text. The six that are usually mentioned by the Mīmāṃsaka are *pratyakṣa*, *anumāna*, *śabda*, *upamāna*, *arthāpatti*, and *abhāva*.

6. Again, it should be noted that the Gauḍapāda *Bhāṣya* appears to be confused concerning epistemological issues. Usually comparison, presumption, probability, etc., are discussed as varieties of inference, although sometimes comparison is also discussed as a variety verbal testimony. Negation (or nonapprehension) is discussed in terms of inference or perception, and only tradition is included within verbal testimony. In view of the inconsistencies throughout this section of the *Bhāṣya*, one is tempted to think that the present text of Gauḍapāda is corrupt.

17. Vyāsa

1. Chakravarti B6381; RB9596, 138ff.

2. Frauwallner B8590; RB12160, Vol. 1, 482.

18. Yuktidīpikā

1. Chakravarti, ed., B1046A; RB2207.
2. Pandeya, ed., RB1370.
3. Albrecht Wezler RB2213, 434-455.
4. Pandeya RB1370, xiv.
5. Wezler RB2213
6. Frauwallner B8590; RB12160, Vol. 1, 287.

7. Allen W. Thrasher, "The dates of Maṇḍana Miśra and Śaṅkara," *Wiener Zeitschrift für die Kunde Sudasiens* 23 (1979): 117-139.

8. Pandeya RB1370, xv.

9. This is not always the case: verses 13, 15, 28, 33, 41-43, 46, 49, 51, 53, 56, 58, 64, and 68 are not broken down into parts.

10. The author designates the discussion thus far as the introduction (*upodghāta*) to the commentary. It might be noted that the mode of presentation in terms of the "basic characteristics of a *tantra*" (*tantraguṇa* or *tantrayukti*) is reminiscent of that found in chapter 65 of the *Uttara Tantra* of the *Suśrutasamhitā*, also entitled *tantrayukti*. Similar accounts of *tantrayuktis* may also be found in *Carakaṣaṃhitā*, *siddhisthāna*, chapter 12; *Aṣṭāṅgasaṃgraha*, *uttara*, 50; and Kauṭilya's *Arthaśāstra* 15, chapter 1.

11. The compounding of the word "*tad*" with "*apaghātaka*", though not permissible (see Pāṇini 2.2.15), is justified by such other usages as in Pāṇini 1.4.55, Kātyāyana 4.1.44, and *Mahābhāṣya* 5.1.59.

12. *Vākyapadīya* 2.426-427.

13. Compare *Nyāyabhāṣya* 1.2.9 and *Nyāyavārttikatātpāryaṭīkā* 1.1.5.

14. For example, Patañjali's *Mahābhāṣya* 5.1.119 and 1.1.57.

15. Cf. *Mahābhāṣya* 2.1.1.

16. Pāṇini 3.1.87 and *Mahābhāṣya* 111.2.

17. In other words, having a locative *tatpuruṣa* compound between *sarvapramāṇa* and *siddhatva*, by Pāṇini 2.1.41.

18. Cf. *Nyāyasūtra* 1.1.6.

19. All of these varieties of perception are implied in the compound *prativiṣaya* by construing it as an *ekaśeṣadvandva*.

20. In *Kārikā* 25 the *sattva* and *tamas* forms of *buddhi* were described, and it was said that both these forms derive from *taijasa*, which probably means *rajas*. Possibly, the theory of the five *karmayonis* fits into the Sāṃkhya analysis as an explanation of the *taijasa* or *rajas* form of *buddhi*.

21. The basic meanings for the contentments and attainments may be found in *Sāṃkhyakārikā* 50-51, and see the commentaries of Gauḍapāda, Vācaspati Miśra, and Paramārtha's Chinese version for variant listings of the ancient names. A precise characterization of each of these ancient lists is no longer available. The interpretations of the ancient terminology in each of the commentaries appear forced and fanciful.

19. Jayamaṅgalā

(notes 5-45 by R. S. Bhattacharya)

1. Chakravarti B6381; RB9596, 166.

2. *Ibid.*, 167.

3. Calcutta Sanskrit Series 19 (1926), 1-9.

4. *Quarterly* Journal of the Andhra Historical Research Society (October 1927): 133-136.

5. "*Muni*" in this verse may refer to the author of the text, i.e., Iśvarakṛṣṇa. But since such an assertion does not appear to be supported by any authority it is quite reasonable to take "*muni*" as referring to the first teacher of Sāṃkhya, i.e., Kapila, the first enlightened being (*ādividvas*). The term may, however, refer to Pañcaśikha, the well-known Sāṃkhya teacher (mentioned in SK 70), as he is said to have transmitted *lokottarajñāna* to Janaka (*Śāntiparvan* 320.38).

6. The definitions are derived from the commentary on SK 53.

7. The printed reading appears to be corrupt. Because "*pradhāna*" and "*prakṛti*" are synonymous, *prakṛti* cannot be said to be a product of *pradhāna*.

8. Yāska's *Nirukta* 2.4.

9. Jayamaṅgalā reads "*ca*" (showing emphasis) in the third foot instead of "*tu*."

10. Vācaspati in his commentary on *Nyāyavārttika* I.1.5 quotes a verse:

"*Mātrā nimitta saṃyogiviyogisahacāribhiḥ*
Svasvāmivadhyaghātādyaih sāṃkhyānāṃ saptadhānumā."

It is attributed to the *Sāṃkhyavārttika* by Vardhamāna in his *Prakāśa* (BI edition, p. 671). There is a slight difference of opinion between the Jayamaṅgalā and this verse.

11. The *Jayamaṅgalā* appears to read *prasiddhi* in place of *pratīti*.

12. This contention of the *Jayamaṅgalā*, that *puruṣa* must not be held as *eka* owing to its plurality, is wrong. The epithet "*eka*" must be applied to *puruṣa* as the aforesaid statement demands. But we are to take "*eka*," not in the sense of number, but in the sense of *ekarūpa*, having one form or one aspect, i.e., immutable or isolated (*kevala*), unmixed, without having any subdivision (*svāgatabhedaśūnya*). The same word "*eka*" will be applied to the unmanifested also in the sense of "one" and to *puruṣa* in the sense of *kevala* or *ekarūpa*.

13. The printed reading of the commentary on the fourth foot of this verse is slightly corrupt.

14. The passage "*tatra siddhe . . . .vedāntavādinaḥ*" is printed as a part of the commentary on SK 17. It is actually the *pāṭanikā* of SK 18.

15. How the *pratiniyama* of birth, death, and organs prove the plurality of *puruṣas* is not clearly shown here.

16. The expression "*anyatra vicāritatvāt granthagauravabhayāt*" clearly refers to another work by the commentator. The identity of the work is yet to be determined.

17. The printed reading quoted for describing these seven forms is corrupt and not fully intelligible.

18. The two illustrations seem to indicate that this connection has some cause and that it can be destroyed by proper means.

19. The reason for the former name appears to be its imperceptible aspect, i.e., the *avyakta* or the *guṇasamya* form. Ancient teachers used the term "*tamas*" for *prakṛtis*; see *Jayamaṅgalā* on SK 70 and also Durga's commentary on *Nirukta* 7.3. "*Avyākṛta*" is used in *Bṛhadāraṇyaka Upaniṣad* I.4.7.

20. The printed reading "*atiśaya*" is wrong.

21. *Jayamaṅgalā* seems to read "*tanmātrapañcakam*." According to us the original reading of the second half of this *kārikā* is "*ekādaśaśca gaṇaḥ tānmātraḥ pañcakaś caiva.*" The sentence shows that there are two groups evolving from *ahaṃkāra*: one group (*gaṇa*) consisting of eleven members (of the organs), the other consisting of five members of the nature of *tanmātras*. "*Tānmātra*" means "concerning or pertaining to the *tanmātras*."

22. The *Jayamaṅgalā* notes that the word "*upastha*" is masculine in gender and that it belongs to both sexes. The seat of *vāc* is in the throat.

23. The passage "*anena dvāreṇa tu . . .ity uktam*" is not quite intelligible. The printed reading seems to be corrupt.

24. *Pakti*: the printed reading "*patti*" is corrupt.

25. It is possible that this verse does not deal with the subtle body but with the *liṅga* that is mentioned in verse 20. In verse 40, the word "*liṅga*" is not an adjective meaning that which goes to destruction (*layaṃ gacchati*) but a substantive. This *liṅga*, not being a product of the *viśeṣas*, is quite distinct from the subtle body, which is positively a product of the *viśeṣas*. Had verse 40 treated of the subtle body mentioned in verse 39, one might have expected plural number and masculine gender, while using the adjectives of the *sūkṣmaśarīra*, as are found in verse 39. The *liṅga* is of the nature of a whole of which the internal and external organs are the parts. The five *tanmātras*, though not parts of the *liṅga*, are attached to it so long as creation exists.

26. The printed reading of the explanation of the term "*kārya*" is corrupt.

27. The *Jayamaṅgalā* seems to read "*guṇavaiṣamyavimardena*" instead of "*guṇavaiṣamyavimardāt.*"

28. The second explanation, "*dharmo vā pratyayah sargaḥ*," is not quite clear.

29. The name for the third *uparama* is wanting in the commentary. The commentary on this seems to be lost.

30. The reading "*śakteḥ*" should be corrected to "*aśakteḥ*" in the passage"*teṣāṃ śakter antarbhavati* . . . ."

31. It is remarked that *siddhi* is *jñanājñānalakṣaṇa*, which seems to be a corrupt reading.

32. The printed reading of the alternative name of the third *siddhi* is corrupt.

33. The printed reading of the passage containing the names of these *asiddhis* is corrupt. Properly speaking, *ūha*, etc., are the cause of *siddhi* (cf. *ūhahetukā prathamā siddhiḥ*).

34. In this connection, the *Jayamaṅgalā* has quoted a verse from a treatise named "*Saṃgraha*". "*Saṃgrahakāra*," however, may mean an author of a *saṃgrahaśloka*, a verse in which a long discussion is summarized in the briefest words.

35. It should be noted that the characteristic features of these species are not stated by the commentator.

36. The *Jayamaṅgalā* remarks that the *bhautikasarga* is of two kinds. The reading "*dvividhaḥ*" appears to be wrong and should be corrected to "*trividhaḥ*," i.e., "of three kinds."

37. The argument is not quite clear.

38. The printed reading of the explanatory passage on the expression "*svārtha iva*" is corrupt.

39. What these kinds of objects are is not mentioned.

40. The sentence "*vyaktātmanā* . . . ." is to be connected with the commentary on SK. 61.

41. The verse "*guṇānām* . . . ." quoted here is also quoted in the *Vyāsabhāṣya* 4.13 (with slight variation) with the remark that it is a *śāstrānuśāsana*. According to Vācaspati, this verse belongs to some work by Vārṣagaṇya, an exponent of yoga; see *Bhāmatī* 2.1.3.

42. The printed reading of the explanatory sentence "*liṅga bhautika* . . . ." is corrupt.

43. The import of the word "*bheda*" is obscure. It may be "veda." Thus, "*āgrya*" would mean that this doctrine (i.e., the knowledge propounded in Sāṃkhya) surpasses the Vedas (i.e., the path of action, the *karmakāṇḍa*). As the *tattvas* are realized through *samādhi* only, *Sāṃkhya* must have its basis in Yoga, which is regarded as higher than the path of action. Cf. *Bhagavadgītā* 6.44.

44. A statement of *pradhāna* and *puruṣa* is quoted here that seems to be an aphoristic statement of some ancient Sāṃkhya teacher. According to Durga, it is a *pāramarśa sūtra*; see his commentary on *Nirukta* 7.3.

45. This shows that the last two verses were composed by the author to glorify himself and his work.

20. Śaṃkara

1. Gerald J. Larson RB1378, 209-235.
2. Allen W. Thrasher, "The dates of Maṇḍana Miśra and Śaṃkara," 117-139.

21. Māṭharavṛtti

(notes by Harsh Narain)

1. The commentary under this *kārikā* contains a number of quotations from the *Brāhmaṇas* and *Śrauta-Sūtra* texts and also one quotation from the *Bhāgavata Purāṇa* bearing upon the slaughter of animals in Vedic sacrifices.

2. The commentary also makes a passing reference to the threefold classification of the operations of words (*śabdavṛtti*): primary signification (*abhidhā*), secondary signification (*lakṣaṇā*), and suggestion (*vyañjana*).

3. The expression "*guṇalakṣaṇena*" in the text appears to be a misreading of "*aguṇalakṣaṇena*" which alone can restore sense to the passage.

4. "*Dvyaṅgulakaśayoḥ*" in the text is meaningless. "*Dvyaṅgulyoḥ*" (between two fingers) would be a better reading.

5. The sentence is not clear. Action capacities (*karmendriya*) cannot be said to know or sense anything.

6. The commentator on SK.33 makes a reference to the incarnation of Viṣṇu named Kalkī, which detracts from the antiquity of the commentary.

7. This is cited as a pro-Sāṃkhya verse, but it fits the Cārvāka materialism better.

8. *Kārikā* 73 (see summary under *Sāṃkhyakārikās* above) is absent in other editions of the *Sāṃkhyakārikās*.

22. Vācaspati Miśra

1. Karl H. Potter RB9446, 453-455.

2. S. A. Srinivasin, ed. (RB3878), *Vācaspatimiśras Tattvakaumudī: Ein Beitrag zur Textkritik bei kontaminierter Überlieferung* (Hamburg: Cram, De Gruyter, 1967), 60-63.

3. Umesha Mishra (RB12387), *History of Indian Philosophy*, vol. 2 (Allahabad, 1966), 100.

4. Richard Garbe, trans. (B732; RB1315), *Der Mondschein der Sāṃkhya Wahrheit* (Munich, 1891).

5. Srinivasan RB3878.

6. (B737; RB1317) *The Tattvakaumudī: Vācaspati Miśra's Commentary on the Sāṃkhyakārikā*, Poona Oriental Series No. 10. (Poona, Oriental Book Agency, 1965).

7. With these poetic verses, Vācaspati Miśra is making several significant allusions to the older intellectual tradition. On one level, he is paraphrasing an old verse from the *Śvetāśvatara Upaniṣad* (IV.5). Vācaspati's paraphrase indicates, however, an important shift in conceptualization. In *Śvetāśvatara Upaniṣad* IV.5 reference is made to a feminine "unborn one" and to a masculine "unborn one." Vācaspati retains the feminine "unborn one" but changes the masculine "unborn one" to many "unborn ones," thereby stressing the classical Sāṃkhya notion of a plurality of *puruṣas*. On another level, Vācaspati is probably also alluding to the Vedānta tradition, and specifically to *Brahmasutrabhāṣya* I.4.8-10 in which Śaṃkara discusses the meaning of *Śvetāśvatara Upaniṣad* IV.5 and in which Śaṃkara argues, interestingly, that the old Upaniṣadic passage is *not* a reference to Sāṃkhya notions. On yet another level, Vācaspati is possibly also alluding to *Chāndogya Upaniṣad* VI in which Being (*sat*) is described as having three constituents, namely, fire, water, and food, which are referred to as being characterized by the colors red, white, and black respectively. Here again, however, the Vedānta tradition of Śaṃkara denies that the old *Chāndogya* passage refers to Sāṃkhya notions. Finally, on still another level, Vācaspati is probably alluding to *Ṛg Veda* I.164.20 (the famous "two birds" passage) and X.129 (the hymn that refers to "that one," or *tad ekam*). Both of these passages were claimed by the followers of Sāṃkhya as references to the Vedic sources for Sāṃkhya philosophy, but the followers of Vedānta (and especially Śaṃkara) denied such claims. Vācaspati, therefore, by making these obvious allusions and by then linking these with the tradition of Sāṃkhya teachers is most likely engaging in an intellectual double entendre. The informed reader knows that this is an appropriate manner to begin a treatise on Sāṃkhya philosophy, but the informed reader also knows that a Vedāntin would not take these traditional allusions very seriously. One is tempted to think that Vācaspati wants to eat his cake and have it too. More likely, however, is that Vācaspati is indicating at the outset that although he is composing a treatise on Sāṃkhya philosophy, he is himself approaching the task from the perspective of Vedānta.

8. Although Vācaspati does not appear to draw any ultimate conclusions with respect to this final set of arguments, the upshot would appear to be that both interpretations of the problem of cause and effect, namely, the Sāṃkhya *satkārya* and the Nyāya-Vaiśeṣika *asatkārya* , appear to require some kind of regress. The Sāṃkhya theory of the manifestation of an existent effect, however, is superior, because it at least allows one to maintain an intelligible relation between cause and effect and to interpret that relation in terms of causal operation, even though it also entails an endless regress of continuous transformation. This problem of an endless regress of continuous transformation is dealt with in Sāṃkhya in terms of one of its two basic postulates, namely, *prakṛti* and its transformations.

9. It is to be noted that Vācaspati does not comment on the issue of *puruṣa* being "one" (*eka*) or "plural" (*bahu*) in his interpretation of these two verses. See, however, the *Bhaṣya* of Gauḍapada, *Jayamaṅgalā*, *Māṭharavṛtti* and the Chinese commentary for differing interpretations.

10. This quotation from a so-called *Rājavārttika* is the same as verses 10-12 of the introductory verses to the *Yuktidīpikā*.

11. B340; RB1121.

23. Bhojarāja

1. E. Frauwallner B8590; RB12160, vol. 1 288.

24. Tattvasamāsasūtra

1. Frauwallner B8590; RB12160, vol. 1, 475.
2. As collected and discussed in Frauwallner B6431A; RB9627, 123-137.
3. And see S. N. Dasgupta B7653; RB11303, vol. 2, 171ff.
4. Garbe B3574; RB5524, vii.
5. Ibid., viii.
6. Max Müller B7625; RB11286, 225-229.
7. Chakravarti B6381; RB9596, 168-169.

25. Kramadīpikā

1. Chakravarti, ibid., 168-170.

26. Sāṃkhyasūtra

1. B3574; RB5524, vii-ix of the preface.

27. Aniruddha

1. Garbe B3574; RB5524, viii-ix.
2. Ibid., xxiv.
3. That is to say, bondage is caused only on the basis of a fundamental nondiscrimination that takes place when consciousness and materiality come in contact or proximity (*saṃyoga*) with each other. Bondage, in other words, is *not* an ontological problem vis-à-vis such issues as essential nature (*svabhāva*), time (*kala*), place (*deśa*), action (*karman*), etc., because ontologically, consciousness and materiality are completely distinct. It is, rather, an epistemological problem of nondiscrimination when consciousness and materiality are in contact or proximity.
4. In other words, the assertion to be proved is so broad as to include literally everything. Hence, nothing can be cited as an illustration or documentation that is not already included in the original assertion to be proved. Put into modern terms,

the statement "everything is momentary" has no nonvacuous contrast by means of which its truth can be judged one way or another.

5. It should be noted that Vijñānabhikṣu, Nāgeśa, and Mahādeva reverse the order of *sūtras* 53 and 54. Presumably, this reversal is because of the particle "*iti*" that appears at the end of *sūtra* 53. Vijñānabhikṣu argues that the use of *iti* indicates that the discourse on bondage in the *sūtras* has now been completed. Because *sūtra* 54 also deals with bondage, evidently Vijñānabhikṣu solves this discrepancy by simply reversing the order of the two *sūtras*. Aniruddha, however, who is the oldest commentator, does not reverse the order, nor does he suggest that the discourse on bondage has been concluded at this point.

6. Presumably, 'internal organ" here refers to the intellect.

7. That is to say, the atomic theory and the theory of primordial materiality are alike in the sense that both are intellectual constructs for purposes of systematic, philosophical reflection and so are first principles functioning more or less as heuristic devices or limiting parameters in which that which is knowable can be talked about.

8. It should be noted that this *sūtra* appears to make *manas* equivalent to *buddhi* or *mahat*. If this is the case, however, then one cannot easily account for the reference in *sūtra* 61 to the "aggregate" of twenty-five. It is probably the case, therefore, that *manas* in this context is not the same as the *indriya* referred to by that name in *Sāṃkhyakārikā* 27. At least, Vijñānabhikṣu argues in this way. Possibly, however, we have here an example of the conflation of traditions. That is to say, different schools of ancient Sāṃkhya speculation may have interpreted *manas* differently and in the *Kārikā* as well as in the *Sāṃkhyasūtra* traces remain here and there as in this instance of the attempt to resolve such divergencies. Compare, for example, the views of Vindhyavāsin as set forth in the *Yuktidīpikā*.

9. In other words, there is no convincing inference that the world does not exist, nor can it be argued that our perception of the world is mistaken, as it is when we perceive a mirage, etc. Indeed, the very possibility of a mistaken perception—as for example in hallucination or mirage—can be accounted for only on the basis of the experience of a nonmistaken perception that corrects the error. If the world were unreal, there could be no rational criterion for even identifying a "mistaken" perception.

10. It should be noted that if one construes *sūtras* 92-99 as dealing with the issues of the existence and functioning of God, the Sāṃkhya position appears to be the following: not only is the existence of God logically untenable, but even more than that, all of the conventional beliefs about God are more adequately accounted for by other means. Thus, God's agency, his controllership, his apparent Vedic attestation, and his discriminative capacity can all be accounted for in terms of the functioning of the *antaḥkaraṇa* or internal organ vis-à-vis the proximity of passive consciousness (*puruṣa*). But compare Vijñānabhikṣu for a varying interpretation of these *sūtras*. Also, see Book V.112 for further comments on the problem of God.

11. That is to say, a jar becomes manifest by the work of a potter, or it becomes destroyed by smashing it with a hammer, etc. In all cases, however, a jar, or clay, etc., are possibilities within a certain causal environment, and in that sense they are always existent effects. Hence, it is quite possible to hold to the theory of *satkārya* and at the same time make relevant distinctions regarding prior absence, posterior absence, etc., of particular manifestations. The latter are verbal characterizations within certain contextual environments and depend on a given manifestation.

12. That is to say, the preceding objections in *sūtras* 119-123 concerning respectively the problems of sequence, of destruction, and of vicious regress likewise arise with respect to the theory of *asatkārya*.

13. That is to say, presumably, space and time presuppose the quantitative measure of distance and duration and, thus, can only be relevant notions when the gross world has been constituted. In other words, space and time in Sāṃkhya are consi-

dered to be phenomenal derivatives of the fundamental principles and are not in themselves real in the sense that the twenty-five fundamental principles are real.

14. It should be noted that the term "*vaikṛta*" is evidently an ancient technical term the precise significance of which is unclear. See Introduction.

15. That is to say, in a given state the designations "primary" and "secondary" are always based on the various functions that have to be performed on various levels of government. Overall, however, it is the governor who retains an ultimate superiority.

16. That is to say, although it is possible to discuss the sun as an intelligible entity in and of itself, any accurate characterization of its functioning must always take account of what is illumined and sustained by it (namely, the manifest world of nature illumined and supported by it). Moreover, because the subtle body is inextricably related to the gross body, therefore, the subtle body cannot be considered to be the Self or contentless consciousness, which by definition can have no such dependence or relation.

17. The *sūtrakāra* does not appear to object to the alternative explanations of the makeup of the gross body, and hence it can perhaps be assumed that these varying interpretations were legitimate positions within the network of Sāṃkhya "schools."

18. That is to say, discrimination and nondiscrimination are the necessary *and* sufficient conditions for liberation and bondage respectively.

19. Just as dream constructions are derived from our experience of waking objects and are judged to be dream constructions precisely because of that, so also the conceptual constructions of accomplished Yogins are to be interpreted. Put simply, the experience of waking awareness is the primary criterion for identifying and assessing other kinds of awareness.

20. Although materiality is eternal and self-sufficient, it nevertheless serves the needs of consciousness in terms of experience and liberation. Materiality, therefore, is the locus for nondiscrimination.

21. It should be noted that there is an interesting contrast between Sāṃkhya and Yoga on the problem of God. Both systems deny the notion of God in a traditional theistic sense, but both accept "God-talk" as it were in a limited way. For Yoga, God is a particular *puruṣa*; for Sāṃkhya, "God" is simply another term for *buddhi* in its apparent manifestation as omniscient and omnipotent.

22. The expression "for the sake of" should be construed in the light of the clarification given by the *sūtrakāra* in II.1.

23. The analogy holds only for the milk and not for the cow. See II.37 for the use of the analogy of the cow.

24. That is to say, action need not be considered a primary cause either of bondage or liberation as it is according to the Mīmāṃsā.

25. For those of middle-level capability, even after discrimination, *prārabdha-karman* or "action that is in the process of being worked through" continues to operate for a time and, hence, there is a kind of experience (*upabhoga*).

26. There is one source of this ancient tale that would indicate that "*Piśācaka*" is a proper name of a person rather than an imp. The source is *Naiṣkarmyasiddhi* 2.3; see the commentary by Jñānottama.

27. Śuka is the narrator of the *Śrīmad Bhāgavatam*. The story is in the *Śāntiparvan* of the *Mahābhārata*.

28. One attains the final goal (*kṛtakṛtyatā*) by means of the knowledge of the principles (*tattvajñāna*), which is brought about through devotion to an authoritative teacher (*gurūpāsanā*), according to Aniruddha.

29. That is to say, if God should have such personal need, then He could not be God, and if He had no such need He would not engage in action or work.

30. The principles of *puruṣa* and *prakṛti*, according to Sāṃkhya, are established by means of inference. *Puruṣa* is inferred by means of *saṃghātaparārthatva*, etc., as set forth

in I.146. On the basis of these effects, which establish *prakṛti,* and the resulting implications, which establish *puruṣa,* however, a God cannot be inferred. All of the functions of God can be more adequately accounted for with respect to the notions of *puruṣa* and *prakṛti.* At best, *puruṣa* or consciousness can be called "God" when, under the influence of nondiscrimination, consciousness appears to be an agent, but such a God is nothing more than a convenient verbal characterization and is certainly not an independently existing entity. Thus, neither perceptual nor inferential grounds exist for establishing the existence of God.

31. The *sūtrakāra* asserts that the existence of God cannot be established by either perception, inference, or reliable authority, and, according to Sāṃkhya, there is no other means for reliable knowing. Hence, the existence of God cannot be established. Compare Vijñānabhikṣu's commentary wherein the *bhāṣyakāra* makes a valiant, albeit unconvincing, attempt to soften the Sāṃkhya denial of God. See especially his commentary on V.12. Finally, it should be noted that, for a full account of the Sāṃkhya denial of God, one should read and compare I.92-99 with V.2-12.

32. Both Aniruddha and Vijñānabhikṣu construe "*sukha*" in this *sūtra* to mean satisfaction, and they then proceed to show how satisfaction is established on the basis of the fivefold inference.

33. An inference may work both ways vis-à-vis that which is to be proved, or only one way. For example, in the inference "all transitory things are produced," the inference works both ways, so that it is equally valid to assert that "all produced things are transitory." In the inference "where there is smoke there is fire," however, the inference only works one way, or on one side, for there are examples of fire without smoke.

34. It should be noted that Vijñānabhikṣu interprets this *sūtra* as applying only to the Veda or *āptavacana.* If construed in this way, then the *sūtra* should be taken with the preceding *sūtras* in which the authority and authorship of the Veda have been discussed.

35. The Prābhākara theory of error is usually called "*akhyāti*" or "*vivekākhyāti*" and not "*satkhyāti.*" The latter designation is usually given to the Vijñānavāda theory of error. The *sūtra* V.53 (*na, sato bādhadarśanāt*) could be taken as referring to Vijñānavāda, and the argument against the theory would be that it entails the denial of the incontrovertible perceptions of an external world. All of the commentaries, however, take the *sūtra* as referring to Prābhākara, and both Garbe and Nandalal Simha agree.

28. Vijñānabhikṣu

1. In S. N. Dasgupta B7653; RB11305, vol. 3, 445-495.
2. Richard Garbe B6227; RB9527, 100-105.
3. A. B. Keith B6291; RB9548, 112.
4. M. Winternitz, *Geschichte der indischen literatur* vol. 3, 454-457.
5. Udayavira Sastrin, *Sāṃkhyadarśan kā itihās,* 303-304.
6. Chakravarti B6381; RB9596, 171.
7. Vijñānabhikṣu, *Yogavārttika,* translated by R. T. Rukmani, 5-7.
8. The author gives two meanings of *sūtra* 152, but philosophically speaking both the meanings are identical. Here he cites a verse of the Buddhist Bhāvaviveka and wrongly attributes it to the *Viṣṇu Purāṇa.*
9. It should be noted that Aniruddha accepts the classical doctrine of the eighteenfold subtle body, thus construing this *sūtra* to mean "seventeen plus one more make up the *liṅga.*" Vijñānabhikṣu says that the subtle body is seventeenfold, the reference to "one" in the *sūtra* alluding to the uniform aggregate that appears at the beginning of creation.

10. This is a unique view of Vijñānabhikṣu's that is not in keeping with classical Sāṃkhya.

11. That is to say, there is (a) a subtle body (*liṅga*), (b) a subtle form of the five gross elements that provides a cover or wrap for the *liṅga* in the process of transmigration, and (c) a gross body born of father and mother. Such an interpretation appears forced and awkward.

29. Bhāvāgaṇeśa Dīkṣita

1. No gloss by Pañcaśikha has been published as yet. As indicated earlier, the reference may be to the *Kramadīpikā*.

30. Mahādeva Vedāntin

1. Keith B6291; RB9548, 112.
2. Mentioned by Garbe in B3574; RB5524, v.
3. Ibid., 5.

33. Nāgojī, or Nāgeśa Bhaṭṭa

1. Keith B6291; RB9548, 112.
2. Cf. *Bibliography* (B) pp. 327-328 (RB, p. 452), for citations of his works.
3. Keith, 112.

34. Vaṃśīdhara Miśra

(notes by R. S. Bhattacharya)

1. See the Sanskrit Introduction to the edition by Rāmaśāstrin. The surname mentioned in the introduction is Punataṃkara, which seems to be a variation in spelling only. Gopinath Kaviraj places Mahādeva in the second half of the 17th century. See G. Kaviraj B6007; RB9253, 80.

2. See the commentary on *Sāṃkhyakārikā* 55.

3. Vaṃśīdhara takes the word "*sāṃkhya*" as a word of the *yogarūḍha* class, i.e., as a word in which both the etymological and customary meanings are partly retained, and shows its two meanings clearly.

4. For elucidation of this view see *Vyāsabhāṣya* on *Yogasūtra* 3.14.

5. As Vaṃśīdhara does not criticize this view we may surmise that he was in favor of the Vedāntic view.

6. As shown in *Yogasūtra* 3.13.

7. As the Vedāntic view has not been criticized by Vaṃśīdhara, it appears that he did not consider the Sāṃkhyan view valid.

8. For the nature of *bhoga* and *apavarga* see *Vyāsabhāṣya* on *Yogasūtra* 2.18.

9. "*Udbhid*," as a source of beings, does not in fact mean a seed or soil as is sometimes supposed. "*Udbhid*" means *udbhedana*, the act of breaking through or shooting out. Because trees, etc., appear as a result of breaking through the earth they are called "*udbhijja*." See Nīlakaṇṭha's commentary on the *Bhīṣmaparvan* of the *Mahābhārata* 4.14, and Lakṣmīnṛsiṃha's commentary on *Śivagītā* 32-33.

45. Pramathanātha Tarkabhūṣana

(notes by Kalidas Bhattacharya)

1. Pramathanāthatarkabhūṣaṇa is unnecessarily worried about interpreting *sūtras* 10 and 11 as though they are in the context of bondage and liberation. May they not

be understood plainly in the context of *sūtra* 9, purporting to show that in the case of a white sheet of cloth changing into red, or a seed germinating, there is no destruction of its nature (*svabhāva*)?

2. Under *sūtra* 26, there is another reading for "*āptavādāt*" in the passage Aniruddha quotes. It is "*apravādāt*," "*apravāda*" meaning "statement without justification." "*Āptavāda*" means a statement for which justification is believed to have been given.

3. One wonders why the meaning of a word should change so often and so soon.

4. Here, "*arthakriyā*" is taken by Pramathanāthatarkabhūṣaṇa to mean "cause."

After elaborating Aniruddha's argument against the Buddhists, Parmathanāthatarkabhūṣaṇa refers to an alternative reading for "*uttarayogāt*" in *sūtra* 39. But he observes that in that case another word, viz., "*kāle*" has to be added after "*pūrvāpāye*," meaning that, if only at the moment a cause is destroyed its effect arises, then that cause can never be a material cause, even through the postulation of anything intermediately extra (*atiśaya*).

For "*hetukāle*" in Aniruddha's commentary on *sūtra* 40 there is an alternative reading, viz., "*hetuhetumatkāle*." According to Pramathanāthatarkabhūṣaṇa this reading is unacceptable.

5. This, according to Pramathanāthatarkabhūṣaṇa, is what Aniruddha means by "*ubhayavyabhicārāt*."

6. Those to whom Aniruddha is referring by the name "*viśeṣavādin*" are just the Sāṃkhyists. The word "*ābhāsa*" in "*kāryatvābhāsa*" in Aniruddha's commentary means a fallacy of the *hetu*.

The expression "*vidhivākyottambhanaya*" in Aniruddha's commentary on I.95 is not found in all texts.

7. But is such an interpretation at all necessary? "*Yoga*" may well mean contact in both cases; and is not this contact the cause of *sṛṣṭi*—manifest nature, nonattachment (*virāga*) being itself a part of that *sṛṣṭi*?

8. But did Aniruddha really understand *vikalpa* to be doubt? He has simply said "It touches both." One has only to note that immediately before that he spoke of *pramāṇa* (instrument of knowledge)and *viparyaya* (error or misconception). So, he may well have meant that *vikalpa* touches both correct knowledge and error. Is this *vikalpa* different substantially from Vyāsa's and Vijñānabhikṣu'ṣ?

9. Why Pramathanāthatarkabhūṣaṇa brings in the subtle body here is not clear, for it has no relevance for the next *sūtra*. For the word "*pariṣvakta*" in III.6 there is an alternative reading. It is "*parimukta*" meaning "in bondage" (the prefix "*pari*" meaning "contrary to").

10. As Aniruddha states III.21, it reads "*prapañcatvādyabhāvaś ca*," where by "*prapañcatva*" he means death. But there are two other alternative readings. One that Vijñānabhikṣu accepts is "*prapañcamaraṇādyabhāvaś ca*" and the other is "*prapañcasyābhāvaḥ*."

Under *sūtra* IV.21, for "*tatsvarūpopāsanāt*" in Aniruddha's commentary there is an alternative reading, "*tatsādṛśopāsanāt*." Pramathanāthatarkabhūṣaṇa is definite that it is a wrong reading.

11. Was this interpretation, with the same word taken to be used so differently in two successive sentences, at all necessary?

12. But, as so interpreted, whose view is it after all? It could be imputed to the Vijñanavādin or the Śūnyavādin or the Advaita Vedāntin. But, as the context suggests, it belongs to none of them.

13. But was this necessary? From the context it appears that "*ubhayatra*" here means as much in the case of "white cloth" as in that of "this horse is running" or "this is a cow."

14. But this clarifies nothing.

46. Kṛṣṇanātha Nyāyapañcānana

(notes by Kalidas Bhattacharya)

1. Evidently, all these are cases of passing from the knowledge of *x* to what is *analytically involved* in *x*.
2. But even then things do not clear up.
3. But are they? Are they immediately experienced at all? Earlier in their commentaries both Vācaspati Miśra and Nyāyapañcānana had said that they are not immediately experienced.
4. In other words, right predispositions alone are either innate or acquired, acquisition being effected through other factors. Wrong predispositions are always acquired ones.
5. Nyāyapañcānana refers to another reading for "*ādhyātmika.*" It is "*ādhyātmikya,*" found, he says, in some manuscripts. But Nyāyapancānana holds that this reading is unacceptable because it spoils the rhythm of the first line of the verse. Again, for "*pañca ca*" he refers to another reading, viz., "*niścakara,*" and rejects it on similar grounds.

He refers to another alternative reading for "*hastacandārdhacandrajam*" in the śloka quoted by Vācaspati Miśra. The other reading is "*cañcaccandārdhacandrajam.*" "*Cañcat*" here means "extended."

49. Pañcānana Tarkaratna

(notes by Kalidas Bhattacharya)

1. There is an alternative reading for "*ete namasyāmaḥ.*" It is "*etān namasyāmaḥ.*"
2. Vācaspati Miśra has quoted a passage "*Akke cenmadhu* . . . ." Pañcānanatarkaratna says there is an alternative reading, viz., "*Arke cenmadhu* . . . .", "*arka*" meaning a kind of plant.
3. Vācaspati quoted a passage from Pañcaśikha, viz., "*svalpasaṃkaraḥ saparihāraḥ,* etc." Pañcānanatarkaratna writes that in some quotations there are some additional explanatory words between "*svalpasaṃkaraḥ*" and "*saparihāraḥ.*" They are "*svalpena paśuhiṃsādijanmanā anarthahetunā apūrvena saṃkaraḥ.*"
4. He does not specify which Sāṃkhyan.
5. This equation is valid for Pañcānanatarkaratna and many others, not necessarily for all Sāṃkhyists.
6. According to some, the Sāṃkhya *tattvas* are twenty-five in number; according to others, twenty-four, *puruṣa* being no *tattva*—"*tattva*" meaning whatever is conducive to the interest of *puruṣa.*
7. Perception being the starting point and the paradigm of knowledge.
8. Pañcānanatarkaratna refers to two alternative readings of the first sentence in Vācaspati's commentary, according as the word "*samākhya*" or "*samākhyayā*" is found after "*pramāṇam iti.*" "*Samākhya*" means definition. "*Samākhyayā*" indicates that the definition is obtained indirectly (not literally).
9. In many editions of the *Tattvakaumudī,* Vācaspati's analysis of the term "*prativiṣayam*" reads as "*viṣayaṃ viṣayaṃ prati vartate.*" Pañcānanatarkaratna writes that the correct reading should be "*visayaṃ prati* . . .," the word "*viṣayam*" being stated only once, not twice.
10. The first alternative obviously, is an attempt to accommodate the Nyāya theory of *pramāṇas.* So far as the Sāṃkhya theory of *pramāṇas* is concerned, all later Sāṃkhya interpreters, from Vācaspati onward, have been heavily influenced by Nyāya.
11. When it is a question of objective certainty, rather than of subjective assu-

rance, it would be of the form "This is such and such." As distinguished from both subjective assurance and objective certainty, an operation of a sense capacity (specifically, of mind [*manas*]) would be of the colorless form "This is such and such" without any emphasis on any part of the sentence.

12. Evidently, *saṃkalpa* falls short of *niścaya* (*adhyavasāya*). But how exactly? Vācaspati has never shown that. Pañcānanatarkaratna has made an attempt.

13. This is with regard to intellect (*buddhi*) as will in which Vācaspati somehow appears to be exclusively interested. Pañcānanatarkaratna, however, as will become evident later, admits a corresponding theoretical side in addition.

14. Orthodox Hindus believe in such periodic dissolutions followed by new creations.

15. "*Gavaya*" is the name of an animal that looks very much like a cow.

16. The whole point is to convince the Naiyāyika even though he holds that universals are perceived.

17. It is doubtful, however, if a Sāṃkhyist will accept this theory. See above.

18. Alternative to the reading "*buddher adhyavasāyasya*" there is (as Pañcānanatarkaratna notes) another reading—"*buddher adhyavasāyaḥ sa.*" According to Pañcānanatarkaratna, this reading is wrong.

19. Vācaspati in the *Tattvakaumudī* writes "*Naiyāyikanayair udbhāvanīyam.*" Pañcānanatarkaratna points out that there is another alternative reading. It is "*Naiyāyikatanayai* . . . ." He rejects this alternative reading as childish and practically out of context.

20. To present the case in this way in the English language is indeed grotesque. In English, objects are satisfying, frustrating, or confusing, rather than satisfaction, frustration, and confusion. But such usage is permitted in Sanskrit.

21. All these points have been stated in Rāmeśacandra Tarkatīrtha's subcommentary *Guṇamayī* on this *kārikā*.

22. It is not known who this teacher is.

23. These points have been made by Rāmeśacandra Tarkatīrtha in his *Guṇamayī*.

24. See the concept of "specious present."

25. Pañcānanatarkaratna refers to three alternative readings for Vācaspati's *Tattvakaumudī* regarding three of the five kinds of contentment—*ambhas*, etc. They are (a) *Yā tu prakṛtyāpi . . . . yā tuṣṭiḥ sā upādānākhyā*, (b) *Yā tu pravrajyāpi . . . . yā tuṣṭiḥ sā kālākhyā*, and (c) *Yā tu na kālāt . . . yā tuṣṭiḥ sā bhāgyākhyā*.

26. These have each been interpreted by Vācaspati in two alternative ways.

27. But has Patañjali, or even Vyāsa, said what is attributed to them here?

51. Kṛṣṇavallabhācārya

(note by R. S. Bhattacharya)

1. Strictly speaking, *pravṛttinimitta* is the limiter of the state of being the thing denoted by the denotative function of a word. It is also called "*śakyatāvacchedaka*," See *Siddhāntamuktāvalī* 8.

53. Rāmeśacandra Tarkatīrtha

(notes by Kalidas Bhattacharya)

1. This distinguishes Sāṃkhya from all forms of Vedānta and aligns it with Nyāya, Vaiśeṣika, and Buddhism.

2. These interpretations will be taken up later in relevant contexts.

3. Vācaspati Miśra begins his commentary on this verse saying "*atra ca pramāṇam*

iti samākhyāya lakṣyaparam." Rāmesacandra adds that there is another reading of this sentence of Vācaspati Miśra, viz., ". . . . *samākhyalakṣapadam,*" and, whereas the former relates to "those that are meant" (*lakṣya*) the latter relates to their defining characteristics (*lakṣaṇa*).

4. *Tanmātras* are *aviśeṣa.*

5. Like the contact of the axe with the tree when an axe (qua axe) is taken as the instrumental cause of the cutting of a tree (qua tree).

6. What precisely is gained by this starting assumption is not clarified by Rāmeśacandra.

7. Obviously gross elements (*sthūlabhūta*) do not have to be inferred. According to Vācaspati Miśra they are *perceived* as gross things like pots and linens.

56. Harirāma Śukla

(notes by R. S. Bhattacharya)

1. *Asādhāraṇa* is a variety of *savyabhicāra*. It occurs where the *hetu* is absent from every *sapakṣa* and from every *vipakṣa,* but is present only in the *pakṣa. Svarūpāsiddhi* occurs where the *hetu* is absent from the *pakṣa.*

2. There must be a corrupt reading here. It appears that verse 60 is to be taken as the example of subservience (*pārārthya*) and not of duration (*śeṣavṛtti*). Since Harirāma explains the verses of the *Rājavārttika* following its order of enumeration, verse 60 must be taken as an example of *pārārthya.*

INDEX

abhāva (absence, non-existence) 171-72, 254, 256, 274, 293, 391, 513, 520, 527, 534
abhibuddhi (pertaining to the function of the *buddhi*; five in Samāsa-Sāṃkhya: reflective discerning, self-awareness, intention, sensing, acting; *vyavasāya, abhimāna, icchā, kartavyatā, kriyā*) 34, 319, 324, 415, 447, 465
Abhidharmakośa (of Vasubandhu) 139
abhimāna (self-awareness) 24, 52, 70, 88, 144, 157, 260, 262, 347, 589. *See also ahaṃkāra, antaḥkaraṇa, trayodaśakaraṇa*
Abhinavarājalakṣmī (of Sītārāma Śāstrī) 17, 31, 613
ābhiṣyandika (potential knowledge) 266
abhyāsa (continuing practice) 29, 81, 162, 191
"accumulation theory" of derivation 51, 137, 260, 559
acetana (non-conscious) 100. *See also prakṛti, mūlaprakṛti*
action (*karman*). *See karman*
action capacity (*karmendriya*). *See karmendriya*
adharma (demeritorious behaviour or vice, a fundamental predisposition or *bhāva*, residing in *buddhi*). *See bhāva*
ādhibhautika (external frustration). *See duḥkha*
adhibhūta (external) 60-61, 319
adhidaiva or *adhidaivata* (celestial or caused by fate) 60-61, 319
ādhidaivika (celestial or cosmic frustration). *See duḥkha*
adhiṣṭhāna (overseeing) 79, 156, 344
ādividvas, ādividvān ("primal wise man," Kapila) 108
adhyātma (internal or personal) 60-61, 319
adhyātmavidyā (science of liberation) 29
ādhyātmika (internal or personal frustration). *See duḥkha*
adhyavasāya (reflective discerning) 24, 52, 69, 88, 144, 153, 157, 242, 260, 262, 280, 303, 322, 347, 512, 540, 596, 601. *See also antaḥkaraṇa, buddhi, trayodaśakaraṇa*
Āditya 61
advaita (non-duality), Sāṃkhya critique of 363, 484, 485
Agni 61, 111, 112
ahaṃkāra (egoity or ego; threefold structure: "modified," "energetic," "producing the elements"; *vaikṛta, taijasa, bhūtādi*) 6, 12, 24, 38, 49-65, 65-73, 76-77, 83, 87, 99, 100, 122, 130, 144, 146, 152, 157, 158, 159, 170, 171, 181, 187, 201, 202, 211, 218, 261, 279-81, 295-97, 308-310, 322, 324, 338, 339, 347, 348, 372, 387, 388, 395, 406, 422, 453, 495-96, 503, 535, 573, 583, 584. *See also abhimāna, antaḥkaraṇa, trayodaśakaraṇa*
āharaṇa (seizing) 53, 158, 174, 188, 202, 219, 263, 280, 296, 309, 454-55, 541, 629n
Ahirbudhnyasaṃhitā 108, 118, 125, 126
aiśvarya (power, a fundamental predisposition or *bhāva*, residing in *buddhi*). *See bhāva*
Aitareya Brāhmaṇa 109
Ājīvikas 113, 293
ajñāna (ignorance, a fundamental predisposition or *bhāva*, residing in *buddhi*). *See bhāva*
akartṛbhāva (non-agency, inactivity) 81, 93, 156, 258. *See also mūlikārtha*
ākāśa ("space," ether). *See mahābhūta*
akliṣṭa (unafflicted) 28, 348
ālocanamātra (mere sensing, i.e., awareness unaccompanied by intellectual elaboration) 24, 32, 52, 158, 187, 218, 262, 280, 296, 454, 553
Amalā (of Pramathanātha Tarkabhūṣaṇa) 17, 35, 473-86
anaiśvarya (impotence, a fundamental predisposition or *bhāva*, residing in *buddhi*). *See bhāva*
anātman (no-self) 74, 75
aṇḍaja (egg-born) 53, 63
Aniruddha 16, 35, 84, 317, 327, 333-373, 474, 487, 545, 651-54n. *See also Sāṃkhyasūtravṛtti*
anirvacanīya (Vedānta theory of error) 362
antaḥkaraṇa (internal organ; threefold: intellect, egoity, mind; *buddhi, ahaṃkāra, manas*; with three separate functions: reflective discerning, self-awareness, purposive intellectual activity; *adhyavasāya, abhimāna, saṃkalpaka*) 25, 52, 62, 76, 77, 87, 100, 158, 188, 231, 383, 506, 583, 589, 607
See also buddhi, ahaṃkāra, manas, adhyavasāya, abhimāna, saṃkalpaka

Library of Congress Cataloging-in-Publication Data

Sāṃkhya : a dualist tradition in Indian philosophy.

(Encyclopedia of Indian philosophies ; 4)
Bibliography: p.
Includes index.
1. Sankhya. 2. Sankhya—Bibliography. I. Larson, Gerald James. II. Bhattacharya, Ram Shankar, 1926- . III. Series: Encyclopedia of Indian philosophies (Princeton, N.J.) ; vol. 4.
Z7129.I5E52 1983 vol. 4 818′.4′0321 s 87-16892
[B132.S3] [181′.41′0321]
ISBN 0-691-07301-5 (alk. paper)